**Stigmatization, Tolerance and Re**

Society is faced with a variety of
conditions such as crime, mental and p~,
disabilities, that usually provoke different responses in people
such as emotions of anger, fear or pity. In our evolutionary
past, these emotions adaptively motivated the repair of interpersonal relationships, whereas more recently they may also
result in other types of social control such as stigmatization or
tolerance. Dijker and Koomen show, on the basis of elementary
psychological processes, how people's responses are not only
dependent on type of deviance but also on personality, situation, historical period and culture. They also examine the implications of these responses for the well-being and coping of
people with deviant conditions or stigmas. This book provides
conceptual tools for developing interventions to reduce stigmatization and offers a deeper understanding of the psychological basis of social control as well as opportunities to influence
its potentially harmful consequences.

ANTON J. M. DIJKER is a social psychologist and works
for the Faculty of Health, Medicine and Life Sciences in the
Department of Health Education and Promotion at Maastricht
University.

WILLEM KOOMEN is a social psychologist and works
for the Faculty of Social and Behavioral Sciences in the Department of Social Psychology at the University of Amsterdam.

# STUDIES IN EMOTION AND SOCIAL INTERACTION
## Second Series

Series Editors

Keith Oatley
*University of Toronto*

Antony Manstead
*University of Amsterdam*

This series is jointly published by the Cambridge University Press and the Editions de la Maison des Sciences de l'Homme, as part of the joint publishing agreement established in 1977 between the Fondation de la Maison des Sciences de l'Homme and the Syndics of the Cambridge University Press.

Cette collection est publiée co-édition par Cambridge University Press et les Editions de la Maison des Sciences de l'Homme. Elle s'intègre dans le programme de co-édition établi en 1977 par la Fondation de la Maison des Sciences de l'Homme et les Syndics de Cambridge University Press.

*Titles published in the Second Series:*

*The Psychology of Facial Expression*
Edited by James A. Russell and José Miguel Fernández-Dois

*Emotions, the Social Bond, and Human Reality: Part/Whole Analysis,* by
Thomas J. Scheff

*Intersubjective Communication and Emotion in Early Ontogeny,* by
Stein Bråten

*The Social Context of Nonverbal Behavior,* by
Pierre Philippot, Roberts S. Feldman, and Erik J. Coats

*Communicating Emotion: Social, Moral, and Cultural Processes,* by
Sally Planalp

*Continued on page following Index*

# Stigmatization, Tolerance and Repair

*An integrative psychological analysis of responses to deviance*

Anton J. M. Dijker
Willem Koomen

CAMBRIDGE
UNIVERSITY PRESS

CAMBRIDGE UNIVERSITY PRESS
Cambridge, New York, Melbourne, Madrid, Cape Town, Singapore, São Paulo

Cambridge University Press
The Edinburgh Building, Cambridge CB2 8RU, UK

Published in the United States of America by Cambridge University Press,
New York

www.cambridge.org
Information on this title: www.cambridge.org/9780521793681

First published 2007

Printed in the United Kingdom at the University Press, Cambridge

*A catalogue record for this book is available from the British Library*

ISBN 978-0-521-79019-2 hardback
ISBN 978-0-521-79368-1 paperback

# Contents

*List of figures*                                                    *page* x
*List of tables*                                                           xi
*Preface*                                                                 xiii
*Acknowledgments*                                                         xvii

**1  Introduction**                                                         **1**
  1.1  Introduction                                       1
  1.2  Three types of social control: repair, stigmatization,
      and tolerance                             3
      *Repair*                                  4
      *Stigmatization*                          6
      *Tolerance*                              10
      *Empirical distinctions among the three types of social control*   14
  1.3  The present theoretical approach to social control   16
  1.4  Practical implications                         19
  1.5  Chapter overview                               21
  1.6  Summary                                        23

**2  Evolutionary origins of social responses to deviance**               **24**
  2.1  Introduction                                      24
  2.2  The evolution of social control                   27
      *Self-preservation and the evolution of the fight-or-flight*
        *system*                      30
      *Altruism and the evolution of the care system*   34
      *Additionally evolved psychological mechanisms*
        *for social control?*         44
      *Societies and social control*           46
  2.3  The functioning of adaptive psychological
      mechanisms for social control              48
  2.4  Neurophysiological evidence for the FF-C network   55
  2.5  From adaptive psychological mechanisms to
      mental content and process                 58
  2.6  Discussion and comparison with other theories    62
  2.7  Summary                                        64

**3  Mental representations of deviance and their emotional
and judgmental implications**                                    **67**
3.1  Introduction                                                 67
3.2  The content of mental representations
of deviance                                                  69
*Methods to reveal the content of people's thoughts*          69
*Mental representations of deviant conditions*                71
*The dimensional structure of rejection hierarchies*          77
*Emotional implications of mental representations
of deviance*                                               81
3.3  The effects of additional or salient information on
perceptions of deviance                                      86
3.4  Effects of mental representations and behavioral
information on judgments of deviant individuals              92
*The effects of behavioral information on judgments
of individuals with passive deviance*                      98
*The effects of behavioral information on judgments
of individuals with active deviance*                       104
3.5  Summary                                                      105

**4  Meeting individuals with deviant conditions:
understanding the role of automatic and controlled
psychological processes**                                        **107**
4.1  Introduction                                                 107
4.2  Extending dual-process models of responding to
deviance                                                     110
*Dual-process views of stigmatization and prejudice*         110
*An integrative model of automatic and controlled processes
in responding to deviance*                                 114
*Variables affecting the nature and strength of the initial
motivational state and its associated expectancy*         117
*Motivation and opportunity to influence the motivational
impact of deviance*                                       120
*Examining the social psychological literature to find support
for the extended dual-process model*                       122
4.3  Doing what you want to do: when aggression,
helping, or avoidance are possible                           124
*Aggression*                                                  126
*Situational influences on aggression: room for displacement
or scapegoating*                                           130
*Helping*                                                     133
*Situational influences on triggering care and helping*       137
*Escape and avoidance*                                        140
*Situational influences on triggering and "displacing" fearful
responses*                                                 143

4.4 Not knowing what to do during unfocused
     interactions between non-deviant and deviant
     individuals                                            144
4.5 The relation between automatic and controlled
     responses in the absence of interpersonal
     contact                                                152
     *How are automatic reactions to deviance measured
        in the psychological laboratory?*                   152
     *Why and when are automatic and controlled responses in the
        psychological laboratory more or less dissociated?* 156
4.6 Summary                                                 160

**5  Individual differences in responding to deviance       163**
5.1 Introduction                                            163
5.2 Individual differences in the FF and C system and
     ideological orientations in responding
     to deviance                                            164
5.3 Authoritarianism and social dominance orientation
     as reflections of the FF and C system                  171
5.4 Gender, education, and negative responses to
     deviance                                               178
5.5 Summary                                                 182

**6  Variations in social control across societies, cultures,
    and historical periods                                  184**
6.1 Introduction                                            184
6.2 Understanding how cultural and historical
     differences in social control emerge                   188
6.3 A qualitative analysis of cultural and historical
     differences in responding to deviance                  196
     *Category 1 societies*                                 197
     *Category 2 societies*                                 204
     *Category 3 societies*                                 208
6.4 A quantitative analysis of differences in
     responding to deviance across contemporary
     Western and non-Western societies                      212
6.5 Idiosyncratic cultural influences and temporary
     factors in responding to deviance                      227
6.6 Summary                                                 232

**7  A focus on persons with a deviant condition I: their
    social world, coping, and behavior                      234**
7.1 Introduction                                            234
7.2 Social world                                            236
     *Obesity*                                              236

|  |  | *Homosexuality* | 240 |
|  |  | *Mental illness* | 243 |
|  |  | *Physical disabilities* | 244 |
|  |  | *Old age* | 246 |
|  | 7.3 | Disclosure | 250 |
|  |  | *The reveal-conceal dilemma* | 250 |
|  |  | *Disclosing one's deviant condition: to whom, how, and when?* | 253 |
|  | 7.4 | Ways of coping with one's deviant condition and negative reactions | 257 |
|  |  | *Coping responses to specific negative reactions* | 257 |
|  |  | *Long-term strategies of coping with one's deviant condition* | 259 |
|  | 7.5 | Perceiver-dependent and other negative reactions of deviant persons in social interactions | 267 |
|  |  | *Self-fulfilling prophecies in social interactions between persons with a deviant condition and others* | 267 |
|  |  | *Interactional difficulties of persons with a deviant condition and their determinants* | 272 |
|  | 7.6 | Summary | 276 |
| **8** |  | **A focus on persons with a deviant condition II: socio-economic status, self-esteem and well-being** | **279** |
|  | 8.1 | Introduction | 279 |
|  | 8.2 | Mechanisms mediating lowered outcomes | 280 |
|  |  | *Affiliation and power loss* | 280 |
|  |  | *Discrimination* | 283 |
|  |  | *Stigma endorsement* | 284 |
|  |  | *Performance deficits* | 285 |
|  | 8.3 | Outcomes of having a deviant condition | 290 |
|  |  | *Socio-economic status* | 291 |
|  |  | *Self-esteem* | 294 |
|  |  | *Subjective well-being* | 301 |
|  | 8.4 | Summary | 304 |
| **9** |  | **Theorizing about interventions to prevent or reduce stigmatization** | **307** |
|  | 9.1 | Introduction | 307 |
|  |  | *What is the nature of the response that we would like to influence?* | 308 |
|  |  | *What should be the ultimate goals of interventions aimed at reducing or preventing stigmatization?* | 310 |
|  |  | *What are the proximal psychological mechanisms responsible for stigmatization and stigma reduction?* | 312 |
|  | 9.2 | Tailoring stigma-reduction interventions to type of deviance | 313 |

|  | *Type 1: Uncontrollable-active deviance* | 313 |
|---|---|---|
|  | *Type 2: Controllable-active deviance* | 316 |
|  | *Type 3: Uncontrollable-passive deviance* | 317 |
|  | *Type 4: Controllable-passive deviance* | 318 |
| 9.3 | Common intervention strategies and their underlying assumptions | 319 |
|  | *Perceiver-directed strategies* | 319 |
|  | *Target-directed strategies* | 325 |
|  | *Focusing at interpersonal contact between perceiver and target* | 327 |
| 9.4 | Reconciling stigma reduction with basic principles of social control | 331 |
|  | *Tailoring stigma reduction strategies to current social control practices* | 331 |
|  | *Raising awareness of basic principles of social control as a generally acceptable and useful strategy of stigma prevention and reduction* | 338 |
|  | *Exploring the usefulness of negotiation as a general strategy to prevent or reduce stigmatization* | 340 |
| 9.5 | Summary | 343 |
|  |  |  |
| *Notes* |  | 345 |
| *References* |  | 363 |
| *Index* |  | 402 |

# Figures

2.1  Four basic types of deviance, commonly used labels,
     and major emotional responses.                          *page* 32
2.2  A psychological mechanism for adaptively
     responding to deviance.                                      48
3.1  Two-dimensional configurations of deviant conditions
     obtained in six multidimensional scaling studies.

     A  Frable, D. E. S., *Personality and Social Psychology*
        *Bulletin, 19*, pp. 370–380 (Figure 1, p. 372)
        copyright 1993 by Sage Publications Inc. Adapted
        and reprinted by permission of Sage Publications Inc.
     B  Deaux, K., Reid, A., Mizrahi, K., & Ethier,
        K. A. Parameters of social identity. *Journal of*
        *Personality and Social Psychology, 68*, pp. 280–291
        (Figure 3, p. 289), 1995, American Psychological
        Association, adapted and reprinted with permission.      73

4.1  Schematic representation of factors that influence the
     extent to which responses to deviance are unitary
     (or integrate automatic and controlled aspects)
     or dissociated.                                            115
6.1  Combined rejection scores for the six deviant conditions
     (based on data from the World Values Survey).              214
6.2  Rejection as neighbor of six deviant groups, compared
     to responses to immigrants (based on data from the
     World Values Survey).                                      216
6.3  Variables used to explain the rejection patterns shown
     in Figure 6.2 (based on data from the World
     Values Survey).                                            218

# Tables

6.1   Social control in three categories of societies.          *page* 191

# Preface

How people respond to undesirable or deviant conditions such as illness or crime has always been of great interest to scientific disciplines such as sociology, social psychology, anthropology, history, or political science. Inescapably, the way these responses are studied and understood is influenced by prevailing explanatory concepts, and characteristic features of social control in the society in which scientists happen to live. Thus in modern Western society, the common and social psychological vocabulary used to describe responses to deviance strongly favors terms such as *stereotype, prejudice, labeling, stigmatization*, or *discrimination* to emphasize that these responses are primarily derived from mental constructions and malicious motives, and that deviant conditions themselves rarely pose objective problems for society and hence demand behavioral responses. These descriptions also reflect the fact that current Western society basically values tolerance or self-control as the major way of responding to deviance, while delegating the actual work of prevention, conflict resolution, punishment, or healing to formal institutions such as the police, court rooms, or centers for disease control and health promotion.

Although we believe that tolerance is a great good in our modern individualistic society, we have become increasingly concerned with certain theoretical and practical disadvantages when responses to deviance or social control are primarily analyzed in terms of modern forms of tolerance and its psychological aspects. From such a perspective, people's main business when encountering deviance seems to be to suppress their negative feelings, feel guilty about them, and intensify their normal degree of "civil inattention," to borrow an expression from Erving Goffman. Many social scientists consider perceptions and thoughts that directly address deviance, and failures to control successfully the associated negative feelings, as evidence for intolerance or stigmatization; whereas expressions of positive feelings tend to be seen as mere compliance with norms and insincere. Unfortunately, such a view prevents one from understanding the motivational implications of different types of deviance, and the social function of accurately

xiii

perceiving and distinguishing them, and from attempting to classify the multitude of potentially deviant conditions in meaningful ways. Indeed, what we see is that deviant conditions are usually treated as interchangeable and merely as objects for illustrating general psychological processes (e.g., information processing) that seem to have little basis in the reality of everyday social control processes.

There also is a practical disadvantage of not clearly distinguishing tolerance from other types of social control, such as the repair of relationships on the basis of realistic perceptions of deviance, or stigmatization and social exclusion. Specifically, programs that are aimed at stigma reduction may violate people's basic needs to engage in repair and may also make certain functional forms of social control such as crime and illness prevention less effective. Conversely, programs focusing on improving the prevention and reduction of crime or illness may unwittingly increase stigmatization. For example, current health promotion efforts that use ill people or people "at risk" for certain illnesses as "bad examples," may need to reconsider their potentially stigmatizing strategies in light of the increasing number of people in society who are unable to stay healthy, such as the elderly or chronically ill.

In struggling with these theoretical and practical issues, we have found it useful to start our psychological analysis of responding to deviance or social control in a very basic manner, adopting an evolutionary perspective according to which deviance should be seen as a threat to fitness or reproductive success. Specifically, we asked ourselves what the basic types of deviance are that any society, from hunter-gatherer to modern Western ones, needs to adaptively prevent or reduce; and which psychological mechanisms would enable or motivate individuals to generate these adaptive responses. We arrived at a remarkably small number of universal types of deviance (e.g., relatively active ones such as crime or mental illness versus relatively passive ones such as physical illness or neediness) and of underlying motivational mechanisms related to experiencing anger, fear, and care/tenderness in response to these types. To our excitement, we discovered that alone or in combination, these mechanisms, in interaction with personal, cultural, historical, and situational influences, could very well explain the great variation in thinking, feeling, and behaving with respect to individuals associated with deviance.

Our psychological analysis also allowed us to better distinguish between three basic types of responding to deviance or social control that seem characteristic for different societies or cultures: repair (characteristic for small groups of individuals related through kinship or other affective ties), stigmatization (typical for hierarchically organized societies, and for serious and permanent forms of deviance within large societies), and tolerance (typical for egalitarian and individualistic Western societies). Practically, our approach implies that attempts to develop interventions to reduce stigmatization first have to establish what type of social control one would like to target (is there really evidence for stigmatization?), and with what type of social control it should be replaced (with more tolerance or repair of relationships?). What our classification of deviant conditions and distinction between types of social control implies for the well-being and coping of people associated with deviant conditions or stigmas is also examined.

Most studies discussed in this book are taken from the field of social psychology and psychology in general. However, in our endeavor to test the generality of our theory, we also cover material from many other disciplines such as anthropology, sociology, biology, and history. We cannot claim expertise in all those different fields and recognize that our use of sources from these disciplines may have been somewhat selective.

Because of its integrative nature, we hope this book will be of interest to students of a variety of scientific disciplines studying deviance, as well as to lay persons and practitioners desiring to gain a deeper under-standing of the psychological basis of social control and of opportu-nities to influence its potentially harmful consequences. Although sometimes, our treatment of certain issues may be somewhat technical, we hope this will not discourage the reader from continuing until an impression is formed of the whole approach and its merits, including the practical implications outlined in the final chapter.

We finally note that in discussing the large number of physical, mental, and behavioral conditions that people may consider deviant, we tried to select descriptive terms that would be generally agreeable and non-offensive, sometimes using the different available terms interchangeably. However, as these terms quickly tend to change as a consequence of medical knowledge, normative considerations, or "political correctness," we may not have been entirely successful in adopting a vocabulary that is acceptable to all.

# Acknowledgments

We would like to express our gratitude to the following persons who, each in their own way, have stimulated and facilitated the writing of this book. We thank Antony Manstead for encouraging us to continue with this project and for his patience and confidence in us, despite the many delays and broken promises to finish the book. We also appreciate his detailed comments on earlier versions of several book chapters. We also profited from the comments that were made on several chapters by Arjan Bos and Rob Nelissen. Anton Dijker thanks Maastricht University and especially Nanne de Vries, head of the Department of Health Education and Promotion, for allowing him to work on the book during a sabbatical leave. In addition to the sabbatical, however, Nanne has shown tremendous tolerance when it became clear that this period was too short for finishing the book, and while listening to the many excuses for not finishing "such a complex" book that were to follow. Willem Koomen thanks the Department of Social Psychology of the University of Amsterdam and particularly Joop van der Pligt, head of the Department, for hosting him, offering him essential facilities and making him still feel welcome after his retirement.

Tolerance was also shown to a great extent by our first editor at Cambridge University Press, Sarah Caro, who was frequently faced with our reluctance to complete and hand over our manuscript. We thank Cambridge's present editors Andrew Peart, Carrie Cheek, Joanna Breeze and Sara Barnes for their help and support.

On a more personal note, Anton Dijker would like to express his love and gratitude to the most important contributor in both his work and life, Marianne van den Maegdenbergh. This book could not have been written without her tolerance for his deviant behavior such as using the weekends for writing and parasitizing on her love for cooking and nurturing, her willingness to accept his promises for future reparations, and her reluctance to stigmatize. Willem Koomen would like to thank his wife Gonny for her understanding, tolerance and care, particularly during the downs in the writing process. She missed some of the fruits that retired husbands usually can offer, but refrained from pointing to them.

## CHAPTER 1

# Introduction

## 1.1 Introduction

People are regularly confronted with a wide variety of features and behaviors in others that they may find undesirable or deviant, such as a bleeding wound, a missing leg, a harelip, depression, bullying, leprosy, cowardice, theft, unwillingness to work, low intelligence, or some threatening feature of a racial or ethnic minority or outgroup, to name only a few examples. Different deviant conditions may evoke different kinds of responses. For example, individuals who display selfish behavior such as hurting others, stealing property, or lack of motivation to cooperate, tend to be punished; others who are incapable of cooperating and contributing to group life due to illness or injury, usually receive care and medical treatment; and still others with abnormal facial features, may primarily evoke fear and avoidance rather than punishment or care and protection. Furthermore, the same deviant condition may also trigger widely different responses in different situations, historical periods, and cultures, ranging from extreme moral outrage and harsh physical punishment to "softer" treatment and forgiveness, and from extreme tenderness and care to "less soft" and more aggressive and authoritative forms of nurturance and therapy. Pretending not to be affected by a particular deviant condition, and the suppression and indirect expression of one's emotional reactions to the condition, or the consistent avoidance of a deviant individual in order to prevent experiencing these emotions, may be considered as further variants of how individuals respond to deviance.

The main goals of this book on responding to deviance can be summarized in three words: classification, explanation, and application. The general goal of this book is to present a theory that enables us to classify the many deviant conditions that are possible, to explain people's responses to them, and to indicate how this theory can be applied in influencing these responses. In our approach, classification and explanation are closely linked scientific activities. Specifically, in explaining responses to deviance, we will look for a limited set of

1

universal psychological mechanisms that cause people to respond in the way that they do. For example, we will argue that some deviant conditions activate a psychological response mechanism that causes people to experience fear and hence motivates them to protect themselves against the deviant individual. In contrast, other deviant conditions may activate in people a mechanism for feeling tenderness and a tendency to protect and care for the deviant individual. We will use knowledge about these and other psychological mechanisms to classify the wide variety of deviant conditions in a psychologically meaningful and universal way. That is, we argue that in any relationship, social group, society, or historical period only a limited number of universal *types* of deviance are possible; and that different conditions that can activate the same (combination of) psychological mechanisms can be assigned to the same type of deviance. To put it differently, our psychological mechanisms can be seen as universal *concepts* that allow people to interpret and classify the wide variety of deviant conditions that are possible, and to provide meaning to the specific language that they use to describe these conditions and their reactions to them. For example, on the basis of the above mechanisms for experiencing fear and tenderness, people are able to distinguish a type or category of relatively uncontrollable and threatening conditions (e.g., madness, contagious disease, a strange group encroaching the territory) from a type of relatively uncontrollable and more passive or dependent conditions (e.g., various instances of illness and neediness).

Our explanation, however, does not only serve to develop a typology and semantic theory of people's representations of deviance, but also to account for variation in people's responses to deviance as a function of type of deviance, differences in personality, and situations or societies. The psychological mechanisms that we use to classify deviant conditions can be more or less strongly activated in particular individuals or societies. For example, some individuals tend to feel more easily threatened by a particular type of deviance (seeing more crime around them), and therefore respond with more fear and aggression, than others. In a similar way, situations, societies, cultures, and historical periods influence the likelihood with which relevant psychological mechanisms in people will get activated. For example, in some situations or societies, the psychological mechanism responsible for reacting with fear to a threatening deviant condition, may already be strongly "primed" or activated (e.g., due to famine, plague, warfare, more permanent structural and cultural features, or simply having seen a scary movie), increasing the chance that an encounter with that condition actually results in fear and defensive aggression. We will not only examine in detail how people respond to deviance in different situations, but also distinguish three characteristic ways in which societies tend to deal with deviance or engage in social control – repair, stigmatization, and tolerance.

Although we emphasize in this book the perspective of the perceiver who responds to deviance, we will also pay attention to the responses of the target. This will give a more complete picture of responses to deviance with their antecedents and consequences. Targets, for example, may affect responses of the perceiver, and they often have to cope with negative responses, which may determine their psychological and social fate. In addition, we add to the perspective of the target relevant elements from our perceiver framework, such as differences between types of deviant conditions.

In sum, the theory we propose in this book systematically explains responses to deviance as a function of type of deviance, individual differences, and contextual influences of situations, societies and historical periods. In addition, responding to deviance or social control is analyzed in terms of three major types of social control – repair, stigmatization, and tolerance. This theory not only integrates a wide variety of facts about responding to deviance, but also has important practical implications for developing interventions to influence people's responses to deviance. We start with introducing and discussing the main concepts and terms that have been used to describe and explain social responses to deviance.

## 1.2 Three types of social control: repair, stigmatization, and tolerance

Scholars from such diverse research disciplines as sociology, anthropology, history, evolutionary biology, and social psychology have used a wide variety of terms to describe and explain social responses to deviance, often without clearly defining them and distinguishing them from one another. To anticipate an important conceptual disagreement in this field of inquiry, some disciplines such as social psychology and sociology vigorously deny the usefulness of the term *deviance* – a term that we find essential as our book title suggests – and would like to replace it by terms such as *stigma* or *label*. These disciplines similarly advocate to analyze responding to deviance entirely in terms of *stigmatization* or *labeling*, rather than, for example, *social control*. In contrast, in other disciplines that have shown interest in describing how small communities respond to deviance, such as anthropology, we rarely encounter the terms *stigma* or *stigmatization*. So let us look in greater detail at the main explanatory terms in the relevant research disciplines, and try to unravel their different and common meanings.

In order to organize this discussion, but also to introduce our inte-grative psychological approach to the subject, it is helpful to use the term *social control* as a general term for social responses to deviance, and distinguish three major types of social control, namely, repair, stigma-tization, and tolerance. Social control can be defined as the process by which individuals and societies attempt to prevent or reduce deviant conditions or their consequences, induce and monitor compliance with their major values and norms, and hence maintain social order and morality (e.g., Black, 1984, 2000; Boehm, 1999; Campbell, 1982; Horwitz, 1990). Repair can be seen as the most basic type of social control that may, dependent on the circumstances, transform into stigmatization or tolerance.

## Repair

A crucial type of social control is the *repair* of disturbed relationships or group life as a consequence of deviance, for purposes of continuing cooperative and reciprocal interactions with deviant individuals. Major strategies of repair are: punishment in order to change the deviant individual's behavior and mind; care, medical treatment, or therapy in order to cure the deviant individual; compensation for suffered losses to the victims of deviant behavior; forgiveness of deviant indivi-duals, negotiation, reconciliation, and allowing and motivating perma-nently disabled individuals to adopt useful social roles and letting them re-integrate; and prevention of deviant conditions or their conse-quences by means of warning and education, or isolation of individuals if their conditions seem dangerous and uncontrollable (e.g., madness or contagious disease). As we will argue later, especially when preventive activities take place outside the safe environment of a group of closely related individuals such as a family or small community, they may easily result in stigmatization.

In considering repair processes, it is impossible to avoid using the term *deviance* to refer to the objective social problems that are caused by particular conditions or behaviors of individuals; and that other indi-viduals or society need to notice, distinguish, and respond to in appro-priate ways. For example, it is difficult to imagine a society in which individuals in general would not be able to distinguish crime from illness, and would not respond effectively to the former in more punish-ing, and the latter in more caring and nurturing ways. Thus the sociol-ogist Goode (2003) argues that deviance is "a fundamental element in all social relations. It's there, it's real, it's important, it is in need of investigation" (p. 519). Goode further notes that our personal feelings toward particular responses to deviance, however justified according to our own values and norms, should be irrelevant to the objective study of these responses and the conditions that give rise to them. Although "some of us don't like the way the word 'deviance' sounds" (2003, p. 520), it remains an indispensable concept for scientific inquiry.

Of course, the specific manifestations of crime and illness may vary across societies and cultures, as do the particular standards or norms used to "define" them as undesirable or deviant. Thus in the 1985-edition of the *Handbook of Social Psychology*, D. Archer usefully defines deviance as "a perceived behavior or condition that is thought to involve an undesirable departure in a compelling way from a putative standard. These behaviors and conditions are seen either as merely regrettable or as objectionable in the sense that they produce the belief that something ought to be done about them" (1985, p. 748). D. Archer further emphasizes that "deviance refers to behaviors or conditions that are the subject of *negative* imputations" (p. 747, our italics) and that the perception of deviance motivates efforts at social control and the emergence of social institutions that specialize in doing something about it.

Although in this book we pay great attention to cultural and historical differences in perceptions (or "definitions") of, and responses to, deviance, we emphasize at the outset that deviance may have more objective and universal physical and behavioral manifestations than is usually recognized by sociologists and social psychologists. Thus some universal examples of crime are murder, adultery, and theft (Black, 1984, 2000; Horwitz, 1990; Roberts, 1979); some universal examples of physical illness or injury are weakness, lethargy, loss of interest, sleeping during normal periods of wakefulness, increases in temperature, bleeding, diarrhea, vomiting, or coughing (Fábrega, 1997, p. 56); and some universal examples of mental illness are excessive violent conduct, wandering around naked, or talking non-sense (Helman, 1994, p. 252).

Repair seems most characteristic for relatively small groups of closely connected and interdependent individuals, such as a family or small nomadic group of hunter-gatherers, which engages in face-to-face social control or "mutual monitoring" (Campbell, 1982). In order to see the distinction between this and other types of social control, it is important to emphasize that repair focuses on behavior or temporary physical or mental conditions or states (e.g., acute suffering and illness), rather than on persons and their entire configuration of deviant as well as non-deviant features. Furthermore, societies that engage in repair explicitly notice and clearly respond to deviance (even when apparently doing nothing for strategic reasons) until the normal pattern of cooperation and social order have been restored. The latter may happen, for example, when individuals associated with deviance actually change their undesirable condition or behavior, or society manages to socially accept and assimilate them without such changes (e.g., when disabled persons learn to cope with their condition and adopt useful social roles). We will argue later that repair is best characterized in psychological terms as a balanced way of responding to deviance; neither too harsh, nor too soft, motivating the parties involved to solve the problem and allowing sufficient room for mutual adaptations and negotiation. Sometimes, the ways of letting deviant individuals know that their behavior might be unacceptable may appear stigmatizing; for example, when it consists of staring, explicit withdrawal of social attention (ostracism), or gossiping (Roberts, 1979). Yet, as long as these patterns of response are aimed at changing the deviant's mind, behavior, or condition, in the service of prevention of deviance and re-integration, these social control strategies are different from stigmatization.[1]

## Stigmatization

In contrast to repair, *stigmatization* is a type of social control that does not distinguish between a person and his or her deviant behavior or temporary condition, and that is aimed at excluding the person from a relationship or society. Social control may turn into stigmatization when a deviant condition is increasingly perceived and responded to as a defining or essential attribute of the "whole" person or social group, or of the person's or group's reputation, character or identity. It goes at the cost of discovering the individual's or group's *non*-deviant and useful attributes, and treats the victim as "essentially" or morally bad, thereby withholding giving him or her a "second chance." More formally we define stigmatization as: the process by which an individual's or group's character or identity is negatively responded to on the basis of the individual's or group's association with a past, imagined, or currently present deviant condition, often with harmful physical or psychological consequences for the individual or group. The deviant condition may or may not actually be present; what is important is that the individual is *associated* with a past or present deviant condition and hence that the perceiver cannot but respond to the motivational implications of that deviant condition, imagined or not.

Stigmatization can be seen as a functional form of social control when repair would be desirable but is not possible; for example, when a deviant condition poses a relatively permanent threat to the community and is unlikely to change in response to repair. For example, in relatively large social groups or societies people need to identify and label particular individuals in terms of their (association with a) deviant condition in order to warn each other of these individuals' bad or shameful reputation or dangerous character. Probably the most characteristic feature of stigmatization is to *publicly* associate a person with a shameful deviant condition (or stigma), thus preventing the person from engaging in a repair process and from adapting his or her behavior. Of course, the deviant condition itself may increasingly lose its relevance or truly harmful consequences in this process. The latter is especially likely to occur when, in hierarchically organized societies, stigmatization is *used* by those in power in order to maintain and legitimize their power, mainly by publicly associating those who threaten their power and values with a bad reputation and exposing them as "bad examples" and objects of public punishment. Thus the history of the European Middle Ages is full of examples of the literal use of stigmas (e.g., badges for distinguishing the "worthy" poor who were allowed to beg, ear-boring or branding of recidivous rogues, and a wide variety of recognizing marks to be worn by heretics, Jews, lepers, and homosexuals; see Jutte, 1994; Moore, 1987), elaborate public floggings, tortures, and denigrations in which the dominated public is encouraged to take part and allowed to "displace" its aggression and "enjoy" itself (Foucault, 1975/1977; Le Goff, 1984/1987; Moore, 1987; Stiker, 1999; Vanhemelryck, 2004). More recent examples of such practices can be found in totalitarian systems such as Nazi Germany. Despite the obvious "misuse" of stigmatization under particular circumstances, we do not stipulate in our definition that a deviant condition with which a person gets associated needs to be "irrelevant" or even merely the product of prejudiced perceivers. As noted above, people may need to be warned about individuals with relatively permanent, immutable, and serious deviant conditions such as those with lethal and contagious illnesses, or those engaging in pathological forms of cheating and harmful behavior.

Our definition of stigmatization shares important elements with the common usage of the term. For example, Jones *et al.* (1984, p. 8) propose that "impression engulfment is the essence of stigma" and that when people specifically respond to a deviant attribute (e.g., a past psychiatric treatment) and do not make it "the most important single thing about his personality," their response should not be considered stigmatizing. In other places these authors speak of the deviant attribute or "mark" having a "master status." However, our definition adds a new and, in our eyes, fundamental element to current usage – the concept of *deviance* – thereby allowing researchers to explicitly address the similarities and differences between stigmatization and other types of social control. It sharply contrasts with efforts of social psychologists to downplay the role of deviance in stigmatization by, for example, maintaining (quite inconsistent with D. Archer's definition) that deviance can also refer to something that is positively evaluated (e.g., Crocker, Major, & Steele, 1998, p. 506; Stangor & Crandall, 2000, p. 80) or by equating deviance entirely with rather trivial distinguishing features such as skin color. Crocker *et al.* (1998, p. 506) even mention the possibility that individuals such as women may be stigmatized in particular contexts without being deviant. We cannot think, however, of a single situation in which women would be stigmatized without the perception of some deviant feature or condition. Typically, in situations in which women are judged in terms of male standards (cf. D. Archer's definition cited above) and found to depart from these standards in an undesirable way (e.g., men may see women as unskilled at technical jobs, or unfit for leadership), they are seen as deviant.

Now, the consequence of stigmatization is usually that an individual associated with a deviant condition is also associated with a *stigma*; and it is this term in particular that invites researchers to ignore the role of deviance in stigmatization. A stigma refers to an attribute or symbol (e.g., a word referring to that attribute) that is known to be negatively evaluated by a social group or society, in such a way that individuals or groups associated with the attribute tend to be denigrated and socially excluded and hence stigmatized (Crocker *et al.*, 1998; Goffman, 1963b).[2] In principle, it should be possible to objectively verify if a deviant condition can be considered a stigma or not. That is, the more the condition is negatively responded to (in the sense of stigmatization) by a group of people or society at large, the greater the likelihood that the reputation, character, or identity of an individual being associated with that condition will be spoiled.[3] If we realize that stigmatization can also be defined as the application of an existing stigma when perceiving and responding to another person, the definition of stigmatization comes very close to terms that emphasize the mental, subjective, or top-down aspects of the process, and the triviality of objective reasons or bottom-up aspects for negative responses. For example, stigmatization is used almost interchangeably with the social–psychological terms of *prejudice* or *stereotyping*.[4] In addition, sociologists tend to use the closely related term of *labeling*, arguing that individuals primarily become deviant and a problem for social control once others and society have labeled and responded negatively to their ("primary") deviance; something these individuals in turn respond to with starting a "deviant career" and hence acquiring "secondary" deviance (Becker, 1963; Link & Phelan, 2001; Orcutt, 1983). Thus, according to common understanding, to stigmatize someone is to view and respond to a trivial attribute of the person in light of society's image, stigma, label, prejudice, or stereotype about that attribute, assuming that the stigma is somehow mentally available or represented in the subject's mind.

In addition, *discrimination* refers to the behavioral side of this process; the unequal treatment of individuals on the basis of features that are considered irrelevant for the decision to deliver that treatment. Although there may be a strong consensus about the irrelevance of features such as skin color, sexual orientation, or religion, any doubt that is cast on their irrelevance will result in uncertainty about the correct application of the term discrimination.

It is our guess that the general unwillingness of social psychologists and sociologists to use the term *deviance* may be due to its being easily equated with *stigma* and hence with both the primarily subjective or mental aspects of stigmatization and the less benign aspects of social control in general. However, although stigma logically implies deviance, the reverse is not true: deviance does not logically imply stigma. For example, in the context of repair (but also of tolerance; see below), deviant individuals are not usually stigmatized, although under some circumstances, these types of social control may have stigmatizing side-effects.[5]

Although we recognize that stigmatization has important subjective and biasing elements, resulting in decreased attention to a person's non-deviant attributes, self-fulfilling prophecies, and "deviant careers" (cf. Becker, 1963), these are not sufficient reasons for us to dispose of the term deviance. Indeed, we maintain that deviance plays a fundamental role in social control in general (see especially our earlier discussion of the role of deviance in repair), and therefore also in stigmatization. First, unlike the often used example of skin color as being merely a trivial cue for categorization and differentiation between social groups, deviant properties are usually motivationally relevant and far from trivial. For example, it is obvious that a person sitting in a wheelchair cannot walk and requires (or "affords," cf. McArthur & Baron, 1983) assistance, and that the uncertain and careful behavior of a blind person motivates an even greater concern (for arguments against such a view, see Crocker *et al.*, 1998). Furthermore, even if stigmatization is focused on entire groups rather than specific individuals, it is usually not simply the "cues for categorization" such as skin color or other trivial ethnic attributes such as an islamitic head shawl, that are of interest to people. For example, groups may also respond to the specific cultural or ethnic differences that each of them actively advertises in order to be recognized and respected by the other (L. Brown & Lopez, 2001; Park & Judd, 2005). In addition, minority groups are frequently associated with a low socioeconomic but protected status, which implies a particular type of deviance that is related to perceived social parasitism and laziness (see Chapter 2). Finally, even if racial or ethnic features cannot be seen as deviant or conflicting conditions in the usual sense, intergroup relations frequently involve a situation in which a strange ethnic minority is potentially threatening and a problem for social control during the *initial* stages of contact. Especially when members of an ethnic minority enter the territory of a particular majority group or society (e.g., immigrant workers from North African countries arriving in Europe), acceptance of their presence may only be realized when these groups have carefully observed particular requirements that are related to fear reduction and the need to exercise control by the host country. Although these requirements are little recognized by social psychologists studying the benefits of intergroup contact, their importance can be derived from anthropological studies on stranger-incorporation rituals and general mechanisms of fear reduction that are addressed in Chapter 9. Fortunately, the dominant "color-blind" approach to interracial and interethnic relations does now seem to be waning (L. Brown & Lopez, 2001; Park & Judd, 2005).[6]

A second reason for allowing deviance to play an important theoretical role in stigmatization is that a failure to do so easily results in the error of equating stigmatization with social control in general rather than seeing it as a particular type of social control. For example, in a recent attempt to apply evolutionary theory to the explanation of stigmatization (Kurzban & Leary, 2001), relatively recent examples of stigmas are used to argue that stigmatization must have been an adaptive form of responding to deviance in our evolutionary past (i.e., increasing our reproductive success); thereby forgetting that other forms of social control such as repair probably might have been more adaptive for our human ancestors living in small groups of hunter-gatherers (see the next chapter, for a critical discussion). The practical implications of confusing deviance and stigma, and denying that deviance may exist as an objective social problem, are even more serious. That is, well-intentioned attempts to reduce stigmatization may then be similar to attempting to reduce social control all together; thereby ignoring and frustrating people's need to respond to deviance (see below).

## Tolerance

Let us finally turn to a third major type of social control: *tolerance* (or *toleration* as philosophers tend to call it). Although, since the Wars of Religion during the sixteenth and seventeenth centuries, tolerance is a frequently used word in modern Western society, it remains a difficult to define and much debated term (e.g., Heyd, 1996b). Furthermore, the term does not appear to exist in social psychology as an established psychological term around which a distinguishable research tradition has developed (although particular psychological aspects of tolerance are increasingly well-studied, as we will see in a moment). Let us first try to determine what tolerance is *not*. Tolerance is not the same as indifference with respect to the behavior and beliefs of other individuals, although in practice, it may look like that. At a minimum, tolerance requires that we *do* care about the behaviors or beliefs of others, and respond negatively (e.g., fearfully, aggressively) to them, but also attempt to suppress and control these responses. Therefore, tolerance is not the same as a positive attitude toward individuals associated with the particular deviant condition, a general reluctance to categorize or stereotype people and see them as "different," "non-prejudice," a general kindness toward people, or a "liberal personality," as some authors have implied (e.g., Allport, 1954/1979; Phillips & Ziller, 1997). However, it cannot be denied that a caring and empathic attitude certainly helps to tolerate irritations aroused by others' behaviors or beliefs.

However, tolerance is more than simply suppressing negative responses and exercising restraint. It seems to be associated with a feeling that it is *good* to allow others to think and act in ways that one disapproves of. Tolerance is thus seen as a value and virtue. Now, here is where it gets paradoxical: tolerance "required someone to think that a certain belief or practice was thoroughly wrong or bad, and at the same time that there was some intrinsic good to be found in its being allowed to flourish" (Williams, 1996, p. 25). The solution that philosophers such as Williams (1996) and Heyd (1996a) have proposed, is that we have to separate an individual's thought and behavior from "the person" or character, and respect the latter; i.e., value his or her "autonomy," "dignity," "integrity," "independence," or "authenticity." This makes it possible to approach tolerance more positively as: *In spite of your wrong or deviant behaviors or beliefs, I accept you as a person.*

Thus in contrast to stigmatization, but similar to repair, tolerance implies that we should separate deviant conditions and behaviors from the person. But in contrast to repair, tolerance is not aimed at inducing the deviant individual to change his or her behavior or mind. Indeed, tolerance requires us to look the other way, and interact with the deviant individual as if his or her deviance did not exist.

How is tolerance psychologically possible? First, a caring or protective attitude toward the deviant individual may help to tolerate the irritation that the deviant individual arouses, and also may motivate (via the emotion of guilt; see Chapter 2) to suppress hostile and punishing responses to the individual. However, the meaning of tolerance demands that the caring attitude cannot be so strong that the deviant condition goes unnoticed or that the deviant individual is "unconditionally" accepted or loved. In Chapter 2, we argue that there is one particular type of deviance that lends itself ideally for tolerance; tendencies to make use of others' strong motivation to care, commonly referred to as "laziness," free riding, or social parasitism. The behaviors and beliefs of individuals associated with these conditions are tolerated as long as their free riding and demands do not become too obvious and costly for the caregiver.

Second, tolerance may also be possible because individuals suppress hostile responses to deviant others out of fear of retaliation by them or the social group or state. Interestingly, several social psychologists argue that the two main motives for suppression of hostile responses to deviant individuals or groups are guilt (associated with "internal reasons") and fear (associated with "external reasons"); with both reasons to suppress negative responses further strengthened by egalitarian social norms (e.g., Crandall, Eshleman, & O'Brien, 2002; Fazio & Hilden, 2001; Monteith, Devine, & Zuwerink, 1993; Plant & Devine, 1998).

A third important pre-condition for tolerance is that it may only be possible in a particular kind of society in which individuals are increasingly reluctant to exercise ("informal") social control, leaving it entirely to the state and its institutions which specialize in law enforcement (the police, lawcourts, prisons) and mental and physical health care ("formal" social control); with the exception of certain domains of social life such as the family, workplace, or schools (Horwitz, 1990). Additional important features of such a society, of which the modern, individualistic, and urbanized Western world is the main example, are that individuals should be free to pursue their aspirations and have the right to "privacy," and should avoid becoming too closely involved in each other's affairs (Milgram, 1992). As will become clear in later chapters, tolerance easily breaks down when individuals or groups associated with deviant behaviors and thoughts become too close or demanding (e.g., ethnic minorities too strongly advocating their traditional religious values, drug users claiming the use of public space, or people on welfare complaining about insufficient support). Alternatively, it may transform into an asymmetric relationship in which the deviant individual is primarily seen as a medical problem or needy patient. In addition, tolerance tends to break down in situations or societies where individuals show a strong tendency to respond with fear, aggression, or care for other reasons than deviance, and "displace" these emotions on to deviant individuals.

In sum, tolerance is a special type of social control, implying that individuals try to deny the very existence of deviance and show restraint in responding to it, and leave it to others to engage in the actual process of repair or stigmatization. Ironically, although it is often assumed that tolerance goes together with respect for the deviant individual's person or "autonomy," we believe that in its usual form, it is more often associated with negative feelings and behavior that resemble stigmatization. Especially during face-to-face contact with deviant individuals, tolerance comes with characteristic psychological consequences such as dissociations between automatically triggered emotional and non-verbal responses to deviance and efforts to suppress these responses and to hide them by explicitly subscribing to social norms; tenseness, nervousness, ruminations, or lack of spontaneity as a result of these efforts at self-control; and tendencies to avoid the deviant individual in order to prevent experiencing these unpleasant and stressful consequences. Hence, tolerance may also come with a prize for the deviant individual as he or she may respond negatively to the other's self-focused attention and resulting psychological problems, and may want *more* than tolerance: to be spontaneously chosen and truly accepted as a relationship partner or responsible member of society on which one can rely for cooperation. What is unfortunate, however, is that social psychologists refer to these more complexly determined aspects of tolerance as *stigmatization*, although now frequently adding that it is "subtle," "modern," "unconscious," or "unintended" stigmatization, prejudice, or discrimination. Thus in a recently published book on stigmatization (Heatherton, Kleck, Hebl, & Hull, 2000), all contributors consistently use the terms "stigmatizer" and "(non)stigmatized" when describing, for example, the content of people's thoughts about deviant conditions or the awkward and tense moments described above, thereby placing on one line tolerance and social exclusion during, for example, the European Middle Ages or Nazi Germany. The literature is full of examples illustrating how the term stigmatization is overused and poorly defined. For example, it is maintained that stigmatization is equivalent to the normal psychological processes by which individuals hold each other responsible for bad conduct (Weiner, 1995); professionals in health care avoid contact with lethal contagious diseases such as AIDS (Crawford, 1996); or people choose healthy rather than chronically ill or disabled persons as dates or marriage partners (e.g., Bishop, 1991; Crandall & Moriarty, 1995).

Again, not clearly distinguishing one type of social control from another has undesirable theoretical consequences. Specifically, it may obscure the true psychological mechanisms behind both types of social control, with tolerance, as we will argue in the next chapter, fundamentally depending on a motivation to care for individuals seen as vulnerable, and stigmatization, more on fearful and aggressive tendencies that are more typically activated in competitive or hierarchical social structures or situations.

To conclude, much conceptual confusion in this vast area of research may be resolved by first realizing that any social group or society needs to engage in social control, and that, on the basis of universal psychological mechanisms (probably with evolutionary origins) and historical developments, social control may take three major forms: repair, stigmatization, and tolerance. Although each of these three types may be characteristic for different societies or historical periods, it is important to emphasize that within the same relationship or society, people may engage in all three types of social control. For example, although tolerance seems typical and functional for individualistic Western and urban society, the same society shows evidence of more blatant stigmatization in situations where deviance does not seem controllable by means of repair processes, or people can get away with it (e.g., when they are allowed to use punishment to teach the deviant individual a lesson; see Chapter 4); and as illustrated in Chapter 5, on the basis of personality differences, some individuals in that society may be more stigmatizing than others. Furthermore, small communities and families within modern Western society *do* engage in repair in which they explicitly address deviance. Moreover, although the European Middle Ages are characterized by extremely stigmatizing measures employed by those in power (Moore, 1987), care and tolerance (e.g., as preached by religion) were never entirely absent (Jutte, 1994). Lastly, in small communities characterized by repair, more stigmatizing responses to deviance may also occur, especially when deviant conditions are serious and unresponsive to repair (e.g., serial killings, madness) or under particular conditions (e.g., famine, warfare). It is our hope that the theoretical model presented in the next chapter helps to specify the circumstances and types of societies in which a particular type of social control will be especially likely.

## Empirical distinctions among the three types of social control

Although it is important to distinguish between the three types of social control for theoretical reasons, it should be acknowledged that it may not always be easy to distinguish them on empirical grounds. Specifically, the same response to deviance may have different reasons and consequences, dependent on the particular relationships with the deviant individual. This is especially likely to occur with preventive activities in the context of repair. For example, in modern Western society, and on the basis of current medical knowledge, an obese or heavily smoking person may receive aggressive responses by those who care for his or her well-being and fear that the person is a danger to his or her own health. In the context of an intimate relationship or family, these preventive repair responses certainly cannot be considered stigmatizing as the target can be reasonably sure that they are not directed at his or her character or moral reputation, do not require him or her to leave the relationship, and allow room for mutual adaptation and re-integration. However, when similar responses are directed at *strange* obese and smoking individuals outside a particular relationship or community, they normally can be interpreted as blaming and as imputing these individuals with an immoral character or bad reputation. After all, it is not clear if those criticizing their behavior really care about their well-being, want them back, or merely exercise power for their own benefits (e.g., because they do not want to spend health care money on these individuals, or do not want to be exposed to irritating and perhaps dangerous smoke). Finally, it may also not always be clear that those who are "tolerant" with respect to the observed eating behavior or smoking of individuals effectively suppress their negative responses and "respect" the persons involved; or actually engage in covert forms of repair or stigmatization (e.g., they may silently complain about their irresponsible behavior, appear less spontaneous, make ambiguous remarks in their presence, or gossip about them).

Other examples of the thin line between prevention in the context of repair and stigmatization can be derived from situations in which individuals associated with deviance are more seen as a danger or a nuisance to others than to themselves. Consider, for example, a severely injured person who, with the aid of modern medicine and years of extensive nurturing and training, has managed to adapt to his situation and is now able and motivated to look for a job primarily demanding intellectual skills. Unfortunately, the person remains in important respects dependent on the help of others because, for example, he needs to move around in a wheelchair and be assisted daily with several essential activities (e.g., carrying to the bathroom, washing, transporting, etc.). Are his prospective employers "stigmatizing" him when they deny him a job that primarily demands intellectual skills? Do they see the physical disability as an "essential" property of a bad person? Or do they engage in repair, simply by preventing the expected burden for the company and co-workers in adapting to the disabled person's presence?

And how about a person with a criminal record who is not allowed to become a police officer; a person with limited eyesight who cannot become an airline pilot; a pedophile who is denied a job as a baby sitter by a mother who also warns the whole neighborhood of his presence; or chronically ill or disabled persons who are not chosen as partners for dating or marriage? Are these individuals stigmatized? On the one hand, the answer is no; people respond in a functional and self-protective way to a specific deviant property of an individual, and do not necessarily want to exclude these individuals on a permanent basis from society. On the other hand, yes; these individuals are not given "a second chance" or specific aids in order to adapt themselves to the new situation, and may experience responses to their condition as exaggerated and denigrating, causing others to neglect their non-deviant and potentially positive attributes.

To conclude, although it is theoretically useful to distinguish repair, stigmatization, and the interpersonal consequences of tolerance it may sometimes be difficult to distinguish the three empirically. When in doubt, therefore, we will use the generally valid expressions "social responses to deviance" or "social control."

## 1.3 The present theoretical approach to social control

Until now, researchers tend to ignore commonalities as well as differences between repair, stigmatization, and tolerance; resulting in different researchers from the same or from different scientific disciplines independently producing a large amount of facts that appear difficult to integrate at a theoretical level. We believe that such an integration may be accomplished by first taking a step back to the basic psychological and evolutionary principles of social control. We argue in this book that, as a consequence of evolution, humans are endowed with psychological mechanisms that allow them to form relationships and societies in which deviance can be responded to in each of three ways, dependent on the type of deviance, individuals involved, and situational and cultural factors.

Our analysis starts with a classification of deviant conditions in terms of several basic types. We assume that certain psychological mechanisms evolved because they allowed group-living individuals to respond adaptively to these basic types. Specifically, from an evolutionary perspective, deviance may be considered a threat to the (inclusive) fitness or reproductive success of genetically related group members. Although we will make a distinction between different subtypes, the main categories of deviance that we will distinguish are "passive" deviance or reduced states of fitness (e.g., due to illness or injury) and "active" deviance or behaviors that threaten the fitness of others (e.g., aggression, bullying, stealing, lying). We assume that early mammalian evolution has resulted in brain mechanisms that helped individuals to respond adaptively to these main forms of deviance. Specifically, passive deviance can be responded to adaptively with the (parental) care system, a motivational system that motivates individuals to protect, nurture, and care for vulnerable others. Active deviance can be responded to adaptively with the fight-or-flight system, a system that motivates individuals to respond with escape and/or aggression to the selfish behavior of others. Because of their adaptiveness, these motivational systems, like most of an organism's other physical attributes and organs, were selected, retained, and inherited as a result of natural selection. Consequently, they will continue to play a causal role in behavior in later generations, even in environments that differ considerably from the environment in which these mechanisms originally evolved.

We attempt to show that, if these two motivational systems are combined into a neural structure in which they mutually inhibit or compete with each other for expression, a mechanism results that allows organisms to respond in flexible ways to a wide variety of threats to (inclusive) fitness, without needing more specific and advanced reasoning or "computational" procedures at higher cortical levels. However, the input and output to these motivational mechanisms may be further modified and stored in memory by an expanding neocortex capable of language use, symbol manipulation, and reasoning. This expansion may also result in relatively "cold" cognitions or beliefs, capable of influencing our thinking and behavior without fully activating the underlying motivational systems. We believe that a large number of psychological phenomena in relation to responding to deviance can be explained and integrated in terms of our proposed mechanisms. We also suggest that our use of language to describe the input, output, and functioning of these mechanisms may be responsible for the misleading impression that these mechanisms are essentially procedures for manipulating words or other symbols, a view that is common both in traditional cognitive psychology and in evolutionary psychology. Thus in our view, motivational systems like the fight-or-flight and care system can be conceived as language-independent *concepts* for the meaningful language that we use to describe the properties of deviant individuals and our emotional and behavioral reactions to them, in a manner that is both universal and independent from language and other culturally produced symbol systems.

How do the above motivational systems enable individuals to generate adaptive responses when confronted with deviance? First, taken separately, these mechanisms enable individuals to realize their goals by quickly adapting their current behavior to objective properties of the environment. Specifically, these mechanisms enable individuals to (a) accurately perceive, recognize, and differentiate between certain objective features of deviance (e.g., a threatening move forward, taking away food, a bodily injury, a cry for help); (b) get into the right motivational state or emotion at the right moment (e.g., fear, anger or tenderness), urging them to do the right thing (e.g., to flee, aggress, or protect) once these features occur; and (c) adapt their responses to the particular behavior of the deviant individual (while learning from past failures and successes) and persevere in responding until the harmful consequences are reduced (e.g., run until a safe distance has been reached, punish until the other changes his or her behavior or begs for forgiveness, nurture and heal until the other is cured and less dependent). Under the circumstances in which these mechanisms evolved and proved to enhance fitness, they normally allowed individuals to confirm the validity of their initial responses to the individual and to build up accurate internal representations of the environment (the vulnerable child or ill person usually starts crying when handled too roughly; a person with selfish motives will eventually act selfishly).

A second way in which the proposed mechanisms help group members to produce adaptive and fitness-promoting responses to deviance is through mutual competition. That is, the particular way in which the fight-or-flight and care system may compete with each other for expression, allows for considerable fine-tuning to the deviant individual's behavior and to the particular context in which the individual is encountered. For example, as we will argue in the next chapter, forgiveness of a selfishly acting individual who shows remorse (which involves displaying infantile and submissive behavior) may be caused by the inhibitory influence of the care system on the fight-or-flight system, resulting in a "softer" response. Similarly, mildly angry responses to vulnerable or ill persons who appear to neglect their health or fitness, or exaggerate or fake their dependency, may be explained in terms of the care system being partially inhibited by the fight-or-flight system. Especially when groups consist of genetically related individuals, the production of moderated or balanced responses to deviance seems highly adaptive, preventing group members from responding too violently to active deviance and too softly to passive deviance.

As shown extensively in the chapters which follow, this relatively simple network of two motivational systems may not only help to understand differences in responses to different deviant conditions; it also enables us to explain individual, situational, and cultural differences in responding to deviance in terms of the likelihood with which the two relevant motivational systems are activated in different individuals, situations, and societies. For example, we will argue that, due to a relatively strong activation of the care system, egalitarian societies are likely to engage in either repair processes when confronted with deviance (especially in small societies based on kinship) or tolerance (especially in modern and individualistic Western society). In contrast, due to a relatively strong activation of the fight-or-flight system, stigmatization is especially likely in hierarchically organized societies.

One theoretical advantage of our theory is its integrative power. Social scientists have independently studied responses to a wide variety of deviant conditions, without systematically comparing them with one another. Deviant conditions were usually classified on empirical grounds; for example, by letting research participants judge the similarities and differences between different conditions. As explained in Chapter 3, however, the "dimensions" and classifications found by this approach depend on the deviant conditions that happen to be included in the stimulus set, and the particular verbal labels the researcher uses to interpret these dimensions. In contrast, we offer a psychologically meaningful and theoretically derived typology of deviant conditions and show that, when carefully interpreted, a variety of empirically derived classifications is quite consistent with our typology. As noted above, this universal typology also allows us to compare in a much more systematic fashion how different societies or cultures deal with deviance.

Another distinctive feature of our theoretical approach is the systematic inclusion of caring or positive responses to deviance. We even explain certain negative responses to deviant conditions such as illness in terms of frustration of, and anger about, a basic motive to care for individuals associated with passive deviance (e.g., when these individuals appear to fake their illness, behave irresponsibly, or take a free ride). Our inclusion of care as one of the most important social motives in responding to deviance, sharply contrasts with other recent attempts to apply evolutionary theory to social control and stigmatization (e.g., Fishbein, 2002; Kurzban & Leary, 2001; Neuberg, Smith, & Asher, 2000).

## 1.4 Practical implications

Finally, our integrative approach has important practical implications. For most social scientists, the main reason for studying stigmatization is to get rid of it. Unfortunately, a failure to appreciate the importance of social control for any relationship or society, and not seeing stigmatization as a special type of social control, may actually result in interventions aimed at the extinction of social control, and frustration of those who need to engage in it. The reverse is also true. Those social scientists and practitioners developing interventions aimed at improving a society's repair processes may unwittingly help to promote the stigmatization of particular groups of people. Our approach may help to analyze this problem in greater detail and to adopt intervention strategies that limit undesirable social side-effects.

In the last chapter of this book, we show how our psychological theory of social control allows us to think about interventions aimed at stigma reduction in a more systematic way than has been common in this field. In particular, we will propose that the interventions should be tailored to the prevalent or appropriate type of social control and type of deviance involved.

First, consider tailoring to type of deviance. Type of deviance determines which motivational systems and corresponding emotions have to be targeted in order to influence responses to particular deviant conditions. For example, responses to active deviant conditions such as psychiatric illnesses or contagious and lethal diseases may only be successfully influenced when the underlying fight-or-flight system (responsible for fear) can be de-activated; e.g., by asking the deviant individual to display predictable and less threatening behavior or by other fear-reducing strategies. Similarly, the desire to care that tends to be evoked by conditions such as chronic illness or disability may be satisfied by an ill or disabled individual who sometimes asks for help but who also shows a strong motivation to cope effectively with his or her condition and to get well. Our theory suggests that effective ways to influence responses to deviance should take into account the needs and emotions of both perceivers and individuals with deviant conditions.

Now consider the additional tailoring of interventions to prevalent social control practices. When we attempt to reduce or prevent stigmatization, we may try to replace it with one of the two more benign types of social control: repair or tolerance. (Clearly, reducing stigmatization should not be equated with the elimination of responses to deviance or social control.) However, which of these two types is chosen should depend on the prevalence of the three types of social control in the individuals, situations, or societies concerned. For example, interventions aimed at increasing tolerance by alluding to general norms to be kind and to exercise self-control, may be effective when the prevalent type of social control is tolerance; for instance, when unrelated individuals are only required to have superficial contact with each other. Similarly, interventions aimed at increasing repair by letting deviant and non-deviant individuals explicitly address and negotiate over the consequences of a particular deviant condition, may be effective when repair is a main social control strategy in that particular setting; for instance, when the intervention is targeted at an existing egalitarian and intimate relationship or small community of mutually dependent individuals. In that situation, we may expect the individual associated with a deviant condition to become fully socially integrated (although the type and seriousness of deviance should also be taken into account).

In contrast, as Chapter 9 will extensively illustrate, we may expect less desirable effects when we try to increase tolerance when people are used or motivated to engage in repair processes or stigmatization. For example, current interventions that are focused on the prevention of illness and crime regularly make use of repair strategies that may be potentially stigmatizing, such as identifying and labeling certain individuals or groups "at risk" (young offenders, ethnic minorities, obese individuals, smokers), and educational programs that present these individuals to the public as "bad examples" and encourage it to adhere to self-control and responsibility in order to avoid illness and norm violations (Guttman & Salmon, 2004). Furthermore, repair processes in the community may also be unintentionally activated, for example, when a neighborhood is suddenly confronted with human service facilities attracting large groups of individuals associated with salient deviant conditions (e.g., drug users, homeless people). Clearly, in these different cases it does not make sense to focus stigma-reduction interventions primarily at increasing tolerance without first explicitly addressing people's desire to engage in repair which may conflict with tolerance.

To conclude, we propose that social scientists studying and intervening in social control adopt a broad theoretical perspective; based both on a sound psychological theory and knowledge of contextual, cultural, and historical influences. In general, it is unrealistic to assume that "contact" with individuals associated with deviance implies that one can accept these individuals and become friends without addressing the particular nature of deviance, and simply by looking more closely at their non-deviant and unexpected attributes; an assumption that forms the basis of the immensely popular "contact hypothesis" (Allport, 1954/1979; R. Brown & Hewstone, 2005) and which will be critically analyzed in Chapter 9.

## 1.5 Chapter overview

In the next chapter, using an evolutionary approach, we first attempt to classify the basic types of deviance that can occur in a small group of individuals, and then examine which psychological mechanisms are needed for the group to respond adaptively to these basic types and engage in effective social control. In addition, we examine the neurobiological evidence for these mechanisms, and closely consider how they can be responsible for expectancies, the content of representations, and emotions in general, and emotions (e.g., pity) and goals (e.g., nurturing) that are relevant for responding to deviance in particular. In Chapter 3, we attempt to show how the way people think and communicate about deviant conditions and about the emotional and behavioral responses to them, can be parsimoniously explained and organized in terms of our proposed psychological mechanisms. In Chapter 4, we explore in considerable detail, and primarily on the basis of social psychological experiments, how responses to deviance are caused by interactions between psychological mechanisms and the particular social context in which they are activated. In addition, we will outline how activated motivational systems and other variables, such as norms, operate to shape perceptions and behavior with respect to these individuals. In Chapter 5, we discuss how individual differences in responding to deviance (e.g., as related to personality or sex) may be explained in terms of differences in activation of basic psychological mechanisms. For example, we will argue that the negative responses of "authoritarians" to a wide variety of deviant conditions may be explained by the ease with which the fight-or-flight system can be activated in these individuals. In contrast, more compassionate or forgiving responses in "egalitarian" individuals may be due to the relative strong contribution of the care system. Chapter 6 discusses in broad terms how structural and cultural differences between societies and historical periods may influence the intensity of aggressive, fearful, and protective or kind responses to individuals with deviant conditions. Here we will construct a typology of societies that primarily cope with deviance in terms of repair, stigmatization, or tolerance, respectively. Chapters 7 and 8 examine in detail how, in current Western societies, individuals with deviant conditions cope with negative responses to their conditions, and what the tangible and psychological outcomes are that eventually result from those conditions. These issues are relevant not only to reveal the specific needs and ways of coping with stigmatization of individuals with deviant conditions; but also because, as our previous analysis suggests, it is not self-evident that people primarily respond in stigmatizing ways to deviance. Hence, deviant persons' self-esteem or well-being should be complexly determined by the nature of their deviant condition, their coping, and the particular way in which different responses to them are perceived. Finally, Chapter 9 explores the practical implications of our approach. We will propose and illustrate that a broad theoretical perspective that integrates issues of repair, stigmatization, and tolerance, may be useful to examine the different consequences of attempts to reduce stigmatization or improve a society's repair potential. In addition, we demonstrate that a more detailed understanding of how our proposed psychological mechanisms are involved in responding to particular types of deviant conditions, may help to more effectively influence the responses to these conditions.

## 1.6 Summary

In this introductory chapter, we outlined our approach to study social responses to deviance and the plan of this book. In this approach we distinguished between three patterns of social control or responding to deviance: Repair, stigmatization, and tolerance. Social control is unavoidable and functional in any relationship or society and aims at changing deviant conditions or reducing their harmful consequences. In intimate relationships, families, or small communities, social control can be viewed as a process directed at repairing relationships, often on the basis of negotiation and making mutual adaptations between the different parties involved. Stigmatization represents responses that are often functional in the context of hierarchical relationships, and more directed at a person's character or identity and that are related to prejudice and discrimination. Finally, tolerance is also founded on elementary processes of social control that are triggered by the perception of deviant conditions, but that, due to internal restraints and social norms, express themselves only in a limited way in behavioral responses.

Although repair, stigmatization, and tolerance have unique psychological aspects – this is one of the reasons why they are often treated separately, also in an applied sense – they have important psychological mechanisms in common. More specifically, we distinguish two major motivational systems that produce adaptive responses to deviance. In the case of active deviance, which threatens other persons (e.g., criminality), the fight-or-flight system is activated, motivating individuals to escape or aggress. Passive deviance, which implies reduced fitness (e.g. illness), on the other hand, activates the motivational care system, which brings persons to protect and care for vulnerable others. Under particular circumstances, e.g., when threats unrelated to deviance occur, the activated motivational systems may give rise to phenomena more commonly associated with stigmatization. Under other circumstances, internal restraints and social norms result in suppression of the behavioral output of these motivational systems.

This approach can integrate quite diverse research findings and provide us with a theoretically based classification of deviant conditions. It also allows insight into how relevant meanings and the content of representations of deviance are established. In addition, positive or caring responses to deviance are not neglected. Furthermore, context effects due to culture or situation can easily be explained in terms of activation of the motivational systems, and finally a number of practical implications result. This chapter also discussed important conceptual and terminological issues concerning deviance and stigma, and attempted to offer a more precise definition of stigmatization.

## CHAPTER 2

# Evolutionary origins of social responses to deviance

## 2.1 Introduction

What is the best way to classify the many deviant conditions that are possible in human societies? Is it possible to distinguish between basic or universal types of deviance that can be found in any society or historical period? And how can we organize and explain the wide variety of responses that can be observed across different types of deviance, individuals, situations, and societies? Is it possible that these different responses can be explained in terms of a limited number of psychological mechanisms? Answering both kinds of questions – about categorizing deviant conditions and the responses to them – would greatly assist us in organizing and integrating the enormous amount of facts about social responses to deviance that are available.

We believe that current evolutionary theorizing could be of great help in simultaneously answering these two kinds of questions. In particular, it should be possible to describe the basic features of early human societies, argue that these societies needed to cope with a limited number of basic types of deviance in order to function effectively, and speculate about the psychological mechanisms that should have been selected for (or "designed") by evolution to make these adaptive responses possible, and that were retained or genetically inherited by later generations. For example, we may describe these early societies as small groups of genetically related and cooperating individuals engaged in simple subsistence activities, note that a common type of deviance consists of a variety of selfish behaviors such as the non-sharing or stealing of food, and infer that, in order to respond adaptively to this type of deviance, group members should have had the psychological capacity to recognize it, get angry about it, and punish the responsible individuals. Although basically this will be the way in which we will proceed in this chapter, two problems associated with such an evolutionary approach, especially when applied to human mental and behavioral processes, should be noted.

First, we have to be clear about the nature of the psychological mechanisms that we are looking for, and of their inputs and outputs.

Are we looking for procedures for thinking and reasoning *about* the world with the use of words or other symbols ("software" programs)? Or is it neural mechanisms (instincts, motivational systems) that we are looking for; mechanisms that do not need symbols for their functioning, yet are somehow responsible for the meaning of the words or other symbols that we use to describe the content of our thoughts, emotions, and behavior with respect to deviance? Recent attempts to combine evolutionary theory with cognitive psychology, resulting in the field of *evolutionary psychology* (Buss, 1999; Pinker, 1997; Tooby & Cosmides, 1992), tend to equate psychological mechanisms with reasoning or symbol manipulation according to rules or instructions (an attitude that is associated with mentalism or mind-body dualism), and are not bothered very much with finding neurophysiological evidence for the existence of the proposed mechanisms (this point will receive more attention at the end of this chapter). Consequently, these theoretical developments may result in postulating more "specifically designed" psychological mechanisms than actually needed to properly explain observed variability and context-dependency of human behavior. Although evolutionary psychologists acknowledge the importance of adaptive perceptual and motivational mechanisms that are much older than the environment in which typically human traits would have evolved, and which evolved to solve adaptive problems faced by mammals in general (e.g., Duchaine, Cosmides, & Tooby, 2001), they tend to play a minor role in evolutionary psychology's explanations of currently observed social behavior. Reading evolutionary psychology's account of the origin of "typically human" psychological mechanisms, one gets the impression that most proposed adaptations were newly invented some 150,000 years ago (during our existence in small groups of hunter-gatherers), and that the brain of our human ancestors would allow the evolution of virtually every specific psychological adaptation imagined to be adaptive in that particular environment. This is strange as some very old motivational mechanisms such as those involved in aggression, defense, and parental care seem so universally adaptive that they must have been used in later evolved mechanisms. Currently, the view of a multi-modular, Swiss-army-knife kind of mind, consisting of a theoretically unlimited number of computational procedures, is much criticized (e.g., Fodor, 2000; Holcomb, 1998; Lloyd, 1999; Panksepp & Panksepp, 2000). Our position in this debate is that we should proceed in a parsimonious way, starting with a limited set of evolutionary very old and important psychological mechanisms, and then see how far we get in explaining more complex mental phenomena that are based on language or other symbol systems (cf. Grossberg, 1980).

A second problem in applying evolutionary theory to explain social responses to deviance is that it is tempting to focus exclusively on the evolution of negative (e.g., fearful, aggressive) responses, thereby forgetting that caring and more positive responses to deviance may have been equally adaptive in our evolutionary past. As will be argued below, most evolutionary views of social control and stigmatization concentrate on how genetically unrelated individuals in large social groups respond to failures to cooperate or reciprocate; either because individuals are unmotivated to sufficiently cooperate (and "cheat"), or are unable to do so, for example because they are ill or disabled (e.g., Cosmides & Tooby, 1992; Kurzban & Leary, 2001; Neuberg *et al.*, 2000; Tooby & Cosmides, 1996). Unfortunately, such a perspective neglects to show that particular types of deviance such as illness should also receive care (e.g., because the deviant condition implies reduced fitness of kin), that "cheating" or social parasitism may only occur in light of a strong motivation to care for the former type of deviance, and that true cases of criminal cheating among kin may also be responded to in more caring, forgiving, or "softer" ways.

In order to address the problem of mentalism and neglect of caring tendencies in evolutionary accounts of social control and stigmatization, we decided to return to the most basic questions that can be asked with respect to social control: how can individuals who are essentially selfish in a genetical sense, but also share copies of their genes, live together, share, and cooperate (cf. Campbell, 1982)? What are the main types of threats to fitness or reproductive success (i.e., types of deviance) that can occur in such a social group, and what are the basic psychological mechanisms needed to respond adaptively to these threats? In answering these questions, we will be extremely parsimonious. That is, we go back to Hamilton's (1964) elementary genetic principles of inclusive fitness or kinship-based altruism and Dawkins' (1976, 1982, 1989) applications of them, and only allow psychological mechanisms that are known to have motivational or emotional implications, and that can use non-symbolic events as input and output (although, of course, interacting with language and other symbol systems). Furthermore, these psychological mechanisms should have a neurophysiological basis and such a fundamental evolutionary importance (e.g., rooted in mechanisms for defense, aggression, or parental care) that they are likely to constrain later evolutionary and genetic influences. In this book, we will attempt to show that these mechanisms not only are necessary, but often also sufficient to explain the great variation in responses to deviance that can be observed across deviant conditions, individuals, and societies. Thus, rather than assuming the evolution of a specific psychological mechanism for each and every problem of social control that would have bothered our ancestors, we demonstrate how far we get in accounting for variation in responding by using only a few basic motivational mechanisms and a few elementary evolutionary principles of social living.

## 2.2 The evolution of social control

To gain a basic understanding of the adaptations that are necessary for social control, it is useful to distinguish four levels of analysis and to try to understand the relationships among them: the level of genes, individual organisms with their specific adaptive physical and behavioral properties, relationships between individuals, and societies consisting of different types of relationships. In general, social control refers to solving the problem of how relationships and societies are possible while there is essential selfishness at the level of genes and individuals.

Genes are the smallest chemical units with a capacity to replicate or make copies of themselves. Genes produce effects on their environment, resulting in bodies or organisms with particular physical and behavioral properties that help to protect them against their environment (which consists of other genes) and to make use of opportunities offered by this environment to replicate. It is illuminating to consider genes or "replicators" as essentially "selfish" in their endeavor to make as many copies of themselves as possible, at the cost of other genes. Genes can be considered to be in competition with each other for "food" (they may also be used as "food" themselves) or other resources for replication. Thus successful replication of one gene may result in other genes becoming less numerous and eventually their extinction (Dawkins, 1976, 1982, 1989).

Importantly, genes do not "want" to replicate; they just do it whenever possible. Instead, they happen to exist in bodies that "are motivated" and have the capacity to help them replicate under the right conditions, and thus increase their frequency. On an extremely large time-scale, evolution "selects" individual organisms with those properties (or "phenotypes") that happen to increase the genes' success to replicate in the particular environment in which these organisms live, and that are coded for by the particular genes that happen to be present in the selected organisms. It is in this sense that we can say that genes try to "predict" which properties or phenotypes will best serve their selfish tendency to replicate.

At the level of individual organisms, it also useful to speak of the "selfishness" of individuals that are complexly produced by multiple genes that code for the many different physical and behavioral properties that make up a single organism; and hence of their reproductive success or fitness as the number of offspring produced that live long enough to reproduce themselves. (We leave out the problem of how multiple competing genes manage to build a single organism with a body and properties that help all the genes involved in this process to replicate. For a discussion, see Dawkins, 1976; 1982.)

The general problem of the genes and evolution in "designing" bodies that help genes to replicate can be analyzed in terms of three subproblems that have to be solved: self-preservation (eat and prevent from being eaten), reproduction (make as many copies of genes as possible), and altruism (promote self-preservation and reproduction of organisms carrying copies of one's genes). Self-preservation refers to the problem that genes and the organisms they code for, should have some stability or longevity; at the very least, they should live until they manage to replicate successfully. This implies that organisms should have adaptive physical and behavioral properties that help them to find and consume food (prey), and to prevent contact with other organisms that have the same goal (predators). Reproduction in its sexual form requires finding a suitable mate. At the very least, this mate should have "good" or "healthy" genes that help to code for properties that increase the chances of the new combinations of genes, and the new properties in offspring the latter code for, to self-preserve and reproduce.

Altruism basically refers to the problem of *not* letting self-preservation goals prevail during contact with organisms carrying copies of one's genes, such as the products of previous reproduction (offspring) and other kin. That is, kin should not be eaten and not be damaged in the process of defending oneself against *their* self-preservation needs. In addition, altruism should result in properties that help promote the self-preservation and reproductive success of offspring and other kin. The "ruthless selfishness" of genes (cf. Dawkins, 1976) allows us to appreciate one of the most basic but counterintuitive insights of neo-Darwinism: that altruistic properties of individuals and eventually individuals' capacity to form social relationships and live in societies, derive from the selfish tendencies of genes actually helping and cooperating with their own copies.

Together, physical and behavioral properties beneficial for self-preservation, altruism, and reproduction are said to enhance the fitness or reproductive success of genes and individuals. Because this not only involves the fitness of a single individual but also the fitnesses of all other individuals with which the individual shares the same genes, this is also called *inclusive* fitness (Hamilton, 1964). At an elementary evolutionary level, we see deviance as a threat to inclusive fitness and will distinguish *active* deviance or behavior that reduces the fitness of others (e.g., crime, madness) from *passive* deviance or actual states of reduced fitness in others (e.g., illness, injury), which are often a consequence of active deviance.

Before examining the nature of adaptive properties that make self-preservation, altruism, and reproduction a success for organisms and their genes, it is important to introduce the third level of analysis: relationships. Organisms that have the opportunity to repeatedly interact and hence form a relationship with each other, are generally better able to enhance their fitness because they (and their genes) will be better able to predict and hence control the fitness consequences of these encounters. In terms of self-preservation, antagonistic relationships will be formed between prey and predator, or weak and strong opponents. Altruism results in relationships between parents and offspring, brothers and sisters, nephews and nieces, and kinship in general. Finally, sexual reproduction results in relationships between males and females.

Relationships, in turn, result in the evolution of mutual adaptations that allow interacting individuals to make better use of the predictable fitness consequences, also called "evolutionary arms races" (Dawkins, 1976, 1982). For example, the more evolution selects predators with properties that allow them to effectively spot, hunt down, and kill their prey, the more it will favor prey that are effective in hiding, camouflaging, detecting predators, and escaping from them. The latter tendency, in turn, favors the selection of predators that are still more effective in preying, and so on. The concept of arms races is also helpful to understand how mutually adaptive properties evolve in relationships between dominant and submissive individuals, parents and offspring (or caregivers and recipients in general), and males and females.

Finally, a society organizes these different relationships in particular ways and attaches particular values to them. For example, some societies highly value a reproductive system based on male dominance and therefore not only suppress the freedom of females but also systematically engage in stigmatization of a variety of deviant conditions that threaten the prevalent dominance relationships. Other societies strongly value a reproductive system based on egalitarian relationships and, dependent on the level of kinship or individualism, primarily engage in repair in response to deviance or adopt a tolerant attitude.

Let us now have a closer look at the nature of the behavioral properties that help individual organisms to successfully enhance their fitness or reproductive success. We will call these properties *psychological mechanisms* as they cause or motivate the organism to respond in the right (fitness promoting) way under the right (fitness promoting or threatening) circumstances. For present purposes, it is not yet important to distinguish sharply between cognitive (e.g., perceptions, expectancies, interpretations, beliefs), emotional or motivational, and behavioral aspects of these responses. We simply assume that cognitive, emotional, and behavioral aspects are three aspects of one and the same motivational state of the organism, caused when an underlying psychological mechanism (motivational system, instinct) is triggered by the perception of certain key environmental features or trigger stimuli. We will now examine psychological mechanisms that generate adaptive responses to deviance in the context of self-preservation and altruism.[1]

### Self-preservation and the evolution of the fight-or-flight system

In order to survive until reproduction is possible, organisms should have a neural structure or motivational system that we shall call the *fight-or-flight system* (FF system, for short). Such a system allows individual organisms to (a) attack other individuals and feed on them, (b) escape from others who want to attack or feed on them, and (c) prevent others from attacking and feeding on them by threatening and attacking them. (Neurophysiological evidence for the fight-or-flight system will be discussed later in this chapter.) It is easy to see why the latter two aspects make the FF system one of the psychological cornerstones of social control, enabling the prevention of fitness loss or deviance in groups of individuals (the other cornerstone being the ability to restore actual states of reduced fitness due to attacks or illness; see below). A tendency to escape or feel fear is necessary to sense a threat to fitness, while a tendency to aggress, feel anger, and punish is necessary to prevent these threats from materializing into actual injury or harm.

But how do individuals decide when to attack or escape? Assuming that all selfish individuals involved are endowed with the same FF system, and hence able to induce fear and an expectancy of attack in others, the following three decision rules seem to make sense. (Importantly, we are not suggesting that these rules are expressed in terms of symbols, and logical relations among them, let alone in terms of language, and that organisms engage in symbolic reasoning. What we suggest is that organisms behave *as if* they follow these rules.)

(1) If you cannot predict how another individual will attack, escape as soon as the other comes in sight. This is a useful rule when other individuals are strangers to you and you have no opportunity to learn about their habits and predict their behavior.
(2) If you have had the opportunity to observe other individuals for a while and learn about their behavioral patterns, habits, or

behavioral "rules" they follow, then make an unpredictable attack on them. However, since attacking is costly and may result in counterattacks, it would be better for preventive reasons, to merely *suggest* a capability and motivation to attack. That is, follow their habits, keep a close eye on them, and show only a little aggression while merely suggesting an attack (e.g., stare, growl, frown, or move a little forward) when you suspect and fear they will deviate from their habits or "rules"; but increase your aggression and actually punish, once the deviation gets more serious and they really need to be taught a lesson. This rule already introduces one of the elementary senses in which deviant individuals are "held responsible" for the fitness-reducing consequences of their behavior, and explains why we get more angry at deviant individuals the more we see them as responsible. That is, the more individuals are predictable and controllable in terms of the habits or "rules" they follow, and the more they should know that I keep a close watch on them and have already slightly warned and punished them, the more they ought to foresee that deviations from these "rules" arouses anger in me, and the more responsibility or self-control I may demand. Getting angry at controllable or "responsible" deviant individuals is like saying "stick to what you usually do and on which we agreed" or "conform to the expectations or norms." In contrast, associating behavior with unpredictability, impulsivity, and immutability, is similar to holding deviant individuals less responsible for their behavior and its consequences. (When we later discuss passive deviance, we will encounter two additional meanings of responsibility.)

(3) Launch a counterattack if another attacking individual has already physically contacted you and injury is unavoidable. Here, aggression is used as a last resort to escape from bodily contact with a predator or opponent, and therefore should be vigorous, all-or-nothing, panic-like, furious, or "hysterical."

To summarize, based solely on individuals interacting in terms of the FF system, one can distinguish two major types of active fitness threats or active deviance: threats that are rather unpredictable and those that can be predicted and controlled on the basis of knowing or guessing the other individual's habits, behavioral plans or strategies, states of mind, or "intentions." Examples of uncontrollable-active (Type 1) deviance include all kinds of opportunistic attacks by invisible predators (e.g., contagious and dangerous bacteria or viruses, larger predators lying in ambush) or opponents, and can generally be associated with "crazy" behavior or "madness"; and more diffuse threats signaled by abnormal

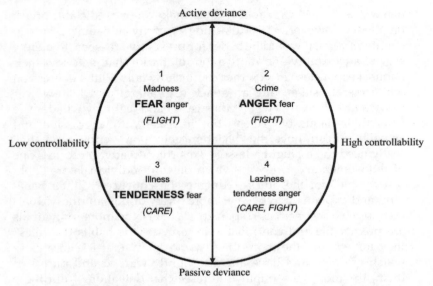

**Figure 2.1** Four basic types of deviance, commonly used labels, and major emotional responses. (Capitalized and bold faced emotion words express relatively strong emotional intensity. The main motivational systems involved are mentioned within parentheses.)

and strange physical or "crooked" appearance. Examples of controllable-active (Type 2) deviance include all kinds of intentional or pre-meditated attacks on others and their resources for reproduction such as stealing or destroying their food, territory, or mates (i.e., "criminal" behavior), but also behaviors that are inconsistent with norms and values. Note that, of the four types of deviance that we distinguish, Type 2 deviance probably represents the most heterogeneous category as there are as many norm violations possible as there are specific behavioral norms to be violated across different societies and cultures.

Figure 2.1 shows how these two types of deviance are associated with different kinds of emotions and also what their relationship is with the other two major types of deviance that we will distinguish in this book. As can be seen, the four types of deviance are distinguished in terms of active versus passive deviance and low versus high controllability, and associated with a unique pattern of emotions due to the activation of the underlying motivational systems. Active deviance is especially associated with anger and fear because the underlying FF system is relatively strongly activated. In the case of passive deviance, the care system is more strongly activated than the FF system, resulting in the experience of tenderness (see below). Finally, controllable types of deviance result in relatively strong levels of anger, while uncontrollable types are more associated with fear than anger.

In the absence of kinship-based altruism, it is already instructive to examine what type of active deviance is the most common among a group of individuals who primarily control each other's behavior on the basis of the FF system. Among these individuals, relationships between prey and predator, or weak and strong opponents are likely to evolve that are based on inheritable differences in the capacity to harm and subdue others, and that are signaled by their size, strength, or armor. As noted above, evolutionary arms races between prey and predator result in the selection of physical and behavioral properties that help the two to mutually adapt to each other's selfish tendencies. Dominance relationships between opponents of the same species can also be viewed as emerging from an evolutionary arms race, resulting in an asymmetry in the physical properties and behavioral strategies with which less and more powerful opponents, who also have the most resources for reproduction, adapt to each other's behavior.

For the strongest or dominant opponents, the main problem is that they can better prevent than predict an attack from weaker or submissive opponents. For the latter, the main problem is that they can better predict than prevent an attack from the dominant ones. Specifically, being strong and dominant, busily exercising and maintaining one's power (e.g., patrolling one's territory, punishing petty thieves), implies that one is highly visible and predictable to other individuals who try to steal resources or take over power. Therefore, because of their greater opportunity to watch and observe the dominant opponent, the main strategy of submissive individuals will consist of planning opportunistic attacks on him, keeping a low profile, and testing him once in a while for weak spots and moments. In contrast, the general strategy of the dominant individual at first may consist of hysterical punishments directed at the deviant individual, with vigorous attacks, chasings, and furious beatings and bitings (cf. Clutton-Brock & Parker, 1995). But to the extent that other dominated individuals are around, a more efficient strategy would be to issue *general* and public warnings that others should not steal or attack and keep their place. The latter strategy may be considered the most elementary form of stigmatization in a competitive or hierarchical social system. First, dominant individuals will try to increase the predictability of attacks or deviance by singling out, remembering, or "labeling" individuals once they commit a deviant act. Second, they will punish these individuals extensively, not only to make sure they will refrain from any future attempts to question or overthrow their power, but also to teach others present a lesson. The public nature of the elaborate and time-consuming punishments by the dominant individual also has another useful function. It allows the submissive and fearful public to take part in the lengthy beatings, tortures, and denigration; directing or "displacing" its aggression more at the deviant individual than those in power. In sum, stigmatization in a hierarchical relationship is not simply a brief act of aggression, but a process by which the individual is exposed to public aggression and associated with a shameful identity, reputation, and label or stigma. When killed, the killing itself is not as important as the public exposure of the criminal's harm and suffering. This pattern of punishment and stigmatization is exactly what we see in many non-human animals (e.g., Clutton-Brock & Parker, 1995) and many hierarchically organized human societies (e.g., Black, 1984; Horwitz, 1990; Moore, 1987). As we will see below, although stigmatization serves an important function in hierarchical relationships, it is not unavoidable in human relationships, especially not in particular egalitarian relationships based on altruism and kinship.

As the society increases in complexity and size due to division of labor, and dominated individuals get increasingly out of sight and start to engage in more differentiated relationships, a hierarchical system can only be maintained by imposing an increasingly differentiated set of rules or laws to be obeyed and by alluding to internalized restraints in adhering to these rules (cf. Campbell, 1982). In a relatively simple, face-to-face hierarchical system, uncontrollable and opportunistic forms of active deviance should be more frequent than the more predictable and controllable forms, because the latter are mainly used by the few individuals who are in power. In contrast, in more complex and individualistic hierarchical systems, controllable-active deviance should be more common because now, dominated individuals can commit a variety of intentional norm violations or crimes. Consequently, their punishment will increasingly take place away from the public and be primarily directed at getting confessions, mental change, brainwashing, and indoctrination. Indeed, it can be argued that the main modern function of punishment by those in power is to shape and monitor the behavior of (potential) criminals in and outside "correction" centers (cf. Foucault, 1975/1977).[2]

## Altruism and the evolution of the care system

Properties that promote altruism toward offspring and kin should first of all help promote the self-preservation and reproductive success of offspring; hence result in a capacity for parenting. Equally fundamental should be a tendency of *not* letting self-preservation needs prevail during contact with organisms carrying copies of one's genes such as offspring and other kin. This would argue for the evolution of a motivational system that can operate independently from the FF system and can overrule it. Like the FF system, it should also be triggered in a relatively unconditional manner; this time the only conditions being that the other is kin and urgently needs assistance and protection. We will call this motivational system the care system (C system for short), associate it with the emotion of tenderness (see Figure 2.1), and discuss its neurophysiological correlates later in this chapter.

It seems likely that the general property to protect and help needy kin in general, has evolved from the more specific motivational mechanism involved in parental care. Dawkins (1989, p. 281) argues that there may not have been a single mutant gene responsible "for" an entirely new behavioral pattern characteristic for altruism toward kin in general, but a step-by-step genetic alteration of pre-existing neural structures controlling parental care. For example, altruism toward brothers and sisters may simply occur because the parental care system is allowed to start firing at a much younger age in offspring once they perceive the infantile and vulnerability cues in their brothers and sisters. Perhaps, parental care itself has evolved from a self-healing mechanism motivating organisms to restore fitness loss caused by injuries from attacks by predators or opponents. For example, it is known that in many species, wounded individuals rub afflicted parts, take rest, and even eat medicinal plants (Fábrega, 1997). Once this mechanism is in place, it can further evolve into a mechanism that is also triggered by recognizing states of reduced fitness in offspring. Dawkins (1976, see also Axelrod & Hamilton, 1981) has also suggested that principles of kin selection and parental care help explain the evolution of generalized reciprocity among strangers, first independently establishing patterns of cooperation in multiple smaller groups of kin or families, then spreading throughout the population when cooperation among members of different groups would prove successful too.

The most important goal of care is to prevent fitness reduction in vulnerable offspring (the most attractive target for predators or strong opponents) and to raise them as soon as possible to maturity and independence so that they can start taking care of themselves. Many species display a minimal amount of parental care such as temporary feeding and protection of offspring. But parenting is most powerfully developed in mammals who considerably invest time and energy in raising offspring (Bell, 2001; MacLean, 1985).

It is important to emphasize that the mechanism responsible for parenting is entirely different from, and in certain respects opposite in nature to, the adaptive solution to the problem of active deviance. That is, if there is one outstanding feature of mammalian parental care, it is that it often lacks any signs of aggression and is associated with such behaviors as gentle and tender handling, licking, giving warmth, embracing, feeding, and so on. Clearly, parents act as if their infants have a label attached that reads "Fragile! Handle with care!"

Just as self-preservation, altruism is also associated with the problem of predictability and controllability of fitness loss, yet this time with respect to potential fitness loss in *others* such as offspring and kin. Predictability of these threats to fitness first depends on the two types of deviance introduced above. That is, vulnerable offspring may be attacked in more or less predictable ways by predators or strong opponents. The response of parents would be the same as when these attacks are directed at themselves; hence, they may aggressively defend their offspring against predictable dangers, but flee in the face of unpredictable ones.

However, an entirely new type of fitness threat or deviance (Type 3, see Figure 2.1) is introduced when the offspring actually suffer fitness loss that could not have been prevented, but which may still be reduced by care, healing, and nurturing that is explicitly directed at the offspring. Examples of this type of deviance include illnesses and injuries due to the sudden or invisible attacks by predators such as bacteria or viruses, or by opponents from the same species, or injuries due to "accidents" caused by the offspring's carelessness. Clearly, this type of deviance, due to its fear-arousing properties, should activate both the care system and the flight component of the FF system; and the more the latter is activated, the greater the likelihood that the parent will experience less care and more fear (a motivational state that we call *pity*, see below), and may even abandon or kill the offspring. Usually, care not only involves preventing these accidents from happening but also responding with healing efforts that are likely to restore the other's reduced fitness (e.g., licking afflicted parts; relaxation) and "education" and punishment in order to teach offspring how to prevent these events from happening again.

The evolution of care not only results in the emergence of Type 3 deviance within relationships and societies, but also in changes in the frequency with which Type 1 and 2 deviance occur in relationships between genetically related individuals and in the manner in which they are responded to by kin. That is, any aggressive or deviant behavior and the punishment for it should now take into account that it may be directed toward copies of one's own genes. This would necessitate the evolution of mechanisms allowing individuals to both induce aggression-inhibition or care in others (e.g., showing remorse, offering apologies) and responding in softer ways to these attempts (e.g., to forgive).

The problem of altruism and care also introduces a fourth type of fitness threat or deviance that is the most difficult to understand because it lies on the border between Type 3 deviance, which involves a relationship between caregiver and care recipient, and a symmetrical, reciprocal, and cooperative relationship between adults. It is important that we try to explain this type of deviance and the responses to it as well as possible because it is one of the most dominant types in a modern and caring Western society, but is often confused with the three other types and therefore incorrectly explained. Whereas the first three types consider deviant individuals who are perceived as crazy, criminal, or ill, respectively, the fourth type essentially deals with individuals perceived as lazy or "pathetic" or as social parasites or free riders; those who continue to arouse our care and generosity but at the same time anger us because they seem capable of taking care of themselves and to engage in reciprocal relationships (and once in a while can be observed performing well in these relationships), but do not seem sufficiently motivated to do so on a continuous basis. Here, predictability and controllability refer to a perceived lack of motivation to engage in reciprocal relationships (see Figure 2.1). Thus the anger that the lazy person or free rider arouses is usually not as intense as the anger aroused by Type 2 deviance such as stealing from, or harming others, because it is mixed with tenderness. We call the composite emotional state of moderate levels of care and anger, *disrespect*. (Note that in Figure 2.1, this state is seen as equivalent to a moderate activation of both the C system and the fight component of the FF system.)

Throughout this book we will examine extensively social responses to three important categories of Type 4 deviance. First, individuals with chronic illnesses and physical or mental disabilities who manage to engage in a limited form of reciprocity with a few other individuals (e.g., parents, friends, teachers), but who are easily viewed by strangers as social parasites, especially in situations where they cannot be observed performing socially valued tasks. Two other and more recent forms of Type 4 deviance also belong to this category: individuals who do not seem to care about their own health and fitness (e.g., the obese, smokers), and those who claim to be patients and therefore deserving of care and medical treatment, but who suffer from relatively unreliable, vague, unexplained, or invisible physical or mental symptoms (e.g., chronic fatigue syndrome or fibromyalgia, cf. Looper & Kirmayer, 2004).

The second important category of Type 4 deviance consists of individuals who are forced into a role of permanent dependency by relationship partners or societies who are willing (if reluctantly) to care for them, but can or want to do little to get them out of their care-receiving role. Specifically, in these relationships, which are more similar to parent-offspring than to dominant-submissive or power relationships, both parties gain sufficient benefits. One, because the benefits of receiving help from others are obvious; the other, because giving help or engaging in charity satisfies a strongly activated care system and reduces guilt. At the level of societies, this category of Type 4 deviance consists of a wide variety of groups with low socioeconomic statuses which are produced by an increasing division of labor in society, with associated differences in fitness and satisfied need states. The most salient are beggars, the poor, and the homeless. Yet, according to the prevalent views and reactions of those with high socioeconomic status (e.g., the well-to-do, those with non-manual and intellectual jobs, academics, and urbanites), a wide variety of other groups with low socioeconomic statuses (e.g., manual laborers, peasants, and ethnic minorities who are likely to occupy these economic roles such as guest workers from African countries in Europe or African-Americans and Mexicans in the USA) are also associated with Type 4 deviance. These individuals tend to be disrespected by those who structurally care for them (e.g., in the form of institutionalized systems of charity, or provisions made by the welfare state) and viewed as strong but stupid, pleasure-loving, childlike, lazy, loud, and dirty (LeVine & Campbell, 1972, pp. 156–157; Lott, 2002; Smedley & Bayton, 1978).

Finally note that the two categories of Type 4 deviance often appear in combination. That is, the second category is likely to create illness and disability, whereas the well-to-do and those with non-manual jobs manage to stay relatively healthy. Clearly, the more individuals associated with social parasitism can be viewed as suffering and needy (cf. the beggar in the street), the more guilt about leaving them in this situation will be felt. It is not surprising that since the Middle Ages, almsgiving and charity, are not only institutionalized in order to provide for the poor, but also to give the well-to-do the opportunity to conform to religious altruistic duties and to reduce guilty feelings (Jutte, 1994).

Similar to hierarchical relationships and societies that start to stigmatize Type 2 deviance for functional reasons, care-based or egalitarian relationships and societies may want to single out, label, and stigmatize individuals associated with Type 4 deviance, in order to warn people of their suspected lazy and cheating character. Furthermore, we may expect that in our circle of deviance (see Figure 2.1), Type 4 deviance increasingly migrates to Type 1 and 2 deviance. For example, as soon as individuals associated with Type 4 deviance stick together, protest against their bad situation, and make demands for improvement, they will be seen as a threat to the social order and easily associated with madness or crime.

In order to further understand the nature of Type 4 deviance or social parasitism, its strange position on the border between Type 3 deviance and true reciprocity, and the tolerance of caregivers and others for incomplete reciprocity (giving more than receiving back), it is helpful to appreciate that normal reciprocity itself may be based on a care-based tolerance for moderate levels of non-reciprocity, cheating, or even "stealing." So, what exactly are the psychological mechanisms behind reciprocity, cooperation, or sharing; interactions in which people are usually *not* considered deviant but "normal"? Although other theorists acknowledge a strong relation exists between reciprocity in strangers and kinship-based altruism (e.g., Dawkins, 1989; Humphrey, 1997; Krebs, 1998), this relationship has never been fully analyzed in terms of the proximate psychological mechanisms associated with the care system.

At first sight, the involvement of kinship-based altruism, let alone parental care, in reciprocity, sharing, exchange or cooperation among adults is hardly visible, because the need states of both individuals are often not acute, and helping and sharing is not costly and primarily involves sharing surplus fitness resources with others, or letting others profit from one's own fitness-promoting behavior without any additional costs. We argue, however, that the care system may be involved in a rather subtle way, enabling individuals to tolerate the gaps and time-delays that are inherent in cooperation and reciprocity. During patterns of cooperation and reciprocity, individuals doing or giving a little less than others because others do or give a little more, find (perhaps associated with some guilt) that they do not immediately restore the associated reduced fitness of others. Yet, they are first allowed to restore the other's fitness or "pay back" the other's investment when the latter is temporarily doing a little less or explicitly asks for assistance. (A quite different pattern of often hostile reciprocity will emerge when individuals give gifts that are unsolicited and meant to induce an unpleasant obligation to pay back.) We believe that these delays in reciprocity can only be tolerated on the basis of a chronic background activation of the care system (i.e., activation caused by other sources than deviance, such as aspects of the situation or society), and that involvement of this system is needed to explain a wide variety of psychological phenomena associated with reciprocity, which are not well understood.

First, the involvement of the C system seems to explain the psychological basis of what is considered to be the evolutionary most successful behavioral strategy for reciprocity: Tit-for-Tat or being nice or trusting on the first move (i.e., give something to others without being entirely sure that you will receive something in return), followed by simply responding in the way your partner responded (i.e., be nice again if your partner also proved to be nice, but punish once he or she cheated on your kindness and did not reciprocate. See Axelrod & Hamilton, 1981;

Dawkins, 1989). It seems plausible to assume that reciprocity starts with the activation of care in the individual who makes the first move, followed by activation of care or guilt in the recipient of help, and again care or forgiveness when non-reciprocating is explained in terms of certain uncontrollable or external causes (i.e., Type 3 deviance). Second, people engaged in established patterns of reciprocity often strongly object when their partner starts to explicitly analyze the exchange pattern in terms of "bookkeeping," thereby suggesting that the relationship is actually not care-based but competitive or hierarchical, and based on fear of cheating and aggressive punishment (Silk, 2003). Third, in a recent revolutionary experiment, it was shown that nasal administration of oxytocin, the central hormone involved in parental caregiving in mammals (see below), increases trust in making the first move in a typical social dilemma game (Kosfeld, Heinrichs, Zak, Fischbacher, & Fehr, 2005). Finally, there are strong personality differences in trust, cooperativeness, and competitiveness in experimental games with which cooperation is studied (Van Lange, 2000), which are likely related to genetic differences in the strength with which the FF and C system is developed in individuals.

In contrast to our explanation, the evolution of reciprocity is normally explained independently of kinship-based altruism, and by emphasizing that individuals are not close kin and have no inherent reason to care about each other's fitness or well-being (Boyd & Richerson, 2005; Cosmides & Tooby, 1992; Ridley, 1996; Trivers, 1985). It is said that *if* parental care is involved in reciprocity in non-kin, then surely it must be a "mistake," or misfiring of the psychological mechanism that would certainly result in fitness loss for the caregiver. However, because such mistakes are unlikely from an evolutionary point of view (it would primarily result in fitness loss in the caregiver to spend energy in helping non-kin), it is argued that reciprocity is based on expectancies that others will return favors, formed on the basis of observations of habitual or predictable patterns of exchange. Indeed, it seems implicitly assumed that reciprocity is based primarily on a *norm* of reciprocity that operates outside the influence of particular psychological mechanisms and is publicly available for inspection once individuals start to interact.

In addition to neglecting the role of kinship-based altruism in reciprocity among strangers, theorists also seem to assume that reciprocity necessarily takes place in the context of competitive or hierarchical relationships in which fear and aggression rule, and care and trust are absent. In this context, it is not surprising that research has predominantly focused on people's ability to detect and predict if another individual is likely to cheat or free-ride, on the manner in which they punish the other in the case of cheating (e.g., by aggressing or letting the other feel ashamed), and on the rather unpleasant emotion of gratitude as a motive for repaying received help or gifts (Cosmides & Tooby, 1992; Kurzban & Leary, 2001; Ridley, 1996; Trivers, 1985). Yet, gratitude is an undesirable motivational state caused by *un*expectedly receiving help (McCullough, Kilpatrick, Emmons, & Larson, 2001), for example, by a dangerous or dominant individual (McDougall, 1908/1948). In addition, shame rather than guilt is an emotional response by a sub-missive individual to the disapproving and aggressive reactions of authorities or the public to non-reciprocity (Gilbert, 2003).

We do not deny that reciprocity may be based on distrustful book-keeping, an obsession with detecting cheaters, and excessive punish-ment for non-reciprocity or cheating. What we suggest is that this pattern of reciprocity is characteristic for FF-based or hierarchical rela-tionships in which the non-reciprocator is primarily seen as a criminal (Type 2 deviance) and the only acceptable excuse for his or her crime would be an allusion to madness or Type 1 deviance. As proposed above, in egalitarian or care-based relationships, the non-reciprocator is not criminal but lazy, and an acceptable excuse when caught would be to refer to an illness or dependency (Type 3 deviance). Once the role of care in reciprocal relationships is taken seriously, reciprocity stops being a mystery and care can hardly be seen anymore as an evolution-ary mistake.

To conclude, Type 4 deviance lies on the border between true reci-procity and legitimate dependency or illness, and tolerance for its existence can be explained by assuming that there is relatively strong background activation of the care system already present in reciprocity itself and that makes random violations of reciprocity tolerable. In addition, social parasitism is especially likely to occur when its negative fitness consequences for caregivers can be equally shared among all individuals of a society, and thus effectively reduced in each individual involved. If arousing interest at all, individuals will certainly not be obsessed with cheater detection here. But the situation can change drastically under circumstances where the FF system starts to play a more significant role.[3]

Interestingly, starting from different theoretical perspectives, several other theorists have arrived at similar conclusions, with respect to social responses to Type 3 and 4 deviance, as we do. For example, Parsons (1951) has argued that sick individuals can only expect to receive medical help and treatment when they carefully fit certain role descriptions that are characteristic for a generally accepted "sick role" in society. Thus the occupant of this role is exempted from normal social role responsibilities and is not considered responsible for the incapacity and may demand to be taken care of; but he or she must also recognize that the illness is inherently undesirable and must want to get well and seek technically competent help and to cooperate in the healing process. Although Parsons was not particularly concerned with disability but acute forms of suffering, we can easily see that the sick role is violated when a disabled or chronically ill person appears to be able to engage in reciprocal relationships, yet does not show evidence of actually trying it. For example, when an unfamiliar disabled person sitting in a wheelchair is met and shows both signs of enjoyment and dependency, but does not yet reveal how he or she has coped with the normal demands of reciprocity or cooperation, the person may be viewed as unwilling to contribute to a reciprocal relationship and as unnecessarily arousing our care and pity; an angry reaction may be the result. Similarly, as Weiner has shown in multiple experiments (Weiner, 1995; Weiner, Perry, & Magnusson, 1988), it is fairly easy to change the pity that we feel for the disabled and ill into anger by simply suggesting that these individuals might have been responsible for their deviant condition. With some deviant conditions related to illness such as heart failure or lung cancer we do not even need to be reminded of the individual's responsibility, because we spontaneously do so our self (i.e., we suspect that these individuals must have engaged in careless and irresponsible behavior such as working too hard or smoking). In contrast, some labels for disabilities so obviously make one think primarily about dependency and neediness (e.g., paralysis, blindness) rather than some kind of cheating, that they will spontaneously be associated with Type 3 deviance (see Chapter 3). Many other theorists also see perceived responsibility or controllability as a major determinant for angry or stigmatizing responses to deviance, although they often fail to see that the meaning of responsibility may differ for passive and active deviance (Crocker *et al.*, 1998; Jones *et al.*, 1984). As noted earlier in this chapter, in the case of active deviance, controllability refers to the extent to which perceivers can predict and control deviant individuals' behavior and its consequences. Complementarily, it refers to attributing a property to the target, called *responsibility*, expressing the extent to which this sense of controllability would be possible. In contrast, passive deviance does not refer to behavior that threatens the fitness of the perceiver but to conditions that are primarily threatening to the deviant individual's *own* health and fitness. Here, controllability has two additional meanings: responsibility for the onset and responsibility for the offset of a deviant condition. Being informed that a deviant condition was caused by other people's faults or accidents (low onset responsibility) makes the deviant individual appear vulnerable and activates the C system. In the case of an illness or disability, pity may then be aroused (and in the case of Type 2 deviance or crime, aggression may be inhibited and perhaps forgiveness felt; see below). Interestingly, in the case of Type 4 deviance, onset and offset responsibilities are highly related. That is, individuals associated with this type of deviance do not take enough care of their own health and fitness, either by behaving in a careless or risky manner and consequently getting ill or dependent; or by showing lack of motivation to get well once they have got into this situation.[4]

In an interesting extension of Parsons' sick role concept, Brickman *et al.* (1982) distinguish the legitimately ill person (*medical model*; our Type 3 deviance) from the lazy one who is seen as responsible for both the onset and offset of the condition (*moral model*; our Type 4); the deprived who should be motivated and mobilized to take control over their situation (*compensatory model*; also our Type 4); and those seen as responsible for the onset of but not the offset of their condition such as alcoholics and drug addicts and who demand disciplined treatment (*enlightenment model*). As more fully illustrated in Chapter 3, however, we view different addictions as being on the boundary between controllable active and passive deviance since they have both passive and active elements. (In passing, we also note, that other deviant conditions such as mental disability are viewed by us as lying on the border between *un*controllable active and passive deviance; i.e., as having both threatening mental and care-arousing physical aspects; see Chapter 3.)

A final attempt to classify passive deviant conditions (in addition to desirable attributes of social groups) that we would like to mention is the one recently proposed by S. Fiske and colleagues (Fiske, Cuddy, Glick, & Xu, 2002). These authors suggest that deviant and non-deviant groups in society can be sufficiently distinguished in terms of two theoretical dimensions; their "warmth," indicating their intent, friendliness, or trustworthiness, and their "competence" or intelligence and independence. Although they tried to represent deviant and positively valued groups within the same two-dimensional space, making their results difficult to compare with our two-dimensional model, S. Fiske *et al.*'s interpretation of two of their clusters is partly consistent with the present proposal. Specifically, their distinction between groups who are seen as warm and incompetent (e.g., blind, disabled, elderly) and groups who are seen as less warm and incompetent (e.g., welfare recipients, the poor) is similar to our distinction between Type 3 and 4 deviance. Importantly, just as our theory would predict, they found that people responded with more pity and less "contempt" (a composite of contempt, anger, frustration, and hate) to the former than the latter cluster. We doubt, however, Fiske *et al.*'s theoretical interpretation of their two dimensions. For example, why would a distinguishing property of disabled people be their "warmth" (with poor people relatively "less warm" than disabled people) and a distinguishing attribute of homosexuals and blue-collar workers (belonging to a third cluster) be their greater "competence." We believe that the former two clusters can be more meaningfully distinguished in terms of our concept of controllability, and that it is additionally important to distinguish active from passive deviance and hence to include fearful responses to active deviance; a category of responses that is missing in S. Fiske *et al.*'s model.

The psychological states associated with occupying a role associated with Type 4 deviance as well as with a role of the perceiver have been brilliantly analyzed by both Goffman (1963b) and Murphy and associates (Murphy, Scheer, Murphy, & Mack, 1988). Both have emphasized that during everyday encounters with "normals" the disabled, for example, are constantly faced with the dilemma of behaving in accordance with the sick role in which they acknowledge their dependency, or actively proving that they count as normals. The perceiver faces the similar dilemma of expecting either too little or too much from the disabled. According to Goffman, it is almost impossible for the disabled to do it right in the eyes of normals. In the words of Murphy, the disabled have a *liminal* or transitional status; they are neither ill nor healthy, and make it difficult for perceivers to decide how to behave toward them (see also Silver, Wortman, & Crofton, 1990). The psychological consequences of perceiving this type of deviance have been further analyzed in terms of *ambivalence* by Katz (1981) and other social psychologists (see Chapters 3 and 4).[5]

*Additionally evolved psychological mechanisms for social control?*

Several evolutionary theorists argue for the presence of a specific psychological mechanism to adaptively avoid contact with group members infected with contagious bacteria and parasites. This mechanism would be responsible for the arousal of the emotion of disgust. It is assumed that infected individuals show relatively unambiguous signs of the presence of these contagious predators (e.g., bleeding injuries or abnormal or asymmetrical facial or behavioral features) that can unconditionally activate the particular mechanism (Cottrell & Neuberg, 2005; Kurzban & Leary, 2001; Park, Jason, & Schaller, 2003). We are, however, not entirely sure what such a mechanism would theoretically add to our evolutionary analysis in terms of self-preservation and altruism; an analysis that has resulted in only two basic motivational systems; the FF and C system, and their different combinations.

First, fear of being contaminated with a contagious and lethal disease, an example of our category of uncontrollable-active deviance, seems to us a more adequate preventative emotional response than disgust upon noticing or imagining that the responsible germs or parasites have already entered the mouth. Second, there may not be physical features that reliably indicate that individuals suffer from the presence of contagious parasites. That is, there are many abnormal physical features (not particularly disgusting but fear-arousing) that may signal both the presence of infectious parasites and a wide variety of "bad genes," such as those responsible for mental handicaps (Kowner, 2001), which should be avoided for evolutionary reasons, especially when looking for a mate. It seems to us that the potential contagiousness of hidden diseases can only be inferred from knowledge about the infectious or lethal *consequences* of interpersonal contact, rather than from stable physical features; consequences that are either directly observable (e.g., seeing other people getting ill after contact) or taught by means of education. Third, it may be argued that a too eager avoidance and exclusion of individuals infected with parasites would prevent the group from building up immunity (cf. Traniello, Rosengaus, & Savoie, 2002).

Instead of linking disgust to a specific type of deviance such as the presence of infectious parasites, it seems more plausible to treat it as a fairly general reaction to a wide variety of immoral behaviors (Rozin, 1999), that originates from an evolutionarily very old emotion that is present in many other mammals than humans, and that is not specifically related to social control. That is, disgust is a reaction that motivates the organism to expel noxious substances from the mouth, and that can be triggered by, and conditioned to, taste, smell, appearances, and a wide variety of immoral qualities (cf. Rozin & Fallon, 1987).

Several theorists have also argued that there would be an evolved psychological mechanism to specifically respond with fear and aggression toward outgroups. They usually derive this possibility from principles of kin selection, assuming that outgroups are suspected to exploit the normal altruistic tendencies in one's own group (e.g., Fishbein, 2002; Kurzban & Leary, 2001). Probably for this reason, renowned evolutionary psychologist Pinker (1997, p. 376) remarks that "foraging tribes can't stand one another. They frequently raid neighboring territories and kill any stranger who blunders into theirs." Fishbein (2002) goes so far to assume that responding to any kind of deviance within a social group or society (e.g., mental or physical handicaps) is based on our natural tendency to feel animosity toward genetically unrelated outgroup members (for a related argument, see Kurzban & Leary, 2001; Neuberg *et al.*, 2000). We even find these suggestions among the originators of principles of kin selection themselves. That is, kin selection would originally require for its evolution mechanisms that help individuals discriminate kin from non-kin, thereby introducing reluctance to let non-kin, "strangers," or "outgroups" exploit kin-directed altruism (Dawkins, 1976; Hamilton, 1975). However, this notion fails to take into account that the main product of kin selection in mammals – proximate mechanisms for parental care – may have fundamentally changed the nature of our sociality and responses to deviance in general. To be sure, it is adaptive to be suspicious and wary with respect to unfamiliar individuals (from other groups) who have not yet proven to be altruistic themselves (cf. Hamilton, 1975). However, a "soft" attitude presumably originating from parental care may be additionally adaptive to inhibit defensive and aggressive tendencies, thereby paving the way for sharing of resources, trade, and group expansion. Thus ingroup altruism, especially when founded on parental care, does not necessarily predict outgroup hostility, except when one considers hierarchically organized societies in which aggressive tendencies tend to overrule caring tendencies, or societies of ants with almost complete ingroup altruism without parental care in the usual sense (cf. Dawkins, 1976). (For a different argument against assuming a strong positive relation between ingroup love and outgroup hate, see Brewer, 1999).

## Societies and social control

Societies are groups of at least a small number of individuals engaging in the different types of relationships that are produced by evolutionary problems associated with self-preservation (e.g., strong vs. weak, dominant vs. submissive), altruism (e.g., parent-child, brother and sister), and sex (male vs. female). How are these possible relationships organized in a society? The answer will depend in complex ways on different ecological factors such as how food can be obtained, division of labor, and the presence of predators in the particular environment in which a species evolves. However, without addressing these issues in any detail, and in focusing especially on the evolution of primate and human societies, our above analysis suggests that a crucial factor for social organization and control is the extent to which the FF or C system will be involved in sexual reproduction. First note, that at the moment mammals were faced with the problem of forming relationships between parents and offspring (at first, primarily meant for raising offspring), sex and the competition and conflicts with which it is associated pose a serious threat to these relationships. One solution to this problem is that males and females (aggressively) depart after having mated, leaving it all to the female to raise offspring. Yet, within primate and especially human societies, two solutions for merging sexual and other relationships have emerged. Either the males take control over sexual reproduction and establish male dominance hierarchies and a polygamous mating system, resulting in social control primarily based on a strong activation of the FF system. Or egalitarian relationships are established based on kinship in which males and females primarily engage in monogamous relationships ("marriages"), resulting in social control primarily based on a strong activation of the C system.

In a hierarchically organized or FF-based society, dominant and polygamous males not only control access to females but also to resources for self-preservation (food, safety, territory). Consequently, such a society frequently consists of dominant males defending their territory and harem, surrounded by a large group of submissive males who opportunistically try to mate with straying females, steal food, or dethrone those in power. In contrast, in small egalitarian societies, individuals aspiring a dominant status are actively prevented from doing so by the group. In these societies, the output of the strongly activated C system is able to combine with the output of the sexual system, resulting in pair formation, bonding, and love between mates (cf. McDougall, 1908/1948), and extensive patterns of reciprocity, cooperation, and sharing between adult kin (Boehm, 1999; Knauft, 1991).

In Chapter 6, we explore in considerable detail how egalitarian and hierarchical societies, when combined with different degrees of collectivism or individualism, differ in the manner in which they respond to different deviant conditions and in their characteristic way of social control. Here, we point out that small egalitarian societies based on kinship tend to engage in repair, that larger collectivistic and hierachically organized societies employ stigmatizing social control strategies, and that current egalitarian and individualistic society highly values tolerance as a major attitude toward deviance. As explained in Chapter 6, we also have to take into account that cultures may differ in their assignment of specific deviant conditions to the universal types of deviance, and that historically evolved values, norms, and education contribute to "defining" what is deviant and how to respond to it.

To summarize, our evolutionary approach suggests that humans have an evolved psychological capacity to respond in both a "hard" and "soft" way to both active and passive forms of deviance, with plenty of room for individual differences and contextual influences. Societies may respond to deviance with repair, stigmatization, or tolerance. We now need to start to examine in greater detail the psychological plausibility of assuming that only a few motivational systems would be both necessary and sufficient to explain the wide variety of cognitive, emotional, and behavioral responses that can be observed when people are confronted with deviance.

## 2.3  The functioning of adaptive psychological mechanisms for social control

Figure 2.2 depicts a simplified neural network that we will use to explain in a parsimonious way the occurrence of different responses to the different types of deviance, as well as the influence of contextual factors on these responses.[6]

The network consists of two motivational systems – the fight-or-flight (FF) and the care (C) system. For particular purposes it may be helpful to speak of a separate aggression and escape system which also compete for expression. Yet, the two are triggered by highly similar stimulus features and are so closely connected functionally and anatomically, that we refer to them as a single system. Each of these systems has a specific input unit connected to it that responds specifically to the presence of perceptual stimuli that can trigger the particular system. The FF system will be activated when its input unit is sufficiently

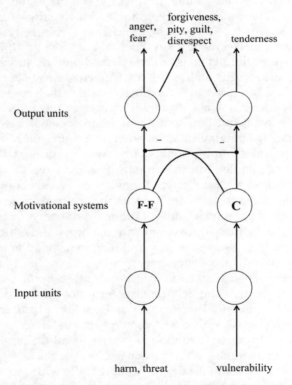

**Figure 2.2** A psychological mechanism for adaptively responding to deviance.

activated by the presence of harm or threat cues (e.g., an alarm call, the sight of a suffering group member, someone stealing one's property). The FF system will propagate activity to output units that will cause the emotions of fear or anger, and different kinds of escape and aggressive defense behaviors. Which of these emotions will be aroused, depends on various situational factors. The care system will be activated when its input unit is sufficiently activated by the presence of vulnerability cues (e.g., baby features, smallness, harmlessness, dependency). It will propagate activity to output units that will cause the emotion of tenderness and a motivation to nurture and care for the object. Both the C system and FF system can also be activated when the input units register evidence that these systems are activated in *other* persons. That is, witnessing other people's expression of fear, anger, or tenderness may induce the same emotions in us (McDougall, 1908/1948).

A crucial feature of the network in Figure 2.2 is the inhibitory relationship between FF and C. That is, the output of one system can inhibit or negatively influence the output of the other, resulting in the systems competing with each other for expression. An alternative way of expressing this is to say that the network is engaged in "decision making" at a subcortical level. As explained later, this should not be confused with reasoning in terms of symbolically represented behavioral outcomes. When the two systems are about equally activated they may, dependent on the strength of the inhibitory connections, produce no output at all (a state of indecision) or produce output that can only weakly activate the two output units, resulting in responses that are less clearly identifiable as belonging to either system, and perhaps represent new emotional and motivational qualities. For example, an individual perceived in a particular situation may contain both trigger stimuli that can activate FF (e.g., the individual bleeding and crying fearfully) and trigger stimuli that can activate C (e.g., the individual lying in a vulnerable posture on the ground). However, if one of the systems gets slightly more activated than the other, it may win the competition; it may first successfully inhibit the other system after which the latter system will be prevented from producing inhibitory activity, resulting in an outstanding and, compared to its previous output, extreme response of the first system. Importantly, the competition may be won by either adding more activation to the input unit of a particular system (e.g., by successively activating or "priming" that system with different trigger stimuli) or by taking away input from the competing system. An example of the former would be when seeing a suffering victim especially frightens us when the flight component was already somewhat activated in a previous situation, resulting in enough inhibition of C that the victim's vulnerability cues are incapable of activating C and hence cannot trigger a helping response. Attending more closely to the vulnerable features of the victim rather than the fearful properties of the situation may produce enough input activation for C, resulting in helping behavior. An example of the latter would be when the victim decreases the emission of distress signs, thereby lowering the inhibitory activation of FF on C's output, and hence giving C an opportunity to express itself. We will later use this property of the network to explain context-dependent variability in responding to deviance.

The principle of lateral inhibition, as displayed by the present network, has been recognized by many theorists as a universally adaptive brain mechanism. It would not only enhance perceptual contrast (Lindsay & Norman, 1977) but also promote decision making (or "motivational contrast", cf. Grossberg, 1980) in a complex world that often contains trigger stimuli relevant for more than one motivational system (Ludlow, 1980; Toates, 1986). The competitive network recognizes that the different systems are equally important for fitness enhancement and should be partly allowed to function independently from one another, but also allowed to overrule each other when the situation requires this. This has especially important social consequences in the case of the C system. This system can be considered the true basis for altruistic behavior because it forces individuals to unconditionally and uncritically help each other in emergency situations, without first needing proof that the other will pay them back on a later occasion, as common views of reciprocal altruism would require. Although the systems need to work independently from one another, their activity can be immediately inhibited when the situation requires this. Thus helping others can be stopped when cheating is suspected or helping becomes too dangerous, and aggression can be stopped and forgiveness experienced when vulnerability cues are perceived (e.g., when the other shows remorse; see below). A competitive relationship between the FF and C system creates a qualitatively new mammalian behavior; a kinder form of punishing active deviants and a firmer, critical, and authoritative mode of care giving (for an evolutionary perspective on parenting styles that is particularly consistent with the present view, see Maestripieri, 1999).

Different research findings are consistent with the view that activity of the C system negatively influences aggressive responses to deviance. For example, it has been shown that infantile bodily (Alley, 1983) and facial features (Berry & McArthur, 1986) can inhibit aggressive tendencies and arouse pity when they go together with signs of distress (Dijker, 2001). Other evidence for a negative relationship between activity of care and aggression comes from studies showing that focusing on another person's dependency and suffering inhibits aggression and antisocial behavior in general (Baron, 1977; Björkqvist, Österman, & Kaukiainen, 2000; Miller & Eisenberg, 1988) and responding aggressively to active deviants such as criminals (Batson *et al.*, 1997).[7]

Let us have a closer look at the nature of the different composite or "secondary" (the term is McDougall's 1908/1948) emotions or motivational states that may result from the simultaneous or successive activation of, and resulting competition between, the FF and C system. In particular, let us look at the emotions of pity, guilt, forgiveness, and disrespect that are especially important for social control.

When output of the C system is moderated by simultaneous activation of the flight component of the FF system (or *vice versa*), *pity* may be experienced. That is, pity for a suffering person can be seen as felt distress or fear tinged with tenderness (Dijker, 2001; McDougall, 1908/1948). When you feel pity you experience the suffering of an individual as being undesirable in light of your motivation to protect the individual against harm and suffering, making indistinguishable your motivation to relieve the suffering for "selfish" (i.e., to relieve your own unpleasant feeling state) and "unselfish" reasons (i.e., to improve the other's well-being). A first empirical demonstration of the relation between protective or caring tendencies toward healthy and non-suffering individuals and pity was provided by Dijker (2001). He not only showed that tendency to protect and pity have a U-shaped relation with age-related vulnerability cues, but also that the two variables are highly correlated. More recently, Batson, Lishner, Cook, and Sawyer (2005, Experiment 2) also used McDougall's proposal that parental care should be an important ingredient of pity, and argued that students' higher levels of pity (or empathy; see below) for a suffering child or dog than for a student reflect a greater tendency to protect or nurture the former two than the latter (unfortunately, these researchers did not measure a protective tendency).

It is important to indicate briefly how the present view of pity relates to the meaning of several other terms that are frequently used by psychologists in relation to altruistic behavior such as empathy, concern, or sympathy; all terms that we believe have feelings of tenderness and hence an activated C system in common. The way in which Wispé (1986, p. 318) defines sympathy ("a heightened awareness of the suffering of another person as something to be alleviated") seems highly similar to our description of pity (see also Eisenberg & Miller, 1987). However, sympathy also seems to be used when another individual is in a healthy and non-suffering state, and liked for his or her tenderness-arousing, "cute," and altruistic features.

In an extremely influential and fruitful line of research, Batson (1987; 1998) has consistently used the term *empathy* to refer to an altruistic emotion which he measures with such adjectives as *tenderness, warmth,* and *softheartedness*; clearly, feelings that we associate exclusively with activation of the C system and that do not yet imply the perception of suffering. There are two main conceptual problems with Batson's use of the term *empathy* for this emotional state. First, the term suggests that some cognitive understanding or "perspective taking" would be necessary in order to trigger the C system. Indeed, most other theorists use the term empathy to refer exclusively to the *cognitive* process of understanding another person's feelings (Wispé, 1986). We argue, however, that the C system and hence feelings of tenderness are rather automatically triggered by the perception of elementary, age-related morphological features, postures, and behaviors of healthy and non-suffering individuals (Dijker, 2001). According to our perspective, tenderness essentially is a pleasant emotional state with the primary goal of *preventing* other individuals from suffering by offering them protection – behavior that is, of course, much more adaptive than starting to help and nurture individuals once they are physically harmed and can be empathized with. Yet, some additional understanding of situational threats to the fitness of vulnerable beings (e.g., young offspring) is needed to worry about the other's fitness, to get angry at predators, or feel pity when fear also starts to play a role.

Second, the experimental manipulation most often used by Batson to induce empathy also incorrectly suggests that one needs to take the perspective of suffering victims in order to feel empathy or tenderness. In virtually all of Batson's studies, the effects of perspective taking on empathy are studied by comparing responses of participants who are either asked to ignore another person's need state (inducing them to remain objective and detached) or concentrate on the other's feelings and imagine how the other person feels. Batson associates the latter condition with "perspective taking," and typically finds that here, people respond with more empathy than fear or distress to the needy other (although often, fear is also somewhat increased); even to persons with threatening contagious diseases or criminals. In addition, he has often demonstrated that empathy motivates helping behavior, even when people are offered an easy opportunity to avoid the other person (Batson, 1987). Batson's experimental procedures and findings, however, are consistent with a simpler explanation. People who are not induced to take the other's perspective simply ignore or intellectualize the stimuli that are necessary to activate the C system, whereas those who are induced to take the victim's perspective simply have a chance of being optimally exposed to these trigger stimuli. Because

Batson's research on empathy has influenced much research on responses to deviance (to be reported in later chapters of this book), and terms like sympathy and concern are also frequently used in this area of research, we will use all these terms, along with pity and tenderness, interchangeably in the rest of this book. The main idea that we should keep in mind is that they all relate to activation of the C system.

In addition to pity, we also see two other important emotions as the result of the mutual involvement of the FF and C system: guilt and forgiveness. In contrast to the other emotions discussed in relation to social control, guilt is a response to the perception and evaluation of one's own behavior rather than a response to the perception of another person's behavior or state. Guilt is crucially dependent on activation of the C system, first inducing a desire to protect others and avoid doing harm to them (e.g., because they are vulnerable, friends, or family members), then noticing that one has harmed them and reduced their fitness, and is subsequently motivated to repair the damage (Gilbert, 2003; McDougall, 1908/1948). Of course, in the context of social control, one may also feel guilty about having been too punitive or hostile to individuals associated with deviance (see Chapter 4). It is important to distinguish guilt from shame. According to Gilbert (2003), although shame too may follow from harming others or norm transgression in general, it is typically aroused in the context of a hierarchical relationship in which it is associated with fear of punishment by dominant others or a powerful crowd, submissive behavior, and avoidance rather than with a motivation to repair the harm done. Gilbert also notes that there are situations in which both guilt and shame are aroused.

Forgiveness is highly similar to guilt except that it also depends on the deviant individual's own behavior, in the form of apologies or remorse when receiving or anticipating a punitive response to his or her deviance. Specifically, when output of the fight component of the FF system is moderated by simultaneous activation of C (e.g., when an active deviant shows remorse and infantile suffering, declaring "I feel terrible about what I did"), aggression may be inhibited and forgiveness experienced. In sum, pity, guilt, and forgiveness may depend on the same underlying psychological mechanism, expressing the central involvement of the care system, with care moderating fear (pity) or aggression (guilt, forgiveness). Presumably because of their relation with care, true altruism, and sociality, these three emotions have been called "moral" emotions (McCullough *et al.*, 2001). The close association of these emotions is supported by the strong correlations between measures of forgiveness, guilt, and Batson's empathy measure (McCullough *et al.*, 2001; McCullough, Worthington, & Rachal, 1997).

Furthermore, an experiment by Gold and Weiner (2000) revealed that, compared to a no-remorse condition, remorseful norm transgressors evoked *both* more forgiveness and sympathy and less punishment, and that forgiveness was positively correlated with sympathy but nega-tively with anger. In light of our typology of deviant conditions, it could be argued that remorse first emphasizes that active deviance was controllable (with the perpetrator taking full responsibility) and then changes it into submissive and norm-conforming (and also con-trollable) behavior. Also note that feelings of sympathy motivate people to punish offenders in "softer" ways; that is, to rehabilitate them, whereas other forms of punishment are driven by responsibility attri-bution and anger arousal, or fearful expectations of future wrongdoing and hence deterrence (Graham, Weiner, & Zucker, 1997). The involve-ment of the C system in forgiveness is finally supported by findings of Karremans, Van Lange, and Holland (2005), who showed that forgive-ness of a specific target is associated with a stronger generalized pro-social orientation resulting, for example, in greater willingness to engage in volunteering. Probably forgiveness activates the C system it is related to, and that activation leads to more general prosocial behaviors.

A final composite emotional state that we consider important in the context of social control is disrespect, a state that we associate especially with the perception of controllable-passive or Type 4 deviance, and with the activation of both the C system and the fight component of the FF system. Specifically, when a deviant individual appearing ill or dependent evokes care in others but also aggression because of his or her apparent exaggeration or social parasitism, this may (due to mutual inhibition) result in a relatively weak activation of both care and aggres-sion, resulting in disappointment about not being able to increase the other's fitness (frustrated care), and in the withdrawal of attention. That is, the other is not seen anymore as a responsible and respectful group member who is in control of his or her responses, but a "pathetic" or "pitiful" creature (Sennett, 2003; Solomon, 1976). Disrespect seems to be related to the emotion of *contempt*, but we believe, partially on the basis of McDougall's (1908/1948) analysis of this emotion, that there are two important differences. First, although both disrespect and contempt imply an asymmetrical relationship with the target, the former is based on caregiving and the latter exclusively on power and hierarchy that motivate to "look down" on someone. Second, contempt may be associated with disgust. To the extent that Type 4 deviance is often associated with lack of grooming or self-care, bad smell, and filth, and a hierarchical relationship with the target is implied, disrespect may thus transform into contempt.

## 2.4 Neurophysiological evidence for the FF-C network

The fight-or-flight system belongs to one of the most studied motivational mechanisms in ethology and psychology (Archer, 1976; Eibl-Eibesfeldt, 1989; Panksepp, 1998), and can be anatomically associated with the brain stem and what MacLean (1985) termed the *protoreptilian brain*. Studies using electrical stimulation or lesions suggest that fight and flight responses in mammals are controlled by neural activity of specific adjacent sections of the hypothalamus. This structure of the brain is not only related to defensive and aggressive behavior, but also to other activities directly responsible for self-preservation like feeding, respiration, blood circulation, and sex. It is also recognized that, although escape and aggression should act as partly independent motivational systems and hence compete with each other for expression, they are also two sides of the same coin, accounting for rapid oscillation between the two tendencies when individuals fight (Archer, 1976). Furthermore, it seems now indisputable in psychology that anger and fear are basic emotions with distinct and opposing behavioral tendencies (attack and escape, respectively), that belong to the most frequently self-reported emotional experiences. In addition, self-reports of anger and fear are highly correlated; an object that arouses fear normally also arouses anger, and *vice versa* (Dijker, 1987; Dijker & Koomen, 2003).

Modern brain-imaging technology suggests that especially the amygdala may be implicated in triggering and generating responses of the FF system (cf. LeDoux, 1996). Relevant for responses to deviance, Phelps and colleagues (Phelps, O'Connor, Cunningham, Gore, & Banaji, 2000) measured activity of the part of the amygdala involved in triggering defensive reactions to threat and found stronger activity in response to black than white faces. They also found that, after exposure to these faces, participants with stronger amygdala activity in particular tended to show a stronger eyeblink response when startled (a defensive reflex to, and indication of being prepared to respond to, threat), and responded faster with assigning negative trait names to black faces than to white faces (an often used implicit measure of negative responses discussed more fully in Chapter 4). Moreover, Whalen, Shin, McInerney, Fischer, and Rauch (2000) demonstrated that the amygdala showed slower habituation to black than to white faces.[8] Amodio, Harmon Jones, and Devine (2003) also found differential eyeblink responses to black and white faces, but only for those with primarily external reasons to suppress negative responses to blacks (e.g., because of what others might say).

Activity of the FF system can also be clearly distinguished at the endocrine and physiological level. First, following Cannon's (1929) influential work, the fight-or-flight response, mobilizing the organism for vigorous action, has been considered the most characteristic mammalian response to threat or stress. It is associated with an activation of the sympathetic adrenomedulary system, resulting in increased cardiac output, bloodflow to skeletal muscles, myocardium and brain, increased heart rate, and dilation of the blood vessels. Triggering of the adrenal medula causes the release of norepinephrine and epinephrine, ACTH, and cortisol. Feelings of arousal, vigilance, fear, and aggression are also associated with this response pattern (Panksepp, 1998; Taylor *et al.*, 2000; Uvnäs-Moberg, 1998). A clear fight-or-flight reaction is often preceded by an episode of "freezing," characterized by intense alertness or vigilance, enhanced muscle tone, suppressed respiration, and particularly high blood pressure. This seems to reflect a moment of indecision in which it is not yet clear if the nature of the danger demands fighting or fleeing (Uvnäs-Moberg, 1998).

The neurophysiological aspects of the motivational system responsible for parental care, associated by us with a more general care system, are also increasingly well documented. The system is anatomically located in what MacLean has termed the *limbic system* or *paleomammalian brain* (for a detailed discussion of brain structures associated with the FF and parental care system, see Panksepp, 1998); a structure that is generally associated with warm-bloodedness and social bonding. Activation of the parental care system produces physiological and hormonal changes that contrast with the output of the FF system. Much attention has been given to the role of oxytocin in mammalian parental care. It is released by another paraventrical part of the hypothalamus where it acts on the parasympathetic nervous system, producing a fall in blood pressure and cortisol levels, inhibition of flight and fear, calmness, and feelings of relaxation. It is also responsible for increased tolerance for pain stimuli. It is widely associated with health consequences such as the body's healing capability after injury (Uvnäs-Moberg, 1998). It seems plausible to assume that a bodily state of calmness and relaxation underlies the subjective experience of tenderness and softheartedness. Curiously, although parental care is recognized as an important motivational system with unique neurophysiological and behavioral output, emotion theorists usually do not recognize tenderness as a distinguishable emotion. Perhaps, because the feelings and expressive behaviors associated with this emotion are especially strongly connected with maternal care for offspring, its occurrence in males or in other situations has been less salient to emotion theorists (Frijda, personal communication).

While the activity of both the fight-or-flight and parental care system can be observed in both males and females, activation of the parental care system is more typical for females. This should not be surprising, as in most mammals females are often more closely involved in parenting than males. Indeed, one of the characteristic hormones of the parental care system – oxytocin – is released during such maternal activity as breastfeeding, giving warmth, and tender care. Another cause for the clear sex difference in release and influence of oxytocin is the male sex hormone testosterone, which appears to be closely linked to sympathetic activity and fear and aggression. However, the stress and fear-reducing effects of oxytocin have been observed in both males and females after injection or relaxation massage (Bell, 2001; Taylor *et al.*, 2000; Uvnäs-Moberg, 1998).

Different studies suggest that men predominantly respond with FF-activity (evidenced in higher testosterone, increased signs of stress, and lower reported tenderness) to distress or separation calls in infants, whereas women primarily respond with activity of the parental care system. However, mothers and fathers respond to these cries with greater sympathy than non-parents (Maestripieri, 1999). Fleming, Corter, Stallings, and Steiner (2002) showed that level of testosterone is negatively related to self-reported feelings of sympathy and felt need to respond to the infant. Storey, Walsh, Quinton, and Wynne-Edwards (2000) showed that holding a baby doll decreases testosterone in expectant fathers (it was not measured in this study if handling of dolls is also associated with increased levels of oxytocin). Furthermore, marriage and having children seem to decrease testosterone level in men (Gray, Kahlenberg, Barrett, Lipson, & Ellison, 2002). Thus although men are more adverse to distress cues, these responses may, under the right circumstances, be downregulated by experience with children. (Chapter 5 will explain sex differences in responding to deviance partially in terms of these differential neurophysiological aspects.) Finally, it is of interest to mention that the positive influence of pets on human health has also been associated with the possibility that pets reduce stress and cardiovascular problems because their human baby-like features may automatically activate caring and nurturing behaviors (Allen, 2003; Archer, 1997).

In sum, there is considerable neurophysiological support for the existence of the presently proposed psychological mechanism responsible for reacting to deviance. Whereas an activated FF system prepares the individual for energy mobilization and vigorous activity, an activated parental and presumably more general care system produces calmness, muscle relaxation, and a state of openness. The antagonistic nature of these systems, with one activating the sympathetic and the other the parasympathetic nervous system (for a discussion of this downregulation, see Panksepp, 1998), supports our representation of these systems in terms of a competitive network.[9]

## 2.5 From adaptive psychological mechanisms to mental content and process

At this point it is important to indicate clearly how we use the term *emotion* and see its relationship with more cognitive terms such as *expectancy, internal representation,* and *thinking* or *reasoning.* In the present view, an emotion is a motivational state preparing and urging an organism to engage in adaptive goal-directed behavioral and mental activity – a state that is caused by the activation of one or more evolved motivational systems that can be neurophysiologically identified. The more strongly the underlying system is activated by its characteristic trigger stimuli, or by a high activation level left over from a previous emotion-arousing situation, the more the "total" organism is involved in emotionally responding (with the involvement of cognitive, physiological, motor, and expressive elements), and the more likely the emotion is consciously experienced. It seems conceivable that weaker activations of the underlying systems are less likely to be consciously experienced, and therefore can be less easily verbally reported. The present view is consistent with many theoretical perspectives on emotion stressing the evolutionary origins, adaptiveness, and dual nature of biased and fast emotional responses to important events (generated by activated motivational systems or instincts), and their discrepancy from, or correction and control by, slower thought processes (LeDoux, 1996; McDougall, 1908/1948; Tooby & Cosmides, 1990. So-called "dual-process" models have also been proposed to explain responses to deviance, see Chapter 4). This view assumes that, without demanding much cognitive elaboration, motivational systems can be triggered in a reflex-like manner by perceiving relatively simple stimulus configurations. For the emotions and behaviors that are caused by the activation of a motivational system to be fitness-enhancing, it is only required that these simple triggers are correlated with the objective presence of fitness problems in the environment in which the system evolved (e.g., a strange looming creature is likely to be an attacking predator; a vulnerable and crying creature is likely to be a suffering family member in need of help). It is not necessary (perhaps even maladaptive because it would take too much time) for perceivers to have an explicit understanding of what is objectively behind the presence of simple trigger stimuli. What is important is that perceivers get into the right motivational state at the right moment in the long run. Of course, experience will often confirm that the arousal of an emotion was based on the true presence of threats and challenges to fitness (e.g., the looming creature really was a dangerous predator, the crying individual indeed was a needy family member). And even in those cases in which the emotion proved to have been based on wrong perceptions or "false alarms," it was still a sensible response in terms of evolutionary adaptedness (for discussions, see Tooby & Cosmides, 1990). That activated motivational systems may have a biasing influence on perception, but are rooted in the objective properties of the world, was nicely illustrated in a neural network simulation to explain how people judge the (un)attractiveness of human faces (Zebrowitz, Fellous, Mignault, & Andreoletti, 2003). Specifically, these researchers showed that the attractiveness of faces and the particular properties that we associate with them such as health, intelligence, dominance, and dependency are based on the extent to which these faces are objectively similar to anomalous faces (e.g., as a result of birth defects) and to the faces of healthy babies.

Clearly, interaction with the objects that are able to activate motivational systems will result in the formation of internal representations that are much richer in content than the original ("unconditioned") stimuli that are necessary to activate those systems. This will be especially the case when we start to represent and describe these objects and their emotion-arousing properties in terms of language (Frijda, 1993; Lerner & Keltner, 2000).

Thus we propose that activation of a motivational system results in the experience of an emotion that includes both having a particular expectancy and a goal or desire with respect to the properties behind the presence of the simple trigger stimuli that caused the activation of the system. In Chapter 3, we will use this feature of motivational systems to explain the perceiver's reactions to specific behaviors of deviant individuals during everyday interactions. For example, an encounter with a person associated with a dangerous condition (e.g., a contagious disease, a past treatment for schizophrenia) may activate the flight component of the FF system, resulting in an expectancy that the person may soon start behaving dangerously (e.g., infect or attack you), and a desire that the other behaves safely. Behavior that is congruent with this expectancy (e.g., the other suddenly moves forward) will increase your fear; behavior that is incongruent (e.g., the target is able to reassure you with his or her self-controlled and quiet behavior) will reduce it.

Although the expectancies and desires associated with an activated motivational system are essentially non-verbal (they can also be found in human infants and in species without language), they can be described in terms of language (e.g., the deviant person is associated with trait terms like unpredictable, dangerous, helpless, ungrateful, obtrusive, and so on). Similarly, the motivational state caused by activated motivational systems can be described in terms of words referring to emotional responses to deviant individuals. Additionally, the use of both words referring to emotional reactions and to properties of deviant individuals should be highly correlated (see Chapter 3). To put this differently, we believe that the motivational systems responsible for the arousal of motivational states function as language-independent *concepts* that supply the *meaning* of the words that people use to describe their emotional reactions to deviant conditions and the (expected) properties of these conditions (see Chapter 3). For example, consider the meaning of the word *responsibility* when used to indicate that an ill person is personally responsible for getting ill. In our view, this meaning is caused by a motivational mechanism motivating us to care for ill or dependent individuals (together with representations of the particular consequences of its activation in various contexts), with *irresponsibility* referring to persons who endanger or neglect their own health and fitness against the wishes of caring others, and *responsibility* referring to persons who take care of their own health, obey caregivers and authorities, and grow independent as soon as possible.

Such a semantic explanation in terms of motivational mechanisms helps to address the pervasive problem of mentalism or mind-brain dualism so typical for current cognitive psychology and evolutionary psychology.[10] Briefly, mentalism refers to the tendency to equate psychological mechanisms with symbolic representations of the world and manipulation of symbols (usually seen as words) that refer to, or are *about*, the world; the latter process being identified with reasoning. Yet, it is this "aboutness" that puts us in serious trouble if we want to causally explain mental content and process (note that nobody would deny *that* the most distinctive quality of thought is that it uses symbols). Specifically, staying exclusively at the level of symbolic representation and reasoning, the mediating processes between inputs (e.g., objective features of deviance) and outputs (e.g., thoughts, emotions, and behavioral decisions) can only be described in terms of a reasoning process by which thoughts *about* the input are combined with thoughts *about* some internal state (a feeling, bodily condition, or another thought) in order to arrive at new thoughts (or "conclusions") *about* the output. Such a description of symbol manipulation is commonly referred to as "information processing," "reasoning," or "computation" and is frequently compared to running programs (sets of computational instructions) on a computer. Correspondingly, internal representations are assumed to consist of the same words and sentences that people themselves use to describe the content of their thoughts about the world or their bodily reactions to it. These representations, therefore, are commonly referred to as "representations of meaning," "knowledge representations," or more generally "symbolic representations" (cf. Rumelhart & Norman, 1988).

If a person's main business is to use symbols that refer to (or are about) the "real thing" (or other symbols), how can the person ever make contact with the real thing itself (i.e., the world out there, or the body); be influenced by it and affect it in the form of output (e.g., muscle twitches, behavior)? Clearly, saying that we manipulated or computed symbols according to a set of rules or instructions is not the same as offering a *causal* explanation for an underlying process, as such an explanation should be grounded in some material, and in the present case the neurophysiological mechanism that forces us, according to natural laws, to do what we do (Bunge & Padilla, 1987; Hempel, 1966). Returning, for example, to a semantic explanation of the term *responsibility*, it hardly reveals a causal mechanism to say that the meaning of this word can be expressed in terms of other words such as *could foresee that the illness would result from his or her behavior; did nothing to prevent it*, etc.

Although we obviously do not pretend or even aspire to solve the problem of mentalism here, we suggest as a working hypothesis that, in order to understand how the symbolic content of representations of deviance can have any causal connection with objective features of deviant conditions, and in turn can affect the body and behavior in general, the universal concepts for understanding deviance may be equated with the motivational systems of our FF-C network (for a similar view on semantics, see Morris, 1946).

Also note that this proposal may be applied to causally explaining the serial process of reasoning and decision making. Specifically, the functioning of our FF-C network can be described in terms of explicitly formulated decision or computational rules of the kind: "Always help vulnerable or needy others to increase their lowered fitness state, unless your own individual fitness is too much endangered (e.g., when you need to escape) or you need to attack and punish (e.g., when the other seems to hurt you or cheat)" or complementary: "Always promote your own individual fitness (e.g., by escaping, aggressing, and doing other things that are important), unless the fitness of others is too much endangered." In principle, humans can use these symbolic rules to think and communicate about the social world, and cognitive scientists may use them (in the form of programs or sets of if-then instructions) to simulate social decision making on a computer. Yet, it is important to keep in mind that these simulations may not represent a valid model of the underlying causal mechanisms but only the symbolic capacity of the scientist (cf. Clancey, 1997; Grossberg, 1980). Our discussion also makes clear how, in the hands of evolutionary psychology, mentalism and computational psychology may easily lead to an explosion of assumed adaptive "software" modules (Pinker, 1997; Tooby & Cosmides, 1992) when the plausibility of these modules is not systematically checked against available neurophysiological evidence (cf. Panksepp & Panksepp, 2000).

To conclude, the involvement of motivational systems explains how internal representations of deviance can have meaningful content. Furthermore, it must be assumed that symbolic descriptions of deviant conditions can only causally influence behavior when these descriptions are capable of activating underlying motivational systems or concepts. Thus the use of language-independent mechanisms underlying meaning may function as an antidote against mentalism and mind-body dualism. However, although our theory assumes that temporary network states (emotions, expectancies, desires) can result in more stable internal representations or memories (e.g., attitudes) that can be referred to by words or other symbols, we refrain from addressing the difficult question of how activity of the network at a subcortical level specifically relates to mental activity with the use of language at higher cortical levels. Yet, our explanatory model may help to understand how truly material and causal mechanisms can be responsible for the meaning of the words that people use to describe their thoughts about social properties.

## 2.6 Discussion and comparison with other theories

Our evolutionary approach consists of identifying a small number of language-independent motivational systems that function as universal concepts with which people, independently of society or historical period studied, can classify and interpret the many different deviant conditions that can be encountered in society. We attempt to test this part of the theory in Chapters 3 and 6, where we will review studies examining how people in different cultures classify and judge deviant conditions. Another important aspect of our theory is that we specify how the activation and application of these motivational systems or concepts are dependent on the particular social context in which they are activated. This aspect is tested in Chapter 4, in which we study experimentally produced context or "displacement" effects on responding to deviance; and in Chapter 6, in which we examine cultural and historical differences in responding to deviance. Here we briefly summarize how our approach differs from other evolutionary approaches to social control and stigmatization.

First, we agree with most of the other approaches (Cottrell & Neuberg, 2005; Kurzban & Leary, 2001; Neuberg *et al.*, 2000; Tooby & Cosmides, 1992, 1996) that social groups need to respond to a wide variety of active threats to sociality such as cheating or non-reciprocity, exploiting outgroups, and contagious illnesses; and that fear and anger are adaptive emotional reactions in these cases. We differ, however, in three important respects. First, we do not assume that these responses require the evolution of "extremely specific" (Kurzban & Leary, 2001, p. 188) mental procedures (see also Tooby & Cosmides, 1992). Instead, evolutionarily much older non-symbolic motivational systems might do the same job. For example, if we look at the main responses to deviance that Kurzban and Leary (2001) attempt to predict from an evolutionary perspective – disgust, anger, and fear – we fail to see why these would refer to "highly specialized" computational machinery. To be sure, anger is different from fear with respect to their input and output, and both are therefore "specific." Yet, each of these emotions is fairly "general" in that the latter is triggered by a wide variety of threats (e.g., to physical safety or property) and the first to a wide variety of obstacles to be removed with some form of aggression. Furthermore, we argue that the relatively simple neural network of motivational systems that is responsible for these emotions, although by itself capable of functioning independently of language or other symbol systems, is responsible for the meaningful content of our thoughts about deviance, and even for guiding more complex serial processes of reasoning.

Second, and more importantly, all these approaches neglect deviant conditions that specifically activate a care system, and primarily analyze responding to deviance in terms of almost criminal failures to cooperate or reciprocate. Even illnesses and disabilities are framed entirely as inabilities to reciprocate (Kurzban & Leary, 2001). Cottrell and Neuberg (2005, p. 772) stretch the concepts of pity and reciprocal altruism to the limit when they propose that the function of pity would be to generate "gratitude from the recipient and subsequent reciprocity of the assistance back to the helper in the future." We do not deny that chronic illnesses and disabilities may pose a problem for cooperation and reciprocity, and that people may want to help ill or disabled persons for this reason. However, as argued above, the function of care and tenderness which is aroused by children and other dependent individuals such as the ill or disabled is to cope with an acute state of reduced fitness or vulnerability. Being concerned with the prospects of future reciprocity would be highly maladaptive in most cases. Yet, pity may be moderated by activation of the independently functioning FF system once evidence suggests that further care is useless or the care recipient cheats. (As illustrated in Chapter 3, Cottrell and Neuberg (2005) could leave out the involvement of the care system because they primarily studied relatively active deviant conditions.) In Chapter 6, we will illustrate that, depending on the circumstances and societies, parents with a maturing disabled child, or individuals with a disabled or chronically ill partner, may be satisfied with quite different levels of non-reciprocity (sometimes receiving a simple smile seems sufficient), and may allow disabled persons to play respected social roles when the negative fitness consequences of incomplete reciprocity can be shared with other family members or the community.

Third, the above mentioned authors neglect contextual influences on responses to deviance, making it impossible to distinguish, for example, responses that would have been originally adaptive in hunter-gatherers from those that are observed in more recent hierarchical or egalitarian societies. In our view, it is not fruitful to sample in rather arbitrary ways evidence for hostile or exclusionary responses to ill or disabled persons in such diverse circumstances as chimpanzee societies, the European Middle Ages, and the modern Western welfare state, in order to demonstrate that stigmatization must have been a universally adaptive strategy in our evolutionary past (see Kurzban & Leary, 2001). We are happy to discover that several of the evolutionary-inspired researchers discussed above, are now beginning to explore how contextual activation or priming of, for example, fear may influence responses to deviant conditions (Maner *et al.*, 2005. This study will be described in Chapter 4).

To conclude our discussion of evolutionary approaches, one of the most fascinating implications of our theory is a rather counter-intuitive one. Unlike theories that predict all stigmatizing responses to deviance from primarily aggressive or fearful tendencies in humans that are associated with the FF system, our theory, firmly based on principles of kin selection, predicts that many negative responses nevertheless involve the deeply social tendency to care for our fellow group members.

## 2.7 Summary

After discussing several general problems related to current evolutionary psychology, the present chapter set out to sketch a scenario for the evolution of psychological mechanisms enabling small groups of genetically related individuals or families to engage in social control, and in particular, in repair processes. Starting from Hamilton's inclusive fitness model, it was proposed that deviance can be seen as referring to those behaviors and features of group members that threaten inclusive fitness. Correspondingly, strategies to control deviance can be considered adaptations that enhance inclusive fitness. The enhancement of inclusive fitness is related to two major problems each caused by a particular form of deviance requiring a particular solution or adaptation. First, there is the problem of how to prevent genetically related individuals from decreasing each other's fitness or chances to reproduce by behaving in selfish ways (active deviance). The second adaptive problem that occurs for relatives living together is how to help increase the fitness of individuals who relatively lack fitness (passive deviance). We further argued that these two major types of deviance can be adaptively responded to by means of two evolutionarily very old motivational systems, for which we also provided neurophysiological evidence. That is, on the basis of the fight-or-flight (FF) system, group members are generally able to recognize accurately key features of active deviance, and to respond in time with fear and/or defensive aggression. In contrast, the motivational system, originally evolved to secure the fitness and health of vulnerable and needy offspring by means of protection and tenderness (which we referred to as the care or C system), allows individuals to adaptively respond to objective signs of passive deviance; also when associated with unrelated or unfamiliar individuals of increasingly larger social groups.

We also distinguished two controllability subcategories of active and passive deviance, thus resulting in four basic types of deviance. When active deviance is seen as intentional and controllable, it arouses particularly angry and punishing behavior; when seen as uncontrollable and unpredictable, it arouses particularly fear and less anger. In the case of passive deviance, when it is seen as controllable, the protective feelings are mixed with anger. Finally, when passive deviance is seen as uncontrollable, tenderness, protection, and pity are aroused.

In light of inclusive fitness, however, group members are faced with a third adaptive problem with respect to social control among relatives: how not to respond too aggressively to individuals engaging in active deviance (their fitness should not be reduced too much by the punishment as this may harm copies of one's own genes), and how not to be "too soft" on passive deviance (those individuals should not misuse other people's motivation to care by exaggerating their illness symptoms or by a lack of motivation to get well). We argued that this problem is solved by a negative or inhibitory relationship between the FF and C system, allowing the two systems to moderate each other's activity and output, and to experience such emotions as guilt and forgiveness, and to engage in a more authoritative form of caring.

On the basis of this evolutionary analysis, we argued that people in all societies and historical periods are not only motivated to respond to deviance but also use the underlying motivational systems as (universal) *concepts* for classifying and interpreting deviant conditions in terms of the proposed deviance typology; independently from language or other kinds of culturally defined symbol systems, that is. Furthermore, it was also illustrated how the functioning of these motivational systems may help to understand the process of responding to deviance in considerable detail. For example, in addition to type of deviance, the influence of situations, societies, historical periods, and individual differences on responding to deviance can be explained in terms of the likelihood with which the FF and C system are activated.

In comparing ours with other evolutionary approaches to social control or stigmatization, we concluded that the latter place too much emphasis on reciprocal altruism at the cost of inclusive fitness, neglect the crucial role of the C system in responding to passive deviance and "softening" aggressive responses to active deviance, confuse psychological mechanisms with symbolic reasoning, and pay insufficient attention to contextual influences on responding to deviance. This last aspect in particular causes theorists to incorrectly assume that stigmatization is the main form of social control in any society and thus must have been originally adaptive for our human ancestors. In contrast, we maintain that stigmatization is a specific type of social control in a particular context or society, and that the oldest type of adaptive social control is not stigmatization but repair in the context of small groups of genetically related hunter-gatherers.

# Mental representations of deviance and their emotional and judgmental implications

## 3.1 Introduction

How does the activity of the psychological mechanisms proposed in the previous chapter (the network consisting of the fight-or-flight and care system; our FF-C network) influence the way people mentally represent, think, and talk about deviant conditions and the individuals associated with these conditions? Is the content of their thoughts about deviance, and about their emotional reactions and behavioral impulses felt, consistent with the operation of these mechanisms? In this chapter, we are not so much concerned with the bodily and experiential aspects of emotions, and with the motor aspects of "real" and observable behavior (these are examined in more detail in Chapter 4), as well as with the way people think and talk about their emotions and behavior with respect to deviance. That is, we will treat not only thinking or cognition, but also emotion and behavior, as products of the mind or mental content, and assume that the common language that people use to describe these products generally corresponds with their true internal representations, actually felt emotions, and observable behaviors. More generally, we propose that the same (language-independent) motivational mechanisms that are responsible for the content of representations of deviance are also responsible for the causal role of these representations in influencing bodily, emotional, and behavioral responses (see also Chapter 2, for a discussion of how our approach deals with the problem of mentalism). However, although our motivational systems can be conceived as universal concepts that are responsible for the meaning of people's mental representations and their causal role, the activation of these systems, and hence the use of concepts, is also sensitive to contextual and cultural influences and can bias people's responses to deviance (see Chapters 4 and 6). Yet, because we assume that all responses to deviance are similarly determined by the universal aspects of meaning and content of representations, this chapter will not distinguish among stigmatization, tolerance, or repair.

Describing relationships between thoughts about properties of objects (expectancies, beliefs, stereotypes, mental or symbolic representations in general) and thoughts about emotions and about past or future (or "intended") behavior is the most dominant way in which behavior is "explained" in both everyday life and psychology; commonly referred to as "expectancy-value models" (Ajzen & Fishbein, 1980) or "belief-desire" psychology (Sterelny, 1990). For example, we normally assume that our expectancies about a fragile object (i.e., that it will break when handled too roughly), influence the way we feel about it (tenderness or care), that these feelings in turn influence our motivation or intention to behave in particular ways in relation to the object (e.g., gently handling the object when picking it up); and that normally this intention will be translated into observable behavior (e.g., a researcher may demonstrate that the tension of the muscles in our hand indeed decreases during lifting of the object). Individuals may, of course, not always be accurate in reporting their thoughts or beliefs and in predicting behavioral consequences. This may, for example, happen when they hardly pay attention to the objects or situations to which these thoughts refer, or are motivated to lie about what they think. Yet generally, it seems likely that measuring the thoughts of a group of people in an aggregate manner will reveal accurately the content of group members' internal representations with respect to particular objects, and its emotional and behavioral implications.

In this chapter, we will use two complementary ways to demonstrate that the motivational systems or concepts of our FF-C network are responsible for the content of people's mental representations of deviance. First, we will examine how people mentally represent multiple deviant conditions and the similarities and differences between them. We will test the hypothesis that people generally use two dimensions or concepts to interpret and classify these conditions (see Figure 2.1 in Chapter 2); and that this two-dimensional structure can be independently derived from the way people think about properties of these conditions and about their behavioral responses to them. In addition, we examine the hypothesis that the location of deviant conditions in two-dimensional mental space is associated with unique patterns of emotional reactions.

Second, we will study how people interpret, evaluate, and judge the behavior of individuals associated with deviant conditions. We will show that mental representations of deviance function as expectancies in terms of which information about a deviant individual's behavior is judged; and that behavior that is seen as ambiguous or as expected is assimilated to the relevant expectancy, whereas behavior that is seen as unexpected often creates a "contrast effect." In addition to a purely

cognitive account of these phenomena in terms of schema-based processing or stereotyping, however, we will also illustrate that people not
only expect but also desire particular behavior from deviant individuals once the relevant motivational systems are activated by the
perception of deviance; and that in light of these desires the particular
behavior is negatively or positively evaluated. For example, whereas
the unexpected behavior of a "mad" person (e.g., self-controlled rather
than unpredictable behavior) may result in a reduction of fear, relief,
and a positive evaluation, the unexpected behavior of an acutely ill and
needy person (e.g., behaving self-confidently and showing happiness)
may cause a negative evaluation and anger because the person frustrates our need to care for him or her. We will show in detail that several
ambiguities in this field may be resolved once we force ourselves to
explain expectancy-based perception and judgment on the basis of a
detailed understanding of the motivational mechanisms that underlie
particular expectancies.

## 3.2 The content of mental representations of deviance

*Methods to reveal the content of people's thoughts*

Researchers have used different methods to study people's thoughts
about deviant conditions, each having particular advantages and
disadvantages. First, they may ask people to spontaneously report as
many details as they can about a single deviant condition, only slightly
helping them to structure their thoughts and to organize the interview.
Clearly, self-reports that are generated with open-ended questions and
a minimum of help from the interviewer will be relatively unbiased
and therefore highly valuable. However, they are limited in the sense
that they will not reveal aspects of internal representations that are
less easily verbalized or important differences in representations of
different deviant conditions. Two other methods have been employed
to get a more complete picture of the content of representations of
deviant conditions. First, still making use of people's spontaneous
thinking about deviance, researchers may present research participants
with different labels referring to different deviant conditions, and ask
them to indicate how similar or dissimilar these conditions appear to
them, using whatever criteria they consider appropriate. After having
compared all the different conditions with each other (and sometimes
sorting them into piles of more or less similar ones), researchers may
construct a (dis)similarity matrix revealing the subjective "distances"
among the different conditions, and use a statistical technique to
uncover the different criteria, concepts, or "dimensions" that participants

must have used in thinking about these distances. Second, researchers may also supply participants with a particular selection of words for describing the properties or attributes on which the different deviant conditions may differ (e.g., "How dangerous, warm, responsible, etc. do you perceive condition X to be? (1) not at all ... (7) very much."). Subsequently, on the basis of profiles of mean attribute ratings of the different conditions, they may use a similar statistical technique to reveal the underlying dimensional structure. However, one disadvantage of this method is that the dimensions revealed and their interpretation will be dependent on the property words that have been chosen by the researchers in order to measure participants' thoughts. In contrast, the advantage of the first method is that researchers do not guide or bias participants in their thinking about the perceived properties. However, in order to aid interpretation of the obtained dimensions, researchers may use the former and latter method in combination, asking participants first to judge (dis)similarities among deviant conditions on intuitive grounds, and subsequently ask them to rate these conditions on pre-formulated attribute scales. In order to interpret the spontaneously produced dimensions, the latter ratings then are correlated with the locations of the different conditions on those dimensions (Kruskal & Wish, 1978; Schmelkin, 1988).

Two particular disadvantages of using (dis)similarity and attribute ratings in order to reveal underlying dimensions or concepts should be mentioned. First, the matrix of distances among deviant conditions and the dimensions that are finally obtained are dependent on the conditions that are included in the stimulus set. It is evident that a particular dimension can only be revealed if the set includes examples of conditions that saliently differ on that dimension. For example, in order to reveal an active-passive dimension, the stimulus set should include both active (e.g., crime or threatening contagious diseases) and passive deviant conditions (e.g., disabilities). For our purposes, this implies that we should be especially interested in studies that employ not only spontaneous (dis)similarity judgments but also a heterogeneous set of deviant conditions to judge.

Second, asking participants to compare different deviant conditions with each other, and encouraging them to focus on their most important differences, may obscure certain complexities in participants' mental representations that may only become apparent if they concentrate on interacting with a particular deviant individual. For example, without specifying an interaction or relationship with the deviant individual, an illness like cancer may appear close to mental illness in terms of high activity (think about the similarity between fear-arousing, malignant cell growth and unpredictable aggressive behavior), but closer to less dangerous and more passive physical illnesses and disabilities when associated with the suffering, vulnerability, and need state of a concrete patient. However, the possibility that cancer may have both these active and passive aspects may be neglected when, in comparing it with other deviant conditions, research participants try to establish how cancer is generally different from, or similar to, these other conditions (see also our suggestion in Chapter 2 that, for certain purposes, active and passive deviance may be seen as two independent dimensions rather than the opposite poles of a single dimension). To reveal this more complex or ambivalent nature of representations of deviant conditions, we also need to study them in isolation within a specified context. For example, asking participants to imagine interacting with a person with a particular lethal and contagious disease (i.e., using *vignettes* or scenarios to trigger self-reports) may result both in the perception that the person can be dangerous to them (high activity) and is dependent on their care (high passivity). Given the different advantages and disadvantages of the different research methods used to reveal the content of thought about deviance, it seems best to use studies that employ these different methods in a complementary way to construct a complete picture of people's thinking about deviance.

## Mental representations of deviant conditions

As suggested above, the most valuable studies for testing our general hypothesis that differences in deviant conditions will be reflected in the internal representation of deviant properties are those that have employed a heterogeneous set of conditions and asked participants to judge the (dis)similarities among these conditions on intuitive grounds and as unconstrained as possible. To facilitate comparisons among studies, they also should have analyzed these perceived similarities by means of multidimensional scaling analysis (MDS for short). We could locate only three studies that satisfied these requirements. In order to relate the results of these and later discussed studies to our theoretically derived two-dimensional classification of deviance, we sometimes rotated the obtained configurations (which, with a few exceptions, were always two-dimensional) 90 or 180 degrees and/or displayed their mirror images in such a way that their vertical dimension matched with our active-passive and their horizontal dimension with our controllability dimension. It is important to note that, in this process, we did not rotate the dimensions independently from the data points. Surely, this is a rather conservative method of testing our hypothesis. That is, each MDS analysis results in a relatively arbitrary orientation of the two orthogonal dimensions that sometimes may be better fitted to the data points by rotating them. Yet, because this rotation may easily result in a biased confirmation of our expected dimensions, we decided to accept the obtained and reported orientations of the two dimensions as given. Of course, in this way particular deviant conditions could accidentally fall in the "right" as well as "wrong" quadrants of our proposed two-dimensional space.

In two highly similar studies, Frable (1993b, Study 1) and Deaux, Reid, Mizrahi, and Ethier (1995, Study 2) asked American students to make pairwise similarity judgments of eleven and fifteen deviant conditions, respectively. The resulting distance matrices were analyzed by means of MDS, resulting in two dimensions (see Figure 3.1 (A and B)). To help interpret the obtained dimensions, Frable (1993b) and Deaux *et al.* (1995) obtained additional ratings on ten and six attributes, respectively. In each study, the authors interpret the horizontal dimension as "commonness" or "visibility" (e.g., smokers, blacks, or fat people are perceived as more "common" or "visible" than retarded or homosexual people) and the vertical one as "evaluative connotation" (e.g., criminals and persons with AIDS are seen as relatively bad, threatening, and active). Thus both Deaux *et al.*'s and Frable's interpretation of the vertical dimension appears similar to our active-passive dimension. However, we do not agree with their interpretation of the horizontal dimension as reflecting the concept of "visibility." Why, for example, would an amputee or mentally retarded individual be less visible than a fat or black person? (Below we discuss another MDS study that offers a quite different interpretation of visibility.) Instead, we propose that our interpretation in terms of controllability makes more sense. Specifically, active deviant conditions will be judged in terms of the amount of mental or behavioral control the deviant individual has over his or her threatening behavior and its consequences, with, for example, a criminal having more, and a mentally ill person having less, control. Passive deviance will be judged in terms of the amount of control individuals have over the onset and/or offset of their conditions, with obese persons and those on welfare having more control over their situation than clearly dependent and disabled individuals. (The ambiguous position of addictions on the active-passive dimension will be addressed below.)

Schoeneman, Segerstrom, Griffin, and Gresham (1993) employed a free sorting task with forty-eight mental disorder descriptions, mixed with labels for severe norm transgressions and addictions, and obtained three dimensions. Our presentation of their results (see Figure 3.1 (C)) is based on the coordinate values of the conditions on the first and third dimensions presented in their Table 2. Only conditions that were most often mentioned spontaneously in a preliminary study,

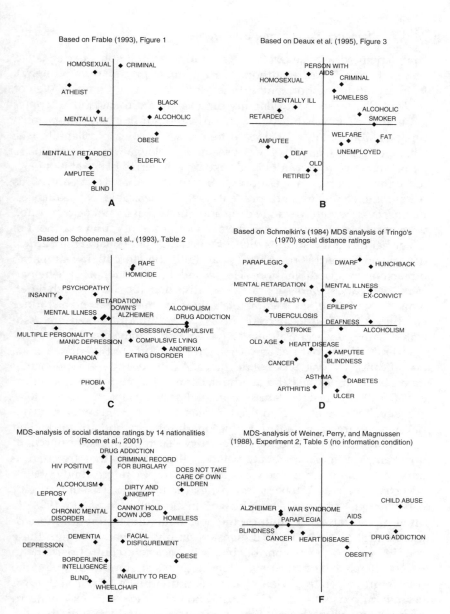

**Figure 3.1** Two-dimensional configurations of deviant conditions obtained in six multidimensional scaling studies. Vertical dimension is interpreted as Active vs. Passive, horizontal dimension as Low vs. High Controllability. Original configurations of studies were sometimes rotated 90 or 180 degrees, or displayed as a mirror image to aid interpretation. For the plots in B and D, coordinates of conditions had to be estimated by taking measurements from graphs without clear metric units.

complemented with several others to aid interpretation, are displayed in our Figure 3.1 (the authors use a similar presentation strategy). In interpreting the horizontal dimension, the authors refer to Weiner *et al.*'s (1988) onset controllability dimension; a dimension that comes close to our controllability dimension, although our two-dimensional representation allows for three different senses of controllability (see Chapter 2). For example, it does seem less relevant for lay persons to judge an active form of deviance like rape in terms of onset responsibility than in terms of the individual's ability and duty to control his behavioral impulses and prevent their undesirable consequences. Furthermore, when we judge drug addiction we may not be concerned with onset but with offset; i.e., the individual's motivation to get out of his or her deviant condition. Schoeneman *et al.* (1993) label the vertical dimension "severity" or "potency" and it is therefore highly similar to our active-passive dimension. (The second dimension that Schoeneman *et al.* (1993) uncovered, separated cognitive deficits, such as Alzheimer, Down's syndrome, and mental retardation, from the rest, yet the former conditions were all located in our left upper quadrant, and are associated with our uncontrollable-active type of deviance.)

Overall, the above three studies seem to support our two-dimensional classification of basic types of deviance. All three studies locate mental illness in the upper left hand quadrant. Because the study by Schoeneman *et al.* (1993) also includes labels for mental problems that are clearly fear-arousing because of their unpredictable nature (e.g., insanity, psychopathy), we are confident that this quadrant corresponds to deviant conditions that are uncontrollable-active. Turning to the upper right quadrant, we find threatening behavioral conditions that are controllable and punishable such as crime or rape. Interestingly, being addicted to alcohol, tobacco, or drugs (or to any other substance or behavior, cf. "obsessive-compulsive" in Schoeneman *et al.*, 1993) is often placed far to the right on the horizontal dimension but more or less neutral on the vertical dimension, implying that, although these conditions are seen as controllable, it is unclear if control pertains to passive deviance (i.e., the deviant individual's attempt to get out of the condition) or active deviance (i.e., the individual's responsibility for behavioral consequences of the condition and the perceiver's concern with coping with these threatening effects). We also find that the different studies are in agreement in placing physical disabilities (e.g., amputation, blindness), as well as mental conditions that are associated with mental suffering, weakness, and dependency (depression, phobia), in the lower left quadrant. Finally, our hypothesis that the lower right quadrant would contain deviant conditions that, while still triggering the care system because of their implied dependency on others, are associated with less suffering and a greater responsibility for the onset and/or offset of illnesses or disabling conditions, also seems to be supported. We may associate the latter conditions with the perceiver's skeptical attitude or doubt about their seriousness and the legitimacy of soliciting his or her help and care. This hypothesis is more specifically supported by the finding that all three studies place obesity, a condition that is generally seen as disabling and associated with immaturity, a lack of willpower, and laziness, in this quadrant. (Interestingly, Schoeneman *et al.* more generally speak of "eating disorder" and include anorexia as well.) Deaux *et al.* (1995) also add to this quadrant being on welfare and unemployed, and Schoeneman *et al.* (1993) compulsive lying (which may be seen as related to disobedience to caregivers and unwillingness to mature). It must finally be admitted that despite the impressive similarities between the results of the three different studies, they sometimes differ with respect to the placement of particular deviant conditions.

A recent study (Towler & Schneider, 2005), in which participants card-sorted fifty-four deviant conditions after which they rated the conditions in terms of a variety of properties offers further support for our two-dimensional interpretation. Cluster analysis revealed seven clusters and MDS revealed three dimensions which were labeled "controllability," "general pity," and "social undesirability." However, the way these three dimensions are interpreted, does not suggest that they are independent. In fact, the authors' interpretations seem to be consistent with our active-passive and controllability dimension. (Note that the authors do not present MDS configurations, and discuss their results in terms of the direct ratings of the seven clusters.) Specifically, consistent with our Type 2 deviance, the cluster Social deviants (e.g., murderers, sex offenders) was rated high on both social undesirability and controllability, and low on pity; consistent with our Type 3 deviance, the cluster Physically disabled was rated low on both social undesirability and controllability, and high on pity; and consistent with Type 4 deviance, the clusters Economically disadvantaged (e.g., the homeless, the unemployed) and Physical appearance (e.g., the obese, the unkempt, people with body odor) were rated moderately on social undesirability and high on controllability and pity. Finally, note that the authors' cluster of Racial identity was seen as similar to our Type 3 deviance (presumably because participants emphasized the disadvantaged status of the ethnic groups involved), and that the location of the cluster with mental illness was not clearly associated with one of our four types of deviance; presumably because it contained both active (suicidal, schizophrenics) and passive instances (depressed).

In sum, although our horizontal and vertical dimensions are often differently labeled and interpreted, they can be clearly recognized in the two-dimensional configurations that have been obtained in different studies by asking participants to think about differences and similarities among deviant conditions. Studies examining the internal representation of individual deviant conditions in greater detail further support our interpretation. For example, with respect to cases of Type 1 deviance, Corrigan and colleagues (Corrigan *et al.*, 2000) report that schizophrenia is predominantly seen as unpredictable and dangerous. Furthermore, when judged without a vulnerable patient in mind, cancer has the same perceived properties. For example, a respondent in an interview study reported that "cancer eats up the body. I visualize it as a packman. It eats whatever it comes across. It has an open mouth with teeth and it bites off everything. The body is fallen apart" (Weiss, 1997, p. 461). And in some cultures, especially the unpredictability of physical illnesses may be emphasized. For example, Whyte (1995) found that people in Tanzania associate epilepsy with uncontrollable-active or threatening deviance, indicating that the convulsions of epileptics are caused by a worm or lizard crawling from the spinal cord to the brain, and appear similar to the erratic fluttering of a beheaded chicken. Additionally, they may tell that it is dangerous to approach a person having a seizure, and especially warn against contact with the person's saliva.

With respect to cases of Type 2 deviance it is found that these conditions are seen as both dangerous and anger-arousing, and as potentially alterable through threat, punishment, learning, and mental change. It is noteworthy that we tend to be most upset by harmful behavior that is planned against vulnerable group members such as children, females, and elderly persons varying from smokers harming children by side-stream smoke (Rozin, 1999) to pedophiles or child abusers abducting children (Archer, 1996; Weiner *et al.*, 1988). Similarly, we also find that aggression against child abusers, wife beaters, or those who are hostile toward vulnerable social groups is relatively acceptable (Crandall *et al.*, 2002).

With respect to cases of Type 3 deviance, Walkey, Taylor, and Green (1990) found that the concepts "cancer patient" and "coronary heart patient" in comparison with the concept "average man" were both perceived as delicate, tense and slow, reflecting dependence, according to the investigators. Investigating images of wheelchair users, Fichten and Amsel (1986) found that the five traits most attributed to disabled students were isolated, lonely, helpless, silent, and depressed, traits that largely seem to reflect dependency (although in a college or performance context they may additionally reflect poor coping with their disadvantaged situation and hence an association with Type 4 deviance; see later).

Finally, with respect to cases of Type 4 deviance, Harris, Walters, and Waschull (1991) found that college students were perfectly willing to describe overweight men and women as lazy, sexless, ugly, self-indulgent, and sloppy. Similarly, Tiggeman and Rothblum (1997) found among American and Australian college students that fat people were seen as substantially less happy, self-confident, and attractive, and more self-indulgent and lazy. Klesges *et al.* (1990) found that, in simulated job decisions, employees expected both a mildly obese and a diabetic "job applicant" to have poorer work habits than a healthy one. While the diabetic was rated as more likely to have medically-related job absences, the obese applicant was expected to have other absences such as "abusing company privileges by feigning illness" (p. 527).

Other examples of controllable-passive deviance are conditions with apparently mild or not clearly visible physical symptoms that appear to be rather psychosomatic, not to be taken completely seriously, and implying a certain extent of exaggeration or malingering (for a discussion, see Looper & Kirmayer, 2004). It is noteworthy that in a Dutch national survey, asthma, diabetes, arthritis, and migraine were associated by 33 percent (diabetes) to 40 percent (arthritis) of the respondents with the possibility that patients may "sometimes use their illness to get something done" (Rijksvoorlichtingsdienst, 1993). Finally note that there is much evidence that the poor and homeless and individuals associated with low socioeconomic status are also perceived in a way that is quite consistent with our Type 4 deviance (see Chapter 2). Furthermore, when these individuals start to pose a threat to others, they may also be associated with more than one deviance. For example, people who risk their health such as smokers (Rozin, 1999) or ethnic or racial minorities who engage in organized protests against their discriminatory treatment (Rothbart, 1976) may be increasingly associated with criminality or uncontrollable violence.

## The dimensional structure of rejection hierarchies

Several researchers have asked people to indicate their social acceptance or avoidance of individuals with different deviant conditions in different settings (e.g., as neighbors, teachers, friends, or marriage partners), on the basis of which they constructed a social distance or rejection hierarchy. Although the main focus of these researchers is usually on examining social distance rankings for their own sake or to compare them across different cultural groups, their interpretation may be enhanced by using our categorization of deviant conditions in terms of the motivational mechanisms that these conditions tend to activate. Specifically, we would expect that deviant conditions in the upper half of our two-dimensional space would be more socially rejected than conditions in the lower half because the former are more threatening to the perceiver's well-being while the latter evoke a caring response (sometimes moderated by fear or anger). This is indeed what has been found by many researchers. For example, in a study by Westbrook, Legge, and Pennay (1993), informants (health practitioners) from six Australian ethnic communities indicated the degree to which twenty different disabilities and illnesses were socially rejected in their community. The researchers found the greatest rejection of persons with AIDS, people with a variety of mental or brain problems, and alcoholics, and the lowest rejection of asthma and diabetes. Employing a similar method (this time using informants from fourteen different countries), Room, Rehm, Trotter, Paglia, and Ustun (2001) obtained a similar ranking, additionally finding relatively strong rejection of ex-criminals and drug addicts, and the lowest rejection of wheelchair users and the blind. Furthermore, Juvonen (1991) found that schoolchildren showed more rejection of a classmate engaging in bragging or aggression or with a high activity level than one who was shy, obese, or physically ill. Using a more subtle measure, Rozin, Markwith, and McCauley (1994) found that people showed the greatest and about equal resistance to wearing a sweater that was previously worn by a murderer, a person with AIDS (irrespective of the origin of the illness) or one with tuberculosis; followed by a sweater worn by a homosexual and a person who had lost a leg in an accident.

With a set of primarily physical deviant conditions (presented as drawings) social distance hierarchies have also been examined with children from Western and non-Western cultures (Harper, 1995, 1999; Richardson, 1971). Among the deviant conditions, a child with an amputated hand or foot or with a facial disfigurement (cleft palate) was most rejected, a person with a crutch or in a wheelchair the least. Whereas Western societies rejected an obese child even more, several non-Western ones rejected that child the least (probably due to an association with shareable wealth) and a foot amputation the most. Although the author explains this hierarchy differently, it may be proposed that a crutch or wheelchair accentuates the passive nature and dependency of the deviant person and that children are scared by a visible amputation or facial scar.

Interestingly, the above social distance hierarchies are also reflected in how socially acceptable or desirable people find it to openly express rejection, avoidance or discriminatory behavior in settings such as dating, employment, or housing. Thus it is considered relatively acceptable to express negative feelings against drug users, ex-convicts, or child abusers, but not against welfare recipients, fat people, and black Americans and other disadvantaged ethnic minorities (see Crandall *et al.*, 2002). It is interesting to mention that, on the basis of an almost perfect correlation between these acceptability ratings and people's negative evaluations or prejudice of these deviant conditions, Crandall *et al.* argued that the latter must be derived from the former or norms. However, this correlation is equally consistent with the opposite view that these norms are derived from the motivated responses that objective features of deviance universally tend to trigger. Specifically, in terms of our theory, Crandall *et al.*'s (2002) pattern of findings can be interpreted as reflecting the universal disapproval of hostility toward passive deviance (e.g., the blind, minorities when they are seen as disadvantaged) and the universal approval of defensive and punishing responses toward active deviance (e.g., those who are guilty of hostilities toward passive deviance, such as racists, child abusers, wife beaters, and so on). The adherence to norms of social acceptability of expressing negative evaluations may follow from this universal truth.

In a relatively unknown article, Schmelkin (1984) makes the important point that studies computing rejection hierarchies may give the misleading impression that people's reasons for their relative rejection are organized in a one-dimensional manner. Indeed, as far as we know, she has been the first and only researcher who tried to uncover the multi-dimensional structure of a social distance hierarchy. In particular, Schmelkin (1984) performed a multi-dimensional scaling analysis on the correlations among social distance ratings of twenty-one deviant conditions as obtained by Tringo (1970, reported in Schmelkin, 1984). Interestingly, as shown in Figure 3.1 (D), of the three dimensions she identified, the first and third seem similar to our theoretically proposed dimensions.[1] The fact that a paraplegic, together with a dwarf and hunchback, is located high on the vertical dimension, suggests that in this stimulus set, the former is not primarily seen as passive (e.g., due to paralysis) but as strange and threatening (e.g., due to a strange and spastic posture of the limbs). In contrast to Frable (1993b) and Deaux *et al.* (1995), Schmelkin does not interpret our horizontal but vertical dimension in terms of visibility, arguing that several threatening conditions such as dwarf or hunchback are more visible than certain passive conditions such as ulcer, asthma, and diabetes. In addition, she reports difficulty with interpreting the horizontal dimension but suspects that it may contrast more (e.g., hunchback, alcoholism) versus less ostracized conditions (e.g., old age, cancer). As may be evident from the above discussion, we believe that these interpretations make less sense than our theoretically derived dimensions.

Inspired by Schmelkin's (1984) secondary MDS analysis of social distance ratings, we performed one ourselves on the social distance rankings reported by Room *et al.* (Room *et al.*, 2001, Table 9), treating the mean ratings provided by the fourteen different countries as cases. The result is the configuration displayed in Figure 3.1 (E), which fits remarkably well on our theoretically derived two-dimensional representation. However, this time, alcoholism and drug addiction seem to be especially associated with active forms of deviance.

Finally we would like to pay attention to a very influential study on responses to a heterogeneous set of deviant conditions. In two different studies, Weiner *et al.* (1988) asked American and Canadian students to rate ten deviant conditions not only in terms of behavioral tendencies (assistance and charitable donations) but also in terms of perceived responsibility, blame, likeability, pity, and anger. In Study 1, origin of these conditions was left unspecified; in Study 2, an experimental manipulation was included, contrasting conditions that were presented as uncontrollable, controllable, or without information about origin. The authors used the results to compare mean ratings between the deviant conditions and between the three information conditions. We performed an MDS-analysis on the means of the above rating scales obtained in Study 2 and as presented in Weiner *et al.*'s Table 5 (no information condition). Interestingly, although Weiner *et al.* force their research participants to judge deviant conditions primarily in terms of controllability (no other property than responsibility was measured), our results indicate that participants also made use of our vertical active-passive dimension (see Figure 3.1 (F)). For example, passive conditions (e.g., blindness, heart disease, and cancer) are located in the lower left quadrant, obesity in the lower right quadrant, and the very threatening but punishable (anger-arousing) "child abuse" in the upper right quadrant. Also, like in many other studies, drug abuse is located at the right hand side and very close to the horizontal dimension. Finally, war syndrome, like Alzheimer, may have been associated with a somewhat scary mental condition. When we performed an MDS analysis on our replication of Weiner (Dijker & Koomen, 2003, discussed below), we found a highly similar configuration as in Figure 3.1 (F).

*Preliminary conclusions*   Our analysis thus far warrants the conclusion that, despite several disagreements among studies with respect to the specific location of individual deviant conditions in the two-dimensional space, the different studies reveal a common two-dimensional structure that shows a good fit with our theoretically derived dimensions. This is remarkable because the different studies not only employed different stimulus sets but also different methods of presenting them to participants, with some using an unconstrained sorting procedure, others attribute ratings, and still others a more behavior-like response in terms of social distance or relative rejection. Because it is well known how sensitive many kinds of verbal responses are to context effects caused by instructions, the presence of other stimuli, and the wording of labels and rating scales (cf. Schwarz & Sudman, 1992), one would have expected greater disagreement among the studies. Our secondary analysis of the results of the cross-cultural study by Room *et al.* (2001), additionally suggested that our two dimensions may have some universal status. That is, by performing an MDS analysis on social distance rankings provided by participants in fourteen different countries, we were able to obtain a similar two-dimensional structure as in single national samples. Finally, it is worth repeating that we did not rotate the dimensions to obtain a better fit with the configuration.[2] In sum, until now, our analysis leads us to conclude that our hypothesized dimensions are very robust against major variations in method, analysis, and samples employed. Also remember from Chapter 2 that the meaning of many other dimensions that are suggested in the literature on social control and stigmatization, such as visibility, disruptiveness, or aesthetics, as well as the different meanings of responsibility, are well captured by our active vs. passive and controllability dimension.

## Emotional implications of mental representations of deviance

*Emotion profiles*   In Chapter 2, we proposed a combined hypothesis for the content of representations of deviance and the emotions experienced in response to deviance. Specifically, because elementary features of deviance would be able to activate the FF or C system, activation of these systems would not only cause people to categorize and interpret deviant conditions in terms of the active-passive and controllability dimension, but also to feel specific (combinations of) emotions in response to the different categories of deviance. Thus it was hypothesized that active deviance would arouse more fear and anger, and less tenderness/pity than passive deviance, because the former activates the FF system, and the latter the C system (see Figure 2.1, Chapter 2). Due to the moderating influence of controllability, it was additionally hypothesized that uncontrollable-active deviant conditions would arouse more fear and less anger than controllable-active conditions; and that uncontrollable-passive conditions would arouse more fear and hence pity (especially when the condition is associated with suffering and distress), and less anger, than controllable-passive conditions. As may be remembered, we theorized that controllable-passive conditions arouse anger and less pity because, in light of the activated C system, people get angry at individuals they care for but who do not seem to take enough care of their own health and fitness and behave immaturely. Although people may feel anger at these deviant individuals (and perhaps also look down on them when showing no motivation to behave responsibly), and will feel a lack of motivation to help them, they may nurture these individuals if given a chance and they show motivation to get well. Thus, overall, aggression and avoidance in the lower half of our two-dimensional space would not be as extreme as aggression and avoidance in the upper half.

Unfortunately, we have been unable to locate studies in which the emotions of pity, fear, and anger were simultaneously measured for deviant conditions representing all four basic types of deviance. Instead, the available studies concentrate on one or two of the three emotional responses (sometimes in terms of related emotion words) to only some types of deviance. In particular, we miss information about emotional responses to our category of uncontrollable-active deviance, especially in terms of fear. Nevertheless, the above hypothesized emotion profile tends to be supported by a number of studies. In particular, these studies support the hypothesis that, when going from the lower left, to the lower right, to the upper right quadrant in Figure 2.1, mean intensity of anger responses tend to increase, but mean intensity of pity reactions decrease. For example, Weiner *et al.* (1988, Table 1) found for several typical examples of Type 2, 3, and 4 deviance that, on a 9-point scale, anger intensity could be ordered from low to high when comparing, for example, blindness (1.7), obesity (3.3), and child abuse (7.9); and that pity intensity could be ordered in the reverse way when comparing blindness (7.4), obesity (5.1), and child abuse (3.3). In a replication of Weiner *et al.* (1988), Dijker and Koomen (2003, Study 1) found a similar ordering. Again, anger intensity could be ordered from low to high when comparing blindness (1.54), obesity (2.43), and child abuse (8.21), whereas mean pity scores could be ordered in the reverse way when comparing blindness (6.79), obesity (5.12), and child abuse (3.10). Although Menec and Perry (1995) did not present their participants with deviant conditions with labels only but with additional information about the origin of the condition and age of target person, their results are relevant too. In particular, for deviant individuals of younger age, they found that, on a 9-point scale, anger intensity could be ordered from low to high when comparing blindness presented as uncontrollable (1.93), obesity presented as uncontrollable (2.74), and unemployment presented as being caused by unreliability and fighting with coworkers (4.93); and that pity intensity could be ordered in the reverse way when comparing blindness (7.26), obesity (6.02) and an unreliable and aggressive unemployed person (4.10). (The effects of Menec and Perry's age manipulation will be discussed below.) Finally, using a 5-point scale, Fiske *et al.* (2002, Study 4), found that the mean pity ratings for uncontrollable-passive (their cluster of high warmth, low competence) and controllable-passive deviance (their cluster of low warmth, low competence) were 3.66 and 3.39, respectively. In addition, on the authors' composite measure of contempt that included anger, frustration, and hate, the first cluster was rated lower (M = 1.70) than the latter (M = 2.50).

To our knowledge, we have been the only ones to measure fear responses to a heterogeneous set of deviant conditions. The results of our replication of Weiner *et al.*'s (1988) study (Dijker & Koomen, 2003, Study 1) suggest that a typical controllable-active deviant condition such as child abuse evokes more fear (5.47) than conditions in the lower half of the circle shown in Figure 2.1 (except for drug addiction with a mean fear score of 4.81 and AIDS with a mean of 4.08, all other conditions received a mean fear rating lower than 3.58). However, of the two conditions found in our uncontrollable-active quadrant (see Figure 3.1 (F)), war syndrome (3.58) and Alzheimer (3.01) received higher fear ratings than blindness (2.77).

Using more limited stimulus sets, two recent studies provide additional information about the relative importance of fear, anger, and pity responses. Cottrell and Neuberg (2005) measured anger, fear, and pity (together with disgust) to examine responses to several social groups that seemed to differ primarily on an active-passive or threat dimension. Specifically, these researchers found that strong threat, fear, and anger, and less pity was aroused by African-Americans, Mexican Americans, fundamental Christians, and activist feminists; and less threat, fear and anger, and more pity by European Americans, Asian Americans, and non-fundamental Christians. Homosexuals occupied an ambiguous position on this dimension, being the only group that aroused relatively strong disgust as well as pity, the latter probably because of their association with ill health (in Chapter 6 we suggest that, due to its inherent ambiguous nature, responses to homosexuality may vary greatly across cultures and historical periods). Corrigan *et al.* (2005) found that among their four deviant conditions, mental illness received more intense fear and less intense pity responses than leukemia, while anger ratings did not differ for these two conditions. However, presenting mental illness more like a medical condition ("a brain tumor that makes him act like he has a mental illness sometimes") resulted in similar fear and pity ratings as leukemia. In this study, presenting the target as having a drinking problem resulted in higher levels of fear and anger, and lower levels of pity than mental illness (note that in this study, the presentation of mental illness may have emphasized certain non-deviant and harmless aspects by stating that the target is a new student in class who is "transferring from a special school").

To conclude, the available evidence on mean emotion ratings seems to offer preliminary support for the hypothesized differences in emotion intensities as shown in Figure 2.1.

*The relative importance of different emotions*    An alternative way of establishing associations between deviant conditions and emotions is to compute the relative contribution of different emotions in predicting behavioral tendencies or general evaluations evoked by these conditions. Taken over the whole range of deviant conditions that were included in Dijker and Koomen's (2003) replication of Weiner *et al.*'s (1988) Study 2, pity and anger had an independent but opposite influence on tendencies to help a deviant individual. Moreover, when fear was added, anger did not explain these tendencies anymore, while pity ($p < 0.001$) and fear ($p < 0.07$) did. This suggests that both the FF and C system are independently involved in responding to deviance in general (Weiner *et al.*, 1988, do not report regression analyses in which these two emotions were included as predictors).

We expect that the extent to which individual emotions predict behavioral tendencies will be dependent on the deviant condition's potential to trigger the FF or C system. This has been examined for a few of our basic types of deviance. With respect to uncontrollable-active deviance (those conditions that are primarily threatening because they imply unpredictable danger or contagiousness) we would expect that the flight component of the FF is activated and that its output in the form of fear would exert a stronger influence on responding than anger. To the extent that these conditions also have passive elements (i.e., can be associated with patients who suffer from the particular condition), pity can also be expected to have an influence. Consistent with this expectancy, when Angermeyer and Matschinger (1997) regressed a measure of social distance from schizophrenia on aggressive emotions (including anger), fear, and pro-social responses (including sympathy), they found that aggressive emotions exerted "a very minimal" (no significance for the regression coefficient was reported), but fear and pro-social emotions a strong influence on social distance. In a recent study (Corrigan, Markowitz, Watson, Rowan, & Kubiak, 2003), the same pattern of relations was observed. These researchers found that, of the three emotions measured, fear and pity did, but anger did not independently predict a tendency to help mentally ill persons. Furthermore, with respect to social avoidance of persons with tuberculosis, Jaramillo

(1999) found that regressing avoidance on anger, fear, and pity only resulted in a positive influence of fear.

With respect to controllable-active deviance, there is sufficient evidence that tendencies to punish are independently determined by anger and pity (e.g., Graham *et al.*, 1997; Weiner, 1995). Note that ethnic outgroups may represent both active and passive elements. On the one hand, they may be seen as threatening, unpredictable, but also as planning to compete and take advantage of the ingroup. On the other hand, to the extent that perceivers are concerned about their unequal treatment and discrimination, they may be perceived as disadvantaged and passively deviant. It is probably for this reason, that attitudes toward minority groups in the Netherlands can be very well predicted from a linear combination of fear, anger, and pity (Dijker, 1987, although here, pity was combined with a number of positive emotions into a composite of "positive emotions" ).

There is considerable evidence suggesting that responses to passive deviant conditions varying in controllability and that involve both elements of suffering and danger to the perceiver (because the illness is associated with serious or lethal consequences, or with contagiousness), may be independently determined by all three emotions. For example, Dijker and Koomen (2003, Studies 2 and 3) found that a tendency to avoid a patient with one-sided paralysis due to brain hemorrhage or a tendency to help a patient with chronic heart disease, were independently influenced by anger, fear, and pity. Moreover, Dijker, Kok, and Koomen (1996) reported that social avoidance of persons with AIDS could be predicted by an additive combination of anger, fear, and pity. Finally, Reisenzein (1986) demonstrated that the helping responses to a scenario in which a victim collapses in a subway and remains lying on the ground were independently determined by pity and anger.

*Correlations among emotional responses* We also need to consider how the pattern of intercorrelations among the three emotions can be interpreted as providing additional support for the presently proposed motivational network. In the studies that measured all three emotions, anger and fear are normally positively correlated (e.g., Dijker, 1987; Dijker, Kok *et al.*, 1996; Dijker & Koomen, 2003), suggesting that both emotions may be evoked simultaneously or alternately by the deviant condition's potential to activate the FF system. Furthermore, consistent with an inhibitory relationship between the C and FF system, the same studies showed that anger correlates negatively with pity (see also Reisenzein, 1986). The relationship between pity and fear is more complex and dependent on whether the deviant condition is passive or active. In the case of passive deviance like illness, fear and pity are positively correlated, indicating that the suffering of others activates both the fear aspect of the FF system and the C system (Dijker, Kok *et al.*, 1996; Dijker & Koomen, 2003, Studies 1–3). However, fear may also inhibit the output of the C system, for example, when one imagines interacting with a threatening active deviant. This is consistent with the finding that fear and pity responses to ethnic minorities are negatively correlated (Dijker, 1987). It is, however, quite conceivable that when people have a greater opportunity to reflect on the disadvantaged position of a minority group, fear and pity may also be positively correlated, as is the case for illnesses.

*Emotions as mediators of the influence of mental representations on behavior* In different studies it was shown that (self-reported) emotions can be seen as mediating the influence of the active-passive and controllability dimension on (self-reported) behavioral tendencies. For example, Dijker and Koomen (2003, Experiments 2 and 3) demonstrated that experimental manipulations of the seriousness of an illness and its controllability influence both the emotions of fear, anger, and pity, and participants' willingness to care for a patient (with the emotions being strongly correlated with the willingness to care). In addition, a path analysis revealed that controlling for emotions partly removed the influence of perceived seriousness and controllability on willingness to care (for similar analyses with respect to controllability only, see Reisenzein, 1986; Weiner *et al.*, 1988). In sum, we have shown that, at least at a mental or verbal level that can be reported by research participants to investigators, thoughts about the properties of deviant conditions may causally affect emotional as well as behavioral responses to individuals with those conditions.[3]

### 3.3 The effects of additional or salient information on perceptions of deviance

In responding to deviance or deviant persons people sometimes have extra information about the deviant condition (e.g., they may learn that it is uncontrollable), about the deviant person in question (e.g., he had an unhappy childhood), or may pay, because of a particular focus, more attention to some facts about the deviant person rather than to other facts. How these three factors may affect our responses will be described in the present section. Generally, the effects of these informational factors will reflect the motivational systems that they activate. Of course, these responses may also be affected by the behavior shown by the deviant person. This issue, however, will be treated in the next section.

We start by describing some effects obtained by informing people about the specific nature of deviant conditions. For example, the threatening nature of Type 1 deviance may be emphasized by informing people that mental illness is caused by biological and genetic factors, thus accentuating its uncontrollable and immutable nature (Mehta & Farina, 1997; Walker & Read, 2002). In contrast, in presenting mental illness as psychosocial in origin (being caused by childhood or environmental factors), one may emphasize dependency. The former information appears to result in more negative responses to persons suffering from mental illness than the latter (for a related discussion of the undesirable side-effect of stressing a genetic basis for mental illness, see Phelan, 2002). A similar effect can be observed with homosexuality, which may also be partly associated with Type 1 deviance. Stressing the biological basis of this condition may increase its threatening nature, especially for those with negative attitudes. Indeed, males with negative attitudes toward homosexuals tend to respond negatively to information suggesting that homosexuality is due to uncontrollable and immutable biological factors (Hegarty, 2002), and maintain that homosexuals are responsible for controlling their behavior (Whitley, 1990) or "choose or learn to be that way" and therefore punishable (Ernulf, Innala, & Whitam, 1989). (Note that for those with positive attitudes, stressing the uncontrollable and biological nature of homosexuality would be desirable, because it avoids seeing it as Type 2 deviance, and implies acceptance of the other person. See also Hegarty, 2002.)

People may also learn more about specific deviant persons. An illness may be quite serious or less serious. Increasing seriousness of an illness may enlarge fear and avoidance. For example, when Crandall and Moriarity (1995) informed research participants that a seriously ill person suffers from fever, frequent bouts of diarrhea, and a persistent cough, participants responded with more rejection. However, these investigators did not specify under what conditions the ill person would be met and whether there was a dependency of the patient on the perceiver. In contrast, when Dijker and Koomen (2003, Experiment 2) asked university students to imagine that during their vacation they worked in a nursing home, assisting the staff with the care, social support, and revalidation of a particular patient, they did not find a relationship between a similar manipulation of seriousness and the participants' unwillingness to care for the patient. In addition, they showed that seriousness had a positive influence on both anxiety and pity, and that anxiety positively and pity negatively affected reluctance to care for the patient. Thus, another person's suffering may also arouse pity when the person is seen as dependent, and the more pity is felt the greater the likelihood that the other will be cared for.

If people are confronted with a deviant person, and they learn that the person also happens to have another deviant condition, the two sets of information or the two mental representations are likely to be combined, especially when concrete, salient individuals are involved. For example, combining specific information about, on the one hand, suffering and dependency and, on the other hand, old age is likely to result in extra activation of the care system and to increase pity. Viewed in isolation, old age is spontaneously associated with incapacity to work and contribute to the community, chronic illness, suffering, depression, and death (e.g., Slotterback & Saarnio, 1996). Furthermore, on the basis of age information alone, people generally favor younger adults over the old for a life-saving but scarce (medical) treatment (Burnstein, Crandall, & Kitayama, 1994; Furnham & Ofstein, 1997). Yet the response may change dramatically when health practitioners decide on a life-saving medical treatment on the basis of the specific need state of patients (Wetle, Cwikel, & Levkoff, 1988). Furthermore, when people are exposed to signs of suffering of target persons who are presented in a clearly visible way, exposing their age-related physical vulnerability cues, elderly individuals (together with toddlers, adolescents, and adult females) arouse more protection and pity than younger adult males (Dijker, 2001). In contrast to most studies on "ageism," the latter study indicates that negative responses to the label "old age" may be reduced by exposing individuals to concrete visual information about the fragility of old bodies, or by an easily imagined everyday interaction with an elderly person (see also, Burnstein *et al.*, 1994). This is also suggested by Menec and Perry (1995) who showed that after giving age information about vividly described ill patients, participants felt more pity for old than for young (adult) persons.

Another important piece of information that people may have is whether the deviant person is responsible for his or her condition. Weiner *et al.* (1988) examined the effects of changes in this onset responsibility in considerable detail. In general, compared to conditions in which ill or disabled individuals are presented without additional information, information that those individuals had onset responsibility for their condition increased feelings of anger and decreased feelings of pity. But there is a caveat here. In these experiments, it is not clear if this effect is due to associating the responsible patients with socially undesirable attributes with a more active component, or with foreseeability and intentionality in bringing their illness upon themselves; something we see as typically associated with Type 4 deviance. For example, in Weiner *et al.* (1988), individuals highly responsible for their illness are presented as having engaged in negatively valenced behavior that could hurt others (paraplegia was caused by colliding with the rear of a car stopped at a traffic light; AIDS caused by a promiscuous sex life) whereas in the case of low responsibility a behavioral cause was entirely absent (e.g., illnesses caused by other people's faults, accidents, or hereditary factors). Similar problems can be noted in many other experimental manipulations of controllability in which the controllable and behaviorally caused need state or illness was caused by behavior associated with such things as alcoholism or harassment of others (e.g., Alicke & Davis, 1990; Crandall & Moriarty, 1995; Reisenzein, 1986).

In order to disentangle the effects of the valence of the behavioral cause (or controllable-active nature of deviance) and true onset responsibility for a deviant condition, we (Dijker & Koomen, 2003, Study 1) performed an exact replication of Weiner *et al.*'s (1988) study but now with the potentially confounding variable "valence of behavioral cause" also measured. In addition, we (Dijker & Koomen, 2003, Studies 2 and 3) conducted two experiments in which we manipulated both a pure form of onset controllability (the stimulus person either did or did not know that he had a slumbering medical condition – an aneurysm – that needed special behavioral precautions, and did or did not choose to ignore the doctors' warnings and behavioral advice) and valence of behavioral cause (prior to getting ill, the stimulus person acted negatively, neutrally, or positively toward others). In general, the results showed that both in our replication of Weiner *et al.*'s study and our experiments, onset responsibility and valence of behavioral cause exerted an independent or additive influence on pity, anger, and helping or avoidance tendencies. Furthermore, in the two experiments it was shown that, irrespective of having previously engaged in socially desirable or undesirable behavior, perceivers judged an ill person more negatively when the illness was foreseeable and avoidable. Thus these experiments reveal for the first time in a relatively pure way the truly remarkable aspect of onset controllability, namely that we can get angry at strangers who appear to willfully neglect their own health, and are associated with Type 4 deviance. As mentioned earlier, we reason that, endangering your own health (especially after having been warned by a person who cares about your health) arouses anger (and decreases pity) because it is inconsistent with an automatically triggered desire of the perceiver to care for a sick and dependent individual.

Furthermore, the same information about a deviant person may, particularly dependent on people's focus, be emphasized or not. If it is emphasized, it will more strongly activate relevant motivational systems. This is particularly evidenced by many studies conducted by Batson (1987) in which participants were asked to focus on the other person's psychological suffering (how does she feel, how is she affected), instead of distancing themselves from the suffering. Focusing on suffering resulted in more pity or helping responses. As a more recent example of this line of research, Batson *et al.* (1997) showed that, in comparison with a more objective and detached attitude, focusing attention on information indicating that a murderer (Type 2 deviance) had little control over his deed and previously was seriously provoked and angered, increased feelings of pity (as discussed in Chapter 2, we doubt if this process should be termed "perspective taking"). Importantly, this effect was not found immediately but several weeks later during an interview in which participants were first presented with a series of questions on "prison reform" (e.g., about the inhumanity of prisons and the rights and needed rehabilitation of criminals). Probably this context strengthened pity responses. Similarly, in a study by Batson and Ahmad (2001), participants played a prisoner's dilemma game with a person who was always presented as somewhat distressed because of a recent break-up with her boyfriend, and as having made an uncooperative and selfish first move during the game. Earlier, participants were either asked to ignore the other person's need state (inducing them to remain objective and detached) or concentrate on the other's feelings and imagine how the other person felt. It appeared that, after having previously ignored the other's suffering (or when no communication at all took place), participants punished the target by starting with an uncooperative move themselves. Yet, they reduced their punishment and behaved more cooperatively after having concentrated on the other's need state.

In the case of Type 3 deviance, which normally activates some care and fear, the focus on threatening aspects may increase fear and decrease care responses, whereas a focus on vulnerability and dependency may result in the reversed responses. It seems likely that asking people to focus on seriousness or suffering *per se* may primarily activate the flight component of the FF system (and hence arouse fear or distress), whereas the simultaneous perception of serious suffering and vulnerable and dependent aspects of a concrete patient may activate the care system and, in combination with fear, pity. For example, Batson *et al.* (Batson, Early, & Salvarani, 1997) found that perceivers who were required to focus on how they instead of a suffering target would feel, experienced more distress or fear than perceivers asked to focus on how the situation would affect the victim. Also, Pyszczynski *et al.* (1995) argue that when perceivers have the opportunity to become aware of their own vulnerability rather than being concerned with the other person's plight, such a focus will lead to "defensive distancing" from the victim. Consistent with this they found that, although perceivers' immediate response to a person with a serious illness (cancer) was more sympathetic than to a person with a less serious condition (a sprained ankle), this difference disappeared when responses were measured after a short delay suggesting that their own vulnerability became involved. In addition, evidence was found that perceivers in the delay condition saw themselves as more dissimilar to the victim than in the no-delay condition. The activation of the FF system also seems especially likely when perceivers feel vulnerable to a specific deviant condition. Such a focus on own vulnerability may strengthen fear and avoidance responses. For instance, Katz *et al.* (1987) found that the more people are afraid about getting cancer themselves, the more they responded negatively to a cancer patient.

The described informational effects may particularly occur when complex deviant conditions, which have diverse aspects, are involved. Because of their heterogeneity, quite divergent information may be relevant and processed into responses. Take as an example the complex image of AIDS. As different studies have shown, the image of persons with AIDS contains both active (AIDS is lethal and contagious) and passive elements (these persons are suffering from a disease and are dependent on the help of others). In addition, they may also be seen as intentionally violating social norms; engaging in risky sexual encounters or homosexual conduct (Pryor, Reeder, Vinacco, & Kott, 1989). The complexity of the image accounts for varying effects observed in responding to persons with AIDS. For example, when nurses expect to inject patients, the contagiousness of AIDS determines their tendencies to avoid the patient. However, when they expect to have a conversation with patients, the lethal character but not the contagiousness of AIDS influences their willingness to do so (Dijker & Raeijmaekers, 1999). Furthermore, sexual orientation does not seem to influence people's responses when thinking about interacting with someone with a deadly infectious disease, but does when the disease is not contagious. In the latter case, a homosexual is more negatively judged than a heterosexual (Bishop, Alva, Cantu, & Rittiman, 1991). Probably, in the former case fear is so strong that other aspects of the person with the deviant condition are quite irrelevant.

As another example take the complex image of black people, which contains both active and passive elements, with the active ones referring both to uncontrollable physical aspects (e.g., they are seen as muscular, tall, antagonistic, and as speaking loudly), and to more controllable aspects such as criminal behavior (e.g., Nieman, Jennings, Rozelle, Baxter, & Sullivan, 1994). A similar finding was reported with respect to the perception of black Surinamese people living in the Netherlands (Dijker, Koomen *et al.*, 1996). On the other hand, black people may be seen as the victims of discriminatory treatment and stigmatization, and hence in acute need of help (Type 3 deviance).

However, perceiving them as disadvantaged and as having low socioeconomic status in turn may invite the view that they should actually show more responsibility in getting out of their bad situation (Type 4 deviance). Interestingly, Crandall (1994) notes that the stereotypes associated with fat people and blacks are remarkably similar in this respect. Both groups are regarded as lazy, sinful, and lacking in discipline. Fat people are seen as eating too much and black people as violating important other social values such as hard work. Both groups are also seen as responsible for their condition, although in a somewhat different way. Fat people are responsible for their overweight condition and black people of course not for their being black, but for their low social position in society. Information and judgmental dimensions (e.g., discrimination and vulnerability) may activate the corresponding parts of such complex representations, which is the reason that we categorized blacks in varying types of deviance.

Because African-Americans and disabled persons are among the most frequently employed stimulus groups in research on stigmatization (see the next section and Chapter 4), it is finally important to stress that in certain contexts, disability or chronic illness too may be viewed as Type 4 deviance. That is, especially when disabled individuals are judged in terms of reciprocity or performance in an everyday situation which does not involve an acute need state or request for help, they may be blamed for insufficient coping with their condition (see our discussion of incomplete reciprocity and parasitism in Chapter 3). Consistent with this, performance expectations of disabled persons are generally low (Hastorf, Northcraft, & Picciotto, 1979). Yet, to the extent that their dependency on others and similarity with acute illness are stressed (and a comparison is made with more salient examples of Type 4 deviance such as low socioeconomic status, unemployment or obesity; see Figure 3.1), they may primarily evoke caring responses, which is more characteristic for Type 3 deviance.

## 3.4 Effects of mental representations and behavioral information on judgments of deviant individuals

One of the most fundamental and most frequently tested assumptions in current cognitive and social psychology is that people use their mental representations or expectancies (beliefs, stereotypes, opinions) to interpret, judge, and evaluate the behavior of others (cf. Fiske & Taylor, 1991; Lindsay & Norman, 1977). Indeed, it is hard to imagine that the tremendously adaptive property of the brain to internally represent and organize the external world – enabling individuals to think and plan in ways that are relatively independent of the actual state of the environment – would not be put into use (Sommerhoff, 1974). Although these internal or mental representations will be usually accurate, they may, of course, also color and bias the way we process information about events. In general, when the behavior of a deviant individual is ambiguous or consistent with an expectancy, it tends to be assimilated to the expectancy, and perceived, interpreted, judged, or remembered in a way that is congruent with its content. However, when the behavior of the individual is inconsistent with an expectancy and hence unexpected, the behavior may be relatively extremely judged and a contrast effect may occur.

Let us first consider the different ways in which mental representations or expectancies may influence information processing when the behavior of a deviant individual is ambiguous or consistent with an expectancy and hence can be "assimilated" to the particular contents of these representations or expectancies. In a classic experiment by Duncan (1976; for a replication and refinement, see Sagar & Schofield, 1980), white participants looked at a (what they thought to be a life) dyadic interaction between a white and black individual displayed on a television monitor. When, during an argument, one of the individuals gave the other an ambiguous shove, it was more likely to be interpreted as being aggressive in intent in the case of a black than a white actor. This indicates that the particular content of expectancies about deviant conditions influences what we see and how we interpret ambiguous information about the behavior of a deviant individual. As another example, imagine that you see a woman walking out of a store without paying for a hat. If you share with many others the expectancy or stereotype that older people are forgetful, you would probably attribute the woman's behavior more to forgetting when she is old, whereas stealing seems to be a better option when she is young. This is exactly what Erber, Szuchman, and Prager (2001) found in two experiments with slightly different scenarios. In addition, when a particular expectancy or stereotype is invoked, people may actively seek out stereotype-relevant information. For example, in a study by Carver and de la Garza (1984), participants read a brief description of an auto accident, which involved either an elderly or a young driver as its protagonist. They then were given an opportunity to indicate what additional information they would prefer to obtain if they were trying to ascertain causal responsibility for the accident. As predicted on the basis of the stereotype of the elderly, the "old driver" condition led to the seeking of information concerning the physical and mental adequacy of the driver and possible impairment of his vision, whereas the "young driver" condition led to the seeking of information as to whether the driver had been drinking.[4]

Expectancies do not only influence the encoding or perception but also the retrieval of information from memory, usually in a way that is consistent with the content of the expectancy (cf. Fyock & Stangor, 1994). For example, in a study by Davidson, Cameron, and Jergovic (1995) children ranging in age from about 7 to 11 were asked to recall descriptions of, and additional statements about, individuals labeled elderly or not labeled at all. For the additional statements, these children having negative stereotypes about the elderly recalled more negative statements about them than they did about individuals not labeled elderly. Interestingly, memory was not only selective but also more actively distorted in a stereotyped way. About 30 percent of the children remembered positive information about the elderly in a negative form, for example, recalling a healthy elderly individual as being sick. Another form of memory distortion due to stereotyping was demonstrated by Van Knippenberg and Dijksterhuis (1996). Labeling a person (e.g., a soccer-hooligan) or activating a stereotype after a behavioral description had been given led to deteriorated recall of stereotype-inconsistent behaviors that were part of the description. Their research also made it plausible that stereotype activation essentially makes it more difficult to access behaviors organized in a stereotype-inconsistent trait (e.g., soccer hooligans are intelligent). Via facilitation of access to stereotype-consistent information, inhibition of access to stereotype-inconsistent information, and transforming specific information in agreement with the stereotype, retrieval content can be made a reflection of the stereotype.

In view of the effects of mental representations or expectancies on encoding, perception, and memory, it stands to reason that they will also influence more complex processing of information, such as judgment and decision making, that is based on encoding and memory. An example can be found in a study by Bodenhausen (1988). In this study, participants were asked to play the role of a juror who had to determine the guilt or innocence of a defendant accused of criminal assault. The defendant about whom one of two types of case evidence was provided was either "Carlos Ramirez," which was assumed to activate a Hispanic stereotype of aggressiveness, or "Robert Johnson" not related to a relevant stereotype. The stereotyped defendant was seen as more likely to be guilty than the non-stereotyped one, irrespective of the favorability of the case evidence. As will be shown in Chapter 4, not only judgments but also behaviors are affected by mental representations and expectancies.

Mental representations or expectancies often operate in an assimilative way, but under some conditions they can also produce contrast effects (see, for a review and explanation, Stapel & Koomen, 2001). The latter, for example, is especially likely to happen when these representations involve images of specific individuals (or "exemplars") that can be used as standards of comparison. For instance, Stapel and Koomen (1998) showed that a specific woman was seen by their participants as less dependent (a contrast effect) when participants were first made to think about specific dependently behaving individuals, but as more dependent when a general representation of the trait "dependency" was first activated. Explanations for the former contrast effect hold that individuals are more distinct and more relevant to compare the target person with than traits. When forming a judgment about the target woman, one needs a comparison standard, and for that standard individuals can be more easily used than traits. Thanks to these contrast effects persons with deviant conditions may sometimes be seen as ducking out of their condition. An old person may be perceived (in comparison with prototypical members of his or her category) as quite vigorous and independent.

It should be noted that the evaluative aspects of assimilation and contrast effects have also been explained in motivational terms rather than in terms of expectancy-based information processing. Why do people judge or evaluate the same negative behavior of a deviant and non-deviant individual more negatively in the case of the former than the latter (assimilation)? And why do they evaluate the same positive behavior of a deviant and non-deviant individual more positively in the case of the former than the latter (contrast)? Referring to these phenomena as *response amplification*, Katz (1981) has argued that people judge the negative and positive behavior of a deviant individual in a relatively extreme or amplified way *in order to* reduce ambivalence or conflict and create a psychological state that is more in accord with the perceiver's self-esteem. Specifically, he assumed that people may have ambivalent attitudes toward deviant individuals, with a negative component associated with some perceived threat, and a positive one associated with seeing the deviant person as needy or disadvantaged. Noticing particular behavior of the deviant individual and responding negatively or positively to it may make this conflict more salient, and would threaten the perceiver's self-esteem. For example, when a relatively poor performance of a disabled or black person is negatively judged, this judgment conflicts with, and is not acceptable in light of the sympathy felt for a person who is relatively disadvantaged. By accentuating the negative component of the attitude and responding very negatively toward the deviant individual, the perceiver reduces the experienced conflict (with the target now being seen as an unworthy person), and consequently reduces the threat to self-esteem. Similarly, the relatively good performance of the disabled or black person may be very positively judged in order to reduce a conflict with the negative feelings felt for an unworthy object. (According to Katz, salience of conflict, with similar consequences for response amplification, may also be caused by first behaving oneself in a negative or positive way toward the deviant individual, rather than by first perceiving and responding to negative or positive target behavior.)

Although we refrain from using the concept of self-esteem and its associated psychodynamic aspects, our explanation of response amplification shares some important elements with Katz's account. First, we believe that it is no accident that in all studies performed to test his theory, Katz (1981) has used African-Americans and disabled persons in performance contexts as stimulus persons; targets that we associate with the ambivalence or conflict between care and anger typical for Type 4 or controllable-passive deviance. Specifically, white Americans tend to see black persons as low in socioeconomic status, disadvantaged and needy, misusing welfare and the care they trigger in others, and as unmotivated to cope with and improve their disadvantaged situation (hence as lazy). This may be especially the case when these individuals are viewed in a job-related or performance context; it seems likely that in other judgmental contexts, associations between black skin color and active deviance involving physical threats and crime may more easily come to the fore. Above, we argued that when disabled persons are similarly viewed in a job related or performance context, they too may be associated with Type 4 deviance. That is, people may generally expect poor performance and incomplete reciprocity, and may similarly associate this with insufficient coping with the deviant condition under everyday conditions. As we will see below, Katz sometimes explicitly interprets very positive responses to black persons in terms of positive appraisals of good coping.

As proposed in Chapter 2, the moderate levels of care and aggression typically aroused by Type 4 deviance seem to keep each other in balance, resulting in disrespect. In contrast, we argued that needy or fragile individuals who are primarily associated with an acute need state and demand for help will primarily arouse care, pity, and assistance. Chapter 4 will show that disabled or ill individuals who explicitly ask for help indeed tend to receive considerable assistance from others.

Now, when individuals with Type 4 deviance behave in ways that are consistent with the general expectancy associated with this type of deviance (e.g., their poor performance frustrates the perceiver's own goals or values), they may further increase the activity of the FF system which was already somewhat active due to the perception of this particular type of deviance. That is to say, the deviant individual will be more negatively judged than a non-deviant individual displaying the same behavior. However, in the case of a black or disabled target person, good performance or reciprocity during interaction not only appears relatively unexpected and draws attention but is also especially consistent with a desire (related to an activated C system) that the person should make the best of his or her disadvantaged situation and try to get out of it, no longer motivating us to care for him or her. As a consequence, one may feel sympathy or respect for the person, and this may further de-activate the FF system. Hence, given the same positive behavior, the deviant person will be more positively judged than the non-deviant one.

Probably, our explanation of response amplification in terms of activation of the FF and C systems may not lead to entirely new predictions compared to expectancy-based judgments. However, in addition to pure expectancy effects, our motivational perspective helps us to understand how expected and unexpected outcomes are differently appraised by perceivers, dependent on the motivational implications of the particular content of the expectancies about different types of deviance (for a recent comparison of different theoretical interpretations of response amplification, see a brief review by Fleming, Petty, & White, 2005). For example, whereas the expected behavior of individuals associated with Type 1 or 4 deviance may result in heightened fear or anger/disrespect, respectively; the unexpected behavior of these individuals may result in feelings of safety/reassurance, or respect, respectively. Furthermore, the unexpected behavior of individuals associated with Type 2 deviance (e.g., showing remorse and willingness to repair the damage of a criminal act), may reduce aggression and induce forgiveness.

Interestingly, in contrast to the good coping of an individual with Type 4 deviance, the unexpected behavior of individuals with Type 3 deviance may not always be positively evaluated. First, especially if we care strongly about the well-being and health of ill persons, we expect them to ask for help and let themselves be cared for. When these persons act in ways that suggest independence and happiness, they may frustrate our desire to care for them and arouse anger and perhaps a more imposing way of caring. Second, there is probably also a more general mechanism involved in our negative evaluation of persons associated with different types of deviance who behave independently or assertively during interpersonal encounters. In particular, to the extent that these persons are stigmatized and have a lower status, they are generally expected to be modest and submissive. As Goffman

(1963b, p. 146) observed: "The stigmatized are tactfully expected to be gentlemanly and not to press their luck; they should not test the limits of the acceptance shown them, nor make it the basis of still further demands. Tolerance, of course, is usually part of a bargain. (. . .) The nature of a 'good adjustment' (. . .) requires that the stigmatized individual cheerfully and unself-consciously accept himself as essentially the same as normals." Unfortunately, it may not always be easy to tell if "positive" behavior of individuals associated with Type 3 or 4 deviance will be interpreted as good coping with their particular deviant condition, or as undesirable immodesty. Let us have a closer look at the different meanings that the behavior of deviant individuals may have in light of the representation of deviance.

### The effects of behavioral information on judgments of individuals with passive deviance

A remarkable number of experiments appear to have examined judgments of the expected or unexpected behavior of individuals associated with, what we have termed, Type 4 or controllable-passive deviance. Examples of this type include racial or ethnic minorities, or disabled and obese persons when judged in a socioeconomic or performance context or during everyday interactions. In general, we argue that people expect these individuals to succumb to their need state and dependency on others and to cope poorly with their situation. This combination arouses some care and pity but also hostility for not doing enough to get out of a disadvantaged situation and parasitize on the perceiver. First, consider clear demonstrations of response amplification for white participants judging the behavior of a black or white target person. For example, when the target is presented as a high school dropout and rebellious social misfit with no plans for the future (Dienstbier, 1970), a job applicant wearing an old sports jacket and pants and speaking in non-standard English (Bettencourt, Dill, Greathouse, Charlton, & Mullholland, 1997), or a law-school applicant with marginal qualities (Linville & Jones, 1980), a black person is more negatively judged than a white person. However, when both the black and the white target person are portrayed in a more positive way (i.e., as ambitious, with good scholarly credentials, wearing a formal suit and speaking in correct English), the behavior of the black person is seen as unexpected and more positively judged than the behavior of the white person. Importantly, Bettencourt *et al.* (1997) demonstrated that expectancies indeed mediated the observed assimilation and contrast effects.

This pattern was recently confirmed by Barden, Maddux, Petty, and Brewer (2004) using a primarily visual presentation of target persons and their attributes. In each of their studies, white participants responded to black or white faces presented against a meaningful background, either by explicitly evaluating these pictures with a questionnaire or in terms of a priming procedure (the latter procedure will be discussed in Chapter 4). In the different studies, a black target was evaluated more negatively than a white target when the picture suggested (poor) intellectual performance (a face against the background of a technical classroom) but more positively than a white target when the picture suggested high intellectual competence (a face of a man in a business suit against the background of a prison, apparently a lawyer), or a strong motivation to work (a face against the background of a factory). This pattern of findings is consistent with our view that individuals associated with Type 4 deviance are associated with laziness and social parasitism, and should behave in more responsible ways and overcome their disadvantaged situation by successful coping. Katz, Cohen, and Glass (1975) gave a similar interpretation of the greater willingness of white participants to being interviewed by a black rather than a white interviewer when the interviewer presented himself as having a part-time job in a "Self-Help Program for Negro/White students at the university." These authors argue that the Protestant work ethic motivates perceivers to value highly the black interviewer's efforts to work his way out of his disadvantaged position (this study on helping behavior is discussed in more detail in the next chapter).

Let us now examine evidence for response amplification in the case of disabled persons who are not acutely suffering or ill, but still may show signs of incomplete reciprocity, partial dependency, and relatively poor performance in everyday situations. As argued in Chapter 2, this group may also be associated with Type 4 deviance and expected to cope poorly with their condition. Hence, we should expect similar assimilation and contrast effects as in the case of black Americans. For example, in a study by Gibbons *et al.* (1980), participants tried to solve anagrams while a fellow student (either disabled or not) performed the same task, and their combined performance would be compared with the performance of other dyads. When she succeeded in contributing to a positive outcome, the disabled target was judged more positively than the non-disabled one. However, when she failed, the disabled target was judged more negatively than the non-disabled one. One of the experiments showed that this was especially the case when the target worked with the participant as a teammate rather than independently. Thus the results of this study suggest both assimilation and contrast effects in the case of a disabled target person.[5]

An important question, both from a theoretical and practical point of view, is what people see as good or bad coping in the case of Type 4 deviance. What do they actually want from a disabled person who is largely able to interact and cooperate with them but who still shows some evidence for dependency and need? That certain behaviors can be readily interpreted as lack of coping and will be negatively responded to seems self-evident because they clearly obstruct interpersonal interaction and reciprocity. Research indeed confirms that signs of depression and chronic lack of coping in disabled persons are especially disliked (e.g., Elliot & MacNair, 1991). Using one's condition of passive deviance as an excuse for poor performance similarly may invite negative responses. For example, Ryan *et al.* (2002) showed that using age as an excuse for memory failures in the elderly increased reactions of worry and frustration, especially in younger perceivers. Furthermore, Hebl and Kleck (2002) found that, in a simulated job interview shown on video, an obese person who explicitly refers to or "acknowledges" her condition (stating "when people meet me, one of the first things they notice is that I'm overweight"), is more negatively evaluated than an obese person who does not refer to her condition. Interestingly, in another study these researchers demonstrated that a physically disabled person who was responsible for his condition (i.e., ignored the advice of a doctor to have surgery), and who also mentioned his condition, thus emphasizing Type 4 deviance, similarly received less sympathetic and more hostile responses than one who did not explicitly refer to it. In contrast, the handicapped person who was not responsible for his disability received more positive responses after explicitly referring to his condition.

Helplessness of disabled persons in long-term relationships may also not be valued. For example, studying social support received by breast cancer patients from significant others, Bolger *et al.* (1996) found that, although physical impairment positively affected received support, patient's distress had a negative effect on support. The authors explain this difference by noting that significant others view the patient's physical impairment as beyond, but her distress as under, her control: "Given that patients show no emotional improvement over time, perhaps significant others see the patient's distress as increasingly unjustifiable and therefore reduce their support provision" (p. 290).

Unfortunately, little research has been conducted on perceptions of good coping with a disability or illness. In one study (Schwarzer & Weiner, 1991), when positive coping was straightforwardly manipulated by informing participants that the ill target person stuck to a healthy diet and adhered to the medication prescribed by doctors, the target received relatively positive evaluations. Interestingly, this study also suggests that efforts to offset a chronic illness by means of good coping are judged as more important than responsibility for the onset of the deviant conditions. Schwarzer and Weiner (1991) supplied participants first with information about a target's onset responsibility (similar to Weiner *et al.*, 1988) and then informed them about the target's coping efforts. In contrast to Weiner *et al.* (1988), Schwarzer and Weiner (1991) found that onset responsibility had no effect on anger (a finding which remarkably receives no special attention from the authors), but that lack of coping increased anger, irrespective of whether the target was or was not responsible for the origin of the condition. A similar pattern was found for expected social stress in interacting with the deviant target, with more expected stress for a poorly coping target. In addition, Schwarzer and Weiner (1991) found that onset controllability decreased but good coping increased pity for the target. These findings suggest that people are interested in the target offsetting his illness and that they respond positively (with less anger and with more care and pity) to learning about it. Thus, once we know about a person's good coping, his or her past careless behavior seems to matter less; apparently, what we do care most about is that the person gets well as soon as possible.

In another study, good coping involved much more than dealing with a disabling physical condition. Hastorf, Wildfogel, and Cassman (1979) exposed participants to different videotaped interviews with disabled persons and found that the disabled person who acknowledged his handicap was favored for future interaction above one who did not talk about his disability when questioned about his personal experience or made a personal disclosure that was irrelevant to his disability. It is important to mention, that in these experiments, the acknowledgment involved a complex mixture of information indicating problems with the handicap, acceptance and learning to cope with it, and encouraging others to ask questions about it (1979, p. 1792). In one of the experiments, this disclosure even proved effective when the disabled person showed non-verbal signs of nervousness and distress. Similar positive results of these kinds of balanced acknowledgments have been obtained by Silver *et al.* (1990). They showed that providing female participants with information about a breast cancer patient's "balanced coping" with her distress (representing a balance between acknowledging distress and effectively dealing with the illness), increased supportive responses to the patient, compared to a condition in which she was presented as coping poorly with her illness (conveying substantial distress) or a condition in which no information was supplied. The condition in which only positive coping was stressed also invited more positive responses than the poor coping or no information condition, although in certain respects (e.g., distress, desire for future interaction) not as positive as the balanced coping condition.

The above results suggest that people may respond positively when being informed about good coping behavior of a deviant individual. However, as noted above, as good coping is partly demonstrated by showing independence and self-reliance, it may be confused with obtrusiveness which is generally disapproved of in case deviant individuals are stigmatized. Several studies indeed suggest that people desire deviant individuals to show modesty and humility at the interpersonal level. First, disabled persons themselves report a higher tendency to conform, ingratiate, and show dependency in their daily interactions than non-disabled persons (Colella & Varma, 2001; Orr, Thein, & Aronson, 1995, Study 1). Other studies confirm that submissive behavior may prove an effective social strategy. For example, socially accepted mentally handicapped children are frequently those who engage in friendly but submissive behavior rather than in friendly and assertive behavior (Siperstein & Leffert, 1997). Furthermore, a study by Ryan *et al.* (2000), in which nursing home staff and residents judged nurse-resident conversational scenarios in which a resident responded to a patronizing nurse reveals a similar process. Both staff and residents evaluated the direct and assertive response of the resident more negatively than passive and humorous responses. Humorous responses to patronizing speech were the most appreciated in terms of both competence and politeness.

Also, Katz *et al.* (1978) found that participants were less willing to help and interact with a handicapped than a non-handicapped person when he or she administered a test to participants in a friendly but assertive and achievement oriented manner. Participants were also more angry at the former than the latter target. The reverse was true for a target who administered the test in a submissive and apathetic manner. Here, participants were less angry at the handicapped than the non-handicapped target. It is interesting to mention that Katz *et al.* were surprised with these results because they generally expected that "positive" (being achievement oriented) versus "negative" behavior (lacking in achievement) would result in response amplification, with the former receiving extremely positive and the latter extremely negative responses. Yet, their unexpected results made them recognize that these behaviors in the case of handicapped persons may receive a unique meaning and evaluation in terms of idiosyncratic role expectations for sick and partially dependent persons. For example, showing assertiveness or achievement in the case of a handicapped person may violate the person's sick role and hence may not constitute "positive" behavior.

Furthermore, Orr *et al.* (1995, Study 2) presented participants with a videotaped interaction between a disabled (wheelchair) and non-disabled individual playing a particular cooperative game. Four different versions of the tape were constructed, with each participant judging only one version. On two tapes, both actors behaved assertively or submissively, respectively; on two other tapes, the able bodied actor behaved assertively and the disabled one submissively, or *vice versa*. The main question of interest was which individual participants would choose as a teammate to play a similar cooperative game with. Although a non-disabled individual was generally favored as a partner over a disabled one, the only condition in which this pattern was reversed (with 72 percent choosing the disabled and 28 percent choosing the non-disabled target) was when a conforming disabled person interacted with an assertive able-bodied one. In addition, the condition in which the disabled person was the least favored as an interaction partner occurred when he behaved assertively towards a submissively behaving able bodied person. Here, only 13 percent of the participants selected the disabled individual. Apparently, the complementary nature of the interaction may have highlighted both the desirable nature of the disabled person's conforming interaction strategy and the undesirability of his dominant behavior.

Finally, Colella and Varma (2001, Study 1) conducted a simulation study in which participants worked as "supervisors" together with a disabled (using a wheelchair) or non-disabled "employee" who did or did not act in an ingratiating and clearly dependent way. They found that ingratiation only affected participants' rating of the quality of the relationship with the disabled employee. Specifically, whereas there was no difference between the ratings of a disabled and non-disabled employee when he or she acted neutrally, more positive ratings of the disabled than non-disabled employee were obtained when he or she adopted different ingratiating tactics. In a subsequent field study, with true supervisors and subordinates with varying disabilities working in different companies, Colella and Varma (2001, Study 2) found a similar positive influence of ingratiation on the experienced leader-employee relationship.

To conclude, there is some evidence suggesting that response amplification may occur when individuals associated with Type 4 deviance cope poorly (in which case they are very negatively judged) or well (in which case they are very positively judged) with their need state during everyday encounters. However, once these individuals overstep the perceiver's tolerance for reduced reciprocity and apparent lack of competence by translating their successful coping with their condition into dominant or threatening interpersonal behavior, they may become the target of increased hostility and more negative judgments. Yet, it should be clear from our discussion of the literature that much more research is needed to understand how people interpret and evaluate the deviant individual's behavior in light of expectations about coping with, or getting rid of, the deviant condition.

## The effects of behavioral information on judgments of individuals with active deviance

People expect individuals associated with active deviance to show threatening and dangerous behavior in either uncontrollable (Type 1 deviance) or controllable ways (Type 2 deviance). Especially, in the former case, controlled, predictable, or submissive behavior that increases a sense of safety will be highly valued, but is relatively unexpected; whereas behavior that is consistent with the characteristic expectancy (e.g., impulsive behavior) will appear threatening and is extremely negatively judged. Several studies provide support for this predicted pattern.

With respect to mental illness, a classic study by Gergen and Jones (1963), which appeared to have inspired Katz's (1981) view on ambivalence reduction, showed that only when a mentally ill person displayed unpredictable behavior with negative affective consequences for the perceiver, he was more negatively evaluated than a non-deviant person. Riskind and Wahl (1992) found that a psychiatric patient who was described as active and moving, was seen as more threatening and aroused more fear than one who was described as passive and at rest. Although in the case of a non-threatening individual (a clown or ordinary person) an increase in activity also led to an increase in fear, this effect was much smaller than in the case of the psychiatric patient. This phenomenon is described by these authors in terms of "loomingness." Similarly, Dijker et al. (1997) showed that participants' anxiety in response to an imagined interaction with a colleague with AIDS increased when the colleague's behavior changed from a predictable and self-controlled style to an unpredictable and impulsive one. Furthermore, the predictable colleague with AIDS did not arouse more fear than a healthy colleague. Participants were also less willing to have indirect physical contact (e.g., sharing the same coffee machine) with the unpredictable than the predictable person with AIDS.

The study by Barden et al. (2004) described earlier in this chapter, also suggests assimilation of negative behavior (crime) to the negative expectancies associated with active deviance. Thus when participants were presented with black or white faces against the background of a prison, they evaluated the black target more negatively than the white one. This was in contrast to other backgrounds such as a church interior (against which black and white faces received equally positive evaluations) or a basketball court (against which black faces received more positive evaluations than white faces).

We finally note that assimilation to negative expectancies is also evidenced by the many studies showing that information about intentionality or controllability may increase anger, blame, and different negative judgments (Fincham & Jaspars, 1980; Weiner, 1995). In contrast, behavior indicating remorse may be relatively unexpected and give room to activation of the C system and forgiveness (Gold & Weiner, 2000. See also Chapter 2).

## 3.5 Summary

People think and talk about a wide variety of deviant conditions, as well as about their emotional and behavioral responses to these conditions, and a main question addressed in this chapter was if the rich content and meaning of these symbolic expressions can be explained by a limited number of psychological mechanisms. Examining many different studies asking people to indicate differences and similarities among deviant conditions, or to directly describe or judge these conditions, strongly suggests that people categorize and represent these conditions in terms of only two basic motivational mechanisms – the fight-or-flight (FF) and care (C) system – which thus seem to function as language-independent concepts. In particular, people distinguish deviant conditions that tend to activate the FF system (active deviance) from conditions that activate the C system (passive deviance). Yet, they also differentiate among the active conditions those that more strongly activate the flight component (uncontrollable-active deviance such as madness) from those that more strongly activate the fight component of the FF system (controllable-active deviance such as crime). Furthermore, within the passive conditions, people distinguish conditions that, in addition to the C system, also activate the flight component (uncontrollable-passive deviance such as illness) from those that also activate the fight component of the FF system (controllable-passive deviance such as laziness).

It is important to emphasize that we obtained these results not only by analyzing what properties people associate with deviant conditions (e.g., tendency to violate norms, contagiousness, neediness, poor coping with condition) but also by inquiring about their behavioral tendencies with respect to individuals associated with these conditions. Moreover, the emotional reactions that people report about the different types of deviance could be well predicted on the basis of the underlying motivational mechanisms or concepts. Thus active deviance evokes more anger and fear than passive deviance, while the latter evokes more care and pity. Furthermore, the uncontrollable forms of active and passive deviance trigger more fear than the controllable forms, while the latter are associated with more anger than the former. Together, the discussed studies confirm the validity and usefulness of the basic types of deviance that were derived from our evolutionary perspective presented in Chapter 2.

We also discussed more complex forms of deviance that seemed to be combinations of several basic types (e.g., persons with AIDS who are perceived as ill, responsible for their illness, and as dangerous), and a variety of contextual influences on the perception of deviant conditions. For example, people's representation of "old age" primarily contains negative attributes while their representation of "old people" may, in addition, also contain care-arousing features. Similarly, emphasizing that a person associated with controllable-active deviance has a "bad childhood" or that an ill person responsible for the onset of his or her illness also harmed other people, tends to accentuate passive or active aspects of deviance, respectively.

Finally, we discussed the various ways in which representations of deviance influence perception and judgment of the behavior of deviant individuals. On the one hand, we analyzed these influences in terms of expectancy effects or stereotyping, illustrating how ambiguous behavior of deviant individuals is assimilated to the content of expectancies, while behaviors violating these expectancies are relatively surprising and often produce contrast effects. On the other hand, we illustrated how our motivational perspective may contribute to a better understanding of people's evaluative and emotional reactions to expected and unexpected behavior of deviant individuals, and of what people actually want from deviant individuals. This allowed us to explain negative and positive reactions to behavior in terms of social responses to poor or good coping with deviant conditions. However, we also noted that being associated with deviance more generally seems to require that one presents oneself in a modest and humble way to others, which may contradict information suggesting that one is coping well and in a mature or autonomous fashion with one's condition.

# Meeting individuals with deviant conditions: understanding the role of automatic and controlled psychological processes

## 4.1 Introduction

In the previous chapter, we used our motivational perspective to explain the contents of people's mental representations or images of deviant conditions. We also showed how these representations are related to different emotional qualities, the way people think or reason about the behavior of deviant individuals, and about their own responses to them.

At first sight, it seems self-evident that these representations and emotional implications will play an important role in motivating and guiding people's "real" behavior when exposed to deviant individuals. For example, it seems reasonable to expect that in certain situations the protective and caring tendencies that an ill person arouses result in behavior that improves the person's health, while additionally getting angry because the person insufficiently copes with his or her condition, may stimulate the person to get better and stay well. Similarly, fear responses to a person with a particular mental illness or behavioral problem may be translated into demands at the person not to endanger his or her social environment.

That representations and underlying motivational systems may be functional for this type of social control (which we have termed *repair*) also follows from our evolutionary perspective on the general role of motivational systems. To repeat from Chapter 2, in light of an evolutionary perspective, motivational systems help organisms to adapt to the environment because they (1) are automatically activated by the perception of certain key environmental features, forcing organisms to interrupt ongoing activity, pay attention to and analyze these features, and start solving the urgent adaptive problems implied by these features; and (2) coordinate and focus the different cognitive, emotional, and behavioral aspects of responding until the characteristic ultimate goals of these systems (e.g., to escape from danger, to improve the well-being of another individual) have been realized.

Thus characteristic of this process is the unified nature of the organism's responding to the environment; integrating fast and automatic or bottom-up processes that are responsible for biased or selective attention, and top-down or controlled processes that, with knowledge about previously successful courses of action and situational opportunities, help to analyze or "reason about" the environment and decide on possible courses of action.

Surprisingly, looking at the vast amount of social psychological studies of stigmatization and prejudice that have been conducted during the last three decades, one gets a completely different impression about the nature of responding to deviance. In particular, people's automatic responses appear unrelated to the particular nature of the deviant condition and its internal representation (i.e., they seem "irrational" or prejudiced) and are so undesirable for the deviant individual and society, that they need to be altered, suppressed or expressed in covert ways. Yet, because this regulation usually is not entirely successful, the automatic and controlled aspects of behavior seem to be incongruent or dissociated. Consequently, clearly negative goal-directed behavioral responses to deviant individuals tend to be viewed as failures to exercise control, while positive responses (which apparently are generally desirable for the deviant individual) tend to be seen as controlled or suppressed negative tendencies that are unlikely to be based on truly positive feelings.

We believe that the above sketched phenomena may partly reflect a type of social control that we have termed *tolerance* and associated with individualistic and modern Western societies (see Chapters 1 and 6); and that social psychology has contributed to improving our understanding of the psychological aspects of this type of social control. That is, in modern Western societies in which people try not to get involved too much in each other's affairs (aptly termed "civil inattention" by Goffman, 1963a) and leave it to authorities or formal institutions to engage in social control, it is generally functional not to attend too much to deviance, to look the other way, to correct or suppress negative responses, and to be generally nice to each other. Furthermore, the revealed processes underlying tolerance may also be relevant for understanding interpersonal processes when the concept of deviance can be less easily applied. For example, most North American social psychological research on stigmatization and prejudice has focused on relationships between European-Americans and African-Americans, social groups that are often assumed to differ only with respect to skin color. To the extent that people consider this to be the only relevant cue inviting negative responses or stigmatization, they may actively try to suppress their discriminatory tendencies for the sake of tolerance.

Unfortunately, the social psychological research paradigm that has been developed around the psychological aspects of tolerance may be less suitable for understanding what happens when people get so closely involved in each other's affairs, are confronted with such clear cases of deviance or conflict (e.g., crime, illness, dependency, intergroup competition), or simply associate apparently trivial cues such as skin color with relevant deviant conditions that demand social control (e.g., crime or lack of motivation to contribute to society or laziness), that they may want to engage in blatant social exclusion or repair processes. Under these circumstances, traditional "dual-process" models of stigmatization and prejudice that assume frequent dissociation between automatic and controlled aspects of responding to deviance, may appear less useful and need to be extended. After the next section describes such an extended dual-process model, we use it to integrate and re-interpret the wealth of empirical studies on responding to deviance that have been conducted by social psychologists. In particular, in one section, we discuss studies that offer support for our view that, given relevant response options, what people do during interactions with deviant individuals is simply to intelligently try to realize the characteristic goals of the motivational systems that are triggered by a particular deviant condition. For example, people will seek out situational opportunities to punish or aggress against individuals associated with active deviance but will help individuals associated with passive deviance such as illness or disability.

In two subsequent sections, we discuss phenomena that we interpret as psychological aspects of tolerance. There, we distinguish studies of unfocused or unstructured interactions between non-deviant and deviant individuals in which dissociation between anxiety (and its bodily symptoms) and "normalizing" or friendly behavior can be observed; and studies in which participants are not required to interact with deviant individuals and in which measures of automatic, reflexlike or "implicit" responses closely related to FF-C activity are pitted against controlled or "explicit" verbal responses.

Unfortunately, because current social psychological research has primarily focused on short-term responses to deviance, it is usually difficult to tell if, for example, observed aggressive or helping behavior serves repair processes or stigmatization. It is even more difficult to tell if, in situations with little response options, automatic responses as measured, for example, in terms of reaction times, heart rate, or sweating, amount to stigmatization or even "subtle racism." In order to decide how the automatic or relatively controlled responses are relevant for different types of social control, we need to study how they affect long-term patterns of responding, interpersonal relationships, and societal processes; an issue that we will take up more fully in Chapters 6 and 9.

## 4.2  Extending dual-process models of responding to deviance

*Dual-process views of stigmatization and prejudice*

Many theoretical approaches to stigmatization and prejudice empha-size that responses to deviant individuals are based on two essentially different processes. On the one hand, initial responses are triggered that are primarily negative, emotional (in particular referring to bodily arousal and "gut" feelings), uncontrollable, based on little information or on unconscious or difficult to access ("implicit") internal representa-tions, and therefore inaccurate, irrational, or prejudiced. On the other hand, more positive and controlled responses are generated that are based on more extensive processing of the "true" attributes of indi-viduals, and correction or suppression of the initial responses. Complementarily, when negative responses are seen as more control-lable, they also tend to be conceptualized as independent additions to the relatively "raw" initial perceptions and responses and referred to as rationalizations, justifications, or displacements that may serve a vari-ety of needs such as self-enhancement or power, or that are motivated by certain features of personality (Allport, 1954/1979; Crandall & Eshleman, 2003; Kunda & Spencer, 2003; Tajfel, 1969). A wide variety of more specific theories of prejudice and stigmatization in social psy-chology associate the restrained aspects of responding to deviance with the strong influence of egalitarian norms in modern Western society. For example, conceptions such as "aversive racism" (Gaertner, 1976; Gaertner & Dovidio, 1986; Gaertner & Dovidio, 2005) or "subtle pre-judice" (Pettigrew, 1985; Pettigrew & Meertens, 1995) stress that con-trolled responses to deviance have become more positive and in accordance with the egalitarian principles of modern Western society, while people remain essentially stigmatizing or prejudiced at a rela-tively automatic level; necessitating them to "cover up" their negative responses and express them in more subtle and covert ways (Crosby, Bromley, & Saxe, 1980). It is also proposed that many people may not personally harbor hostile feelings toward deviant individuals but that some deviant conditions may be so widely associated with negative feelings and beliefs within society as a whole that even people who strongly adhere to egalitarian norms cannot escape from automatically associating these individuals with these stigmas (Devine, 1989; Fazio & Olson, 2003). Alternatively, well-intentioned people may show both friendliness and anxiety in behavior because they may anticipate that individuals associated with deviance *see* them as prejudiced during everyday encounters (e.g., Devine, Evett, & Vasquez-Suson, 1996; Plant & Devine, 2003; Poskocil, 1977).

In attempting to specify the psychological characteristics of automatic and controlled processes of responding to deviance, theorists have made different assumptions with respect to at least three important issues: (a) the nature of, and differences between, automatic and controlled aspects of responding to deviance; (b) the motives that underlie the control or regulation of automatic processes; and (c) the social consequences of the regulation and suppression of automatic processes.

Several dual-process models of prejudice (e.g., Fazio, 1990; Fazio, Jackson, Dunton, & Williams, 1995) subscribe to the view that the automatic aspects of responding that may need regulation are essentially affective or evaluative in nature and have minimal content or meaning (see also Murphy & Zajonc, 1993). Relatedly, other approaches to dual-processes focus on the regulation or inhibition of bodily and non-verbal signs of nervousness during everyday encounters with deviant individuals (e.g., Dovidio, Kawakami, & Gaertner, 2002; Kleck, 1968; McConnell & Leibold, 2001). Other researchers, however, tend to associate automatic processes with the activation of internal representations or stereotypes and the manner in which they (automatically) influence perception and judgment. For example, in Fiske and Neuberg's (1990) model, people's initial and automatic, stereotype-based impressions of deviant individuals may, under certain conditions, be corrected or replaced by judgments formed on the basis of more effortful and controlled processing of information about a person's neutral or non-deviant attributes. Also, Devine (1989) has proposed that egalitarian people's responses to deviance may be automatically influenced by stereotypes that they do not really believe in and that do not seem to be associated with strong affect or prejudice.

Several recent and more general dual-process models of social behavior emphasize that the relation between automatic and controlled processes should be seen as a relation between two kinds of representations or memories. In these models, well-learned, "routinized," or "implicit" associative networks are contrasted with "explicit" or propositional representations (Hofmann, Gschwendner, Nosek, & Schmitt, 2005; Smith & DeCoster, 2000; Strack & Deutsch, 2004). Associative networks allow for parallel and therefore fast processing of different internal or external sources of information, resulting in a judgmental or behavioral response on the basis of "constraint satisfaction" (Kunda & Thagard, 1996; Smith & DeCoster, 2000). Controlled processes mainly differ from the functioning of these associative networks in that they make use of rules for serially combining information that is "retrieved" from the associative store to form propositions about the world or future behavior. By implication, these processes would be slower than automatic processes and demand more attention and cognitive resources to keep the different units of information active in working memory while they are serially combined (see also Feldman Barrett, Tugade, & Engle, 2004).

Sometimes, propositional representations may not accurately reflect information represented by associative networks because, for example, people are unaware of that information, base their propositions on additional information, or are motivated to present socially desirable opinions. These problems of "translation" (cf. Hofmann *et al.*, 2005) may be studied by comparing measures that are specifically designed to tap into implicit and explicit representations. For example, reaction time measures may be used to assess implicit, and traditional self-report measures, explicit representations. Later in this chapter, we illustrate, however, that it is difficult to interpret the often low correlations between these measures because, in the absence of detailed assumptions of the contents of internal representations, it may be unclear to what extent the dissociation between these measures is due to methodological factors (e.g., implicit and explicit measures may not correlate because they happen to assess different aspects of the same internal representation).

While some theorists stress the affective, and others the cognitive nature of automatic processes, it is clear that a sharp distinction between affective and cognitive aspects is untenable. For example, Smith and DeCoster allow for associative networks to have an "affective or emotional tinge" (Smith & DeCoster, 2000, p. 124), while Strack and Deutsch assume that these networks interact with "motivational orientations" (Strack & Deutsch, 2004, Figure 6). Therefore, on the basis of our motivational perspective and borrowing from views on emotion-regulation (Frijda, 1986; Gross, 1998), one may also choose a more inclusive way of thinking about the automatic aspects of responding to deviance that may need to be controlled. In particular, what may need regulation are the different attentional, cognitive, experiential, bodily, and behavioral aspects of a complex motivational state, response tendency, or emotion, that is automatically aroused by the perceptual activation of certain motivational mechanisms. For example, one may try not to think about certain emotion-arousing aspects of a deviant condition, divert attention away from the deviant condition, re-interpret the meaning of the individual's behavior and try to modify one's expectancy or stereotype, or inhibit or modulate expressive or motor activity associated with the emotional reaction (cf. Gross, 1998). The advantage of thinking in terms of motivational states that need to be regulated is not only that affective and cognitive interpretations of dual processes may be integrated, but also that it offers a more comprehensive view of the different desirable and undesirable aspects of controlled processes. For example, while suppression of emotional impulses may temporarily protect a deviant individual from aggressive behavior, it may also increase arousal and deteriorate information processing (Gross, 1997; Richards & Gross, 2000).[1]

A second important challenge for dual-process models of responding to deviance is to understand people's motives for controlling or regulating automatic processes. Typically, the motives that are postulated to underlie control are unrelated to the kind of deviant condition that is encountered and always work to prevent automatic processes from influencing behavior. For example, people are assumed to suppress prejudiced or stereotype-based responses in order to present an unprejudiced image, to avoid reputation loss, to conform to egalitarian norms or standards, or to arrive at a more complex or balanced representation or judgment of deviant individuals (Fazio *et al.*, 1995; Fiske & Neuberg, 1990; Monteith & Voils, 2001). In addition, people may have instrumental reasons to pay more attention to certain functional characteristics than deviant features of the deviant individual.

While not denying the importance of these motives, however, our motivational approach argues for a greater role of the motivational implications of the deviant condition in regulating and modifying responses to deviant individuals. First, as argued at the beginning of this chapter, control and intelligent decision making is an inherent component of most adaptive motivated behavior, hence also of behavior that one tends to label as prejudiced or stigmatizing. This may not be readily apparent in situations that offer people sufficient response options to realize their goals because here, both automatic and controlled aspects of responding seem to work in the direction of one and the same goal (e.g., to punish individuals with active, or help individuals with passive deviance). Second, when the deviant individual triggers both the incongruent FF and C system, behavior may appear less smooth and more hesitant. For example, an obtrusive disabled person may activate both caring and hostile tendencies or a criminal showing remorse may reduce people's felt aggression via activation of the C system (see Chapter 2). During interaction with a deviant individual, an automatically activated C system may continue to motivate people to keep a close watch on their behavior, produce guilt when harm to the deviant individual is anticipated or inflicted, and motivate to compensate the harm done with extra protection or nurturance. We recognize, however, that the C system may also be activated by egalitarian norms or standards. However, to the extent that these norms are said to be "internalized," truly believed in, and are associated with guilt about violating them (Monteith *et al.*, 1993; Plant & Devine, 1998), they are difficult to distinguish from activity of the C system. Anyway, we believe that true care is ignored as an important source of motivation for the regulation of automatic activity related to the FF system.

Dual-process models in social psychology finally need to say something about the social consequences of regulating or suppressing the automatic reactions that are triggered by deviance. Most social psychologists appear interested in dual-process views of stigmatization because these views promise to reveal how negative responses may be reduced or avoided by motivating people to exercise more control over their automatic responses (e.g., Monteith & Voils, 2001); thereby assuming that automatic processes are generally based on representations with little basis in reality, and with behavioral consequences that are generally socially disruptive, dysfunctional, or undesirable for deviant individuals or society. However, knowledge about emotion regulation and social control in general alerts us that this may not be a generally valid and practically useful view. As noted above, and illustrated later in this chapter, suppression of emotions may have certain socially disruptive consequences, and under certain conditions tolerance, which relies on suppression, may be a less desirable mode of social control than repair.

*An integrative model of automatic and controlled processes in responding to deviance*

Figure 4.1 presents a simplified model describing how different variables influence the extent to which responses to deviant individuals have a unified nature (i.e., integrate automatic and controlled aspects of responding to deviance) or instead are relatively dissociated. The model generally assumes that an integration of automatic and controlled aspects of responding to deviance is especially likely when a clear and moderately strong motivational state is aroused during exposure to deviance that coordinates and integrates the different cognitive, bodily, and behavioral aspects of responding in the service of realizing the characteristic goal associated with that state, and given situational opportunities and skills or knowledge to realize that goal. With a "clear" motivational state we mean that this state points to an unambiguous goal, either because the C system or the flight or fight component of the FF system is exclusively activated (and people primarily intend to help, escape, or punish), or the activity produced by the combined activation of these systems can be integrated into a qualitatively new state or emotion (e.g., pity or forgiveness; see Chapter 2). Moreover, the "moderate" strength of the motivational state refers to a certain optimum level of emotional intensity. That is, this state should not be that

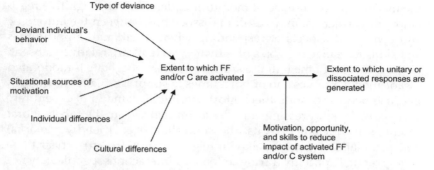

**Figure 4.1** Schematic representation of factors that influence the extent to which responses to deviance are unitary (or integrate automatic and controlled aspects) or dissociated.

strong that it prevents people from exercising control, or that weak that it cannot be integrated with consciously controlled processes. Furthermore, a crucial condition for integration of automatic and controlled aspects of responding is that people pay close attention to the deviant condition in order to confirm the validity and usefulness of their initial reactions, and to determine the condition's implications for interacting with the deviant individual in the current situation. Perhaps the most important message of our model is that controlled attentional and cognitive processes do not necessarily result in dissociation between automatic and controlled aspects of responding but may be integrated in the course of adaptation to situational opportunities for goal realization.[2]

In contrast, the model makes a distinction between two different ways in which the control of automatic processes may result in incongruent or dissociated responses. First, and receiving little attention from traditional dual-process models, responses may be viewed as dissociated when no efforts are made to monitor, regulate, or integrate automatic processes but conflicting motivational systems that are simultaneously activated during exposure to a deviant individual, independently exert influence on behavior. For example, while helping a needy person with an offputting facial deformity, people may also reveal a tendency to avoid contact, which may be evidenced by incomplete or nervous helping. Yet, when one of the motivational systems gains dominance over the other due to neural competition or reciprocal inhibition (see Chapter 2), alternatively it may be said to gain control over the other.

Second, even when a clear and moderate motivational state is initially aroused by exposure to a deviant individual (see above), control in the more traditional sense of monitoring, deliberation, cognitive regulation, or correction, may result in dissociation between the automatic and controlled aspects of responding when situational opportunities and skills to realize the goals of activated systems are relatively absent, or the influence of the initially aroused motivational state is moderated by additional motives and opportunities to suppress or alter its impact. Because people, despite their efforts and ability, may not be entirely successful in suppressing automatic influences on their behavioral reactions to deviant persons, the controlled (e.g., friendly remarks) and automatic aspects of behavior (e.g., an angry frown) appear to be incongruent. Especially during unfocused interactions, people may not only need to control or cover-up automatic responses closely associated with type of deviance (e.g., escape tendencies in the face of active deviance or nurturing tendencies in response to passive deviance) and the associated increase in attention to the deviant condition; but also the bodily and behavioral effects of attempts to inhibit these responses such as tenseness, trembling, speech errors, increased heart rate, or sweating. Indeed, these unfocused interactions seem to offer the most compelling reason for assuming that responding to deviance essentially consists of a mind struggling to gain control over an independently behaving body. Yet, it is easy to forget that these kinds of apparent mind-body dissociations may not be representative for the integrated nature of behavior in many other interaction situations in which people have opportunities and skills to realize goals relevant to the deviant condition.

Finally note, that an additional sense in which control may result in dissociated responses is when automatic and stereotype-based responses generated by a category label are diluted or replaced by more informed judgments when people force themselves to spend more time and energy processing information about a deviant individual's non-deviant attributes (cf. Fiske & Neuberg, 1990).

The extended dual-process model shown in Figure 4.1 distinguishes two important classes of variables that determine the extent to which responses to deviant individuals will be unified or dissociated; variables that, in combination, determine the nature and strength of the aroused motivational state and its associated expectancy (grouped at the left side of the horizontal arrow), and those that moderate the influence of this state or expectancy on finally observed behaviors (grouped below the vertical arrow). Of the latter moderating factors, the role of the C system deserves special attention in light of our motivational perspective. As argued above, the C system may immediately start to inhibit activity of the FF system when deviant individuals are initially responded to, and continue to motivate "carefulness" and regulation during later stages of interpersonal contact. Alternatively, activity of the FF system may dominate initial responding because the triggering stimuli of the C system become available at a later stage, when people have the opportunity to reflect on their protective tendencies and become aware of egalitarian standards. As noted later in this chapter, several studies in which negative relations were found between negative implicit responses and explicit protective responses may be interpreted in this way. We repeat that especially when social norms are interpreted as "internalized" standards that are associated with guilty feelings, it is difficult to distinguish them from activation of the C system and truly felt protective tendencies. As explained below, our alternative interpretation of normative influences in terms of activity of the C system has consequences for interpreting the influence of most variables in our model. Let us now examine these variables, listed in Figure 4.1, in more detail.

*Variables affecting the nature and strength of the initial motivational state and its associated expectancy*

*Type of deviance*   As proposed in previous chapters, salient or strong forms of active deviance (e.g., child abuser, psychopath) are likely to exclusively activate the FF system, whereas salient and strong forms of passive deviance (e.g., an abused child, a molested handicapped person) are likely to exclusively activate the C system. If given sufficient response options, therefore, automatic activity arising from these systems will be integrated with controlled processes, resulting in relatively unified responses (e.g., clear evidence for aggression and nurturance, respectively). However, more complex forms of deviance that immediately activate both the FF and C system are likely to cause a conflict between these systems and hence a less intense motivational state and a greater sensitivity to contextual and normative influences. For example, in the previous chapter we argued that African-Americans and ethnic minorities in Europe are associated with controllable-passive or Type 4 deviance, triggering both the C system because of their relatively dependent and needy situation, and the fight component of the FF system because they are perceived as doing too little to cope with, or get out of, their low socioeconomic position and disadvantaged situation. In addition, these groups may also trigger fear reactions because of aggressively protesting against their situation or subscribing to anti-democratic values. Consequently, complex deviant conditions make ambivalence or dissociation more likely.

Many researchers argue that differences in responding to different deviant conditions can be explained in terms of different normative prescriptions for expressing negative responses to them, or alternatively, for protecting individuals associated with these conditions. Relatedly, these prescriptions would be largely responsible for making controlled and positive responses to deviant individuals. For example, the fact that child abusers or criminals receive strongly negative, but abused children or handicapped persons, strongly positive responses, is explained by assuming that it is considered normatively acceptable to express negative responses to the former, but unacceptable to express them to the latter individuals (e.g., Crandall *et al.*, 2002; Franco & Maass, 1999). But clearly, people do not only judge the normative appropriateness of expressing negative feelings or "prejudice." They are also likely to *feel* that the child abuser should be punished and the abused child be protected or cared for. Hence, the strongly activated FF system in the former, and the strongly activated C system in the latter case, may also account for a strong correspondence between expressive norms and negative or protective behavior.[3]

However, it is quite possible that especially strongly passive forms of deviance may be responsible for controlled protective tendencies later in the response process. This may, for example, be the case when brief exposure to the deviant condition primarily activates the FF system and its associated aggressive or fearful responses, but people's subsequent and more elaborate reflection on their responses makes them aware of the deviant individual's disadvantaged status or the existence of egalitarian norms. Consequently, they may be motivated to explicitly express strongly protective behavior or opinions.

*Deviant individual's behavior*    As argued in Chapter 3, the deviant individual's behavior may facilitate or impede activation of the motivational systems associated with a particular type of deviance. For example, a mentally ill person or ex-convict showing threatening behavior, may increase the likelihood that the FF system actually gets activated; and a disabled person sitting in a wheelchair and asking for help may overwhelm others with pity and a desire to help. In contrast, the more people attend to and process information about behavior that is neutral or inconsistent with respect to the deviant condition (e.g., an ex-convict returns a lost wallet, a child abuser expresses strong remorse, a handicapped person behaves obtrusively), the less likely the relevant motivational system, and the more likely a competing system, will get activated.

*Situational sources of motivation*    Situational factors may also facilitate or impede activation of the FF and C system. Sometimes, these factors may help to focus attention on the motivational aspects of the deviant condition as is the case with encouraging people to take the perspective of and empathize with a deviant individual associated with passive deviance (see Chapter 2). At other times, irrelevant motivational influences may be present that may help to "displace" activity of the FF or C system on the deviant individual. For example, an aggressive response to active deviance becomes especially likely when previous unrelated events make one angry. Sometimes, these additional sources of motivation may be responsible for triggering a moderate motivational state that integrates automatic and controlled aspects of responding; for example, when the deviant condition or the individual's behavior are insufficient to activate the relevant motivational systems on their own account. At other times, situational sources of motivation may, in combination with a certain type of deviance and the deviant individual's behavior, cause such a strong emotional state that its control becomes more difficult.

*Individual differences*   Individual differences additionally contribute to the activation or de-activation of the motivational systems that are involved in responding to deviance. Although this factor will be discussed in detail in Chapter 5, it is important to say a few words here about its possible relationship with the activation of the FF and C system when being exposed to deviance. We argue that individuals who have been commonly classified as conservative or authoritarian respond with relatively strong fear and hostility to the active or threatening aspects of deviance because in these individuals, the FF system is relatively strongly developed and has a low activation threshold. In contrast, individuals commonly classified as "liberal" (in the particular North American sense of the word) or egalitarian, tend to respond with greater "softness," pity, and forgiveness especially to the passive aspects of deviance due to a relatively strongly developed C system. (Below, we will also assume that individuals who are classified as extremely hostile or extremely protective toward deviant individuals on an explicit verbal measure of negative responses or prejudice, will similarly have a strongly developed FF or C system, respectively.) As will become evident, these hypothesized relationships between individual differences and the FF and C system will prove useful in trying to understand how individual differences moderate responses to deviance.

Again, the alternative explanation in terms of the regulating influence of social norms or standards pops up. Specifically, many researchers argue that liberals respond positively to deviant individuals because they would like to comply with standards prescribing egalitarian behavior. When given the opportunity to follow their negative feelings, and the relevance of social norms is less clear, their behavior would be indistinguishable from that of conservatives (Gaertner & Dovidio, 2005). However, we note that the influence of "internalized" egalitarian norms of liberals, in particular, is conceptually similar to a low activation threshold or strongly developed C system in these individuals. Consequently, as illustrated later in this chapter, the positive responses of liberals may also be interpreted as being motivated by truly felt care.

*Cultural influences*   A final factor influencing the activation of the FF or C system that we distinguish in Figure 4.1 is culture or society. This factor will be extensively discussed in Chapter 6. Here, we would like to emphasize that cultural values and structural features of society influence responses to deviance through their potential to chronically activate the FF or C system. For example, whereas in many hierarchically organized collectivistic societies the FF system is more strongly activated in response to deviance, in modern Western societies the C system is relatively more strongly activated than the FF system. Consequently, in the latter societies, people tend to respond less aggressively and in a more caring manner to a wide variety of active and passive deviant conditions. Again, differential activation of the FF and C systems may be alternatively interpreted in terms of social norms or their underlying values.

## Motivation and opportunity to influence the motivational impact of deviance

Let us now turn to factors that moderate the influence of an initially aroused motivational state on behavior. We propose that such moderation is especially likely when, despite the triggering of a motivational state, people have little opportunity or ability to realize the goals of the relevant motivational systems and thus may need to re-direct or suppress their initial responses. In addition, people must have *both* specific motives and opportunities or skills to control the automatically triggered responses associated with the activation of the FF and/or C system. Clearly, without opportunity or skills, even strong motives to correct or suppress automatically produced responses will fail to result in behavioral control (cf. Fazio, 1990; Fazio *et al.*, 1995). It should be emphasized that, unlike most dual-process views, we do not assume that there is a straightforward relation between moderation of automatic responses and the reduction of stigmatization or prejudice. For example, while it may be desirable that suppression may result in less aggressive behavior toward deviant individuals, controlled behavior associated with tolerance may be interpreted as lack of spontaneity or coldness by the deviant individual. In addition, tendencies to divert attention away from the deviant condition in order to "individuate" the deviant individual may prevent people from engaging in repair processes.

*Motives to influence the motivational impact of deviance*   We make a distinction in motives to suppress the different aspects of the triggered motivational state or emotion, epistemic motives to process information about the deviant individual, and instrumental motives to use the deviant individual's attributes to realize a particular goal. First, as illustrated earlier, people may try to suppress or regulate various aspects of the motivational states or emotions triggered by deviance; for example, because they fear social disapproval or reputation loss, want to conform to egalitarian standards, or sincerely desire to protect a vulnerable person.

Second, people may have certain epistemic motives to pay more attention to the deviant individual's non-deviant than deviant attributes, resulting in images or judgments that are relatively individuated (Fiske & Neuberg, 1990) and incongruent with the initially aroused response. For example, when people are held accountable for their final impressions and judgments, they may form more complex representations of the deviant individual.

A third class of motives that may prevent the motivational aspects of deviance from gaining control over people's behavior is related to the importance of realizing interaction goals that are unrelated to the particular deviant condition. Specifically, one may want to use certain qualities of the deviant individual in order to get a particular job done. Although this "outcome dependency" has been primarily discussed in terms of increased attention to the target's non-deviant attributes (Erber & Fiske, 1984; Fiske & Neuberg, 1990), additional cognitive strategies may also be involved here. For example, one may reason that it is important to temporarily ignore the target's threatening or aggression-arousing features in order to efficiently cooperate with a colleague. Similarly, for the sake of defending one's country one may temporarily favor certain attributes such as aggressiveness that under normal circumstances would be considered undesirable or deviant. These possibilities would imply that short-term cooperation between non-deviant and deviant individuals on specific tasks may not necessarily promote harmonious long-term relationships in which the deviant individual is truly integrated.

*Opportunities for influencing the motivational impact of deviance*   In order to reduce the influence of the FF or C system or their associated expectancies on behaviors, people should both be motivated to control these influences and have the ability to do so. Obviously, a general way of preventing realization of the goals of the activated motivational systems is to take away most situational opportunities for realizing these goals. In addition, the three classes of motives introduced above are associated with specific opportunities and skills. For example, people should be able to pay attention to interaction norms or aroused guilt. If they have a lot of other things on their mind, they may not be able to suppress negative feelings effectively. They should also be able to realize their epistemic motives, for example, by allowing them sufficient time to process information about the deviant individual (Fazio & Olson, 2003; Fiske & Neuberg, 1990). Together, motivation and opportunity have been recognized as important factors in reducing the influence of expectancies or stereotypes on forming impressions of other persons (see also our discussion of expectancy-based perception and stereotyping in the previous chapter).

*Examining the social psychological literature to find support for the extended dual-process model*

In our extensive reading of the social psychological literature on stigmatization and prejudice we have uncovered three large clusters of research, two of which will be especially relevant for present purposes. First, researchers may provide participants with rich and meaningful stimulus configurations or scenarios and ask them to describe and summarize their responses in terms of meaningful actions (e.g., to punish, to forgive, to defend) and goals (e.g., to change the deviant individual's behavior or mind, restore relationships, realize safe conditions of interaction). A special case would be when participants are allowed to deliberate on the similarities and differences among multiple deviant conditions, thereby extensively making use of the contents of their internal representations. Studies falling in this cluster of research were presented in the previous chapter. Although these studies primarily address mental content, "mind stuff," reasoning, or imagination, rather than "real" behavior, they have the advantage of allowing the measurement of (self-reported) responses that are relatively unconstrained by situational opportunities to realize the goals of activated motivational systems. Therefore, the question of dissociation between automatic and controlled processes did not come up in the previous chapter. Indeed, we showed that, insofar as self-reports are concerned, thinking, feeling, and doing with respect to deviant conditions are strongly correlated.[4] Thus, these responses may give us important clues about their function in stigmatization and repair processes. For example, we interpreted positive responses to certain behaviors of deviant individuals as satisfaction with their efforts to cope well with their condition, which suggest that these efforts may also become important in repairing relationships between deviant and non-deviant individuals (see Chapter 9).

A second cluster of research consists of studies actually providing participants with opportunities to behave in such a way as to realize the goals of motivational systems activated by the particular deviant condition. Thus, in these studies people are allowed to aggress, help, or avoid deviant individuals, thereby intelligently making use of the opportunities offered by the researchers. We believe that in these studies one can frequently witness responses that integrate automatic and controlled aspects of responding in effective ways. However, again it is difficult to indicate to what extent these responses play a role in stigmatization or repair processes.

In our view, a third cluster of studies primarily addresses the psychological aspects of tolerance as displayed by people living in modern Western society, with strong evidence for dissociation between the automatic and controlled aspects of responding to deviance. One subcluster contains studies primarily attesting to people's incapacity to deal effectively with deviance during unfocused everyday encounters in which people have little opportunity to realize the goals of deviance-relevant motivational systems. Here, we witness nervousness combined with efforts to normalize the interaction and be friendly. Another subcluster consists of a rapidly increasing number of studies in which automatic or reflexlike responses are measured while people are presented with relatively impoverished stimuli (e.g., very brief exposure to the faces or names of deviant individuals flashed on a computer screen), and compared with "explicit" verbal response measures. Again, researchers find much evidence for dissociation between these automatic and controlled responses.[5]

To summarize, while the first cluster primarily deals with mental content but gives important clues about what kind of actions people, under ideal circumstances, may want to perform in relation to deviant individuals, the second cluster shows how mental content may actually translate into goal-directed behavior, while the third one impresses us with evidence not only for tolerance but also for clumsy behavior, anxiety, exaggerated self-focused attention, and dissociation between automatic and controlled aspects of responding. Unfortunately, the second and third cluster of studies seem to function as two incompatible research paradigms in light of which researchers are only able to find evidence for either unified or dissociated responses. Thus, research strategies employed within the third cluster seldom allow one to study unified goal-directed responses to deviant individuals that integrate automatic and controlled aspects, because participants are rarely allowed to realize the goals of deviance-related motivational systems during interaction. On the other hand, the second cluster employs a research paradigm in which dissociation normally cannot be systematically studied.

In the remaining part of this chapter, we will use the second and third research clusters in the following ways to find support for our extended dual-process model of responding to deviance. We use the second cluster of studies to find evidence for the role of deviance-related motivational systems in producing unified goal-directed responses toward deviant individuals. In addition, we discuss the influence of different situational factors on the triggering of these motivational systems. The third cluster will be used to examine the factors that may moderate the influence of automatically activated motivational states on behavior. However, within the latter cluster, we will also look for evidence for the operation of our FF-C network and for conditions under which automatic and controlled aspects of responding are less dissociated than normally assumed by researchers. After we have presented both research clusters or paradigms, it will hopefully be apparent how important the situation is for observing unified or dissociated responses, and how modern research on stigmatization in particular may obscure the motivational and unified nature of responding to deviance outside the psychological laboratory.

## 4.3  Doing what you want to do: when aggression, helping, or avoidance are possible

We now attempt to demonstrate that when people have the opportunity and skills to express the emotions and desires triggered by a deviant condition in terms of meaningful and relatively controlled behavioral sequences, their behavior will be congruent with the motivational implications of type of deviance involved. In particular, we hypothesize that in these situations people are likely to aggress against individuals associated with active deviance, and refrain from helping them when encountered in a needy condition; but help individuals associated with passive deviance and inhibit aggression when required to punish them. In addition, when possible, people may generally avoid deviant individuals, for example, because active deviance is feared, aggression or helping is not possible, or anxiety during unstructured contact is anticipated. Thus, avoidance does not seem uniquely related to the flight component of the FF system but may occur for other reasons.[6] We also examine the hypothesis that in the above situations people's behavior will reflect, in particular, the motivationally relevant aspects of deviance when additional sources of motivation such as the deviant individual's behavior, situational influences, or individual differences contribute to activating the relevant motivational systems.

Before discussing the relevant studies, it is important to emphasize once more that our thesis of the motivational and unified nature of goal-directed behavior towards the deviant individual does not imply the absence of controlled processes. In particular, we argue that people will make use of situational opportunities to adapt their behavior to the situation in the service of goal-realization and need satisfaction, even if their behavior appears rather elementary, habitual, or "subtle." Take the three behaviors that figure prominently in this section: pushing a button with which to deliver electric shocks to a needy deviant individual, selecting a particular physical distance from the individual, or helping an individual with intimidating attributes.

One commonly used laboratory procedure to study interpersonal aggression is the teacher-learner paradigm in which research participants are required to teach a particular task to a learner (always a confederate of the experimenter) by means of punishment in case of errors and in the form of electric shocks or noise blasts (which obviously are never actually received). In an alternative paradigm for studying physical aggression (the Taylor Aggression Paradigm) participants engage in a competitive reaction time task with a fictitious opponent in which shocks are administered to the slowest responding opponent (participants themselves also receive shocks from their opponent on a predetermined number of trials). In both research paradigms, participants may vary both the intensity of shocks (by selecting buttons with labels indicating how mild or powerful the corresponding shocks will be) and their duration. Shock intensity is usually interpreted as involving direct, volitional, and controlled behavior, whereas shock duration is associated with indirect, covert, and less volitional aggression (for general discussions, see Baron, 1977; Giancola & Chermak, 1998). As shown below, especially when participants interact with deviant individuals, their direct and clearly visible aggression is highly sensitive to situational influences. For example, when exaggerated aggression can be retaliated by the learner or when others disapprove of it, people may refrain from direct aggression but still choose exceptionally high levels of indirect aggression to punish a deviant learner. Yet, we argue that, in the case of indirect aggression, covert or "less volitional" may not only mean "strongly motivated" but also intelligently adapted to the particular situation. Indeed, we expect that those individuals who are dispositionally hostile toward a particular type of deviance, in particular, will strategically vary between direct and indirect aggression in order to express their hostility. In addition, we hypothesize that in situations in which the shock intensity is known to the learner and others present (or when the learner and others can retaliate), people will not distinguish between explicitly punishing non-deviant and deviant individuals, but will choose a longer shock duration in the case of active (e.g., mentally ill person, black person in a competitive or threatening context) and a shorter shock duration in the case of passive deviance (e.g., person in a wheelchair). That is, we expect that in these situations, covert aggression reflects what people really want with respect to active (more aggression) and passive (less aggression) deviance, while at the same time communicating with overt aggression and for different reasons (e.g., fear of retaliation or reputation loss) that with both types of deviance, deviant individuals should not be treated differently.

Although selecting a particular seating distance from a deviant individual also tends to be interpreted as indicating an absence of controlled processes (e.g., Bessenoff & Sherman, 2000), it may similarly involve an integration of automatic and controlled elements of responding. Suppose that you enter a waiting room with one row of chairs placed against the wall, and have to choose how many chairs to leave empty between your and a deviant individual's seat. Of course, you will not make it too obvious that you actually want to leave as many chairs as possible between you and the individual. So, you may quickly calculate what still seems to be a socially acceptable amount of space to leave. However, you will also assume that everyone would agree that people should be free to choose where to sit, and hence that no one can blame you if you leave a few more seats free than you usually do in the case of non-deviant persons. Thus physical distancing from a deviant person may be a subtle or covert way of avoiding in the sense that the deviant individual or others present will not be harmed or provoked. However, this behavior may also reflect people's controlled strategies for intelligently realizing their desires. Of course, the less molar and more emotionally expressive distancing behavior becomes (e.g., leaning backwards), the more difficult it will be to control (for a related discussion, see Dovidio *et al.*, 2002).

We finally note that, in particular when helping individuals in need, and refraining from helping them out of fear or aggression, are also behaviors that, in order to be effective, must make use of situational opportunities and decisional processes. Indeed, it seems hard to imagine that behaviors can ever be interpreted as "helpful" when not firmly based on both motivational and controlled processes.

## Aggression

The teacher-learner paradigm has been extensively used by Donnerstein and colleagues to study aggression of white teachers toward white and black (African-American) learners (for a detailed discussions of these experiments, see Crosby *et al.*, 1980; Donnerstein & Donnerstein, 1976). It is generally found that when the situation is "safe" for the teacher (i.e., the learner can not retaliate or the punishment is delivered anonymously), participants deliver shocks of both higher intensity (direct aggression) and duration (indirect aggression) to black than white learners. However, in "unsafe" situations (i.e., with the expected opportunity of the learner to switch roles and to retaliate or with publicly known punishments), participants only show more *indirect* or subtle aggression toward black than white learners, delivering longer but not more intense shocks toward the former.

Using a Taylor paradigm in which participants aggressed against each other by delivering noise bursts, Beal, O'Neal, Ong, and Ruscher (2000) also found that white participants who were previously identified as experiencing strongly negative feelings about blacks (as measured on the Modern Racism Scale), expressed less direct but more covert aggression against a black than a white opponent, especially at a high level of provocation. In contrast, participants previously identified as relatively positive about blacks, used less covert aggression against a black than white opponent. In an interesting second experiment, these researchers tested the hypothesis that using covert aggression by the strongly negative participants may be a strategic process that requires cognitive capacity. They found that under high cognitive load (participants had to memorize a complex number), these participants showed considerably less covert aggression against the black opponent than under low load, while their overt aggression was unaffected by this manipulation. Relatively positive respondents were also not influenced by this manipulation.

In sum, the above aggression experiments employing white and black target persons suggest that negative responses may be strategically expressed and adapted to the available situational opportunities. Equal or reduced overt aggression may be functional in situations in which the deviant individual or others are expected to retaliate, or one truly feels positive about the target. (Interestingly, in contrast to the Donnerstein studies employing a teacher-learner paradigm, participants in the Beal *et al.* study actually experienced the target's aggressive retaliation, which may have motivated them more strongly to actively reduce their aggression toward the black person.) Increased covert aggression may always be functional when one truly feels negatively about the target.

One experiment suggests that also in the teacher-learner paradigm, direct provocation increases whites' aggression toward blacks. Rogers and Prentice-Dunn (1981) arranged for the white or black "learner" to either insult (e.g., referring to the teacher's stupidness) or not insult the teacher before engaging in the learning task. The results showed a clear interaction between the learner's skin color and insult, such that after a previous insult, the black learner received shocks of both higher intensity and duration than the white learner. The reverse was true for the no insult condition, with the black learner receiving shocks of lower intensity and shorter duration than the white learner. The authors explain this pattern of results by suggesting that anger arousal through an insult by the deviant individual may function as an additional instigator of aggressive tendencies aroused by blacks, in a similar way that anonymity or inability of the target to retaliate may disinhibit aggressive tendencies. Presumably, this also results in a convergence of subtle and overt aggression, without participants being sufficiently able or motivated to regulate and dissociate these two kinds of aggression. Although the authors explain the reduced aggression toward the black learner in the no insult condition in terms of "reverse discrimination" and "egalitarian norms," it is unclear why participants also showed reduced *indirect* aggression (i.e., in terms of shock duration); a finding that is inconsistent with the robust results of the Donnerstein studies suggesting more indirect aggression toward blacks than whites. It is worth noting that in the no insult condition in Rogers and Prentice-Dunn's experiment, the learner did not merely refrain from insulting the teacher but remarked that he had no objection to this particular person shocking him. So, perhaps, he may have presented himself unexpectedly as a non-retaliating, submissive, and harmless individual, causing a true reduction of aggressive feelings and increase in non-violent behavior in the case of the black target. Such a pattern is consistent with the finding that pain or suffering cues effectively reduce interracial aggression, even when the target has no power to retaliate and thus should invite relatively high levels of aggression (Griffin & Rogers, 1977).

Other deviant conditions that are also associated with active deviance such as mental illness and homosexuality have also been subjected to aggression studies. For example, using a teacher-learner procedure, Farina, Thaw, Felner, and Hust (1976) demonstrated that male teachers, in particular, show more indirect as well as direct aggression against male learners associated with mental illness. In this study, females showed less aggression toward a mentally ill than a non-deviant female. Employing the Taylor Aggression Paradigm, Bernat, Calhoun, Adams, and Zeichner (2001) first measured participants' attitudes or aggressive tendencies toward homosexuals and subsequently assigned participants scoring high ("homophobic") or low ("non-homophobic") on this scale randomly to an apparently

heterosexual or homosexual opponent. Homophobia appeared to interact significantly with the target's sexual orientation, such that homophobic participants demonstrated both more direct (intensity of shock
level) and indirect (shock duration) aggression in response to a homosexual opponent than non-homophobic participants, but did not differ
in aggression in response to a heterosexual one. In order to examine if
homophobic and non-phobic participants responded differently to
homosexual and heterosexual targets in terms of shock intensity and
duration, we computed four $t$-values on the basis of the authors' Table 3.
Homophobic participants appeared to deliver shocks of longer duration to homosexual than to heterosexual individuals ($t(24) = 2.45$,
$p = 0.02$) and also tended (yet non-significantly so) to select a higher
shock intensity for the former than the latter target ($t(24) = 1.59$,
$p = 0.12$). The pattern for the non-homophobics was exactly the opposite. They gave shocks of both lower intensity ($t(24) = 2,14, p = 0.04$) and
shorter duration ($t(24) = 3.67, p = 0.001$) to a homosexual than a heterosexual target. These findings suggest that for individuals with a negative or aggressive disposition toward homosexuals, homosexuality is
viewed as active deviance, triggering the fight component of the FF
system when actually met. In contrast, for those without negative
attitudes, homosexuality may be associated with passive deviance or
a disadvantaged status that needs protection and aggression inhibition.
That homophobic and non-homophobic participants showed this
pattern on both a direct and indirect and more subtle measure of
aggression, suggests that aggression and aggression inhibition may
correspond with participants' truly felt emotions. Interestingly, a recent
study by Giancola (2003) revealed that the employed behavioral aggression measure is also sensitive to feelings of empathy or care. That is,
individuals with a high level of dispositional empathy or care display
lower levels of physical aggression toward their opponents, and do not
increase aggression after having consumed alcohol; a substance known
for its aggression-facilitating effects.

We know relatively little about aggressive behavior toward individuals primarily associated with passive deviance such as disabled
persons. Yet, a series of experiments performed by Farina and colleagues may offer some clues. For example, in the above cited study by
Farina *et al.* (1976), both males and females gave shocks of the lowest
intensity and shortest duration to mentally handicapped learners. An
earlier study by Farina, Sherman, and Allen (1968) more clearly illustrates reduced aggression toward individuals with passive deviance.
These investigators found that a severely handicapped learner (sitting
in a wheelchair with one leg amputated above the knee) received
shocks of shorter duration than a less severely handicapped one (who

walked with a slight limp). Furthermore, no differences were found in direct aggression or shock intensity. This pattern thus suggests sincere aggression *reduction* in the case of somewhat more passive deviance, together with a desire to treat the handicapped even-handedly in overt ways (see also Farina *et al.*, 1976, p. 41).

While the latter experiment did not employ a control condition with a truly non-deviant person, Titley and Viney (1969), compared aggressive responses toward a male or female target with or without crutches, this time requiring participants to estimate the target's pain threshold, using a shock switch numbered from 0 to 100 (which may be tentatively interpreted as a similar subtle or covert measure as shock duration). The researchers found an interaction between physical condition and participants' sex such that females aggressed less toward the disabled than the non-disabled target, but males showed the reverse pattern. As proposed in Chapter 2, females may have a more strongly developed or more easily activated C system than males (see also Chapter 5).

Finally, note that aggression may also be expressed by negatively evaluating a person's performance on a particular task (Pedersen, Gonzales, & Miller, 2000). Again, we expect people to strategically take the situational opportunities into account. For example, Moreno and Bodenhausen (2001) selected participants who had egalitarian attitudes about gays, but were either low or high in negative feelings towards them. These participants read an essay advocating gay rights that either did or did not contain numerous spelling and grammatical errors. Participants with strong negative feelings toward gays derogated the essay position and the writer as compared to participants with less negative feelings, but only when the essay was poorly written. Their negative feelings about gays may have instigated them to be vigilant and critical and to look for negative behaviors, which was easy in the poor writing quality conditions, but more difficult in the good writing quality conditions.

In sum, we tentatively interpret studies in which aggressive behavior toward deviant individuals is possible and even required, as showing that active deviants strongly activate, relatively speaking, the FF system resulting in increased aggression, and passive deviants strongly activate, relatively speaking, the care system, resulting in inhibition of aggression. With both types of deviance, covert or indirect aggression seems to reflect relatively accurately what people want with respect to deviant individuals.

*Situational influences on aggression: room for displacement or scapegoating*

Is there evidence indicating that additional input to the FF system *not* stemming from type of deviance or the deviant individual's provocation, also increases aggression toward deviance; "displacing" the aggression so to speak toward a target who was not causally responsible for arousing it? Fortunately, researchers show renewed interest in the once popular account of prejudice and intergroup hostility in terms of displaced aggression or scapegoating (Marcus-Newhall, Pedersen, Carlson, & Miller, 2000; Miller, Pedersen, Earleywine, & Pollock, 2003). Interestingly, their theoretical explanation in terms of triggered displaced aggression fits very well with our general principle of threshold lowering of the motivational systems that are associated with deviance. Although the meta-analysis by Marcus-Newhall *et al.* (2000) establishes fairly well that "negativity" associated with the target or situation moderates displaced aggression, only a few studies suggest that displacement is especially likely when targets of aggression themselves have stable undesirable or deviant features. For example, Berkowitz and Frodi (1979) asked female participants to play the role of parents disciplining their 10-year-old child when doing his or her homework. After being provoked or not provoked by disparaging statements of a confederate, participants were required to punish the child for mistakes, using the teacher/learner paradigm discussed earlier. The child was either fairly good looking or made to look unattractive and unkempt, with shadows under her eyes and greasy, stringy hair. The results showed that, although there was only a main effect for attractiveness on the intensity with which the child was punished, with the unattractive child punished harsher than the attractive one, this was especially true when participants had been initially provoked.

In another study (Fein & Spencer, 1997), participants ascribed more negative, stereotype-relevant traits to a homosexual than a heterosexual person, or a Jewish than Italian person (the former belonging to a relatively stigmatized group in participants' subculture), but only when they had previously learned that they had relatively low scores on an intelligence test. In a recent replication of the Fein and Spencer (1997) experiment by Mikulincer and Shaver (2001, Experiment 4), in which participants were only mildly annoyed by failures on cognitive puzzles (no intelligence test was administered), the same displacement pattern was obtained.[7]

Motivational systems relevant for responding to deviance such as the fight system need not necessarily be activated by exposure to the concrete trigger stimuli of these systems. It may be enough to think about the general goals that are typically motivated by these systems, commonly called *values*, or the manner in which they can be realized (i.e., "instrumental" values). For example, thoughts about the importance of norms and responsible behavior may activate the fight component of the FF system, especially in individuals with a dispositionally low threshold of that system. Consistent with this possibility, Katz and Hass (1988) found that priming participants with thoughts related to the Protestant ethic (e.g., "Most people who don't succeed in life are just plain lazy," or "Anyone who is willing and able to work hard has a good chance of succeeding") increased negative or accusatory responses to blacks (e.g., "Most blacks [do not] have the drive and determination to get ahead"). An alternative interpretation of this effect is, of course, that the prime directly confronted participants with general aspects of deviant conditions of our Type 4 or controllable-passive deviance (see Chapter 3).

Another situational factor that may be relevant to activation of the FF system is the presence of a hierarchical interpersonal structure. (An alternative but related interpretation of a hierarchical relationship, that we discuss in Chapter 5, is that it may inhibit activity of the C system through some other factor than the FF system, such as tendency to dominate or compete with others.) In one of their studies, Guimond, Dambrun, Michinov and Duarte (2003) did or did not place French participants in a dominant social position by giving them feedback that they had a high leadership rating or not. Subsequently, and in an ostensibly unrelated study, participants with a high leadership score showed more bias against Arabs and blacks on a prejudice measure than participants with a moderate leadership score. In another study, participants were in a random way – they clicked on a dice – assigned to high or low status positions, i.e., director or receptionist of an organization. Again, directors having a high status position showed more bias against North Africans than receptionists with the low status position did.[8] A study by Richeson and Ambady (2002) showed similar effects on an implicit (see below) measure of negative responding in an interracial interaction situation. These researchers found that white participants who expected to hold a position of relatively high power in an interaction situation with a black person were more negatively biased against blacks than participants expecting to hold a relatively low power position.

In sum, the above studies on aggression suggest that when people have the opportunity to aggress meaningfully against others, aggression is especially likely when (a) active deviant features are present (e.g., black skin color, homosexuality in the eyes of homophobics, unattractiveness, mental illness, annoying features of passive deviance), (b) an active deviant shows behavior that is congruent with his or her deviant condition (e.g., harms the perceiver), and (c) being in an angry or self-assertive mood because of prior provocation or the opportunity to exercise power in the context of a hierarchical relationship.

*Helping*

We have seen that individuals associated with active deviance are more likely to be the recipient of aggression than non-deviant individuals, especially when the aggression is strongly motivated and/or made possible by the situation. In contrast, aggression toward individuals associated primarily with more passive forms of deviance such as a mental or physical handicap seems to be inhibited. In this section, we will argue that the latter individuals are also more likely to be helped than non-deviant individuals because the deviant condition can activate the C system. Before addressing help received by the latter category, however, we would like to examine more closely how much help individuals associated with active deviance receive when apparently needy. This question has been primarily addressed in the context of interracial helping.

According to our motivational perspective, although the C system may be activated upon perceiving passive aspects of African-Americans (e.g., a disadvantaged status) or a particular need for help (the victim drops a bag of groceries), white people may also need to overcome the fear that may be aroused by certain active aspects of the deviant condition (e.g., association with crime) or long-term tendencies to avoid contact. Overcoming such fears may be especially likely when different factors influencing activation of the C system can be combined, such as individual differences, guilt arousal, or aspects of the situation indicating that it is safe to help. Let us first consider the role of individual differences in the likelihood with which the C system is activated. In Gaertner's (1973) field experiment, conservatives and liberals were called by a white or black individual (race was manipulated through the individual's voice and speech characteristics, according to a pilot study) who was apparently stranded with his car while having only one dime for calling his garage but now dialed the wrong number. It appeared that while conservatives helped a black phonecaller less frequently than a white phonecaller (65 percent vs. 92 percent), liberals did not distinguish between the two (76 percent vs. 85 percent). However, unlike conservatives, liberals showed a stronger tendency to hang up the phone before the request by a black phonecaller was fully made. In line with his theory of aversive racism (Gaertner, 1976; Gaertner & Dovidio, 2005), Gaertner (1973) interprets these findings as suggesting that prematurely hanging up the phone reflects liberals' strategy to safely express their negative feelings and avoid contact without feeling normatively compelled to help the target. In contrast, after full exposure to the request for help, liberals must prove to themselves or others that they subscribe to egalitarian values. Consequently, helping merely functions as a token (Gaertner, 1976). To support his interpretation, Gaertner (1976, p. 198) also re-analyzes an experiment by Wispe and Freshley (1971) in which white passersby were confronted with a white or black person leaving a supermarket and dropping his or her packages in front of them. In his re-analysis, Gaertner found that the proportions of white bystanders clearly not helping a black or white individual did not differ. Yet, only 30 percent of the white bystanders who offered some assistance to the black victim, displayed "positive help" (i.e., helping with picking up all the dropped groceries), whereas 63 percent gave this kind of assistance to the white victim. Furthermore, 70 percent of the white bystanders offered "perfunctory help" to the black victim (i.e., helping the victim only with a few groceries and then hurrying on), whereas only 30 percent offered this small amount of assistance to the white victim. Gaertner argues that the latter pattern, in particular, would support the view that liberals or aversive racists desire to interpret contact situations as "no help needed" or "less help needed" and to feel no concerns about acting in non-egalitarian ways.

As indicated earlier in this chapter, our position with respect to the nature of positive behavior toward individuals associated with deviance is less cynical and acknowledges the activation of the C system, resulting in true feelings of tenderness and a desire to protect or help others. In particular, "perfunctory" or "token" help can also be interpreted as fearful helping (i.e., simultaneous activation of the FF and C system), complete helping as being too scary to practice, and helping in a remote situation (e.g., making the phonecall for the black phonecaller in Gaertner, 1973) as a safe form of helping. Moreover, reluctance to help the black victim by the conservatives in Gaertner (1973) may be interpreted as strategically solving a conflict between aggression and fear in the absence of care. That is, conservatives may have felt relatively safe enough to let the threatening victim make his full request after which they decided that an aggressive refusal would be appropriate.

A recurrent pattern in the literature on interracial helping is that black and white victims with salient need states are equally likely to be helped during face-to-face contact, whereas in remote situations they are less likely to be helped (Crosby *et al.*, 1980; Saucier, Miller, & Doucet, 2005). This pattern is also found in field experiments in which Germans were asked to help a confederate who was ostensibly a member of the migrant-worker population or a refugee/asylum seeker (Klink & Wagner, 1999). In terms of our motivational approach, we speculate that, although remote situations may decrease both the activation of the C and FF system, the latter may still be strong enough (e.g., due to the anticipated danger of helping or aggressive or revengeful thought) to successfully inhibit the former. Furthermore, because exposure to vivid need states during face-to-face contact may strongly activate the C system, differential activation of the FF system by black and white victims seems to be prevented. A complementary explanation would be that face-to-face contact more strongly activates norms not to stigmatize and to convey a non-prejudiced impression to the deviant person. Also, in face-to-face situations, noticing the person's individual and non-deviant attributes may dilute or decrease activity of the FF system.

There are, however, also a number of interracial helping studies showing that black victims are more frequently helped than white victims, suggesting an especially strong activation of the C system in the case of the former victims. In particular, these studies suggest that certain passive elements (e.g., disadvantaged status) of the otherwise quite active image of blacks, in combination with other features of vulnerability or harmlessness such as explicit submissiveness and a salient need state, may lower the threshold of the C system thus producing more output of that system in the form of care or helping than in the case of a white victim. For example, Katz and colleagues (Katz *et al.*, 1975, Experiment 1) examined under what conditions black or white interviewers would be more or less successful in requesting white subjects to take part in a brief consumer-survey conducted by telephone. In making the request, interviewers were instructed to adopt either an attitude of high assertiveness ("I'm sure you can give me five minutes of your time"), medium assertiveness ("I'm sure you won't mind ..."), or low assertiveness or high politeness ("Would you mind answering a few questions about ...?"). As predicted, black interviewers obtained more compliance than white interviewers, presumably because they appeared to cope well with their disadvantaged socioeconomic status (see Chapter 3). In addition, the assertiveness variable had a linear influence on helping, with the submissive attitude resulting in the highest compliance scores. Yet, this was especially true for the black interviewer. Specifically, whereas there was no difference in compliance between the white and black interviewer when they adopted a highly assertive style, the black one received increasingly more help as he behaved more submissively.

In another study manipulating the hierarchical status of participants, Dovidio and Gaertner (1981) asked male college students to work with a black or white target person (a confederate of the experimenter) and assigned them to a role implying a higher ("supervisor") or lower ("worker") status than the target. Before starting the task, the target person "accidentally" knocked over a container filled with pencils, scattering them over the floor. The main dependent variable was the likelihood of help given to the target person with picking up the pencils. It appeared that in the low status condition, the black and white target person was helped equally (58 percent vs. 54 percent). However, in the high status condition, the black person was helped almost twice as often as the white person (83 percent vs. 42 percent). Again, our interpretation would be that for a white perceiver, low status of the deviant individual in combination with a salient need state and certain passive elements in the image of blacks, signals that the individual is harmless and vulnerable, thus more strongly activating the C system. In addition, this may also help to reduce activation of the fear responses generated by the FF system, which in turn would allow a stronger activation of the C system.[9]

To summarize, there is some evidence that equal or greater observed helping of blacks than whites may not only be due to a concern with social norms or reputation loss, but also with more salient perceived vulnerability, subsequently activating the C system, and triggering spontaneous helping. Such a view is consistent with the observed reduction of both direct and indirect aggression (with the latter being relatively less sensitive to normative concerns) when blacks show vulnerability or pain cues (Griffin & Rogers, 1977; Rogers & Prentice-Dunn, 1981).[10]

Let us now turn to helping individuals primarily associated with passive deviance. Our theoretical model predicts that when there is clear evidence for passive deviance such as dependency or need state, and people have an opportunity to engage in helping and expect that helping can be useful, they will show more nurturance and helping toward a passive deviant than a non-deviant individual. However, this tendency to help may be reduced when the passive deviant condition (e.g., sitting in a wheelchair) also contains active and threatening elements such as a salient physical or facial disfigurement. The contribution of passive and active elements may explain the considerable variation that has been obtained in studies in which people's helping behavior towards apparently disabled persons has been examined. Here, we concentrate on evidence for increased helping of individuals with relatively "pure" forms of passive deviance such as sitting in a wheelchair, without additional abnormal or unattractive features (reactions to the latter additions are discussed in a later section of this chapter where we discuss escape and avoidance). First note that disabled persons are universally helped simply because of their disability and apparent need state. This was, for example, demonstrated on a massive scale by Levine *et al.* (1994), who performed hundreds of field experiments in each of thirty-six cities scattered around the USA in which experimenters acted, for example, as a blind person with cane and dark glasses standing near a traffic light waiting to cross the road. Although the percentage of helping differed across geographical area, the mean percentage of assisting the blind person by informing him that the traffic light turned green or helping him across the street, was 70 percent. Levine and colleagues (Levine, Norenzayan, & Philbrick, 2001) found similarly high percentages in cities across different cultures. (The variability in helping rates across cultures will be examined in Chapter 6.)

In a field experiment by Piliavin, Piliavin, and Rodin (1975) it was found that 86 percent of New York City subway riders who saw a white male carrying a cane stumble and fall to the floor came to his aid. Noteworthy, when an "easy escape" opportunity or excuse for not helping was offered in the form of a bystander with a medical jacket, people did not help less; something they did, however, when an active deviant element (an unsightly facial birthmark) was added to the victim (see below). Furthermore, we know from a lot of other research that once people feel pity they tend to go out of their way in order to help needy others, even when they have an easy opportunity to "escape" and avoid the victim (Batson, 1987).

It is also known from reports by disabled persons themselves that they often receive assistance when help is not solicited or required by the particular situation (Braithwaite & Eckstein, 2003). Furthermore, a number of field studies show that disabled persons are also often helped for reasons unrelated to their particular disability; for example, when they ask others to take part in a survey interview (Cacciapaglia, Beauchamp, & Howells, 2004), to donate money (Slochower, Wein, White, Firstenberg, & Diguilio, 1980), to give a coin in order to make a phonecall (Taylor, 1998), or to sell alcohol to a 20-year-old male without asking for his license (Stiles, 1995).

In sum, when situations allow people to offer assistance to others, individuals associated with passive deviance seem to receive more help than non-deviant individuals (because of the involvement of the C system and/or egalitarian norms), although this tendency is weakened the more the deviant condition or the situation contains active or threatening elements.

## Situational influences on triggering care and helping

From our theoretical perspective it can be predicted that activation of the care system by events unrelated to deviant individuals (e.g., remembering having been in need oneself and being supported) should also lower that system's threshold and hence will increase the likelihood of that system becoming fully activated when subsequently being exposed to concrete signs of passive deviance, resulting in greater feelings of tenderness and pity and an increased tendency to nurture and help. Alternatively, prior activation of the care system may cause people to respond with less aggression and fear to signs of active deviance because the care system may increase its inhibitory influences on the FF system. Fortunately, a series of experiments conducted by Mikulincer and colleagues, in which responses to both passive and active deviance were examined, offers the opportunity to put this hypothesis to empirical test. Mikulincer *et al.* (2001) were interested in the influence of individual differences and situational activation of "attachment security" on people's emotions of pity and fear (both measured by Batson's empathy and distress scales; see our interpretation of these scales in Chapter 2) when confronted with a needy or disabled person. Individual differences in attachment security were operationalized, among other things, as general lack of anxiety about being abandoned and not supported when in need. Examples of the situational activation of attachment security include recalling situations in which one was helped when in need, exposure to pictures of needy and distressed individuals being helped, and subliminal priming with the words *closeness, love, hug,* and *support* (priming is discussed in detail in Section 4.5). The results of different experiments showed that pity in response to a needy other (e.g., a person in a wheelchair with amputated legs) was negatively, and fear positively, influenced by individual differences in anxiety. Furthermore, pity for the needy other was consistently positively influenced by the situational activation of attachment security when compared with a positive mood induction or neutral condition. The researchers interpret these findings as supporting the view that, whereas insecure attachment with a caregiver chronically activates fearful and hostile tendencies, making one relatively sensitive to threat stimuli such as another person's distress, these tendencies may be reduced when the situation stimulates one to think of a secure attachment and reassuring events of being supported by others. An additional consequence of secure attachment may be that the need of the other person becomes more salient. Although this interpretation is consistent with our view that deactivation of the FF system (e.g., by means of reassurance) may result in less inhibition and hence stronger activation of the care system, it is interesting to note that Mikulincer *et al.* (2001, p. 1223) also mention an alternative explanation of their findings. Specifically, all representations they used to prime attachment security might have equally activated the care system directly. Although the authors dismiss this interpretation, we believe that it does not exclude but may complement the first one, because in our view, the FF and C system reciprocally inhibit each other (see Chapter 2).

In another series of studies, Mikulincer and Shaver (2001) extended their paradigm to responses to different kinds of active deviance. In different experiments they compared the responses of Israeli Jewish university students to an Israeli Arab, ultraorthodox religious Jew, Russian immigrant, homosexual, or individual with anti-Israeli attitudes, with responses made to a non-deviant individual (e.g., Israeli Jewish ingroup member or heterosexual). Again, some participants were primed with attachment security, others with a positive mood induction or assigned to a neutral condition. The results showed that, although the deviant individual generally received more hostile evaluations than the non-deviant one, the priming manipulation was effective in removing this bias, and that this effect was mediated by a reduction of threat/anxiety. Interestingly, the effects of the security manipulation were strong enough to improve the evaluation of a homosexual even after participants were previously made to fail at a cognitive task, a manipulation intended to increase negative responses to deviance, and to replicate the study by Fein and Spencer (1997) mentioned above. Their interpretation is very close to ours in terms of reduction of fear for threat cues associated with active deviance, or increased pity for the disadvantaged target groups employed. In sum, these studies highlight the importance of thinking in terms of two competing motivational systems when confronted with deviant conditions that can be differentially activated by the active and passive elements of these conditions.

Again, prior activation of a relevant motivational system may also be accomplished by thinking about the goals of that system; i.e., values. Thus Katz and Hass (1988) found that participants primed with thoughts related to Humanitarianism-Egalitarianism (e.g., "Those who are unable to provide for their basic needs should be helped by others") responded more positively to blacks.

Other situational aspects may also increase activation of the care system and hence motivate helping. In two studies, Katz (1981) showed that when people are induced to do a small favor to a handicapped person, they are more likely to help a second time. This was not the case for a non-handicapped target, where there was a tendency to help less on the second occasion. We also noted earlier that in other studies performed by Katz and colleagues, people who are made to feel guilty about hurting a deviant individual are more likely to subsequently help the individual. This has not only been observed in the case of whites responding to blacks, but also to handicapped persons. As noted in Chapter 2, feeling guilty implies activation of the C system, and hence motivates helping, even when the deviant individual is somewhat threatening.

Finally, the C system may also be activated by asking people to focus their attention on the vulnerable and needy aspects of a deviant condition itself; a process that has often been referred to as "perspective taking" and which is normally contrasted with taking a more analytical or objective attitude toward a needy individual (see our critical discussion of this concept in Chapter 2 and our review of relevant findings in Chapter 3).[11]

### Escape and avoidance

As noted earlier, of the three behaviors typically studied during contact between non-deviant and deviant individuals, avoidance is the most difficult to specifically relate to the motivational systems of the FF-C network. On the one hand, avoidance could suggest fear for the active aspects of deviance, on the other hand, people's anticipation or experience that unfocused everyday contact will be anxiety-arousing. Also as suggested, avoidance, like aggression and helping, may integrate automatic and controlled aspects of responding to deviance, smartly taking account of the available response options.

Suggestive evidence for fearful avoidance in response to active deviance was provided by several of the Donnerstein studies presented earlier, in which a black "learner" was shocked less intensely than a white learner when the learner had the opportunity to retaliate. In addition, there is suggestive evidence for fearful avoidance in helping studies when passive deviant conditions also have active or threatening elements. In the studies we found it makes sense to distinguish relatively disturbing (e.g., large facial scar, hunchback) from less disturbing physical conditions (e.g., an eye patch) or other threatening aspects (e.g., a beggar may arouse suspicion about his or her true need state or motives). What is important is that these kinds of additions, while increasing fear, do not seem to be clearly associated with dependency on others, and hence likely to trigger avoidance tendencies that will be translated into behavior whenever situational opportunities are present. For example, adding a large birthmark on confederates' faces in the New York City subway study by Piliavin *et al.* (1975) discussed earlier, reduced the percentage of help received from 86 percent to 61 percent. The largest decrease (from 85 percent to 48 percent) was observed when help could be delegated to a bystander with an apparent medical profession and avoidance was easier (remember that the presence or absence of the medically competent bystander did not affect helping a stumbling victim without a birthmark).

This pattern was replicated in a study involving people riding in an elevator. Walton and colleagues (Walton *et al.*, 1988), being primarily interested in finding out if pregnancy behaved as a physical stigma, observed responses to a female victim (a confederate appearing pregnant, non-pregnant, or with a facial scar) who "accidentally" dropped three loose keys. The victim was or was not accompanied by a female or male (indicated by briefly speaking to the victim upon entering the elevator) who ostensibly focused attention somewhere else and apparently did not notice the need situation. Our re-analysis of the helping rates for the victim with or without a facial scar indicates that reduced helping of the individual with the facial scar was clearly dependent on having an excuse not to help. Specifically, when the individual was not accompanied, the deviant and non-deviant female were equally likely to be helped (10 percent and 7 percent, respectively; $Chi^2 = 0.22$, $p = 0.64$), but when she was accompanied by a male or female, the one with the facial scar was helped significantly less (2 percent and 12 percent, respectively; $Chi^2 = 4.82$, $p = 0.03$). (Parenthetically, except when accompanied by a male, the pregnant women was helped most, suggesting a relatively strong activation of the C system which may, however, not influence helping in the presence of another potential protector.)

Perhaps a hunchback would be equally as threatening as a facial scar. Soble and Strickland (1974) asked a female interviewer, with or without a hunchback, to persuade people to let themselves be interviewed in the future either by herself or by another female. The researchers found a higher rate of compliance with the non-deviant female, irrespective of whether the interview would be conducted by the female herself or someone else. However, in the hunchback condition, people more often choose to be interviewed by another female than by the hunchbacked female.

Perhaps somewhat less offputting than a facial scar or a hunchback is an eye-patch. In a study by Doob and Ecker (1970), housewives were asked either to fill out a questionnaire and return it through the mail or to submit to an interview. The person making the request either wore an eye-patch or not. In the questionnaire condition, the eye-patch made participants comply much more, almost 70 percent versus 40 percent. This more positive behavior disappeared, however, when expecting a face-to-face interview, where the eye-patch made no difference. Likely, when the request involved more intense and perhaps fearful social interaction, the expected discomfort increased, and neutralized the positive effect of tendencies to help the deviant individual. In another field study by Ungar (1979), subway riders were given an opportunity to correct misinformation provided by a confederate to a second confederate, the victim, who again wore either an eye-patch or not. In the low effort condition, the victim stood almost directly beside the participant, whereas in the high effort condition the participant was compelled to pursue the victim who was walking away. It was found that in the low effort condition the deviant person received somewhat more help, whereas in the high effort condition clearly less help was given to this person. Note that "high effort" may be interpreted as actively approaching a mildly intimidating deviant individual, while "low effort" implies little opportunity to avoid contact and readiness to emit a care-based helping response.

One study in particular nicely illustrates how people actively make use of situational opportunities to avoid stressful unfocused encounters with a disabled person. Snyder, Kleck, Strenta, and Mentzer (1979) had participants choose between sitting with a handicapped or a non-handicapped person while watching a movie, or choose between two movies, one of which entailed sitting next to a handicapped person, the other of which entailed sitting next to a non-handicapped person. Snyder *et al.* found greater avoidance of the handicapped person when the choice between individuals was also a choice between movies. Apparently, in the movie-choice condition, participants could conceal their desire to avoid the handicapped person by choosing a particular movie. (Parenthetically, in the movie-choice condition during debriefing no one said that the movie choice was based on avoiding the handicapped person. This might have been a result of impression management, but it is also possible that for a number of participants, excuses for avoidance of deviant individuals can be found relatively automatically and may be sincerely believed in.)

Sometimes, people help although they appear to want to do something else such as avoiding the victim. A field study by Slochower *et al.* (1980) illustrates how care may be simultaneously activated with escape tendencies. These researchers observed that passers-by more often donated money to a female collector in a wheelchair than to a non-disabled collector. Interestingly, in the disabled condition almost all participants, whether they donated or not, showed avoidance tendencies and signs of discomfort, such as walking by with head held stiffly away from the collector or patting their hair, reactions that were absent in the non-deviant condition. This study emphasizes that two different responses may occur in parallel and that it is not necessarily the case that a controlled response "corrects" or wipes out a spontaneously produced and motivated response.

Let us now turn to evidence for physical distancing and avoidance of individuals with deviant conditions with active aspects. For example, in a study by Kleck and colleagues (Kleck *et al.*, 1968), participants chose a larger interaction distance to a person assumed to be an epileptic than to a non-deviant person. A similar pattern was demonstrated by Barrios, Corbitt, Estes, and Topping (1976) for persons assumed to be bisexual and by Mooney, Cohn, and Swift (1992) and Bos, Dijker, and Koomen (2007) for persons with AIDS. Heinemann *et al.* (1981) found that participants chose greater personal distances when their interaction partner was assumed to be homosexual or handicapped than a non-deviant. Rumsey, Bull, and Gahagan (1982) measured how far strangers in a street setting would stand from two types of facially disfigured persons as compared to a non-deviant person. Pedestrians arriving first in each trial and waiting for a traffic light stood further away from the facially disfigured persons than from the non-deviant person. In particular, they especially stood further away when the other person had a more permanent birthmark rather than more temporary bruising and scarring. Apparently, a more permanent mark is a more essential characteristic and therefore more threatening. Finally, a study by Sigelman and colleagues (Sigelman, Adams, Meeks, & Purcell, 1986) showed that, although children were quite willing to approach a disabled person, their parents tended to stand closer to their children (apparently to protect them) than in the case of a non-disabled person.

## Situational influences on triggering and "displacing" fearful responses

Just as in the case of aggression and helping, fearful behavior may also be motivated by irrelevant situational sources of motivation that specifically activate the flight or fear component of the FF system. Usually this activation pertains to threats from events that can happen in the future and that are difficult to control. While increased anger results in aggression displacement on deviant targets that can be safely attacked, increased fear will not result in attack but escape and the perception of danger, unless no escape and only defensive aggression is possible. However, the cognitive effects of anger and fear induction may be similar in that both may be associated with expectancies and perceptions of hostility in others. For example, in different experiments, Maner and colleagues (Maner *et al.*, 2005) either exposed participants to a fear-arousing, romantic, or neutral film clip and subsequently asked them to judge the emotions expressed in different faces of European-Americans, African-Americans, or Arab people. It appeared that male participants who were previously exposed to the fear-arousing film clip (as opposed to the neutral film) were more likely to perceive anger (but not other emotions) in black and Arab than white male faces.

Also consistent with the above prediction is a study reported by Schaller, Park, and Mueller (2003) in which Canadian students rated "people from Iraq" as more dangerous (but not more negative in terms of danger-irrelevant traits) when doing the rating in near-total darkness than under normal illumination. According to the researchers, exposure to darkness made participants feel particularly vulnerable to danger cues in general. Interestingly, Schaller *et al.* also report a study in which this effect was especially strong for participants with a strong belief in a dangerous world. Similar results have been reported by Dijker, Koomen, *et al.* (1996) in their content analysis of reasons mentioned for experiencing fear in everyday encounters with members of different minority groups. It appeared that especially in the case of the then most threatening group, black people from the former Dutch colony of Surinam, people frequently mentioned experiencing fear and threat when encountering them at night or in dark alleys.

Two more specific mechanisms may be involved in mediating the relationship between fear aroused by irrelevant situational factors and negative responding to deviance or fear displacement. First, fear may selectively direct attention to those aspects of the environment that are likely to imply danger, resulting in a tendency to make false alarms or *hypervigilance* (Eysenck, 1992). Second, and partially as a consequence, high levels of fear and worrying about potential dangers, may impair the processing of information about fear-irrelevant or neutral information about the environment. Yet, shallow information processing may, in turn, increase the use of simple and general expectancies or heuristics which, in the case of deviant individuals, may often refer to threatening properties. The general effects of threat or fear arousal on the use of expectancies or stereotypes was, for example, demonstrated in a study by Schimel and colleagues (Schimel *et al.*, 1999). These researchers observed that letting American students first think about a fear-arousing event, their own mortality, increased the attribution of stereotypical traits (both negative and positive) to Germans. Also supporting the more general impairment of information processing of threatened people, Wilder and Shapiro (1989), showed that research participants who anticipated socially embarrassing or physically painful experiences, were less likely to recall specific negative or positive information about a deviating member of a jury.

## 4.4 Not knowing what to do during unfocused interactions between non-deviant and deviant individuals

Unlike most of the above discussed interaction situations, in which people pay close attention to deviance and can act according to their needs, many public settings lack a clear structure and merely require strangers to be in each other's presence while paying minimal attention to each other. Sometimes, these strangers may also engage in brief and rather superficial conversations with each other. In this section, we argue that these kinds of situations are especially likely to cause a dissociation between the automatic and controlled aspects of responding to deviant individuals. Returning to our model presented earlier in this chapter, we propose that during these unfocused encounters with deviant individuals, type of deviance automatically activates particular motivational systems together with a desire to realize the goals associated with these systems, but that the nature of the situation also motivates people to inhibit or suppress their initial response tendencies. Furthermore, as this may cause visible bodily evidence of tension and nervousness, the additional problem that has to be solved is how to control and hide these disruptive bodily signals. As a consequence of overcompensating for their leaking signs of nervousness, people may end up responding in an overly friendly manner toward deviant individuals and in a way clearly not matching their unpleasant psychological state.

While the unfocused nature of the interaction seems to be an important precondition for this dissociation between automatic and controlled aspects of responding, our model also points to several additional factors that will contribute to it. In particular, nervousness and dissociation are especially likely when type of deviance or the availability of additional information about the deviant individual activates both the FF and C system, thus causing an ambivalent motivational state. For example, people will feel more need to adopt a friendly posture toward a person with a threatening disability than one with a known criminal record. Furthermore, it may also be expected that a strongly developed C system or internalized egalitarian norms, and hence an increased likelihood to feel guilty about hurting or offending a deviant individual, will additionally motivate people to control their bodily signs of nervousness. Unfortunately, these factors have seldomly been manipulated or measured in studies on unfocused interactions between non-deviant and deviant individuals.

Let us first try to understand the particular problems that are experienced by non-deviant individuals during unfocused interactions with deviant individuals. We believe that these problems are closely dependent on the more general problem that in many public settings in modern Western society people are required to move among strangers while actively trying to be "disinterested without disregard" (Hirschauer, 2005). For example, while passing them on the sidewalk, traveling by bus or train, riding an elevator, or sitting in a waiting room, people need to look briefly at each other (or use peripheral vision), acknowledge and respect each other's presence and personal space, but prevent appearing to have a special interest in each other, thus often quickly bowing their head or looking away. According to Hirschaurer, elaborating on this phenomenon that was termed "civil inattention" by (Goffman, 1963a):

> "The gazes in close proximity gain their typical quality from a double avoidance: They should neither signal a 'recognition,' promising an openness for contact, nor should they be full of distrust and hatred"(Hirschauer, 2005, p. 41).

These behavioral adjustments in public places are so commonly expected that their violation tends to be experienced as unpleasant and impolite. For example, Zuckerman, Miserandino, and Bernieri (1983) found that after an elevator ride, passengers reported more discomfort after a confederate had either stared at them for the full ride or completely avoided looking at them than the normative condition in which passengers received a single glance. Clearly, during these unfocused encounters, people may also briefly chat with each other.

Now, for different reasons, the presence of individuals associated with deviant conditions in these kinds of situations may pose additional problems for people, and is likely to increase the self-focused attention, self-control, and tension that already tend to be experienced. In particular, specific negative emotions may be aroused, the desire to stare that needs to be suppressed may be stronger than usual, and people may feel even more uncertain how to behave. First, the particular type of deviance with which the other individual is associated may be responsible for the arousal of specific emotions such as fear, anger, or tenderness, or, in case the motivational implications are less clear, general curiosity. As studies on unfocused interactions usually do not vary type of deviance, little is known about these different emotional qualities.

Second, in light of these emotions, the desire to pay attention to the other person may be stronger than usual. That is, in the presence of deviance, people may want to know more about the important, motivationally relevant, and attention-drawing aspects of their environment in order to adapt their behavior accordingly. However, as the deviant individual may also be engaged in civil inattention and thus does not provide a special reason to treat him or her differently, people now have to put more effort in controlling their behavioral tendencies. In trying to inhibit their desire to look, they may end up saliently looking away.

Both the desire to look and its inhibition during close contact with deviant individuals are evidenced by research. For example, Langer, Fiske, Taylor, and Chanowitz (1976) found that participants looked longer at pictures of a cripple or hunchback than of a normal individual, especially when staring was unobserved by others present. Similarly, Thompson (1982) observed that in a shopping mall, people looked longer at handicapped than non-handicapped individuals. Importantly, Thompson found the opposite during closer interaction. While handicapped and non-handicapped persons were served in restaurants, waitresses made less eye contact with the former than the latter. (Parenthetically, handicapped customers also had to wait longer till they were approached by waitresses.) In relation to the pattern of attention received by handicapped persons, Murphy, Scheer, Murphy, and Mack (1988, p. 239) refer to "the paradox of nobody 'seeing' the one person in the room of whom they are most acutely, and uncomfortably, aware."

Attempts to solve the conflict between acting according to certain motives and the desire to withdraw attention from the deviant individual is likely to result in tension, nervousness, or stress. However, because this psychological state may co-occur with visible bodily and socially disruptive phenomena such as trembling, sweating, and speech errors, people are also faced with the additional problem of controlling or hiding these phenomena, the more so if these phenomena are expected to be misinterpreted as unfriendliness or prejudice (Devine *et al.*, 1996; Poskocil, 1977).

A final reason why unfocused interactions with deviant individuals may exacerbate problems already experienced as a consequence of civil inattention is that sometimes people need to intensify their involvement with these individuals and behave in ways that are incongruent with their activated motivational systems. Imagine, for example, how you would feel if you were required to chat about the importance of sports with a person with a missing leg, about the art of painting to a blind person, or about aggression and self-control to a person with a particular mental illness. (As illustrated below, researchers seem to have recognized that these embarrassing behaviors during casual contact offer ideal opportunities for demonstrating nervousness and dissociation in the psychological laboratory.) More generally, people may be uncertain about the rules that should be followed in interacting with deviant individuals and may not know how to behave.

Let us now look more closely at the psychological consequences of the above painted problems of everyday interactions with deviant individuals. Everyday contact with deviant individuals is generally described in terms of discomfort, awkwardness, interaction uneasiness, strain, tension, anxiety, or not knowing what to do (Davis, 1961; Fichten, 1986; Goffman, 1963b; Hebl & Kleck, 2000; Hebl, Tickle, & Heatherton, 2000; Jones *et al.*, 1984; Stephan & Stephan, 1985). In addition, there is experimental evidence for this psychological state. For example, Ickes (1984) observed white participants while waiting with a white or black individual, and engaging in minor casual conversations, and noted more non-verbal signs of nervousness and awkwardness in the case of the black individual. Furthermore, and consistent with the role of the C system in our model, Nail, Harton, and Decker (2003) found that liberals but not conservatives displayed greater physiological arousal (indicated by decreased skin resistance and increased heart rate) when being touched by a black as opposed to a white experimenter in order to take their pulse. In this study, participants believed that the researchers were studying peoples' physiological reactions to pictures that were displayed on a computer monitor. Similarly, Devine *et al.* (1996) showed that anticipated anxiety about meeting a homosexual person was unrelated to hostile feelings in people with positive attitudes toward homosexuals, but was positively related to hostility in those with strong negative attitudes. Hence, these authors argue for two qualitatively distinct kinds of interaction anxiety in these two groups of people: one, more self-focused and associated with concerns about responding in harmful ways, the other, more focused at the negative motivational implications of the deviant condition.

That people tend to be self-focused or self-conscious during meetings with the handicapped has also been frequently inferred (e.g., Fichten, 1986; Fichten, Amsel, Robillard, & Tagalakis, 1991). Osborne and Gilbert (1992) showed that anticipated contact with a disabled person may result in so much preoccupation with the consequences of one's behavior, that people fail to attend to situational influences on the person's behavior. Richeson and Shelton (2003) recently demonstrated that cognitive busyness during interracial encounters may exhaust people so much that it deteriorates their cognitive performance on a subsequent and unrelated task. In general, it is also known that inhibition of negative emotions in general may have negative cognitive consequences such as an increase in bodily arousal and poorer memory (Gross, 1997; Richards & Gross, 2000). A final negative cognitive consequence of self-regulation and suppression of negative thoughts or behavioral impulses may be that these negative responses return with more insistence once participants stop actively controlling them. This phenomenon is aptly called a "postsuppression rebound effect" (Macrae, Bodenhausen, Milne, & Jetten, 1994). Under certain conditions, however, stereotype rebound is less likely. As suggested by Monteith, Sherman, and Devine (1998), rebound effects may occur less when there are social norms or personal prescriptions prohibiting the use of stereotypes.

Several studies allow us to draw a more complete picture of the psychological consequences of casual contact with deviant individuals, revealing both stresslike aspects and attempts to control them, hence suggesting dissociation between the automatic and controlled aspects of responding. For example, Kleck, Ono, and Hastorf (1966, Experiment 2) showed that during initial exposure to their interaction partner, non-handicapped participants showed lower skin resistance or greater stress when their partner was approaching in a wheelchair (apparently due to an amputated leg) than when normally walking. Additionally, while participants exchanged potentially embarrassing information with their partner, they took relatively longer to select their questions (apparently to avoid sensitive questions), showed less variability while answering these questions, and terminated the interview sooner in the case of the handicap. Moreover, suggesting dissociation, compared to their answers given to the opinion questions on a different occasion (and apparently reflecting their true opinions), participants interacting with the disabled person expressed relatively less favorable opinions about sports and physical appearance, and more favorable attitudes toward academic achievement. (For similar results, and additionally demonstrating greater motoric inhibition in the case of a handicapped interaction partner, see Kleck (1968).)

A similar research strategy was followed by Heinemann *et al.* (1981), who let participants interview a physically disabled, homosexual (apparently a member of a gay liberation movement), or non-deviant confederate, asking him such questions as "Do you sometimes buy an erotic magazine?," "Do you have a girlfriend?" (a provocative question in the case of the militant homosexual), "What is your greatest problem in life?," and "Do you believe that good looks are important for a man?" While the embarrassing questions were asked, both the handicapped and the homosexual target aroused lower skin-resistance or stronger stress responses and more non-verbal signs of discomfort than the non-deviant target. Although a meeting with an active and passive deviant thus produced equally high levels of stress, participants explicitly reported more positive reactions to the two deviant targets.

Additional evidence for dissociation during unfocused interaction is provided by two other studies. Weitz (1972) found that the less friendly or positive the voice tone of white participants toward blacks and other behavioral responses such as closeness of selected tasks, the more favorable the verbally expressed attitudes of these participants toward blacks were. Similarly, Dovidio *et al.* (2002) found that an explicit verbal attitude measure was uncorrelated with white participants' non-verbal nervousness and unfriendliness during an unstructured conversation with a black person, but was correlated with their (presumably more controlled) verbal behaviors. Finally, consider a series of experiments conducted by Blascovich, Mendes, Hunter, Lickel, and Kowai-Bell (2001), who exposed their research participants to a confederate with or without a large facial birthmark, a low (disadvantaged) or high socioeconomic status, or with white or black skin color, and, after a short conversation, asked them to prepare a speech about working together; a speech that would later be reviewed by their partner. Noteworthy, in this speech, participants had to address the issue of how well they thought their partner would work with people and how well they thought the two of them would work together; clearly, a task that may create considerable tension if one assumes that participants would rather like to avoid these kinds of unstructured or unpredictable interactions. The researchers found that especially during confrontation with the three deviant individuals, cardiovascular activity typical for threat or stress was observed (e.g., increased blood pressure). Interestingly, the greatest physiological stress responses were observed when participants were confronted with a black person with low socioeconomic status. In contrast to this pattern of bodily responses, participants reported more positive reactions to their deviant than non-deviant partner, which the authors' interpret in terms of impression management and self-presentation motives (see also Guglielmi, 1999). Worth noting, in one of their studies, Blascovich *et al.* (2001) could also demonstrate that confederates with a birthmark (of which they were unaware) rated participants' behavior toward them more positively than confederates without a birthmark.

An important consequence of the behavioral manifestations of interaction anxiety such as looking away or lack of spontaneity is that the deviant individual may notice them and interprets them as impoliteness or unfriendliness whereas the non-deviant individual remains primarily focused on attempts at self-control. For example, in the study by Dovidio *et al.* (2002) discussed above, while the black confederates' ratings of friendliness were based on non-verbal signs of unfriendliness, participants' perceptions of their own friendliness were primarily related to their controlled verbal behavior. Clearly, such a discrepancy in judgments may contribute to strains during everyday interaction between deviant and non-deviant persons; a point extensively discussed by Davis (1961) and Goffman (1963b) who spoke of an infinite regress of mutual considerations and a growing mutual uneasiness (see also our earlier discussion of the impoliteness that may be generally associated with entirely avoiding eye contact in public places). The negative interpersonal consequences of suppression of negative feelings are also known from studies on emotion. For example, Butler *et al.* (2003) found that anger suppression during conversation resulted in increased stress responses in both the suppressor and her partner, and decreased interpersonal liking.

Only a few studies seem to support the idea that interaction anxiety may be crucially linked to the unfocused nature of the interaction and will be reduced when people are encouraged to direct attention again outwardly in the course of realizing specific interaction goals. For example, Langer *et al.* (1976) found that after allowing them to stare unobtrusively at a handicapped person, participants chose to sit closer to the person and apparently felt more at ease. Richeson and colleagues demonstrated that participants provided with an interaction script or with a positive rather than suppressive and self-focused attitude, did not show poorer cognitive performance on a subsequent task, suggesting that they had been struggling less with self-regulation (Richeson & Trawalter, 2005; Trawalter & Richeson, in press). Furthermore, Fichten *et al.* (1991) showed that people report less self and other-directed negative thoughts and interactional tensions in situations in which they could offer disabled persons some assistance than in unstructured everyday encounters with them. Similarly, Belgrave, and Mills (1981) found that when disabled persons actually ask for assistance in relation to their disability, people feel more relaxed and more willing to interact. A related observation was made by Goffman (1963b, p. 144) when he noted how disabled persons may employ dependency in everyday interaction by citing a cripple as stating: "Innumerable times I have seen the fear and bewilderment in people's eyes vanish as I have stretched out my hand for help, and I have felt life and warmth stream from the helping hands I have taken." Motivation to reduce interaction anxiety may also partially explain people's desire to interact with relatively submissive deviant individuals (see Chapter 3).

Given the different problems and unpleasant psychological consequences associated with unfocused interactions with deviant individuals during which people need to give evidence for tolerance, it should come as no surprise that people will try to avoid these encounters whenever possible (e.g., Plant & Devine, 2003). Finally, we should not forget that avoidance of these kinds of situations is, of course, also motivated by the particular nature of the deviant condition. Thus people may also be worried about the specific implications of particular deviant conditions such as the threatening aspects of mental illness or physical disability or simply the expectation that interacting with the deviant individual will demand relatively more time and energy.

To summarize, unfocused encounters with deviant individuals may cause considerable stress or anxiety in non-deviant people due to, for example, the threatening nature of the deviant condition, not knowing what to do, and fear of not being entirely successful in hiding these negative feelings. These feelings and attempts to control their expression are often visible in behavioral and bodily signs such as increased heart rate and motoric inhibition. Typically, these bodily and experiential stress symptoms may be dissociated from explicit attempts to normalize the interaction and to appear friendly or at least neutral. While tolerance for deviance and civil inattention in modern Western societies on which the former seems to be based are functional and desirable for deviant individuals in certain situations, its side-effects may turn out to be undesirable when people want more than tolerance and thus need to engage in repair processes during which deviance is explicitly addressed by the different parties involved (see Chapter 9).[12]

## 4.5 The relation between automatic and controlled responses in the absence of interpersonal contact

While the previous section concentrated on the relation between automatic and controlled responses during unfocused and strained interactions with deviant individuals, this section discusses what is known about this relationship in the absence of interpersonal contact, while research participants are merely required to react to signs of deviance.[13] Instead of focusing on the relatively uncontrollable bodily signs of nervousness that can be observed during unfocused interactions, the automatic aspects of responding in the latter studies are often measured in terms of response times, while research participants are seated behind computer monitors. We first describe these "implicit" measures of automatic processes and illustrate how different implicit measures are related. We then address the relationships between these measures and more "explicit" measures in terms of verbal self-reports or other controlled behaviors, and ask how our model may contribute to understanding that relationship.

*How are automatic reactions to deviance measured in the psychological laboratory?*

A fundamental property of implicit measures used in the psychological laboratory is that they tend to capture reflex-like reactions to deviance much like an eyeblink startle response. That is, these responses are usually taken relatively immediately after motivational systems and/or their associated expectancies are activated by exposure to deviance, and before the resulting neural and mental state can be integrated with more complex information about the deviant individual and the situation, and be translated into adaptive actions. This has two important implications. First, to the extent that different automatic measures capture the reflex-like aspects of similar motivational systems or expectancies, they should be positively correlated. Second, the relationship between these measures and more controlled or "explicit" behavior should be more varied. For example, while the firing of an isolated group of neurons somewhere in the brain or response latencies of about 100 milliseconds may show little relationship with a complex goal-directed action such as expressing an opinion about the social treatment or protection of deviant individuals, such a neuronal pattern (especially when observed in the amygdala; see below) may predict controlled aggressive behavior when aggression is the only response option available to people. Let us have a closer look at two of the most widely used "implicit" measures of automatic processes.

Priming is a method often used to study how particular responses are facilitated and psychologically determined by previous events or primes, without participants being aware that these processes are being studied. In many such studies, primes are presented outside awareness or subliminally (e.g., flashed very briefly on a computer monitor). It may be expected that, to the extent that deviant conditions are strongly associated with particular motivational systems and their associated expectancies, using these conditions as primes may also facilitate responses that are representative of these systems or expectancies. For example, if participants are primed with pictures of active deviance or threatening conditions, they should respond faster with negative evaluations or characteristic descriptions (e.g., *threatening*) than when primed with pictures of non-deviant or "normal" conditions. On the other hand, priming with deviant conditions should interfere with making positive or uncharacteristic semantic responses, resulting in slower responses. For example, Fazio *et al.* (1995) asked white participants to judge how good or bad adjectives such as *pleasant* and *awful* appeared to them, either after priming them with white or black faces. They found that, compared to the pattern observed for white faces, previous priming with black faces facilitated responding to negative adjectives and interfered with responding to positive adjectives. In another study, Bessenoff and Sherman (2000) primed participants with pictures of fat and thin women and of neutral objects, and found that they could more quickly determine if negative words were indeed words (vs. non-words) when preceded by pictures of fat women.

A second but similar technique that has been widely employed to measure implicit responses to deviance is the Implicit Association Test or IAT (Greenwald, McGhee, & Schwartz, 1998). Here, pictures of deviant and non-deviant conditions or labels referring to them are not used as primes but are repeatedly presented together with negative or positive attributes. What is measured is how fast participants are in associating these conditions with negative or positive words. Bias against deviance is indicated when participants are relatively slower to associate positively valenced words with deviant than non-deviant conditions; and relatively faster in associating negatively valenced words with deviant than non-deviant conditions. Since response latencies typically are very short, it is assumed that a bias in terms of these latencies is difficult to control by participants (for a general discussion of differences between priming techniques and the IAT, see Fazio & Olson, 2003). Priming techniques, the IAT, and similar implicit measurement techniques have revealed negative biases toward individuals associated with a variety of deviant conditions, such as ethnicity or race, homosexuality, old age, and obesity (for reviews, see Blair, 2001; Dasgupta, 2004; Dovidio, Kawakami, & Beach, 2001; Fazio & Olson, 2003; Hofmann, Gawronski, Gschwendner, Le, & Schmitt, 2005).

Implicit bias has also been compellingly demonstrated using responses that are even more reflex-like and less controllable such as brain activity revealed by brain scanning techniques. For example, passive exposure to the faces of black individuals (Phelps *et al.*, 2000) or the faces of unattractive, transsexual, or pierced individuals (Krendl, Macrae, Kelley, Fugelsang, & Heatherton, 2006) tends to increase neural activity in the brain's threat or fear center located in the amygdala, compared to exposure to white or non-deviant targets. Furthermore, Pryor *et al.* (2004) found that participants' relatively reflex-like, mouse-controlled movements of the computer cursor toward or away from pictures of individuals were affected by the particular deviant condition with which the displayed individuals were associated. That is, participants showed the strongest avoidant reactions toward individuals associated with threatening deviant conditions such as crime, child abuse, or drug addiction, and stronger approach toward more passive conditions such as AIDS due to blood transfusion, blindness, or paralysis. Finally, Vanman, Paul, Ito, and Miller (1997) measured movements in the *corrugator supercilii* or brow muscle (a frowning gesture that is generally associated with anger) and activity in the *zygomaticus major* cheek muscle (a smiling gesture associated with positive feelings) when white participants had to imagine engaging in different types of cooperation with a partner who was incompetent to perform the joint task. Participants showed relatively more frowning and less smiling in the case of a black than a white partner in response to these kinds of annoying situations.

As suggested above, to the extent that different implicit measures capture reflex-like reactions relatively immediately upon activation of the same motivational systems or expectancies, they should be closely associated with each other. This seems to be supported by different studies. For example, individuals who respond relatively fast to negative words such as *aggressive* when exposed to faces of black persons, also tend to show increased neural activity in the brain's threat or fear center (Phelps *et al.*, 2000), and are relatively easily startled when a puff of air is blown in their eyes (Amodio *et al.*, 2003). Furthermore, Neumann, Hülsenbeck, and Seibt (2004) demonstrated that implicit responses to persons with AIDS correlated with rather elementary and automatic approach and avoidance behaviors. Specifically, in their experiment, participants were not only required to respond on an implicit measure to photos of individuals apparently associated with AIDS, but also to respond to these pictures by moving a computer mouse along a rail towards (approach) or away from themselves (avoidance). The results indicated that the more strongly participants associated persons with AIDS with negative evaluations (relative to associating healthy persons with positive evaluations) on an IAT, the faster they were at moving the mouse away from their body.

Implicit measures obtained behind a computer monitor have also been shown to predict awkwardness, nervousness, or strain observed during unfocused interactions discussed earlier. For example, McConnell and Leibold (2001) first asked white participants to complete an explicit and implicit (IAT) measure of responses to blacks (these measures were taken by a white experimenter) and then let a black experimenter interview them about their experiences during that stage of the study; clearly a potentially awkward situation. Behavioral measures taken while answering the interviewer's questions indicated that implicit but not explicit measures of racial bias predicted non-verbal signs of nervousness such as more speech errors and hesitations, and less smiling. In another relevant study, discussed earlier, Dovidio *et al.* (2002) similarly found that a previously taken implicit but not explicit measure of racial bias predicted non-verbal unfriendliness while white participants were required to have an unstructured conversation with a white or black confederate (see also Fazio *et al.*, 1995). Remember, however, that stress during unfocused contact may not only be caused by perceiving certain motivationally relevant aspects of a deviant condition or prejudice, but may also be a consequence of self-control or behavioral inhibition.

Our model predicts that, given relevant response options, implicit measures should also correlate with elementary or "subtle" motivated and goal-directed behaviors triggered by deviance-related motivational systems. Consistent with this view, Bessenoff and Sherman (2000) found that participants with stronger negative implicit evaluations of obese women chose to sit further away from a particular obese woman (see our earlier discussion of the relative contribution of automatic and controlled elements in distancing behavior). We similarly speculate that other behavioral responses such as direct as well as indirect aggression discussed earlier in this chapter will also be related to implicit indicators of activation of the FF system, as long as people are allowed to do what they want to do.

We finally note that, while implicit measures specifically predict certain automatic behaviors that seem to be related to interaction strain or activity of the FF system, explicit or self-reports measures have been shown to be good predictors of controlled behavior. For example, Dovidio, Kawakami, Johnson, Johnson, and Howard (1997) found in one study that explicit attitudes toward blacks were correlated with ratings of guilt of a black defendant (the latter were not related to implicit measures; see also Fazio *et al.*, 1995) and in another that they predicted relative evaluations of black and white interviewers.

*Why and when are automatic and controlled responses in the psychological laboratory more or less dissociated?*

A common thread running through most studies employing implicit measures of biased responding to deviant individuals, is the notion that these implicit and presumably reflex-like biases are difficult to demonstrate at the level of explicit evaluations, verbal judgments, or attitude measures. For example, Vanman *et al.* (1997) found that the black target person was generally more positively evaluated than the white target, despite the former's stronger anger arousal. In many other studies discussed in the previous section it was similarly found that implicit biases were not paralleled on explicit measures. In addition, generally low correlations (usually between 0.20 and 0.35) between implicit and explicit measures are reported (Blair, 2001; Dovidio *et al.*, 2001; Fazio & Olson, 2003; Hofmann, Gawronski *et al.*, 2005).[14]

In studying the relationships between implicit and explicit measures, two different perspectives may be adopted. First, one may ask to what extent representations about deviant conditions can be accurately measured by implicit and explicit measures. The answer to this question partly depends on the assumptions one makes about the nature and content of these representations. In terms of our motivational approach, internal representations represent properties of the world in general, and of deviant individuals in particular, by means of expectancies that are associated with motivational systems. In principle, using the right measurements, important aspects of the content and meaning of these expectancies may equally well be captured by implicit and explicit measures. Suppose, for example, that one would like to measure the content of people's representations of poor people. Because the representation of poor people is likely to contain both attributes related to activation of the FF system (e.g., poverty, having no money to buy food) and attributes related to the C system (e.g., being helped by rich people), the implicit and explicit measures should invite responses to both kinds of attributes. Clearly, if the implicit measure primarily asks participants to respond to the negative attributes of poverty and the explicit measure focuses on tender and protective feelings aroused by poor people, both measures insufficiently tap into the underlying representation. Moreover, these measures would presumably also be little correlated with each other (cf. Nosek, 2005). On the basis of the extensive content analysis presented in Chapter 3, we believe it is plausible to assume that many deviant conditions are complexly represented by expectancies that are associated with activation of both the FF and C system. Clearly, this complexity or ambivalence can only come to the fore when we present research participants with stimuli that can activate both motivational systems. That, in principle, it should be possible to examine these representations in terms of implicit measures is suggested in a study by Moskowitz, Salomon, and Taylor (2000) who found that participants with relatively strong egalitarian values responded relatively fast with egalitarian-relevant words to black faces and did not show implicit bias to black and white faces. Sometimes, the context in which implicit responses to deviant individuals are measured may additionally facilitate automatic activation of the C system. For example, Barden, Maddux, Petty, and Brewer (2004) found that when white participants responded to black or white faces presented against the background of a church interior, the black and white targets were judged equally positively on an implicit, reaction time measure. The researchers interpret this as being consistent with the idea that exposure to a "churchgoer role" activated egalitarian norms or considerations, a proposal that is consistent with our view of the role of the C system.

A second and theoretically more interesting approach to the relationship between implicit and explicit measures taken in the psychological laboratory is to ask what this relationship tells us about the active and motivated regulation of the automatic aspects of responding to deviance. As proposed by our extended dual-process model of responding to deviance, the C system and its associated protective tendencies should play an important role in this regulation, either immediately upon first exposure to the deviant condition, or at later stages when people are provided with opportunities to express protective tendencies. We have the impression that in many studies, implicit measures of responses to deviance primarily assess FF-related activity and expectancies, while explicit or self-report measures allow participants to reflect on care-arousing aspects of the deviant individual or on normative considerations, and to compensate for their automatic negative reactions, perhaps motivated by guilt. (As implied by our earlier discussion of the methodological problems involved in correlating implicit and explicit measures, however, we are unsure to what extent this phenomenon may also be due to the inaccurate implicit assessment of representations of deviance.) This involvement of the C system or egalitarian or protective norms, and hence dissociation between the automatic and controlled aspects of responding, will be especially likely when the deviant condition has passive aspects or people have a strongly developed and easily triggered C system. In contrast, we expect that for strongly active deviant conditions or people with a strongly developed FF system, automatic (negative) and controlled responses will be positively related. Take the following illustrations.

Franco and Maas (1999) first established that among their Italian participants, it was relatively unacceptable to express hostile responses to such groups as Jews and the handicapped but quite acceptable to express such responses to, for example, Islamic fundamentalists or Mafiosi. In a subsequent study, they observed that for Islamic fundamentalists, their three explicit measures (two assessing allocation of funding to the deviant and non-deviant group, one measuring liking) were positively correlated with their implicit measure. In contrast, for the strongly normatively protected Jews, two of their three explicit measures were negatively related to the implicit measure. Similarly, Dambrun and Guimond (2004) first showed that the deviant condition of concern – Arab minorities in France – was strongly normatively protected, and then assessed both implicit and explicit reactions to this and a non-deviant condition with only the explicit measure containing issues relevant to the protection of minorities. They found a negative correlation between the explicit and implicit measures. Although Franco and Maas (1999) and Dambrun and Guimond (2004) interpret the negative correlations exclusively in terms of self-presentational strategies to appear unprejudiced, we have reason to believe that true care and protection activated by deviant conditions that are saliently associated with passive deviance (e.g., particular ethnic minorities) may also be involved.

Fazio *et al.* (1995) probably were the first to more directly demonstrate that a dissociation between implicit and explicit responses to black target persons primarily occurs when white people are motivated to suppress negative responses. For those with little motivation to suppress, explicit responses could be well predicted from implicit ones.

That dissociation between automatic and controlled aspects of responding is especially likely when exposure to deviance labels first activates the FF system and only after some reflection on the potential passive aspects of deviance (i.e., disadvantaged status, suffering), the C system, is more directly suggested in a study by Pryor and colleagues (2004), discussed earlier. These researchers found that initial and relatively automatic movements with a cursor on a computer screen away or toward pictures of labeled deviant individuals were primarily predicted by negative attitudes or prejudice, whereas later movements were relatively more influenced by a motivation to suppress these responses for internal reasons.

Finally, consider evidence suggesting that the regulating influence of the C system may also be associated with certain individual differences in responding to deviance. For example, to the extent that liberals have an especially well developed or easily triggered C system (see the next chapter), we should expect a strong tendency to dissociate implicit and explicit responses. This is strongly suggested by a recent study of Nosek, Banaji, and Greenwald (2002) who found a differential linear influence of conservatism-liberalism (measured in terms of five categories, from strongly conservative to strongly liberal) on an implicit and explicit bias measure. In particular, while liberalism only weakly influenced responses on the IAT (the effect size linearly decreased from 0.85 for strong conservatives to 0.60 for strong liberals; we estimate these values from the authors' Figure 2), it influenced much more strongly explicit bias (the effect size linearly decreased from 0.75 for strong conservatives to 0.15 for strong liberals). Alternatively expressed, dissociation seems to increase linearly with increasing liberalism. In Chapter 5, we present more direct evidence suggesting that liberal or egalitarian people tend to suppress negative responses to deviance for "internal reasons" that are motivated by a strong C system and associated guilty feelings.

Let us finally turn to the role that our model assigns to epistemic and instrumental motives in dissociating automatic and controlled aspects of responding to deviance; a role that has been primarily studied in the context of forming impressions of other individuals. For example, it has been shown that the influence of expectancies or stereotypes on impressions can be reduced, and the influence of non-deviant attributes increased, when people are held accountable for their judgments or are generally motivated to form more detailed or balanced impressions (Fiske & Neuberg, 1990). Furthermore, certain instrumental reasons may motivate people to be especially interested in the non-deviant attributes of individuals associated with deviance, especially when they expect that cooperation with these individuals will be rewarding

(Erber & Fiske, 1984). It should be noted that individuation may not imply exclusive attention to non-deviant features and complete denial of the presence of deviance; something which is, however, suggested by models describing situational influences on stereotyping (cf. Fiske & Neuberg, 1990). Increased attention and processing may as well involve the formation of a more complete image of the target in which *both* deviant and non-deviant features are integrated. For example, one may learn to see a mentally ill person as one with certain problems that need to be realistically dealt with in interpersonal interaction, and as one with certain competencies. It seems likely, however, that brief periods of anticipating contact with the deviant individual are insufficient to allow the formation of these more complex representations.[15]

We also argued with other dual-process models (Fazio, 1990; Fiske & Neuberg, 1990), that people should have the opportunity to let different motives influence their automatic responses. The importance of these opportunity factors is suggested, for example, by studies showing that if people have little opportunity to process individual attributes of a deviant person (e.g., because those attributes are not presented or one has little time to process them), responses tend to be determined by the emotional implications of the deviant condition, whereas adding attributes that contradict the initial expectancy and allowing more time to process them, increases attention to non-deviant features and the positive tone of judgments (Dijker & Koomen, 1996), especially when held accountable for one's judgments (Kruglanski & Freund, 1983). Such a process also agrees with the finding that implicit and explicit measures are more associated when people spontaneously generate explicit verbal self-reports about others (Hofmann, Gawronski *et al.*, 2005). Alternatively, more deliberate self-reports will increase dissociation between implicit measures and these responses.

### 4.6 Summary

In this chapter, we primarily examined how peoples' thoughts and emotions about deviance express themselves in behavior while actually meeting or interacting with deviant individuals. We first noted that addressing this issue calls for a dual-process view according to which people regulate or control certain automatic aspects of responding to deviance. We criticized the tendency of current dual-process models of stigmatization and prejudice to equate negative responses with automaticity and the absence of control, and positive responses with self-control and lack of spontaneity, mostly in the service of self-presentation and conformity to egalitarian norms. We extended these models by specifying factors (e.g., type of deviance, individual differences) responsible for the triggering of clear and moderate motivational states which, given sufficient response options, would result in relatively unified responses to deviance; and by assigning a greater role of the C system in moderating negative responses to deviance.

In the chapter's largest section, it was shown that in many situations that offer people opportunities to realize the goals of the motivational systems activated by deviance, people take these opportunities and spontaneously, yet not without intelligent adaptation to the situation, act in ways that are congruent with these systems. That is, whenever possible, people tend to aggress against or avoid individuals associated with active deviance (and who primarily activate the FF system), but assist and nurture those associated with passive deviance (and who primarily activate the C system). Suggesting the reciprocal relation between the FF and C system, people also seem to inhibit aggressive responses to individuals with passive deviance, and refrain from helping individuals with active deviance when encountered in a needy condition. In addition to an influence of type of deviance on these behaviors, we examined the influence of the deviant individual's behavior, the interaction situation, and individual differences in responding to deviance.

It was also argued that an important motive for controlling emotions and expectancies associated with activation of the FF system arises from activation of the C system and its association with guilt about harming those one wants to care for. It was proposed that guilt-related motives may both be activated by deviant conditions containing elements of passive deviance, and by egalitarian norms. We suggested that these motives and norms may be responsible in particular for people's attempt to regulate and suppress automatic negative responses to deviance, when they engage in unfocused everyday interactions with deviant individuals which offer few opportunities to realize the goals of the activated motivational systems. We illustrated this with research demonstrating people's anxiety, nervousness, self-awareness, and struggle with their bodily reactions in these kinds of situations.

In the last section of this chapter, we discussed recent advances in measuring automatic or reflex-like aspects of responding to deviance, and their frequent dissociation from controlled responses. Although in these studies, participants usually do not interact with deviant individuals but merely respond to implicit (e.g., in terms of reaction times) and explicit (e.g., self-report) measures, we showed how the results of these studies can be well interpreted in terms of the regulating influence of the C system on the FF system. In particular, implicit measures often primarily registrate activity of the FF system while explicit measures allow people to respond to stimuli activating the C system and to express protective tendencies with which they may compensate harm inflicted on deviant individuals.

In this chapter, we also pointed out how little is known about the social consequences of the control and suppression of negative responses to deviant individuals. We expressed doubt about the validity and practical usefulness of the common assumption that self-control and suppression in the service of tolerance is always desirable for the deviant individual and society and pointed out that a long-term perspective on different types of social control makes it possible to evaluate the social consequences of self-control.

## CHAPTER 5

# Individual differences in responding to deviance

## 5.1 Introduction

As noted in Chapter 1, the social psychological literature uses the term "prejudice" to refer to an individual's tendency or disposition to respond negatively to deviant individuals or groups. Following the relevant literature, we will use this term, in addition to terms such as negative responses or responding to deviance, quite frequently in this chapter. Now suppose one is asked to predict the degree of prejudice of an arbitrary inhabitant of our earth. A likely answer is to say that "it depends" and that more information about that person will make for a better prediction. We agree and will attempt to present in this chapter some of that information. We will discuss effects of individual differences and demographic characteristics on prejudice and responses to deviance. Most readers will know some people with rather strong negative responses to many deviant individuals or groups and who may even dislike all kinds of people with deviant conditions. We will attempt to demonstrate that such negative response tendencies can be seen as resulting from the operation of two important motivational systems, namely the FF and C system, which were introduced in Chapters 2 and 3, and which are supposed to underlie different types of social control, such as stigmatization and repair.

The most convincing way of demonstrating relationships between the FF and C system, on the one hand, and negative response tendencies to deviance, on the other hand, would be to have direct measurements of the strength of those systems and relate these to responses to deviance. In these measurements, the habitual experiences of the emotions of anger and fear should be targeted for the FF system, and the emotions of pity and tenderness for the C system. This would give a good indication of the activation threshold of these systems. This approach, however, has not often been followed; some illustrations can be found in Chapter 3. Another approach to understanding individual differences in negative response tendencies is to view these differences as expressions of different underlying value systems. These

163

values or motivational goals, for example security or benevolence, can be rather general and abstract, but they can also be more specific and concrete. We call the latter type *ideological orientations*, which can be seen as more specific expressions of values or goals that are translated to social reality. For example, the value or goal of benevolence could express itself in politically liberal, humanitarian views. This approach, we will argue, brings us in a more indirect way to the role of the FF and C system in prejudiced responses. We will particularly focus on relevant ideological orientations, because they have probably received the most attention in the existing literature and enable us to present a quite systematic picture of individual differences in prejudice. For several reasons, we will also address the role of the much less researched more abstract and general values and goals in prejudice or responses to deviance. One of these reasons is that they can elucidate the nature and role of ideological orientations. Moreover, they can be used to relate the FF and C system to ideological orientations.

Furthermore, we will attempt to show that our FF and C system conceptualization enables us to differentially predict prejudice against persons with active and passive stigmas. As for the demographic characteristics, we will consider effects of gender and education on negative response tendencies to deviance. Explanations for these effects of differences in gender and education on prejudice may be found again in the FF and C system underlying prejudice as individual characteristics.

In the present chapter, we will discuss, more specifically, the role of individual differences in FF and C system and corresponding ideological orientations in prejudice and their differential effects on attitudes toward persons with an active and a passive deviant condition. Then we will discuss the ideological orientations of authoritarianism and social dominance orientation and the prominent role they play in explaining individual differences in negative response tendencies to deviance. Also, we will argue that the FF and C system are strongly related to respectively authoritarianism and social dominance orientation. Finally, we will discuss and interpret the effects of differences in gender and education on prejudice, particularly in terms of the FF and C system.

## 5.2 Individual differences in the FF and C system and ideological orientations in responding to deviance

As mentioned before, one approach to understanding individual differences in negative response tendencies to deviance is to view these differences as expressions of different underlying value systems or goals. This is also our perspective here and we will argue that this approach fits nicely with our conceptualization of the motivational FF and C system underlying responses to deviant behavior and conditions. One prominent theory on values is that of Schwartz (e.g., 1994). In this theory, values are seen as desirable, trans-situational goals that result from basic requirements of human existence such as biological needs, coordinated social interaction and group life. This is quite similar to our underpinning of the FF and C system, as described in Chapter 2. According to Schwartz, the structure of those values or motivational goals can be seen as organized in terms of two basic dimensions. One dimension is called Openness to change versus Conservation and contrasts stimulation and self-direction value types with security, conformity, and traditional value types. The other dimension is called Self-Transcendence versus Self-Enhancement and opposes benevolence and universalism to power and achievement.

The goals included in these two dimensions seem to be similar to goals served by the FF and C system. We contend that the motivational goals of security, conformity, and tradition characterizing the Conservation pole of the first basic dimension can also be seen as goals of the FF system, as preluded in Chapter 4. Also, the motivational goals of benevolence and universalism representing the Self-Transcendence pole of the second dimension can be seen as goals of the C system. Because we are focusing on responses to deviant behaviors and conditions, the other poles with their associated goals of the two basic dimensions seem to be less important here. However, we shall see later that according to some theorists the Self-Enhancement (power) pole of the second basic dimension may play some role in explaining individual responses to deviance. In short, important parts of Schwartz's basic dimensions correspond to goals of the FF and C system.

We assume that confrontations with deviance will activate the FF and C system and thus their goals, which are an essential part of these systems. One way to investigate whether individual differences in the strength of the motivational FF and C system and their goals can predict differences in responding to deviant behavior and conditions – the main subject of this chapter – is to relate individual differences in the strength of goals associated with those systems to such a response. As mentioned before, this research, unfortunately, has not been done more frequently. What has often been done is to investigate the relationships between individual differences in ideological orientations, i.e., the more specific expressions of goals translated into social reality, and negative response tendencies to deviance. We further assume that deviance may both activate the FF and C system goals and their corresponding ideological orientations. Because the main ideological orientations, as we will attempt to demonstrate, can be seen as closely related to the basic value dimensions proposed by Schwartz and to the FF and C system, this research is highly relevant here.

We choose as our point of departure for this research Lambert and Chasteen's (1997) conceptualization of two ideological orientations that are important determinants of prejudice or responses to deviance. The first, which they called a liberal/humanist/egalitarian dimension (for brevity here referred to as a liberal/egalitarian dimension) reflects a political liberal ideology, a commitment to the ideals of equality and a desire to assist disadvantaged or oppressed persons in society. The second, called a conservative/authoritarian dimension, reflects a conservative political ideology, a general dislike of "norm-breakers" and an affinity for persons whose behaviors epitomize traditional values. It is not difficult to see these ideological orientations as corresponding respectively to Schwartz's self-transcendence and conservation values and also as clearly related to the C and FF system. As was described in Chapters 2 and 3, confrontation with passive deviance may often activate the C system, which is likely to underlie a desire to assist disadvantaged or oppressed persons in society. Confrontation with active deviance can be seen as a social threat that will activate the FF system, which is likely to be highly related to a dislike of "norm-breakers" and a preference for traditional values. The stronger a person's motivational system is, the more easily it will be activated by relevant cues or the lower will be its activation threshold. Thus the stronger the C system with its associated goals or values and ideological orientation is, the more protective and positive responses to deviant persons will be, particularly if those persons have a passive stigma or deviant condition. And also, the stronger the FF system with its associated goals or values and ideological orientation is, the more negative responses to deviant persons will be, particularly if those persons have an active stigma or deviant condition.

Lambert and Chasteen (1997) also had an eye for this active-passive difference in deviant conditions. More specifically, and in more operational terms, they proposed that when a deviant group is seen as dependent and having a disadvantaged status, or in our terms has a passive stigma, individual differences in liberalism should be positively correlated with attitudes toward this group. Incidentally, when a (passive) deviant group is not only seen as deviant but also as conventional and exemplifying traditional values, conservatism/authoritarianism will be positively correlated with responses toward this group as well. However, when a deviant group is seen as violating norms and traditional values, or in other words has an active stigma, individual differences in conservatism/authoritarianism should be positively correlated with negative responses toward this group. In our concep-tualization, through the FF system, people will negatively respond to persons or groups with an active deviant condition, and the stronger their FF system the stronger their responses. This will result in positive relationships between the ideological orientation of authoritarianism associated with the FF system and negative responses to those persons or groups. On the other hand, when persons or groups with a passive deviant condition are involved, the C system is more likely to be activated. Thus, similarly, individual differences in liberalism/egalitar-ianism should be positively related to responses toward those persons or groups. Furthermore, authoritarianism will not, due to a lack of FF-activation, be systematically related to responses to persons or groups with a passive deviant condition. Liberalism/egalitarianism, however, may sometimes be related to responses to persons or groups with an active deviant condition, because, due to active deviants harm-ing other people, activation of the C system may occur. Pity with the victims may give extra activation of the FF system, already activated by the active deviants, and lead to increased anger against those active deviants. The stronger the C system is, the more pity and thus the more anger will be shown.

As for the controllability dimension in terms of which deviant con-ditions can be conceived, as was explained in Chapter 2, we repeat here that controllable active deviant conditions tend to activate the fight component of the FF system more. Uncontrollable active deviant con-ditions, on the other hand, tend to activate the flight component more. Thus we would predict that the relationship between authoritarianism, combining fight and flight, and negative response tendencies is not much moderated by the controllability of active deviant conditions. For passive deviant conditions, we noted earlier that controllable pas-sive deviant conditions tend to activate the fight component of the FF system more than uncontrollable passive deviant conditions. Thus, we would predict that the positive relationships between authoritar-ianism and negative response tendencies are stronger with controllable passive deviant conditions. Research on these questions is, however, sparse.

In their research, Lambert and Chasteen measured liberalism/egali-tarianism by Katz and Hass's (1988) Humanitarianism-Egalitarianism scale and responses to specific liberal issues/groups. Conservatism/authoritarianism was measured by Altemeyer's (1988) Right-Wing Authoritarianism Scale and responses to specific conservative issues/groups. Four groups with a deviant condition were included in the research, i.e., blacks, the elderly, gays, and physically handicapped per-sons. The results of that research showed that liberalism/egalitarianism,

controlling for conservatism/authoritarianism, was positively correlated with the attitude towards each of the four groups, which were
perceived by the participants as highly disadvantaged. In contrast,
conservatism/authoritarianism was differentially correlated with the
group attitudes. For blacks and gays, perceived as quite unconven-
tional, there was, controlling for liberalism/egalitarianism, a negative
relationship between conservatism/authoritarianism and attitude; the
more conservatism or authoritarianism, the less positive was the attitude towards these groups. For the elderly, perceived as rather conventional, conservatism/authoritarianism predicted a positive attitude.
However, for the physically handicapped, persons seen as more conventional than blacks and gays but less conventional than the elderly,
and thus as having a more or less average rate of perceived conventionality, there was no correlation between conservatism/authoritarianism
and attitude.

A related prediction with regard to the active-passive distinction in
deviant conditions is that when a deviant group has both passive and
active elements, people's C system will predict responses to the passive
elements, and their FF system will predict responses to the active
elements. Katz and Hass (1988) obtained supporting evidence for this
prediction with blacks as a target group having both passive and active
deviant elements. They found that the ideological orientation of the
Protestant ethic, emphasizing achievement, discipline, and related to
conservatism and thus rather similar to authoritarianism/conservatism,
was more related to anti-black attitudes, which particularly focused on
deviant, disqualifying attributes of blacks. Their Humanitarianism-
Egalitarianism variable, however, was more related to pro-black attitudes, which focused especially on the disadvantaged position of blacks.
Priming these ideological orientations gave similar results and indicated
that the relationships can be seen as causal.

There are other results concerning effects of individual differences
on prejudice that can be interpreted in terms of the strength of the
C system. We focus here on differences in suppression of negative
responses. Liberal/egalitarian people, who value equality, and help
and support of needy deviant groups and persons, are likely to
suppress the stereotypes and negative affect with respect to those
groups. Plant and Devine (cf. 1998), for example, measured people's
"internal reasons" for the suppression of negative responses, and found
that this factor (measured by items like "Because of my personal values,
I believe that using stereotypes about black people is wrong") significantly correlated $(r = 0.45)$ with Katz and Hass' (1988) measure of
Humanitarianism-Egalitarianism (see also Fazio & Hilden, 2001,
Note 1). Also, motivation to suppress negative responses to blacks is

positively related to feelings of guilt when one has inadvertently made a negative and harmful response to black people (Fazio & Hilden, 2001; Monteith *et al.*, 1993); guilt being an emotion that we strongly associate with activation of the C system.[1]

This suppression may have contributed to the positive correlation between liberalism/egalitarianism and the attitude towards a number of disadvantaged or deviant groups, as found by Lambert and Chasteen (1997). Positive correlations between suppression of negative responses and attitudes toward deviant groups have been found by Crandall, Eshleman, and O'Brien (2002). Crandall *et al.* developed a Suppression of Prejudice Scale, designed to measure individual differences in internally motivated inhibition and targeting multiple deviant conditions. For groups having at least in part a deviant condition with passive elements, such as fat people, people with AIDS, black Americans, elderly people, mentally retarded people, deaf people, and blind people, more suppression was related to a more positive attitude. Persons who are highly internally motivated to respond without prejudice and who are likely to be liberal/egalitarian, can be supposed to have a strong C system, which results in less negative responses to deviant conditions, particularly if these conditions have passive aspects. One can, however, question whether Crandall *et al.* succeeded in measuring pure internally motivated suppression; we come to that later. Research by Devine, Plant, Amodio, Harmon-Jones, and Vance (2002) suggests that by better distinguishing internal and external motivation to suppress negative responses and analyzing these two motivations together, suppression of prejudice can be operationalized as a autonomously performed activity without external conformity motivation. Devine *et al.* found that participants who were highly internally motivated to respond without prejudice and not motivated for external reasons, responded with lower levels of hard to control implicit race bias (see Chapter 4) than all other participants. Such pure internally motivated suppression seems to be more highly related to the C system, because externally motivated suppression is excluded. Furthermore, Plant, Devine, and Brazy (2003) showed that people who want to suppress negative responses primarily for internal reasons, are relatively unaffected by an experimental manipulation varying the extent to which participants believe that their true feelings can be detected by the researcher.[2] These results suggest that internal reasons may indeed be related to truly felt care and tenderness. Obviously, suppression may not only be based on internal reasons, but also on external reasons.

Interestingly, Crandall *et al.* also found that for groups having a strongly active deviant condition, such as child abusers, men who don't pay child support, men who go to prostitutes, people who sell marijuana, and porn stars, more suppression was related to a more negative attitude. These relationships are in conformity with a hypothesis advanced earlier and concerning the relationship between liberalism/egalitarianism or the C system and negative responses to persons or groups with an active deviant condition. As explained before, child abusers and the other groups mentioned strongly violate values of benevolence and universalism presumably cherished by high suppressors because of their liberal/egalitarianism orientation, or in other words, people with a rather strong C system. Therefore this strong C system will be frustrated, which may provide extra activation of the FF system. According to Lambert and Chasteen (1997), liberalism/egalitarianism is not correlated with attitudes toward non-disadvantaged groups. However, if those groups are seen as strongly violating norms and traditional values, or in other words have a strong active deviant condition, Crandall *et al.*'s results support our hypothesis that liberalism/egalitarianism may be negatively correlated with attitudes toward those groups.

Crandall *et al.* advance a different explanation of the relationship between suppression and negative responses toward groups having a strongly active deviant condition. They explain this relationship in terms of adherence to social norms. High suppressors of negative responses are hypersensitive to perceived cultural norms. Prejudice against or a negative response toward people who very strongly violate social norms and values is normatively appropriate. Therefore, high suppressors' adherence to social norms makes for prejudice against groups with a very strongly active deviant condition. In support of this explanation, Crandall *et al.* showed that high suppressors are indeed strong norm followers. When high suppressors saw other people condemning or condoning racist conduct, they conformed more than others to this behavior. In other words, high suppressors expressed more tolerance of negative responses than others, when they had seen other people condoning prejudicial behavior, whereas condemnation of prejudicial behavior led to the expression of less tolerance of negative responses. Apparently, suppression of negative responses, as measured by Crandall *et al.*, is also motivated by an attempt to conform to perceived social norms. Our interpretation of the relationship between suppression and negative responses toward groups having a strongly active deviant condition in terms of the C system and the normative interpretation of Crandall *et al.* may complement each other, the former focusing more on internal motivation and the latter on external motivation to suppress prejudiced responses, which is related to conformity behavior. In conclusion, the more negative responses to strongly active deviant conditions may both result from the operation of the C system and an external motivation not to suppress prejudice because of perceived social norms encouraging condemnation of such active deviance.

## 5.3 Authoritarianism and social dominance orientation as reflections of the FF and C system

Lambert and Chasteen's (1997) conceptualization of two ideological orientations, that are important determinants of social prejudice, a liberal/egalitarian orientation and a conservative/authoritarian orientation, has what at first sight may be seen as an important rival, advanced by among others Altemeyer (1998). This rival conceptualization consists of one dimension shared with Lambert and Chasteen's conceptualization i.e., authoritarianism, and one other dimension, social dominance orientation. We will argue that the two conceptualizations are in fact highly similar, and both can be seen as addressing respectively the FF and C system. But before doing this, we will first address more extensively the nature of these two dimensions and their importance in predicting negative responses to deviance.

Turning to authoritarianism, much research on individual differences in prejudice has for long found authoritarianism to be related to rejection of many deviant groups and persons.[3]

We already mentioned the negative relationship between authoritarianism and attitude toward blacks and gays, as found by Lambert and Chasteen (1997). Other examples of relationships between this factor and responses to deviance can be found with respect to fat people (Crandall, 1994) and people with AIDS (Witt, 1989). Such relationships have not only been found in Western countries but also in non-Western countries. Authoritarian Russians, for instance, showed more negative reactions to Americans (Stephan, Ageyev, Coates Shrider, Stephan, & et al., 1994). In Romania authoritarianism was positively related to specific prejudices against Arabs, Hungarians, and homosexuals, and to generalized prejudice (Krauss, 2002), and authoritarian Koreans held more negative attitudes toward prisoners (Na & Loftus, 1998).

Pratto, Sidanius, Stallworth, and Malle (1994) proposed another individual difference measure predicting prejudice. This measure, social dominance orientation, refers to a general orientation toward intergroup relations, reflecting whether one generally prefers such relations to be equal versus hierarchical (p. 742). Pratto *et al.* showed that social dominance orientation was positively related to anti-black and anti-Arab attitudes. Pratto *et al.* (2000) studied the relationships between social dominance orientation and attitude toward deviant groups in four cultures. In Canada social dominance orientation was positively related to ethnic prejudice, and negatively related to support for gay rights. In Taiwan it was positively related to ethnic prejudice against aborigines. In Israel a higher social dominance orientation was related to a more negative view of low-status Jewish ethnic groups; this relationship held for members of both high- and low-status groups. Finally, in China social dominance orientation was not related to endogamy preferences, i.e. marriage within one's ingroup, but it did relate to sexism, as was also the case in the three other cultures.

In an important review, Altemeyer (1998) presented research on the nature of authoritarianism and social dominance orientation and their relationships to prejudice. He included research in which the predictive power of a large number of individual difference measures with regard to prejudice against blacks, women and homosexuals was investigated. The results showed that these negative responses could be quite well predicted by authoritarianism and social dominance orientation, being moderately correlated with each other; the remaining measures, among which need for structure, often thought to be related to prejudice, did not really contribute to the predictions. To study the differences between authoritarianism and social dominance orientation, Altemeyer developed a Personal Power, Meanness, and Dominance scale, which appeared to correlate highly ($r = 0.61$) with social dominance orientation, whereas the correlation with authoritarianism was very low ($r = 0.08$). From this and other results, Altemeyer concluded that people with a high social dominance orientation see life as "dog eat dog" and are determined to do the eating. They tend to reject equality and consider weak minorities as easy targets for exerting power, for being mean, and for dominating others. Authoritarians, on the other hand, seem to be prejudiced mainly because they were raised to travel in tight ethnocentric circles; they fear that authority and conventions are crumbling so quickly that civilization will collapse. These are the roots of their believing strongly in submission to established authorities and the social norms that these authorities endorse. Authoritarians also believe in aggressing against whomever these authorities target. These pictures of authoritarianism and social dominance orientation were corroborated in research by Heaven and Connors (2001) in Australia. Relating value domains to authoritarianism and social dominance orientation, it was found that authoritarianism was best predicted by national strength and order, propriety in dress and manners, religiosity, secure and satisfying relationships and honesty. Social dominance orientation was best predicted by low support for international harmony and equality, low honesty, low religiosity and getting ahead. Interestingly, these values and goals associated with authoritarianism and social dominance orientation strongly resemble two poles of the two basic Schwartz's dimensions respectively, namely Conservation with the value types of security, conformity and tradition, and Self-Enhancement with power and achievement value types. This resemblance was supported in a more direct way by Altemeyer (1998), who reported correlations between authoritarianism and social dominance orientation, on the one hand, and value types on the Schwartz value inventory, on the other hand. Authoritarianism, but not social dominance orientation, correlated with traditionalism and conformity, whereas social dominance orientation, but not authoritarianism, correlated with power.

Earlier research from a somewhat different perspective by Crandall and Cohen (1994) on personality variables involved in prejudice can also be seen as supporting Altemeyer's (1998) view of the importance of authoritarianism and social dominance orientation as determinants of prejudice. Social distance from a number of stigmas, for example amputated leg, obesity, and schizophrenia, could be predicted by two personality variables, constructed by factor analysis, namely Cynical World View and Conventionalism. Faith in people had the highest (negative) factor loading on the Cynical World View factor, whereas Authoritarianism had the highest factor loading on the Conventionalism factor. The similarity to social dominance orientation and authoritarianism is rather obvious, although we prefer to speak of ideological orientations rather than personality variables. Recent research among American and White Afrikaner students by Duckitt, Wagner, du Plessis, and Birum (2002) also underscores the role played by authoritarianism and social dominance orientation in determining prejudice. Their research provides support for a model in which two basic motivational goals, namely control or security motivation, on the one hand, and dominance or superiority motivation, on the other hand, are expressed in authoritarianism and social dominance orientation respectively, which in turn lead to prejudice. This part of the model is quite similar to our conceptualization. Furthermore, those motivational goals are seen as driven by the personality dimensions of social conformity (measured by items such as conforming and conventional) and toughmindedness (measured by items such as ruthless and hard). We think that these personality dimensions of social conformity and toughmindedness can, however, also be conceived in terms of value. There is considerable overlap in content, and they show similar correlations with other variables. For example, Altemeyer's correlations between value types on the Schwartz value inventory, on the one hand, and authoritarianism and social dominance orientation, on the other hand, and reported above, mirror Duckitt *et al.*'s results with respect to the personality dimensions of social conformity and toughmindedness.

Interestingly, very recently, Duckitt (2006) went one step further and predicted in a differential effect account similar to the one presented previously that authoritarianism would result in prejudice against socially threatening groups, and social dominance orientation against socially subordinate or socially disadvantaged groups. Duckitt's results with regard to deviant target groups with active and passive conditions showed that authoritarianism, but not social dominance orientation, was negatively related to attitude to drug dealers, an active deviant condition, whereas social dominance orientation, but not authoritarianism, was negatively related to attitude to physically disabled persons and unemployment beneficiaries, both passive deviant conditions. Furthermore, the authoritarianism effect was mediated by perceived threat from the drug dealers group, and the social dominance orientation effects were mediated by competitiveness toward physically disabled persons and unemployment beneficiaries. Half of the (reverse coded) items of the competitiveness measure were items expressing a cooperative, altruistic attitude to the target group. Therefore the latter mediation can also be interpreted in terms of altruism, which fits still better with our framework.

As noted previously, Lambert and Chasteen's (1997) liberal/egalitarian ideological orientation underlying prejudice, is quite similar to the social dominance orientation of Pratto *et al.* (1994), considered in reverse. Although Pratto *et al.* found the correlation between social dominance orientation and Katz and Hass's Humanitarianism-Egalitarianism scale to be quite modest ( $r = -0.34$ ), social dominance orientation correlated on average moderately with Concern for others ( $r = -0.46$ ), and quite strongly ( $r = -0.57$ ) with a hierarchy-attenuating ideology, called noblesse oblige, i.e., those with more resources should share them with those who have fewer resources. Concern for others and noblesse oblige are important aspects of Lambert and Chasteen's liberal/egalitarian dimension, indicating a commitment to the ideals of equality and a desire to assist disadvantaged or oppressed persons in society. Moreover, recent research by Lambert, Payne, Jacoby, Shaffer, Chasteen, and Khan (2003) found the correlation between Humanitarianism-Egalitarianism and social dominance orientation to be $-0.72$. Apart from this empirical similarity, there is also the similarity with Schwartz's basic value dimension Self-Transcendence versus Self-Enhancement, which opposes benevolence and universalism to power and achievement. In other words, the liberal/egalitarian ideological orientation may be seen as an opposing pole of social dominance orientation. Both measures seem to contrast equality and inequality, although in a somewhat different way. Humanitarianism-Egalitarianism consisting of only items favoring equality is more directed at the measurement of the equality pole of the dimension, whereas the social dominance orientation measure including items favoring equality and items favoring inequality is more directed at both the measurement of the equality and inequality pole. This may mean that social dominance orientation provides relatively more differentiated measures of the inequality pole of the dimension, that it shows more differences in preferences for inequality, in willingness to exert power, in being mean, and for dominating others. If one thinks, as we do, that a lack of a well developed C system does not necessarily imply such characteristics as meanness and unrestrained exercise of power, social dominance orientation as a proxy for the measurement of the C system adds some noise to this measurement. This difference between the Humanitarianism-Egalitarianism and the social dominance orientation measure may also explain why sometimes relationships between these measures are not strong.

Theoretically, according to Pratto *et al.* (1994), social dominance orientation reflects a motivational power system. We think, as noted before, that at least as a measurement it also, but not completely, reflects a rather weak C system. Incidentally, the use of social dominance orientation or liberal/egalitarian measures will be quite dependent on one's theoretical predilections, emphasizing power and, our predilection, care motivation respectively. More research seems to be needed to establish definitively whether and to what extent both variables represent poles of and thus measure the same construct, or whether there is some independence. In the rest of this chapter, we will, because of the measure used in most research, often use the term social dominance orientation, but assume its high similarity to the liberal/egalitarian dimension and consider it as a rough reflection of a rather weak C system.

From the more extensive information presented on the nature of authoritarianism and social dominance orientation or the liberal/egalitarian dimension more support can be obtained for considering these ideological orientations as highly related to the FF and C system.[4] As for the FF system, fear, on the one hand, and anger and aggression, on the other hand, are essential components of that system, but they also seem to underlie authoritarianism. Indeed, as we noted above, Altemeyer's (1998) description of authoritarians includes fear and aggression. They fear that authority and conventions are crumbling and that civilization will collapse and they believe in aggressing against whomever the established authorities target. A different way of describing the relationship between the FF system and authoritarianism is by focusing on their goals. Our approach here is in part similar to the approach of Duckitt *et al.* (2002) described above. As noted above, the values or goals of security, conformity, and tradition are distinguished by Schwartz as characterizing the Conservation pole of the first basic dimension, and thus the values or goals of the FF system are quite characteristic for authoritarians.

Confrontation with passive deviance may often activate the C system and result in feelings of tenderness and pity. These positive emotions also seem to play an important role in Lambert and Chasteen's (1997) liberal/egalitarian dimension, which reflects, as noted above, a political liberal ideology, a commitment to the ideals of equality and a desire to assist disadvantaged or oppressed persons in society. Describing also the relationship between the C system and liberalism/egalitarianism or social dominance orientation in terms of their goals, the most important goals associated with the C system seem to be benevolence and universalism representing the Self-Transcendence pole of the second basic dimension of Schwartz. As was noted above, these values are quite characteristic for people high on liberalism/egalitarianism (or low on social dominance orientation).

Our interpretation of authoritarianism and social dominance orientation as resulting from the FF system and the C system respectively also fits nicely with the view presented above that authoritarianism and social dominance orientation as individual difference variables are the main determinants of negative responses to deviant conditions. As argued previously, the FF system and C system are the primary motivational systems activating responses to deviant conditions. So, as also suggested by Schwartz's two basic value dimensions, there is little room for other important values as determinants of prejudice.

Interestingly, authoritarianism and social dominance orientation or liberalism/egalitarianism seem to have a clear genetic component as can be inferred from data reported in Tesser (1993). Tesser also mentions that aggression and altruism, that can be seen as highly important aspects of the FF and C system respectively, have such a genetic component. As explanation for attitude heritability he proposes that attitudes have a more or less direct biological substrate. This is wholly consistent with our view that underlying (biological) motivational systems, which are likely to be partly heritable, give rise to the ideological orientations of authoritarianism and social dominance orientation. It also qualifies Altemeyer's (1998) conclusion that authoritarians seem to be prejudiced mainly because they were raised to travel in tight ethnocentric circles. Of course, ideological orientations do have social and cultural determinants, but apparently they also have a genetic basis.[5]

In this context, the question of the role of personality traits with regard to prejudice and ideological orientations may be raised. Ekehammar, Akrami, Gylje, and Zakrisson (2004) studied the relationships between authoritarianism, social dominance orientation and the classic Big Five personality factors, namely conscientiousness, extraversion, openness to experience, agreeableness, and neuroticism. Authoritarianism showed the highest correlations with conscientiousness ($r = 0.25$) and openness to experience ($r = -0.28$), whereas, social dominance orientation was only related to agreeableness ($r = -0.25$). It is not hard to interpret these correlations in terms of the nature of these two ideological orientations, as described previously. In further analyses the investigators obtained support for a model in which the effects of the Big Five personality on prejudice were mediated by authoritarianism and social dominance orientation. Overall, the effects of the two ideological orientations were markedly stronger than the effects of the Big Five factors.

Because negative responses to and prejudice against deviant groups can be conceived of as expressions of the FF and C system, or of their underlying values or goals, it can be expected that based on these systems and their associated values individuals have a consistent tendency to be prejudiced against those groups or their members. As already noted by Allport (1954/1979, p. 68), if an individual is prejudiced against one deviant group, he is likely to be prejudiced against other deviant groups. Let us give some examples of this consistent tendency. For one, in the study by Crandall and Cohen (1994), undergraduate participants rated an obese person, a person with an amputated leg, convicted of theft, having AIDS, and having a history of schizophrenia, on a number of social distance questions. Whereas these deviant persons were presented in the form of vignettes, measurement of prejudice against homosexuals took place using a scale. Factor analysis of social distance scores for these six deviant conditions, all of which have at least active aspects, revealed a single "Stigma" factor, supporting the notion that rejection of deviant persons or persons with a stigma is a generalized tendency with, in this case, probably particularly the FF system as the underlying mechanism. Cunningham, Nezlek, and Banaji (2004), following a similar approach, demonstrated such a generalized tendency not only for explicit, but also for implicit attitudes. Another example can be found in a study by Bierly (1985) in which the interrelatedness of attitudes toward four outgroups, namely blacks, women (acceptance of traditional sex roles), homosexuals, and old people (two measures) was investigated. Nine of the ten possible intercorrelations were significant beyond the 0.01 level. Interestingly, attitudes toward old people tended to correlate less (average correlation 0.19) with attitudes toward blacks, women, and homosexuals, which had a correlation average of 0.48. For Bierly, the low intercorrelations of the two old people scales with the other scales were unexpected. These low intercorrelations could, however, have been expected in light of our conceptualization of the FF and C system as two different systems underlying prejudice or negative responses and their focus on respectively active and passive deviant conditions. The elderly seem to have a passive deviant condition with hardly active aspects, activating the C system, whereas attitudes toward blacks, homosexuals, and traditional women can be seen as expressions of the FF system. On the basis of the FF and C system underlying prejudice, it can thus be predicted that the tendency to exhibit negative responses against deviant groups will show more empirical consistency when the groups involved have either an active or a passive stigma. When target groups with active and groups with passive stigmas are involved, this general tendency will be less consistent.

## 5.4  Gender, education, and negative responses to deviance

Much research has shown that women are less likely than men to express negative responses or prejudice against deviant groups. For example, in a study by Chesler (1965) women showed more acceptance of physically disabled persons, and in the study by Bierly (1985), women expressed more tolerance toward homosexuals, blacks, and the aged. Also, women have been found less likely to endorse antifat attitudes (Perez-Lopez, Lewis, & Cash, 2001). Although there are also many studies that have not found gender differences, those showing men expressing less prejudice than women are rare. Explanations for these gender differences can be looked for in a difference in the C system and its associated values underlying prejudice. In Chapter 2, we presented evidence indicating that women have a more strongly developed C system. Consistent with this, recent research by Costa, Terracciano, and McCrae (2001), analyzing data from twenty-six cultures, found women to be higher in nurturance. More specifically, women scored higher on such traits as warmth, trust, and altruism. Men were found to be higher in assertiveness. These more positive inclinations of women and their lesser assertiveness are also quite consistent with gender differences in social dominance orientation that emphasizes inequality and getting ahead without concern for others. Men often appear to have a stronger social dominance orientation than women (Pratto *et al.*, 2000). Thus, gender differences in prejudice may be explained in terms of gender differences in the C system and, relatedly, social dominance orientation. Research by Whitley (1999) has confirmed this mediating role of social dominance orientation in gender differences in prejudice. Investigating prejudice against African-Americans and homosexuals, Whitley found that the percentage of variance in a number of prejudice measures accounted for by gender was substantially reduced (by an average of 77 percent in two samples of psychology students) when social dominance orientation was controlled. In other words, women's lower prejudice against African-Americans and homosexuals could be explained to a large extent by their lower social dominance orientation. Furthermore, gender differences in social dominance orientation were larger than gender differences in the other important orientation underlying prejudice, namely authoritarianism, thus excluding strong involvement of the FF system. Indeed, in one of the two samples, there was no significant gender difference in authoritarianism, a result that has also been reported by Altemeyer (1998). Moreover, in the other sample women were found to be slightly more authoritarian than men, which makes a mediating role of authoritarianism in explaining gender differences in prejudice still more unlikely. Because, as proposed earlier, the mediating C system or social dominance orientation factor is particularly related to attitudes toward deviant groups with a passive stigma, gender differences in prejudice can be expected to occur especially with regard to those groups.

As for education, the type of education is of course an important determinant of responses to deviance. Education in the humanities and social sciences, for example, is likely to result in more liberal or "politically correct" views of deviant groups than most other types of education (cf. Goode, 2003). But considering education in general, it has often been found that people with less education show more negative responses towards deviant groups. As with gender differences in prejudice, there are, however, also many studies that have found no educational differences in prejudice; but again, those that show less educated people expressing less prejudice than more educated people are rare. Let us give some examples of studies showing that more education tends to mean less prejudice. Dekker and Mootz (1992) found in a general opinion survey of the Dutch population that well educated people were more accepting of AIDS patients than less educated people. Loftus, (2001) using United States survey data from 1973 to 1998, found that a higher educational attainment reduces the likelihood that an individual will condemn homosexuality. Brockington, Hall, Levings, and Murphy (1993) concluded on the basis of a large opinion survey in two English districts that the more educated were in several aspects more tolerant of the mentally ill.

The relationship between education and prejudice against ethnic minorities has been extensively investigated by Wagner and Zick

(1995). They demonstrated, using seven representative samples from four European countries, namely West Germany, Netherlands, France, and Great Britain, that across three indices of ethnic prejudice and across various ethnic target groups the more highly educated respondents indicated a lower rejection of the relevant minorities than did the less educated respondents. Sometimes it is proposed that such differences in prejudice do not reflect "true" differences in attitudes, but are expressions of differentially endorsed norms to evaluate outgroups positively, with the group with more education endorsing those norms more. In additional analyses, Wagner and Zick found little support for this argument. In one of those analyses they compared results on blatant and subtle prejudice scales, the latter developed with the aim of detecting more hidden and socially accepted forms of ethnic prejudice (cf. Pettigrew & Meertens, 1995) with each other. Although they did find that the educational differences were smaller on the subtle prejudice scale than on the blatant scale, suggesting social desirability effects, the educational differences on the subtle scale remained highly significant. Thus, the evidence they found for social desirable response tendencies seemed not strong enough to explain the attitudinal differences between the educational groups. Moreover, Wagner and Zick also used the bogus pipeline procedure, where participants believe a machine will reveal their true attitudes and thus can disclose deception; therefore they tend to reveal their true attitudes. Wagner and Zick found in that study that the bogus pipeline procedure compared to a paper and pencil procedure did not result in a reduction of the educational difference in ethnic prejudice; it even enlarged the difference.

Explanations for these educational effects on prejudice may again be looked for in the FF and C system and their associated ideological orientations. The relationship between education and social dominance orientation, however, is rather unclear (Pratto *et al.*, 1994) or non-existent (Altemeyer, 1998), which makes this factor and relatedly the C system less likely candidates for mediation. In contrast, the relationship between education and authoritarianism and thus the FF system has frequently been found (Altemeyer, 1998; Duriez & Van Hiel, 2002); more education means less authoritarianism. It can be easily argued that more education provides in terms of the first basic Schwartz dimension – Openness to change versus Conservation – more room for stimulation, and self-direction goals or values and lays less emphasis on goals of security, conformity, and tradition (cf. Prince-Gibson & Schwartz, 1998). Another explanation for educational effects on prejudice, which is compatible with the previous one, can be found in differences in stress between socioeconomic status levels. Lower socioeconomic status with less education as a highly important aspect is

related to more stressful experiences, such as social conflict and financial limitations. It is also related to a lack of resources, tangible but also
personal and social such as social support that may buffer those stress
experiences (see Gallo, Bogart, Vranceanu, & Matthews, 2005). Stress in
turn can be seen as a threat that may strengthen the FF system and
amplify negative responses to deviance as we described in Chapter 4
and which will be further illustrated in Chapter 6. In conclusion, with
regard to this second explanation, lower socioeconomic strata with less
education as an important characteristic are exposed to more stress,
which results in more authoritarianism and directly or indirectly in
more prejudice.

Suggestive evidence for a mediating role of authoritarianism was
obtained in a study by Agnew, Thompson, and Gaines (2000). These
investigators found among undergraduates that a Tolerant Personality
factor, containing measures that can be thought to tap tendencies
toward authoritarianism and Conservative Beliefs, played a mediating
role in the relationship between Family Status, including one's father's
or parents' education as an important element, and a generalized measure of prejudice. This prejudice measure included such target groups
as homosexuals, elderly people, and foreigners. In other words, a
higher social status of family of origin, with education as an important
aspect, is conducive to a more tolerant or less authoritarian personality
and less conservative beliefs, which in turn lead to less prejudice.
Analyses for specific outgroups supported the distinction between
active and passive stigmas. Whereas the path between Conservative
Beliefs and prejudice was quite strong for target groups having a more
active stigma like homosexuals, it was essentially non-existent for the
elderly, having a more passive stigma. This difference can be explained
again by assuming that authoritarianism is much more positively
related to prejudice against groups with an active stigma than against
groups having a passive stigma. In the latter case even a negative
relationship may be found. Wagner and Zick (1995), combining their
samples, also found some evidence for the mediating role of authoritarianism in the relationship between education and ethnic prejudice.
Wagner and Zick did measure education of the respondent rather than
of his or her family, but their conservatism measure focused on the
respondents' position on the left-right political spectrum, which does
not seem to be the core of authoritarianism. All in all, more research is
needed to examine the mediating role of the FF system and authoritarianism in the relationship between education and prejudice. Anyhow, a
mediating role of authoritarianism in the relationship between education and prejudice seems more likely than mediation by social dominance orientation or liberalism/egalitarianism. Because, as suggested

earlier, the mediating authoritarianism factor is correlated with attitudes toward deviant groups with an active stigma, educational differences in prejudice can be expected to occur particularly with regard to those groups.

## 5.5 Summary

In the present chapter, we addressed the role of individual differences in FF and C system and corresponding goals and ideological orientations underlying prejudice. We argued that the goals served by the FF and C system underlying responses to deviance correspond with value types or goals distinguished by Schwartz's theory on values, namely security, conformity, and tradition for the FF system and benevolence and universalism for the C system. Confrontations with deviance will activate the FF and C system and thus their goals, which are an essential part of these systems, but supposedly also ideological orientations, the more specific expressions of goals translated to social reality. The stronger a person's FF and C system, their corresponding system goals, and ideological orientations are, the more easily they will be activated by relevant cues or the lower will be their activation threshold. Furthermore, passive stigmas or deviant conditions will activate the C system, whereas active stigmas or deviant conditions will activate the FF system. Thus the stronger the C system is, the more positive responses to deviant persons will be, particularly if those persons have a passive stigma or deviant condition. And also, the stronger the FF system is, the more negative responses to deviant persons will be, particularly if those persons have an active stigma or deviant condition. Research using, as ideological orientations, a liberal/egalitarian value dimension and a conservative/authoritarian value dimension found support for these predictions.

Operation of the C system can also be seen in suppression of earlier acquired negative stereotypes and affect. Positive relationships between suppression of prejudice and attitudes toward groups with a passive stigma have been found. Interestingly, for groups having a strong active stigma more suppression of prejudice was related to a more negative attitude, which can be interpreted as partly due to the operation of the C system. Groups with a strong active stigma such as child abusers strongly frustrate the C system with its goals of benevolence and universalism. Stronger C systems will be more frustrated and may result in more negative attitudes toward those groups.

Another ideological orientation predicting prejudice is social dominance orientation referring to a general orientation toward intergroup relations, reflecting whether one generally prefers such relations to be equal versus hierarchical. Research has shown that prejudice or negative responses can be quite well predicted by authoritarianism and social dominance orientation. Research has also painted more specific pictures of authoritarianism and social dominance orientation. Authoritarians seem to be prejudiced especially because they were raised to be committed to traditions and conventions. They fear the impairment of authority and conventions and believe strongly in submission to established authorities and the social norms that these authorities endorse. They also believe in aggressing against whomever these authorities target. People with a high social dominance orientation, on the other hand, tend to reject equality, like to exert power and consider weak minorities as easy targets for exerting power. The liberal/egalitarian orientation is quite similar to the social dominance orientation. On the basis of these results and conclusions, authoritarianism and to a large extent social dominance orientation can be seen as ideological expressions of the FF and C system respectively.

Due to the FF and C system, which, as genetically based individual characteristics underlie prejudice, individuals have a consistent tendency to be prejudiced towards members of deviant groups.

Women appear to be less likely than men to express prejudice towards deviant groups. These gender differences in prejudice may be explained in terms of gender differences in the C system and, relatedly, social dominance orientation or liberal/egalitarian orientation.

People with less education have often been found to show more prejudice towards deviant groups than better educated people. People with more education are often lower on authoritarianism and stress and thus can be supposed to have a less developed FF system. This may explain the relationship between education and prejudice.

# Variations in social control across societies, cultures, and historical periods

## 6.1 Introduction

In the previous chapters, our particular psychological approach served us quite well in explaining and integrating many different factors that influence responses to deviance, such as the motivational aspects of different types of deviance, the behavior of the person associated with a deviant condition, the situation in which interaction with the person takes place, and certain individual differences in responding. It is important to realize, however, that most of the psychological phenomena discussed thus far have been primarily observed and documented in modern Western societies. The goal of this chapter is to demonstrate that our psychological approach may also be useful to explain and integrate what is known about differences and similarities in responding to deviance in different cultures and historical periods. Let us first consider different approaches that can be used to describe and explain the influence of culture or society on responding to deviance.

First, we may treat each society as relatively unique and offer fine-grained descriptions and interpretations of patterns of social control in each and every culture, society, or historical period encountered; thereby not pretending to generalize interpretations and conclusions to other societies. This clearly is a much preferred method as the literature is full of rich ethnographic and historical descriptions that have been independently produced by researchers working in a wide variety of disciplines, but unfortunately resulting in extreme fragmentation of this field of inquiry. To be sure, researchers sometimes try to identify broad principles that might help explain certain similarities and differences in cultures in responding to deviance, but usually these principles are tested with only one particular deviant condition in mind. A broad distinction can be made between, on the one hand, anthropologists, sociologists, criminologists, and students of law extensively studying how particular cultures respond to deviant behavior such as crime, adultery, or cheating (for reviews, see Black, 1984; Roberts, 1979); and, on the other hand, medically interested anthropologists concentrating more on culture-dependent interpretations and responses to acute forms of passive deviance such as illness and injury (e.g., Fábrega, 1997; Helman, 1994; Shweder, Much, Mahapatra, & Park, 1997). Other researchers have focused their attention on community responses to more permanent forms of active and passive deviance such as mental illness and different kinds of physical and sensory impairments (e.g., Armstrong & Fitzgerald, 1996; Edgerton, 1970; Ingstad & Whyte, 1995; Jenkins, 1998; Koty, 1934; Neubert & Cloerkes, 2001). Finally, historical analyses are an additional source of information on variation in responding to deviance across societies and cultures, especially with respect to relatively extreme forms of responding such as social exclusion, public shaming, persecution, and execution (e.g., Le Goff, 1984/1987; Vanhemelryck, 2004). As a result of this fragmentation, there has been little attention to developing and testing general theoretical principles explaining *why* different societies and historicial periods respond differently or similarly to deviance. Sometimes, one gets the impression that culture and history are primarily evoked to illustrate and emphasize time and again how idiosyncratic, variable, and easily influenced human beliefs and behavior with respect to deviance are, and how fruitless it seems to search for general explanatory principles in describing this amazing variability.

A second approach to studying cultural differences is to first identify a small number of important "dimensions" on which societies or cultures might differ, and then try to correlate these dimensions with observed social behavior. Although this approach is widely employed in cross-cultural psychology (cf. A. Fiske, Kitayama, Markus, & Nisbett, 1998; Hofstede, 2001; Triandis, 1996), it has seldomly been used to understand cultural differences in responding to deviance or social control. As will become evident later, however, the three major cultural dimensions that have been proposed – collectivism-individualism, egalitarian vs. hierarchical organization of society, and complexity – may be especially relevant for our concerns. In explaining correlations between the positions of societies on these dimensions and behavioral responses to deviance, there are two major challenges. First, one should have enough societies at one's disposal to examine how these three (and perhaps more) dimensions independently as well as interactively influence these responses. Considering only two values of each dimension, this would require enough societies or "cases" to study behavioral patterns in the $2 \times 2 \times 2 = 8$ possible combinations of these dimensions, preferably with at least ten cases for each combination. The importance of studying interactions between cultural dimensions can, for example, be seen from the contradictory statements that are made with respect to the apparent stigmatizing influence of collectivism-individualism.

For example, some authors argue that collectivistic societies show a stronger tendency to exclude or hide disabled individuals than individualistic societies (e.g., Hofstede, 2001; Westbrook *et al.*, 1993). The problem with this comparison, however, is that the collectivistic societies studied in modern surveys are usually represented by developing countries that tend to be hierarchically organized, whereas collectivistic societies that are relatively simple and egalitarian are lacking. As shown later, students of the latter societies frequently report caring attitudes toward, and social integration, of disabled persons (e.g., Hanks & Hanks, 1948; Ingstad & Whyte, 1995; Koty, 1934). Thus, although it is important to study interactions between broad cultural dimensions, it may be difficult to find enough representative examples of the different combinations of these dimensions. In addition, it may be possible that some combinations may not even occur in reality.

A second but related challenge for applying cross-cultural psychology to social control is to understand how the influence of broad cultural dimensions on behavior is mediated by basic psychological mechanisms that operate at the level of individuals. Although an important step in showing the psychological relevance of cultural dimensions is to relate them systematically to the characteristic value patterns of societies (e.g., Triandis, 1996) or individual or personality differences in stigmatization or prejudice (e.g., Duckitt, 2001), these proposals are still not specific enough to understand how different social contexts are responsible for the activation of the mediating psychological mechanisms.

Before presenting our approach to relating culture to social control it is first important to emphasize that the two approaches mentioned are faced with an additional and common problem. In particular, both the particularistic or descriptive and the cross-cultural or explanatory approaches tend to neglect the universal motivational implications of deviant conditions. Indeed, researchers often look at deviance as if each society or historical period uniquely determines whether and how a particular physical or behavioral condition is to be "defined" or "constructed" as deviance, and hence what its social implications will be. We admit that cultural variability in responding is especially likely with respect to the many specific norm-violating behaviors that we assign to our controllable-active or Type 2 deviance; these behaviors are indeed as variable as there are specific norms that can be violated in different societies. However, we will argue that *types* of deviance, because they are constituted by universal motivational mechanisms or concepts (see Chapters 2 and 3), are similarly responded to across cultures and historical periods. For example, each society needs to differentiate between crime and illness if it is to respond effectively to deviance. Indeed, we will illustrate that, in comparing the influence of type of deviance and cultures on responding to deviance, the former has a far more impressive influence than the latter. Nevertheless, we will also illustrate that whether particular physical or behavioral conditions are considered undesirable or deviant, and to which type of deviance they are assigned, depends on the unique motivationally relevant features of these conditions, the extent to which the relevant motivational systems or concepts are activated in a particular society and tend to bias interpretations and responding, and certain beliefs about the nature and social implications of these conditions.

Our alternative to the two approaches to cultural influences on social control consists of a bottom-up and evolutionary approach that first identifies the major psychological mechanisms that are involved in the explanation of these influences, and then proceeds to examine how, in interaction with certain structural features of societies, activation and output of these mechanisms are associated with three major categories of societies, each with a characteristic mode of social control. As may already have dawned upon the reader, we will use the same psychological mechanisms in classifying societies that we see as responsible for our universal typology of deviant conditions and for the different psychological processes described in Chapters 3 and 4. In the next section, we explain this approach and show how it relates to the three major cultural dimensions that have been proposed by cross-cultural psychology. In particular, we will argue that these cultural dimensions and their associated value patterns emerge from the way the FF-C network functions in different social structures varying from small collectivistic groups of egalitarian hunter-gatherers to large individualistic modern societies. However, our approach emphasizes that a particular category of society is more than a combination of broad different cultural dimensions, and represents a unique configuration of ecological, economic, and social conditions of living and their associated values (see also A. Fiske, 2002).

After we have formulated hypotheses about how the three categories of society, in interaction with types of deviance, influence social control, we test them in two complementary ways. First, using a wide variety of anthropological and historical sources, we will describe and illustrate differences in social control between the three categories of societies in a qualitative way. This also allows us to address a major concern of this book, namely: How do some societies, social groups, or relationships manage to engage in repair processes with respect to deviance, while others merely tolerate deviant individuals, and still others actively stigmatize and socially exclude them? This question cannot be answered by merely considering the influence of a few broad cultural dimensions on responses to deviance, but should include an understanding of the mutual and long-term adaptations between deviant and non-deviant individuals within a particular social group or relationship. Note that in the previous chapters, this question could not be satisfactorily answered because we primarily looked at the universal aspects of mental representations of different types of deviance (Chapter 3) and short-term cognitive, emotional, and behavioral responses to deviant individuals (Chapter 4). Although it may be plausibly argued that certain individual or personality differences predict stigmatizing or tolerant tendencies (see Chapter 5), individuals can first translate these tendencies systematically into behavior in particular social settings or societies. Thus, only when we look at long-term patterns of responding and the consequences for the deviant individual it becomes possible to establish if particular deviant conditions are responded to with stigmatization, repair, or tolerance.

Second, we also perform a quantitative analysis of cultural influences on responding to deviance, by re-analyzing several data sets in which responses to deviant conditions in different cultures could be measured by means of modern survey techniques and standardized response measures.

Before we start we would like to issue a warning. The reader should only expect tentative answers and insights from our approach to the field of cultural and historical influences on responding to deviance. The complex way in which societies and cultures influence the behavior of individuals should make one cautious in formulating general conclusions about the overall extent to which particular societies stigmatize, engage in repair, or exercise tolerance. In addition, there are many gaps in the literature and our reading of it will, to a certain extent, be selective and incomplete. A major shortcoming of the field is the lack of studies comparing responses to a variety of deviant conditions in many different cultures, using the same cognitive, emotional, and behavioral response measures. Our approach to this field, therefore, should be seen as a first and modest attempt to understand how universal psychological mechanisms may mediate the influence of culture on responses to deviance and patterns of social control; and hence to bring causal explanation of behavior to this field rather than sticking to endless descriptions of the observed variability in responding across societies and cultures.

## 6.2 Understanding how cultural and historical differences in social control emerge

In explaining cultural differences in responding to deviance we will distinguish three major categories of societies in which particular activation patterns of the FF-C network are responsible for qualitatively distinct ways of responding to deviance or social control. We derive these categories from our evolutionary perspective that was introduced in Chapter 2. There, we argued that early human societies were faced with the problem of how interpersonal relationships that are based on self-preservation (dominant-submissive) and kinship (parent-child, brother-sister, etc.) are to be combined with relationships based on sexual reproduction (male-female). Two solutions were proposed. Either the males take control over sexual reproduction and its pre-conditions (e.g., food supply, safety, or territory), and establish male dominance hierarchies and a polygamous mating system, resulting in social control primarily based on a relatively strong activation of the FF system. Or egalitarian relationships are established based on kinship in which males and females primarily engage in monogamous relationships ("marriages"), resulting in social control primarily based on a strong activation of the C system.

In a hierarchically organized or FF-based primate society, dominant and polygamous males not only control access to females but also to resources for self-preservation (food, safety, territory). Consequently, such a society frequently consists of dominant males defending their territory and harem, surrounded by a large group of submissive males who opportunistically try to mate with straying females, steal food, or dethrone those in power (perhaps because of its strong association with conflict, however, polygamy became increasingly rare in later hierarchical societies). For social control this implies that active deviance is the most salient type of deviance in these societies, that the response to it primarily consists of fear and aggression, that the threatening aspects of passive deviance such as illness are emphasized or interpreted as active deviance, that the political and economic aspirations of females are suppressed by males, and that, on the instigations of dominant males, groups and societies frequently engage in intergroup warfare.

In contrast, in egalitarian societies, the C system is relatively strongly, and the FF system relatively weakly, activated due to the presence of kin-related individuals who are strongly motivated not to engage in selfish behavior and to rise to a dominant status (cf. Boehm, 1999). Furthermore, the output of the strongly activated C system is able to combine with the output of the sexual system, resulting in pair forma-tion, bonding, and love between mates (cf. McDougall, 1908/1948), and extensive patterns of reciprocity, cooperation, and sharing among kin. For social control, this implies that passive deviance is the most salient type of deviance in these societies, that the response to it consists of care-based tenderness and protectiveness, that the relatively infrequent cases of active deviance tend to be treated as passive deviance, that the political and economic aspirations of females are less suppressed by males, and that groups are connected to each other through an extensive network of intergroup marriages, resulting in a general willingness to share economic resources, trade, and cooperation.

Different evolutionary theorists have argued that the latter, egalitarian social structure would be most characteristic for early human societies, consisting of small groups of genetically-related hunter-gatherers (families), whereas a hierarchical organization would emerge once groups settled down and increasingly engaged in agriculture and food storage, thus growing rapidly into larger societies consisting of multiple families or clans (Boehm, 1999; Knauft, 1991; Whiten, 1999). A strong hierarchical organization kept the mosaic of groups together but also maintained patterns of economic and political inequality, as well as intergroup tensions and hostilities that, together with more fear-arousing conditions (e.g., due to warfare, poverty, famine, and plagues), were responsible for selective and chronic activation of the FF system. Thus in Knauft's (1991) evolutionary reconstruction of primate sociality and violence, a U-shaped trajectory of primate violence is proposed, with great apes (especially chimpanzees) showing a high, small and simple human societies a low, and more complex middle-range societies (village-level societies, chiefdoms, prestates) a high intensity and frequency of violence. Consistent with the present approach, Knauft argues that the high incidence of violence in both chimpanzee and middle-range human societies can be attributed to the existence of competitive male dominance hierarchies and their associated power conflicts, sexual rivalry and lack of food and resource sharing (see also Whiten, 1999).

We will refer to early egalitarian societies as Category 1, and to societies with a male-based dominance system, as Category 2 societies, and associate a characteristic activation pattern of the FF-C network with each of them. Specifically, in Category 1 societies, the C system normally is strongly activated and the FF system, partially because of its inhibitory relationship with the C system, is only weakly activated. This pattern would be responsible for a type of social control that we have referred to as *repair*. In contrast, in Category 2 societies, the FF system is relatively strongly activated and, again following a "winner-takes-all" principle, able to mostly inhibit the C system. Thus rather than "softly" responding to deviance, these societies tend to respond primarily fearfully and aggressively to it; a pattern of responding that we have associated with stigmatization (see Table 6.1).

In extending this analysis, we can see that increasing division of labor, together with increasing industrialization and technological developments, result in modern, in particular Western societies that

Table 6.1 *Social control in three categories of societies.*

| | Category 1 societies | Category 2 societies | Category 3 societies |
|---|---|---|---|
| Characteristic input-output pattern of motivational systems[a] | (FF)—(C) | (FF)—(C) | (FF)—(C) |
| Main type of social control | Repair | Stigmatization | Tolerance (with unintended stigmatization) |
| Characteristic type of deviance in society | Uncontrollable-passive (e.g., illnesses, misfortunes caused by dangerous environment) | Active (e.g., madness, predatory violence, heresy, conflicts of power, contagion) | Controllable-passive (e.g., laziness, being on welfare, low socioeconomic status) |
| Typical examples | Small group of egalitarian hunter-gatherers | European Middle Ages, current developing countries | Modern Western societies |
| Relation with cultural dimensions | Egalitarian, collectivistic, simple | Hierarchical, collectivistic, moderately complex | Egalitarian, individualistic, highly complex |

[a] FF refers to fight-or-flight system, C refers to care system. Thickness of arrows indicates weak, moderate, and strong activation (input/output) of systems, respectively.

are much larger and more complex than Category 2 societies, and that, like Category 1 societies, are also egalitarian but in a more impersonal manner. Specifically, as these societies, which we classify as Category 3 societies, need to encourage the employment of individual competencies and aspirations, as well as to care for its vulnerable members (children, the elderly, disabled), "soft" egalitarian responding to deviance is less based on kinship-based personal involvement with deviance (as the state has taken over social control) and more on generalized values of equality and justice. The motivational power of these values and formal rules, however, remains crucially dependent on a chronic activation of the C system, something which may suddenly become evident when people in modern Western societies respond with extreme pity and distress when exposed to vivid cases of vulnerability (e.g., the image of a child in some African country suffering from starvation). Expressed in terms of patterns of activation of the FF-C network, we could say that Category 3 societies are characterized by a relatively low activation of the FF system (due to the relative absence of internal and external conflicts, and favorable conditions of living) and a somewhat higher activation of the C system; a pattern that we associate with tolerance. Although we argue that the C system in Category 1 societies is more strongly activated than in Category 3 societies, we will also show that in the former category of societies this does not usually result in exaggerated care and pity but a practical and problem-focused outlook on helping others. In contrast, in Category 3 societies, involvement of the C system, in combination with weak interpersonal ties, may imply pity responses to needy others that are more self-focused.

A final distinguishing feature of individualistic Category 3 societies that should be noted is the increasing attribution of personal control for the onset and offset of deviant conditions. In particular, a complex society that cares for its vulnerable members will be especially keen on distinguishing "deservingly" ill or disabled individuals from those with more controllable forms of passive deviance (e.g., those who are perceived as staying dependent for an unnecessarily long period).

We realize that we simplify matters considerably, especially when talking in a general way about Category 3 or modern Western societies. First, modernization and individualism may also result in strongly hierarchically organized societies as is evidenced by twentieth century National Socialism and Communism, which are far from tolerant with respect to a wide variety of deviant conditions. Second, it may be necessary to distinguish between two subcategories of modern Western societies which can both be considered egalitarian and relatively tolerant. That is, it is useful to make a distinction between welfare states with a predominantly caring attitude toward the vulnerable of society (typical for European social democracies) and countries which are strongly individualistic and competitive (e.g., the USA). In the latter countries, we witness a tendency to more aggressive and conservative law-and-order responses that are so characteristic for Category 2 societies.

Let us now examine the similarities and differences between our typology and the broad cultural dimensions that have been proposed by cross-cultural psychology (see Table 6.1). First consider collectivism-individualism. With collectivism it is meant that a society is primarily organized in terms of altruism, mutual aid, and loyalty based on family ties, kinship or other affectionate interpersonal ties, whereas individualism refers to interactions among strangers who do not frame their relationships and obligations in terms of genetic relatedness or affective bonds. People in collectivistic societies adapt their thought and behavior largely toward other members of society, lack an autonomous sense of self, and feel dependent on others. Individualism develops when societies grow in size and complexity due to division of labor and urbanization, and individuals need to increasingly interact on the basis of individual aspirations, competencies, merits, and exchangeable products and services. To regulate these interactions, norms derived from kinship, tradition, and religion are less suitable than a general competence to apply a wide variety of situation-specific rules and to exercise internal restraint (Riesman, Glazer, & Denney, 1955). Consequently, individualistic societies highly value self-expression, independence, autonomy, competition, and differentiation from others (for recent discussions of this dimension, see A. Fiske, 2002; A. Fiske *et al.*, 1998; Hofstede, 2001; Triandis, 1989; Triandis & Gelfand, 1998). In our typology, Category 1 and 2 societies should both be considered collectivistic whereas Category 3 societies are individualistic.

However, Table 6.1 also suggests a relation between our typology and a second cultural dimension that has been found relevant; the extent to which societies are organized in an egalitarian vs. hierarchical manner. Although both Category 1 and 2 societies are collectivistic, Category 1 combines this feature with an egalitarian, and Category 2 with a hierarchical social organization. Furthermore, although both Category 1 and 3 societies are egalitarian, the first is collectivistic and the second individualistic.

The reader may now ask why we did not simply draw up a $2 \times 2$ table by crossing the egalitarian-hierarchical with the collectivistic-individualistic dimension, resulting in four categories of society. In fact, such an analysis has been proposed by an influential theorist in the field of cross-cultural psychology (Triandis, 1996). The answer is that, for our purposes, these two dimensions are not sufficient to characterize social control in each of the four combinations, and may also result in a problematic assignment of illustrative societies or cultures to each of them. First, notice that we also used a third cultural dimension to distinguish the three categories of society; one that we believe is intrinsically confounded with the first two dimensions and without which the meaning of the first two dimensions cannot be understood. Students of community responses to disabilities, in particular, emphasize that the extent to which societies are *simple vs. complex* should determine whether cultures respond with social exclusion or integration to deviance (e.g., Armstrong & Fitzgerald, 1996; Dinitz, Dynes, & Clarke, 1969; Scheer & Groce, 1988; Whyte & Ingstad, 1995). The idea behind the influence of this dimension is as follows. In relatively simple and small societies, people have the opportunity to observe disabled persons performing multiple tasks, thereby allowing them to compensate in one way or the other for their functional impairment, contribute to the community, and prevent the disability from receiving a "master status" that would define in a negative way the person's identity. This would often be possible in societies in which a small group such as a family functions as an economic unit. In contrast, in larger and complex societies a person is often only allowed to develop expertise in one particular role, and hence is only known by unfamiliar others to perform tasks in that particular role. When, under these circumstances, a person is associated with disability, this would more easily result in seeing the disabled condition as the person's central and defining attribute that disqualifies the whole person.

In our typology, Category 1 societies can only be egalitarian and collectivistic because they are relatively simple, whereas the hierarchical-collectivistic nature of Category 2 societies is partly due to their larger complexity. Finally, it is not possible to understand the growth of modern individualistic and egalitarian tendencies without appreciating how Western countries have transformed into extremely complex societies.

Yet, there are still other cultural aspects that differentiate our three categories of societies, suggesting that even three cultural dimensions are insufficient to characterize them. Most importantly, our Category 1 society is not only simple, egalitarian, and collectivistic; it is also based on a strong activation of the C system due to kinship or family relationships. This would imply that it may not be simplicity per se that is responsible for relatively inclusionary responses to, for example, disabled persons in these societies (Scheer & Groce, 1988; Whyte & Ingstad, 1995). In particular, these societies should not only be flexible in allowing the deviant individual to play different roles, but also adopt a relatively caring or supportive attitude that is associated with relatively low levels of irritation about incomplete reciprocity or cooperation (see below). Furthermore, as may already be clear, complexity does not necessarily imply more social exclusion of the disabled because, together with welfare programs organized by the state, it may create greater tolerance. Finally, egalitarianism in the case of modern Category 3 societies is accomplished in different ways from egalitarian tendencies in Category 1 societies. In sum, because many cultural variables seem to be intrinsically related, we prefer to analyze cultural influences on social control in terms of three categories of qualitatively different types of society that can be derived using an evolutionary perspective on the origin and development of human societies.

Our approach is also generally consistent with the emphasis that cross-cultural psychology places on values as mediators of the influence of cultural dimensions on social behavior. In general, it may be argued that structural and temporary features of a society cause some motivational systems in the FF-C network to be more frequently and easily activated than others. Consequently, individuals living in a particular society will start to value the states of affairs and policies that are congruent with these motivational systems, and reject those that are inconsistent. For example, societies that tend to respond fearfully to deviance because of temporary (e.g., famine, plague, or war) or more structural factors such as a hierarchical organization associated with mutual suspicion and power struggles, will highly value security, stability, and conformity, whereas societies in which the FF system is less, and C more frequently, activated will highly value care for the needy members of society and mutual trust and support. Importantly, the activation of motivational systems and the functioning of values should be seen as a reciprocal process. That is, values not only originate from frequently activated motivational systems, they may also help to activate these systems in turn in different segments of society. For example, where power relationships are seen as quite natural and associated with particular values, such values will be shared and translated into behavior in the family, professional associations, and political organizations, so that people not only learn the same values and norms in a wide variety of social situations but also follow them as guidelines for their behavior.

Interestingly, a more detailed look shows that the activation patterns of the FF-C network that we consider characteristic for the different categories of societies can be readily translated into the values that have been proposed by Schwartz (Schwartz, 1992; Schwartz & Bardi, 2001), and which we discussed in the previous chapter. For example, in Triandis' (1996) view, egalitarian-collectivistic societies are characterized by Schwartz' benevolence or altruism directed at individuals in one's immediate social environment (typical for small Category 1 societies), whereas more individualistic-egalitarian societies are associated with Schwartz' universalism or altruism and care directed at people in general (typical for large Category 3 societies). As shown in greater detail below, we believe that the difference between benevolence and universalism adequately describes how Category 3 societies, in contrast to Category 1 societies, engage in a care-based but impersonalized form of social control that is crucial for tolerance but which prevents individuals from engaging in repair processes. Furthermore, Triandis associates hierarchically-collectivistic Category 2 societies with Schwartz' value pattern of security, tradition, and conformity. Although Triandis associates hierarchical-*individualistic* societies (e.g., the USA) with a value pattern of achievement, competition, and hedonism, we believe this pattern to be characteristic for all modern Western societies. Yet, we agree that the less individualistic European welfare states, in particular, are associated with greater universalism.[1]

To conclude, it can be argued that the hierarchical-egalitarian and the collectivism-individualism dimensions influence responses to deviance through their association with activation patterns of the FF-C network, which some authors prefer to describe in terms of values or other individual differences. Yet, we assume that these value patterns are crucially dependent on basic motivational mechanisms and the specific social conditions under which they are activated.

In the next two sections, we will examine the hypothesis that, due to a relatively strong activation of the C system and weak activation of the FF system, Category 1 and 3 societies respond with less stigmatization and hostility toward deviance than Category 2 societies that are generally associated with an opposite input-output pattern of the FF-C network, namely strong activation of the FF system and weak activation of the C system. However, in Category 1 societies, this tends to result in true integration of deviant individuals, whereas in Category 3 societies, tolerance, formal kindness, and lack of personal involvement seem to be the best deviant individuals (when they are not family members) can hope for. Furthermore, within Category 3 societies we hypothesize considerable differences between extremely and more moderately individualistic societies, with the former showing some resemblance with Category 2 societies (e.g., an aggressive and blaming attitude, subscribing to conservative values).

The next section discusses these hypothesized differences in social control primarily in a qualitative way. After a subsequent section has presented a quantitative assessment of these hypotheses, we address two remaining issues. First, we illustrate that cultural differences in responding to deviance are also dependent on the particular meanings that specific deviant conditions may have in light of prevalent value and belief systems. Second, we also discuss the influence of relatively temporary social and economic conditions on responding to deviance that may, for example, result in scapegoating.

## 6.3 A qualitative analysis of cultural and historical differences in responding to deviance

We now discuss in some detail the psychological characteristics of responding to deviance in the three categories of societies. We are especially interested in how ecological, economic, and social-organizational features of these societies are responsible for particular input-output patterns of our FF-C network (together with their distinctive value profiles), and how these patterns, in turn, explain the prevalent types of social control in these societies. For several reasons, we will pay relatively more attention to Category 1 societies. First, these societies best reveal the mechanisms of social control that would have been adaptive in our evolutionary past (cf. Chapter 2). Second, understanding how these societies manage to combine social control with the prevention of stigmatization will be especially important when we address stigma-reduction strategies in Chapter 9. As discussed in that chapter, an implicit assumption underlying interventions to reduce stigmatization through "contact" between deviant and non-deviant individuals is that interpersonal relationships without stigmatization would be characterized by tolerance or unconditional acceptance of individuals with deviant conditions or attributes. In order to critically evaluate this assumption, it is important to gain a realistic understanding of the conditions under which social control in relationships or small groups is possible without people engaging in stigmatization. As will become clear, it is neither warranted to associate Category 1 societies such as hunter-gatherer societies with the inhuman and cruel stigmatization that some authors have attributed to them, nor with the more romantic and unconditional kindness thought by others to be characteristic for them.

## Category 1 societies

We argue that Category 1 societies that combine egalitarian and collectivistic values typically engage in repair processes when confronted with deviance, and that this is made possible through a relatively strong activation of the C system and a relatively weak activation of the FF system. Specifically, through a strong activation of the C system, people in these societies are both relatively reluctant to engage in active deviance and to respond to the deviance of others with strong aggression inhibition. In addition, people's fear responses to the active elements of deviance are buffered through the stress-reducing influence of social support and cohesion. Furthermore, people's care for those with passive deviant conditions tend to be practical in outlook and different in quality from more fearful or self-focused patterns of distress or pity that we might find in other societies. We believe that the specific ecological aspects and features of social organization of small groups of genetically-related hunter-gatherers are the ideal basis for such a pattern of activation and output of the FF-C network and its associated values. We base the characterization of these simple and collectivistic societies on reviews by Boehm (1999), Fábrega (1997), Johnson and Earle (1987), Kelly (1995), Knauft (1991), Roberts (1979), and chapters in Lee and DeVore (1968).

First, consider the different factors that may be responsible for a generally low activation of the FF system in these societies. A hunter-gatherer way of living can be characterized as an immediate return economy with little food storage, absence of landownership, and a lifestyle that has been described as relatively slow, happy, and fatalistic, with little concern about what tomorrow will bring (see Lee & DeVore, 1968). Other factors that prevent activation of jealous, competitive, or aggressive tendencies are the extensive sharing of food and resources among all group members, monogamy (reducing sexual competition among males), absence of dominance hierarchies and formal leaders, a strong egalitarian ethos, and the relative absence of intergroup conflict and war.

Second, a hunter-gatherer way of living also seems responsible for a generally strong activation of the C system which is, according to our approach, an additional reason for a lowered output of the FF system. According to our evolutionary perspective, the C system is most strongly activated by egalitarian relationships among kin-related individuals or family members, and frequent exposure to the most vulnerable ones such as children, females, and the elderly. Indeed, children are clearly present in hunter-gatherer society and tend to be socialized in mixed-sex and mixed-aged groups, and in non-punitive, playful, and supportive ways. A climate of visible care and mutual support would further strengthen nurturance and egalitarian values. This contrasts sharply with the same-sex and authoritarian socialization in more complex hierarchical-collectivistic societies in which boys tend to be prepared for warfare (Knauft, 1991).

Let us now illustrate how this characteristic input-output pattern of the FF-C network may be involved in repair processes in the case of active and passive deviance. If there is one thing on which most ethnographers of hunter-gatherer life tend to agree it is that active deviance within the group is generally responded to in non-aggressive and peaceful ways. The ability to control anger, which in our view is related to the negative influence of the C on the FF system, belongs to one of the most valued moral qualities of group members. Consider the following examples of repair processes. When food is stolen or not shared, people may re-interpret it in terms of "borrowing," gossip about it, or temporarily withdraw attention or ostracize the deviant individual. It is important to stress that, although ostracism (also aptly called "silent death") is frequently seen as equivalent to stigmatization (e.g., Alexander, 1987; Neuberg et al., 2000), it is essentially a non-aggressive and effective social control strategy that strongly motivates group members to conform to group norms and restore harmony (see Boehm, 1999). Indeed, the strategic use of attention withdrawal is also practiced by caring parents in response to deviant behaviors of their children. Furthermore, although it may involve the triggering of shame in the face of a powerful majority that threatens to exclude the deviant individual, it may also induce guilt about previously harming the group (see Chapter 2 on the differences and similarities between shame and guilt). Ostracism may not result in the repair of relationships in larger and complex societies. As groups increase in size and increasingly consist of unrelated individuals, and deviance cannot be changed easily (e.g., in the case of mental disabilities or abnormal physical appearance), or is associated with more benefits than costs (e.g., when crimes are difficult to detect), ostracism and public shaming may have the adverse effects of humiliating and isolating deviant individuals, making their behavior even less controllable.

Other non-aggressive and non-escalating modes of conflict resolution known in hunter-gatherers include leaving the group for another group (e.g., when a murderer is faced with revenging actions of the family of the victim), material compensation, use of mediators who may jokingly divert attention away or explicitly try to settle conflicts, and the offering of apologies and receiving forgiveness (Boehm, 1999; Horwitz, 1990; Roberts, 1979). Yet, it should not be forgotten that very serious offenses that threaten the whole community (e.g., serial killings) may motivate the group to decide to execute the deviant individual. However, Knauft (1991) has noted that attempts to physically punish others in hunter-gatherer societies are relatively uncommon and appear unintentional, unpracticed, impulsive, and clumsy.

The consequences of social control motivated by the C system and exercised through face-to-face social control (cf. Campbell, 1982), would be that the actual occurrence of active deviance would be relatively rare, further decreasing input to the FF system. This kind of social control also seems to make Type 4 deviance or social parasitism or laziness less likely. Unsurprisingly, given the evolutionary importance of sex and its strong motivational implications, active deviance based on sex such as jealous behavior, rape, and adultery remain a major reason for extreme punishments of males and females in both egalitarian and hierarchical societies (see Knauft, 1991, who also mentions that strong aggression inhibition may go together with individuals running amok once in a while).

The most important type of deviance in simple egalitarian-collectivistic societies seems to be uncontrollable-passive deviance; the occurrence of unpredictable injuries and illnesses due to predators, hunting accidents, zoonotic infections with parasites (from plants or animals to humans), a wide variety of skin diseases, and different kinds of fever. Epidemic viral diseases (plagues) due to person-to-person infections, and so-called "diseases of civilization" (e.g., chronic heart problems, cancer) are probably absent (Fábrega, 1997; Kelly, 1995). Furthermore, death is a normal and public aspect of hunter-gatherer life, especially in light of the usually high child mortality. In general, these acute forms of deviance are both responded to with explicit and mutual care and with a practical and fatalistic outlook on recovery and the usefulness of care. First, note that, unlike in modern individualistic societies, deviant features and behaviors are of great interest to the community and are explicitly attended to and gossiped about. Yet, this "discrimination" is aimed at exploring possibilities for integrating the individual associated with these deviant aspects into the community rather than excluding him or her. For example, a study of the Kenya Maasai shows that variations in physical condition are explicitly used to describe individual group members without derogatory undertones, hence suggesting a general acceptance of differences (Talle, 1995). Second, the healing of illnesses is something that is of concern to the entire group. Fábrega (1997) mentions different examples of groups publicly discussing the causes of illness, engaging in public healing sessions, and constantly relating deviance to an examination of the quality of their interpersonal relationships (for an extensive recent examination of helping the needy in hunter-gatherers, see Sugiyama, 2004). Compare these responses with modern individualistic societies in which public attention to deviant physical features is considered highly inappropriate because it is primarily seen as hurtful. Third, group members consider themselves to be relatively helpless in face of the dangerous forces of nature, thereby not attributing personal control for illnesses and misfortune but supporting each other in coping with this environment. This was nicely illustrated by Robarchek and Robarchek (1998) for the Semai, a hunter-gatherer society in Malaysia, and reminds us of the importance of "attachment security" in reducing fearful responses to disabled persons (Mikulincer *et al.*, 2001, see Chapter 4).[2]

A final characteristic aspect of responding to passive deviance in simple collectivistic societies is its practical (and seemingly cold) outlook. The acute nature of illnesses and injuries invites a practical response to healing focused on concrete and direct relief from suffering, which is not associated with elaborate expectations or theories about their seriousness, origin, or chances for recovery (Fábrega, 1997). Brief observations may suggest that the discontinuation of nurturance and abandonment are motivated by selfish motives while in fact they may be based on activated care. As discussed below, a realistic assessment of the likelihood that care and help will be useful has altruistic implications as care may be re-invested in other individuals with higher chances of healing and surviving.

While we know a great deal about cultural explanations and healing practices with respect to acute illnesses and injuries in Category 1 societies, we know relatively little about social responses to more permanent disabling conditions which pose greater demands on the caring resources of a community and may more easily result in social exclusion (cf. Edgerton, 1970; Scheer & Groce, 1988). Two important

German exceptions to the scarcity of studies on responding to disability in simple societies (Koty, 1934; Neubert & Cloerkes, 2001), and a number of more recent studies of social integration of disabled persons in simple societies (Ingstad & Whyte, 1995; Jenkins, 1998) suggest that social responses to illnesses and injuries that cannot be cured and hence result in permanent disability may be determined by tolerance for incomplete reciprocity, based on a strongly activated C system.

Small egalitarian and collectivistic societies may allow disabled persons considerable latitude for compensating their limitations not only because these societies are economically simple and therefore make it possible for the deviant individual to switch roles, preventing the deviant condition from receiving a master status; but also because their egalitarian values make them respond with patience and care rather than irritation. This makes it likely that even impairments that we tend to consider relatively attention drawing and disabling do not stand out in these kinds of communities, and will not automatically be associated with low expectancies about a person's contributions to the group. For example, while a mobility-impaired or mentally disabled person would not be able to hunt or gather food, he or she may assist in baby sitting, herding, or preparation of meals. A person may not be judged in terms of the deviant condition alone but primarily in terms of his or her attributes that are valuable and useful to the social group. Only more serious cases would be disturbing to the community and may require some form of confinement (Edgerton, 1970; Neubert & Cloerkes, 2001). Whether a physically impaired person is able to compensate for disabling consequences or not, seems to depend more on a complex combination of factors involving the nature of the deviant condition, the person's present coping with the condition and self-reliance, his or her past behavior and present contribution to the group, and social and economic opportunities to contribute in alternative ways to the community, than on general cultural dimensions. Indeed, it has been noted that in many simple societies people have no separate concept for disability due to its limited practical relevance (for further illustrations, see Hanks & Hanks, 1948; Rensel & Howard, 1997; Whyte & Ingstad, 1995). Dependent on the nature of the deviant condition, individuals may also be invited or forced to play exceptional roles, such as shaman or spiritual healer in the case of mental illness or epilepsy, a leader in artistic and ritual practices in the case of homosexuality, or a (harmless and funny) court jester in the case of dwarfism (Benedict, 1935/1961).

A second phenomenon illustrating the role of caring and integrating tendencies in responding to deviance is the ambivalence and uncertainty with which the killing, abandonment, or assisted suicide of disabled or sick loved ones, parents, friends, or other familiar group members is surrounded; a phenomenon that, when incompletely described or primarily in the context of Category 2 societies or temporary economic hardship, may be mistakenly interpreted as evidence for structural stigmatization and exclusion.[3]

In understanding killing or abandonment in egalitarian-collectivistic Category 1 societies, it is first important to distinguish it from the impulsive killing of, or fleeing from, individuals with fear-arousing physical and mental abnormalities that strongly activate the FF system (see Schlosser, 1952, on infanticide of fear-arousing congenital abnormalities). The responses under consideration here, however, are not impulsive but surrounded with considerable ambivalence, uncertainty, and behavioral indecision; perhaps due to the simultaneous activation of the FF and C systems in these kinds of communities. Consider the following examples.

Edgerton (1970, p. 530) reports on a member of the East African Pokot telling about his intention to drown his mentally retarded daughter aged 4: "Two years ago I decided that she was useless. As you can see, she cannot do anything but sit there and eat dirt [feces] and laugh all the time. But when I took her to the river to drown her, she looked up at me and smiled and laughed. I couldn't do it then. So, I took her home and here she is." Also consider cases that suggest that abandonment may not be practiced without reluctance. For example, Woodburn (Woodburn, 1968, p. 91) reports on the response of the nomadic Hadza in Tanzania to a boy who became paralyzed below the waist:

> He was carried for quite a number of camp moves. Then, on one occasion, the people of the camp moved to a site where they had expected to find water and found none. They were perhaps only about four or five miles from water, but they had reached the point at which it had become rather tedious to carry him for the unexpected move when they were rather tired and rather thirsty. So they left him behind with food and water and with his bow and arrows – not that these were of much use to him – and he did not survive. Those who abandoned him included his own mother and certain other close relatives.

Thus the support may have been finally withdrawn because a combination of competing motives fostering selfish behavior passed a certain threshold. However, the paralyzed boy was not left behind in a totally uncaring manner. We have found much more evidence in the Human Relations Area Files for ambivalent abandonment of the elderly or sick among nomadic hunter-gatherers (*www.yale.edu/hraf*; OCM 730, Ona and Chukchee; see also Koty, 1934).

It is of interest to note that the Human Relations Area Files also contain many examples of voluntary death in the case of disability or old age. For example, an observer of a North Asian group of reindeer hunters called the Chukchee noted twenty cases of voluntary death (*www.yale.edu/hraf*; OCM 730, Chukchee) in which a seriously ill or old person asked to be killed. The same observer notes that group members often appear reluctant to fulfil this request and may only succeed in killing the person after several clumsy efforts. Other references to this phenomenon in different groups of Eskimos can be found in Koty (1934) and Kropotkin (1914/1955). We believe that both the request for assisted suicide and the reluctant response to it provide evidence for the strong involvement of the C system, motivating a strong aware- ness of mutual dependency and sense of mutual responsibility in egalitarian-collectivistic societies. As Kropotkin (1914/1955, p. 103) observes: "When a 'savage' feels that he is a burden to his tribe; when every morning his share of food is taken from the mouths of the children ... when every day he has to be carried ... he [says] 'I live other people's life: it is time to retire!'" (the quotation marks around 'savage' are by the author). Finally, note that while infanticide may be directly motivated by activation of the FF system by fear-arousing congenital abnormalities, its function may also be rooted in social decision making based on an activated C system. In particular, under harsh conditions of living, infanticide may ensure that scarce resources go to infants with higher life expectancies.

Interestingly, infanticide may be practiced for entirely different reasons in less egalitarian and strongly violent societies. For example, the Yanomama of South America – a village-level society frequently engaged in warfare with neighboring tribes – practice infanticide because they fear the ridicule that physical abnormalities may invite (*www.yale.edu/hraf*; OCM 730, Yanomama file).

In sum, infanticide, abandonment, or euthanasia, should not be taken as evidence for the absence of a caring attitude in hunter-gatherers. These practices appear to be associated with choices that do not need to be made any more in modern Western societies, that should be seen as a last resort, and that are probably motivated by a deep sense of social responsibility.

To conclude, simple egalitarian-collectivistic societies may engage in social control without stigmatization and with much effort to repair relationships in the case of both active and passive deviance. A dominant caring attitude, primarily combined with some appre- hension of the unknown forces of nature, but buffered by social sup- port, and strong aggression inhibition, may be responsible for this pattern of social control. The deviant individual is attended to and "discriminated" (even in the case of strategic withdrawal of attention or ostracism), required to make his or her deviant state public, and to engage in re-integration.

For practical purposes, it is important to examine to what extent modern conditions of living may still contain elements of Category 1 societies that will promote repair processes and prevent stigmatization. We will return to this question in Chapter 9.

## Category 2 societies

We argue that Category 2 societies that combine hierarchical and collectivistic values typically engage in stigmatization when confronted with deviance, and that this type of social control is motivated by a strong activation of the FF system (especially its flight or fear-producing component) and a weak activation of the C system, resulting in responses that are primarily fearful and/or aggressive with little trace of tenderness, protectiveness, and forgiveness. Consider how such an activation pattern may have been typical for early hierarchically organized but still collectivistic societies. The introduction of agriculture and food storage would have motivated individuals to distribute surplus resources unequally and hence to increase and maintain their reproductive success through a polygamous mating system, dominance hierarchies, and kinship-based dynasties (clearly, polygamy, at least in the powerless majority of Category 2 societies, was soon to be suppressed, e.g., by means of religious prescriptions). Another characteristic of these societies is that, in contrast to the simple egalitarian societies discussed above, child rearing and socialization often took place in same-sex and same-age groups which were isolated from the rest of society, preparing males primarily for a life as warrior and praising violence and courage as desirable masculine attributes (Knauft, 1991). Consequently, in these societies, children were less encountered in the context of egalitarian relationships and also less available as triggering stimuli for the C system.

As in Category 1 societies, responding to deviance in Category 2 societies is a function of the activation of motivational systems and their associated values both by factors unrelated to deviance and by the nature and prevalence of particular deviant conditions. As argued in Chapter 2, in the context of dominance relationships, deviant behavior appears opportunistic and unpredictable, and is punished in such a visible, shameful, and severe way that others will be deterred from engaging in the same behavior. In addition, the dominated public was often actively involved in venting its aggression during the public punishments and torturing of criminals and others who were believed to threaten the power of the rulers. Thus a general climate of fear would be established which would be further enhanced by an enormous increase in passive deviant conditions in the form of infectious and debilitating illnesses due to the poor hygiene of villages and cities; illnesses that were largely absent in simple egalitarian-collectivistic societies (Fábrega, 1997). As if this were not enough, famine and war among villages and early states would further contribute to activation of the FF system. To complete the picture of input stimuli to the FF system, imagine the large and heterogeneous group of outcasts or vagrants, rejected by their own family or group (out of fear, shame or economic burden), mostly living on begging, wandering between the villages and cities, and consisting of poor, disabled, and sick individuals, as well as active deviants such as unoccupied soldiers, thieves and heretics (Le Goff, 1984/1987; Moore, 1987). It is not difficult to imagine how threatening this group must have appeared to "law-abiding" and relatively well-to-do citizens behind their fortified dwellings.

The literature on social control in the European Middle Ages provides ample evidence that social responses to deviance were primarily motivated by the FF system and hence resulted in stigmatization (for extensive descriptions of public torture, ridicule, execution, and labeling, see, for example, Foucault, 1975/1977; Le Goff, 1984/1987; Moore, 1987). For purposes of identification by the authorities and the rest of the community, criminals might be stigmatized by branding or earboring, heretics by yellow crosses, and Jews by stars or yellow circles, often together with more explicit announcements of their status; other badges were invented for prostitutes, hangmen, and lepers, as were many different insulting nicknames (Jutte, 1994). These stigmas in turn were used without hesitance by courts of law to establish the guilt of criminal suspects (cf. Horwitz, 1990).

Social exclusion created the new problem of how to control the heterogeneous group of outcasts created by this system. This problem was answered by further labeling for purposes of identification and differentiation. For example, Jutte (1994) illustrates how the authorities of many late medieval cities tried to distinguish by means of clothing and badges the "worthy" from the "unworthy" poor, the latter not being allowed to beg because of their association with cheating and social parasitism (see also the multiple examples in Vanhemelryck, 2004, of how professional beggars in medieval Flanders, indeed, may have skillfully faked various disabilities in order to receive alms). In addition, we see the appearance of different kinds of "correction centers" (e.g., Jutte, 1994) in which the large group of "masterless men" could be confined, reformed, or placed under long-term surveillance.

As noted, Category 2 societies are also associated with an enormous increase in passive deviance in the form of infectious and debilitating illnesses due to the poor hygiene of villages and cities (Fábrega, 1997). If there is one thing that distinguishes the image of deviance in these kinds of societies from that in the other two categories of societies, it is their diffuse and threatening character, combining both an expectancy of evil deeds with a terrifying, "crooked" and "impure" physical appearance.[4]

Anyone studying the literature on hierarchical-collectivistic societies which could, for example, be found during the European Middle Ages, will be impressed by the strong influence of religion on virtually every aspect of social life. However, how religion is related to social control and stigmatization appears to be a complex matter. For our approach, it is especially interesting to explore briefly the roles of the FF and C system in mediating the influence of religion. These roles are especially evident in the manner in which religion, used by those in power as an instrument of social control, motivates people to prevent deviant behavior and stick to the rules. First, by means of an elaborate set of stories, prescriptions, and rituals, religion induces complete obedience to a Deity and his representatives or priests on earth. Better than any actual ruler, an omnipresent, omnipotent, and omniscient God is highly effective in controlling deviant behavior by letting individuals constantly feel ashamed or guilty about their basic (or "original") and less basic sins, fearfully anticipate an afterlife with eternal punishment for selfish behavior, or eternal reward for an unselfish and restrained life on earth. How convenient for those in power to claim the exclusive interpretation of God's prescriptions and his exclusive support (for a discussion, see Raven, 1999). Second, in addition to inducing fearful obedience, and as noted especially by Campbell (1975), by preaching unselfish behavior and altruism (e.g., turning the other cheek, helping needy others) and clearly defining what is selfish (e.g., stinginess, greed, gluttony, envy, theft, lust, promiscuity, anger, rage, dishonesty, and pride), religion serves to curb the genetic selfishness of, and stimulate harmony and cooperation among, individuals of large and complex social groups. In combination, obedience to authorities (involving the FF system) and altruistic tendencies (involving the C system) may promote stability in large and complex hierarchical systems.

While the usefulness of religion as an instrument of social control for those in power seems clear, the implications of religion for social responses to deviance are less clearcut. On the one hand, we find suggestions in the Bible for the required negative or FF-based response to specific deviant conditions such as homosexuality and heretic attempts to spread doubt on the validity of religious beliefs (cf. Moore, 1987). Yet, some of these conditions were supposed to be responded to in both negative and positive ways. For example, the Bible warns that "If you do not carefully follow His commands and decrees ... all these curses will come upon you and overtake you: the Lord will afflict you with madness, blindness, and confusion of mind. At midday, you will grope around like a blind man in the dark" (Deuteronomy 28: 15, 28–29). It seems likely that seeing disability as God's punishment makes it easier to adopt a disapproving and perhaps stigmatizing attitude toward illnesses and disabilities in general. On the other hand, the same Bible encouraged people to show consideration and compassion: "Thou shalt not curse the deaf nor put a stumbling block before the blind" (Leviticus 19:14); " ... I command you to be openhanded toward your brothers and toward the poor and needy in your land" (Deuteronomy 15: 11). These prescriptions may have helped the institutionalization of charity and almsgiving to the poor and needy by the rich, and the building of "hospitals" (cf. Jutte, 1994). In sum, although the effects of religion on the prevention of, and response to, deviance seem to be mediated by activity of the FF and C system, the relative influence of these systems in social control is not entirely clear.

We believe that many current and developing non-Western societies also qualify as hierarchical-collectivistic Category 2 societies. Here too we often find a mosaic of multiple social groups tied together in a hierarchical social organization that still primarily engages in agriculture, with considerable overpopulation and poverty. An increasing number of studies indicate that in these societies different chronic illnesses and disabilities are associated with shame, contempt, and social exclusion in the manner described above. This is, for example, demonstrated for epilepsy in China (Kleinman *et al.*, 1995), schizophrenia in India (Raguram, Raghu, Vounatsou, & Weiss, 2004), physical disability in Hong Kong (Holroyd, 2003), and HIV/AIDS in both Africa and Asia (Aggleton & Warwick, 1997). Further evidence on stigmatization in developing countries is presented below when we systematically compare them with modern Western societies.

To summarize, hierarchical-collectivistic Category 2 societies tend to engage in social control *through* stigmatization. The actual prevalence of crime, poverty, illness, handicap, and vagrancy, and the continuous invention of new forms of deviance (e.g., with the aid of religion) create a diffuse and threatening and perhaps impure or disgusting image of the deviant individual, further generalized by fear of contact and contamination, and associated with defensive hostility. Consequently, in these societies most deviant features and behaviors will be categorized as active deviance and perhaps also as relatively unpredictable and uncontrollable. In addition, the fact that collectivism combines with a hierarchical and conflictual social organization in Category 2 societies may be seen as responsible for the tendency of contemporary collectivistic societies to be quite hostile toward a variety of outgroups and to be (overly) generous when dealing with friends (Triandis, 1989). An interesting question with respect to Category 2 societies that we will address later is to what extent their collectivistic tendencies, which surely motivate mutual care within the family and community, influence help giving to needy strangers. We will argue that, although Category 2 societies may generally stigmatize relatively permanent disabilities, the threshold of giving aid in case of emergencies may be relatively low.

## Category 3 societies

Individualism and egalitarianism often go hand in hand in the modern Western world, and this is because egalitarian and democratic values are highly profitable for individual success in a free-market economy (Riesman *et al.*, 1955). Although certain modern Western societies combine extreme individualism with authoritarian elements and hence a relatively stigmatizing mode of social control, we first concentrate on modern European social democracies that have managed to combine individualism with a truly egalitarian and protective attitude toward deviance and social control. Specifically, it can be argued that in a modern egalitarian and individualistic society, the FF system typically is only weakly activated because of the relative absence of war, power struggles, famine, plagues, and serious health problems, and the generally improved standard of living in comparison with Category 2 societies. Additionally, the C system seems to be relatively strongly activated, as is evidenced by the high value placed on care for the needy and even criminals, the importance of non-punishing and supportive socialization of children, and welfare provisions in general. Interestingly, in modern societies we also witness an enormous increase in pets that probably also serve to both activate and satisfy our caring tendencies (Archer, 1997). Indeed, our general "sensitivity" to the suffering of vulnerable beings in society is best expressed by our moral indignation about the cruel treatment of "innocent" animals.

Importantly, we argue that the C system is not as strongly activated as in the small egalitarian-collectivistic communities discussed earlier, and that it is this relatively moderate level of activation that accounts for the phenomenon of tolerance. Specifically, this moderate level of activation seems to be primarily sustained by the relatively weak activation of the FF system, which is thereby prevented from inhibiting the output of the C system, and relatively abstract and impersonal *norms* prescribing to behave in egalitarian and protective ways to people *in general* (aptly termed *universalism* by Schwartz and Triandis; see above). Furthermore, as social control is largely taken over by formal institutions (e.g., the police, health care centers), taking it out of the hands of citizens, individuals in these societies are prevented from being exposed to concrete evidence of passive deviance such as illness and need states. This contrasts with small egalitarian-collectivistic Category 1 communities in which social control is mainly of an informal or face-to-face character and people are exposed to the salient stimuli that have been originally "designed" by evolution to trigger caring tendencies (see Chapter 2). Given the relatively weaker activation of the C system in modern egalitarian societies, it can be expected that, due to an equally moderate level of fear and aggression, the resulting motivational state in response to deviance is rather ambivalent and fragile, easily directed in opposing ways when conditions change. Indeed, as was abundantly demonstrated in previous chapters, tolerance in contemporary Western societies is characterized by a general willingness to behave kindly toward individuals associated with deviance, accompanied with tenseness and akwardness during everyday interaction, efforts to suppress negative feelings, and rather extreme negative or positive responses to particular behaviors and in certain situations. Thus, as argued in Chapter 1, tolerance is not the opposite of intolerance, and does not imply social acceptance in close interpersonal relationships. Nevertheless, deviant individuals who are tolerated in Category 3 societies may be "better off" than in hierarchically organized Category 2 societies.

We argue that relatively the most salient type of deviance in Category 3 society is Type 4 or controllable-passive deviance (e.g., social parasitism/laziness), rather than the three other types of deviance. As illustrated in Chapters 2 and 3, a wide variety of deviant conditions are assigned to this category, such as being overweight, homelessness, incomplete reciprocity, poverty, and low socio-economic status in general; all having in common that individuals associated with these conditions arouse some care and receive some formal assistance, but are incapable or unmotivated to leave their dependent role, thereby also arousing some aggression and disrespect. This is not only because in these societies people tend to "medicalize" active deviance such as behavioral problems and crime (Conrad, 1975) and transform it into passive deviance; but also because individuals associated with Type 4 deviance are often encouraged to stay dependent (Sennett, 2003) and a complex society makes it relatively easy to cheat and stay longer on different forms of welfare than actually necessary.

Furthermore, advances in medical science are responsible for the survival of an increasing number of individuals with typical "illnesses of civilization" and of old age (e.g., cancer, heart problems, diabetes), in addition to a wide variety of other treated or partially treated physical and mental illnesses or disabilities. As these individuals are required to re-integrate into society and be rehabilitated, they can be increasingly encountered in everyday situations. Several developments help to see these individuals not merely as passive and needy but also as being themselves in control of their deviant status (i.e., Type 4 deviance), resulting in considerable ambivalence, blame, and interactional tension noted above. First, epidemiology in combination with health education allows us to see illness increasingly as being caused by behavior, hence as preventable by sticking to the behavioral guidelines of health educators. For example, lung cancer, obesity, diabetis, or cardiovascular diseases, may be increasingly attributed to a failure to behave in responsible ways (e.g., stop smoking, exercise, dieting). Second, integration of chronically ill, handicapped, or elderly persons in society who cope well with their condition creates considerable ambivalence with respect to the true nature of their deviant condition and their real dependency and autonomy. They are both dependent and may demand help and special treatment from others; *and* show themselves as increasingly independent when demanding equal treatment on, for example, the job market, and criticize special attention to their deviant condition (which is considered discriminating). As was noted in Chapter 3, although good coping with illness and disability are appreciated by others, assertive behavior by deviant individuals is not welcomed (in Chapter 9 we argue that a complete denial of dependency and "empowerment" may not work out well for disabled persons in an egalitarian and caring society).

As noted above, some countries belonging to Category 3 societies can be characterized as extremely individualistic, resulting in punitive or law-and-order attitudes or conservative values. In a later section of this chapter, we will test the hypothesis that the most individualistic societies among the modern Western ones such as the USA, will respond with more aggression to deviance than the European social democracies; especially when it concerns deviance that is seen as controllable. While these countries do not formally have a hierarchical social and political organization and value democracy, they tend to subscribe to Category 2 strategies of social control. Specifically, countries like the USA are characterized by a unique combination of, on the one hand, extreme modernity, individualism, and competitiveness, and on the other hand, adherence to authoritarian values associated with religion, conservatism, nationalism, and militarism (Inglehart & Baker, 2000).

How this value pattern translates into social control can be seen from the death penalty for criminals in the USA (to a limited extent a public affair, as is the case in truly hierarchically organized Category 2 societies like medieval Europe or contempory China), frequent sentencing with life imprisonment, and stigmatizing forms of rehabilitation and probation. There is also much evidence that USA judges increasingly apply public shaming in their sentencing. For example, they may order a perpetrator to wear a T-shirt announcing the particular norm violation committed or to place ads making similar announcements (for examples and discussions, see Kahan & Posner, 1999). In addition, it seems as if Type 4 deviance (e.g., poverty, being on welfare) in this society is associated with so much personal responsibility that it is treated as criminality. We also hypothesize, however, that despite these relatively aggressive reactions to deviance, extremely individualistic societies can be considered tolerant in comparison to contemporary developing countries.[5]

Let us finally pay attention to the considerable variation that a complex individualistic and modern society allows in individualistic tendencies and consequently in responding to deviance; not only across individuals (see Chapter 5) but also across different geographic areas and settings. Understanding this variation is especially important when it comes to developing effective interventions for influencing stigmatizing responses to deviance, as we will show in Chapter 9. First, note that the tolerance that we associate particularly with modern and individualistic Western societies seems more characteristic for large cities than for rural areas within these societies. For example, Wilson (1985) showed that in the USA, social acceptance of such groups as atheists, communists, and homosexuals increased as size of community increased. In addition, he was able to demonstrate that migration from rural to urban areas, but not in the opposite direction, increased tolerance, leaving him to speculate that frequent encounters with alien ways of life is an important factor in increasing tolerance. Furthermore, a German study of rural-urban differences in responding to psychiatric problems (Angermeyer, Beck, Dietrich, & Holzinger, 2004) suggests that, while the frequency of experienced stigmatization did not differ, patients with schizophrenia and depression anticipated more stigmatization when living in a small town than in a city.[6] Perhaps it is by inducing these expectations that social control in rural communities is so effective that the expression of deviant behavior is suppressed effectively, precluding experiencing the actual occurrence of negative community responses.

On the other hand, we also know from a meta-analysis (Steblay, 1987) that in the case of acute need states, individuals are more likely to be helped in rural than urban areas. In other words, rural communities seem to engage in a form of social control that is similar to hierarchically organized or authoritarian collectivistic societies. They show a strong orientation to interpersonal relationships and a readiness to help and support each other, yet their pressure to conform may easily result in stigmatizing or exclusionary responses to those who pose a threat because of their refusal or inability to conform. In contrast, life in the big city is characterized by little informal social control and much tolerance for variation in behavior and appearance (see also Horwitz, 1990). Perhaps an additional factor explaining differences in social control between rural and urban areas is educational level (see Chapter 5).

Another reason for variation in social control in modern Category 3 societies is the relative isolation of different social settings with their own characteristic kind of social control. For example, while families or certain institutions specializing in care may engage in long-term asymmetrical and care-based relationships with chronically ill or disabled individuals, this lack of reciprocity may be considered highly undesirable in work settings or many intergroup relations.

## 6.4 A quantitative analysis of differences in responding to deviance across contemporary Western and non-Western societies

In the previous section, we primarily used ethnographic and historical materials to describe qualitative differences in responding to deviance across different categories of societies, making it difficult to directly compare responses to deviance across different societies. In this section, we re-analyze and re-interpret several recent studies in which different categories of societies are more systematically compared in terms of the same psychological response measures. As will become apparent, these studies primarily permit a comparison between Category 2 and 3 societies, and within the latter category, a comparison between typical welfare states such as European social democracies and extremely individualistic and competitive countries such as the USA. As far as the data permit, we will test the following hypotheses. First, as suggested by the previous qualitative analysis, Category 2 societies will respond with more rejection or stigmatization to both active and passive deviance than Category 3 societies. Unfortunately, with a few exceptions, the collectivistic societies that have been studied are usually developing or third world countries with a hierarchical orientation. To our knowledge, no systematic attempts have been made to compare the responses to deviance in these societies with those in small communities that we see as truly representing Category 1 societies. Second, as proposed in Chapter 2, there will be a strong main effect of type of deviance with the more active forms of deviance being more socially rejected than the more passive forms; and within passive deviant conditions, controllable conditions are more rejected than uncontrollable ones.

In different waves of representative national surveys on all six continents, the World Values Survey (WVS) has sampled information about people's values, beliefs, and attitudes with respect to a wide variety of topics through face-to-face interviews. Its results are available to the scientific community for analysis via tables of means (Inglehart, Basanez, & Moreno, 1998), and the world wide web (*http://nds. umdl.umich.edu*). Because the WVS includes questions about responses to six deviant conditions, it offers a unique opportunity to examine cross-cultural differences in social control and stigmatization, although it should be realized that the six deviant conditions are primarily active in nature and do not include explicit descriptions of passive disabilities. To our knowledge, information about responses to deviance in the WVS data have not yet been examined in a systematic way by other research ers.[7] In our analysis we will use data that have been sampled during the 1990–91 and 1995–98 waves (for a similar choice, see Inglehart & Baker, 2000), but for reasons mentioned (see Footnote 7), we excluded data from the ex-communist countries, and from several regional sur veys within countries. For reasons that become apparent below, we additionally excluded Ireland (which cannot be clearly classified as English speaking or European) and South Africa (which cannot be clearly classified as African, English speaking, or European). Thus our sample consists of the data that have been sampled once or twice in 38 countries during two waves, with a total of about 84,000 respondents. We will primarily use countries as units of analysis or "cases." The mean scores for these countries were computed with the statistical program and data made available on the website of the World Values Survey (*http://nds.umdl.umich.edu*), after which we further analyzed them with SPSS. In order to code the countries in terms of collectivism-individualism, we used the 10-point scale proposed by Triandis (see Suh, Diener, Oishi, & Triandis, 1998). For only a few Latin American countries we had to estimate the score by looking at the values for other countries in the same cultural region and (when possible) by using Hofstede's (2001) coding. The countries and their score on the collectivism-individualism dimension can be found in Figure 6.1.

Our main variable of interest is the extent to which respondents reacted negatively towards individuals with different deviant conditions. The WVS enabled us to examine this by providing respondents with a card on which different groups were described and asking respondents to "sort out any that you would not like to have as neighbors" (see V51–V60 in the WVS codebook). The following six deviant

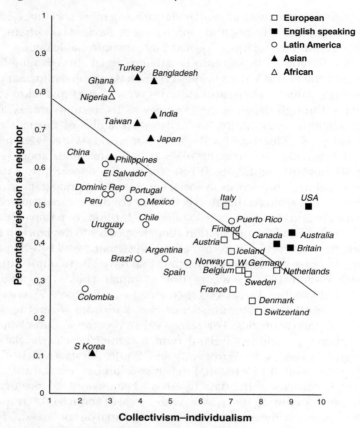

**Figure 6.1** Combined rejection scores for the six deviant conditions (based on data from the World Values Survey).

groups were included: people with a criminal record, heavy drinkers, mentally unstable people, people with AIDS, drug addicts, and homosexuals. In our view, these conditions primarily contain active elements, although the label "mentally unstable" may partially refer to passive aspects (e.g., depression) and AIDS may be seen both in terms of threatening contagion, and illness and dependency. Additional groups included in the question were: people with a different race, political extremist, Muslims (in Non-West-European countries, the interviewer was allowed to test for alternative small but salient minority groups), and immigrants/foreign workers. Although all these groups may have different meanings in different societies, we decided to use the latter category as a baseline condition with mildly deviant elements.

Figure 6.1 shows that rejection of the deviant conditions (taking the mean percentage of all six deviant conditons), decreases as individualism increases ($r = -0.44$, $p < 0.01$).[8] Figure 6.1 also indicates that differences in collectivism-individualism are mainly due to the large difference between Western and non-Western countries, with less differences on this variable within these two categories. Furthermore, also taking account of social rejection, four clusters of countries can be distinguished: Asian and African countries respond the most, non-English speaking European countries the least, negatively toward the six deviant conditions, while Latin American and English speaking countries occupy a middle position (Inglehart and Baker (2000) consider the latter three categories as large and distinct "cultural regions"). Although we did not have particular predictions regarding Latin American countries, we will use these four cultural categories in our further analyses (although Japan and Taiwan are clear exceptions to the large category of relatively poor and developing African and Asian societies, the results are not influenced by excluding them from the analyses). This will also allow us to compare within Category 3 societies the extremely individualistic, English speaking countries with the less individualistic, European countries.

In order to examine how deviant condition interacts with cultural category, we performed an analysis of variance with cultural category as a "between-subjects" (four levels) and deviant condition as a "within-subjects" variable (seven levels). We left out South Korea. This resulted in a strong main effect of deviant condition, $F(6, 192) = 139.07$, $p < 0.001$, revealing the strongest rejection of a drug addict ($M = 0.69$), alcoholic ($M = 0.58$), and criminal ($M = 0.52$), and less rejection of a homosexual ($M = 0.42$), person with AIDS ($M = 0.37$), and mentally unstable person ($M = 0.38$). Immigrants were the least rejected as neighbors ($M = 0.14$). Consistent with our construction of the variable, we also obtained a strong main effect for cultural category, $F(3, 32) = 42.71$, $p < 0.001$, showing that the African/Asian countries responded the most ($M = 0.67$), and the European countries ($M = 0.31$) the least, negatively. Latin American ($M = 0.41$) and English speaking countries ($M = 0.38$) responded about equally negatively. The size of the difference in rejection between the Asian/African and European countries in particular is remarkable (except between the Latin American and English speaking countries, all differences among the four cultural regions are significant; all $ts > 3.01$, all $ps < 0.01$; the difference between European and English speaking countries is marginally significant, $p = 0.078$, and this may be partially due to the small number of cases in the English speaking category). An interaction between cultural category and deviant condition also turned up, $F(18, 192) = 8,61$, $p < 0.001$, and Figure 6.2 may help to interpret its nature.

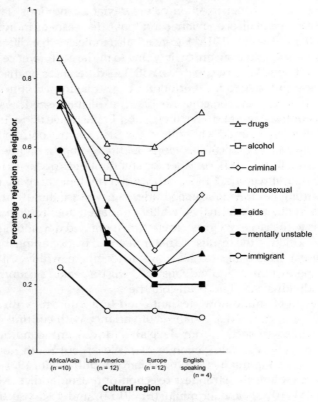

**Figure 6.2** Rejection as neighbor of six deviant groups, compared to responses to immigrants (based on data from the World Values Survey).

First, note that in all four cultural categories, people associated with drug and alcohol addiction are the most negatively responded to. Furthermore, all four cultural categories appear relatively accepting of foreigners in general. Second, Figure 6.2 shows that African and Asian countries not only respond the most negatively to the six deviant conditions, but also tend to lump these conditions together, responding in a similarly negative way to deviant conditions like AIDS, homosexuality, psychiatric problems, and crime. In contrast, European countries respond the least negatively to most of the deviant conditions (including crime), apparently seeing them as similarly non-threatening or passive. In addition, they seem to differentiate more in their response to the various deviant conditions.

Several differences within the two collectivistic and two individualistic cultural categories are important to note. First, the Latin American countries are considerably less negative toward the deviant conditions than the Asian/African countries. In fact, they behave quite similarly as the more hierarchically oriented and individualistic (i.e., English speaking) societies. Perhaps the relatively positive responses of the Latin American countries can be attributed to their so-called *simpatia* culture, a combination of collectivism, Roman Catholic values, a strong value attached to treating others generally kindly, and more broadly defined ingroups than Asian collectivistic cultures (cf. Malloy, Albright, Diaz-Loving, Dong, & Lee, 2004). Within the two individualistic cultural categories, we can also observe several differences in responding to particular deviant conditions. Specifically, the English speaking countries in particular respond more negatively to mental and behavioral problems than the European ones (for crime and mentally unstable, $ps < 0.05$; for alcohol addiction, $p = 0.07$, for drug addiction, $p = 0.11$), whereas homosexuals, persons with AIDS, and immigrants are similarly responded to.

In order to explain in an exploratory fashion the pattern of responses to the six deviant conditions we selected the following items from the WVS: *Personal control* measured by V66 (asking the extent to which respondents feel freedom of choice and control over the way their life turns out; 1: none at all, 10: a great deal); and *Subjective well-being* ("all things considered, how satisfied are you with your life as a whole these days?" 1: dissatisfied, 10: satisfied). In addition, we constructed a measure of *Authoritarianism*, resembling Altemeyer's (1998) conception of this construct, from the items V9 (importance of religion in the respondent's life; 1: very important, 4: not at all important), V24 (the importance of obedience as a quality that children should be encouraged to learn at home; 1: important, 2: not mentioned), V114 (whether greater respect for authority would be a good or bad thing: 1: good, 3: bad), and V190 (how important is God in the respondent's life; 1: not at all, 10: very). After appropriate recoding and standardization, the Cronbach's alpha of this scale appeared to be 0.83. Higher scores on this scale imply greater authoritarianism or conservatism.[9] All scores were transformed into z-scores and submitted to one-way analyses of variance, resulting in significant F-values (all $Fs > 4.30$, all $ps < 0.01$). The patterns of means are shown in Figure 6.3.

First, consider differences between the two categories of collectivistic and two categories of individualistic countries. Contrast coding shows that the collectivistic countries are more authoritarian ($t(34) = 2.88$, $p < 0.01$) and less satisfied ($t(33) = 3.76$, $p < 0.001$) with their lives than the individualistic ones, while both categories do not differ on the personal control measure ($p = 0.76$). Second, among the individualistic countries, the English speaking countries are more authoritarian than

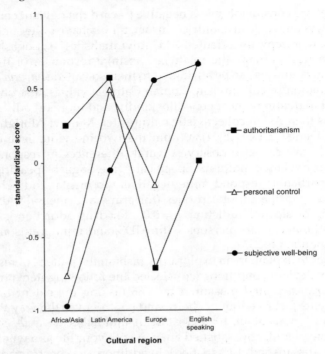

**Figure 6.3** Variables used to explain the rejection patterns shown in Figure 6.2 (based on data from the World Values Survey).

the non-English speaking European ones ($t(34) = 1.69$, $p = 0.10$) but almost as conservative as the Asian/African countries ($p = 0.59$; note that we use the degrees of freedom associated with the total error term). Furthermore, the more hierarchically oriented or English speaking countries also believe more strongly in personal control than the small European ones ($t(34) = 1.61$, $p < 0.12$). Both categories of individualistic countries, however, do not differ in subjective well-being ($p = 0.82$). Third, among the collectivistic countries, the Asian/African countries believe less strongly in personal control ($t(34) = 3.20$, $p < 0.01$) and are less satisfied with their lives ($t(33) = 2.56$, $p < 0.05$) than the Latin American ones. Yet, the two categories of collectivistic countries do not differ in authoritarianism ($p = 0.31$).

We finally examined to see if differences in social rejection of deviant individuals across the four different cultural categories are mediated by one or more of the explanatory variables. First, note that in the total sample of 38 countries, social rejection is significantly related to authoritarianism ($r = 0.38$) and subjective well-being

$(r = -0.67)$. Attribution of personal control is negatively associated with social rejection of deviance $(r = -0.34)$, which is primarily due to African/Asian countries scoring extremely low on personal control (and apparently being fatalistic) and extremely high on social rejection. In a first mediational analysis (Baron & Kenny, 1986), we examined to what extent the influence of the collectivism-individualism dimension on social rejection was accounted for by these three variables. When we regressed percentage rejection on collectivism-individualism, a significant influence of the latter showed up *(Beta* $= -0.56$, $p < 0.001$). When we added authoritarianism and personal control to the regression equation, we obtained some evidence for partial mediation by these variables, with the new Beta for the cultural dimension being $-0.40$ $(p < 0.01)$; for authoritarianism, *Beta* $= 0.29$ $(p = 0.054)$, and for personal control, *Beta* $= -0.36$ $(p < 0.01)$. Interestingly, adding subjective well-being to the equation removed the influence of the above variables $(p > 0.12)$ and showed that subjective well-being was the main explanatory variable *(Beta* $= -0.47$, $p < 0.05$). (We will return to the influence of this factor at the end of this chapter.)

However, an additional analysis suggests that authoritarianism may be somewhat important in mediating the influence of Category 2 vs. 3 society on social rejection. When we regressed percentage rejection on a dummy representing a category of society (with African/Asian countries coded 0 and all Western countries coded 1), the dummy had a significant influence *(Beta* $= -0.92$, $p < 0.001$). (Leaving out the Latin American countries from this analysis seemed reasonable to us because, unexpectedly, it behaved similarly to the English speaking countries and, due to its combination with Roman Catholicism, may have a unique status among the collectivistic countries.) When we added the three explanatory variables to this regression, we obtained some evidence for partial mediation by authoritarianism, with the new Beta for the dummy being $-0.72$ $(p < 0.001)$ and for authoritarianism, Beta $= 0.22$ $(p < 0.01)$; the Betas for the personal control and subjective well-being were non-significant $(p > 0.21)$.

Finally, it was important to explain why the extremely individualistic English speaking countries respond more negatively to deviance than the less individualistic European ones. When we regressed percentage rejection on a dummy variable representing these two cultural categories, the latter had a significant influence on the former *(Beta* $= 0.49$, $p < 0.05$). However, after adding authoritarianism to the regression, the influence of the dummy variable reduced substantially *(Beta* $= 0.23$, $p = 0.41$), while the influence of authoritarianism remained marginally significant *(Beta* $= 0.46$, $p = 0.11$).[10] Similar analyses with personal control and subjective well-being as potential mediators failed to reveal any evidence for mediation. Thus this analysis suggests that social rejection in individualistic countries may be primarily mediated by authoritarian or conservative values.

To conclude, as hypothesized, current collectivistic Category 2 societies, probably also due to their hierarchical nature, respond with greater social rejection to (active) deviant conditions than individualistic societies. Furthermore, African/Asian countries tend to respond in an undifferentiated and hostile manner to all tested deviant conditions (apparently reflecting a bias to respond primarily in terms of a strongly activated FF system), whereas the European countries, in particular, tend to respond in an undifferentiated and relatively friendly manner to the different deviant conditions (apparently reflecting a bias to respond in terms of a stronger activated C system). The more hostile responses of the extremely individualistic Western countries seem to be associated with authoritarian or conservative values.

We were relatively unsuccessful in finding support for the idea that beliefs about personal responsibility mediate the influence of individualism on responding to deviance. However, several other studies may help to fill this gap. For example, Crandall and Martinez (1996) not only found that obesity is more disvalued in an individualistic culture like the USA than a collectivistic culture like Mexico, but also that in the former but not in the latter, evaluation of obesity was strongly negatively related to attributions of responsibility. In a more recent study, Crandall *et al.* (2001) did not find that individualistic cultures responded more negatively to obesity, but that only within the individualistic cultures (USA, Australia, Poland), controllability influenced responses when people evaluated obesity negatively (for additional support, see Cogan, Bhalla, Sefa Dedeh, & Rothblum, 1996). Illustrating that differences between hierarchical-collectivistic societies and individualistic societies may be mediated by egalitarian values and care, a study by Furnham and Murao (2000) found that, consistent with the WVS, British participants viewed people with schizophrenia as less dangerous and abnormal than Japanese participants; and were additionally much more concerned about the rights of these people, such as the right to be released when their behavior is acceptable to society and the right to be treated sympathetically. Moreover, Loftus (2001) found that the increase in liberal values in the USA since 1990 goes together with a greater unwillingness to restrict the civil liberties of homosexuals.

Unfortunately, the WVS does not allow us to examine in greater detail responses to clearly passive deviant conditions such as illnesses and disabilities across different cultures. Two studies, using a quite similar methodology, may provide relevant information on this issue. First, in a study by Westbrook *et al.* (1993), health practitioners from several collectivistic communities in Australia (Chinese, Greek, Arabic, and Southern Italian) as well as from the German and Anglo-Australian community used social distance scales to estimate the attitude of people in their communities toward twenty disabilities. Interestingly, as was the case for relatively active forms of deviance in the WVS, the German community (which was included among the European countries in the WVS) generally responded more favorably than the Anglo-Australian community (an example of an English speaking nation in the WVS), and the latter somewhat more favorably than the four collectivistic communities. Although these differences were significant (the total sample was N = 665), they were small compared to the differences between the different deviant conditions. Specifically, on a 5-point social distance scale (with higher scores indicating greater social approval), the Anglo-Australian community had a mean score of 3.34 for all twenty deviant conditions together, whereas the Chinese (with eleven out of twenty comparisions with the Anglo-Australian community being significant), Greek (ten significant differences), Arabic (eleven significant differences), and Italian communities (five significant differences) had scores of 3.19, 3.15, 3.02, and 3.19 respectively. By comparison, the "main effect" of deviant condition seemed much stronger (unfortunately, no mixed analysis of variance was conducted in which the deviant condition was included as a repeated measure). Specifically, across different communities, relatively passive conditions such as heart disease (M = 4.42), amputed leg or arm (M = 3.94), cancer (M = 3.75) or blindness (M = 3.64) were rated much more positively than relatively active and threatening conditions like cerebral palsy (M = 2.20), mental retardation (M = 1.97), or psychiatric illness (M = 2.01). In this study, AIDS (M = 1.97) also appeared to be treated as active and threatening deviance.

That differences among the studied deviant conditions were relatively independent from cultural group or relatively universal was especially evident from the rank order correlations computed by the authors. The correlations between the ratings in the Anglo-Australian and the other communities were all higher than 0.94. Similarly high rank order correlations were obtained when Westbrook *et al.* (1993) correlated their rankings with those obtained in four studies conducted in the USA. Note that these high levels of cross-cultural agreement may be more strongly influenced by agreements on the relative positions of deviant conditions on the active-passive dimension than on the influence of the controllability dimension. This may be due to a greater social and perhaps evolutionary importance of the former dimension, as well as to the fact that the deviant conditions included in most studies varied less in terms of the latter dimension.

In a replication of Westbrook *et al.*'s study, Saetermoe, Scattone, and Kim (2001) presented Asian-, Latin-, and European-Americans living in Southern California with nineteen disabilities and found that Asian-Americans responded the most negatively to all disabilities, except mental illness (which was the most rejected by all three groups). Interestingly, like in the World Values Survey, Latin or sympatia cultures and Americans responded similarly to the different disabilities.

Using a similar methodology as Westbrook *et al.* (1993), but with a greater variety of active and passive deviant conditions and cultures, Room *et al.* (2001) recently asked key informants from fourteen different countries (with a mean number of fifteen informants per country) to report the degree of social disapproval in their culture for eighteen deviant conditions, using a response scale running from 0 (no social disapproval) to 10 (extreme disapproval). In each country, six informants held jobs in different health professions (e.g., physicians, social workers), three were policy makers, and six had particular disabilities or health conditions themselves or were represented by their caregivers. The authors examined in detail, on a country-by-country level, the similarities and differences in the rank orders of the deviant conditions (see their Table 9, p. 276), and note that, despite some differences, the countries tend to agree on relatively high acceptance of physical conditions (e.g., confined to a wheelchair or being blind) and the relatively high disapproval of conditions like alcohol and drug addiction, criminal record, and HIV.[11]

In order to test our theoretical perspective, we examined Room *et al.*'s data in greater detail by means of analysis of variance.[12] We first constructed scales representing responses to our four categories of deviance. Specifically, we included chronic mental disorder, leprosy, and HIV positivity in the category uncontrollable-active deviance (we left out the conditions dementia and facial disfigurement which are somewhat ambiguous with respect to our typology); alcoholism, drug addiction, and criminal record for burglary in the category controllable-active deviance; wheelchair bound, blindness, inability to read, borderline intelligence, and depression, in the category uncontrollable-passive deviance; and obesity, cannot hold down a job, homeless, dirty and unkempt, and does not take care of children in the category controllable-passive deviance. Second, in a similar way to our re-analysis of the World Values Survey, we treated China, Egypt, Greece, India, Japan, Nigeria, Tunisia and Turkey as examples of hierarchical-collectivistic Category 2 societies (N = 136),

and distinguished two categories of individualistic Category 3 societies, namely the strongly individualistic (and relatively hierarchically
oriented) United Kingdom and Canada (N = 25), and the less individualistic (and more egalitarian) The Netherlands and Luxembourg
(N = 26 ). To allow comparison with our analysis of the WVS, we left
out Spain (the only example of a *simpatia* culture in this study) and the
former communist country Romania.

In order to examine how type of deviance interacts with cultural
category, we performed an analysis of variance with cultural category
as a between-participants (three levels) and type of deviance as two
within-participants variables (active-passive and controllability), each
with two levels. This resulted in strong main effects for active-passive,
$F(1, 184) = 321.07$, $p < 0.001$, and controllability, $F(1, 184) = 110.90$,
$p < 0.001$, revealing stronger disapproval of active (M = 7.36) than passive deviance (M = 4.65), and stronger disapproval of controllable
(M = 7.10) than uncontrollable deviance (M = 4.91). The means for
uncontrollable-active, controllable-active, uncontrollable-passive, and
controllable-passive were 6.72, 8.01, 3.11, and 6.18, respectively, all
differing significantly from one another. Although a main effect of
cultural category, and an interaction between the two deviance dimensions also turned up, these effects were qualified by an interaction
between all three factors, $F(2, 184) = 5.40$, $p < 0.01$. The pattern of
means reveals two noteworthy features. First, for uncontrollable-active
and uncontrollable-passive deviance, the pattern of means of the three
cultural categories were highly similar, with the African/Asian and
English speaking countries equally disapproving of these deviant conditions, yet significantly more so than the European ones. The means
for controllable-active deviance did not differ between the three cultural categories. Second, all three cultural categories differed significantly in their disapproval of controllable-passive deviance, with
African/Asian countries showing the least (M = 5.16) and English
speaking countries the most disapproval (M = 7.42), while the
European countries occupied a middle position (M = 5.96).

In interpreting these findings it should be noted that the methods
used by Room *et al*. (2001) and the WVS differ considerably, with
the latter asking respondents to report on their own reluctance to
have deviant individuals as neighbors, and the former to report on
responses that they, as informants closely involved with health problems, believed to be typical responses for their country or culture.
Perhaps, the latter procedure may result in less differentiation in
responses across different countries, as most informants may have
been generally concerned with stigmatizing tendencies in their society.
This may explain why certain salient differences in responding that

appeared in the WVS did not show up in the study by Room *et al.* (2001). For example, while in the WVS all active deviant conditions such as drug addiction and crime were much more strongly rejected by the African/Asian than English speaking countries, these differences did not appear in the Room *et al.* study. Nevertheless, the WVS and the study by Room *et al.* are similar in showing that the English speaking countries are more negative than the European ones in their response to uncontrollable-active deviance such as mental illness. More importantly, the Room *et al.* study contributes to our understanding of cultural differences in responding to passive deviance. Specifically, we found suggestive evidence indicating that the strongly egalitarian European countries showed the least disapproval of uncontrollable-passive deviance, and controllable-passive deviance was judged more negatively as individualism increased, moving from African/Asian, to European, to English speaking countries.

The above finding of a strong main effect of type of deviance or a universal tendency to respond more negatively to active than passive deviance was also found in several studies conducted by Harper and colleagues (1995). In these studies, children in the USA, Nepal, Antigua (a British colonial island in the Caribbean), Yucatan (Mexico), and from the indigenous Maori of rural and urban New Zealand, were asked to rank pictures of children appearing normal, with a crutch, with a missing hand, or with a facial abnormality in terms of social acceptance (the six studies differed in the inclusion of two additional deviant conditions, namely sitting in a wheelchair and a foot missing, although all also included obesity, which will be discussed below). While the researchers concentrate on cultural differences and do not quantify the similarities, all cultures ranked the four conditions in the order presented above (mean $r = 0.92$), with the exception of Yucatan which placed the crutch at last place, and the facial scar at second (the rural Maori slightly differed from the rest by switching the position of the crutch and the missing hand). This relatively universal ranking seems to indicate that a facial scar was perceived as the most threatening or unattractive (directly followed by a missing extremity), and the use of a crutch as relatively harmless and perhaps vulnerable. Interestingly, when obesity is taken into account, a clear cultural difference does emerge. Specifically, children from all non-Western cultures placed obesity at second place (next to the non-disabled child), whereas in the USA sample, obesity was least accepted (interestingly obesity received a fifth-place ranking by the urban but not rural Maori group, suggesting an influence of modernization in urban areas). The latter finding again supports the view that obesity receives more negative evaluations in individualistic Western than collectivistic non-Western societies.

Also working with children, Crystal, Watanabe, and Chin (1997) studied how children in the USA, Japan, and China responded to vivid descriptions of children with six deviant conditions with a more behavioral character. On the basis of the mean acceptance scores, and showing again a strong influence of the nature of the deviant condition, the six conditions could be ranked in the following way in all three cultures (from most to least accepted): unathletic, learning disabled, withdrawn, poor, aggressive, and mean. However, China formed an exception in reversing the acceptance of the poor and unathletic child, and showing the strongest acceptance of the poor one. Furthermore, consistent with the earlier results, with the exception of the poor child, Chinese children responded the most negatively to all deviant conditions.

Let us finally consider how different cultures respond to acute forms of passive deviance that require immediate helping. We argued that hierarchical-collectivistic or Category 2 cultures are expected to respond in a relatively stigmatizing manner to permanently disabling conditions because being associated with these conditions may imply status loss and an activation of the FF system, which in turn would help to inhibit activation of the C system. However, a collectivistic nature would also imply a readiness to respond with care to the visible need states of others. The question is whether this help is extended only to individuals belonging to one's own family or group, or also to unknown individuals who belong to outgroups.

Findings from a large-scale cross-cultural study on helping behavior in different cultures may be able to find an answer to this question. Levine, Norenzayan, and Philbrick (2001) conducted field experiments in twenty-three large cities around the world to measure how often strangers were helped who were blind (with cane and dark glasses) and standing near a traffic light waiting to cross the road, physically handicapped (walking lamely with metal leg brace) and dropping a pile of magazines a few meters in front of passers-by, or able bodied and simply dropping a pen. Although the authors expected greater helping in collectivistic cultures, they did not find a relation between overall helping rate and collectivism-individualism (the latter scored in the manner we used in the analysis of the WVS), $r = -0.17$. They concluded that only some collectivistic cultures – the typical *sympatia* cultures such as Brazil and Costa Rica – showed more helping than non-*sympatia* cultures. However, in plotting their data, we found that there were four clear outliers among their twenty-three countries that behaved "atypically." Specifically, among the countries that helped least there were four collectivistic countries (Thailand, 61 percent helping; Taiwan, 59 percent; Singapore, 48 percent; and Malaysia,

40 percent). When these countries were removed, the correlation between helping and collectivism-individualism rises to $r(19) = -0.56$, $p < 0.01$.[13] If we additionally drop the ex-communist countries, as was done in our analysis of the WVS, the correlation is even higher, $r(15) = -0.67$, $p < 0.01$. It is important to note that this correlation not only indicates that *sympatia* cultures help more than *non-sympatia* cultures, but also that several Asian collectivistic cultures such as India (83 percent) and China (77 percent) as well as an African one (Malawi, 86 percent) help considerably more than certain individualistic cultures (e.g., Sweden, 72 percent; Netherlands, 54 percent; United States, 45 percent), and even more than certain collectivistic *sympatia* cultures (e.g., Mexico, 76 percent El Salvador, 75 percent). Levine *et al.* also found that helping across cultures was inversely related to a country's economic productivity, but this variable cannot be separated from individualism in this study.

That collectivistic cultures, in spite of their rejecting reactions toward deviance in general, respond with more care to acute forms of passive deviance is also suggested by a study of Miller, Bersoff, and Harwood (1990). These researchers asked adults and children in India and the USA to respond to hypothetical situations in which someone failed to help another person in need, independently varying the seriousness of the need and the agent's relationship with the needy other. Indians appeared to use a much broader and unconditional view of interpersonal moral duties than Americans. That is, Indian judgments of the agent's responsibility and their considerations of the victim's welfare were unaffected by the magnitude of the need state (a life-threatening situation was seen as equally deserving of aid as one involving a moderate or minor need) and by the particular relationship between agent and needy person (whether the latter was the agents' child, best friend, or stranger did not make a difference). In contrast, Americans only judged non-helping in moral terms in the case of a life-threatening situation or in the case of parents responding to the need of their children. Thus for Americans, helping was more a matter of personal choice, context dependent, and less easily triggered.

Together, the results of Levine *et al.* (2001) and Miller *et al.* (1990) suggest that collectivism is associated with a low activation threshold of the C system when needy strangers are encountered. (We should, of course, be aware that in the above studies, collectivism is strongly confounded with a hierarchical social organization and that the latter factor may also be related to helping behavior.) However, permanent need states and disabilities may be easily associated with intergroup hostility, status loss, denigration, and shame, and may not reckon with much compassion. In contrast, in individualistic Western societies, the

C system may not easily be triggered when people can easily avoid individuals with acute need states and can diffuse responsibility for helping. Yet, the C system in these societies may be more easily triggered by vivid exposure and close attention to both temporary and more permanent need states and disabilities. Interestingly, these differences between contemporary collectivistic and individualistic societies resemble the ones found for rural versus urban communities in the modern Western world discussed earlier. That is, in rural areas, readiness to help in the case of acute need states is relatively high compared to helping behavior in urban areas, but tolerance for certain permanent disabilities is lower than in cities.

## 6.5 Idiosyncratic cultural influences and temporary factors in responding to deviance

Until now we have primarily discussed the influence of culture and type of deviance on responding to deviance as if these influences are relatively stable and independent of the specific deviant condition under consideration or individual characteristics of the particular culture (e.g., its particular belief system). We believe that the evidence that we presented strongly supports our view that (a) Category 2 societies such as contemporary developing countries generally respond in a more stigmatizing way to all types of deviance (with the exception of controllable-passive deviance) than Category 3 or modern Western societies, and (b) the social rejection of the different types of deviance follows a universal pattern. Although, to the best of our knowledge, no standardized measures have been used to compare Category 1 with Category 2 and 3 societies, our qualitative analysis gave us reason to suspect that the former category tends to respond in the least stigmatizing way to deviant individuals.

However, several factors may somewhat qualify these general conclusions. First, a particular abnormal condition may receive a rather unique interpretation and response in a particular culture due to the culture's idiosyncratic belief system or conditions of living. Second, rather than by stable cultural features, responses to deviance may be influenced by temporary ecological or economic circumstances. We already came across several examples of the first possibility. For example, the fact that obesity is more negatively responded to in Western than non-Western societies may be partially dependent on the former's greater knowledge about health risks associated with that condition (e.g., heart problems, diabetes), and the latter's worse economic conditions, making a large body size a sign of wealth and potential to share resources. Furthermore, Crystal *et al.* (1997) explain the tendency of

Chinese children to respond more positively to a poor child than children in the USA and Japan in terms of Chinese Communist beliefs about the moral superiority of poor peasants and laborers. These authors propose similar interpretations for the tendency of children in the USA to respond especially negatively when imagining to work together with a child with a learning disability (more than Japanese and Chinese children, American children would value competition in the classroom) and for Japanese children to be especially negative about the unathletic, but positive about the aggressive, child (Japanese culture would attribute a beneficial social role to fighting ability). Consistent with the latter finding, Room *et al.* (2001) found that of all fourteen countries studied, informants reported Japanese society to be the most negative toward wheelchair users and blind people (for comparison, the Japanese were the least negative about an esthetic imperfection such as a facial disfigurement).

Ethnographic and historical sources attest to the influence of culture-specific values and beliefs on responding to a variety of other mental and behavioral conditions. With respect to homosexuality, first note the great variation in responding that can be observed across cultures. For example, Broude and Greene (1976) presented data on a variety of sexual attitudes and practices for a large number of societies. In 21 percent of forty-two societies homosexuality was accepted or ignored, in 12 percent there was no concept of homosexuality, in 14 percent it was ridiculed, scorned, but not punished, in another 12 percent it was mildly disapproved, considered undesirable, but not punished, whereas in 41 percent of the societies it was strongly disapproved and punished. One explanation of this diversity is that the different behavioral manifestations of homosexuality have different cultural meanings and are differently evaluated. For example, according to Herdt (1997) in ancient Greece a man could honorably engage in sexual relations with a boy so long as he remained in the socially dominant or senior position of being the penetrator for phallic pleasure. However, homoerotic relations between adult free citizens were generally ridiculed. Also, the Azande, living in southern Sudan, allowed for age-structured sexual relations between boys and men, but penalized any other form of homosexuality that did not conform to this pattern (Herdt, 1997). In Europe, after a long period of relatively indifferent societal responses, homosexuality suddenly was strongly negatively responded to during the European Middle Ages, due to a combination of increased salience of a specific religious norm defining homosexuality as sinful, and the increased presence of many other threatening deviant groups in society such as lepers, Jews, and heretics (Moore, 1987). As previous chapters have shown, although it is not persecuted anymore, homosexuality continues to arouse ambivalent responses in modern Western societies, that under particular circumstances may grow violent again.

Another elucidating example of a specific cultural meaning of a deviant condition relates to deafness (Winzer, 1997). The Greek philosopher Aristotle viewed speech and hearing as arising from a common site. So he concluded that men who are born deaf are also dumb. Moreover, because he assumed that hearing contributes heavily to intelligence he considered deaf people no better than animals in the forest and unteachable. With these views, accepted without reservation by medical scholars, Aristotle may have influenced the fate of deaf people in Europe for nearly 2,000 years. Only in the eighteenth century did views about deafness change and more positive treatment approaches were followed.

Finally, consider mental illness and epilepsy. Whereas in modern Western society, "crazy" behavior may (despite its frightening aspects) be interpreted as signs of illness and dependency, certain non-Western societies may interpret and value it as evidence for a capacity to communicate with the spiritual world of the ancestors or shamanism (Helman, 1994). In a quantitative study of responses to different disabilities in Ethiopia (Mulatu, 1999), it was found that schizophrenia and epilepsy were strongly associated with ideas about supernatural retributions and that these in turn motivated more negative attitudes.

Despite the clear idiosyncratic influence of cultural values and beliefs, however, we would like to speculate briefly about the importance of objectively present physical features and behaviors that may, because of their universal motivational relevance, constrain the variation in evaluations and beliefs. For example, certain "crazy" behavioral aspects of mental illness (cf. Helman, 1994) predict that most people and cultures will respond with some apprehension to it and, because of the involvement of the flight component of the FF system, consider it Type 1 or uncontrollable-active deviance. Yet, some societies may manage to employ these frightening aspects in the form of shamanism, whereas others consider it dangerous madness to be avoided or contained. Similarly, although the response to deafness may have been influenced by the work of Aristotle, we should not forget the universal stimulus features of the relatively uncontrolled speech behavior of deaf people that may appear weird and unintelligible to normally hearing people, despite knowledge of more accurate biomedical theories and caring attitudes. In this respect it is interesting to note that blindness, a deviant condition that appears relatively harmless, vulnerable, and associated with old age and wisdom (yet, to our knowledge, not linked to any particular theory), usually has received much more tender responses throughout history (Winzer, 1997).

With respect to cultural differences in responding to obesity, we also suspect that the physical appearance of an overweight person (e.g., slow and unbalanced locomotion, easily out of breath) may, in combination with certain ecological factors, constrain the possible interpretations and responses. In poor agricultural societies in which being overweight is rare, this condition may be envied and longed for, as it signals satisfaction and wealth ("does not need to work"), and perhaps the ability to share food with others. However, when obesity is more common and interpreted from a Western and individualistic perspective, emphasizing work and staying healthy, the same image of the overweight person may be associated with illness, unwillingness to work, laziness, and lack of will power. Again, these are not merely arbitrary theories or beliefs, but interpretations that are forced upon perceivers by the particular stimulus configuration of being overweight, in light of motivational systems or concepts that are activated by particular motivationally relevant features of societies or cultures.

As a final example, we speculate that the ambiguous nature of homosexuality (involving the simultaneous presence of masculine and feminine qualities, yet without clear physical dangers or functional limitations attached to the condition) may be partially responsible for the observed cultural variation in responses. For instance, among different nineteenth-century tribes of North American Indians, the combination of feminine and masculine aspects was highly valued as a spiritual go-between between males and females or *Berdache* who dressed in female cloth, often lived with women, and excelled in creative roles (Benedict, 1935/1961). As noted above, homosexual *behavior* was valued in ancient Greece when it was associated with the penetrating activity of a male in the dominant role of teacher *vis à vis* his pupil; and more generally in different cultures as a valuable sign of male dominance. In contrast, the receptive and more feminine side of homosexual behavior is generally not valued in a masculine culture.

Finally we would like to address briefly the role of relatively temporary rather than structural or cultural factors in responding to deviance. A dominant idea, often termed "scapegoating" or "displacement," is that some form of environmental stress due to, for example, famine, plague, economic crisis, natural disaster, or war, activates the motivational systems normally activated by deviant conditions, thus making it easier for the latter to trigger full-blown emotional responses when encountered, and hence for people to "displace" their relatively irrelevant emotions (e.g., Dollard, Miller, Doob, Mowrer, & Sears, 1939; Edgerton, 1970; Frazer, 1922/1993; Koty, 1934). We described the psychological aspects of this process in considerable detail in Chapter 4. Such a view was already espoused long ago. As eloquently expressed by Tertullian, an early Christian author, commenting at that time on the plight of Christians in the Roman empire: "If the Tiber reaches the walls, if the Nile does not rise to the fields, if the sky doesn't move [i.e., no rain] or the earth does, if there is famine, if there is plague, the cry is at once: 'The Christians to the lion!'" (as quoted in Berelson & Steiner, 1964, p. 492).

More systematic studies, employing archival and survey techniques to examine the relationship between economic distress and responses to deviance, provide mixed support for this idea, however. For example, in a classic analysis, Hovland and Sears (1940) found some evidence that declining cotton prices in the American South, in combination with other indicators of economic growth, were related to the lynchings of blacks. Yet, in re-analyzing these data, Green, Glaser, and Rich (1998), found little support for these relationships. Furthermore, their analysis of hate crimes in New York City in the recent past also provided little support for a relationship between racial, religious, ethnic, or homophobic incidents and fluctuating economic conditions. However, because thresholds for aggressive behaviors such as hate crimes are quite high, a relationship between economic threats and subjective negative responses may be more easily established. This was first suggested by our re-analysis of the World Values Survey in which we found a negative correlation between subjective well-being and unwillingness to accept individuals with deviant conditions as neighbors. Furthermore, using a large pooled sample of an annual survey conducted in the USA between 1972 and 1994, Persell, Green, and Gurevich (2001) found that attitudes toward African-Americans and homosexuals became more negative the more respondents reported low economic security and greater anomia (the authors controlled for differences in education).

Moreover, Doty, Peterson, and Winter (1991) measured economic and social threat by using public opinion polling data and "objective" social and economic indicators, and obtained some evidence suggesting that racial prejudice among American high school students decreased in the less threatening time period. However, they did not take into account possible long-term trends in prejudice reduction.

Threats can have an economic character, but, of course, a more social character as well. Twenge (2000) found that self-reports of anxiety and neuroticism by American college students and children increased substantially from the 1950s to the early 1990s. Interestingly, anxiety levels were correlated with low social connectedness indicators such as divorce rate and percentage of people living alone, and overall threat as measured by indicators such as crime and suicide rate. Economic conditions appeared to be a much less important determinant of anxiety levels. These results suggest that social disintegration may be a stronger threat for people than economic strain, and thus may to a larger extent affect negative responses to deviant conditions.

## 6.6 Summary

While the previous chapters demonstrated that the functioning of the FF-C network helps to explain the influence of type of deviance, individual differences, and situations on responding to deviant individuals, the present chapter attempted to show how this network may also help to understand cultural and historical influences on social control. In particular, we distinguished three categories of societies in terms of the characteristic input-output patterns of these motivational systems, argued that these patterns are associated with certain structural properties and value patterns of these societies, and illustrated how these patterns are responsible for the manner in which societies tend to engage in social control. Thus in Category 1 (roughly simple-egalitarian-collectivistic) societies, due to a strong activation of the C system and a relatively low activation of the FF system, people usually respond with repair to deviance; in Category 2 (roughly moderately complex-hierarchical-collectivistic) societies, due to a reversed input-output pattern of the FF-C network, with a stronger FF than C activation, people usually engage in stigmatization; and in Category 3 (roughly very complex-egalitarian-individualistic) societies, due to a moderate activation of the C system (that we tend to associate with more universalistic altruistic tendencies) and a low activation of the FF system, we found evidence for a pattern of social control that is best described as tolerance.

We first illustrated the viability of this analysis by means of a qualitative analysis of differences in social control between different societies and historical periods. In particular, we discussed as main examples of Category 1, 2, and 3 societies, hunter-gatherers, the European Middle Ages, and modern Western societies, respectively. We showed that hunter-gatherers tended to respond in relatively balanced ways to deviance, neither too aggressive, nor too soft, but that in the European Middle Ages, responding to deviance was strongly determined by fear and aggression. An entirely new quality of social control emerged in modern, egalitarian, and individualistic societies in which people tend to delegate social control to formal institutions, behave according to egalitarian norms, and, as discussed in Chapter 4, respond in a self-controlled and dissociated manner during interpersonal encounters with deviant individuals.

As a second and more quantitative demonstration of the usefulness of our cultural analysis of social control, we looked closely at the results of several surveys employing standardized measures of responses to deviant conditions in contemporary Western and non-Western societies. On the basis of a secondary analysis of these results, we concluded that social control in current Western and non-Western or developing countries appears similar to social control in Category 3 and 2 societies, respectively. That is, current non-Western countries respond far more negatively to different types of deviance than modern Western societies. However, we discovered two important qualifications. First, among the Western societies, the more individualistic and authoritarian English speaking countries tend to respond more aggressively to deviance than most European countries. Second, English speaking Western societies appear to respond especially negatively to deviant conditions that belong to Type 4 deviance such as obesity, homelessness, and unemployment.

It is important to emphasize that in most studies we found that type of deviance not only had an independent but also a stronger influence on responding to deviant individuals than culture. Furthermore, the ranking of deviant conditions in terms of negative responding appeared relatively invariant across cultures. These findings seem to confirm that our typology of deviant conditions has universal validity.

We closed this chapter with an examination of more idiosyncratic cultural influences on responses to specific deviant conditions. For example, we illustrated that responses to such conditions as obesity, homosexuality, and mental illness are dependent on interactions between specific beliefs, values, and the particular nature of the condition.

CHAPTER 7

# A focus on persons with a deviant condition I: their social world, coping, and behavior

## 7.1 Introduction

In earlier chapters, it became clear that the negative reactions frequently received by persons associated with deviant conditions may turn into a type of social control that we have termed *stigmatization*. Although, as shown in Chapter 6, people in modern Western societies often show relatively strong egalitarian tendencies and disapproval of stigmatizing and prejudiced responses, persons with a deviant condition neverthe-less frequently meet with stigmatization in these societies, with a social world that is at least in part chilly, cold, and hostile. As we have noted in Chapter 1, under these circumstances, where a deviant condition is stigmatized and generally seen as a shameful or discrediting attribute, it can be useful to denote deviant conditions with the term *stigma*. Nevertheless, for different reasons it may not be possible to sharply distinguish stigma from deviant condition. First, as will become clear in this chapter, the person associated with a deviant condition contributes to shaping the responses of the social environment. For example, a person with a minor facial abnormality may unwarrantly expect severe negative or stigmatizing responses from others, and accordingly behave in rather tense or defensive ways when meeting strangers. Clearly, in these cases the term *stigma* will be used prematurely when referring to the deviant condition. Second, as noted in previous chap-ters, it is often difficult to determine empirically to what type of social control observed negative responses belong. At any rate, there are many kinds of experienced negativity that should not be automatically connected to stigmatization or social exclusion. As argued in Chapter 1, in addition to repair (e.g., getting angry at unhealthy behavior) or tolerance (e.g., appearing nice but self-controlled and rather tense), people's negative responses to deviance may also reflect mechanisms of interpersonal attraction or sexual selection (e.g., not choosing an unattractive or unhealthy person for dating or marriage). For the above reasons we often have chosen this for the term deviant condition, which is more generally applicable.

In this chapter, we will start with a sketch of the negative social world of people with deviant conditions. We will do this for a number of deviant conditions, some more active and others more passive. These descriptions will elucidate the world persons with a deviant condition live in and enable us to better describe and explain, which is the major part of this chapter, how those persons cope with this social world and their deviance and how they behave in interaction with others. As will be clear from earlier chapters, deviant conditions often strike in two ways. On the one hand, they confront the persons involved in a direct way with specific problems related to the condition in question. Having a passive deviant condition implies not only a form of dependency and incapacity but also often forms of physical and psychological suffering. People suffering from chronic illnesses, for example, may be quite incapacitated and dependent on others, but often they also have to endure much physical pain and psychological stress. Having an active deviant condition usually implies potentially harmful behavior toward others, which may also result in psychological stress. Convicts or ex-convicts, for example, may experience guilt and remorse. On the other hand, deviant conditions often confront the persons involved with negative reactions and stigmatization, elucidated in our description of their social world. The main general question for persons having a deviant condition is how to cope with that condition and such a negative world. In this book, coping with negative reactions and stigmatization is a much more central topic than coping with deviant conditions. Often, however, coping efforts and strategies cannot be unequivocally seen as either resulting from the deviant condition or the negative world, but may be focused on both simultaneously.

The general question of how to cope includes a number of more specific questions and topics. One of the more specific questions is whether people with a deviant condition, given there is a choice, will disclose their condition to others. Why would they, and why would they not? And relatedly, to whom will the condition be revealed and how and when? This chapter presents relevant information to these questions. Another question concerns how persons cope when they are confronted with specific negative responses; they may, for example, attempt to find original ways to deal with a negative reaction of others, or they may pay attention to their own positive qualities in order to compensate mentally for the negativity. However, they do not only cope directly when confronted with a specific negative and stressful event, but they also show habitual long-term responses or strategies to cope with their condition and a negative social world; they may, for example, attempt in different ways to reduce their deviant condition or they may attribute their negative outcomes to prejudice and discrimination. Furthermore, social interactions between persons with a deviant condition and others often do not run smoothly and can have a rather negative tone. The previous chapters sketched the negative contributions of others in this respect. In the present chapter, we will describe these interactions in terms of self-fulfilling prophecies elicited by the expectations and responses of those others, but also sketch the more independent contributions to these interactions by persons with a deviant condition themselves.

## 7.2  Social world

In earlier chapters, we presented many examples of the negativity of the social world of persons with a deviant condition. In addition to these examples, we will attempt here to present pictures of this negative world and treatment for a number of important social domains, which demonstrate the generality of negative responses; they are often not limited to specific domains. These pictures will be given for a variety of deviant conditions, some more active and others more passive. More specifically, these conditions pertain to obesity, homosexuality, mental illness, physical disabilities, and old age. This will give some indication of the importance of such treatments for society and particularly for the victims in question. In addition, and as noted before, more systematic descriptions of the social world persons with a stigma have to cope with will make it easier to understand those coping efforts. We also present these pictures in view of S. Fiske's (1998) call to social psychologists to better document discriminatory behavior in order to get a more complete picture of stereotyping processes. In such processes "real" behavior is often neglected.

In our presentation, we will provide information regarding negative treatment of persons with deviant conditions in the following important domains: the personal relationships with others, received help, favors and services, the educational field, and the field of work and employment. That in those domains contact and help may often be somewhat costly for other persons, may be an extra reason – as elucidated in Chapter 4 – for less positive treatment of persons with a deviant condition compared to persons without such a condition. This may also explain why positive responses, which were described in Chapter 4, may not be common and only occur under certain circumstances. Finally, the descriptions will pertain to modern Western societies, particularly American society, one reason being that most of the relevant research was performed there.

### Obesity

People's obesity is usually measured by the body mass index (BMI), i.e., weight in kilograms divided by height in meters squared and often defined, for example by the World Health Organization, as a BMI equal to or greater than 30. According to this criterion, in 1999 27 percent of adult Americans were obese, which is an increase when compared to earlier years (Wadden, Brownell, & Foster, 2002). In this book, we will, however, use the obesity concept more loosely and in using it or similar concepts, we refer to weight and body fat levels that exceed normative standards (cf. Roehling, 1999). Imagine now that you have such a deviant appearance, i.e., you are obese or overweight, and also try to imagine how the world will treat you because of this condition. You will probably come up with a number of less positive circumstances and behaviors. Indeed, the world will not be kind to you. Not only the material world, at times giving you problems with seating, but the social world, in particular, can be very troublesome for you. A large United States general population survey indicated that the three most common reasons respondents reported for experienced discrimination were race-ethnicity (37 percent), gender (33 percent), and various aspects (predominantly weight) of appearance (28 percent) (Kessler, Mickelson, & Williams, 1999). Let us present a number of more specific negative experiences of obese or overweight people.

For one, overweight people are less likely to be popular and their social relationships with others are likely to suffer. In Chapter 6, we presented a number of results showing the relatively low popularity of obese individuals in Western societies. More specific results were obtained by Cash (1995), who examined the accounts by female college students of experiences of appearance-related teasing and criticism during childhood or adolescence. Most participants recalled persistent teasing and criticism, whereby facial characteristics and weight were most often targeted. About half of the teased participants had been given one or more nicknames that referred to the physical attribute(s). The perpetrators of the women's earlier appearance teasing and criticism were most often regarded as peers. Similar results have been obtained by Rothblum, Brand, Miller, and Oetjen (1990). In their study, the more obese categories of participants indicated that they had experienced more school victimization, particularly negative weight-related nicknames and exclusion from sports or social gatherings by peers other than the average weight group. Also, interaction with siblings may be less positive. Bullen, Monello, Cohen, and Mayer (1963) asked in their study sampling among obese and non-obese girls for the kind of activities engaged in with siblings. Obese girls mentioned much more frequently "fighting," whereas non-obese girls more frequently described a friendly interaction, such as playing and having fun together.

Being overweight is also an impediment to having dates and finding a partner in life. As found by Sobal, Nicolopoulos, and Lee (1995), high school students, particularly men, reported less comfort in dating overweight people. This is probably one reason that having dates seems to be much more of a problem for obese than for non-obese individuals. In the study by Bullen *et al.* (1963), more than half of non-obese girls, and only 7 percent of the obese girls reported having more than two dates per month. In a study by Sitton and Blanchard (1995), it was investigated how likely it was that men selecting romantic partners would choose an obese person compared to a person with a history of drug addiction. Advertisements in two newspapers depicted a woman who was 50 pounds overweight or with 11 months of sobriety. Thirty men responded to the recovering addict, compared to eight for the obese woman. In both cases a large majority of the men were in the same deviant condition, i.e., former drug addicts or obese persons. A content analysis of 100 personal advertisements in the same papers as the "experimental" advertisements showed that 70 specified a preference for women who were height-to-weight proportional and 10 indicated a distaste for "drinkers or druggies." These results again point to the negativity of the overweight condition. Because of their lessened desirability as dates and life partners, overweight people can also be expected to find life partners less often. This has been found by Gortmaker, Must, Perrin, Sobol, and Dietz (1993) studying the relation between overweight and subsequent (seven years later) consequences such as educational attainment, income, and marital status in a very large (more than 10,000) sample of young people, representative of the United States. Controlling for base-line characteristics such as household income, educational level of respondents and their mother and father, race or ethnic group, it was found that both overweight adolescents and young adults married less often. Such an effect on marital status was not found for a group of young people with asthma, musculoskeletal abnormalities and other chronic health conditions, suggesting that health problems associated with being overweight had not impeded the attainment of marital status by the overweight group.

We all need help, favors, or services in life from time to time. For some categories or groups of people finding such positive treatments is less easy, which makes life more difficult. Because they are less liked or less popular, overweight people are one of those categories facing more prejudicial treatments. In a study by Karris (1977), an obese and normal confederate, instructed to wear shirts, neckties, and jackets, looked for apartments to rent. Landlords appeared to be less willing to rent to the obese confederate. A study by Benson, Severs, Tatgenhorst, and Loddengaard (1980) presents another example of such prejudicial treatment of overweight people. In this study, public health administrators were asked via mail to help a college junior assess her chances of getting into graduate school and finding employment. In two conditions of the study, a picture of a woman with normal body-build or of the same woman with obese body-build (via padding under her shirt) was added to the covering letter and résumé. A returned questionnaire was used as a measure of helping. It appeared that the return rate for the normal (57 percent) and a no picture condition (64 percent) was remarkably greater than for the overweight condition (25 percent).

Within the field of education there is also evidence of negative treatment or stigmatization towards overweight individuals. In the study by Rothblum *et al.* (1990) mentioned earlier, the obese groups gave instances of victimization by teachers, such as humiliation in front of other students, receiving lower grades, and being refused letters of recommendation because of their weight. In the study by Benson *et al.* (1980), public health administrators also devaluated the ability and potential of obese students. The public health administrators who returned the questionnaire were rather pessimistic about the student's chances of getting into a public health graduate program when she was obese, but quite optimistic when she seemed to have a normal body-build or no body-build information was available. Canning and Mayer (1966) comparing two high-ranking colleges with an excellent suburban high-school system found a lesser prevalence of obese, particularly female, students in the college sample. Canning and Mayer (1966; 1967) also, however, found hardly any differences in academic criteria, health records, future plans, or applications rates between obese and non-obese high school students that could explain the differential prevalence of the two student categories in colleges. On the basis of these results, the investigators argued that the discrimination they found was exercised mainly by college interviewers and was not shown in the recommendations by high school teachers.

Also in the field of work and employment evidence of negative treatment and stigmatization of overweight people has been found. For example, Pingitore, Dugoni, Tindale, and Spring (1994) demonstrated in a simulated employment interview study that college students recommended overweight applicants less often for employment than their equally qualified normal weight counterparts. This bias was greater for female than for male applicants. As noted by the investigators, these results are, however, only indirect evidence for stigmatization because the raters were not experienced and empowered to make hiring decisions. In the study by Rothblum *et al.* (1990), the very obese group (50 percent or more above ideal weight) reported more types of weight-related discrimination in the workplace than the obese and average groups. In written comments, very obese individuals indicated, for example, that they had been questioned about their weight or urged to lose weight. Seventeen percent of these individuals said that they had been fired or pressured to resign because of their weight. But self-reported discrimination may, of course, be an attribution to conceal one's real failures. Roehling (1999), however, reviewing the evidence from laboratory and field settings on prejudice and discrimination against overweight individuals in employment contexts, concluded that the evidence of consistent, significant discrimination against over-weight employees is sobering, and found it to be the case at virtually every stage of the employment cycle.

Because the overweight condition may be changed, it is interesting to see what, in a before-after design, the consequences of weight change can be with regard to stigmatization. In a study by Drenick (reported in Allon, 1982), consequences of weight loss after a fasting regimen were investigated. A 21 percent increase in employment after weight loss, and a pay increase for 56 percent of those employed prior to the study were found, suggesting at least in part less stigmatization. Surgery to lose weight has been applied to morbidly obese individuals. A study by Rand and MacGregor (1990) showed that preoperatively these indivi-duals perceived overwhelming prejudice and discrimination, among others in the field of work and employment, whereas 14 months after operation with an average weight loss of more than 45.5 kg little or no prejudice or discrimination was perceived. Again, however, self-reported discrimination may be somewhat subjective, and, for example, partly the result of feelings of well-being due to the loss of weight.

## Homosexuality

In the years 1764 and 1765 nine men were executed in "liberal" Amsterdam because of homosexual behavior. And even today homo-sexuals are imprisoned or worse in some Islamic countries. More gen-erally, as Chapter 6 demonstrated, homosexuals often have a very hard time in the non-Western world. Unfortunately, in the Western world echoes of those treatments and actions still resound in the harassment and violence experienced by homosexuals in their relationships with others. Berrill (1992) compiled results from twenty-six surveys of US city, state, region and national samples of lesbian, gay, and bisexual people and found an astonishingly high level of harassment and vio-lence. In the surveys that reported rates of specific victimization, the median proportion of respondents who were verbally harassed was 80 percent. Forty-four percent said they had been threatened with violence; 33 percent said they had been chased or followed; 25 percent said they had been pelted with objects; 19 percent had experienced van-dalism; 17 percent had been physically assaulted; 13 percent said they had been spat upon and 9 percent had been assaulted with an object or weapon. Unsurprisingly, in the light of these figures, 66 percent of the respondents said that they feared for their safety, and 80 percent that they expected to be the target of such harassment and violence in the future. The general profile of a "gay-basher" is described by Berrill as a young male, often acting together with other young males, all of whom are strangers to the victim. Moreover, victimization by, ironically, law enforcement officials, does not seem to be exceptional. In the surveys mentioned above, 20 percent (median) of lesbians and gay men reported some form of victimization by police because of their sexual orientation.

This negative treatment does not only occur in a street context, but also in supposedly more liberal contexts such as colleges. For example, Berrill (1992) summarized data from four studies about victimization in colleges. Between 3 percent and 5 percent of the respondents reported they had been punched, hit, kicked, or beaten at some point in their college careers. Sixteen to 26 percent had been threatened with physical violence, and 40 to 76 percent had been verbally harassed. Also at the high school and junior high school levels, investigations reported by Berrill (1992) found anti-gay violence and harassment to be widespread. Even in the home anti-gay violence and harassment occur. The surveys compiled by Berrill (1992) and measuring anti-gay abuse by relatives, showed that between 16 and 41 percent of the respondents had experienced verbal insults or intimidation by relatives and 4 to 8 percent had encountered physical violence. Such experiences may have contributed to the alarmingly high rate of suicide attempts among homosexual youths. Waldo, Hesson-McInnis, and D'Augelli (1998) reported for an urban sample that 42 percent were said to have attempted suicide at least once, whereas for a rural university sample this figure was 32 percent. They contrasted these figures with the figure for adolescents in general, namely 8 to 13 percent.

Self-reports by homosexuals or other stigma bearers on treatment experienced may, of course, be biased. The victims may exaggerate, or wrongly interpret behaviors others engage in. Therefore, studying possible perpetrators of those behaviors rather than victims can be enlightening. Franklin (2000) did that for anti-gay behaviors and administered an anonymous survey to community students. For Franklin, the most startling finding of this study was the commonplace nature of antigay behaviors among her sample, a young non-criminal group with more women than men, in a politically liberal and reputedly tolerant geographic region of the United States. Ten percent of her sample reported physically assaulting or threatening people whom they believed were homosexual and an additional 24 percent reported calling homosexuals by insulting names. These findings corroborate the self-reports of gay people.

Homosexuals are also often discriminated against in situations in which people need help, or may expect that services are properly rendered to them. In Chapter 4, we already mentioned less positive responses when asking shoppers for change, and when asking someone to relay a message by telephone. Interestingly, but not unexpectedly, in this latter investigation (Ellis & Fox, 2001), men were more likely to help lesbians than gay men, whereas women made no difference between lesbians and gay men. This finding is consistent with meta-analytically obtained attitudinal results holding that men have more negative attitudes toward gay men than toward lesbians (Kite & Whitley, 1996).

The "renting rooms" paradigm has also been used to investigate stigmatization of homosexuals. Page (1998) observed that reference to being homosexual in telephone inquiries about the availability of rooms or flats led these rooms or flats to be described much more often as unavailable (38 percent vs. 15 percent). This time, sex of the caller or the landlord made no difference. Discrimination has also been found in making hotel reservations. In a study by Jones (1996), hotels and bed and breakfast establishments were sent letters from either a same-sex or opposite-sex couple, requesting weekend reservations for a room with one bed. Same-sex couples were less often granted reservations than opposite-sex couples. The sex of the same-sex couples made no difference; the sex of the decision-maker(s) was unknown. Walters and Curran (1996) investigated the differential treatment of same-sex and opposite-sex couples in retail stores. Trained confederates for each store were randomly assigned to a homosexual or heterosexual couple. All couples displayed the same affectionate behavior (holding hands, smiling, talking). The average time, reliably measured, for sales associates to approach heterosexual couples was considerably less than for homosexual couples. In fact, staff did not assist one third of the homosexual couples at all during the six minutes they remained in the store, whereas all heterosexual couples were helped. Perhaps still more convincingly, observer's ratings of staff demeanor showed large differences. Whereas at no time were heterosexual couples treated negatively by staff, the behavior toward homosexual couples was disconcertingly negative; there was, for example, often staring and talking, about the couple. Furthermore, there was much more staring, talking, and rude treatment for gay couples than for lesbian couples. Again, this is consistent with the greater dislike, at least among men, for gay men than for lesbians.

To examine stigmatization within the field of work and employment, Croteau (1996) compiled nine studies focusing on the work experiences of lesbian, gay, and/or bisexual people. His general conclusion was that discrimination is pervasive in the workplace experiences of the groups in question. In virtually all of the studies, negative actions toward these people due to their sexual orientation were a central feature of participants' self-reported experiences. Asked if they had ever been discriminated against in employment, 25 to 66 percent of the participants reported affirmatively. Discrimination by the employer often involved decisions to fire or not hire persons due to their sexual orientation. More informal discrimination included examples of verbal harassment and property violence. Fear or anticipation of discrimination also seemed pervasive. Participants largely assumed that discrimination would occur if or when their sexual orientation was discovered.

## Mental illness

As noted by Corrigan (2000), mental illness like depression or schizophrenia often strikes with a two-edged sword. On the one hand, the symptoms and skill deficits arising from the illness impede social functioning in a direct way. On the other hand, negative reactions from others that may partly be instigated by the deficient social functioning of mental patients, hamper their social functioning still more. Because negative reactions from others may be elicited by less optimal social functioning of the mental patient, it is often difficult to establish whether the negative reactions to be described below, can be seen as convincing examples of stigmatization and discrimination. These reactions can also be seen as more or less self-evident reactions to negative behaviors of the mental patient; one would respond similarly to negative behaviors of non-deviant persons. However, the more a person is an ex-mental patient, and therefore less plagued by deficient social functioning, the more can negative reactions be seen as forms of stigmatization.

A rather convincing example of stigmatization, pertaining to the relationship of mental patients with others, was presented by Sibicky and Dovidio (1986) in a study in which students took part in a getting-acquainted conversation. In one condition (the client condition) the target was described as a student receiving psychological therapy at the university counseling center. Students in this client condition showed more negative behavior in the form of less enthusiasm and interest, and more insensitivity and unsociableness than students expecting to interact with a "normal" target.

As for help, favors, or services in life, Page (1995) again used the "renting rooms" paradigm to investigate stigmatization of mental patients in this respect. In one condition of this study, telephone calls were made about the availability of rooms or flats, whereas in another condition the caller added that he was currently receiving "some mental health treatment in the hospital" but would soon be requiring accommodation outside of the hospital. In this latter condition rooms were much more likely to be described as unavailable (29 percent) than in the former condition (9 percent). Page also observed that in a number of cases people were unable to be served in certain restaurants, or to open bank accounts once the psychiatric hospital's address was given.

To examine stigmatization within the field of work and employment, Farina and Felner (1973) had confederates present themselves in an employment interview as an ordinary job applicant who had been traveling the preceding nine months, or as a former mental patient having been in a mental hospital for the same period. In the mental illness condition, the interviewer gave a lower estimate of the probability of finding a job, and manifested less friendliness as measured by ratings of surreptitiously made recordings of the interviews. The responses of co-workers to former mental patients were investigated by Farina, Felner, and Boudreau (1973). Confederates related their personal history and behaved in either a calm, relaxed manner or in a tense, somewhat disturbed way. Earlier they had been presented to the participants as a former mental patient, a surgical patient, or a normal person. Male hospital employees rejected the (male) confederate both when he was tense and when he was a former mental patient. For example, they expected to get along less well and recommended him less often for a job in the ex-mental patient than in the ex-surgical patient condition. Interestingly, in two other studies, female co-workers did evaluate the (female) confederate unfavorably when she was tense, but not when she was a former mental patient, which suggests that women are more kind to co-workers who are former mental patients than are males (cf. Farina, 2000). We reported similar sex differences in Chapter 5. Druss, Marcus, Rosenheck, Olfson, Tanielian, and Pincus (2000), distinguished in their study of a national US sample persons with a general medical condition (most prevalent were diseases of the musculoskeletal system and respiratory conditions) and persons with mental disability (most prevalent were anxiety disorders and major depression). Among the respondents with only a mental disability who were currently working, 19 percent reported job discrimination on the basis of their disability within the past five years. The most common form mentioned was difficulty advancing in work (12 percent). As for access discrimination, 4 percent reported being refused employment on the basis of disability.

### Physical disabilities

As proposed by Stone and Collella (1996), the category of disabled persons includes persons with mental conditions, the negative treatment of whom was described before, and those with sensory impairments, learning disabilities, neurological conditions, addictive disorders, and physical conditions. Undoubtedly, the nature of the disability is very important for the kind and extent of negative treatment or stigmatization faced by disabled persons and for other problems they have to face because of their disability. Here, we focus as much as possible on the treatment of people with physical disabilities, for example, paraplegics or persons missing an arm or leg. As extensively discussed in Chapter 4, people often show behavioral discomfort in interaction with physically disabled individuals. For example, Heinemann, *et al.* (1981) found that individuals confronted with a physically handicapped person showed more non-verbally expressed discomfort and less relaxedness than individuals confronted with a non-handicapped person. It can, however, be doubted whether such experiences also characterize the personal relationships of physically disabled persons. Whereas in the study by Druss *et al.* (2000), mentioned before, 19 percent of the persons with a mental disability reported having trouble making or keeping friendships, only 2 percent of the persons with a general medical condition reported so. This suggests that physically disabled persons are not particularly troubled in their social relationships.

Physically disabled persons are often in need of some accommodation in order to function as non-disabled persons do. In the field of education, and work and employment, this may mean modifying the physical environment, for example, to adapt it to a wheelchair, or to reassign job duties. These accommodations, however, ask for extra money or efforts, and are therefore not often made. To give an example from Wertlieb (1985), although 75 percent of US universities and colleges claimed that they would accept intellectually capable handicapped students, only 25 percent had specialized facilities to accommodate those students. This is likely an important reason why physically disabled persons have a lower educational attainment than their non-disabled counterparts. In the field of work and employment, requesting accommodation may have adverse effects. In a study by Hazer and Bedell (2000), a hypothetical disabled (physical or psychiatric) job candidate asked for reasonable accommodation and offered compensation for time off. Participants, among whom were human resources professionals, gave this candidate lower suitability ratings than a disabled candidate not seeking accommodation. Whether the adverse effects of requesting accommodation were due to expected extra efforts for staff or co-workers or to the perceived seriousness of the disability could not be established.

Research in France by Ravaud, Madiot, and Ville (1992) revealed discrimination of physically disabled people seeking employment. In their study, unsolicited job applications were sent to a large sample of branches of French companies. In those applications, a physical disability (paraplegia, with a wheelchair) was mentioned or not. The position applied for was entirely compatible with the chosen disability. A second independent variable was the applicant's qualifications; he was highly or modestly qualified. The investigators found that highly qualified able-bodied applicants had 1.78 more chance of a positive response (obtaining an interview) than their disabled counterparts. For modestly qualified applicants, discrimination was more marked, the corresponding figure being 3.2. Perry, Hendricks, and Broadbent (2000) examined access and treatment discrimination among males and females with and without disabilities who graduated from a large US university. In an analysis controlling for state of health and ability to work, respondents with disabilities, particularly respondents with visual impairments, and in wheelchairs, reported experiencing more access (more difficulty in the job search process) discrimination than respondents without disabilities. A similar analysis showed no significant difference in treatment discrimination, for example, seeing one's income as adequate, reported by individuals with and without disabilities. According to the authors, one of the reasons for this lack of perceived discrimination may be that employees tend to receive similar standard benefits packages. However, the study by Druss *et al.* (2000), mentioned previously, suggested treatment discrimination. Among the respondents with only a general medical condition who were currently working, 24 percent reported job discrimination on the basis of their disability within the past five years. The most common form mentioned was difficulty advancing in work (16 percent). As for access discrimination, 9 percent reported being refused employment on the basis of disability.

## Old age

Are elderly people negatively treated or stigmatized in their relationships and contacts with others? Do, for example, children or young people respond more negatively to elderly adults than to younger adults? Pasupathi, Carstensen, and Tsai (1995) reviewed evidence on these questions. One study revealed that children, working on a jigsaw puzzle with an elderly or younger confederate, sat farther away from, made less eye contact with, spoke fewer words to, initiated less conversation with, and asked for less help from an elderly confederate than from a younger one. In their own research, Pasupathi *et al.* (1995) paired female participants aged 18–21 with other women, who were either the same age or elderly. These dyads were instructed to come to an agreement on a topic about which they held opposite opinions. As gauged by raters, those participants interacting with older partners were more respectful, polite, and directive, and changed their opinions more during the interaction (later, however, they returned to their initial opinions). Furthermore, they moved their chairs closer to their partners. These results were obtained both in groups of European-Americans and Chinese-Americans. The interpretation of these findings is not easy. The behavior exhibited by the children may be seen as negative expressing dislike, but also as positive expressing respect and awe. Their greater directiveness in the conversation may have been a helpful response to the assumed dependency of elderly people. In any event, as noted by Pasupathi *et al.*, the behaviors toward elderly people mentioned above can hardly be seen as hostile or negative, and some behaviors seem to be quite positive and examples of repair responses.

In other relevant research, we have not found clear proof of stigmatization of elderly people in their personal relationships and social contacts either, although the way in which they sometimes are spoken to, may be a case in point. Elderly people sometimes meet with "baby" talk, "elderspeak," or patronizing speech, involving a slower rate of speaking, simplifications in content and formulations, and an exaggerated prosody such as a high, variable pitch. Patronizing speech seems to be particularly used toward institutionalized elders, but also community-dwelling older adults reported to have experienced patronizing speech. Furthermore, such speech is not only found when people communicate with babies or elderly persons, but also in communication with mentally disabled persons, pets or foreigners. What these different targets have in common is that they may be assumed to have problems with understanding "normal" speech. Therefore patronizing speech may usually reflect good intentions on the part of the speakers in their attempts to adapt their speech to the supposed communicative needs of the targets. However, helping people can hurt, because the help may imply an assumed incompetence of the target. Caporael, Lukaszewski, and Culbertson (1983) found that caregivers of aged care receivers with a low expectation of elderly people's behavior in a social sphere were more likely to judge patronizing speech as the most effective for interacting with the elderly and as the most likely to be preferred by the elderly. Relatedly, Caporael *et al.* found that the evaluation of patronizing speech by the elderly depended on their level of functional ability. Residents with higher functional ability tended to like patronizing speech less. It is also disliked by community-dwelling older adults (Hummert, 1994). Kemper and Harden (1999) attempted to develop a form of "patronizing" speech that benefits older adults without being perceived as insulting or patronizing. Providing semantic elaborations and reducing the use of subordinate and embedded clauses improved older adults' performance on a referential communication task, whereas high pitch and slow speaking did not contribute to a better task performance, but did result in a negative evaluation of the speaker. In short, patronizing speech in its full form is often seen, despite the good intentions of the speakers, as stigmatizing by elderly people.

With regard to situations in which elderly people need help or services, research has been particularly focused on health care. In Chapter 3 we noted, that people generally favor younger adults over the old for a life-saving but scarce (medical) treatment, but we also noted that this difference may become smaller when concrete elderly patients expressing vulnerability are involved. As for mental health care, according to Gatz and Pearson (1988), mental health professionals may not hold global negative attitudes toward the aged, but they may have specific treatment biases. For example, Ford and Sbordone (1980) found that psychiatrists regarded older patients described in clinical vignettes as less ideal for their practice and as having a poorer prognosis than younger ones. These judgments may reflect stereotypes of elderly people as less competent and independent. Although those stereotypes may have a factual basis in some situations, they are often likely to result in stigmatizing behavior on the part of the medical practitioners. Those stereotypes may also affect the communication between physician and older patient. In a number of studies, Greene and colleagues (cf. Greene, Adelman, & Rizzo, 1996) found that overall, physician responsiveness (i.e., the quality of question asking, information giving, and support) was better with younger patients than with older patients, and that there was less concordance on the major goals and topics of the visit between physician and older patients than between physician and younger patients. Also, physicians were less likely to be egalitarian, patient, respectful, engaged, and to demonstrate therapeutic optimism with older patients than with younger patients. That older patients were found to be less assertive than younger patients may have been both a cause and an effect of those communication differences. All in all, these communication differences strongly suggest stigmatizing behavior on the part of physicians toward elderly patients. As another example of stigmatization when asking for help, favors, or services in life, Page (1997) also used the "renting rooms" paradigm in two Canadian cities to investigate stigmatization of the elderly. Rooms or flats were significantly more often described as unavailable when the caller was an elderly female than when she was young or the call was made on her behalf.

In the field of work and employment, Perry (1997) reviewed research on age access discrimination and concluded that there is some evidence that older applicants may experience less favorable outcomes than younger applicants. This relationship, however, appears to be moderated by a number of factors. One of these factors, for example, is whether the job in question is age-typed. Some research has indicated that age discrimination is stronger for jobs seen as more typical for young people. Perry also noted that in 1993 age discrimination claims accounted for 23 percent (19,884) of all claims filed by the US Equal Employment Opportunity Commission. Whether all these results are clear examples of stigmatization is hard to tell. Age may at times be a relevant concern for employers considering that younger workers have more years to devote to a job than older workers.

To sum up the aforementioned findings, in spite of occasional positive behaviors, persons with a deviant condition such as obesity, homosexuality, mental illness, physical disabilities, and also old age to some extent, tend to be negatively treated in their social environment, and thus to live in a relatively negative social world. This negativity applies to various domains. For most of those conditions, the quality of their personal relationships suffers. This seems to hold particularly for the overweight and the homosexuality condition, the latter regularly even meeting with physical aggression. Parenthetically, especially in the domain of personal relationships, not all negative behaviors can be seen as examples of stigmatization as we defined it. For example, if overweight persons are more often declined as marital partners, we think that the people who decline cannot be accused of stigmatization. In light of the nature of the relationship, the declination seems to be based on relevant grounds. Also, in the domain of received help, favors and services, there were for most of the conditions clear examples of stigmatizing treatment. Finally, whereas stigmatization has been found for the overweight condition in the educational field, in the field of work and employment such stigmatization has been found to some extent in all five deviant conditions. Furthermore, the five deviant conditions seem to elicit a general negative treatment and stigmatization to a different extent. The overweight and the homosexuality condition, probably due to their rather strong controllable active aspects, seem to instigate the most negative treatment and stigmatization, whereas the passive old age condition seems to instigate the least negative treatment and stigmatization. The mental illness and physical disabilities conditions are in between, with the former instigating somewhat more negative treatment than the latter. However, one should realize that the treatment differences between conditions are also dependent on what the literature has provided us with. Moreover, it is sometimes hard to tell in the examples whether stigmatization or other types of social control are involved, such as self-evident negative responses to negative behavior, for example in the case of mental illness.

## 7.3 Disclosure

Many deviant conditions are immediately apparent to others. To borrow from the ones described earlier in this chapter, people can easily see that a person is overweight, old, or physically disabled. Such conditions are visible and often cannot be hidden; individuals having these conditions are discredited, as Goffman (1963b) put it. The same often holds for ethnic differences that can be apparent from people's appearances. Many other deviant conditions, however, can often be concealed, for example, homosexuality, a history of mental illness, and a large variety of diseases. Such active and passive deviant conditions are concealable, but potentially stigmatizing, and thus individuals having those conditions are discreditable, to borrow from Goffman's terms again. Other people might discover the potentially stigmatizing condition and therefore react as if the condition were visible. Admittedly, condition visibility is not a dichotomous but a continuous variable. Mild instead of severe retardation may be difficult to spot. On the other hand, homosexuality may be discovered from brief observations of dynamic nonverbal behavior (Ambady, Hallahan, & Conner, 1999). And of course, people may try to conceal or reduce their visible deviant condition, using cosmetic surgery or prosthetic devices such as an artificial leg.

### The reveal-conceal dilemma

At first sight, concealing one's deviant condition, if possible, seems the natural thing to do and to be the rule rather than the exception. In this way, one can avoid feelings of shame about having that condition and other people's negative reactions to it. Jones *et al.* (1984) in a classic work on stigma supported this strategy: "concealment would usually seem better" (p. 35).[1] However, in the course of time a number of disadvantages of concealment, some of them already mentioned by Jones *et al.*, have received more attention in the literature (cf. Frable, Platt, & Hoey, 1998).

One disadvantage of concealment is experiencing feelings of guilt and shame because one is not willing to tell others about an important aspect of oneself, but is willing to deceive other people in this respect. This will be particularly the case when revealing the condition could have consequences, for example, not telling an employer about a debilitating chronic disease. Another disadvantage is that one may have to face stigmatization, which is not tempered by rules of decency, against the category or group one belongs to. It seems to be a common experience of closet homosexuals who have to face anti-gay jokes and pretend to like them.

There is also a fear of discovery that may make one anxious and worried and this may spoil pleasant social interactions. To prevent discovery one has to be choosy with regard to the social situations one selects to be in. Situations in which the condition will have conse- quences are unsafe and risky and should be avoided. A homosexual may find himself in trouble when his heterosexual friends are looking for possibilities to meet girls. Ex-psychiatric patients may need to avoid situations where they run the risk of meeting other ex-mental patients, which could lead to discovery of their condition (Herman, 1993). Discovery cannot only be prevented by situation management but also by information management. In social interactions with others one should be on one's guard and manage the conversation. Frable, Blackstone, and Scherbaum (1990) obtained some results indicating that individuals with a concealable condition, such as having been raped or being an incest victim, paid close attention to their conversa- tions with another individual. These individuals, in comparison to individuals with a visible condition, such as blacks and overweight persons, later made frequent references to the conversation and they spontaneously remembered what their partner said. The individuals with a visible condition, on the other hand, recalled minute cued details about the experimental room and their partner's physical appearance. These individuals had to manage an already spoiled interaction, whereas the individuals with a concealable condition had to keep their interaction from becoming spoiled (Goffman, 1963b). Individuals with a concealable condition, for example ex-psychiatric patients, may redirect conversa- tions by changing the subject or answering a question with a question (Herman, 1993). A more active technique is the use of "disidentifiers" (Goffman, 1963b, p. 44), for example, making jokes about one's own deviant condition. To prevent discovery entire periods or domains of one's life may need to be closed off, such as a psychiatric past or one's sexual relationships. This is not easy and perceptive listeners may often become suspicious.

The preoccupation with the embarrassing condition secret is not only stressful, but it also takes a lot of mental energy, and it can even make the condition more accessible. Smart and Wegner (1999) found that, ironically, the accessibility of thoughts related to eating disorders was increased with individuals having the concealable condition of eating disorders who role-played not having that condition. When people try not to think about something, they must monitor whether they succeed and therefore search for the very thoughts that are under suppression, which makes these unwanted thoughts, about the deviant condition in this case, more accessible. This increased condition or stigma accessi- bility may in turn fuel the preoccupation with the condition. In Chapter 4, we described similar rebound effects of suppression for people trying to suppress their stereotypes of deviant persons.

A final major disadvantage of concealment of one's deviant condition is social isolation (Archer, 1985). Concealing one's condition deprives people of the opportunity to interact with similar others sharing one's condition, which frustrates important motives (McKenna & Bargh, 1998). One of these motives is the need to belong. If one does not see or know similar others, one will feel alone and different from other people. Frable (1993a) found that individuals with a concealable condition (e.g., gays) perceived less consensus between their personal preferences and those of others for a number of mundane items than individuals with visible conditions (e.g., obesity) or individuals without a deviant condition. Also, individuals with a concealable condition rated themselves higher on items related to uniqueness than did others. A second motive that is thwarted is reduction of uncertainty about oneself. The absence of similar others will make social comparisons on important aspects of the self (the deviant condition) difficult or impossible; therefore self-knowledge fed by social comparison remains underdeveloped. In addition, uncertainty about oneself is maintained because there is no exchange of information on how to view one's own deviant condition and the social world one is confronted with, and how to act toward that world. These factors are presumably also related to a third motive that is thwarted by the absence of similar others, namely holding a positive self-image. Similar others may provide more positive attitudes about the group or category in question, and useful information about the social world and effective behaviors, which may enhance efficacy-based self-esteem (Frable *et al.*, 1998).

In addition, seeing and knowing similar others will make identification with a social group easier, which may enhance self-esteem (Tajfel & Turner, 1986). Indeed, Frable, Platt, and Hoey (1998) found in an eleven-day experience-sampling study that students with concealable conditions (bisexuality or homosexuality, bulimia, and family earning less than $20,000 each year) reported lower self-esteem and more negative affect than students with visible conditions (blacks, obesity, and stuttering) and those without deviant conditions. In addition, the presence of similar others lifted the self-esteem and mood of students with concealable conditions, but not of students from the other categories. Students with concealable conditions experienced, however, less occasions in which similar others were present than students with visible conditions. In a similar vein, McKenna and Bargh (1998) found that involvement in Internet newsgroups related to concealable conditions such as homosexuality or having deviant sexual interests led to greater self-acceptance, as well as coming out about the condition to family and friends. Here too communication with similar others seems to have salutary effects.[2]

Compared to all the disadvantages of concealment disclosure can often have clear, positive effects. It is therefore not really surprising that Crandall and Coleman (1992) found that HIV-positive people, whose condition was known to significant others, were less depressed and anxious than those who had not disclosed their condition. There is even some suggestive evidence that disclosure may produce observable health benefits. For example, Sherman, Bonanno, Wiener, and Battles (2000) found that children's self-disclosure of their HIV/AIDS status to friends was related to a slowing of their disease progression. And it is also not surprising that disclosure may be experienced as a relief from a heavy burden. Roughly one third of the ex-psychiatric patients studied by Herman (1993) felt that discussing their mental illnesses and past hospitalizations was cathartic and alleviated much of the burden of their loads. Schneider and Conrad (1980), studying epileptics, speak of "therapeutic telling" about the epilepsy condition.

The pros and cons of condition concealment are presumably both greater for active deviant conditions than for passive ones. As argued in Chapter 3, people generally react more negatively to persons who can be related to harmful behavior, e.g., ex-convicts or homosexuals, than to persons who are incompetent or dependent, for example, because of an illness. So the avoidance of those negative reactions presents a greater gain for people who have an active condition than a passive one. On the other hand, because there seems to be more at stake for individuals with an active condition, they may have stronger feelings of guilt and shame because they deceive other people about important aspects of themselves. Also the fear of discovery, and the corresponding situation and information management, may be greater. And last but not least, social isolation may be more severe because one's deviation seems to be greater, at least in the eyes of other people, than in the case of passive condition. All this means is that the reveal-conceal dilemma, as it may be called, is often greater for individuals with an active than a passive condition. This difference, however, may depend on the type of relationships. Due to interpersonal dependency concealment of passive conditions, for example, chronic illnesses, may be quite harmful for others in close relationships because of the burden they may entail in the present or the future. This may reduce the difference in the seriousness of the reveal-conceal dilemma between active and passive conditions for this type of relationship.

### Disclosing one's deviant condition: to whom, how, and when?

If people with a concealable condition choose to reveal, they will mostly selectively disclose, and carefully select other persons whom to tell. Of course, there will be large individual differences in disclosure that will be in part dependent on the social context. Ragins and Cornwell (2001) studied disclosure or "coming out" in a national sample of members of gay rights organizations. Most of their respondents concealed their condition from others at work. Twelve percent reported that they were out to no one at work, 37 percent reported being out to some people, 24 percent being out to most people, and 27 percent reported being out to everyone at work. Disclosure was negatively related to perceived workplace discrimination and greater in organizations that had supportive policies and practices and that were covered by protective legislation.

In general, and reflecting the degree of closeness of the relationship, condition disclosure appears to occur most frequently to family members, followed by close friends, and then acquaintances. Schneider and Conrad (1980) found such a pattern for epileptics and Herman (1993) for ex-mental patients. Important when deciding to disclose is whether the other person is "safe" or accepting, which will often be related to the closeness of the relationship. In a study among topless dancers, an occupation being seen as an active deviant condition, almost all of the dancers indicated that their close friends, spouses or boyfriends, and people they associated with on a regular basis knew their occupation and had no problems with it. Most, however, did not tell new acquaintances, casual friends, or their parents the truth (Thompson & Harred, 1992), which last result suggests that close relationships do not always imply an assumed accepting attitude. But generally, close others are expected to show more positive or understanding reactions. Moreover, concealment to close others will result in more guilt, and situation and information management will be more troublesome because of more frequent and personal contacts with close others. For these reasons, close others will be popular disclosure targets.

However, as hinted before, close others do not always exhibit positive or understanding reactions. In the case of active conditions such as homosexuality close others such as parents may often react negatively, with the disclosed condition being perceived as a crisis by the family (Strommen, 1989). The parents apply their negative conceptions of homosexual identity to their child, which makes that child suddenly a stranger and produces a feeling of alienation from him or her. Moreover, this alienation is accompanied by feelings of guilt and personal responsibility for the child's new identity. D'Augelli, Hershberger, and Pilkington (1998) found that among young lesbians, gays, and bisexuals in US metropolitan areas three-quarters had revealed their sexual orientation to a parent, particularly the mother. One-quarter of fathers and 10 percent of mothers were reported to have shown a rejecting response to their disclosed children. Furthermore, about one-quarter of those who disclosed were verbally abused by parents, and nearly 10 percent experienced threat and physical abuse. Illustrating further the risks of disclosure, one-quarter of those who had disclosed said they had been physically hurt by fellow students because of their sexual orientation compared to, unsurprisingly, none of the non-disclosed. Also, an English study by King (1989) among out-patients with HIV infection showed that one-quarter received negative reactions from at least one confidant. Parents and siblings reacted less rejecting or discriminating than sexual partners and close friends. Rejection by employers and dentists was proportionately most common and was frequently harsh. Differential rejection may in part be explained in terms of the relevance of the condition for the relationship and the nature of the relationship between the patients and the others. For sexual partners, employers, and dentists HIV infection seems to be highly relevant in view of the specific relationships in question.

Whether people reveal their condition to close or more distant others, in both cases a process of "testing the waters" may be involved in which the discloser tests the reactions of the recipient before disclosing more detail. By investigating the attitudes of potential recipients the conceal-ing person can find out whether it is wise to disclose or not (Dindia, 1997). If persons have decided to reveal their condition, the question of what and how to disclose arises. Generally, disclosure does not mean simply revealing the condition, but it often involves adding different kinds of extra information with the aim to influence the listener's perception of the discloser and the condition in a positive way. Schneider and Conrad (1980) and Herman (1993) describe such disclo-sures for epileptics, and ex-mental patients.

In what may be called "beyond-control" disclosures, the actors try to remove blame and responsibility from themselves for the deviant con-dition. About half of the ex-mental patients Herman (1993) studied used "medical disclaimers"; the genes are to blame or past hospitaliza-tions are presented as a side effect of another medical problem or disease. In this way the controllability component, implying one's own contributions, can be discarded from the deviant condition. In what we call "colored" disclosures the actors embellish the conditions or circumstances surrounding the deviant condition. The actors may withhold negative aspects, e.g., distasteful behavior, and emphasize positive aspects of their condition in order to create a positive impres-sion. A third form of disclosure is "normalization" by which actors seek to deny or downplay that their behavior or condition is deviant (Herman, 1993). In their disclosure, ex-mental patients, for example, emphasized that they participated in a full round of normal activities and aspired to normal attainments, thereby presenting a non-deviant conception of self and making their past hospitalization less deviant. A fourth form of disclosure is "education," giving others a more or less factual and unbiased description of the deviant condition to remove all kinds of misunderstandings about that condition. In this way the listeners may be stimulated to redefine their image of the condition and see the actor in a different light.

People with visible conditions may, of course, also use these different kinds of extra information that people with a hidden condition may add to simple disclosure of that condition. These people too may often want to influence the listener's perception of them and their condition in a positive way. For example, Davis (1961) described a particular strategy used by visibly handicapped persons that he called "deviance dis-avowal" and that is highly similar to normalization. These persons recognized their disabling condition but in such a way as to downplay it and prevent it from becoming central or disruptive. For example, they alluded in passing during straightforward conversational exchanges to their involvement in a normal round of activities. Or they interjected taboo or privatized references by way of letting the other person know that they did not take offense at the latter's possible uneasiness.

In addition to the question of whom to disclose to and how to disclose, there is the question of when to disclose. Early disclosure is regularly used as a strategy for minimizing the pain of later rejection (Herman, 1993; Schneider & Conrad, 1980). The argument is that before investing in a relationship, it is good to know whether that is worth-while and the other person will not retreat upon hearing about the condition later. On the other hand, disclosure after meeting someone may backfire unless, of course, it is highly functional, as in an applica-tion interview. It may be considered too intimate and personal given the stage of the relationship, and appearing to be looking for sympathy or understanding. Also, later disclosure enables one to build a more unbiased and positive image of oneself that is not affected by the condition. The association between the stage of the relationship and the positivity of the effects of disclosure is likely to be curvilinear (Kelly & McKillop, 1996). Condition disclosure may occur too soon, but it may also backfire when it occurs after having known someone for quite a long time; in the latter case it may be considered as a lengthy deception and a lack of trust. This may be more the case for active than for passive conditions, because secrecy about the former often can be more easily seen as serving the interests of the concealing person. But note also here that the relevance of the condition for the type of relationships may moderate this difference. Not too early and not too late seems the best although rather vague advice.

Research on the effects of condition concealment and particularly different forms of disclosure has hardly been done. Link, Mirotznik, and Cullen (1991) made a first attempt and studied the effects of secrecy, selective avoidance and withdrawal, and educating others as strategies of ex-psychiatric patients. No positive effects of these strategies on, for example, demoralization of the patients could be demonstrated; there were even some indications of negative effects. Obviously, more research is needed.

## 7.4 Ways of coping with one's deviant condition and negative reactions

If one's deviant condition is visible, disclosed or in other ways known to others, one often has to cope with negative reactions because of that condition. When these negative reactions arise, for example, one is stared at, a coping response is elicited; one might stare back, make a joke, silently curse the other person or ignore the staring. In addition to these short-term coping responses, the relevant literature also describes types of coping responses or strategies that are either not or less tied to specific responses or situations and are more habitual long-term responses to cope with a deviant condition and a negative world. People may reason, for example, that negative stereotypes and treatments associated with their deviant condition are due to prejudice and discrimination. First, we will discuss coping with specific negative reactions.

### *Coping responses to specific negative reactions*

How do deviant people generally cope with all kinds of negative events related to their condition? Myers and Rosen (1999) studied this question for obese individuals and examined the frequency of different types of negative situations, the ways of coping by obese people, and the relation of these variables to psychological adjustment. The most frequent negative situations were hurtful comments by children, other people making unflattering assumptions about the obese person, and encountering physical barriers (such as chairs being too small). Respondents reported facing these situations between "once a year" and "several times in my life." Being stared at and being subjected to unsolicited negative comments were also relatively frequent. The investigators distinguished twenty one types of coping responses to those situations, most of which can be classified in more encompassing categories (cf. Carver, Scheier, & Weintraub, 1989; Tobin, Holroyd, Reynolds, & Wigal, 1989). The category "problem-solving" comprises "heading off" negative remarks (say "hi" to people who might be staring), humor, ignoring situation and making no response, responding positively and/or being "nice." "Cognitive restructuring" includes positive self-talk ("I think, it's who I am on the inside that matters"), using faith, prayer, self-love and/or self-acceptance, see the situation as the other person's problem ("I regard people who have problems with obesity as small-minded and childish"). "Confrontation" includes refusing to hide and being visible, responding negatively, and physical violence. "Venting of emotions" comprises negative self-talk ("I feel really bad about myself"), and cry and/or isolate myself. "Social support" contains support from other people (obese or non-obese) and therapy. Other relevant categories are "avoidance" or "leaving situation," and "education" (wearing buttons with size-positive messages). The three other coping responses pertain to eating, diet and refuse to diet, and seem to be dependent on the obesity condition. The most frequent coping responses were "positive self-talk," attempts to "head off" negative remarks by socially disarming people who might otherwise be critical, and using faith and prayer for self-consolation. These responses were employed from "once a month" to "several times a year." The relationships between types of coping responses and psychological adjustment were weak or non-existent. This may not really be surprising, because often distress increases coping efforts, which will counteract positive relationships between coping and adjustment (Gunthert, Cohen, & Armeli, 1999).

The more encompassing categories that we distinguish, namely problem-solving, cognitive restructuring, confrontation, venting of emotions, social support, avoidance and education, are for the most part quite similar to coping categories distinguished in theories about how people cope with stress (e.g., Carver *et al.*, 1989). This is of course not unexpected, because in both cases people have to cope with a threatening situation which allows for only a limited number of general coping responses. Thanks to this similarity we may assume that the coping categories and responses obtained in the Myers and Rosen (1999) study on obesity stigmatization presumably also hold for other types of deviant conditions. Because other people's reactions to active conditions will often be more negative or hostile than to passive conditions, as explained in earlier chapters, coping responses may also be more negative or hostile in the case of active conditions than passive conditions, assuming that more negative perceptions and behaviors elicit more negative responses. Of course, the above hypotheses have still to be tested. Relevant research is needed on the relationship between types of coping responses and psychological adjustment. Some responses may be maladaptive, whereas others may seem helpful.

*Long-term strategies of coping with one's deviant condition*

By using long-term responses to cope with a deviant condition and a negative world, persons with that condition may alleviate both that condition and recurring negative reactions on a more or less permanent basis. For example, some types of coping responses continuously enable them to control to some extent the negative emotions resulting from the deviant condition and negative reactions. In this way, persons with a deviant condition may maintain a positive self-view and well-being, as we will describe in the next chapter. We will successively discuss the following important types of coping responses: reduction of the deviant condition, group formation and membership, social creativity, attribution of one's negative outcomes to prejudice and discrimination, and social comparison with others.

*Reduction of the deviant condition*    This strategy is focused on removing one's deviant condition or making one's membership of the deviant category less prototypical. Of course, in light of social control and repair processes in particular, this should be a highly common strategy. For some conditions removal is attainable to a large extent; many people who are obese can lose weight and facial disfigurement can often be repaired by plastic surgery. Sometimes people with a deviant condition cannot remove their condition, but by making it weaker they can present themselves as less prototypical members of their category, thereby lessening their deviant condition. Physically disabled persons can use prosthetic devices and elderly people cosmetic surgery to this end. This strategy has often been described as a transition from a deviant condition to a less or no deviant condition. Similar efforts may, of course, be made to postpone or avoid a transition to a deviant condition. People diet in order not to become obese, and use cosmetic surgery to stay or look young.

An interesting question is whether one can get rid socially of one's condition or stigma if elimination of the deviant condition is technically possible. Studying this question, Rodin and Price (1995) found that people who had successfully remedied a deviant condition, such as obesity or facial disfigurement, were accorded more credit for having overcome their condition, but were judged less acceptable as social companions than people who had never had that condition. One of the explanations the investigators mention for this "lingering taint" from the stigma history is the contamination effect described in Chapter 1. Past contact of an object with a negative stimulus makes the object negative. So people avoid wearing a sweater of a murderer or avoid a person that once had a deviant condition (Rozin *et al.*, 1994). As a sad implication of their results the investigators note that in a similar way to people who have a condition to conceal, people who are now "normal" must be on guard to conceal the fact that they have overcome a deviant condition, particularly because it is an accomplishment in which they are likely to take a great deal of pride.

*Group formation and membership*    By forming or becoming a member of groups serving the interests of people with a deviant condition, people in question can enjoy important advantages. Those groups may give them information and support, which may enable them to see their condition in a more accurate and probably positive way and to better cope with the negative reactions to it. Goffman (1963b) mentioned a plethora of such groups, varying from ex-mental patients to the obese and physically handicapped and covering the whole deviant spectrum. Those groups may also function as pressure groups, as agents attempting to change the social evaluation of the deviant condition in a positive way, and to supply their members and members of the deviant category in general with benefits, for example in terms of taxes, facilities, and services. Such groups may be militant and exhibit social protest. Cox and Gallois (1996) described a homosexual rights group engaging in confronting tactics, such as going into heterosexual night clubs and engaging in "kiss-ins" and using slogans like "I hate straights." More moderate group behaviors include lobbying for the formulation of anti-discrimination legislation, signing anti-discrimination petitions or attending protest meetings. Simon *et al.* (1998) studied determinants of willingness to participate in such groups in the context of the older people's movement (Gray Panthers) in Germany and the gay movement in the United States. Their research suggested that important determinants of willingness to participate were calculation of the costs and benefits of participation and identification with the movement. The costs and benefits of participation included the value of the collective goals of the movement for the potential participator and the expected reactions of significant others to one's own participation in the movement.

One may speculate that more militant group behavior by persons having an active condition, for example, homosexuality, may emphasize the potentially harmful character of the group, eliciting anger and fear among other people. On the other hand, militant behavior by persons having a passive condition, for example, physical handicaps, may because of the discrepancy between behavior and expectations elicit ridicule and contempt; those people can be seen as not knowing their place. Taking such consequences into account may make militant group behavior more effective.

*Social creativity*  Social creativity here means mentally manipulating judgmental dimensions so that a more positive view of oneself or one's group is attained. Important social creativity strategies are redefining the value attached to various judgmental dimensions and finding new dimensions on which to judge oneself. An example of value redefining is provided by Simon, Glässner-Bayerl, and Stratenwerth (1991). These investigators found in a questionnaire study among straight and gay men in Germany that gay respondents reevaluated group attributes in favor of their ingroup. More specifically, gay respondents rated negatively valenced straight attributes more negatively and negatively valenced gay attributes more positively than did straight respondents. More generally, dimensions with comparatively negative outcomes for oneself or one's ingroup are devalued and dimensions with comparatively positive outcomes are overvalued. This hypothesis holds true, as the reader may suspect, for people in general and not only for people with a deviant condition or stigma (Rosenberg, 1979). Crocker, Major, and Steele (1998), describing these phenomena from a self-esteem perspective, use the term disengagement to refer to the initial disconnecting of one's self-esteem from one's outcomes in a particular condition-threatening situation. By placing less importance on the negative outcome on a condition-related dimension one can protect one's self-esteem. Outcomes on that dimension become less informative for one's self-esteem that in the face of negative outcomes can more easily be maintained. To refer to the more chronic disconnecting of self-esteem and outcomes, Crocker, Major, and Steele use the term disidentification. People with passive conditions may disidentify with performances central to their condition and people with active conditions may downplay a number of social prescriptions and distance themselves from the majority's social world and its values.

The other social creativity strategy, finding new dimensions, is in line with the value redefining strategy. By finding comparison dimensions on which one obtains positive outcomes, one can maintain and even enhance one's self-esteem. An example was provided by Schulz and Decker (1985), studying the adjustment of spinal-cord-injured persons about twenty years after the disability occurred. These investigators found that the majority of the persons in question ascribed positive meaning to their disability and mentioned most frequently types of meaning related to personal growth such as increased awareness of self and seeing other people as more important. Groups with a deviant condition may even attempt to ameliorate their undivided social identity, for example "black is beautiful" and "gay pride."

Crocker and Wolfe (2001) proposed another creative strategy people with a stigma can use to avoid low self-esteem, namely basing their self-esteem on contingencies such as other's approval, or God's love, that are less related to competencies. If people with a stigma base their self-esteem on God's love, a disadvantaged position and negative reactions of others are made less important. Crocker and Wolfe argue that older people, for example, experiencing losses in important sources of self-esteem such as cognitive capabilities and physical agility, may attempt to selectively optimize their contingencies of self-esteem and base that esteem on religious beliefs and God's love.

*Attribution to prejudice and discrimination*    Another type of habitual long-term responses to cope with a deviant condition or stigma is attribution to prejudice and discrimination (Crocker & Major, 1989). Later in this chapter, we will note that persons with a deviant condition often expect negative views or stereotypes and discrimination from others and that they overestimate the effects of their deviant condition. In this light it stands to reason that those persons tend to attribute negative feedback or poor outcomes of themselves or their group to prejudice and discrimination. By attributing these outcomes not to themselves as causal agents but to discriminating others, those persons protect their self-esteem on the outcome dimension. For example, Crocker, Major, and Steele (1998, p. 523) describe research in which overweight and normal-weight women were led to believe that weight is not controllable and that they had been rejected by a man as a potential date. Overweight women were more likely to blame the rejection on the man's prejudice against their weight than normal-weight women. Interestingly, when overweight women were led to believe that weight is controllable, they blamed the rejection less on the man's prejudice against their weight compared to overweight women believing that weight is not controllable. Presumably, feeling a personal responsibility for one's condition, believing that it is under one's control or is one's own fault, makes out that the negative outcome is seen as deserved and others are not to blame (Crocker *et al.*, 1998). Persons with a deviant condition seem to take the controllability or responsibility factor with regard to their condition into account in the same way as other persons do, which was described in Chapter 3. The more responsibility they feel, the more negative reactions they deserve, and thus the less stigmatization they experience.

It can, however, be argued that there are also psychological costs associated with attributing negative outcomes to discrimination. For example, as found by Kaiser and Miller (2001), people may devalue persons who attribute their failure to discrimination, even if it is quite certain that discrimination has occurred. Therefore, the fear of being negatively evaluated may prevent people with a deviant condition from attributing negative outcomes to discrimination, at least in public.

Research by Dion and Earn (1975) indicated that Jewish undergraduates attributing their failure in a supposedly strategic task to discrimination by gentiles reported feeling more aggression, sadness, and anxiety than those who could not invoke discrimination as an explanation for their failure. Thus, negative emotions also may be costs of attributing failure to discrimination.

Attribution to prejudice and discrimination as a habitual response to cope with a deviant condition is likely then to be dependent on psychological benefits and costs, such as protection of self-esteem, expected social costs and experiencing negative emotions. In addition, there also seem to be cognitive determinants: expecting negative stereotypes and discrimination from others and overestimating the effects of one's own deviant condition. Dependent on these determinants, the net effect on prejudice attribution is likely to differ among types of deviant conditions. Also the relevance of the situation for the expectations related to the condition has to be taken into account. All this means that it is difficult to predict whether there are systematical differences between persons with an active and a passive condition in attributing outcomes to stigmatization.

*Social comparison*  A final type of habitual long-term coping response to a negative condition is social comparison (Crocker & Major, 1989). One of the main reasons for people to compare themselves with others is to evaluate their abilities and other attributes. Generally, they have much freedom to select these others. Important selection criteria are similarity and self-protection. In agreement with the similarity criterion, persons with a deviant condition are more likely to compare themselves with others sharing their condition (Crocker *et al.*, 1998). The performances and attributes of persons sharing the condition seem to be more relevant and informative for evaluating one's own abilities and attributes than the performances and attributes of other persons. In addition, by comparing themselves with others sharing their condition instead of making unflattering and painful comparisons with persons without the condition, they can avoid threats to their self-worth and protect their self. They may still succeed better in protecting their self by preferentially selecting others sharing their condition who are even more disadvantaged than they are themselves. For example, Wood, Taylor, and Lichtman (1985) studying adjustment of breast cancer patients found that these patients' social comparisons were not only almost always to fellow cancer patients, but also overwhelmingly downward, i.e., to worse-off members of their own category. More generally, people facing medical problems are likely to make downward comparisons. Affleck and Tennen (1991) summarized research findings concerning the role of social comparison in coping with three major medical problems: rheumatoid arthritis, newborn intensive care and its aftermath, and infertility. These findings show that the victims of these problems often use downward social comparison as a way of mitigating threats to self-esteem and psychological well-being. Finlay and Lyons (2000) found that for another condition, learning difficulties, the most common comparisons these people made were downward and lateral (i.e., the self is presented as the same as another person). The lateral comparisons involved mostly others who did not have learning difficulties. By noting their similarities with these "normals" the participants could present themselves in a positive light. The downward, flattering comparisons were made mostly with other people with learning difficulties, but also with others who behaved in socially unacceptable ways, such as drunks, beggars, and thieves. These selections of people who break the rules or have active, controllable conditions, as a comparison standard illustrate the freedom people have in structuring their comparison world. In addition, people may not only select persons as a comparison standard, but also prototypes and stereotypes (cf. Miller & Prentice, 1996). And of course – almost everything is mentally possible – one can even create stereotypes that are most useful for comparison purposes. Heckhausen and Brim (1997) demonstrated that when people had problems in social domains, such as money, health or job, they created a representation of their peers as having similar problems but to a larger extent. In this way, they could compare themselves positively to this biased view of their peers. This tendency was most pronounced for older adults.

There may be, however, for various reasons, no downward comparisons. Research by Schulz and Decker (1985), mentioned earlier in this chapter, suggested that there might be important differences between coping in the early stage of the condition and later coping processes. Whereas downward comparisons seem to be important for early stage adaptation (cf. Wood *et al.*, 1985), these comparisons were relatively absent for the spinal-cord-injured persons who had adapted successfully over a long period, and were studied by Schulz and Decker. Possibly, these persons, having made a successful adaptation by ascribing positive meaning to their disability and focusing on attributes that made them appear advantaged, had created a world for themselves in which disability and other disabled people were much less central and therefore superfluous. Therefore, comparisons with unfortunate others were less necessary. Another reason for the absence of downward comparisons may be that persons with a deviant condition sometimes may be very sensitive to being labeled as such. Renick and Harter (1989) hypothesized and found that this held for learning disabled students. In their efforts to see themselves as normal these students were reluctant to see other learning disabled students as their social comparison group and 84 percent of them spontaneously made upward comparisons with normally achieving students in their regular classes. Not surprisingly, these comparisons resulted in perceptions of lower academic competence than the comparisons they were asked to make with other learning disabled students.

Because short-term coping responses to specific reactions and long-term coping responses both are focused on the alleviation of a deviant condition and a negative social world, it will not come as a surprise that they show some overlap. For example, confrontation and education as short-term responses can be recognized as important elements in the long-term strategy of group formation and membership often containing protest and supplying of information. Also, the short-term coping response of cognitive restructuring, including positive self-talk and seeing the situation or negative response as the other person's problem, may contain elements of the long-term coping responses social creativity, social comparison, and attribution to prejudice and discrimination. However, because short-term coping responses are focused on specific reactions to the immediate situation and long-term coping responses on more general aspects of the deviant condition and a negative social world, the overlap is limited.

Short-term and long-term coping responses can also be considered on the more global level of functions which the coping responses serve. This results in an important distinction within both the short- and long-term coping responses that pertains to problem-focused versus emotion-focused coping. As for the short-term coping responses, problem-solving, confrontation, and education can be seen as forms of problem-focused coping. The long-term strategies reduction of the deviant condition and group formation and membership, particularly if pressure groups are involved, can also be seen as forms of problem-focused coping. With these types of responses or strategies persons with a deviant condition attempt to change their deviant condition, influence negative reactions and their social world, and achieve better outcomes. Cognitive restructuring, venting of emotions, and social support, on the other hand, can, as short-term coping responses, be seen as forms of emotion-focused coping, whereas the status of "avoidance" in this respect is less clear. Furthermore, social creativity, attribution of one's negative outcomes to prejudice and discrimination, and social comparison with others, can, as long-term strategies, also be seen as forms of emotion-focused coping (cf. Miller & Major, 2000). With these emotion-focused coping responses and strategies persons with a deviant condition attempt to regulate and control the negative emotions they have to face because of their condition.

These emotion-focused coping responses and strategies may be psychologically beneficial, resulting in less negative emotions and a higher self-esteem and well-being. In the next chapter, we will return to these determinants of self-esteem and well-being of persons with a deviant condition. On the other hand, these forms of emotion-focused coping may undermine the motivation to change oneself and one's social world. If a person with a deviant condition, because of negative achievements, devalues intellectual performance (social creativity), or blames others for these results (attribution to prejudice), or makes a downward comparison to others who failed even more (social comparison), this person has found a psychological alibi for a lack of achievement (cf. Crocker *et al.*, 1998). Similarly, obese people may deal better with a negative reaction such as being stared at by problem-solving and changing the reaction than by cognitive restructuring without attempting to affect that reaction. Emotion-focused coping seems particularly reasonable when changing oneself and one's social world is hopeless.

A distinction relevant for the choice of coping responses is that between deviant conditions that are more individual-related or more group-related. The former conditions, for example facial disfigurements or physical handicaps, are linked less to meaningful groups, and the persons involved do not share a common culture. Furthermore, individuals having these conditions do not interact frequently with each other. In contrast, group-related conditions, for example, ethnic and racial minority groups, or to a lesser extent homosexuality, are more linked to meaningful groups having a common culture and showing much social interaction between group members (cf. Crandall, Tsang, Harvey, & Britt, 2000). As for the long-term coping strategies, individuals with a group-related condition will presumably more often adopt a group formation and membership strategy and attempt to improve the position of their group than individuals having an individual-related condition. Having a common culture and much interaction makes the development of pressure groups relatively easy. Because of the saliency of their group and their greater identification with it, individuals with a group-related condition will also more often make group comparisons, and distinguish between "us" and "them." These comparisons will not always be flattering, and therefore different coping strategies, for example social creativity, may be needed. Further, group saliency and identification may also enhance attribution of one's negative outcomes to prejudice and discrimination. It may, however, be questioned whether, as we will note in the next chapter, this strategy affords protection of one's self-esteem.

Apart from these differences in coping strategies, if a group-related deviant condition is involved, having a link to a meaningful group with a common culture and much social interaction between group members, one's general coping is likely to be more successful than in the case of an individual-related condition. Interacting with similar others sharing one's condition and a condition-related culture serve the need to belong and give social support. It becomes easier to develop an understanding of the deviant condition and to cope with it and with discrimination. Also, the development of a positive self-image becomes easier. Group members provide more positive attitudes about the group in question. Persons with individual-related stigmas lack these advantages.

## 7.5 Perceiver-dependent and other negative reactions of deviant persons in social interactions

Social interactions between persons with a deviant condition and others often have a somewhat negative tone. In Chapter 4, we sketched the negative reactions of those other persons in this respect, and here we will describe the often reciprocal nature of the reactions of persons with a deviant condition and other persons to each other. Moreover, we will describe how persons with a deviant condition may also contribute to the negativity of those interactions in other ways.

*Self-fulfilling prophecies in social interactions between persons*
*with a deviant condition and others*

In the description of the reciprocal nature of the reactions of persons with a deviant condition and other persons to each other a useful concept is that of a self-fulfilling prophecy or expectancy effect. A self-fulfilling prophecy is defined, in the beginning, as a false definition of the situation evoking a new behavior which makes the originally false conception come true (Merton, 1957). Darley and Fazio (1980) outlined a specific social interaction sequence as the process by which interpersonal self-fulfilling prophecies or expectancy effects occur. In this sequence, one person (the perceiver) develops a set of expectancies about another person (the target), for example, that he is unlikable (step 1). The perceiver then acts toward the target in accordance with these expectations and shows somewhat negative behavior (step 2). The target interprets the meaning of the perceiver's negative action (step 3), and responds based on this interpretation by acting negatively (step 4). The perceiver then interprets the target's negative action, which will strengthen his or her expectancies (step 5), and can be regarded as reentering the interaction sequence loop at step 2. In a final step 6, the target interprets his or her action and may internalize that action and change his or her self-concept accordingly, for example as a less likable person. In similar interaction sequences deviant conditions may lead to negative self-fulfilling prophecies. Let us give a number of examples.

In the study by Sibicky and Dovidio (1986), using the mental patient condition and described earlier in this chapter, student perceivers responded in a getting-acquainted conversation more negatively to a student assumed to be a client receiving psychological therapy than to another student not so labeled. These "clients" (unaware that they had been labeled clients) in turn felt less comfortable and enjoyed the conversation less. These targets were also rated by independent observers as behaving less positively than the targets in the student condition. Vrugt (1990) also used the mental patient condition, but focused on specific non-verbal behaviors of the parties involved. In her study, trainee psychotherapists interviewed students about their satisfaction with the study of psychology. Self-descriptions of the interviewees informed the therapist (untruthfully) that either the interviewee was treated for psychological problems (the client condition) or was a well-adjusted, normal person. The therapists interviewing "clients" used more symmetrical arm positions, indicating a lack of relaxation (Mehrabian, 1972). These and possibly other, not-measured, behaviors resulted in reported discomfort in participants introduced as clients. This discomfort was not only a private experience but was also expressed in the use of ah-filled pauses and speech disturbances by the client. Although in a preliminary study trainee psychotherapists appeared to have a more negative attitude toward clients than to people in general, the expectancy effects may have been driven here more by the uneasy and uncomfortable behavior of the therapists than by negative behavior.

Self-fulfilling prophecy studies using children as participants are quite rare. One of these studies was performed by Harris, Milich, Corbitt, Hoover, and Brady (1992), who focused on the attention-deficit hyperactivity disorder (ADHD) condition. ADHD is a common childhood behavior problem with prevalence estimates of up to 10 percent of elementary school children. Another interesting aspect of this study is that the ADHD expectancy was manipulated orthogonally to the actual diagnostic status of the child (having ADHD or not). The ADHD expectancy was created by telling the child (all participants were boys) that their partner in the investigation was in a special class for his behavior and a number of disruptive behaviors (talking when he shouldn't, acting silly) were mentioned. Participants (perceiver and target) performed two tasks together, an unstructured cooperative task and a structured competitive task. Perceivers with an ADHD expectancy were less friendly toward their partners and talked less often. Targets of an ADHD expectancy enjoyed the social interaction less, judged their dyad as doing less well and said their partners were meaner. The effects of expectancy were weaker than the effects of diagnostic status. To mention some diagnostic status effects, ADHD boys talked more and issued more commands, and were found meaner by their normal partners. The effects of expectancy and diagnostic status were largely independent, which means that the most negative outcomes were often experienced by the ADHD boys who had been labeled as such, which is the typical case for the ADHD condition and many other stigmas. In this respect, the investigators make the interesting suggestion that the negative effects of a label such as hyperactivity may be qualitatively different from effects of the disorder itself. As support for this suggestion they note that the effects of the expectancy manipulation were not to make the targets more active or disruptive but to make the perceivers not look forward to the interaction and subsequently withdraw from it. This resulted in lesser enjoyment on the part of the targets. More generally, a deviant condition may lead to a self-fulfilling prophecy in a more global evaluative way, for example, less attractive target behavior, but not necessarily with respect to behavior characteristic of the stigma, such as disruptive or incompetent actions.

Another deviant condition that has been investigated in self-fulfilling prophecy studies is obesity. In a study by Snyder and Haugen (1994), male perceivers were led to believe that the female interaction partner they would speak to by telephone was either of normal weight or obese. In addition, interaction goals were manipulated. If the goal was to find out what kind of personality the target had, the perceivers initiated the behavioral confirmation process and the targets behaviorally confirmed perceivers' erroneous beliefs and acted in a less positive way.

Finally, the elderly condition has been studied as a source of expectancy effects. Harris, Moniz, Sowards, and Krane (1994) performed two related studies and examined how perceivers' expectations about the elderly were translated behaviorally and how these behaviors in turn affected targets. In the first study, students were asked to teach a game task via videotape to a target they believed was either another college student their age or an elderly woman. From ratings of the videotapes it appeared that in the elderly condition teachers were nervous and less friendly. In addition, female teachers believing they were teaching an elderly taught less material than teachers in the college-aged condition. In the second study, the videotapes from the first study were given to other students and these students were asked to complete the task. The elderly expectancy appeared to have harmful effects on its targets. Students watching videotapes made by teachers in the elderly condition identified fewer concepts correctly than students of teachers in the college-aged condition. This effect persisted after controlling for the amount of material taught. Parenthetically, as the investigators note, the adverse consequences of the elderly expectancy may be due to negative affect directed specifically to the elderly but also to a generalized anxiety provoked by the confrontation with a member of a group with a deviant condition or stigma.

The results of the self-fulfilling prophecy studies described here do not all conform to the social interaction sequence formulated by Darley and Fazio (1980). The most essential step in this sequence seems to be step 4 in which the target behaviorally confirms the expectations of the perceiver. This appears to be the case in at least the investigations of Sibicky and Dovidio (1986), using the mental patient stigma in a getting-acquainted conversation, in the Snyder and Haugen (1994) study, using the obesity stigma in conversations, and the Harris *et al.* (1994) studies, using the elderly stigma in a teaching situation. Perceiver expectations of less friendliness or incompetence were translated in less friendly or less competent target behavior. In the study by Vrugt (1990) using the mental patient condition in an interview situation, and the Harris *et al.* (1994) studies, using the elderly condition in a teaching situation, also perceiver anxiety resulting in target anxiety may have played a role in the inter-action sequence. As noted before, the confrontation with a member of a group with a deviant condition may provoke generalized anxiety. According to Devine, Evett, and Vasquez-Suson (1996), the same avoi-dant non-verbal behaviors can be indicators of two very different psy-chological experiences: social anxiety and antipathy. Therefore, avoidant behavior to people with a deviant condition may be a consequence of anxiety and can occur in the absence of antipathy or hostility. Finally, we note that also the results of Harris *et al.* (1992), who used the ADHD condition in a cooperative and competitive task situation, cannot easily be incorporated in Darley and Fazio's social interaction sequence. As noted before, a deviant condition may lead to behavioral expectancy effects in a more global evaluative way, for example less attractive target behavior (e.g., less enjoyment), that does not confirm specific perceiver expectations such as disruptiveness or incompetence (see also Jussim, Palumbo, Chatman, Madon, & Smith, 2000).

Self-fulfilling prophecies or expectancy effects can have an interper-sonal character, but obviously also an institutional or societal character. Deviant conditions or stigmas may be embedded in the culture of a society and therefore reflected in customs, rules, and laws. For example, the elderly stigma of incompetence has made nursing homes foster dependency and loss of control for their residents in their regimes and regulations. This is, for example, reflected in the ways in which nursing home staff members respond to self-care behaviors from resi-dents, as studied by Baltes and Reisenzein (Baltes & Reisenzein, 1986). These investigators coded residents' self-care behaviors (e.g., brushing teeth, dressing) as either independent (performed without help) or dependent (performed with help). Staff responses were coded as either dependence-supporting (e.g., giving assistance), independence-supporting (e.g., praise for independent self-care behavior), no response, or other response. Baltes and Reisenzein found that much more staff support was given for dependent than for independent behavior. Interestingly, for institutionalized children this support pattern reversed, indicating that the support for dependent behavior is more related to age than to institutional setting. This reversal also illustrates that elderly people in contrast to children may be seen as having a passive, uncontrollable condition, as argued in Chapter 3. By the reinforcement of dependency and other factors, such as institutional rules, the elderly people do not then have much choice other than to display the expected behavior. In research by Rodin and Langer (1977) these residents were given the opportunity to make decisions and to feel increased responsibility, which resulted in their becoming more actively interested in their environment, more sociable and self-initiating, and more vigorous, as well as more healthy. Apparently and fortunately, the earlier institutional self-fulfilling prophecy could be defeated. As for another self-fulfilling prophecy with institutional aspects and pertaining to education, there is suggestive evidence that teacher expectations may particularly produce self-fulfilling prophecies among students from lower socioeconomic backgrounds and among African-American students (Jussim & Harber, 2005). This may, of course, result in a lack of social integration and other negative outcomes for those students.

Expectations related to deviant conditions or stigmas will be in different situations differentially relevant for social interaction. For example, an expectation of incompetence, related to passive deviant conditions, will be highly relevant in teaching situations or in other situations in which competence matters, but less so in social situations. Active deviant conditions, on the other hand, will be less relevant in competence situations, but may be more so in social situations, in which a pleasant atmosphere may be endangered by the potentially harmful behavior of the person with an active condition. This suggests that in the case of passive deviant conditions self-fulfilling prophecies will be stronger in competence situations, whereas in the case of active deviant conditions they often will be stronger in social situations.

Self-fulfilling prophecies are often also thought to be stronger when moving from relatively powerful perceivers to relatively powerless targets than in the reverse direction (e.g., Copeland, 1994). One of the reasons may be that powerful perceivers have more resources to affect the interaction than powerless targets, and can therefore more successfully act on the basis of their expectations. This means that in interactions between, on the one hand, people with a deviant condition, who are often relatively powerless, and other people, who are often more powerful and have negative expectations concerning the condition, rather strong expectancy effects may occur. This is likely to apply particularly to institutional or societal self-fulfilling prophecies; the powerful dominant group lacking a deviant condition makes the rules in institutions and society (cf. Link & Phelan, 2001). To this we can add that persons with a deviant condition may not only behaviorally confirm perceiver expectations in response to perceiver actions, but they may also contribute to the negativity of interactions with other people in other ways and for other reasons, questions we now turn to.

*Interactional difficulties of persons with a deviant condition and their determinants*

When persons with a deviant condition and other persons interact with each other, both may experience difficulties in interacting smoothly and both may show less adequate responses, particularly when they do not know each other well. We outlined this for those other persons in Chapter 4. Here, we give a similar description from the perspective of persons with a deviant condition or stigma. Let us begin with describing a number of determinants of the interactional difficulties of these persons.

One important determinant is that persons with a deviant condition are generally aware of or expect negative views or stereotypes held by others about them and discrimination against them (Crocker *et al.*, 1998). Blind people, for example, often think that sighted people perceive them as slightly retarded and hard of hearing (Coupland, Giles, & Benn, 1986). As found by Link, Cullen, Struening, Shrout, and Dohrenwend (1989), current mental patients, former patients, and non-patients agree that mental patients will be rejected by most people. People with HIV, but also the general public, appeared to expect quite negative views about people with HIV, much more negative than these views in fact were (Green, 1995). These negative expectations of people with a deviant condition may lead them to be generally mistrusting and suspicious of other persons' intentions and motives (Devine *et al.*, 1996). For example, in a study by Santuzzi and Ruscher (2002), participants role-played in an interview situation with a confederate the role of a lesbian, and did or did not disclose this status. Compared to a control condition, "lesbian" participants evidenced more negative inferences about their partner's disposition, particularly in the disclosure condition.

A second factor that may contribute to awkward interactions with other people, is negativity and ambivalence about one's own group. On the one hand, the individual with a deviant condition knows and even shares some of the negative stereotypical knowledge applied to his or her category. The obese respondents in a study by Harris, Waschull, and Walters (1990) were not only well aware of the negative societal stereotypes of the obese but also shared them to some extent. Also, 93 percent of these respondents blamed themselves for being overweight, mentioning feelings of being out of control, and feeling responsible and guilty. Crandall (1994) combining results for seven samples found no correlation between dislike of fat people and own weight; in other words overweight persons shared the negative image of fatness. Gibbons (1985) reported research on the reactions of institutionalized mentally disabled individuals to a mentally disabled or non-disabled target person. The mentally disabled target appeared to receive much less favorable evaluation on social distance items (e.g., "have as a friend or roommate"). On the other hand, the ingroup of the individual with a deviant condition is involved which may make his or her views of that group more positive (cf. Goffman, 1963b, p. 131). This explains, for example, why the obese respondents in the Harris *et al.* (1990) study shared the negative societal stereotypes only to some extent. Incidentally, individuals with a deviant condition often view their self rather positively. Obese Italian women attributed rather negative ratings to an obese person, but described their real self as quite positive (modest, kind, warm, and large) (Molinari & Riva, 1995). And in the research described by Gibbons (1985) the mentally disabled individuals saw themselves more favorably than the mentally disabled target and about equal to the non-disabled target in terms of intelligence. However, they evaluated themselves as pessimistically as the mentally disabled target on social behavior dimensions, such as dating and marriage.

A third factor that may play a role in the negativity of interactions with other people is overestimating the importance of one's condition. Persons with a deviant condition often assume that most of the behavior emitted by other persons interacting with them is causally related to their own condition. They give their own condition a master status (Hughes, 1945) that determines the actions of other people toward them. For example, in an experiment in which obese, and non-obese students interacted with a nice, nasty, or neutral confederate, obese students overwhelmingly attributed the confederate's behavior to their own weight (Rodin & Slochower, 1974). These attributions occurred equally often in response to a nice and a nasty confederate. Therefore, these weight attributions cannot be interpreted as defensive in reaction to a threatening other. Rather, as noted by the investigators, it seems that obese persons consistently use their weight to explain the behavior of others toward them. Another example can be found in a study by Kleck and Strenta (1980) in which individuals were led to believe that they were perceived as physically deviant in the eyes of an interactant. The physical characteristic at issue was potentially stigmatizing (epilepsy or a facial scar first cosmetically prepared and then removed without the individual knowing it) or not stigmatizing (an allergy). From descriptions that participants gave of the behavior of the other interactant it appeared that scar and epilepsy participants made statements reflecting a greater impact of their characteristics on the other interactant than allergy participants.

Now think about persons who expect negative views or stereotypes held by others about them and discrimination against them, who may even share some of the negative stereotypical knowledge and that overestimate the effects of their condition. Undoubtedly, all these views make it hard for those persons to interact with others not sharing that condition in a spontaneous and open way. They will have extra concerns during the interaction. They probably want to discover whether in fact the other person has a negative attitude toward them, and therefore have to monitor all kinds of verbal and non-verbal messages that may reveal the other person's attitude. In this monitoring process ambiguous behavior can easily be interpreted as negative because a negative attitude or behavior is expected. Again, according to Devine, Evett, and Vasquez-Suson (1996), the same non-verbal behavior, for example evasion of eye contact, can be an indicator of two very different psychological experiences: social anxiety and antipathy. Therefore, anxious non-verbal behavior emitted by other people – Chapter 4 described why they regularly show this behavior – may easily be seen as an expression of antipathy or hostility. Another concern for people with a deviant condition is how to handle interpersonal encounters with others effectively. How can a person with a deviant condition, assuming that the other person has some negative views about him or her that are perceived as not wholly undeserved and also assuming that the condition is strongly affecting the other person's reactions, successfully break the ice and put the person at ease?

Moreover, during the interaction persons with a deviant condition have to face and deal with so-called attributional ambiguity (Major & Crocker, 1993). If other people in interactions with people with a deviant condition emit positive or negative behavior, the latter have to interpret the meaning of those behaviors (step 3 in the social interaction sequence of Darley & Fazio, 1980). This is often rather difficult because of that condition. Negative behaviors could easily be seen as forms of stigmatization, but they could also be due to actual shortcomings in the behavior or characteristics of the person with a deviant condition and therefore be deserved. On the other hand, positive behaviors emitted by others may reflect the positive qualities of the person with a deviant condition, but they could also be a consequence of the condition, that may regularly elicit feelings of sympathy or normative positive behavior, as described in Chapter 4. Also, important positive behaviors such as giving help may signify that the recipient is inferior. Schneider, Major, Luhtanen, and Crocker (1996) argued that help that is given without clear evidence of need or inferiority on the part of the recipient (i.e., assumptive help) could potentially threaten recipients' sense of competence and self-esteem. This is probably the case for individuals with a deviant condition, and particularly so for individuals having passive deviant conditions signaling incompetence, because they may often feel that they are inferior or are suspected of being inferior. Schneider *et al.* demonstrated in their study that black students who received assumptive help from a white peer reported lower competence-based self-esteem than black students who did not receive such help or white recipients of assumptive help. Note that incompetence is an important element of the condition or stigma of blacks. Furthermore, there were no differences in competence-based self-esteem between blacks and whites who did not receive help.

Further complicating matters is that persons with a deviant condition and others may differ in their perceptions of what constitute positive attitudes and behaviors toward people with a deviant condition. Makas (1988) investigated this issue for disabled and non-disabled persons. For the disabled respondents positive attitudes meant either dispensing with the disability category entirely, or promoting attitudes that defend the civil and social rights of the disabled. For the non-disabled, these positive attitudes reflected a desire to be nice, helpful, and ultimately place the disabled person in a needy situation, which was understandably not appreciated by the disabled persons themselves, who did not want to be helped. Ironically, then, when non-disabled persons try hard to express their positive attitudes, they may actually be perceived by disabled persons as expressing negative attitudes.

All these factors mean that persons with a deviant condition will often experience discomfort in their encounters with other people and will perform less adequately. This was demonstrated in a study by Comer and Piliavin (1972) that employed an interview-like situation in which a confederate either served as a physically disabled or a physically normal person interviewing physically disabled participants. Participants interacting with a normal interviewer as compared to a physically disabled interviewer terminated the interactions sooner, showed greater motoric inhibitions, exhibited less smiling behavior, demonstrated less eye contact, and reported feeling less comfortable during the interview. In Chapter 4, we described that in social interactions between persons with a deviant condition and others, those others showed similar responses indicating stress and discomfort. The responses of persons with a deviant condition and those others are likely to reinforce each other.

Again, as described for self-fulfilling prophecies, expectations related to deviant conditions may be in different situations differentially relevant for social interaction. Therefore, the contribution of persons with a deviant condition to the negativity of interactions with other people is likely to depend on the nature of the deviant condition and the situation. In competence situations, for example, persons with a passive deviant condition may contribute in a more negative way because of their assumption that others expect them to be incompetent.

Occasionally, persons with a deviant condition seem to be able to improve their performance or behavior. In a study by Miller, Rothblum, Felicio, and Brand (1995), obese and non-obese women participated in a brief telephone conversation with another person. The key manipulation was that participants were either led to believe that their partner could see them (on a television monitor) or that their partner could not see them. Partners who could see the obese women rated the social skills of these women as more favorable when these women thought they were visible than when they thought they were not visible. Apparently, the women's belief about whether they could be seen made them alter their behavior in such a way that it influenced their partner's impression. These results can be explained by assuming that the women in the visible condition tried to compensate for their weight stigma by acting more positively. Striving to maintain a positive self-image, as people generally do, people with a deviant condition, like people in general, can follow the direct way and try to prevent the occurrence of negative outcomes, such as obese women acting nicely if rejection is feared. Thus, compensation may bring about that social interactions between persons with a deviant condition and others sometimes have a less negative tone. Nevertheless, as we have explained and described here and earlier, these interactions are often uncomfortable and stressful (cf. also Crocker *et al.*, 1998).

## 7.6 Summary

In this chapter, we described, concentrating on the modern Western world, that persons with a deviant condition of obesity, homosexuality, mental illness, physical disabilities, and also old age tend to be negatively treated in their social environment, and thus to live in a rather negative social world. This negativity of their world applies to a varying extent to the following important domains: the personal relationships with others, received help, favors and services, the educational field and the field of work and employment. The descriptions suggest, however, that the negative treatment elicited by deviant conditions is not uniform. The more controllable overweight and active homosexuality conditions seem to instigate the most negative treatment, whereas the passive old age condition seems to instigate clearly the least negative treatment.

These negative treatment descriptions gave a background to the main theme of this chapter, the description and explanation of how persons with a deviant condition behave and cope with their plight. One of the questions we dealt with is whether those persons, given there is a choice, disclose their condition to others. They are confronted with a reveal-conceal dilemma. With regard to this dilemma, we described a number of disadvantages of concealment such as feelings of guilt and shame because of deception, having to face prejudice not tempered by rules of decency, fear of discovery, and social isolation which will frustrate important motives. These disadvantages may dominate the advantages of concealment, namely avoiding feelings of shame about the deviant condition and other people's negative reactions. The reveal-conceal dilemma is likely to be greater for individuals with an active than a passive deviant condition. Disclosure of the stigma seems to occur most frequently to family members and close others, and often includes extra information aiming to influence the listener's perception in a positive way. Regularly, disclosers have to face negative reactions from others. As for the timing of disclosure, not too early and not too late may have the most positive consequences.

If persons with a deviant condition are confronted with specific negative reactions, their responses may be rather diverse. On the basis of many specific coping responses uncovered among people with the obesity stigma, we have distinguished a number of more encompassing types of these short-term coping responses. These types, namely problem-solving, cognitive restructuring, confrontation, venting of emotions, social support, avoidance and education, are quite similar to the more global coping categories distinguished in theories about how people generally cope with stress. Persons with a deviant condition or stigma do not only have to cope directly when confronted with a specific stressful event, but they also show habitual long-term responses or coping strategies for their deviant condition and a negative social world. As important long-term coping strategies we described reduction of the deviant condition, group formation and membership, social creativity, attribution of one's negative outcomes to prejudice and discrimination, and social comparison with others.

The often somewhat negative social interactions between persons with a deviant condition and others can be seen in terms of self-fulfilling prophecies or expectancy effects. We described a number of self-fulfilling prophecy studies with people having various deviant conditions as targets, such as mental patients, children suffering from ADHD, obese people, and elderly people. Indeed, in a number of these studies perceiver prophecies of less friendliness or incompetence resulted in less friendly or less competent behavior on the part of the person having the deviant condition. Self-fulfilling prophecies may also have an institutional character and be based on institutional customs and rules, driving, for example, institutionalized elderly people to show dependent behavior. Persons with a deviant condition also appear to contribute independently to negative social interactions with others. They expect negative views, stereotypes, and discrimination from others, even partly endorse these views, and overestimate the effects of their condition. This makes them interact with others in a less spontaneous and positive way.

## CHAPTER 8

# A focus on persons with a deviant condition II: socio-economic status, self-esteem and well-being

## 8.1 Introduction

In the previous chapter, we have described that persons with a deviant condition even in the modern Western world, in comparison with other persons, are confronted with a greater number and also more specific problems in life. We also described how those persons cope with their problems. From those descriptions it will have become clear that these problems are often difficult to solve and may leave their marks, be they tangible or psychological, in the lives of those persons. In this chapter, again concentrating on people with deviant conditions in the Western world, we will discuss three highly important marks or outcomes. One of them is more concrete and tangible and refers to socio-economic status, which indicates people's social position in society. The other two are psychological and refer respectively to self-esteem and subjective well-being. These two psychological variables are, as we will note later, empirically highly correlated. Because of, in part, distinct literatures and perspectives, we will treat them separately. Thus, we will attempt to determine whether persons with a deviant condition experience losses in socio-economic status, self-esteem and subjective well-being.

The various coping responses and strategies described in the previous chapter may solve in part problems related to the deviant condition. If people cope well, the effects of their condition may be less strong. Other factors that may mediate the effects of the deviant condition on outcomes can, however, make these effects stronger. Here, we will discuss a number of such factors or mechanisms, namely, loss of affiliation and power, discrimination, stigma endorsement and performance deficits. Due to unpopularity persons with a deviant condition may experience a loss of affiliation and power in their social relationships; they are less welcome in groups and less likely to attain positions of power in those groups. Moreover, they may often experience discrimination and share to some extent the negative view of others about their condition. In other words, they may endorse the stigma. Finally, persons with a deviant condition may regularly perform worse than persons without such a condition, they may show performance deficits. Until now, it has been unclear how such mechanisms as affiliation and power loss or discrimination may lead to specific outcomes for specific deviant conditions. Therefore, we will discuss those mechanisms in a more general way and present them as plausible mediating factors that may lead to lowered outcomes of socio-economic status, self-esteem and subjective well-being. In describing the outcomes, we will attempt to establish to what extent empirical support has been obtained for the operation of the mediating factors.

## 8.2  Mechanisms mediating lowered outcomes

We will start this chapter by discussing a number of mechanisms that may mediate lowered outcomes for persons with a deviant condition and adapt and extend in that discussion the sociological framework of Link and Phelan (2001). They distinguish three important mediating mechanisms: status loss, discrimination, and social psychological processes operating through the person with a deviant condition such as expecting and fearing rejection. Link and Phelan consider particularly the set of outcomes they call the distribution of life chances such as careers, earnings, housing, criminal involvement and health. Those outcomes all seem to be tangible and related to one's social position in society or socio-economic status. We think that for a more complete picture psychological outcomes such as self-esteem and subjective well-being are also relevant and because of the attention they have received in research we will treat them rather extensively. We rearranged, renamed and extended the mechanisms proposed by Link and Phelan somewhat and will discuss successively the following mechanisms likely to be mediating the effects of deviant conditions on outcomes: loss of affiliation and power, discrimination, stigma endorsement, and performance deficits.

### *Affiliation and power loss*

In Chapter 4, we outlined the idea that due to negative affect and stereotypes persons with a deviant condition, for example, overweight people and homosexuals, are relatively unpopular and not seen as desirable interaction partners. Moreover, as we outlined in Chapters 4 and 7, when persons with a deviant condition and others do interact with each other, they both may experience difficulties in interacting smoothly and may show less adequate responses, particularly when they do not know each other well. As a result, these interactions may often be somewhat uncomfortable and stressful, which will lower the popularity of persons with a deviant condition still more. This loss of affiliation may make attaining desirable status positions in society more difficult. To attain such positions membership in relevant groups, for example, fraternities or business associations, and the formation of networks may be important. But if a person with a deviant condition is or feels less welcome in those groups and the formation of personal relationships is more difficult, attaining desirable status positions in society may be hampered. Furthermore, the unpopularity of those persons may impede their developing social skills, which may additionally reduce their attractiveness as interaction partners and their access to groups.

Evidence concerning social skills of people varying in physical attractiveness indicates that beauty is not only skin-deep. According to meta-analyses by Langlois *et al.* (2000), physically attractive adults, compared to unattractive adults, are somewhat more extraverted, and possess somewhat better social skills. One plausible explanation of these attractiveness effects is that attractive and unattractive individuals develop differential traits as a result of differential evaluation and treatment by others, mechanisms that were also demonstrated in the meta-analyses. If unattractive individuals do have different personality characteristics, then individuals likely to have an even more deviant physical appearance, such as overweight individuals and individuals with a cleft lip and palate, can also be supposed to possess different characteristics compared to individuals with a "normal" appearance.

To investigate whether this is the case for obese women, Miller, Rothblum, Barbour, Brand, and Felicio (1990) had obese and non-obese women have a telephone conversation with a college student. Ratings by their telephone partners indicated that the obese women made a less positive impression and were less friendly. Ratings by college student judges, also not aware of the women's weight, indicated that the obese women were less likable and less socially skilled than the non-obese women. The investigators suggest as one important explanation that the obesity stigma involving negative treatment is likely to limit the opportunities of obese women to develop social skills. In addition, the experience of being unpopular and having stressful interactions, as mentioned before, may also have played an important role. With regard to individuals with cleft lip and palate, Richman and Millard (1997) presented results from a longitudinal study indicating increasing levels of social inhibition over the years for girls with the condition in question. According to the authors, previous studies had found similar results suggesting that many adolescent females with cleft lip and palate show inhibition to a degree raising a risk for depression. In short, these examples suggest that a disfigured appearance may lead to less well developed social traits. Earlier we noted that such disfigurement conditions often elicit strong negative reactions that may also explain these outcomes.

In addition to affiliation loss, there may be a loss of power. The unpopularity of persons with a deviant condition also reflects a low social status that is likely to manifest itself in all kinds of hierarchical social relationships. As noted by Link and Phelan (2001), the sociological expectation-states tradition, closely related to the psychological self-fulfilling prophecy approach discussed in Chapter 7, is relevant here. Driskell and Mullen (1990) performed a meta-analysis in which they obtained support for the essential processes posited by expectation-states theory, namely that external status characteristics that differentiate group members lead to the formation of differential performance expectations, which in turn determine inequalities in group interaction. As described by Link and Phelan (2001), a deviant condition, for example membership of an ethnic minority group, will operate as an external status characteristic that may be irrelevant for the group task at hand, but still affect performance expectations. Persons with a deviant condition will be expected to perform less well. Consequently, they will talk less frequently, have their ideas less readily accepted in the group and are less likely to become group leader. This loss of power in relevant groups may further hamper the attainment of a desirable status position in society. Unlike the more powerful members of such groups, they cannot use their power and position in the group to pave their way to a high socio-economic status in society. In addition, less adequate social skills and power loss may also impede attaining desirable status positions in a more direct way. With those handicaps, stigma bearers may be judged less suited for the jobs they apply for.

Affiliation and power loss are also likely to have a subjective component. Experiencing affiliation and power loss will impair people's self-efficacy beliefs, their beliefs that they are able to perform actions to reach their goals, and their expectations of the outcome of their performances. As suggested by Morrow, Gore, and Campbell (1996) for the career development of lesbian women and gay men, those reduced self-efficacy beliefs and outcome expectations may hamper the development of more ambitious career interests. Affiliation and power loss may not only impede attaining desirable status positions, they may also, particularly through their subjective aspects, lead to the psychological outcomes of lowered self-esteem and subjective well-being.

Affiliation and power loss may mediate the effects of both active and passive deviant conditions. For the former type of conditions, however, the underlying unpopularity is especially based on perceived potentially harmful behavior, whereas for the latter type of conditions it is more based on perceived incompetence. Because these different characteristics may be relevant in different situations, situations may play a moderating role. For example, in performance situations in which competence is important, the effects of passive deviant conditions on affiliation and power loss are likely to be stronger than those of active conditions.

## Discrimination

In the previous chapter, many examples were given of discrimination or stigmatization of, for example, overweight and homosexual people. As also noted in that chapter, persons with a deviant condition may experience difficulties in interacting smoothly with others and show less adequate responses. This may have contributed to discriminatory responses by those others.

Discrimination, as described in the previous chapter, pertained among others to housing, education, and work, domains that are highly important in attaining a desirable position in society. In particular, discrimination in the field of education and at work may in a direct way impede attaining desirable status positions in society. In those examples, individuals, such as a landlord, teacher or boss, often engaged in discrimination. Discrimination, however, can also have an institutional or structural character, operating apart from individual forms. According to J.M. Jones (1997), institutional discrimination may work as an institutional self-fulfilling prophecy. Relevant institutional laws, customs, and practices concerning groups with a deviant condition exist because those groups are or were deemed more or less inferior, and institutional discrimination provides actual inferiority. An example of institutional discrimination with regard to the domain of education is not taking into account or openly rejecting the different norms and values held by minority group students, which may place these students at risk of lower educational outcomes.

A useful distinction with regard to institutional discrimination has been made by Sidanius and Pratto (1999), namely overt and covert institutional discrimination. Overt institutional discrimination consists of institutional rules and procedures that explicitly and openly discriminate between members of social groups, South Africa during Apartheid being an extreme example of such differential treatment. In covert institutional discrimination, there are no explicit and open policies for differential treatment. However, the institutional rules and procedures are structured in such a way that differential treatment and outcomes result. As we see it, in many examples we have given previously, covert institutional discrimination may be found. For example, if intelligence or willpower is a criterion for hiring persons, persons with a deviant condition who supposedly do not possess those qualities are less likely to be hired. Covert institutional discrimination is more difficult to spot and perpetrators and targets may often not even be aware of its occurrence.

Discrimination may also operate in its effects through social-psychological processes within persons with a deviant condition. As suggested by Link and Phelan (2001), expecting and fearing rejection, people may lose confidence and act more defensively, which seems to be rather similar to the impairment of self-efficacy beliefs and outcome expectations. Again, related to those social-psychological processes, discrimination can also be supposed to affect the psychological outcomes of lowered self-esteem and subjective well-being.

Discrimination may mediate the outcomes of both active and passive deviant conditions. Because of the greater relevance of passive deviant conditions in performance situations, the mediating effects of discrimination may be larger in performance situations for passive conditions.

### Stigma endorsement

As noted in the previous chapter, persons with a deviant condition know and often even share to some extent the negative views about their condition. This is, of course, not really surprising. Deviant conditions may evoke inherent negative responses, as outlined in Chapters 3 and 4. Seeing one's own disfigured face will immediately lead to rather strong negative reactions and no one else is needed to tell a person that having a missing leg is a strongly deviant condition. In addition, in a long and extensive process of socialization it is almost impossible not to become acquainted with stereotypes and views about relevant groups and categories of people. Mass media are a great help, but also contact with others may be very informative, particularly when those others can be seen as showing negative and stigmatizing behavior. Generally, the whole culture and society to which persons with a deviant condition belong are imbued with those negative views and it seems to be almost impossible not to be to some extent infected by them. This infection may occur more for implicit views, which are rather unconscious, than for explicit views, because the former are more difficult to control and suppress. For example, older people, like younger ones, tend to have negative implicit attitudes toward the elderly. In contrast, the explicit attitude toward the elderly becomes more positive as the age of people increases (Levy & Banaji, 2002). In Chapter 4, we presented other examples of such dissociation, but involving perceivers, such as liberals, who exhibited much more dissociation between implicit and explicit racial bias than conservatives. Similarly, as found by Livingston (2002), African-Americans demonstrated strong overall evidence of ingroup-bias on explicit measures, while they showed no evidence of ingroup-bias on implicit measures. Interestingly, high perceived negativity from whites was associated with low ingroup-bias on implicit measures. Apparently, high perceived negativity from whites may become part of the implicit attitude toward the ingroup itself. In contrast, high perceived negativity from whites was associated with strong explicit ingroup-bias, i.e., more negative views of the outgroup. As noted by Livingston, this finding conforms with the idea that individuals tend to reciprocate negative evaluations and derogate the source of perceived negativity.

Jost and Banaji (1994) stipulate in their system justification approach towards stereotyping a process whereby stereotypes are used to explain and justify the existing social system and the positions and actions of self and others. According to their view, disadvantaged groups may subscribe to negative stereotypes of themselves and others and thereby justify the societal system that produces the disadvantages. In this way, the existing social order is preserved in spite of the psychological and material harm it entails for those disadvantaged groups. In other words, "false consciousness" is produced, the holding of beliefs that are contrary to one's personal or group interest and which thereby contribute to the maintenance of the disadvantaged positions.

Stigma endorsement may contribute, particularly in the case of passive deviant conditions, to reduced self-efficacy beliefs and outcome expectations. Believing that one's group or category is less able to perform well is likely to affect one's self-efficacy beliefs and outcome expectations in a negative way. In this way, stigma endorsement may contribute to the attainment of lower status positions in society. The effect of stigma endorsement on self-esteem and subjective well-being may be more direct. The negative views about one's deviant condition may be directly incorporated into one's self-views.

## Performance deficits

We will treat here rather extensively social psychological processes leading to a decrease in task performance by persons with a deviant condition which were not discussed previously. As we will attempt to demonstrate, relevant research shows that persons with a deviant condition often perform worse than persons without such a condition.

However, people with such a condition or stigma may also try to down-play their condition by compensating for or disproving condition-related characteristics as they do in the normalization form of disclosure that we described in the previous chapter. A decrement in performance is not really inevitable and may turn into an increment. For example, in a study by Farina, Allen, and Saul (1968), students were led to believe that their interaction partner thought that they had been hospitalized for mental illness, were homosexual, or a rather typical college stu-dent. In fact, these interaction partners always thought that the other person was a typical college student. The mere belief that one is viewed as a former mental patient was found to lead to a better task performance compared to the other two conditions. Using anecdotal evidence the investigators speculated that a former mental patient, but not a homosexual, is viewed as inadequate at motor tasks such as the one used. For the participants with "a mental patient stigma" it was therefore worthwhile trying to dispel that stigma. The reader should, however, note that these responses do not necessarily reflect the responses of persons with an actual deviant condition. Incidentally, the social performance of the persons with the stigma label seemed less adequate. Possibly due to an anxious and aloof way of acting, these persons were spoken to less than participants with the college student label were. Farina *et al.* suggested that the mere belief that one is viewed as having a stigma might lead to actions that in turn cause rejection by others.

Without losing sight of the compensation idea, it should be empha-sized, as noted before, that performance decrement is likely to be more common among persons with a deviant condition. These decrements may have their origin in a number of factors. In the previous chapter, we described two of these factors, one of them being the differential treat-ment received from other persons, as in self-fulfilling prophecies with regard to the elderly condition, which often leads to performance deterioration. The second factor we mentioned is loss of motivation. By using self-esteem sustaining emotion-focused coping strategies per-sons with a deviant condition may lose the motivation to perform well, particularly when that fits with the negative stereotype related to the condition. In the case of a poor performance, for example, persons with a deviant condition can control their negative emotions and find com-fort in the idea that performing well is not that important, which legitimizes lack of achievement and lessens motivation.

Here, we will describe a third factor that may lead to performance deterioration of persons with a deviant condition, namely their aware-ness of having that condition. Having such a condition means being deviant in many situations or being a token. Research on the effects of a token status has shown that knowing that one is different may lead to self-preoccupation and divert one's attention from the central relevant task, resulting in performance deficits on memory and problem-solving tasks. Saenz (1994) demonstrated this in a study in which female participants solved anagrams together with three other females who were identified as students from the same school as the participant or a different school. In the latter (token) condition participants were more adept at tracking the performance of the group members and thereby solved fewer anagrams. In a similar way, when persons with a deviant condition think that their condition is revealed instead of concealed, that they are a token, they will act rather differently as shown in a study by Farina, Gliha, Boudreau, Allen, and Sherman (1971). In this study, former mental patients worked with a confederate as a cooperative team on a task. If these patients were under the impression that their co-worker was aware of their condition, they were rated as more tense by their co-worker, who was in fact unaware of their condition. In addition, the former patients reported feeling less appreciation, thought that the task was harder, and performed more poorly.

Awareness of one's deviant condition is not only an awareness of being different and distinctive, but can also be an awareness of being a member of a group or category that is known for its relative incompetence, as will often be the case with passive deviant conditions. In the latter case, what Steele and Aronson (1995) have called "stereotype threat," may occur. Stereotype threat is related to stigma endorsement, which was previously described, but seems to be less focused on the attribution of the stereotype to oneself. Stereotype threat is present when a stereotype is not only known but also presents a framework for interpreting the behavior of the person in question. This poses the threat that one may be seen or treated in terms of the stereotype or that one may confirm the negative stereotype by one's behavior. Stereotype threat may impair performances, but it may also impair aspirations to perform in relevant domains, which may result in disidentification. In the case of stereotype threat people may disidentify with such domains more or less permanently, as we noted before. To demonstrate stereotype threat, Steele and Aronson told African-American and European-American students taking a difficult verbal test that their performance was ostensibly diagnostic of ability or not. In the latter case, the purpose of the research was presented so as to better understand the "psychological factors involved in solving verbal problems ...". In the diagnostic condition, the test performance of the African-American students was significantly worse than in the non-diagnostic condition and than the European-American students' performance in the diagnostic condition, whereas in the non-diagnostic condition differences between these two categories of students were absent. In a further study, Steele and Aronson showed that African-American students expecting to take a difficult, ability-diagnostic test showed, as predicted by the stereotype threat notion, greater cognitive activation of stereotypes about African-Americans, and of concerns about their ability, than students in the non-diagnostic condition. Much earlier, Langer, Rodin, Beck, Weinman, and Spitzer (1979) had included in their study, without realizing the later relevance attached to such a finding, a demonstration of what was most likely stereotype threat. Elderly people living in a nursing home were given memory tests that were presented as memory tests or not. In the test-concealed conditions participants scored better on a pattern recall and probe recall test than in the test-unconcealed condition.

Steele and Aronson (1995) suggested that stereotype threat may impair performance by a number of mechanisms such as anxiety, self-consciousness, distraction, and impaired attention. These mechanisms are similar to those causing inefficient information processing when people are under other evaluative pressures, for example, due to an audience or a token status. Research, however, has also found evidence for a different mechanism in which awareness hardly seems to play a role. For example, Levy (1996) presented old participants subliminally with words related either to a senile (e.g., decline, confused, incompetent) or a wise (e.g., guidance, sage, creative) image of old age and measured their memory performance. When positive stereotypes were activated, participant's memory performance improved, whereas the activation of negative stereotypes led to a worse performance. In other words, without being aware that an elderly stereotype was activated, participants assimilated their behavior to the stereotype. This and other research (cf. Dijksterhuis *et al.*, 1998; Wheeler & Petty, 2001) suggest that a different mechanism than anxiety and impaired attention, as involved in awareness of one's deviant condition, can be at work. The sheer accessibility of cognitive representations related to the deviant condition, for example, incompetent in the case of the elderly condition, may, without mediating anxiety and impaired attention, elicit corresponding, incompetent behavior both for people with and without the deviant condition. Elderly people and people with other passive deviant conditions are likely to have more contacts with or to be more attentive to individuals with similar conditions, or to be in environments (e.g., nursing homes) that all prime the relevant, often negative stereotypes. The so activated stereotypes may then influence the performances of these people. Parenthetically, persons without such deviant conditions but with much exposure to relevant stereotypes, for example, personnel in nursing homes, may be assumed to be liable to similar effects.

An implication of the foregoing is that when stereotypes about (passive) conditions are not negative but neutral or even positive, there will be less or no performance deterioration. This is exactly what Levy and Langer (1994) found when exploring the effects of negative stereotypes about aging on memory loss in old age. Their research participants consisted of old and young Chinese, American Deaf (a cultural community) and American hearing individuals. Members of the Chinese and American Deaf cultures held a more positive view of aging than the American hearing mainstream. More interestingly, the Chinese and Deaf American old participants out-performed the American hearing old participants on the four types of memory studied. For the old participants, the influence of culture on memory seemed to be mediated by the positive view factor. Surprisingly, also in view of the tests traditionally reflecting memory loss with age, there were no significant differences on memory scores between the young and old participants in China. The explanation for this outcome may be the fact that the Chinese reported holding the most positive views of aging across the cultures studied. The authors note that in view of their results the social psychological component of memory retention in old age may be even stronger than they believed.

However, these classic and strong results may be somewhat doubted in view of recent findings by Yoon, Hasher, Feinberg, Rahhal, and Winocur (2000). These investigators studying memory performance among younger and older Anglophone, and matched Chinese-Canadians, found a much smaller cultural effect. Older Chinese-Canadians did outperform older Anglophone Canadians on two of four tests, whereas there were no differences between the two younger age groups on these tests. However, in this investigation the young Chinese-Canadians did outperform the old ones. Moreover, the investigators suggest that the differences they found for the two older age groups may be explained by the nature of these tests, the test stimuli resembling ideographic characters in written Chinese. However, the absence of differences between the two younger age groups is at odds with such an explanation. More research into these cultural effects is sorely needed.

To summarize, performances of persons with a deviant condition may deteriorate by differential treatment received from others as in self-fulfilling prophecies, but also by a loss of motivation resulting from comforting emotion-focused coping strategies. Furthermore, persons' awareness of having a deviant condition may lead to self-preoccupation and divert one's attention from the task performance, resulting in performance deficits. Moreover, awareness of having a deviant condition can also be an awareness of being a member of a group or category that is known for its relative incompetence, which can lead to "stereotype threat" with the effect of underachievement. Finally, even subtle specific situational cues, on the basis of a selectivity principle (e.g., more frequent interactions with persons sharing one's condition) more likely to be present for persons with a deviant condition, may affect performances in a negative way.

Performance deficits of persons with deviant conditions may contribute to the attainment of a lower socio-economic status in society, as performances obviously are related to status positions. They may also be supposed to lead to lower self-esteem and subjective well-being because of an awareness of such deficits. Because more of the determinants of performance deficits, for example, self-fulfilling prophecies and stereotype threat, seem to relate particularly to passive than to active deviant conditions, performance deficits and their effects can be supposed to be larger for passive deviant conditions.

The four mediating mechanisms we have discussed are likely to be dependent on each other. For example, severe discrimination may as a key mechanism enhance affiliation and power loss, stigma endorsement and performance deficits. Conversely, affiliation and power loss, stigma endorsement and performance deficits may, if present, strengthen discrimination by providing the perpetrator with extra reasons to do so.

### 8.3  Outcomes of having a deviant condition

Mediated by affiliation and power loss, discrimination, stigma endorsement and performance deficits, deviant conditions or stigmas may have clear, adverse consequences for one's socio-economic status in society, and for more psychological attributes such as self-esteem and subjective well-being. The strategies people use to cope with their deviant condition and the negative social world, be they problem-focused or emotion-focused, are in case of socio-economic status unlikely to affect those adverse consequences. Obviously, emotion-focused strategies cannot really affect one's socio-economic status, and the effects of problem-focused efforts to change one's condition and the social world will generally be too weak or too indirect to influence that status. For the psychological outcomes of self-esteem and subjective well-being, on the other hand, those coping strategies, particularly the emotion-focused ones, sometimes may sufficiently counterbalance the effects of the other mediating factors such as discrimination. We start our discussion with the socio-economic status variable.

*Socio-economic status*

A crucial determinant or manifestation of one's socio-economic status in society is income, and we will use mainly income as a proxy for socio-economic status. As for the relationship between income and deviant condition, much evidence has been gathered with regard to the ethnic condition of African-Americans in the United States. For example, J. M. Jones (1997) extensively outlined income and also educational disadvantages of this group. He introduced institutional racism, i.e., established laws, customs, and practices adversely affecting groups, as a key mechanism accounting for the leeway in education and income of African-Americans. But, of course, other mechanisms may be involved, such as individual discrimination and performance deficits caused by stereotype threat, as we described earlier.

In the previous chapter, we described the negative social worlds of persons with deviant conditions of obesity, homosexuality, mental illness, physical disabilities and old age. We will attempt here to determine whether those conditions also go together with a reduced income. For those conditions, be it because they are passive and have characteristics such as incompetence and dependency, or active and characterized by potentially harmful or negative behavior, income may lag behind. Also, controllability of the condition may play an important role. A prominent example of a controllable, passive condition is the overweight condition, of which the stereotype includes characteristics such as less intelligence and moral failings such as self-indulgence and lack of self-discipline (Quinn & Crocker, 1999; Rothblum, 1992). Gortmaker, Must, Perrin, Sobol, and Dietz (1993), as already outlined in the previous chapter, studied the relation between being overweight and subsequent (seven years later) income and educational attainment in a very large sample of young people, representative for the United States. Controlling for base-line characteristics it was found that women who had been overweight had completed fewer years of school and had lower household incomes. For overweight men such effects were not found. Nor were they found for a group of young people with chronic health conditions. This last finding suggests that overweight associated health problems had not limited the socio-economic attainment of the overweight women. The investigators suggest that stigmatization or discrimination may account for the lower socio-economic attainment of overweight women. Consistent with this suggestion is that research has shown that American females are more concerned than males about body weight which is likely to reflect that the American culture considers obesity a more negative condition for women than for men (cf. Pliner, Chaiken, & Flett, 1990). Parenthetically, the negative relationship between weight and socio-economic status generally found for women in the Western industrialized countries and often interpreted in terms of a causal influence of status on weight, may therefore be based in part on the reverse effect (cf. Sobal & Stunkard, 1989).

The specific mechanisms involved in the process through which discrimination of the overweight may lead to lowered socio-economic attainment are not known yet. One such mechanism was revealed by Crandall (1995), who found that overweight daughters were less likely to receive financial support from their families for college independent of the families' ability to pay. Furthermore, Crandall found that female college students from politically conservative homes were thinner than those from liberal homes. Additional evidence suggested that this was because conservative families are less likely to send their overweight daughters to college under any circumstances. According to Crandall, this reluctance probably reflects the antifat attitudes of conservatives (see Chapter 5). Conservatives tend to attribute internal controllable causes for fatness, which leads to blaming fat people for their condition, feelings of anger and a reduced willingness to give assistance to fat people.

The consequences of the homosexuality condition for the income of that group in the United States were studied by Badgett (1995). She analyzed pooled 1989–91 data from a national random sample and used questions about sexual behavior as a proxy for sexual orientation. Controlling for economically relevant factors, among which sex, education, occupation, marital status, race and region, Badgett found that behaviorally gay/bisexual men earned from 11 to 27 percent less than behaviorally heterosexual men. For women such a discrepancy was hardly found. As noted earlier, at least in the United States gay men seem to face greater discrimination than lesbian women do. Moreover, heterosexual men, the most important decision-makers in the occupational field, hold a more negative attitude toward gay men than to lesbian women, as noted in Chapter 7. These factors may have contributed to the different effects of sexual orientation on income for men and women.

The adverse effects of mental illness on labor market outcomes have been studied by Ettner, Frank, and Kessler (1997). From their large, national (US) sample, it appeared that 31 percent of women and 26 percent of men experienced at least one diagnosable disorder during the previous twelve months. For women the most common disorders were simple phobias, major depression and social phobia, whereas for men alcohol dependence, major depression and social phobia were most common. Using a large number of control variables, Ettner *et al.* found that recent psychiatric disorders reduced employment rates among both men and women by about 11 percentage points or more. They also found evidence of small reductions in work hours (estimated using employed respondents only) of men and a substantial drop in the income of men and women. With regard to these latter results, they noted that the larger reduction in income than in work hours suggests that psychiatric disorders affect the earnings of workers primarily via a wage effect. To what extent these adverse effects can be seen as results of discrimination and stigmatization or the other mechanisms mediating deviant condition effects is hard to tell, because less optimal functioning is also very likely to have been involved. Adding functional limitations (restrictions of sensory, mental, or physical capacities) to the control variables, Baldwin (1999) still found effects of mental impairments in her analyses of data from the US Survey of Income and Program Participation. Mental impairments, i.e., mental disorders but also mental disability, had negative effects on the probability of employment, suggesting a role for employer discrimination.

Unsurprisingly, employment rates, as a rough indication of socio-economic status, of physically disabled persons are also relatively low. For example, recent estimates suggest that only about 30 percent of physically disabled adults in Britain and Japan are employed (Neufeldt & Mathieson, 1995). Baldwin (1999) also found effects of physical disability on employment rate in her analyses of data from the US Survey of Income and Program Participation. Controlling again also for functional limitations, she found that physical disability had negative effects on the probability of employment, suggesting employer discrimination.

To investigate whether there is age discrimination in earnings, Mueller, Mutran, and Boyle (1989) examined in the US the age-earnings relationship for a panel of older workers in 1966 and 1976. In this study, the investigators controlled for a large number of variables that might account for age effects. Thus they included worker background variables, education, training, health limitations, experience, job characteristics and labor market conditions. Controlling for all those variables, the investigators found age-based discrimination in earnings for workers in the economic core sector, but not in the economic periphery sector. This discrimination became more prevalent as the workers grew older.

In summary, we have found that, controlling for relevant factors, overweight women and gay men lag behind in socio-economic status, as measured by income. Findings also suggest that people with a mental illness stigma and elderly people in the economic core sector suffer a drop in income. Controlling for functional limitations, physically disabled people were found to be less often employed, which also indicates a lowered social position in society. In view of the discrimination, particularly in the field of work, experienced by those groups, as described in the previous chapter, it is highly likely that discrimination has at least in part mediated the lowered socio-economic status. Whether the mechanisms of affiliation and power loss, stigma endorsement and performance deficits have also to some extent contributed to a lowered status is hard to tell.

### Self-esteem

In light of, among other things, discrimination and generally negative reactions experienced by people with a deviant condition and their frequent sharing of the negative stereotypes about their own group or stigma endorsement, a lowered self-esteem among these people would speak for itself. Theoretically, such lowering in self-esteem is predicted, for example, by the old and influential sociological perspective of "reflected appraisal" as proposed by Cooley (1902). In this perspective, the self is a "looking-glass self"; persons develop an image of themselves as they see themselves as seen by others. In other words, the self is reflected or mirrored in the perceived actions and responses of others to oneself. This implies that people with a deviant condition will incorporate the negative responses and stereotypes in their selves, which will lower their self-esteem. Surprisingly, Crocker and Major (1989) reviewing evidence on this question for a variety of deviant conditions, for example, hare lip or cleft lip and palate, mental disability, homosexuality, and mental illness, failed to find consistently lower self-esteem for the members of these groups. It is also questionable whether there is a reduction in self-esteem in old age, although such a reduction has been found in a large-scale study collecting data over the Internet (Robins, Trzesniewski, Tracy, Gosling, & Potter, 2002). Even more surprisingly, the self-esteem of African-Americans is, on average, higher than that of white Americans (Twenge & Crocker, 2002). Crocker and Major (1989) proposed that people with a deviant condition could develop or maintain positive self-esteem by a number of coping strategies, as discussed in the previous chapter. These strategies include attributing negative feedback to prejudice against one's group, comparing one's outcomes with those of one's own group rather than with relatively advantaged outgroups, and selectively devaluing outcomes on which one's own group fares poorly and valuing outcomes on which one's own group excels. As noted in Chapter 7, Crocker and Wolfe (2001) added another coping strategy, namely basing one's self-esteem on contingencies such as others' approval, or God's love, that are less related to competencies. One important explanation for the high self-esteem of African-Americans is, according to Crocker and Wolfe, that African-Americans are less likely to base their self-esteem on others' approval and are more likely to base it on God's love.

However, not finding evidence for a lowered self-esteem among people with a deviant condition may be due in part to the evidence being limited or incomplete. Collecting extensive evidence, Langlois *et al.* (2000) found in their meta-analyses of physical attractiveness that unattractive adults perceived themselves as less competent and less mentally healthy than attractive adults. Also for the obesity condition, a moderately lower self-esteem has been demonstrated in an extensive meta-analysis using seventy-one studies (Miller & Downey, 1999). In their analysis, Miller and Downey introduced a number of variables that, according to research and theory, might moderate the relation between being overweight and self-esteem. These variables include gender, age, socio-economic status (SES), and ethnicity. For these variables there are differences in the standards of thinness, the cultural value placed on being thin and the prevalence or normativeness of obesity within the groups in question. The more thinness is the culturally important standard and is prevalent, the stronger will be the stigma attached to obesity, and the more self-esteem may be expected to suffer. As for gender, the investigators argued that the standards for thinness are both more extreme and rigid for women than for men. We noted such a difference already in our description of the effects of the overweight stigma on income. As for age, appearance seems to be especially important in the dating and mating period of one's life, i.e., adolescence and young adulthood. Socio-economic status is negatively correlated with being overweight; in other words, overweight people are more prevalent in the lower socio-economic strata. As for ethnicity, ethnic minorities are generally disproportionately represented in the lower socio-economic status groups, and therefore obesity should be more common among these minorities. Moreover, for African-Americans obesity is less of a stigma than for white Americans. Consistent with these arguments, the negative relationship between being overweight and self-esteem was stronger for women than for men, for high school and college students than for children, for high socio-economic status than for low socio-economic status samples and for non-minority than for ethnic minority samples.

The relationship between being overweight and self-esteem was also stronger for people who perceive themselves as overweight than for people who actually are overweight. Miller and Downey (1999) suggest that one reason for this difference is that both self-perceptions about being too heavy and self-esteem are self-evaluations that are dependent on each other and therefore more highly correlated. The difference also strongly suggests that the outcomes of deviant conditions may be not only dependent on negative reactions of others but also, as noted before, on stigma endorsement, on how persons with a stigma themselves view that stigma. An important belief in this respect is the controllability of being overweight. As discussed in Chapter 3, the obesity stigma often involves the belief that weight is controllable and therefore being overweight stems from a lack of willpower. When persons with an overweight condition share this belief, it may affect their self-esteem. Testing this hypothesis, Tiggeman and Rothblum (1997) found that overweight women (but not men) who had an internal locus of control for weight, in other words, deemed weight controllable, had lower self-esteem than overweight women having an external locus of control for weight. Interestingly, as noted by the investigators, an internal locus of control for weight can be seen, on the one hand, as a positive asset in getting rid of one's deviant condition and stigma. It may make people confidently engage in weight-loss programs and sometimes predicts success. On the other hand, however, it has its psychological costs, namely a lowering of self-esteem.

Quinn and Crocker (1999) replicated and extended the results obtained by Tiggeman and Rothblum (1997). They showed that, in addition to controllability, having a Protestant ethic ideology, which is related to conservatism (see also Chapter 5), may lead to lowered self-esteem – their measure also included anxiety and depression and in a second study hostility – among overweight women. By making the Protestant ethic salient for their participants, they also established that the causal direction could go from ideology to self-esteem. As explanation they suggested that people use the ideology as a standard for judging themselves. If people fail at controlling their weight, then they judge this failure as being due to moral failings such as self-indulgence or lack of self-discipline. These notions are prominent in the Protestant ethic ideology and by stressing these notions the ideology enlarges stigma endorsement. This enlarged endorsement in turn leads to lowered self-esteem.

The more specific categories distinguished with regard to the overweight condition bring us to a different approach to studying the relationship between deviant condition and self-esteem. In this approach, the focus is not on comparisons between people with and without a specific deviant condition, but on studying the relationships between a number of stressors, particularly stigmatization, and self-esteem *within* the group of people with a deviant condition (cf. Friedman & Brownell, 1995; Meyer, 1995). Let us give a number of examples of this approach. Frable, Wortman, and Joseph (1997) studied responses of homosexual and bisexual men. They developed, through structural equation analyses, a model in which negative reactions for being gay, more specifically, stigma or rejection from own family, stigma or rejection from other gay men, and stigma or rejection in general, lead to lowered positive self-perception, in terms of self-esteem, well-being and distress. Meyer (1995) tested the mental health effects of three stressors in a sample of gay men. Internalized homophobia, i.e., uneasiness about their homosexuality, stigma, i.e., expectations of rejection and discrimination, and prejudice, which was defined and measured here as actual experiences of discrimination and violence, predicted independently a variety of mental health measures, such as demoralization and guilt. Waldo, Hesson-McInnis, and D'Augelli (1998) using structural equation modeling found that for lesbian, gay and bisexual youths antigay victimization, which included among others threats, being chased, and being assaulted, led to lowered self-esteem, which in turn heightened psychological distress. The ultimate negative effect of victimization on distress is consistent with Meyer's (1995) results mentioned before. Westbrook, Bauman, and Shinnar (1992) studied the relationship between perceived stigma, i.e., the belief that having the stigma negatively affects social relationships and interactions, and self-esteem for adolescents with epilepsy. Controlling for biological attributes of epilepsy, such as seizure frequency, they found that perceived stigma was a significant predictor of self-esteem; higher perceived stigma was related to lower self-esteem.

The negative relationship between stigmatization and self-esteem, the latter broadly conceived, that was revealed in all these studies, does not support an important argument of Crocker and Major (1989). These investigators argued that recognizing that one's negative outcomes may have resulted from prejudice – attribution to prejudice – rather than from one's own personal shortcomings can protect self-esteem. The evidence for this seems to be largely based on attributional coping that is specific to a single instance of prejudice. Branscombe, Schmitt, and Harvey (1999) suggested that when attributions to prejudice reflect a more general sense of stable and pervasive prejudice against one's group, they may have negative consequences for self-esteem. A key argument for this suggestion is that a pattern of stable attributions to prejudice is likely to reflect perceived systematic and unaltering exclusion and rejection on the part of the stigmatizing group. Feeling rejected and excluded in this way will harm self-esteem, for humans are motivated to seek inclusion and avoid exclusion. In the previous chapter, we already concluded that attributions to prejudice and discrimination may have important costs such as experiencing negative emotions. In their research Branscombe *et al.* (1999) found in a sample of African-Americans support for a model suggesting a direct negative effect of attributions to prejudice on self-esteem, and an indirect positive effect of attributions that was mediated by minority group identification. The relationship between attributions to prejudice and self-esteem seems, however, to be liable to moderation. Research by McCoy and Major (2003), for example, suggests that for individuals who saw their group as central in their self-concept perceiving discrimination against the self or their group is a threat that may lead to negative emotions. Beneficial effects of perceived discrimination may be more easily obtained for individuals who see their group as less central in their self-concept.

A weakness in virtually all these studies on the relationship between discrimination or stigmatization and self-esteem and recognized by all of them, is that the data are cross-sectional and therefore do not allow causal interpretations of the results. Not surprisingly then, other studies reverse the causal direction and assume that self-esteem affects perceived stigmatization, for instance, a study by Kent (1999) on the vitiligo (a gradual depigmentation of the skin) condition. In this study, self-esteem was found to be a significant predictor of perceived stigma, although Kent too recognizes that it is not possible to ascertain the direction of causation. Phinney, Madden, and Santos (1998) similarly recognized the causality problem but made less reservations in this respect and developed a model in which self-esteem and mastery influence perceived discrimination. They distinguish between discrimination as objectively measurable events and perceived discrimination, which is the individual interpretation of events as discriminatory. Sociologists make a similar distinction between "enacted" stigma – actual incidents of discrimination – and "felt" stigma or the anticipation of rejection (cf. Kent, 1999). Perceived discrimination may be influenced by psychological variables related to one's interpretation of the intentions of others. Phinney *et al.* (1998) expected that higher self-esteem would be related to a generally positive interpretation of events; possible slights would more likely to be seen as misunderstandings than as deliberate discrimination. On the other hand, depression would be expected to lead to a negative view of the world and a greater likelihood of seeing discrimination. Phinney *et al.* developed and tested their model among adolescents from minority and immigrant groups living in the United States. The model showed that individuals with higher self-esteem experienced less depression and in turn also perceived less discrimination.

That perceived discrimination may be influenced by psychological variables was also proposed by Pinel (1999), who measured stigma consciousness for a number of groups that are or can be seen as stigmatized such as women, blacks, Hispanics, gay men and lesbians. This variable reflects the extent to which targets of stereotyping expect to be judged on the basis of their group membership. Pinel found that people high in stigma consciousness were more likely to perceive discrimination directed toward their group and toward them personally. Parenthetically, Pinel also showed that when women high in stigma consciousness believed they would compete against a man as compared with a woman, they were more apt to avoid stereotypically male topics. This effect appears to have been mediated by performance expectancies. Women high in stigma consciousness expected to perform worse on the stereotypically male topics than on stereotype-irrelevant topics when they were competing against a man as compared with when they were competing against a woman. These results suggest that people high in stigma consciousness may forgo opportunities to invalidate stereotypes about their own groups.

A recent study among gay and bisexual men by Huebner, Nemeroff and Davis (2005) took the confounding role of personality characteristics into account and found that the personality characteristics, hostility and neuroticism, were positively related to both perceived discrimination and reported depressive symptoms. More importantly, controlling for hostility and neuroticism perceived discrimination still predicted depressive symptoms, that can be seen as a rough measure of self-esteem. Thus this study, although cross-sectional, gives some evidence for a causal role of discrimination with regard to self-esteem.

Fortunately, some investigations did not use a cross-sectional but a longitudinal design, which alleviates the problem of causal interpretation of the results. For example, in a study by Link, Struening, Rahav, Phelan, and Nuttbrock (1997), men with dual diagnoses of mental disorder and substance use were interviewed at two points in time – at entry of treatment and then again after a year of treatment, when they were far less symptomatic and largely drug- and alcohol-free. Rejection experiences like being avoided and having people feel uncomfortable around the respondent, were, controlling for baseline depressive symptoms and other relevant variables, significantly associated with depressive symptoms that included self-evaluation. These results form evidence that stigmatization may affect self-esteem.

What can we now conclude about the relationship between deviant conditions or stigmas and self-esteem? First, it seems highly likely that, making comparisons between people with and without a specific deviant condition, a somewhat lowered self-esteem is characteristic in the case of some conditions such as physical unattractiveness and obesity. Such a lowering of self-esteem may particularly occur for persons with individual-related stigmas, who, as noted in Chapter 7, lack the support and culture of meaningful social groups. In addition, for more specific categories of obese people, such as women, high school and college students, individuals with a high socio-economic status and from non-minority groups, and individuals having an internal locus of control for weight and a Protestant ethic ideology, self-esteem is predictably lowered to a larger extent. Second, one can also study the relationship between deviant condition and self-esteem in terms of the relationship between a number of stressors, particularly reported or perceived stigmatization, and self-esteem *within* a group of people with a deviant condition. Following this approach suggests that a bi-directional relationship between stigmatization and self-esteem is very likely. That stigmatization lowers self-esteem can be theoretically argued and has not only been found for more global and subjective, but also for behavioral measures of discrimination and victimization, making in the latter case self-esteem as a strong causal factor less likely (cf. Meyer, 1995; Waldo *et al.*, 1998). In addition, longitudinal research has made a causal role of stigmatization more likely. The negative effect of self-esteem on (perceived) stigmatization, on the other hand, can also easily be argued (cf. Phinney *et al.*, 1998). Moreover, it has been shown that manipulating sense of control, a variable related to self-esteem, affected perceived discrimination (Ruggiero & Taylor, 1995). From those within-group approach studies it can, however, not be concluded that groups with a deviant condition in comparison with groups without such a deviant condition are suffering as a whole from a lowered self-esteem. For one thing, the strength of the relationship may be partly due to a causal input of self-esteem. Furthermore, a higher level of discrimination may characterize only a limited number of group members, which does not essentially contribute to the average level of discrimination for the group as a whole.

Results of the within-group approach studies on the effects of discrimination suggest that discrimination is an important mechanism mediating the effects of deviant condition on the outcome of self-esteem. Those results, for example the adverse role played by internalized homophobia, also suggest that stigma endorsement is such a mechanism. The mediating role of stigma endorsement is also suggested by the fact that overweight women having an internal locus of control for weight and a Protestant ethic ideology, which enhance stigma endorsement, lowered their self-esteem. Furthermore, the self-esteem reduction for more specific categories of obese people, for example, women and individuals with high socio-economic status, can easily be explained as mediated by discrimination and stigma endorsement. More research on the possible mediating mechanisms of coping strategies, affiliation and power loss, and performance deficits is needed to establish whether these factors may also have to some extent affected self-esteem.

*Subjective well-being*

For most people subjective well-being or happiness, people's evaluation of their life, is extremely important (cf. Diener, Suh, Lucas, & Smith, 1999). Also, most people, including students of psychology, think that having a deviant condition or stigma, particularly a passive one, may reduce this happiness considerably (Diener & Diener, 1996). Therefore, it will come as a surprise for most people that the majority of individuals having a deviant condition report positive levels of well-being. For example, as reviewed by Diener and Diener (1996), persons with disabilities ranging from quadriplegia to blindness report positive well-being. A more accurate picture may be derived from comparisons between people with and without a specific deviant condition. Let us give some examples. Ramund and Stensman (1988) found no differences in self-reported quality of life between Swedish disabled persons with severely impaired mobility, all using a wheelchair, and non-handicapped matched controls. Schulz and Decker (1985) in a study on the adjustment of spinal-cord-injured persons about twenty years after the disability occurred, and mentioned in the previous chapter, concluded that well-being of these persons was only slightly lower than that of different non-disabled adult populations. Mehnert, Krauss, Nadler, and Boyd (1990), however, found considerable differences in life satisfaction between large samples of non-disabled and disabled individuals. Ninety percent of the former reported that they were at least somewhat satisfied against 68 percent of the latter.

Diener *et al.* (1999), reviewing the relationship between health and well-being, concluded that when a disabling condition is severe or entails multiple or chronic problems, it may negatively influence well-being. Diener *et al.* (1999) also reviewed the relationship between the elderly condition and well-being and found no decline in well-being with age. Diener, Wolsic, and Fujita (1995) conducted three studies among college students to establish the relationship between physical attractiveness and well-being. These studies revealed that physical attractiveness only had a marginal effect on happiness and life satisfaction. Their results also suggested that at least part of the small relation between well-being and physical attractiveness is due to the fact that happy people do more to enhance their appearance beyond their natural state, for example by using cosmetics.

As noted by Diener *et al.* (1999), important explanations for the modest relationship between deviant conditions and well-being are the mechanisms of adaptation and coping. We notice here that for people with a deviant condition feelings of well-being are not only based on stigmatization or other negative experiences, but also on being different in a negative way that often relates to physical and psychological suffering. As for adaptation to the condition and its stigma, people's emotion system reacts most strongly to new events and these reactions dampen over time. This adaptation or habituation can be seen as an automatic passive biological process affecting well-being and probably also self-esteem. In coping with the condition and its stigma, on the other hand, the participant plays a more active role. In the previous chapter, we described a number of habitual long-term responses or strategies that people use to cope with their deviant condition and a negative social world. In this way, those persons can achieve better outcomes or can regulate and control the negative emotions they have to face because of their condition and stigma. It is highly likely that adaptation and coping in combination mitigate distress and further well-being. Interestingly, persons with passive deviant conditions may also unknowingly and from necessity select goals that are conducive to their well-being. Rather than focusing on less attainable extrinsic goals of money and power, they may select more attainable intrinsic goals such as interpersonal relatedness and personal growth. Research by Schulz and Decker (1985) described earlier showed that a majority of the spinal-cord-injured persons studied ascribed positive meaning to their disability, mentioning most frequently types of meaning related to personal growth such as increased awareness of self and seeing other people as more important. Other research has shown that the more importance individuals place on intrinsic relative to extrinsic goals, the more likely they are to report higher well-being (e.g., Ryan *et al.*, 1999). Self-determination theory has offered an explanation. Intrinsic goals can directly satisfy basic psychological needs, such as autonomy and relatedness, which leads to a true sense of personal well-being. In contrast, extrinsic goals can only provide indirect satisfaction of these basic needs and may actually distract from or interfere with their fulfillment, leading to lower well-being (cf. Ryan *et al.*, 1999).

Most of the effects of deviant conditions on well-being, that we described here, may have resulted from sheer inability and incapacity and negative emotions related to those conditions; negative reactions by others may not have been involved. More direct evidence with respect to the relationship between stigmatization and well-being can be found in studies following the within-group approach with stigmatization as a predictor. Because generally a very strong relationship has been found between self-esteem and well-being, it will come as no surprise that these studies paint the same picture as found for stigmatization and self-esteem. For example, Frable *et al.* (1997) found in their research described before that self-esteem and well-being formed, together with distress, a homogeneous variable, called positive self-perception. In their model, this positive self-perception variable was adversely affected by stigmatization. Another example is a study by Markowitz (1998), who conducted a two-wave study of persons with mental illness in self-help groups and outpatient treatment. In this longitudinal study discriminatory experiences had a negative effect on life satisfaction, making a causal role of stigmatization also with respect to well-being more likely.

Particularly because of the very strong relationship that has been found between self-esteem and subjective well-being, our conclusions regarding the effects on well-being of having a deviant condition or stigma can be globally rather similar to the conclusions regarding such effects on self-esteem. At least for some conditions, such as physical unattractiveness (among college students) and more severe disability, somewhat lowered well-being is likely, although for the latter condition stigmatization in the form of negative reactions by others may have played a minor role. For other conditions, such as old age, no loss of well-being has been found. More research is needed to establish whether the effects of deviant conditions on self-esteem, for example, the detailed effects obtained for the obesity condition, and well-being parallel each other. Again, results of the within-group approach studies on the effects of discrimination suggest that discrimination is an important mechanism mediating the effects of deviant conditions on well-being. Results on the role of stigma endorsement for self-esteem in combination with the strong empirical relationship between self-esteem and well-being also suggest a mediating role for stigma endorsement with respect to well-being. More research on the possible mediating mechanisms of coping strategies, affiliation and power loss, and performance deficits is needed to establish whether these factors also affect well-being.

Of course, it would be utterly wrong to infer from the modest or small loss of self-esteem and well-being among persons with deviant conditions that they have little to complain about. The limitation of those losses attests more to the amazing ability of humans to cope successfully with adverse and extreme conditions than to a life without problems. As Solzhenitsyn (1963) noted, describing one miserable day in the life of Ivan Denisovich in a Siberian labor camp, even that day was for Ivan counting his blessings almost a happy day. The days of persons with a deviant condition generally are less miserable than the one described by Solzhenitsyn, but as this book has shown, they frequently can be quite unpleasant. Apparently and fortunately, people with a deviant condition also often succeed in giving their days a positive tone. However, we should not forget that the persons with a deviant condition we focused on are mostly living in the modern

Western world. Looking at these matters from a social comparison perspective, we note that, as Chapter 6 made clear, the plight of similar persons from other parts of our earth is often worse, even much worse. It can be questioned whether these persons frequently succeed in making their days positive.

## 8.4 Summary

As outlined in this and earlier chapters, life is often not easy for people with a deviant condition, even when living in the modern Western world. In that light, it is not surprising that at least some of them or some groups or categories with a deviant condition will also be confronted with more or less permanent marks or outcomes of stigmatization. We started our discussion in this chapter with a number of mechanisms that may mediate such outcomes. As mediating mechanisms we discussed affiliation and power loss, discrimination, stigma endorsement, and performance deficits. Due to unpopularity persons with a deviant condition may experience a loss of affiliation and power in their social relationships; they are less attractive interaction partners, less welcome in groups and less likely to attain positions of power in those groups. Furthermore, the unpopularity of some categories of those persons may impede their developing social skills, which may be an extra contributing factor to affiliation and power loss. Affiliation and power loss are also likely to affect specific self-perceptions. Experiencing affiliation and power loss will impair peoples' self-efficacy beliefs, their beliefs that they are able to perform adequate actions to reach their goals, and their expectations of the outcome of their performances.

Discrimination of persons with a deviant condition can pertain to domains that are highly important in attaining desirable status positions in society, such as housing, education, and work. It can be engaged in by individuals, such as a landlord, teacher or boss, but also have an institutional or structural character, operating by established laws, customs, and practices adversely affecting groups with a deviant condition. Both forms of discrimination are likely to affect the outcomes of persons with a deviant conditions. Because the deviant condition per se may be negative, e.g., a disfigured face, and usually the whole culture and society to which persons with a deviant condition belong, are imbued with negative views about that condition, it seems to be almost impossible for persons with that condition to escape from those views. This often means stigma endorsement, knowing and sharing to some extent the negative views about one's condition. Stigma endorsement can be seen as system justification. Disadvantaged groups subscribe to negative stereotypes of themselves and others and thereby justify and maintain the disadvantageous societal system for themselves.

As a final mediating mechanism that may lead to outcome losses we discussed performance deficits and their determinants, one important determinant being a person's awareness of having a deviant condition or being a token that may lead to self-preoccupation and diverting one's attention from the task. Another determinant we discussed is "stereotype threat," the threat that one may be seen or treated in terms of the negative stereotype about one's group or that one may confirm the stereotype by one's behavior.

The mediating mechanisms, affiliation and power loss, discrimination, stigma endorsement and performance deficits, can be supposed to hamper the attainment of desirable status positions in society. Affiliation and power loss, and performance deficits may do this, because they reduce the own means of persons with deviant conditions to reach such positions. Stigma endorsement may operate more in an indirect demotivating way, by impairing and reducing peoples' self-efficacy beliefs and outcome expectations. Discrimination implies that one's efforts to reach desirable positions are thwarted by societal rules or individual actions, for example, by one's teacher or boss.

These mechanisms may also be supposed to impair one's self-esteem and subjective well-being. Affiliation and power loss, discrimination and performance deficits may, through an awareness of one's limitations, and more specifically impaired self-efficacy beliefs and outcome expectations, lower one's self-esteem and subjective well-being. Stigma endorsement may have a more direct effect on self-esteem and subjective well-being. Sharing the negative views about one's deviant condition is highly likely to affect self-esteem and well-being.

At least a number of groups and social categories with a deviant condition have experienced a lowered socio-economic status, as measured by income. We have found evidence for income losses among overweight women and gay men, people with a mental illness stigma and elderly people. Physically disabled people were found to be less often employed, which also indicates a lowered social position in society. Discrimination is likely to have mediated the lowered socio-economic status.

Due to mechanisms of habituation, adaptation, and coping, a lowered self-esteem and well-being due to having a deviant condition sometimes may be limited or absent. For example, African-Americans seem to have an even higher self-esteem than whites, and there seems to be no relationship between age and well-being. However, unattractive people have a less positive view about themselves and report somewhat lower well-being than attractive people. A lowered self-esteem also has been found for overweight people. Furthermore, for more specific categories of those people, women, high school and college students, individuals with high socio-economic status and from non-minority groups, and individuals having an internal locus of control for weight and a Protestant ethic ideology, a predicted larger effect of weight on self-esteem has been found. Results of the within-group approach suggest that discrimination is an important mechanism mediating the effects of deviant conditions on the outcome of self-esteem and well-being. They also suggest that stigma endorsement is a contributing factor.

CHAPTER 9

# Theorizing about interventions to prevent or reduce stigmatization

## 9.1 Introduction

In Chapter 1 we noted that a major motive for social scientists studying stigmatization is to find ways to prevent or reduce it. Although this interest, as shown in the present chapter, has resulted in the development of several useful intervention strategies, it may have undesirable consequences if not accompanied with a thorough reflection on the nature of stigmatization and its relation to other types of social control. Especially troublesome is the strong tendency among students of stigmatization to see most negative responses to deviance as undesirable, stigmatizing, and requiring intervention, thereby running the risk of intervening in useful social control processes; to implicitly assume that the ultimate goal of interventions should be something like unconditional acceptance of, or even love for, individuals associated with deviant conditions, thereby ignoring other desirable ultimate intervention goals; and that stigmatization and its reduction are primarily based on general psychological mechanisms in the head of "stigmatizers" that are relatively independent of the particular nature of the deviant condition. These tendencies among social scientists are complemented by the activity of a wide variety of advocacy groups for people associated with deviance, protesting against a stigmatizing and discriminating society and attempting to realize legal change and policy implementation through protest, political mobilization, lobbying, and empowerment.

We believe that the theoretical perspective that we have developed and illustrated in this book may help to sharpen our thinking on the usefulness and effectiveness of interventions to prevent or reduce stigmatization. In particular, this perspective raises the following three critical questions with respect to these interventions.[1] First, what is the nature of the response that we want to influence? Is it really stigmatization or is it actually a useful kind of social control such as repair or tolerance of which certain negative aspects may be mistaken for stigmatization? Second, given that it is stigmatization, what should we replace it with? With repair, tolerance, or perhaps with long-term care and protection? To put this question differently: What should be the ultimate goals of intervention aimed at reducing or preventing stigmatization, and are these objectives desirable and feasible in the context of prevalent social control practices? Third, what are the proximal motivational mechanisms that underlie stigmatization (especially those that are specifically related to different types of deviance), which of them can be used to reduce stigmatization, and how do the immediate outcomes of these mechanisms contribute to realization of ultimate intervention goals? Let us examine how our theoretical approach may help to start answering each of these three critical questions.

### What is the nature of the response that we would like to influence?

To fully understand the nature of responses to deviance, we have found it useful in this book to see these responses as resulting from interactions between evolved motivational mechanisms and social situations, societies, or historical periods. We have argued that certain features of deviance automatically trigger motivational mechanisms that give rise to elementary forms of social control. Thus, for example, when people perceive certain signs of controllable-active deviance (e.g., crime), they will experience anger and will be motivated to punish the deviant individual; but when they perceive evidence for uncontrollable-passive deviance (e.g., illness) they will experience pity, which in turn will motivate them to nurture the other person (see Chapter 2). These elementary responses are modified by the particular relationship or society in which these motivational mechanisms are triggered. Specifically, we argued that in close relationships or small groups of kin-related individuals, activation of the relevant mechanisms normally will result in responses to deviance that are neither too hard nor too soft. Here, people address deviance explicitly and focus on repairing their relationships; they neither deny the existence of deviance and are unconditionally nice, nor stigmatize.

We have further argued that, in modern Western societies, the same motivational mechanisms are also automatically activated by the perception of deviance when unfamiliar people engage in a more formal type of social control, and exercise tolerance, often guided by strong social norms not to pay attention to deviance. Here too, some negativity is associated with responding to deviance, yet this time, due also to the suppression of negative feelings, self-control, interactional anxiety, irritation, or stress, and tendencies to avoid these unpleasant experiences through reducing contact. People associated with deviance contribute to this negativity, for example, due to negative expectancies and mechanisms of self-fulfilling prophecies. It would be a mistake to interpret the negative aspects of both repair and tolerance as evidence for stigmatization and to disrupt rather than facilitate these processes. Stigmatization, as we have argued, first arises in larger social groups when people start to advertise a person's bad or unworthy character because of his or her association with a deviant condition; for example, because of the permanent or serious nature of the condition, power motives, or processes of displacement.

Finally, note how several other behaviors in relation to individuals associated with deviance may be mistaken for stigmatization. For example, long-term care of people with particular forms of passive deviance (e.g., the frail elderly, or the mentally handicapped) may appear to have undesirable or even stigmatizing aspects if evaluated against the ideal of reciprocity and mutual respect. But clearly, people with particular dependencies, illnesses or disabilities, are sometimes better off in informal or institutionalized care settings than in an environment that primarily demands them to engage in reciprocal relationships. Also, principles of interpersonal attraction, sexual selection, and partner choice should not be confused with stigmatization of persons who, due to their illness, disability, abnormal physical features or other association with deviance, tend to be less often chosen as friends or relationship partners.

Unfortunately, as noted in Chapter 1, it is often difficult to empirically distinguish if people responding to deviance engage in repair, tolerance, or stigmatization; especially if observations are made only once and the measure employed is one-dimensional. For example, it is hard to tell from single expressions of "dislike" or "negative evaluation" if people are temporarily angry with the deviant individual, feel that their tolerance is pushed to the limit, or truly denigrate or stigmatize the person. Similarly, expressions of "liking" may indicate that people primarily want to protect or care for the other person with little expectation of reciprocity, or that they truly value and respect the other person's competencies and contribution to a reciprocal relationship. In the context of evaluating the need for, and effectiveness of, interventions, the least we can do is to measure qualitatively different emotional aspects of responding (see Chapter 3) and to consider their role in long-term patterns of social control.

To conclude, many different aspects of responding to deviance may involve negative elements, but this should not be enough reason to try to influence them. Furthermore, seemingly positive aspects of responding to deviance may not always be desirable in light of certain ultimate intervention goals.

*What should be the ultimate goals of interventions aimed at reducing or preventing stigmatization?*

As argued above, the absence of stigmatization is not the same as unconditional niceness, liking, or harmony. Yet, although not clearly specifying the ultimate goal of interventions, current thinking on stigma reduction strongly gives the impression that it is. Specifically, it seems as if the ultimate goal of stigma-reduction interventions should be something like a generalized likeability of all members of a particular social category, based on positive feelings about, or personalized contact (or preferably friendship) with individual members of that category (cf. R. Brown & Hewstone, 2005; Dovidio, Kawakami, & Gaertner, 2000; Miller, 2002; Pettigrew, 1998). On the basis of our theoretical approach to deviance and social control, we suggest four ultimate goals that seem more realistic and that refer to different strategies of dealing with deviance in the context of interpersonal relationships or societies. (As illustrated later, we emphasize that certain other ultimate goals of common stigma-reduction strategies, that are related to the correction of certain general shortcomings of human reasoning, seem highly useful and valuable to us.) The usefulness of three of these goals or strategies – tolerance, repair, and long-term care – depends on prevalent social control practices and the nature of deviance. The fourth strategy – raising general awareness of the basic principles of social control and of the complexity of deviance and social control in modern Western society, and using negotiation about mutually agreeable forms of interacting – is seen as a meta-strategy allowing for flexible use of the first three strategies.

Tolerance and repair have been treated sufficiently in this book. To repeat, tolerance implies that the normal motivational systems associated with types of deviance encountered are activated but their output suppressed or transformed, often on the basis of generalized care or egalitarian values. Consequently, the existence and relevance of deviance tends to be denied and social control is delegated to formal institutions. Repair involves mutual efforts of non-deviant and deviant individuals in the context of a relationship or social group to prevent or reduce deviance, for example, by means of punishment, showing remorse, forgiveness, medical treatment, willingness to get better, and generally assigning mutual responsibilities for maintaining social order.

However, while tolerance attempts to deny deviance and repair focuses on relatively acute and short-term deviance, and both are applicable to a wide variety of deviant conditions, long-term care specifically focuses on relatively permanent forms of passive deviance in the context of asymmetrical relationships involving primarily protective and caring non-deviant individuals. Examples are people caring for the very old, chronically ill, severely mentally or physically ill, or any other social category that is unable or not allowed to fully take part in social and economic life. As will become evident later in our critical discussion of interventions, it is important to distinguish long-term care from truly symmetrical or reciprocal relationships that are often seen as an alternative to stigmatization and prejudice in inter-ethnic relationships and conflict. Although deviant individuals may be "liked" in the context of long-term care, this "liking" is not the same as "liking" on the basis of respect for mutual contributions and responsi-bilities in a truly reciprocal relationship. It is important to note that "liking" for ethnic minorities or people with a different skin color may also be based on general protectiveness and care, a tendency that has been termed "political correctness."

Importantly, the desirability and feasibility of the above strategies depends on ethical considerations and their match with existing social control practices in the relationship or society under consideration. As shown in greater detail later in this chapter, strategies to replace stig-matization with tolerance or repair may only be effective in settings in which people see these types of social control as legitimate. Sometimes individuals associated with deviance may not like the idea of tolerance because they do not associate themselves with deviance in the first place. At other times, however, these same individuals may have to face the problem that close interpersonal relationships often require that the deviant condition is explicitly dealt with and that some form of prevention or repair must take place, even if the condition seems irrelevant at first sight (e.g., a crime or disabling accident with which a person is associated happened more than ten years ago and since then, the person underwent considerable changes).

Yet, the desirability and feasibility of the three major alternatives to stigmatization are also dependent on their match with current social control practices. For example, tolerance as a general stigma reduction strategy may work best in settings in which people are able and moti-vated to sustain superficial relationships with each other, while repair may work best when, in the context of a closer relationship, non-deviant and deviant individuals encourage one another to make mutual adap-tations. In contrast, striving for tolerance does not seem to be a good idea in close relationships in which people are used (e.g., family, friend-ship) or temporarily motivated (e.g., a neighborhood confronted with a former child abuser or a facility for drug addicts) to engage in infor-mal social control or repair. Equally non-productive are attempts to realize aspects of informal social control or repair where the normal social control practice is tolerance. As explained later, given these complexities it seems useful to formulate a fourth ultimate intervention goal that can be used as a meta-strategy, allowing people to make flexible use of different social control strategies.

## What are the proximal psychological mechanisms responsible for stigmatization and stigma reduction?

As we will illustrate later in this chapter, social psychologists have proposed a wide variety of intervention strategies that are mostly based on general psychological mechanisms that are relatively independent of the particular type of deviance under consideration. Among these are general principles of information processing, self-control and suppression of negative responses, and conformity to general norms of civil inattention, egalitarianism, or niceness. However, from our theoretical perspective it becomes clear that many of these intervention proposals are primarily directed at non-deviant perceivers and are often motivated by the ultimate goal of improving either tolerance (combined with niceness) or long-term care. (As shown later, even strategies aimed at improving the quality of contact between perceivers and targets, appear to be primarily focused on accomplishing changes in perceivers.) As implied by our theoretical approach to social control, any intervention that wants to realize more than tolerance, striving for a reciprocal interpersonal relationship with repair potential, needs to take into account the motivational mechanisms that are specifically triggered by the type of deviance under consideration. Furthermore, it then also becomes apparent that interventions usually should address both the non-deviant and deviant individual. Take, for example, fear reduction in the case of contagious disease or particular forms of mental illness. It would be insufficient to try to reassure the perceiver by means of education without requiring the deviant individual to refrain from threatening behavior. We will therefore propose later in this chapter to tailor interventions carefully to the specific motivational implications of different types of deviance, with important roles for perceivers as well as individuals associated with deviance and the situations in which they meet.

To conclude, practical thinking on stigma-reduction in social psychology is not embedded in a broad theory of social control in which the relationship between stigmatization and other types of social control is clarified, and allowing us to reflect critically on the desirability and feasibility of different ultimate intervention goals. In addition, proximal mechanisms assumed to underlie stigmatization and its reduction tend to address primarily the perceiver and ignore the specific motivational implications of different types of deviance, aspects of targets, relationships, and society.

This chapter is organized as follows. First, we illustrate how stigma-reduction interventions can fruitfully make use of the deviance typology that was developed in this book, thus tailoring the proximal intervention mechanisms to the motivational implications of different types of deviance. Second, we review the main intervention strategies to reduce or prevent stigmatization that have been proposed by social psychologists and examine their underlying assumptions with respect to proximal mechanisms and ultimate intervention goals. Third, we sketch a broad perspective that allows us to reflect critically on the desirability and feasibility of the ultimate goals of different intervention strategies. In particular, we will look at how proposed interventions may match or mismatch with current social control practices and propose how interventions need to be tailored to these practices in order to be useful and effective. In addition, we propose what we believe to be a generally acceptable and useful meta-strategy for dealing with many deviant conditions and situations, and for both perceivers and targets. Thus our contribution to developing future stigma reduction strategies will consist of both an explicit consideration of ultimate intervention goals and a better specification of deviance-specific motivational mechanisms.

## 9.2 Tailoring stigma-reduction interventions to type of deviance

Our approach strongly suggests that successful interventions, at a minimum, should take into account the specific motivational implications of different types of deviance (see Chapter 2, for a derivation of the four basic types). Here, we will examine how knowledge of these implications may be used to formulate complementary recommendations for individuals engaging in stigmatization (perceivers) and stigmatized persons (targets), as well as for practitioners arranging contact situations in which perceivers and targets meet. We will not attempt to be complete and ignore complex combinations of different types of deviance. Instead, our examples should be seen as illustrations of principles that require further theoretical and empirical examination. Although we especially formulate our intervention suggestions in the context of repair, thus seeing perceiver and target as mutually contributing to stigma prevention and reduction, they may also be more generally applicable.

### Type 1: Uncontrollable-active deviance

This type of deviance primarily activates the flight component of the perceiver's FF system and hence is relatively strongly associated with the experience of fear and the goal of avoiding contact with the target (e.g., by staying at a safe distance or making it impossible for the target to approach). Initial contact, therefore, should be primarily directed at fear reduction. Although fearful perceivers prefer to avoid any physical contact with the target at all, they may find contact acceptable if they experience the conditions under which it is realized as safe.

How is the experience of safety realized when contact with a threatening target is imminent? Although there are different theories of how exposure to a threatening target may reduce fear, three important principles can be distilled from the literature on clinical treatment of simple phobias by means of exposure to the fear-arousing target (e.g., Arntz, Lavy, van den Berg, & van Rijsoort, 1993; Foa & Kozak, 1986; Marks, 1987; Wolpe, 1990). First, the perceiver should be in complete control over the spatial and temporal manner in which the distance between perceiver and target is reduced. This is understandable from an evolutionary perspective (see also Chapter 2). While the fearful organism tends to accept the slightest evidence (from whatever source) for the presence of danger, it is extremely reluctant to accept information indicating the absence of danger. Being able to avoid contact with potentially harmful objects is so important that decisions about safety can only be reliably based on subjective changes in one's own motivational state. That is, it is the perceiver, and only the perceiver, who can experience and determine, on the basis of self-observed changes in fear, that contact is safe. The key words, therefore, are gradual and controlled exposure: "No one else but me is able to tell if the situation is safe. Therefore, I decide when and how the distance between me and the target is further reduced and contact intensified."

Second, as a consequence of personally controlled exposure, the negative expectancy that the target has dangerous properties that are incongruent with safety (e.g., target will suddenly pop up and attack) are replaced by positive expectancies that the target has attributes that enable safe modes of contact (e.g., target's approach and attack can be predicted and responded to in time). "If I approach or manipulate the target in a particular manner, it remains passive or even moves away from me" (see Chapter 3). Luckily, in the case of human fear-evoking targets, perceivers have an important additional way to form safety relevant expectations. That is, these targets may verbally reassure the perceiver that their intentions are harmless and peaceful.

Third, contact with a fear-evoking target that is experienced as safe may result in the discovery of stimuli that can activate motivational states that will start to compete with fear such as interest, admiration, or anger.

It seems plausible to assume that these principles of fear reduction can also be fruitfully applied when people try to gain social control over a threatening deviant target. In particular, while perceivers may be taught to exercise control over the spatial and temporal aspects of the manner in which distance with the target is reduced, targets may be asked to behave in such a way that the perceiver initially feels in control (e.g., targets may be requested to let themselves be inspected, to give information, to refrain from sudden and threatening moves, etc.). We know of only two studies in which the effectiveness of one or more of the above principles of exposure therapy was examined. First, with respect to responding to persons with AIDS, Bean, Keller, Newburg, and Brown (1989) found that techniques such as group desensitization in combination with relaxation training (participants proceeded through a hierarchy of ten scenes involving progressively closer imaginal contact with a person with AIDS), cognitive inoculation (participants were reassured of the safety of different contact situations), or mastery imagery (participants were encouraged to engage in positive self-talk in gradually more stressful imagined contact situations), all tended to reduce fear of persons with AIDS. Unsurprisingly, the presentation of factual information about AIDS enhanced participants' knowledge about AIDS, but it did not reduce anxiety. Bean *et al.* (1989) are doubtful about widespread application of systematic desensitization procedures, although they make an exception for the use of such procedures when fear or anxiety may be highly relevant, for example for nurses or dentists working with AIDS patients.

Also inspired by exposure therapy for phobias, we (Dijker *et al.*, 1997) directed fear-reducing strategies not at the perceiver but at the target. We asked participants to imagine interacting with a person with or without AIDS who varied in personality traits indicating more or less self-control over impulse expression and hence predictability in behavior. This interaction involved different forms of indirect physical contact such as manipulating objects that were previously touched by the target. We found that, the more the target was presented as predictable, the more differential fear and associated behavioral responses to a target person with or without AIDS disappeared. Presenting fear-reducing information about self-control and predictability may also be seen as aspects of the target's disclosure and acknowledgment of his or her deviant condition (see Chapters 3 and 7). Finally, note that the study by Langer *et al.* (1976) described in Chapter 4, can also be interpreted as showing the effectiveness of exposure principles. As may be remembered, when non-handicapped perceivers were first allowed to look in an unobtrusive way at a handicapped target person, they showed greater willingness to sit closer to the target than those without prior opportunity to look. Recognizing the important role of the target, and citing Goffman (1963b), Langer *et al.* (1976, p. 461), make the interesting suggestion that similar exposure principles may have been used by handicapped persons with threatening features themselves: "A 37-year old male whose face is grossly disfigured but who carries a real estate business stated, 'When I have an appointment with a new contact, I try to manage to be standing at a distance and facing the door, so the person entering will have more time to see me and get adjusted to my appearance before we start talking.'"

Additional recommendations for fear reduction may involve implementing the contact situation gradually, with forewarning, and with cooperation of both perceiver and target. Authorities should guarantee and demonstrate that safety will be maintained, and provide response options and simple structure during the interaction.[2]

### Type 2: Controllable-active deviance

When individuals are associated with past criminal behavior, a bad reputation of free riding or non-reciprocity, or not respecting perceivers' safety needs during initial contact (see above), the fight component of the FF system is the most strongly activated, and the emotion of anger will be felt (provided that the perceiver is more in control over the situation than the target). Here, the main immediate objective of interventions should be to reduce anger. Anger is best reduced by being exposed to a mixture of information indicating that targets change and adapt their behavior and actually change their minds and will conform to the perceiver's and group's norms. In addition, anger may be reduced when the target appears to suffer, is vulnerable, and feels remorse ("I feel terrible about what I did"), thus activating the perceiver's C system, thereby promoting pity and forgiveness, and inhibition of aggressive tendencies (see Chapters 2 and 3). We believe that it is less useful to create the impression that targets entirely lack responsibility for their past wrong doings, for example, by "medicalizing" the deviant condition or saying that he has had a bad youth or is generally discriminated by society; dominant tendencies in modern Western societies. On the contrary, a person associated with controllable-active deviance may gain more respect by taking responsibility.

While, in the context of repairing interpersonal relationships, anger should be considered a useful emotion of which the reduction is partly dependent on the behavioral adaptation of the target of anger, one may also exclusively focus on the perceiver in order to reduce anger. For example, just as in the case of the flight or fear component of the FF system, the fight or anger component also seems responsive to relaxation training. As noted by Deffenbacher, Oetting and DiGiuseppe (2002), these approaches, that have been applied in populations such as college students, incarcerated individuals and drivers with anger problems, teach clients relaxation coping skills and their application, and also often use systematic desensitization procedures in which relaxation is linked to situations that provoke anger. Another type of anger management intervention is cognitive. As described by Deffenbacher *et al.*, cognitive interventions aim at changing anger supporting factors such as hostile appraisals and attributions, irrational beliefs, and inflammatory thinking. A meta-analytic review by DiGiuseppe and Tafrate (2003) found moderate improvement among treated participants.

### Type 3: Uncontrollable-passive deviance

This type of deviance primarily activates the C system and hence is relatively strongly associated with the experience of tender feelings and pity, and a desire to nurture and heal the target. Initial contact, therefore, should be primarily directed at respecting and satisfying this need. As was argued earlier, this means that the target confirms but does not disconfirm the expectancy that he or she is needy and dependent on the perceiver by, for example, showing submissive behavior, and especially by asking for specific help. In Chapter 4 we discussed different studies suggesting that the latter strategy may indeed be effective in reducing tension and inducing liking in the perceiver; whereas others suggested an increase in perceiver's irritation when the target did not observe these rules.

A complementary perceiver-directed strategy, that may be especially important in modern Western societies in which the C system is already relatively strongly activated, may be to try to reduce activation of this system by, for example, encouraging the perceiver to be "less careful" with the target and to engage in more spontaneous behavior, and to monitor critically whether the target really wants to get well.

However, as also pointed out, it would be preferable that the perceiver forms a more balanced impression of the target that also incorporates the target's good coping and competence. Although this may be communicated by particular acknowledgments made by the target during initial contact, the deviant condition may be too complex to bring a balanced message across. For example, we saw in the Hastorf *et al.* (1979) and Silver *et al.* (1990) studies discussed in Chapter 3 that the acknowledgment that proved useful in reducing interactional anxiety was quite extensive and complex. These studies certainly need further replication to demonstrate their usefulness. (In the Silver *et al.* study good at coping portrayals may have been primarily effective because the target – a cancer patient – presented herself not only as good at coping with cancer but also as very sociable.) A more effective general strategy would be to encourage long-term and varied interactions between perceivers and targets in which disabled targets can truly present themselves in respectable roles (see also Whyte & Ingstad, 1995).

A special situation obtains when disability is also strongly associated with active deviance such as in the case of contagious disease (e.g., AIDS, leprosy) or abnormal threatening appearance (mental handicap, leprosy). With these deviant conditions, it also seems important to first reduce fear responses.

Finally observe that, irrespective of type of deviance, perceiver-directed interventions may make use of the functioning of the C system in triggering tender and protective responses to deviant individuals (although we expect this strategy to work best for deviant conditions that clearly contain passive elements). This would, for example, be the case when researchers try to evoke empathy with such diverse targets as criminals (e.g., Batson *et al.*, 1997) or ill persons (Weiner *et al.*, 1988. See Chapter 3, for a discussion of contextual influences on representations of deviance). A quite extensive procedure has been employed by Clore and Jeffrey (1972) who had students play the role of a wheelchair user. Participants had to imagine that due to an automobile accident they had to make use of a wheelchair and it was their first day back on campus after the accident. Then they made a trip on the campus in a wheelchair meeting with various kinds of difficulties that are customary for wheelchair users. Four months later these participants responded more positively compared to a control group toward disabled students on an evaluative measure. This effect was also obtained for participants that vicariously role played; they walked behind the role players and their task was to observe the role player's experiences. The vicarious role playing or observer condition seems to be rather similar to perspective taking conditions in which participants are asked to imagine how targets, for example, wheelchair users, feel about their experiences and plight, or what kind of situational factors are responsible for their dependent situation.

## Type 4: Controllable-passive deviance

With this type of passive deviance, not only the C system is activated but also the fight component of the FF system responsible for anger. The resulting motivational state or emotion, therefore, can be described as a mixture of pity and anger; yet, because these two emotions inhibit each other, anger and pity are experienced to a lesser extent than in the case of the other three types of deviance. We alternatively described this emotional state as disrespect.

We suggest two potentially effective strategies for the target. First, the target could admit that he needs help from the perceiver, thereby exclusively and more strongly activating the perceiver's C system. Compare the alcohol or drug addict or the obese person finally admitting that he or she needs therapeutical help. Second, and perhaps simultaneously, the target could also admit responsibility for his or her deviant condition ("yes, it is wrong that I eat or drink too much, causing my family and friends so much trouble; I should have recognized my wrong behavior much earlier"). An advantage of this would be that perceivers now are in the position to forgive targets, allowing protective tendencies to come to the surface that are also needed when the target wants to receive therapeutic help. Another possibility would be to change more directly the image of targets as lazy, complaining, and free riding persons, who lack any self-respect, by letting targets show physical strength, competence, and self-respect (e.g., by carefully dressing or grooming, or self-assertive locomotion and posture). These suggestions are in agreement with self-assertive coping strategies, such as looking confidently at others when entering a room full of people, that some obese persons employ to make themselves feel better and that may result in greater self-respect (cf. Myers & Rosen, 1999. See also Chapter 8). These suggestions should make it clear that simple acknowledgment of one's deviant condition is insufficient and even counterproductive in the case of Type 4 deviance such as obesity or addictions. This is suggested by Hebl and Kleck (2002) who found that acknowledgment resulted in more positive reactions to a physically handicapped but not an obese person (see Chapter 3).

## 9.3 Common intervention strategies and their underlying assumptions

For purposes of reducing or preventing stigmatization and prejudice, social psychologists have focused on three main intervention strategies that may be used in isolation or in complementary fashion. These interventions may be directed at individuals engaging in stigmatization (perceivers), stigmatized persons (targets), or situations in which perceiver and target are encouraged to interact (contact), respectively. In this section, we examine to what extent these strategies take into account the deviance-specific motivational mechanisms discussed above, and what the underlying assumptions are with respect to ultimate intervention goals.

### Perceiver-directed strategies

Perceiver-directed strategies can be divided into strategies that are relatively cognitive in focus and that try to change the internal representation of deviant individuals and its associated emotional consequences, and those that are more affective or behavioral in orientation, attempting to induce self-control or generalized feelings of empathy or sympathy. The first type include educational efforts to correct people's incomplete or false beliefs about people with a deviant condition by means of, for example, leaflets, pictures, presentations by those associated with the deviant condition, or media coverage, and raising the level of general knowledge about the nature and origin of that condition. For example, an educational program about HIV infection (the virus responsible for AIDS) may try to convince people that the virus is not transmissible by shaking hands with an infected person, or that not all infections are related to homosexual behavior but may instead be due to infusion with infected blood, transmission from mother to unborn child, or other accidents. These programs have generally shown improvements in knowledge and more favorable evaluations of HIV-infected individuals or persons with AIDS, at least when measured by means of self-reports and immediately following the intervention (cf. Brown, MacIntyre, & Trujillo, 2003).

Clearly, many educational interventions do not simply raise the level of knowledge but also try to affect the motivational implications of the type of deviance under consideration. For example, presenting accurate information about HIV transmission may reduce the fear-arousing aspects of HIV or AIDS by means of reassurance, or may induce tenderness and pity for infected people by pointing to uncontrollable causes of getting AIDS. Similarly, it has been shown that negative evaluations of, and anger at, norm violators and criminals can be reduced by presenting targets as vulnerable and suffering (e.g., Batson *et al.*, 1997; Weiner *et al.*, 1988).

Representations of deviance may also be altered by presenting targets with attributes and behaviors that are clearly unexpected or atypical in light of expectancies or stereotypes about the deviant condition. For example, one may present targets associated with controllable-passive or Type 4 deviance such as low socioeconomic status or obesity with admirably good coping skills and as strongly motivated to get out of their disadvantaged situation. As illustrated in Chapter 4, one may additionally motivate perceivers to primarily attend to a target's non-deviant attributes, for example, by activating epistemic, self-presentational, or instrumental motives.

While it seems that common intervention strategies take into account certain obvious motivational implications of deviant conditions (in fact, in the case of HIV and AIDS it is difficult to miss fear as a very important motivational aspect; see Chapter 3), this attention may not be systematic enough to correctly predict the more and less beneficial immediate consequences of interventions. Consider how new images or representations resulting from cognitive interventions may sometimes be incomplete and unrealistic. For example, although the educational efforts to reduce fear of HIV infection through casual contact that were discussed above, certainly are relevant, they insufficiently take into account the target's role in triggering and sustaining activity of the FF system. Specifically, in the context of social control, it seems necessary that the new image recognizes that threat is not simply a matter of viruses and transmission routes but an interpersonal quality. Thus as illustrated in the previous section, fear of HIV infected individuals may only be effectively reduced when targets somehow are able to show that they respect the safety concerns of others, thus behaving carefully, predictably, and restrained during physical contact. Clearly, knowledge that certain patient groups of HIV infected individuals claim having "rights" to engage in unprotected sex (cf. Crossley, 1998) does not seem to contribute to fear reduction (see below). Similarly, one may wonder if images of threat can really be changed when there is so much evidence of the real scope of the problem of getting infected in certain African countries where whole populations are threatened to be wiped out by the virus. As another example, interventions addressing the violent behavior of individuals with schizophrenia run the risk of increasing rather than reducing people's fear (Mayville & Penn, 1998).

In Chapter 3, we noted how important but also how difficult it is to present realistic information about the extent to which targets cope with their deviant condition and to let perceivers incorporate information about non-deviant attributes into a credible image of the target. For example, if for educational purposes, a mentally ill person is presented as completely in control of his impulses and without suffering from his mental problems in order to disconfirm a general expectancy about mental illness (e.g., Reinke, Corrigan, Leonhard, Lundin, & Kubiak, 2004), the person may appear as if no deviance would exist at all. More seriously, if a person with cancer is presented as coping exceptionally well with his or her condition, the person may be prevented from receiving social support when actually in need for it (Silver *et al.*, 1990). Furthermore, a person in a wheelchair appearing cheered-up and assertive may arouse more anger than one displaying behavior more consistent with the sick role (Katz *et al.*, 1978). Because perceivers may have different needs and desires with respect to different types of deviance (e.g., safety versus nurturance), perhaps only extensive interpersonal contact, allowing the perceiver to observe the target in a variety of different situations, may create a more realistic and balanced impression of the target and his or her ability and motivation to cope with the deviant condition (below, we argue that negotiation may additionally foster the development of realistic expectations). The importance of creating images that contain both information about deviant and non-deviant attributes is stressed in Langer, Bashner, and Chanowitz's (1985) attempt to increase people's *mindfulness* by inviting them, with explicit reference to a particular handicap to "increase rather than decrease the number of distinctions people make about people to change the relative importance of any particular difference" (p. 113). The authors found some support for the effectiveness of their attempt to "decrease prejudice by increasing discrimination."

Affective or behavioral perceiver-directed strategies may encourage perceivers to suppress negative thoughts and feelings with respect to the deviant condition, for example, by confronting perceivers with the harmful consequences of their responses (Monteith & Voils, 2001. See Chapter 4, for an extensive discussion). A remarkable example in thinking along these lines is a series of studies by Kawakami and colleagues (Kawakami, Dovidio, Moll, Hermsen, & Russin, 2000), demonstrating that training people to "say no" to associating a deviant condition (e.g., skin head) with negative stereotypical attributes (e.g., aggressive) – participants in these studies were required hundreds of times not to make an association between condition and attribute – indeed decreased the likelihood of automatically making these associations when later confronted with the deviant condition.

Other strategies may bypass responding to deviance by directly inducing a variety of positive feelings for targets in general by, for example, inducing admiration for famous individuals with the same condition (Casey et al., 2003; Dasgupta & Greenwald, 2001) or feelings of tenderness, compassion, or empathy for the target (for a general discussion, see Stephan & Finlay, 1999).

Finally, note that principles of social learning and modeling may also be employed to bypass attention to deviance and to directly induce desirable responses to individuals associated with deviance. For example, it may be hypothesized that when a celebrity such as the late Princess Diana engaged in close and friendly contact with persons with AIDS or leprosy, people might have generally responded with more care and support to persons afflicted with these conditions.

Although many perceiver-directed strategies may help to increase tolerance, their effectiveness cannot be evaluated without taking into account the different undesirable side-effects that were noted in Chapter 4. For example, suppression and self-control may result in lack of spontaneity, increased hostility and lack of interpersonal warmth; increased accessibility of deviance-relevant expectancies or stereotypes (and cognitive rebound effects); decreased cognitive and attentional resources for paying attention to the target's non-deviant attributes (thus contradicting attempts to increase more elaborate information processing); and possibly an increase in subliminal or unconscious, and hence less controllable influences, of the motivational implications of deviance.

Let us now turn to assumptions made with respect to the ultimate goals of perceiver-directed interventions. Unfortunately, because these goals usually are not explicitly addressed, it is impossible to assess if one attempts to realize a desirable goal and if the immediate intervention outcomes contribute to its realization. However, we believe that there is at least one useful ultimate goal that many perceiver-directed strategies attempt to realize. That is, these strategies seem to promote a general carefulness in reasoning, motivating perceivers to engage in piecemeal processing of all the available information about deviant individuals, and be critical about first impressions and the validity of generalizations (cf. S. Fiske, 1998; Nisbett & Ross, 1980). In addition, they may promote a general reluctance to act impulsively with respect to deviance. Yet, most of these strategies also assume that old stereotypes or generalizations must be replaced with new and more benign generalizations about the target's likeability. But as noted above, it is unclear if, for example, the liking for mentally handicapped persons which is based on activation of the C system is the same liking that (intellectually competent) physically disabled, elderly, obese or homosexual individuals (let alone individuals from racial or ethnic minority groups) may ultimately want. That is, the latter may primarily desire respect on the basis of reciprocity rather than protection and care.

A particularly good illustration of assuming that generalized liking not only would be a desirable immediate but also ultimate intervention goal, is the following approach. Houlette *et al.* (2004) describe an intervention study in which elementary schoolchildren are presented with a small green circle on a felt board, "representing the world of people who you care about and the people who care about you." The facilitator adds a stick figure to the circle, explaining to the children that it represents themselves, and leaves out several other figures that represent family members. He or she subsequently enlarges the circle to include the self and all family members. Then the children are asked to imagine how it feels to be outside the circle because, for example, of their size or shape, skin color, or gender. The facilitator points out that the "circle of caring and sharing" needs to grow to include others, so that it is large enough to include individuals who are black and white, male and female, or small and large. When comparing several effect measures in the intervention and control group, the investigators found that children exposed to the green circle intervention were more likely to choose as a most preferred playmate children that were dissimilar to themselves with respect to race, weight, or gender, suggesting that the intervention had been effective in developing a more inclusive identity. However, affective or bias measures were not influenced by the intervention and being overweight showed the least benefit from the intervention (children also felt the most unhappy when asked to imagine playing with the overweight child). The authors interpret these findings as generally supporting the effectiveness of increasing the inclusiveness of ingroup boundaries for the reduction of prejudice (see also Gaertner & Dovidio, 2005).

At first sight, inducing general feelings of empathy or pity with individuals who do not belong to one's circle or social group (and in a wider sense are discriminated against) may work well if one's main goal is to motivate young children to choose individuals associated with deviance as playmates. A closer look, however, reveals that both the success and the desirability of such strategies depend on the nature of deviance and prevailing social control practices with respect to these conditions. For example, as discussed in Chapter 3, Gibbons and Sawin (1979) showed that liking for the mentally handicapped tends to be based on paternalism; they are excused when failing on a task, but do not receive credits when succeeding. Consistent with this suggestion, a series of studies by one of us (Dijker, In preparation) increasingly reveals the ambivalent nature of childrens' and adolescents' images of mentally handicapped individuals. It was found that, although 13-year-old school children expressed strong liking for and want to befriend a mentally handicapped individual (even as much as a physically very attractive child!), they nevertheless judged the handicapped child as highly incompetent and threatening. Furthermore, when these school children were asked to imagine a truly reciprocal relationship with the target, they felt more contempt and anxiety for the mentally handicapped than non-handicapped target and desired a greater interpersonal distance from the former than the latter (interestingly, the reverse was the case when the target was presented as dependent and in need of help). Lack of respect for a mentally handicapped target trying to engage in reciprocal contact also seems to be responsible for the result of an earlier study showing that 17-year-old adolescents preparing for manual jobs, tend to reject a mentally handicapped person as a colleague in favor of a non-handicapped one (Dijker, Tacken, & van den Borne 2000), presumably because in these settings lack of competence and hence reciprocity is viewed as more problematic.

To conclude, perceiver-directed strategies generally try to explicitly contradict particular expectations or stereotypes regarding deviant conditions, or to bypass reference or responding to deviance altogether by encouraging exclusive attention to non-deviant and desirable target attributes, self-control, and feelings of unconditional or generalized acceptance, sympathy, pity, or admiration. These strategies seem to be based on the assumption that expectancies regarding deviant conditions are generally invalid or irrelevant, and that negatively responding to these conditions is always undesirable, and generalized sympathy desirable, for the target, interpersonal relationship, or society. However, as illustrated, perceiver-directed educational programs can only hope to be effective when taking into account the motivational implications of different types of deviance. Moreover, certain ultimate intervention goals may not be desirable for targets as originally assumed.

## Target-directed strategies

While we increasingly understand how, by means of a variety of coping strategies, people associated with deviance may improve their situation, well-being, and self-esteem (see Chapter 8), we know almost nothing about strategies that may be employed by targets to influence social responses to their deviant condition and to improve the quality of their relationships with others who respond to their deviance. This is unfortunate because targets, since they are the ones suffering from stigmatization, may have the most to gain in influencing perceivers. As noted by Coleman and DePaulo (1991), stigmatized individuals can contribute to the education of perceivers and to the smoothness of social interaction by explicitly communicating their own preferences and expectations for how they would like to be treated.

As discussed in Chapter 3, only a few studies suggest how targets with certain deviant conditions may disclose and acknowledge their condition in such a way that they will receive supportive and accepting responses from unfamiliar others. For example, it was illustrated how people with chronic conditions such as cancer may try to present a balanced and realistic picture of themselves, with information about dependency and suffering (motivating social support) balanced with information about good coping (cf. Silver *et al.*, 1990). We additionally speculated about useful target strategies when discussing the need to tailor interventions to different types of deviance.

A plausible reason for social psychologists' lack of attention to target strategies may be that people associated with deviance tend to be primarily viewed as victims of stigmatization who only deserve our compassion, rather than responsible members of society who may earn our respect by showing responsibility for repairing relationships and by demonstrating useful competencies. Consequently, strategies directed at the perceiver rather than the target have received the most attention when it comes to thinking about influencing negative responding. Moreover, in light of a focus on the causal role of the perceiver in determining the well-being of stigmatized targets, advising targets how to present themselves and adapt their behavior is likely to be interpreted as "blaming the victim" and yet another sign of stigmatizing tendencies. Reflecting these concerns, there appears to be a strong tendency to advise targets to protest against, rather than adapt to, the responses and demands of the social environment (cf. Corrigan & Penn, 1999), encouraging them to engage in political mobilization, advocacy, lobbying, and empowerment. To be sure, this seems a useful strategy when applied to minority groups that tend to be oppressed and discriminated by those in power, or to accomplish basic levels of participation through legal change.

From our theoretical perspective on social control, however, one may worry about the adverse effects that certain assertive or aggressive tendencies may have on the general social treatment and acceptance of people with chronic illnesses and disabilities. In particular, during the last fifteen years, and especially in Great Britain, a minority perspective associated with protest activities of ethnic and racial groups and women, has also been applied to people with disabilities, arguing that, whatever the nature of their disability, and their special needs, they belong to an oppressed and stigmatized group that can only hope for improvement of their situation by joining forces, empowerment, and aggressively striving for political change (e.g., Barnes & Mercer, 1996; Oliver, 1990; Parker & Aggleton, 2003). Accordingly, it is proposed to replace the traditional "medical model" that views disability as a personal tragedy that should be normalized by means of medical treatment and behavioral change or rehabilitation, with the "social model" that primarily attributes the handicapping aspects of disability to a stigmatizing society, propagates a suspicious and critical attitude toward health care, and even seems to value the state of being impaired.

A useful critique of these tendencies is provided by Bickenbach, Chatterji, Badley, and Üstün (1999), who argue that "the minority group analysis is founded on a forced analogy between racial minorities and disabled people that breaks down at many important points. Not only are the social responses to different forms of mental and physical impairment vastly different, from the other direction, there is almost no commonality of experience, of feelings of solidarity, between people with diverse disabilities" (pp. 1180–81). The authors further point out that "the leaders of the disability movement tend to be highly educated, white middle-class males with late onset physical disabilities and minimal medical needs, a group that is hardly representative of the population of people with disabilities in the world" (p. 1181).[3]

From our theoretical perspective on social control, and closely following Parsons' important concept of the sick role (see also Crossley, 1998), we would like to add to these critical notes on empowerment and the social model of disability that passive deviance, like active deviance, automatically arouses social responses that are often beneficial to both the deviant individual and the relationship or society in which he or she participates, and that are generally necessary to keep a relationship and society functioning. Although it seems important for targets to be critical about too much care, "paternalism," and loss of autonomy, they should also be aware that recognition and displays of dependency are fundamental in sustaining continued care and assistance. Of course, acknowledgment of disability and dependency, will be more difficult to adopt as strategies the more disabled people have managed (with the aid of medical development, health care, and social support) to realize independent living and autonomy and the more strongly they are aware of the condition's irrelevance. Below, we argue, however, that especially in modern Western societies, it is often difficult for perceivers and targets alike to determine the relevance of a deviant condition.[4]

## Focusing at interpersonal contact between perceiver and target

A very influential view in thinking about the causes of stigmatization and prejudice is the idea that these phenomena are based on a lack of contact between the people involved, thus providing people with too much opportunity to form wrong ideas about each other (e.g., stigmas, stereotypes, prejudice) and stick to their initially aroused emotions and behavioral impulses; and that these phenomena can be reduced by bringing people together under particular conditions of contact. This so-called *contact hypothesis*, which is generally associated with Allport's (1954/1979) foundational thinking on prejudice, has received impressive empirical support, especially in Pettigrew and Tropp's (2006) meta-analysis of more than 500 independent studies, involving a variety of deviant conditions, social groups, types of contact, and effect measures. The mean effect size obtained in this analysis ($d = -0.45$, $r = -0.21$) certainly suggests that contact has the potential to reduce negative responses to deviant individuals.

The mechanisms assumed to be responsible for immediate positive outcomes of contact are not essentially different from the mechanisms assumed to underlie the effects of strategies exclusively directed at perceivers discussed earlier. That is, the beneficial effects of contact are usually explained in terms of a change in beliefs or stereotypes due to encountering unexpected and new facts about deviant target persons (e.g., Pettigrew, 1998). Yet a distinct aspect of contact is its potential to establish affective ties or friendships between deviant and non-deviant individuals (see Pettigrew, 1998). In addition, contact may also be effective through reduction of cognitive dissonance. That is, observing one's own positive feelings and (freely chosen) friendly behaviors toward the target may cause cognitive dissonance and consequently attitude change in perceivers ("my friendly tendencies are inconsistent with my initial feelings," e.g., Amir, 1976; Pettigrew, 1998).

Fortunately, researchers increasingly study the emotions that may mediate the effects of contact on the reduction of negative responses to deviance. Thus, consistent with our theoretical framework, it is now well-established that contact reduces negative responses to deviance because it reduces fear or anxiety and increases feelings of tenderness, empathy, or pity (R. Brown & Hewstone, 2005). However, these changes in motivational states are not yet systematically related to specific motivationally relevant features of different deviant conditions or of the particular contact situation studied. Neither is the desirability of an emotion such as pity or empathy checked against explicitly formulated ultimate intervention goals.

As with perceiver-directed strategies, we are concerned with the lack of attention to the seriousness and motivational implications of the type of deviance under consideration, and the unexamined ultimate goals of contact. Although contact researchers seem to be aware of the relevance of considering the nature of the deviant condition or conflict involved, it is unclear when and why particular deviant conditions are more or less suitable for contact interventions. For example, Allport stresses the importance of excluding "extreme" cases of deviance from the domain of the contact hypothesis, remarking that "it is conceivable that a given group may have such a preponderance of offensive or dangerous traits that only a saint would consider it unwarranted to avoid and criticize the group" (Allport, 1954/1979, p. 87). As an example of this, Allport mentions "ex-convicts" (p. 88), in which case we may partially deal with a "well-deserved reputation." Furthermore, the contact hypothesis does not seem to apply in the case of extreme conflicts such as war (Allport, 1954/1979, p. 88; see also Hewstone, 2003). That contact in the case of serious deviance may impact negatively, is further suggested by a study of Seefeldt (1987), showing that increased contact with people with severe dementia results in stronger negative evaluations of these people. Moreover, superficial or casual contact with persons with salient ethnic features may increase irritation and anxiety (Amir, 1976; Dijker, 1987). Although the meta-analysis by Pettigrew and Tropp (2006) also reveals that the nature of the deviant condition moderates the immediate positive effects of contact on liking or acceptance, the nature of, and mechanisms behind, these moderating effects are unclear and left unexplained.[5] Hopefully, our distinction between the different motivational implications of different types of deviance may offer a starting point for analyzing these moderating effects in greater detail in future research.[6]

What should be the ultimate goal of contact between perceiver and target and to what extent does the immediate intervention outcome – interpersonal liking or acceptance – contribute to it? Theorists frequently mention that contact interventions should produce intimate and friendly contact, true social acceptance, and even the formation of long-term harmonious interpersonal relationships (see Dovidio, Gaertner, & Kawakami, 2003; Pettigrew, 1998). However, a closer look at the different types of deviance and different kinds of relationships covered by contact research, reveals that outcome measures of contact studies may not relate to the same ultimate goal. For example, increased positive evaluations due to contact with African-Americans may be related to having established symmetrical, cooperative, and reciprocal relationships in which their different competencies, if any, may be valued and respected. In contrast, many studies examining the contact hypothesis involve contact with elderly, mentally ill, or mentally handicapped individuals under asymmetrical conditions of contact that strongly evoke a motivation to care for and protect the deviant individual rather than increasing respect and expecting reciprocity. For example, Revenson (1989) found a linear effect of contact frequency on rheumatologists' perceptions of dependency of, and felt protectiveness for, elderly people. Interestingly, she did not consider this a "beneficial effect" that would be in agreement with the contact hypothesis, as it would involve more stereotyping of elderly patients; although she noted that contact did not decrease liking for these patients. Lee, Farrell, and Link (2004) showed that increased exposure to the homeless was associated with increased care and tendencies to offer assistance, especially when perceivers had previously provided some form of aid to them. Importantly, there were no effects of contact on perceived competence.

Furthermore, many studies showing positive effects of "mainstreaming" (placement of children with disabilities into educational programs for and with non-disabled children) and of educational attempts to let non-disabled and disabled children cooperate with each other (these studies figure prominently in Pettigrew and Tropp's meta-analysis), deal with interactions between perceiver and target that are essentially unequal. As Fishbein (2002, p. 247), reviewing a great many of these studies mentions: "In the majority of these studies, non-handicapped children felt they helped their handicapped peers but did not feel that those peers helped them." Similar observations are made by J. Katz and Mirenda (2002), although these authors also mention examples of intervention programs resulting in greater reciprocity.

In sum, as with perceiver-directed intervention strategies, contact strategies do not explicitly examine to what extent the immediate intervention outcome of liking or sympathy is desirable for the target or long-term relationship with others. Is it liking primarily based on protection or also on reciprocity and respect?

We have the impression that contact researchers, but also other social psychologists, often implicitly assume that the alternative to stigmatization is a relationship in which participants exhibit a kind of generalized and unconditional liking or sympathy for each other, and in which deviance never needs to be addressed explicitly or perhaps does not even exist. Undoubtedly, requiring targets to behave atypically and creating conditions of contact that are as pleasant, prettified, and harmonious as possible contribute to this (see Bramel, 2004). Although we contend that especially friendship and kinship foster relationships based on unconditional care and restrained aggression, it would be a mistake to equate these relationships with the absence of social control (see Chapter 6).[7]

Perhaps more to the point, it is known that increased contact with individuals with chronic illness or disability within a close relationship or family may be associated with a great psychological burden (for an extensive review demonstrating this for a variety of chronic conditions, see Harris *et al.*, 2003) and interpersonal hostility, especially with decreasing reciprocity. For example, Horwitz, Reinhart, and Howell-White (1996) showed that seriously mentally ill patients receive less support from family members the less they reciprocate it. Similarly, Ybema, Kuijer, Hagedoorn, and Buunk (2002) found that partners of cancer or multiple sclerosis patients are more likely to experience burnout and negative feelings about their partner, the more they feel that they underbenefit from their relationship. Interestingly, caregiving, well-being and health in close relationships are increasingly studied in terms of social control rather than unconditional social support. For example, a study by Lewis and Rook (1999) found that partners who actively engage in social control (e.g., criticizing each others' health behavior) show better health but also irritation and sadness. Clearly, these kinds of studies picture a more complex view of the benefits of contact for targets as well as perceivers than most contact studies do (see also Coyne, Wortman, & Lehman, 1988; Tucker & Mueller, 2000).[8]

## 9.4 Reconciling stigma reduction with basic principles of social control

We believe that current thinking on stigma-reduction strategies should be complemented with a better specification of the motivational implications of different types of deviance (treated at the beginning of this chapter), but also with a thorough reflection on the different ultimate goals of these strategies and how they fit with current social control practices. After we consider how our three major strategies of repair, tolerance, and long-term care can be tailored to these practices, we derive a meta-strategy for stigma reduction which consists of raising general awareness of the basic principles of social control. Finally, we explore how negotiation may be used as a specific intervention technique for raising awareness and finding mutually agreeable ways of interacting between perceivers and targets.

### *Tailoring stigma reduction strategies to current social control practices*

How feasible and desirable are the three major stigma-reduction strategies of tolerance, repair, and long-term care that we have distinguished? Feasibility is dependent on the congruence of a particular strategy with current social control practices and the nature and seriousness of a deviant condition. Desirability, which we will address later, must be established on the basis of ethical or normative considerations. We first examine how the feasibility of efforts to promote tolerance and repair as alternatives to stigmatization are dependent on the extent to which they match with current social control practices. Perhaps unsurprisingly, we expect that attempts to improve tolerance work best in relationships, settings, or societies where tolerance already is a major type of social control (together with formal social control). For example, attempts to induce perceivers to feel guilty about, and suppress negative responses, to deny the relevance of, or change beliefs about, deviance, and concentrate on the targets' non-deviant features, and to be generally kind to them, all fit very well with relationships or settings in which interpersonal contact mainly is superficial, polite, and "civil." Of course, the likelihood that tolerance breaks down increases when the deviant condition gets more serious or contact loses its superficial nature, requiring people to get so much involved in each others' affairs that deviance cannot be successfully ignored anymore.

Similarly, we expect that attempts to improve repair will be most successful in relationships or societies in which people are able and motivated to address deviance in informal ways and in such a manner that it will be prevented or its negative consequences reduced. Normally, this should be seen as a two-sided process. For example, perceivers may be motivated to closely attend to deviance, express fear, anger, care, or disrespect, while targets are induced to disclose, confess, and reduce danger, show remorse, ask for help, and cope well with their condition. In return, perceivers are expected to reduce fear and anger, and increase care and respect, and to consider the target's re-integration. Again, the effectiveness of this strategy is dependent on the severity and mutability of deviance; as pointed out in Chapter 6, sometimes, there are no other options than to publicly label, stigmatize, or abandon deviant targets.

Good examples of mutual repair efforts are to be found in close relationships and families, and in, what we have termed in Chapter 6, Category 1 societies. However, in modern Western or Category 3 societies, similar informal strategies, when carefully implemented, may also be successful. For example, reintegrative shaming (or restorative justice), originally advocated by Braithwaite (1989; see also Strang & Sherman, 2003) and now widely applied in New Zealand and Australia, uses a conference primarily aimed at repairing relationships rather than applying retribution and punishment, in which the perpetrator and victim, along with their families and supporters come together to express anger, remorse, guilt, shame, and forgiveness.[9] Furthermore, Peper and Spierings (1999) describe how community mediation in The Netherlands has been effectively used to reduce annoyances between neighbors and repair relationships.

Attempts to improve tolerance and repair are less likely to be effective when they are not congruent with current social control practices. First, consider how certain social psychological strategies may try to implement aspects of repair in a one-sided, incomplete, and contradictory fashion when tolerance rather than repair is the major form of social control. For example, in order to repair relationships, interventions may require targets to acknowledge their deviant condition (e.g., its implied dependency, dangerousness, or responsibility) and to change their behavior while simultaneously asking perceivers not to care about these changes and to look the other way for the sake of tolerance. Similarly, interventions may induce perceivers to feel generally safe about targets associated with mental illness or contagious disease without sufficiently demonstrating how targets themselves take the necessary precautions to protect perceivers; or interventions may induce perceivers to feel pity, guilt, or forgiveness without telling them what targets' themselves will do to change their behavior and earn respect.

Now consider the undesirable consequences of attempts to increase tolerance in relationships or settings where people are used or motivated to engage in repair with respect to deviance. For example, it would be a gross mistake to require people engaged in close relation-ships or living in small communities to exercise tolerance in the face of deviance (e.g., to deny its relevance and to concentrate only on the target's non-deviant attributes) in favor of explicitly responding to it, making mutual adaptations, and trying to repair the relationship. It would be similarly inappropriate to demand from people living with a chronically ill partner not to critically explore any opportunity for reciprocity that is left in the relationship in order to decrease the burden of caring.

Yet, even in a setting or society in which superficial encounters are common and tolerance the required form of social control, encouraging people to be tolerant with respect to certain deviant individuals may be inappropriate and ineffective when the deviant condition or the man-ner in which deviant individuals are introduced evokes a strong desire to engage in informal social control or repair. Indeed, as will be illus-trated below, the re-introduction of elements of repair may result in stigmatization when implemented in an individualistic society in which social control is primarily of a formal type.

In clarifying the tense relationship between repair and tolerance, it is useful to make a distinction between the intentional and uninten-tional activation of people's desire to engage in informal social control or repair. With intentional activation we mean that a relationship or society strongly values and encourages repair, while unintentional activation refers to events that temporarily motivate perceivers to engage in repair processes, for example, when an otherwise tolerant neighborhood is confronted with individuals with serious and disturb-ing deviant conditions. An example of the former is modern Western society's tendency to increasingly encourage people to respond with greater vigilance, preventative measures, punishment, labeling, "risk management," and public shaming with respect to active deviance such as shoplifting (e.g., posting photographs of former offenders in the supermarket), anti-social behavior, and other norm violations; thereby, making less demands on institutions engaged in formal social control such as the police and the legal system. Similar preventative and punitive tendencies can be observed with respect to passive deviance. For example, health care increasingly demands responsible behavior and changes in lifestyle in order to prevent physical and mental illness, thus paving the way to respond in punishing ways to those who behave "irresponsibly" or get ill (Guttman & Salmon, 2004. See also Chapter 1).

While all these measures may be employed to improve the quality of interpersonal and community relationships (and are too important simply to be replaced by tolerance and kindness), they may result in stigmatization when re-introduced in a modern society that is individualistic at heart, and in which perceivers and targets do not know each other. For example, public shaming may not result in desirable behavioral change but in resentment (cf. Braithwaite, 1989) and disabled and chronically ill people may be financially punished or refused when asking for insurance or medical treatment. Furthermore, health education may create a generally stigmatizing climate by presenting ill or disabled persons, and generally those at risk for getting ill (e.g., smokers, overweight people), as "bad examples" or social parasites. Thus it will be increasingly difficult to be tolerant with respect to people with a weight problem or cancer due to smoking when health educators increasingly demand "responsible" behavior. Therefore, a major task for health education and promotion is to develop interventions that are both effective in preventing illness and stigmatization.

In sum, where in small communities public exposure, punishment, shaming, and gossiping served to induce guilt and behavioral change in addition to shame (see Chapter 6), in large social settings (and currently also on the internet) these responses primarily tend to result in feelings of revenge and Schadenfreude on the side of perceivers, and shame, lack of self-esteem, hostility, or indifference on the side of targets. To the extent that stigmatization actually has taken the place of tolerance, calls for the latter would have entirely lost their effectiveness.

We also see much evidence for the unintentional activation of a desire for informal social control while it is actually tolerance that is wanted. This problem can be vividly illustrated with conflicts about the location of human service facilities or housing projects for people like the homeless, drug users, mentally or physically ill or disabled, asylum seekers or former offenders. (Because we believe that our theoretical approach may make a substantial contribution to thinking about interventions in this area, we discuss this problem at length here.) Generally, what authorities and service providers want is to introduce these facilities as quietly and smoothly as possible, without disturbing the normal level of tolerance present in the neighborhood. Their approach primarily is user- rather than community-centered (Lake, 2001), attempting to educate the public about the needs of users, refuting fears about personal safety, property devaluation, or decline of neighborhood quality, and often seeking the public's "collaboration" by means of public hearings and interviews. Yet, an autonomous approach to facility siting, keeping a low profile during the siting process, focusing on consumers' rights, and seeking support from legislation, is also not uncommon. Thus service providers may also respond to opponents saying things like "You didn't seek permission to move into this neighborhood, so why should we?" (Dear, 1992, p. 294).

However, public attention to the siting of human service facilities and housing projects, instead of quieting neighbors, tends to trigger strong and emotional opposition, sometimes together with blatant stigmatizing tendencies (Dear, 1992; Takahashi, 1997; Zippay, 1997). Remarkably, these community responses tend to be primarily explained in terms of peoples' inherent irrational, fearful, egocentric, unfounded, and prejudiced tendencies to stigmatize and exclude individuals associated with deviance, referring to these responses with the term NIMBY (not-in-my-backyard). Specifically, NIMBY refers to the phenomenon that, while people may recognize the general need for certain human services, such as shelters for the homeless and housing for the mentally ill, they egocentrically want to avoid the undesirable consequences of having to live near these sites, and demand that other neighborhoods should carry the burden.

Rather than describing this phenomenon with the pejorative and value-laden term NIMBY (see Lake's, 2001, proposal to replace the term with *locational conflict*), we suggest a more complete and objective analysis in terms of people's basic need for social control. Specifically, we believe that serious opposition to the siting of facilities and housing projects for deviant individuals may be caused by introducing a problem of social control in the community that is perceived as so serious that it can only be answered with defensive, aggressive, and sometimes stigmatizing responses. Specifically, the sudden introduction of considerable numbers or even *groups* of individuals associated with permanent deviance (often of both an active and passive nature; see below), who have never been part of the particular neighborhood and hence targets of social control, but who are now in need of care and protection, provides clear evidence that society has failed to engage in social control and will do little to help citizens to restore social control and to create a climate of safety, social order, and justice. It is important to remember that we are usually dealing with individualistic citizens who normally rely on authorities and formal modes of social control, together with tolerance, and thus have little experience with engaging in informal social control themselves, except within close relationships or the family. Now, these same authorities leave them unprotected and even forbid to take defensive actions. While repair and demands for behavioral adaptation would be logical community responses that express social concern, service providers and authorities tend to see these as selfish or prejudiced; what they demand is tolerance and to look the other way, mixed with feelings of pity and guilt with respect to service users.

Understandably, given this threatening situation, facility users tend to be seen as dangerous and unpredictable. However, because they are often also associated with what we have termed Type 4 or controllable-passive deviance, they may be seen as social parasites, not doing enough to get out of their dependent position, and earning little respect. The latter perceptions are strengthened by actually observing them in permanently needy and passive roles, without apparent improvement of their situation. For example, drug users leaving a service location providing them with methadon, may be witnessed taking their shots in public; homeless people appear unkempt; or mentally ill or handicapped persons may show all kinds of socially disorderly attributes or behavior. But perceptions of threat, responsibility, and immutability are not by themselves evidence for stigmatization, as is assumed by NIMBY theorists (e.g., Takahashi, 1997).[10]

To summarize, asking for tolerance for deviant individuals when people first want to establish elementary forms of social control, is asking for trouble. Although with most sitings of human services, silence tends to return as time passes (e.g., Zippay, 1997), this does not necessarily imply that education has been effective or people have "come to reason" or "get used" to these projects, let alone accept these facilities in their neighborhood. Indeed, people may aggressively ruminate about their lack of influence, only waiting to respond in openly aggressive ways at the moment an incident involving the interaction between deviant individual and neighborhood occurs. Furthermore, tolerance combined with suppressed irritation does not seem to promote social acceptance.

We generally would like to suggest that a useful strategy to address local opposition to housing projects is to recognize that what is introduced in the neighborhood is not simply a facility for passive individuals with special needs, to which people are expected to respond with compassion, indifference, or tolerance, but a symptom of a more fundamental problem that should be solved by society as a whole (e.g., the existence of poverty, drug addiction, untreatable mental illness, or tensions between culturally different groups who do not want to make mutual adaptations) and that nobody would like to have in his or her backyard if they had a choice; cf. Wolsink, 1994.) (Thus people may be more appropriately called NIABYs, referring to "not in anybody's backyard" than NIMBYs, cf. Wolsink, 1994). This recognition should be communicated by the manner in which the project is introduced in the neighborhood and the further collaborative or "outreach" efforts of the service providers after entry. Thus, dependent on type and seriousness of deviance, service providers may organize an open house, inform the neighborhood how users will try to cope with their problem and attempt to adapt to the neighborhood's wishes for social control, or actually demonstrate that users are able and motivated to engage in repaired relationships with the neighborhood. Examples of the latter would be making extra contributions to quality of life such as participating in community volunteer activities (e.g., neighborhood clean ups or recycling); activities that are often reported by service providers to facilitate social acceptance (see Zippay, 1997). Rather than appeasement strategies (cf. Dear, 1992), we see these activities as essentially contributing to the restoration of social control and reciprocal relationships (see also Sennett, 2003).

To conclude this section, policy makers and careproviders should become aware that modern society is not a small community with self-repairing potential anymore. In choosing for tolerance or repair as stigma-reduction strategies, they should take into account that tolerance may be difficult to realize when informal social control or repair is strongly invited by the occurrence of deviance in particular settings (e.g., family, school, neighborhood). Likewise, relationships are unlikely to be repaired when people are merely required to engage in polite and civil interaction. As illustrated, encouraging people to be tolerant and to engage in repair at the same time, may invite stigmatizing tendencies as a last resort in gaining control over the lifeworld. What we also have learned is that "contact" as a stigma-reduction strategy, despite its impressive positive effects on immediate expressions of interpersonal liking, is a too simplified notion with limited practical value, given the discussed complexities of social control in everyday life (see also Dixon, Durrheim, & Tredoux, 2005, for a similar argument).

In light of these conclusions, the value of long-term care as a stigma-prevention or reduction strategy should be recognized. Care of individuals associated with permanent passive deviance by friends, family, or institutions, with varying degrees of expected reciprocity, is a great benefit to be highly cherished. Although, as illustrated in a later section, targets themselves or their advocates may not always appreciate it, the low expectations with respect to reciprocity prevents perceivers from becoming frustrated and allows them to sustain a relationship, albeit one that is in important respects asymmetrical. We believe it holds for many chronic illnesses and disabilities that people may be worse off when left on their own, merely tolerated or the subject of critical repair efforts.[11] Tolerance, repaired relationships, and long-term care each could be a valuable ultimate goal of intervention strategies, provided that they are tailored to prevalent social control practices and type of deviance. But sometimes these strategies may be undesirable for ethical reasons, related to issues of equality and discrimination. That is, these strategies may not be seen as discouraging but as encouraging stigmatization and discrimination by deviant targets themselves, an issue that we turn to in the next section.

*Raising awareness of basic principles of social control as a generally acceptable and useful strategy of stigma prevention and reduction*

A major objection against our approach, one that may be especially fueled by strong egalitarian norms, individualism, and a civil and human rights perspective, may be that repair and long-term care, and even tolerance, may encourage rather than discourage stigmatization because deviant conditions would not exist or are irrelevant in the eyes of people associated with these conditions. Indeed, if one believes that, for example, one's physical or mental disability is or should be irrelevant in social interaction, one may find it offensive to be required to engage in some kind of repair process and to make behavioral adaptations. Furthermore, the more one is able to cope with the disability and is able to contribute to the community, the more one would also object to asymmetrical forms of long-term care in which autonomy and respect are usually denied. Perhaps, one may even object to the concept of tolerance, because there would seem to be nothing that can be tolerated. As noted earlier in this chapter, people making these complaints tend to identify themselves with minorities that are distinguished only from the majority in terms of apparently trivial cues such as skin color. Yet, social psychologists too may emphasize a perceiver perspective and see political correctness and unconditional acceptance as ultimate intervention goals.

As may be clear by now, we think that this perspective oversimplifies matters considerably. Deviance and social control in modern Western society are too complex to choose for one-sided solutions that entirely focus on changing the mentality and behavior of "stigmatizing" perceivers. A closer look reveals that this complexity is mainly due to the difficulty of determining the relevance of deviance under modern conditions of living. First, consider the different senses in which a deviant condition may appear largely irrelevant. A deviant condition may have been relevant but, due to certain adaptations made by the individual and the environment, is now not anymore. And in that case, it seems inappropriate to advise repair as an intervention strategy. For example, a person may have committed a crime ten years ago but, due to serving a long sentence or making necessary reparations with the victims, he or she is now a different person. Similarly, due to an accident ten years ago, a person may have become paralyzed below the waist but after extensive medical treatment, coping, training, and rehabilitation is able to move around in a wheelchair and perform normal social and intellectual tasks (except if mobility related). When meeting these persons for the first time, should we require them to start all over again; to confess their crime and show remorse or explain their tragedy and admit their losses, partial dependency, and need for help? Also consider conditions and behavioral differences in which it may be even more problematic to apply the concept of deviance and hence to require people to engage in repair processes such as ethnicity or homosexuality. Finally realize that deviance and hence repair may appear even less relevant the more one recognizes that responses to deviance may also be influenced by contextual influences (cf. displaced aggression, conflicts of power) and personality differences (cf. authoritarianism), as was extensively illustrated in Chapters 4, 5, and 6.

Having these cases in mind and from an egalitarian, disability rights, and empowerment perspective, it is understandable to object to interventions that require a two-sided solution, demanding not only perceivers to alter their responses, but also targets to acknowledge their association with deviance, thus demanding mutual adaptations for the sake of social control.

Yet, we argue that it is the difficulty, in particular, of establishing the relevance of deviance under modern conditions of living that requires us to more even-handedly assign responsibilities for stigma prevention and reduction. Modern medicine and health practices have created such a variety of deviant conditions with which people, with the aid of modern appliances, medication, and therapy, are able to continue taking part in everyday life, that perceivers will find it increasingly difficult to appropriately respond. Similarly, behavioral treatments of active deviance such as mental illness, crime, or psychopathology, have also advanced, yet in such a way that it is also increasingly unclear to the lay person how much deviance is actually left and how risky interaction is. Finally, consider how modern Western societies increasingly require social groups which differ widely in cultural backgrounds and values to live side by side, thus creating multiple opportunities for tension and conflict. Add to this that we need to respond to people associated with deviance in different situations requiring different alternatives to stigmatization, and it becomes evident that encounters with individuals associated with deviance demands very complex skills from people. For example, in the context of a close relationship or family, one may respond to an overweight or heavily smoking teenager with criticism, threat, and other measures of social control, but an equally overweight fellow passenger or colleague should be treated with tolerance or kindness. Working as a health practitioner, and meeting these persons in their ill condition, one is supposed to engage in cure and care, and treat them primarily with compassion. Given these complexities, the wisest advice for both perceivers and targets would be to ask for mutual awareness and adaptation and sometimes, if circumstances are favorable, explicit negotiation about mutually agreeable forms of interaction.

We hope that the following general principle is useful and perhaps generally acceptable in dealing with the ethical aspects of the complex relationship between stigma reduction and social control (if not, it has at least the advantage of allowing the reader to critically examine major assumptions that guided us in writing this book):

> In any society, there are deviant conditions that are relevant enough to require social control in the form of repair and occasionally even stigmatization. Sometimes, permanent deviant conditions are to be dealt with in terms of long-term care. However, when deviance is irrelevant, individuals associated with a deviant condition may minimally demand from others that they do not exclude or stigmatize them, and that they tolerate their condition when not having close contact with them. These individuals may similarly demand from society that it facilitates tolerance. But if individuals associated with deviance want more than tolerance and to be included in a close interpersonal relationship or community, and even if the condition seems irrelevant to them, they cannot expect others to behave as if they are not associated with some undesirable or deviant condition. (Obviously, it does not make sense to expect that other people's motivational mechanisms do not become automatically activated upon noticing an association with deviance.) In that situation, it will help to be aware of other peoples' basic needs for social control and perhaps negotiate with them about forms of interacting that are mutually agreeable. Mutual adaptations with which interaction partners potentially can agree can be derived from the three objective, evolutionary-based principles of social control that were introduced in Chapter 2: (1) prevent people from hurting each other, (2) reduce peoples' need states, and (3) in doing (1) and (2), be neither too hard, nor too soft.

Of course, it is especially the term *relevance* that may invite a lot of raised eyebrows and hopefully discussion. This is because, especially in the case of more complex forms of deviance, and given a choice between different ultimate intervention goals – repair, tolerance, and long-term care – (ir)relevance is never self-evident but should be determined every time anew when a relationship between perceiver and target starts. Hopefully, awareness of the general principles of social control, as outlined in this book, can serve as a useful meta-strategy to help prevent or reduce stigmatization. Yet, a more specific technique to be employed in order to find mutually agreeable ways of interacting would be negotiation to which we now briefly turn.

### *Exploring the usefulness of negotiation as a general strategy to prevent or reduce stigmatization*

Social scientists rarely recommend negotiation as a strategy to prevent or reduce stigmatization or prejudice, presumably because they are one-sidedly focused on the perceiver as the main reason for the existence of these phenomena. Only in the case of "realistic" conflicts between social groups, negotiation seems to be acknowledged as a useful intervention strategy (for important applications, however, see R. J. Fisher, 1994; Ross, 2000). But even then, negotiation is expected to fail because negative responding to deviance tends to be exclusively seen as an issue of power. For example, in a recent book on prejudice reduction, Oskamp contends that negotiation "conflicts with the dominant group's usual strong motivation to maintain power over subordinate groups" (Oskamp, 2000, p. 6). We believe, however, that power motives are not always the driving force behind negative responses to deviance, and that even if these motives are involved, a particular approach to negotiation, variously called interest-based, win-win, integrative, or principled bargaining or negotiation, and contrasted with distributive, win-lose, or positional bargaining, may still be very useful in reducing or preventing stigmatization.

We are especially impressed by the approach of principled negotiation taken by R. Fisher, Ury, and Patton's (1991) *Getting to Yes*, the major aim of which is not to reach a compromise between two positions that are vigorously defended in a win-lose battle, but to reach an agreement that is really satisfactory to both parties and that may improve the relationships between parties in the course of negotiating. The advantage of this approach is not only that its principles appear to be readily translated to the basic principles of social control that we have proposed in this book, but also that R. Fisher *et al.*'s (1991) book on negotiation is widely read (more than two million copies sold worldwide), thus increasing the likelihood of their application.

Briefly consider the four main principles on which R. Fisher *et al.*'s (Fisher *et al.*, 1991) approach to principled negotiation is based. *(1) Separate the people from the problem.* This principle is important in allowing parties to address the issues without personally attacking each other and thereby damaging their relationships. Because stigmatization essentially identifies a person with a deviant condition, separating people and issues seems especially relevant when perceivers and targets start negotiating on mutually agreeable ways of responding to a particular deviant condition with which targets are associated. This may imply realistically assessing the relevance of the deviant condition for the current interaction. To what extent does the target need assistance from the perceiver? How harmless is the target's condition after treatment? How motivated is the target to cope effectively with the condition? To what extent is the perceiver (and the community) willing and able to care for, or tolerate the behavior of, the target? *(2) Focus on interests, not positions.* R. Fisher *et al.* (1991) explain that "Your position is something that you have decided upon. Your interests are what caused you to so decide" (p. 42). When a problem is entirely defined in terms of positions this means that at least one party will "lose" the dispute. However, if the parties' underlying interests are identified it may be possible to find a solution which satisfies the interests of both parties. Applied to our problem of dealing with deviance, a focus on interests will imply that targets explain their desire not only to receive responses motivated by the nature of their condition (e.g., assistance, punishment, forgiveness) but also to be accepted as much as possible as equal relationship partners. Also, perceivers should clarify the needs that are triggered by the particular type of deviance, for example, their desire for safety, helping others, or reciprocity. *(3) Invent options for mutual gain.* It is important to think of a wide range of possible solutions to the problem, instead of searching for the one right solution. This may require, for example, techniques such as brainstorming or "look for items that are of low costs to you and high benefit to them, and vice versa" (p. 78). *(4) Insist on using objective criteria.* To resolve differences in interests, parties should first explicitly agree on the criteria that will be used to resolve differences. R. Fisher *et al.* suggest different kinds of objective criteria such as scientific findings, professional standards, or legal precedents. Applied to the present problem, powerful objective standards may be derived from evolutionary principles or mechanisms of kinship-based social control, and their associated emotions (see Chapter 2). When explained to parties, these principles should release the necessary motivation to search for mutual adaptations.

It goes without saying that the decision to apply principles of negotiation as a stigma-preventing or reducing strategy, and its further particulars, depends on the nature of the deviant condition, the particular setting, and the kind of interpersonal relationship that is desired. Briefly consider the following possibilities. The quality of relationships involving a partner with a chronic illness or disability may be improved when partners openly communicate or negotiate about the more or less beneficial forms of helping and the extent of reciprocity expected (cf. Coyne *et al.*, 1988). Similar improvements are to be expected for small group functioning. With the aid of a mediator, the introduction of individuals associated with active or passive deviance in workplaces, schools, or neighborhoods may also be fruitfully accompanied with a negotiation process. Negotiation has the additional advantage that, in the case of ethical or practical objections against a one-sided definition of deviance (e.g., relationships involving social groups with conflicting values, or persons with different sexual preferences), both parties have an equal chance to communicate their own conceptions of the other party's deviance, and their different needs for social control.

## 9.5 Summary

This chapter started with raising three critical questions with respect to interventions aimed at the prevention and reduction of stigmatization: What is the nature of the response that we want to influence? What are the ultimate goals of interventions aimed at stigma reduction? What are the proximal and deviance-specific motivational mechanisms on which stigmatization and stigma-reducing interventions are based? We noted that social scientists too easily regard negative responses to deviant individuals as evidence for stigmatization and hence as targets for intervention; and tend to be unclear about the proximal mechanisms and ultimate goals of these interventions.

In illustrating the practical usefulness of our theoretical model, we first considered how interventions may be tailored to the different motivational implications of the different types of deviance distinguished by our model. For example, one type of deviance seems to ask for interventions specifically designed for fear reduction, whereas other types require interventions that help to satisfy aroused care motives or to manage anger. We then set out to critically discuss common intervention strategies directed at perceivers, targets, and contact situations. In addition to noting that the motivational implications of different types of deviance are often not explicitly taken into account, we also illustrated that the ultimate goals of these interventions are usually far from clear, let alone desirable. For example, when contact interventions produce "liking" for individuals associated with deviance, "liking" for mentally handicapped persons is seen as similar in motivational implications to, and equally desirable as, "liking" for physically disabled but intellectually competent individuals or individuals with, for example, a different sexual orientation or cultural background.

In order to address these problems, we distinguished three ultimate intervention goals or broad strategies for dealing with deviance – repair, tolerance, and long-term care – as well as an additional meta-strategy that would allow people to apply these three strategies flexibly. We proposed that, in order to be effective, these strategies should be tailored to common social control practices. For example, striving to improve repair processes in interpersonal relationships or society at large does not seem to make sense when tolerance is the prevalent type of social control. Similarly, it is problematic to ask people to be tolerant with respect to deviance when the deviant condition or situation strongly motivates people to engage in repair or stigmatization processes. For example, tolerance seems difficult to reconcile with health education emphasizing the responsibility of ill persons and treating them in stigmatizing ways as "bad examples," or with the siting of human service facilities (e.g., for the mentally ill or homeless) in neighborhoods. In contrast, tolerance and repair may be more suitable as ultimate intervention goals or strategies of dealing with deviance in settings or societies commonly practicing tolerance and repair, respectively. We argued that the third stigma-reduction strategy, long-term care, is highly useful to protect and care for individuals with uncontrollable-passive deviant conditions of a permanent nature (e.g., severely mentally handicapped persons, frail elderly), despite the asymmetrical nature of the interpersonal relationships involved.

We closed this chapter with proposing a meta-strategy for dealing in a non-stigmatizing manner with the complexity of deviance and social control in modern Western societies. Specifically, it is often difficult to decide in advance about the suitability of the three general strategies for preventing or replacing stigmatization because the nature of modern deviant conditions may be unclear (e.g., how much dependency and autonomy is implied by current chronic illnesses? how dangerous are partially treated forms of mental illness? how much can and will culturally different groups living side by side adapt to each other's needs for social control?). Furthermore, people encounter the same type of deviance in different situations (e.g., in close relationships, on the train, at work), requiring different types of social control. Finally, individuals associated with deviance may raise ethical objections against each of these strategies, sometimes even objecting to being tolerated. Because of this complexity we suggested that raising awareness of the basic psychological principles of social control, as described in this book, would be a useful meta-strategy in applying in a flexible manner the strategies of repair, tolerance, and long-term care. In line with this strategy, a specific intervention technique would be for perceivers and targets to negotiate about mutually agreeable forms of interacting with each other.

# Notes

## Chapter 1

1. It should be noted that certain kinds of active or threatening deviance may be so serious and immutable that people feel that they can only respond to them with permanent isolation or even execution. With respect to more passive deviant conditions that are also difficult to control or influence (e.g., severe mental disability), however, a society may engage in long-term care. Yet, we do not consider long-term isolation or care as typical examples of repair. We will return to long-term care in Chapter 9 where we present it as one possible ultimate goal of interventions aimed at the prevention or reduction of stigmatization.
2. Parenthetically, the term stigma has its origin in ancient Greek, related to making a mark and, contradicting Goffman (1963b) and others, at that time it lacked its negative connotation. That connotation appears in Latin, where the mark is one of shame and degradation, such as placed on criminals or slaves (cf. Simon, 1992).
3. One reason that stigmas may easily spread through society is that stigmatized persons seem to have the capacity of contaminating others with their deviant condition or immoral quality. Specifically, this quality may be transferred to objects or other persons with which the deviant person has been in contact. This process of "magical contagion" (or "once in contact, always in contact") is well illustrated by a study by Rozin, Markwith, and McCauley (1994) examining people's willingness to wear (fully laundered) sweaters previously worn by a deviant person. Compared to a healthy but unknown man, willingness decreased for a target person having lost a leg or a homosexual, and decreased still further for a murderer or person with an infectious disease such as AIDS or tuberculosis. Similarly, Hebl and Mannix (2003) showed that merely sitting next to an obese individual in a waiting room is sufficient to judge a job applicant more negatively. This more negative judgment was independent of whether the obese woman was seen as the girlfriend of the applicant or as a participant of a different research study, which suggests that a negative evaluation of the obese person is used in a basal associative way in the representation of the job applicant. Of course, this "courtesy stigma" (Goffman, 1963b) or "stigma-by-association" effect (cf. Neuberg, Smith, Hoffman, & Russell, 1994) may also occur because people make different kinds of assumptions about the relationship between non-deviant and deviant individuals. For example, they may assume that both are genetically related (e.g., in the case of mental illness even whole families may be stigmatized) or have similar deviant preferences or an intimate

relationship (e.g., in the case of homosexuality). Whatever the particular processes responsible for these effects, it seems plausible that people may be aware of them and therefore may also be especially reluctant to seek contact with deviant individuals in public places. Indeed, to us, a good test for stigmatization of a particular deviant condition seems to ask research participants to what extent they would object to being seen in a public versus private place with a deviant individual. It also seems likely that (anticipation of) public exposure to a deviant individual contributes to negatively responding to this individual; the latter will not only be increasingly associated with these unpleasant anticipations but may also be blamed for seeking contact with others in public.

4. For our purposes, we find it less important in this book to sharply distinguish between different types of internal representations or expectancies, such as schemas, stereotypes, attitudes, or prejudice. For now it suffices to mention that we use the more encompassing concepts of *internal representation* or *expectancy* to refer to any representation formed by the brain of a deviant property (e.g., criminal disposition, illness, dependency). This internal representation may be a stereotype (when a property is attributed to all members of a social group) or may have the potential to arouse emotions when activated (attitude or prejudice).

5. In a recent discussion of stigmatization by Major and O'Brien (2005), it is increasingly hard to tell the difference between deviance and stigma as the authors propose that stigmas are specific and meaningful attributes that "lead" people to devalue others (p. 395), such as a physical deformity or being a child abuser. However, although these authors even approve of an evolutionary interpretation of these negative evaluations, they do not discuss the theoretical and practical consequences of allowing deviance to play a more important role in stigmatization. Indeed, they try to convince the reader that stigmatization is relatively independent from deviance, and relates to exclusionary attempts of those in power, social construction, and stereotyping.

6. We admit that, for ethical reasons, we should be careful in using the term *deviance* to denote ethnic properties, especially when one fails to clarify according to which cultural perspective the particular group is considered deviant, and requires particular forms of social control. Because people often fail to be aware of the different perspectives that may be adopted, it is best not to use the term deviance in everyday interethnic affairs. Nevertheless, for theoretical reasons, deviance and social control are highly useful theoretical concepts in the area of interethnic relations.

## Chapter 2

1. We leave out a discussion of the implications of sexual reproduction for the perception of deviance and social control because we doubt if a capacity to reproduce sexually is specifically involved in responding to deviance. To be sure, sex is a strong motivational mechanism that may be both responsible for deviance or fitness threats to others (e.g., rape, violence due to jealousy) and for rejecting others as potential mates (e.g., when they appear not to have "good genes" that promise healthy and fit offspring). However, not selecting an unattractive, ill, or disabled person as a mate because of the presence of

"bad genes" does not necessarily imply a particular form of social control or stigmatization. One may simply focus one's attention and behavior on the more attractive individual with the "good genes." Yet, it is conceivable that under particular circumstances, rejection of physically less attractive individuals as mates may combine with more fearful and aggressive responses to them. In a later section, we will propose that, in combination with solving adaptive problems related to self-preservation and altruism, sexual reproduction is responsible for the way societies are organized and engage in social control.

2. In addition to associating stigmatization with power differences it is important to remember that public labeling and shaming will remain important in case repair is difficult to realize (e.g., with permanent forms of deviance or in large societies).

3. An alternative way to understand the nature of Type 4 deviance is in terms of parent-offspring conflict or the dilemma of both parents and offspring to continue an asymmetrical relationship based on care, and to stop the relationship or replace it by a symmetrical one based on reciprocity and cooperation. The conflict arises at a moment at which it is not entirely clear which kind of relationship between parent and offspring will accrue the most genetic benefits to parents and offspring (Trivers, 1985). For the maturing offspring, it is increasingly important to make full use of the benefits of being mature and independent, and to prepare reproducing themselves. On the other hand, it is also tempting to continue to reap the benefits of staying somewhat dependent from the help given by parents. The parents are faced with a complementary problem: What is the right moment not to take the remaining signs of immaturity and dependency of offspring very seriously anymore and to let them stand on their own feet? Observations suggest that in certain species, adolescents may engage in free riding (e.g., adolescent chimps have been observed trying to ride on their mother's back), temper tantrums or even self-mutilation to attract the waning attention and interest of their parents (Trivers, 1985).

4. Can active deviance also be judged in terms of onset responsibility? For example, when Weiner *et al.* (1988, Study 2) and Dijker and Koomen (2003, Study 1) informed their participants that a child abuser had been abused as a child himself ("experiencing severe stress and a nervous breakdown"), or a drug user became addicted due to prior treatment of pain after an injury, they reported more pity (and in the case of the drug addicted, also less anger) than without that information. However, these examples demonstrate that supplying information about a lack of onset responsibility for active deviance, transforms the condition into a more passive one, and that onset responsibility is not an inherent aspect of active deviance. And what about offset responsibility in the case of active deviance? To the extent that active deviance is threatening and potentially harmful to the perceiver, the deviant individual is expected to exercise more self-control, submit to social norms, and stop behaving dangerously. And the less control the individual has over his or her behavior, and the less predictable the harmful consequences of contact with the person are, the more restraining and preventative measures are required. But clearly, believing that active deviance is more or less controllable in this sense, is not the same as attributing more or less offset responsibility in the case of passive deviance. For example, emphasizing that a dangerous person is unable to exercise impulse control and hence is not

348    *Note to page 44*

responsible for his or her behavior is less likely to arouse tenderness than fear (see Chapter 3).

Perhaps, in a highly specific sense, several examples of active deviance lend themselves to an analysis in terms of onset or offset responsibility. For example, a person suffering from epilepsy may be more or less responsible for bringing him or herself into a situation (e.g., drinking alcohol, exposure to stress), in which the active and embarrassing symptoms of epilepsy will manifest themselves. A drug addict may have been warned early on that contact with certain people would expose him or her to the temptation of using drugs. Moreover, taking medication or therapy for a condition representing active deviance may be constructed as a form of offset responsibility. We believe, however, that these represent fairly recent "medical" constructions of cases that people in general tend to perceive primarily in terms of active deviance or as ambiguous with respect to active or passive deviance (see our discussion of the location of several addictions in Chapter 3).

5. Readers familiar with other proposals to classify deviant conditions or stigmas may wonder if our two dimensions are sufficient to classify all types of deviance. For example, what about Jones *et al.*'s (1984) *peril, concealability, disruptiveness,* and *aesthetic qualities* or the often proposed *visibility* dimension (e.g., Crocker *et al.*, 1998; Deaux, Reid, Mizrahi, & Ethier, 1995; Frable, 1993a)? With the exception of *peril* or danger implied by the deviant condition, which is clearly related to our active types of deviance, we doubt that additional dimensions predict other emotional qualities than our two-dimensional representation. Of course, people may distinguish between visible and less visible (or concealable) deviant conditions when presented with conditions that clearly differ in visibility; and relatively visible conditions (e.g., obesity, a scar) may demand different interaction strategies from deviant individuals in order to avoid or reduce negative responses than relatively less visible and concealable ones (e.g., diabetes, a past psychiatric treatment). Yet, concealability does not seem to have a clear motivational influence on the perceiver. Sometimes, knowledge of more concealable conditions (e.g., cancer, contagious disease) is more strongly reacted to than the perception of less concealable ones (e.g., an eye patch). At other times, visible threats (which also tend to be aesthetically displeasing) are more important. For example, based on extensive fieldwork in Israeli hospitals, Weiss (1998) found much more negative parental reactions to newborns with external physical abnormalities (e.g., facial deformities or openings made for excretions or breathing) than with internal problems (e.g., kidney or heart disease). In fact, most of the children suffering external defects were abandoned (68 percent), even though most of them did not suffer from life-threatening illnesses. In contrast, most of the children suffering from internal disease were not abandoned (93 percent) even in cases of serious illness where the chance of recovery is slim.

Of course, the stronger the underlying FF or C system are activated by particular deviant conditions, the more disrupting these conditions are in interpersonal relations. (It should be noted, however, that we find Jones *et al.*'s dimension of *course* an especially important variable to distinguish deviance from stigma as it refers to the extent to which a deviant condition is permanent or can be changed, and the individual can adapt to the demands of cooperation and reciprocity.) Interestingly, when combined with the potential to engage in harmful activity, milder physical abnormalities such as a missing leg or a particularly shaped nose, may contribute to associating individuals with Type 2 deviance; seeing them as "crooked" and unreliable. Alley (1988) discusses the metaphorical use of physical features in person perception, Eagly, Ashmore, Makhijani, and Longe (1991) interpret the social meaning of physical abnormalities in terms of an "ugly-is-bad" stereotype, and Wainapel (1996) illustrates how Charles Dickens used physical disabilities in his novels to emphasize the crookedness or wickedness of his characters.

Finally, consider the differences and similarities between our and Goffman's (1963b) influential classification of deviant conditions. Although his "blemishes of individual character" (different kinds of mental and behavioral problems) are associated with active aspects of deviance, and his "abominations of the body" refer to passive aspects or physical illness, his "tribal stigma" (referring to being a member of a devalued social or ethnic group) does not have a separate place in our typology. That is, given that ethnic or racial minorities often are seen as deviant *because* their members are believed to have a "blemished character," one could well ask why it should be a separate class. Furthermore, Goffman does not distinguish in terms of our controllability dimension between "blemishes" that are in a fearful way unpredictable (e.g., schizophrenia) from those that are intentional and controllable (e.g., crime). Finally, one could ask why "blemishes" such as psychiatric problems are primarily active (in our sense) and are not sometimes closely associated with more passive "abominations of the body" (compare the sadness or depression that can be associated with chronic illness).

6. Although we have been inspired by connectionism and neural network modeling (e.g., Bechtel & Abrahamsen, 1991; Grossberg, 1980) we leave out a discussion of variables that need to be specified in order for the network to be simulated (e.g., input and output functions, number of units to represent the functioning of single motivational systems, connection strength between units, learning rules, and preferably also feedback relations). We hope that our approach motivates future researchers to specify these properties and examine the network's performance with the aid of computer simulation.

7. Aggression inhibition by displaying infantile and submissive features and behaviors may also be involved in politeness rituals and excuse making in the case of norm violations (Scott & Lyman, 1968), young children's attempts to stop interpersonal aggression by looking sad (Camras, 1977), peacemaking and reconciliation in chimpanzees after aggressive encounters (de Waal, 1989), and effectively asking for help from strangers by first emphasizing one's need state (Langer & Abelson, 1972).

8. When Phelps *et al.* (2003) studied a patient with amygdala damage, they still found the biased responding to negative trait names, and concluded that the amygdala may not be crucial in responding in a biased way to blacks since this responding is partly mediated by cognitive processes. However, they allowed for the possibility that the amygdala might still play an important role during the acquisition of negative feelings toward black individuals. (Note that we cannot be sure about the true perceptual antecedents of a fear response, as the measured brain activity may be both a response to certain key features of deviance (e.g., blackness or particular physiognomic features) and general negative views or stereotypes about blacks that happen to be culturally available.)

9. Recent studies employing brain imaging procedures suggest that the com-posite emotions in our model, such as pity and forgiveness, are also asso-ciated with the activation of distinct brain structures (Decety & Chaminade, 2003; Farrow *et al.*, 2001). Furthermore, a recent study employing EEG measures suggests that brain activity associated with pity may downregu-late activity associated with anger in response to active deviance (Harmon-Jones, Vaughn-Scott, Mohr, Sigelman, & Harmon-Jones, 2004). These researchers first successfully induced pity in participants by letting them closely examine someone suffering from multiple sclerosis, after which they either insulted participants or not. They found that brain activity in the frontal brain area, normally caused by insults without prior pity arou-sal, reduced after first experiencing pity.

10. We are aware of other attempts to address issues of mentalism or "embodi-ment" (e.g., Clancey, 1997), but have the impression that since Morris (1946), who identified concepts responsible for meaning with *needs* or motivational systems and *habits*, a motivational approach to mental repre-sentation and meaning has hardly been attempted.

## Chapter 3

1. It is difficult to interpret Schmelkin's (1984) second dimension, which she interprets as contrasting "organic" (e.g., cancer) with "societal" disabilities such as being an ex-convict.

2. Readers may try for themselves to see how rotation of the two dimensions sometimes may result in locations of the deviant conditions that is more in agreement with our deviance typology. For example, a rotation of the two dimensions in Figure 3.1 (E) (obtained from the Room *et al.*, 2001 study) of about 45 degrees counter clockwise (maintaining an angle of 90 degrees between the dimensions), locates "cannot hold down job," "homeless," and "does not take care of own children" in the lower right quadrant associated with Type 4 deviance (with "dirty and unkempt" also very close to this quadrant), referring, together with obesity, to irresponsible or immature behavior and social parasitism; "drug addiction," "alcoholism," and "crim-inal behavior" in the upper right quadrant (Type 2 deviance), with "HIV positive" remaining associated with criminality; while the other conditions largely keep their assignments to the other two quadrants.

3. It is sometimes claimed from similar kinds of analyses that emotions are "more important" than cognitions or beliefs about the properties of deviant individuals or groups in explaining or predicting overall evaluations and behavioral tendencies (e.g., Abelson, Kinder, Peters, & Fiske, 1982; Stangor, Sullivan, & Ford, 1991; Tropp & Pettigrew, 2005). We believe, however, that such a conclusion is mistakenly based on a failure to include in the analysis cognitions or beliefs that function as the cognitive antecedents or appraisals of the studied emotion terms. As we have argued elsewhere (Dijker, Koomen, van den Heuvel, & Frijda, 1996), when cognitions and emotions are matched for correspondence they mainly *share* their influence on evaluations or beha-vioral tendencies. This view agrees with our present view of emotions as motivational states that include expectancies about (emotion-relevant) prop-erties of deviant individuals. This is not to deny that stereotypes may contain a more developed and varied content than references to emotion-arousing

properties. Biernat and Dovidio (2000) suggest a number of factors contributing to the development of such stereotypes. One factor they suggest is "groupiness." If a deviant condition or stigma is based on membership in a definable group, stereotypes are likely to develop and be maintained. This "groupiness" factor is presumably operating because group membership, for example, membership of an ethnic minority, can imply a substantial amount of other (perceived) information about a person. Such well-developed stereotypes may lead people to respond to the targets of those stereotypes in a more differentiating way than they would do merely on the basis of the targets' emotion-arousing properties.

4. Because mental representations may influence information processing at the early stage of encoding and in a relatively automatic way, it may be hard and sometimes impossible for perceivers, if desired, to correct their influence. Sometimes we may even literally see things differently under the influence of mental representations. Stapel and Koomen (1997) demonstrated this by showing that the magnitude of perceptual contrast effects was influenced by social categorizations that have no physical bases. More specifically, the investigators showed this using the Ebbinghaus illusion, in which a target stimulus surrounded by large context stimuli appears smaller than a target stimulus surrounded by small context stimuli. By having participants categorize identical stimuli in different ways – male and female stimuli can be categorized as such but also as students – it could be shown that these different categorizations of surrounding context and target stimuli such as male and female faces affect the perception of the physical size of the target face. In other words, categories and stereotypes may even influence what we actually see or "read off" from immediate sensory experiences, such as the perception of physical magnitude.

5. It should be noted that there are also examples of studies that failed to obtain the complete pattern of response amplification for African-Americans and disabled target persons. For example, Carver *et al*. (1977) found more positive evaluations of a black than white target person irrespective of his behavior; and using similar stimulus materials, Carver *et al*. (1979), found a general "sympathy effect" for a handicapped target person. One interpretation of this failure to obtain more negative evaluations of the negative target behavior may be that this behavior was judged less heavily in light of the relatively strongly activated C system in these experiments. In particular, in both of the above studies, the negatively portrayed target was described as having "few friends," thus emphasizing his neediness.

## Chapter 4

1. Another advantage of the concept of motivational state or emotion is that it does not force us to distinguish between non-symbolic or embodied internal representations and symbolic or propositional representations. In particular, it emphasizes that it is always the meaning or content of representations that we should focus on in order to understand behavior, and that this meaning is constituted by a complex bodily and neural state with cognitive, motivational, and behavioral implications. A closer look at the models proposed by Smith and DeCoster (2000) and Strack and Deutsch (2004) reveals that *both* their implicit associative networks and explicit propositions are symbolic

representations. That is, although their associative networks appear to consist of relatively raw perceptual associations between events (in contrast to the meaningful symbols), they are conceptualized not only as episodic but also as "semantic memories" with units and nodes that are rich in content and meaning (for a similar interpretation, see Erb *et al.*, 2003). Consequently, when it comes to explaining the meaningful content of these representations in terms of underlying motivational or neural processes, one may be faced with mind-brain dualism (see Chapter 2, for a discussion).

2. It should be noted that we do not use the terms "unified" or "lack of dissociation" to refer to the theoretically less interesting cases in which behavioral responses can be considered unified because they either are largely automatic (with hardly any evidence for control) or largely controlled (with hardly any evidence for the influence of automatic aspects). An example of the latter case would be when the deviant condition fails to trigger any motivational system at all. An example of the former case would be when a weak emotional response is aroused during brief contact, perhaps accompanied with a noticeable facial expression, which hardly receives further attention, and is not accompanied by other behavioral reactions to the deviant individual because the perceiver is too much involved in other things. Yet another example would be when a very strong emotion is aroused (e.g., rage) that prevents the perceiver from exercising control.

    Our hypothesis that (moderately) strong initial motivational states or emotions are likely to take control over thinking and behavior, resulting in a unified response with little dissociation between automatic and controlled aspects, bears resemblance to arguments within attitude theories that especially strong, accessible, and relevant attitudes will influence behavior (cf. Fazio, 1990; see also Nosek, 2005). Indeed, internal representations of deviance discussed in the previous chapter may be thought of as emotional dispositions which in turn are highly similar to certain conceptions of attitude. However, whereas theories of attitudes and prejudice tend to see a strong correspondence between automatically activated attitudes and behavior as evidence for the *absence* of control or suppression and the hegemony of affective or primarily irrational impulses, our view stresses that initial automatic responses are not simply "irrational" negative versus positive evaluations but qualitatively different emotions and expectancies that motivate and guide goal-directed behavior toward the deviant target and the situation.

3. As argued in Chapter 3, Crandall *et al.*'s (2002) observation of high correlations between normative approval of negative responses to deviance and tendencies to make these responses, such that, for example, it is more acceptable to respond negatively to individuals associated with active (e.g., child abuse, wife beating, drug use) than passive deviance (e.g., disadvantaged minority or disability), may not only indicate that these tendencies are derived from normative disapproval but may also be the cause of these disapprovals. See Chapter 5, for a more extensive discussion of these findings.

4. Of course, the problem remains that the evaluative implications of qualitatively different verbal responses to deviance may be influenced by desires to present oneself in socially desirable ways.

5. It may appear somewhat strange that we do not discuss in this chapter research inspired by the influential *contact hypothesis* (e.g., Allport, 1954/

1979; Pettigrew, 1998). Because we believe that this research lacks a clear theoretical foundation and often involves the evaluation of broad contact interventions, we discuss it in Chapter 9. Nevertheless, it may be useful to mention here that the contact hypothesis shares with some of the dual-process models discussed in this chapter the assumption that stigmatization or prejudice is based on beliefs or stereotypes that can be corrected by encountering unexpected and new facts about (atypically behaving) deviant individuals.

6. While in this chapter we are particularly interested in behavior that can be specifically explained in terms of our FF-C network, Chapter 7 will discuss discrimination of deviant individuals in a broader sense.

7. Incidentally, the latter study suggests that Fein and Spencer's (1997) assumption that people engage in displacement *in order to* repair lowered self-esteem may not be generally valid as it seems unlikely that the mild provocation used by Mikulincer and Shaver (2001, Experiment 4) would have been sufficient to lower self-esteem. However, we recognize that the repair of lowered self-esteem may sometimes be an additional explanation for the relationship between prior provocation and negative responses to deviance. In particular, a decrease in people's well-being may be remedied through comparison with a less fortunate other or by active derogation of another person or group (Wills, 1981).

8. Interestingly, these studies also found that the influence of hierarchical status on negative responses was mediated by a tendency to compete with, and dominate others, which was measured in terms of an individual difference variable termed social dominance orientation (a measure that we extensively discuss in Chapter 5).

9. Unfortunately, the fact that both Katz *et al.* (1975) and Dovidio and Gaertner (1981) experimentally manipulated the hierarchical status of white helpers, that their main effects were qualified by these manipulations, and that in Gaertner (1973) blacks were helped less frequently *only* by conservatives, is not mentioned in the meta-analysis of interracial helping studies performed by Saucier *et al.* (2005). Furthermore, important moderators, in the six other studies revealing significantly more helping of the black than the white target person, and that we believe to be related to the functioning of the C system, are also not discussed by these researchers. For example, in a study by Thayer (1973), white males more frequently helped a black than a white target, but only when the target claimed to be deaf and asked participants to make a phonecall. Katz, Glass, Lucido, and Farber (1979), first induced white males to make highly insulting vs. neutral remarks about the target before giving them an opportunity to help him, thus likely causing differential helping on the basis of guilt and a desire to care. Similarly, in a study by Dutton and Lake (1973), students with liberal attitudes were told that they appeared hostile and prejudiced on physiological measures, and presumably made to feel guilty before meeting the target person who asked for spare change. Compare this with studies more directly showing that guilt may be aroused when confronting white participants with their negative responses to blacks (e.g., Fazio & Hilden, 2001).

10. Helping patterns with respect to active deviant conditions other than ethnic or racial background have been examined far less frequently. For example, in a field experiment by Tsang (1994), shoppers were asked for change either by an ostensibly lesbian person, as revealed by a slogan on her

tee-shirt, or by a female person wearing an unmarked tee-shirt. The apparently heterosexual person met more often with a positive response than the apparently lesbian person (68 percent vs. 47 percent). In a study by Ellis and Fox (2001) in England, the wrong number technique was used to examine levels of helping behavior shown toward lesbians and gay men. A wrong number telephone call was made by a confederate who self-identified as homosexual or heterosexual by mentioning the first name of his/her partner. The caller requested help by asking the respondent to relay a message to his or her partner by telephone (the caller's mobile telephone battery was running out). Results showed that self-identified lesbians and gay men were less likely to receive help than their heterosexual counterparts.

11. We doubt if other attempts to induce perspective taking can be interpreted in the same way. For example, when Galinsky and colleagues ask participants to write an essay about a typical day in the life of an elderly man as if they were that person (Galinsky & Ku, 2004; Galinsky & Moskowitz, 2000), and found more positive thoughts and feelings toward old age, this may have been caused by taking the perspective of an actor who copes well with his condition; rather than by an observer perspective that is typical for Batson's experiments. Consistent with this speculation is Galinsky and Ku's (2004) finding that this kind of "perspective taking" only results in positive effects when participants are high on dispositional or experimentally manipulated self-esteem.

12. Recently, using a different framework, many of the interaction studies discussed in the current section, were also presented systematically by Hebl and Dovidio (2005), who argue convincingly for a more elaborate use of these kinds of studies.

13. As will become clear, one class of laboratory studies, in which participants' responses are studied while they anticipate future interaction with a target person, forms an exception.

14. To our knowledge, the question whether dissociation between automatic and controlled responses should be established in terms of correlations between implicit and explicit measures or in terms of (differential) main effects of deviance versus non-deviance on implicit and explicit measures has not yet been addressed by investigators. Yet, a recent study by Nosek (2005) in which implicit and explicit responses to fifty-seven objects or issues were assessed shows that these two kinds of operationalization of dissociation may sometimes yield different conclusions.

15. In light of this reservation, the practical implications of a recent study by Wheeler and Fiske (2005) must also be questioned. These researchers showed that automatic responses may be very quickly moderated or diluted. Specifically, whereas a normal categorization task with white and black faces resulted in the usual bias on both a priming task and amygdala activity, instructions to search for a dot somewhere on these faces or estimate the photographed individual's vegetable preferences, reduced this bias. Yet, this should be less surprising if one realizes that merely distracting attention away from the target's deviant features may simply prevent activation of the relevant motivational systems and associated expectancies. More generally, although epistemic or instrumental motives may help to by-pass attention to deviance and the need for social control during anticipated or perhaps brief cooperative contacts, these motives may be insufficient to foster repair processes during long-term contact (see Chapter 9).

## Chapter 5

1. It is interesting to mention that internal reasons are frequently distinguished from "external reasons" to respond positively to deviant individuals (as measured, for example, by an item like "If I acted prejudiced toward black people, I would be concerned that others would be angry with me"), and that the latter motives seem to refer more to activity of the FF system. For example, Plant and Devine's (1998) external motivation to respond without prejudice is positively related to explicitly negative responses to blacks. This is consistent with results obtained by Monteith, Devine, and Zuwerink (1993). These researchers showed that participants with a strong tendency to respond negatively (prejudiced) to homosexuals, experienced anger when made aware of the fact that their negative responses were discrepant with standards prescribing equal treatment. A similar factor proposed by Fazio and Hilden (2001) is also associated with agitated feelings rather than with guilt when participants are made aware of their inadvertent negative responses to blacks.

2. Plant, Devine, and Brazy (2003) used a so-called "bogus pipeline" procedure, letting white participants believe that the experimenter, via some sort of biomedical equipment, had access to their actual feelings about a target person. Participants were required to guess their "bodily" responses to the target, ostensibly in order to examine how well they were in touch with their true feelings. Such a procedure was earlier used by Carver *et al.* (1978) to measure responses to a handicapped, black, or non-deviant individual and may also be informative about the unique role of the C system in responding to handicapped persons. These researchers assumed that the self-report responses of participants connected to the bogus pipeline would reflect their true conscious feelings, whereas those in a control condition who were not attached to a bogus pipeline, would be more likely to fake their responses in case responses to a particular deviant condition would be subject to social desirability and suppression. Indeed, the researchers found that in this control condition, the pattern of evaluations of the target persons could be interpreted in terms of social desirability; responses to both the handicapped and the black target person were more positive than eva-luations of the non-deviant person (responses to the former two did not differ in positivity). However, the presence of a bogus pipeline had an effect on participants' evaluation, but only when they judged a black person, with the black person evaluated more negatively than the non-deviant person. This pattern suggests that normally obtained positive responses to the han-dicapped cannot be additionally raised by inducing participants to be more sincere about their feelings. In contrast, the positive response to the black target may have been controlled and faked under normal conditions and actually more negative than the response to the white person in the bogus pipeline condition.

3. In psychological research, Adorno, Frenkel-Brunswik, Levinson, and Sanford (1950) laid the foundation of the authoritarianism concept in their classic study on the authoritarian personality. Initially, their study, following psychoanalytic concepts and ideas, was focused on the dynamics of anti-Semitism, but later it broadened to prejudice in general, with the personality structure of the prejudiced person being at the center. The study got a very favorable receipt, but later it met with quite a number of methodological and

theoretical objections. Afterwards, researchers, particularly Altemeyer (1988), incorporated important ideas from the study, for example, submission to authorities, in a new authoritarianism concept.

4. Jost, Glaser, Kruglanski, and Sulloway (2003) unite fear or resistance to change, as measured, for instance, by an authoritarianism-scale, and acceptance of inequality, as measured by the social dominance orientation scale, in their conceptualization of political conservatism. From the present chapter it will be clear that such a conceptualization blurring the distinction between the authoritarianism and social dominance concept will make for a less elaborated theory with many imprecise predictions in the field of prejudice and responding to deviance.

5. The genetic basis of authoritarianism and social dominance orientation contradicts a recent proposal by Kreindler (2005) arguing that these individual tendencies are a product of group dynamics. In addition, her model has other questionable assumptions. For example, that the social dominance orientation of members of high status groups originates from social creativity processes, which serve to legitimize an undeserved status. This assumption is conflicting with attributes related to social dominance orientation, as found in the literature, such as meanness or "dog eats dog."

## Chapter 6

1. Reasoning from individual differences in responding to deviance or prejudice, Duckitt (2001) arrives at a similar psychological description of different contemporary political ideologies and societies. (Of course, this should not come as a surprise as we know from Chapter 5 that values and individual difference measures of prejudice are systematically related.) In Duckitt's view, the hierarchical-egalitarian dimension evolves from differences in social dominance orientation (SDO; see Chapter 5), while the collectivism-individualism dimension is associated with authoritarianism (or Altemeyer's RWA construct; see Chapter 5). Thus in hierarchical and collectivistic societies, individuals tend to score high on both SDO and RWA, whereas in hierarchical and individualistic societies people are relatively less traditional and authoritarian but highly competitive, domineering, and valuing inequality. According to Duckitt, societies combining egalitarian and collectivistic values score high on authoritarianism but low on SDO, and egalitarian and individualistic societies (social democracies) score low on both RWA and SDO.

2. Robarchek and Robarchek's (1998) comparison of the extremely peaceful Semai society with the extremely violent Waorani of Amazonian Ecuador makes clear that not all hunter-gatherers can be assigned to our Category 1 society. Although both societies are strikingly similar with respect to conditions of living and social organization, the Semai are truly egalitarian and collectivistic, while the Waorani are extremely individualistic, seeing themselves as self-reliant, independent, and in full personal control over their environment. Furthermore, they are highly suspicious about personal malevolent intentions that may be expressed in sorcery. Indeed, there are no "accidents" and "bad luck," and few "natural deaths" in Waorani society (in contrast, the Semai do not see individuals but the natural world as malevolent, which can only be coped with through social cohesion and mutual care).

Although the researchers explain the endless blood feuds and revenge kill-ings in Waorani society as a consequence of a worldview which highly values individualism and personal control, the reverse causal influence also seems likely; being trapped in a spiral of tit-for-tat violence encourages the attribu-tion of personal control. Whatever the particular reason for extreme indivi-dualism among the Waorani, the consequences for social control in the case of passive deviance are noteworthy. For example, Robarchek and Robarchek (1998) report that the Waorani may leave snakebite victims or laboring women in the forest to fend for themselves while the group continues its hunting expedition or, in the event of a spearing raid, flee for their lives, with men abandoning their wives and women their children. Interestingly, responses to deviance and conflict in this society can also be well described in terms of a personality characteristic that we came to know in the previous chapter as social dominance orientation or "dog eats dog."

3. We have the impression that authors may too easily interpret killing or abandonment as evidence for stigmatization. For example, Winzer (1997) maintains that chronically ill or disabled persons must have been abandoned or killed by prehistoric hunter-gatherers due to their harsh and nomadic way of living, and Kurzban and Leary (2001) seem to assume that such treatment would generally have been evolutionary adaptive or fitness-enhancing. A particularly illustrative example of overseeing prosocial responses to deviance among primates is the case of "Mr McGregor," a polio-stricken and crippled adult chimpanzee male, which is widely cited as evidence that primates, including humans, would have a deep-seated evolutionary ten-dency to primarily respond with stigmatization to disabled group members (e.g., Jones *et al.*, 1984; Kurzban & Leary, 2001). As Goodall (1986a; 1986b) describes the case, group members responded with hostility and ostracism to him when he begged to be groomed by them. However, Goodall also reports that McGregor was not only shunned but also had "a faithful attendant in the younger Humphrey . . . who in defense of his friend, not only dared to attack the higher-ranking and powerful Goliath, but stayed near McGregor for several hours each day throughout the last two weeks of the male's life" (Goodall, 1986a, p. 385). Other examples of both shunning and healing, grooming, nurturing, and defending wounded and sick animals among (sometimes unrelated) chimpanzees are reported by Fábrega (1997, pp. 36–46). As for early humans, skeletal remains from different prehistoric archeological sites strongly suggest the permanent presence of disabled persons among prehistoric hunter-gatherers. For example, an adult Neanderthal male (Shanidar I) found in Shanidar Cave in Iraq showed serious but *healed* bone fractures, suggesting arthritis, blindness, and ampu-tation. This suggests some form of support by other group members. Dettwyler (1991) usefully discusses the different reasons that group mem-bers of prehistoric societies might have had to include individuals with these disabling conditions.

4. That the association between physical abnormalities and an unreliable or evil character may be timeless, is especially well illustrated by many of Charles Dickens' novels, where adult villains tend to be depicted as disabled persons "whose physical deformities are outward manifestations of their inner deprav-ity" (Wainapel, 1996, p. 629), and paralysis and aphasia as a consequence of punishment for wickedness. Interestingly, Dickens also tried to induce pity for the disabled, ill, or poor by presenting them as innocent *children*.

5. It should be noted that many twentieth century totalitarian states such as the communist Soviet Union, the People's Republic of China, and Nazi Germany, that strongly suppressed individualistic tendencies, practiced extreme stigmatization. In addition to public punishments and deterrence that are so typical for hierarchical-collectivistic societies, we here see punishments and torture that are relatively invisible to the public, unpredictable disappearances, and various strategies of indoctrination and brainwashing as social control.

6. Interestingly, consistent with the motivational implications of our deviance typology, patients with schizophrenia (clearly an active type) reported more cases of experienced stigmatization than depressed patients.

7. Although some reference to deviance is made in a recent analysis by Inglehart and Baker (2000), their method of analysis has certain limitations. Specifically, on the basis of factor analysis of a large and heterogeneous set of variables, these researchers constructed two dimensions on which they compared the sixty-four countries included in their sample. One dimension distinguished relatively poor countries with a strong emphasis on materialistic or survival values (e.g., developing and ex-communist countries) from more affluent and mostly modern Western societies that valued self-expression. Because this dimension was also measured in terms of disapproval of homosexuality, it should come as no surprise that it correlates strongly with negative responses to homosexuals, with the former countries responding more negatively to homosexuals than the latter. This dimension also correlates with negative responses to the other deviant conditions included. The second dimension that Inglehart and Baker (2000) found – which they term *tradition vs. secular values* – again distinguished poor developing countries (this time together with a few modern but traditional Western societies) from a large number of ex-communist countries and small European countries, both lacking in traditional values. At the country level, this dimension appeared to be uncorrelated with responses to deviance, which is odd given that conservatism and tradition strongly predict negative responses to deviance (see previous chapter); but understandable if one considers that the large set of ex-communist countries not only lack traditional values but differs from the small European ones in terms of economic hardship and frustration. The fact that the two dimensions of Inglehart and Baker (2000) unclearly differentiate between cultural aspects is also evidenced by Hofstede's (2001) finding that *both* dimensions positively correlate with collectivism-individualism ($r = 0.49$ and $r = 0.74$, respectively; Hofstede, 2001, p. 266). Furthermore, Inglehart and Baker themselves acknowledge that the ex-communist countries are difficult to characterize in cultural terms as these poor and materialistic countries are both non-traditional and recently show salient religious and orthodox tendencies. We believe that it is possible to get a clearer view of the cross-cultural differences and similarities in responding to deviance in the WVS by leaving out the ex-communist countries, by clearly distinguishing the countries in terms of collectivism-individualism, and by a more detailed look at responses to the different deviant conditions included.

8. When the outlier South Korea is removed, a better fit with the regression line can be obtained and the correlation rises to $r = -0.56$, $p < 0.001$.

9. Unfortunately, other potentially useful items in the WVS, measuring opinions about equality, competition, and need states were formulated with

ambiguous anchors, simultaneously expressing different reasons for (dis)agreement.

10. We remind the reader of power problems with this analysis which are especially due to the extremely small number of cases in the English speaking category.

11. See also Chapter 3 for a discussion of rejection hierarchies in modern Western societies and for our multidimensional scaling analysis of the Room *et al.* rankings.

12. We are grateful to Dr. Robin Room, for providing us with the SPSS data file of this study.

13. The reason why these four countries were located at a considerable distance from the regression line is somewhat unclear. Perhaps, the cities in which helping was tested in these countries – Bangkok, Taipei, Singapore, and Kuala Lumpur – have a business-like, commercial, and hence individualistic atmosphere.

## Chapter 7

1. For supporting evidence they referred to Goldberg (1974) who had found that children with invisible heart disease were better adjusted than children with visible facial burns. One can, however, question whether this evidence supports the concealment strategy. As we noted in Chapter 2, facial disfigurement seems to be a much more severe deviant condition than internal diseases. The greater adjustment of children with invisible heart disease than children with visible facial burns studied by Goldberg (1974) may be better explained by condition severity – Goldberg himself mentioned this possibility – than by condition concealment.

2. Unfortunately, the internet provides individuals with a deviant condition not only with beneficial possibilities such as groups consisting of persons with the deviant condition in question or social support groups, but also with information attacking deviant individuals in a highly stigmatizing way. The internet contains a large number of websites spreading hate and stimulating violence to persons or groups with a deviant condition. It is hard to tell whether there is or will be a positive balance now or in the future (cf. Bargh & McKenna, 2004).

## Chapter 9

1. For a useful general discussion of the importance of thinking about the relationships among effect measures, immediate intervention outcomes, and ultimate intervention goals when evaluating the effectiveness of intervention programs, see Rossi, Freeman, and Lipsey (1999, pp. 102–107).

2. An interesting parallel with the above principles can be drawn with attempts to reduce infants' fear of strangers. As Sroufe (1977) concludes from different studies, a stranger is more likely to elicit an infant's exploratory behaviors with a security provider (often the mother) present, adequate familiarization time, and sufficient infants' response options. The approach of the stranger should be delayed, gradual, indirect, and mediated by toys or play. In addition, the infant has to have the opportunity to crawl away; physically restrained infants show more signs of fear (see Sroufe, 1977). The importance

of attachment security in decreasing fear responses to a person with cancer or members of minority groups has been demonstrated in studies by Mikulincer *et al.* (2001) that have been discussed in Chapter 4.

3. Another critique argues that patient empowerment in the case of HIV infected gay men may contradict useful social implications of Parsons' sick role (see Chapter 2) in that it rejects medical knowledge (while simultaneously profiting as much as possible from available therapies), expresses unwillingness to fulfill social obligations to protect others against infection (claiming a "right" to sexual and reproductive freedom), and exaggeratedly claims independence from health services (Crossley, 1998).

4. In light of this, an exclusive focus on the "rights" of individuals associated with deviance does not seem a profitable strategy to us. With Parker and Aggleton (2003) we believe that empowerment, political change, and legislation should have top priority in settings and countries where stigmatization is an instrument to maintain inequality and power such as in many developing countries. (Parenthetically, we find less useful Parker and Aggleton's (2003) suggestion that in the modern and Western world, power and hierarchy should also be the main concepts for explaining responses to deviance; see Chapter 6.) Furthermore, in Western societies legislation too seems fundamental to promote equal opportunities for those associated with deviant conditions. Yet, it remains to be studied how the introduction and implementation of such legal measures as busing, schooling, mainstreaming, affirmative action, and so on, take into account the motivational implications of different types of deviance and hence peoples' basic needs for social control. If one thing is clear, evidence for the effectiveness of legal change is mixed (see, for example, Havinga, 2002).

5. It should be noted that the ranking of the effect sizes for the different deviant conditions very much depends on whether one assumes fixed or random effects in one's statistical analysis. In Pettigrew and Tropp's (2003) original manuscript, which circulated widely on the internet, a fixed-effect analysis was used, and it was found, for example, that the elderly profited almost as well as homosexuals from contact interventions, while the mentally ill and disabled profited the least. In contrast, changing to a random effects analysis of the same data, Pettigrew and Tropp (2006) found that homosexuals profit the most, and both the elderly and mentally ill the least from contact interventions.

6. Another indication of the relevance of deviance-specific motivational systems in explaining contact effects, but one that is similarly not explicitly addressed in this research, is the moderating role of individual differences. For example, Allport (1954/1979) declared the contact hypothesis not applicable to people with "too intense" negative feelings toward others or particular personality characteristics, reserving it for "a population of ordinary people, with a normal degree of prejudice" (p. 281). A rare opportunity to analyze in somewhat greater detail the role of individual differences in explaining contact effects offers a study by Herek and Capitanio (1996) on attitudes toward homosexual men. Although the authors did not find significant interactions between demographic factors and contact (adopting a Bonferroni-corrected, conservative significance level of 0.003), the pattern of attitude means suggests a consistently stronger effect of contact for liberal than conservative individuals. Specifically, on an attitude scale ranging from 3 (extremely favorable) to 12 (extremely hostile), with

an overall mean score of 9.08 (SD = 2.71), political liberals who reported contact with homosexuals were more favorable (M = 6.14) than liberals reporting no contact (M = 9.07). In contrast, for political conservatives, the contact and no-contact means were much closer (Ms = 9.19 and 10.08, respectively). Similar patterns were found when crossing political party, religiousness, and education with contact, with democrats, non-religious individuals, and those with highest education showing the strongest effects of contact. Rather speculatively, on the basis of our FF-C network, it may be proposed that the FF system tends to be relatively easily triggered in conservative, religious individuals with little education (see Chapter 5), motivating these individuals to respond negatively to the features of homosexuality that become evident through contact.

7. In this context, we doubt the usefulness of Allport's following description of family life: "Within a family there are often marked differences of appearance, talent, temperament. Ted is bright and handsome; his brother Jim, dull and homely; his sister Mary extroverted but lazy; and his sister Deborah is 'peculiar'. But each of these oddly assorted sibs may accept their differences and love one another" (Allport, 1954/1979, p. 87). Although we do recognize the importance of care and trust in kin-based relationships, we doubt if, for example, Mary's behavior will not be aggressively corrected when resulting in too many free rides, or Jim's homeliness will not result in conflict and a need for negotiation when the family is planning a vacation. Unsurprisingly, usually strong correlations are found between friendship (as compared to non-friendship), anxiety reduction, empathy or care, and increased liking of different outgroups and deviant conditions (e.g., R. Brown & Hewstone, 2005; Herek & Capitanio, 1996; Paolini, Hewstone, Voci, Harwood, & Cairns, 2006; Pettigrew, 1998). Yet, as suggested, friendship does not imply the absence of social control or explicitly addressing deviance. Furthermore, a key question, especially with respect to problematic forms of deviance, should be how to become friends when deviance cannot be concealed or ignored; unfamiliar targets with salient deviant conditions are generally not selected for relationships and not well liked (cf. Amir, 1976). In sum, although friendship would be a nice consequence of contact between perceiver and target, stigma-reduction interventions would do well to focus on ultimate intervention goals such as tolerance or repair that can be realized with more deviance-specific and realistic immediate intervention outcomes such as feelings of safety or mutual respect.

8. Further attesting to the potential for negative responses to deviance in the context of close interpersonal relationships are the studies on disclosure of homosexuality discussed in Chapter 7.

9. We believe that shaming is not an appropriate label here. As Braithwaite (1989) himself emphasizes, shame may be an undesirable emotion when it primarily motivates the perpetrator to withdraw from attention and to feel resentful. Thus guilt rather than shame (or in combination with shame) may be the effective emotion in repair, as it exclusively motivates perpetrators to redress the harm done (see Gilbert, 2003. See also our Chapter 2, for a discussion).

10. It is interesting to mention that similar community responses have been observed when Turkish immigrant workers entered into neighborhoods of the Dutch city of Utrecht during the 1970s. In a series of detailed ethnographic studies, Bovenkerk, Bruin, Brunt, and Wouters (1985) found that

the most commonly heard complaint of the Dutch was that the foreigners show a lack of *adaptation* and respect for the Dutch way of living. They convincingly illustrate that the wish for adaptation does not imply that the neighborhood wants newcomers to completely assimilate, but that they ought to show some conformity with a few neighborhood customs, thereby showing their willingness to become a potentially controllable part of the social environment. Furthermore, while the autochthonous inhabitants behaved altruistically to the early and vulnerable immigrant workers who came on their own, they showed growing irritation when these initial visitors increased in number (e.g., letting their family come over) and became more focused on their own ethnic group and religion. A large-scale study by Van Oudenhoven, Prins, and Buunk (1996) confirmed that what the Dutch population wants is not assimilation per se, but integration of ethnic groups showing at least willingness to make contact with, and orient to the social control demands of, their hosts.

11. Some deviant conditions are inherently ambiguous with respect to possibilities for repair and reciprocity. For example, as explained in Chapters 2 and 3, many individuals with a mental handicap are neither physically nor mentally ill, yet in varying degrees lack the necessary skills to engage in reciprocal relationships. While they are often passionately cared for by relatives and friends, the opposite may occur when they are required to integrate in the community while living in small-group homes. On the basis of a critical and detailed analysis of the current ideology of deinstitutionalization, according to which mentally handicapped individuals should socially integrate in the general community in which they live, Cummins and Lau (2003) make the suggestion that this tendency may be more beneficial to policy makers and service providers than to mentally handicapped residents themselves. While it may be generally true that living in small-scale housing projects fosters greater well-being than in institutions or hospitals, the most important determinant of residents' well-being appears to be that they feel connected to and supported by service providers, family, and mentally handicapped friends. So the question arises whether requiring mentally handicapped persons to engage in more extensive social contacts with the neighborhood or community at large confers additional benefits to them, especially in light of the individualistic and competitive nature of modern society.

# References

Abelson, R. P., Kinder, D. R., Peters, M. D., & Fiske, S. T. (1982). Affective and semantic components in political person perception. *Journal of Personality and Social Psychology, 42,* 619–630.

Adorno, T. W., Frenkel-Brunswik, E., Levinson, D. J., & Sanford, R. N. (1950). *The authoritarian personality.* New York: Harper.

Affleck, G. & Tennen, H. (1991). Social comparison and coping with major medical problems. In J. Suls & T. A. Wills (eds.), *Social comparison: Contemporary theory and research* (pp. 369–393). Hillsdale, NJ: Erlbaum.

Aggleton, P. & Warwick, I. (1997). *Household and community responses to HIV and AIDS in developing countries: Findings from multi-site studies.* Geneva, Switzerland: UNAIDS.

Agnew, C. R., Thompson, V. D., & Gaines, S. O., Jr. (2000). Incorporating proximal and distal influences on prejudice: Testing a general model across outgroups. *Personality and Social Psychology Bulletin, 26,* 403–418.

Ajzen, I. & Fishbein, M. (1980). *Understanding attitudes and predicting behavior.* Englewood Cliffs, NJ: Prentice Hall.

Alexander, R. D. (1987). *The biology of moral systems.* Hawthorne, NY: Aldine de Gruyter.

Alicke, M. D. & Davis, T. L. (1990). Capacity responsibility in social evaluation. *Personality and Social Psychology Bulletin, 16,* 465–474.

Allen, K. (2003). Are pets a healthy pleasure? The influence of pets on blood pressure. *Current Directions in Psychological Science, 12,* 236.

Alley, T. R. (1983). Growth-produced changes in body shape and size as determinants of perceived age and adult caregiving. *Child Development, 54,* 241–248.

(1988). Physiognomy and social perception. In T. R. Alley & K. A. Hildebrandt (eds.), *Determinants and consequences of facial aesthetics* (pp. 167–186). Hillsdale, NJ: Erlbaum.

Allon, N. (1982). The stigma of overweight in everyday life. In B. B. Wolman (ed.), *Psychological aspects of obesity: A handbook* (pp. 130–174). New York: Van Nostrand Reinhold.

Allport, G. W. (1954/1979). *The nature of prejudice* (25th edn.). Reading, MA: Addison-Wesley.

Altemeyer, B. (1988). *Enemies of freedom: Understanding right-wing authoritarianism.* San Francisco: Jossey-Bass.

(1998). The other "authoritarian personality." In M. P. Zanna (ed.), *Advances in Experimental Social Psychology* (Vol. 30, pp. 47–92). Orlando, FL: Academic Press.

Ambady, N., Hallahan, M., & Conner, B. (1999). Accuracy of judgments of sexual orientation from thin slices of behavior. *Journal of Personality and Social Psychology, 77*, 538–547.

Amir, Y. (1976). The role of intergroup contact in change of prejudice and ethnic relations. In P. A. Katz (ed.), *Towards the elimination of racism* (pp. 245–308). New York: Pergamon.

Amodio, D. M., Harmon Jones, E., & Devine, P. G. (2003). Individual differences in the activation and control of affective race bias as assessed by startle eyeblink response and self report. *Journal of Personality and Social Psychology, 84*, 738–753.

Angermeyer, M. C., Beck, M., Dietrich, S., & Holzinger, A. (2004). The stigma of mental illness: Patients' anticipations and experiences. *International Journal of Social Psychiatry, 50*, 153–162.

Angermeyer, M. C. & Matschinger, H. (1997). Social distance towards the mentally ill: Results of representative surveys in the Federal Republic of Germany. *Psychological Medicine, 27*, 131–141.

Archer, D. (1985). Social deviance. In G. Lindzey & E. Aronson (eds.), *Handbook of social psychology* (3rd edn., Vol. 2, pp. 743–804). New York: Random House.

Archer, J. (1976). The organization of aggression and fear in vertebrates. In P. P. G. Bateson & P. H. Klopfer (eds.), *Perspectives in ethology* (Vol. 2, pp. 231–298). New York: Plenum.

—— (1996). Attitudes toward homosexuals: An alternative Darwinian view. *Ethology and Sociobiology, 7*, 275–280.

—— (1997). Why do people love their pets? *Evolution and Human Behavior, 18*, 237–259.

Armstrong, M. J. & Fitzgerald, M. (1996). Culture and disability studies: An anthropological perspective. *Rehabilitation Education, 10*, 247–304.

Arntz, A., Lavy, E., van den Berg, G., & van Rijsoort, S. (1993). Negative beliefs of spider phobics: A psychometric evaluation of the spider phobia beliefs questionnaire. *Advances in Behaviour Research and Therapy, 15*, 257–277.

Axelrod, R. & Hamilton, W. D. (1981). The evolution of cooperation. *Science, 211*, 1390–1396.

Badgett, M. V. L. (1995). The wage effects of sexual orientation discrimination. *Industrial and Labor Relations Review, 48*, 726–739.

Baldwin, M. L. (1999). The effects of impairments on employment and wages: Estimates from the 1984 and 1990 SIPP. *Behavioral Sciences and the Law, 17*, 7–27.

Baltes, M. M. & Reisenzein, R. (1986). The social world in long-term care institutions: Psychological control toward dependency. In M. M. Baltes (ed.), *The psychology of control and aging* (pp. 315–343). Hillsdale, NJ: Erlbaum.

Barden, J., Maddux, W., Petty, R. E., & Brewer, M. B. (2004). Contextual moderation of racial bias: The impact of social roles on controlled and automatically activated attitudes. *Journal of Personality and Social Psychology, 87*, 5–22.

Bargh, J. A. & McKenna, K. Y. A. (2004). The internet and social life. *Annual Review of Psychology, 55*, 573–590.

Barnes, C. & Mercer, G. (1996). Introduction: exploring the divide. In C. Barnes & G. Mercer (eds.), *Exploring the divide: illness and disability* (pp. 11–16). Leeds, UK: The Disability Press.

Baron, R. A. (1977). *Human aggression*. New York: Plenum Press.

Baron, R. M. & Kenny, D. A. (1986). The moderator-mediator variable distinction in social psychological research: Conceptual, strategic, and statistical considerations. *Journal of Personality and Social Psychology, 51*, 1173–1182.

Barrios, B. A., Corbitt, L. C., Estes, J. P., & Topping, J. S. (1976). Effect of a social stigma on interpersonal distance. *Psychological Record, 26*, 343–348.

Batson, C. D. (1987). Prosocial motivation: Is it ever truly altruistic? In L. Berkowitz (ed.), *Advances in experimental social psychology* (Vol. 20, pp. 65–122). New York: Academic Press.

(1998). Altruism and prosocial behavior. In D. T. Gilbert, S. T. Fiske & G. Lindzey (eds.), *The handbook of social psychology* (4th edn., Vol. 2, pp. 282–316). New York: McGraw-Hill.

Batson, C. D., Early, S., & Salvarani, G. (1997). Perspective taking: Imagining how another feels versus imagining how you would feel. *Personality and Social Psychology Bulletin, 23*, 751–758.

Batson, C. D., Lishner, D. A., Cook, J., & Sawyer, S. (2005). Similarity and nurturance: Two possible sources of empathy for strangers. *Basic and Applied Social Psychology, 27*, 15–25.

Batson, C. D., Polycarpou, M. P., Harmon Jones, E., Imhoff, H. J., Mitchener, E. C., Bednar, L. L., Klein, T. R., & Highberger, L. (1997). Empathy and attitudes: Can feeling for a member of a stigmatized group improve feelings toward the group? *Journal of Personality and Social Psychology, 72*, 105–118.

Beal, D. J., O'Neal, E. C., Ong, J., & Ruscher, J. B. (2000). The ways and means of interracial aggression: Modern racists' use of covert retaliation. *Personality and Social Psychology Bulletin, 26*, 1225–1238.

Bean, J., Keller, L., Newburg, C., & Brown, M. (1989). Methods for the reduction of AIDS social anxiety and social stigma. *AIDS Education and Prevention, 1*, 194–221.

Bechtel, W. & Abrahamsen, A. (1991). *Connectionism and the mind: An introduction to parallel processing in networks.* Cambridge, MA: Basil Blackwell.

Becker, H. S. (1963). *Outsiders: Studies in the sociology of deviance.* New York: Free Press.

Belgrave, F. Z. & Mills, J. (1981). Effect upon desire for social interaction with a physically disabled person of mentioning the disability in different contexts. *Journal of Applied Social Psychology, 11*, 44–57.

Bell, D. C. (2001). Evolution of parental caregiving. *Personality and Social Psychology Review, 5*, 216–229.

Benedict, R. (1935/1961). *Patterns of culture.* London: Routledge & Kegan Paul.

Benson, P. L., Severs, D., Tatgenhorst, J., & Loddengaard, N. (1980). The social costs of obesity: A non-reactive field study. *Social Behavior and Personality, 8*, 91–96.

Berelson, B. & Steiner, G. A. (1964). Human behavior: An inventory of scientific findings. Oxford: Harcourt, Brace, and World.

Berkowitz, L. & Frodi, A. (1979). Reactions to a child's mistakes as affected by her/his looks and speech. *Social Psychology Quarterly, 42*, 420–425.

Bernat, J. A., Calhoun, K. S., Adams, H. E., & Zeichner, A. (2001). Homophobia and physical aggression toward homosexual and heterosexual individuals. *Journal of Abnormal Psychology, 110*, 179–187.

Berrill, K. T. (1992). Anti-gay violence and victimization in the United States: An overview. In G. M. Herek & K. T. Berrill (eds.), *Hate crimes: Confronting violence against lesbians and gay men* (pp. 19–45). Thousand Oaks, CA: Sage.

Berry, D. S. & McArthur, L. Z. (1986). Perceiving character in faces: The impact of age-related craniofacial changes on social perception. *Psychological Bulletin, 100,* 3–18.

Bessenoff, G. R. & Sherman, J. W. (2000). Automatic and controlled components of prejudice toward fat people: Evaluation versus stereotype activation. *Social Cognition, 18,* 329–353.

Bettencourt, B. A., Dill, K. E., Greathouse, S. A., Charlton, K., & Mullholland, A. (1997). Evaluations of ingroup and outgroup members: The role of category-based expectancy violation. *Journal of Experimental Social Psychology, 33,* 244–275.

Bickenbach, J. E., Chatterji, S., Badley, E. M., & Üstün, T. B. (1999). Models of disablement, universalism and the international classification of impairments, disabilities and handicaps. *Social Science & Medicine, 48,* 1173–1187.

Bierly, M. M. (1985). Prejudice toward contemporary outgroups as a generalized attitude. *Journal of Applied Social Psychology, 15,* 189–199.

Biernat, M. & Dovidio, J. F. (2000). Stigma and stereotypes. In T. F. Heatherton, R. E. Kleck, M. R. Hebl & J. G. Hull (eds.), *The social psychology of stigma* (pp. 88–125). New York: The Guilford Press.

Bishop, G. D. (1991). Lay disease representations and responses to victims of disease. *Basic and Applied Social Psychology, 12,* 115–132.

Bishop, G. D., Alva, A. L., Cantu, L., & Rittiman, T. K. (1991). Responses to persons with AIDS: Fear of contagion or stigma? *Journal of Applied Social Psychology, 21,* 1877–1888.

Björkqvist, K., Österman, K., & Kaukiainen, A. (2000). Social intelligence – empathy = aggression? *Aggression and Violent Behavior, 5,* 191–200.

Black, D. (1984). Social control as a dependent variable. In D. Black (ed.), *Toward a general theory of social control* (Vol. 1, pp. 1–36). Orlando, FL: Academic Press.

(2000). On the origin of morality. *Journal of Consciousness Studies, 7,* 107–119.

Blair, I. V. (2001). Implicit stereotypes and prejudice. In G. B. Moskowitz (ed.), *Cognitive social psychology: The Princeton symposium on the legacy and future of social cognition* (pp. 359–374). Mahwah, NJ: Erlbaum.

Blascovich, J., Mendes, W. B., Hunter, S. B., Lickel, B., & Kowai-Bell, N. (2001). Perceiver threat in social interactions with stigmatized others. *Journal of Personality and Social Psychology, 80,* 253–267.

Bodenhausen, G. V. (1988). Stereotypic biases in social decision making and memory: Testing process models of stereotype use. *Journal of Personality and Social Psychology, 55,* 726–737.

Boehm, C. (1999). *Hierarchy in the forest: The evolution of egalitarian behavior.* Cambridge, MA: Harvard University Press.

Bolger, N., Vinokur, A. D., Foster, M., & Ng, R. (1996). Close relationships and adjustment to a life crisis: The case of breast cancer. *Journal of Personality and Social Psychology, 70,* 283–294.

Bos, A. E. R., Dijker, A. J. M., & Koomen, W. (2007). Sex differences in emotional and behavioral responses to HIV+ individuals' expression of distress. *Psychology and Health, 22,* 493–511.

Bovenkerk, F., Bruin, K., Brunt, L., & Wouters, H. (1985). *Vreemd volk, gemengde gevoelens: Etnische verhoudingen in een grote stad. [Strange people, mixed feelings: Ethnic relations in a city]* Amsterdam: Boom.

Boyd, R. & Richerson, P. J. (2005). Solving the puzzle of human cooperation. In S. Levinson (ed.), *Evolution and culture* (pp. 105–132). Cambridge, MA: MIT Press.

Braithwaite, D. O. & Eckstein, N. J. (2003). How people with disabilities communicatively manage assistance: Helping as instrumental social support. *Journal of Applied Communication Research, 31*, 1–26.

Braithwaite, J. (1989). *Crime, shame and reintegration*. Cambridge: Cambridge University Press.

Bramel, D. (2004). The strange career of the contact hypothesis. In Y. T. Lee, C. McCauley, F. Moghaddam, & S. Worchel (eds.), *The psychology of ethnic and cultural conflict: Looking through American and global chaos or harmony?* (pp. 49–67). Westpoint, CN: Praeger.

Branscombe, N. R., Schmitt, M. T., & Harvey, R. D. (1999). Perceiving pervasive discrimination among African Americans: Implications for group identification and well-being. *Journal of Personality and Social Psychology, 77*, 135–149.

Brewer, M. B. (1999). The psychology of prejudice: Ingroup love or outgroup hate. *Journal of Social Issues, 55*, 429–444.

Brickman, P., Rabinowitz, V. C., Karuza, J., Coates, D., Cohn, E., & Kidder, L. (1982). Models of helping and coping. *American Psychologist, 37*, 368–384.

Brockington, I. F., Hall, P., Levings, J., & Murphy, C. (1993). The community's tolerance of the mentally ill. *British Journal of Psychiatry, 162*, 93–99.

Broude, G. J. & Greene, S. J. (1976). Cross-cultural codes on twenty sexual attitudes and practices. *Ethnology, 15*, 419–429.

Brown, L., MacIntyre, K., & Trujillo, L. (2003). Interventions to reduce HIV/AIDS stigma: what have we learned? *AIDS Education and Prevention, 15*, 49–69.

Brown, L. M. & Lopez, G. E. (2001). Political contacts: analyzing the role of similarity in theories of prejudice. *Political Psychology, 22*, 279–292.

Brown, R. & Hewstone, M. (2005). An integrative theory of intergroup contact. In M. P. Zanna (ed.), *Advances in Experimental Social Psychology* (Vol. 37, pp. 255–343). San Diego, CA: Academic Press.

Bullen, B. A., Monello, L. F., Cohen, H., & Mayer, J. (1963). Attitudes towards physical activity, food and family in obese and nonobese adolescent girls. *The American Journal of Clinical Nutrition, 12*, 1–11.

Bunge, M. & Ardila, R. (1987). *Philosophy of psychology*. New York: Springer.

Burnstein, E., Crandall, C. S., & Kitayama, S. (1994). Some neo-Darwinian decision rules for altruism: Weighing cues for inclusive fitness as a function of the biological importance of the decision. *Journal of Personality and Social Psychology, 67*, 773–789.

Buss, D. M. (1999). *Evolutionary psychology: The new science of the mind*. Boston: Allyn and Bacon.

Butler, E. A., Egloff, B., Wilhelm, F. H., Smith, N. C., Erickson, E. A., & Gross, J. J. (2003). The social consequences of expressive suppression. *Emotion, 3*, 48–67.

Cacciapaglia, H. M., Beauchamp, K. L., & Howells, G. N. (2004). Visibility of disability: Effect on willingness to interact. *Rehabilitation Psychology, 49*, 180–182.

Campbell, D. T. (1975). On the conflicts between biological and social evolution and between psychology and moral tradition. *American Psychologist, 30*, 1103–1126.

  (1982). Legal and primary-group social controls. *Journal of Social and Biological Structures, 5*, 431–438.

Camras, L. A. (1977). Facial expressions used by children in a conflict situation. *Child Development*, 48, 1431–1435.

Canning, H. & Mayer, J. (1966). Obesity – its possible costs on college acceptance. *The New England Journal of Medicine*, 275, 1172–1174.

(1967). Obesity: an influence on high school performance? *The American Journal of Clinical Nutrition*, 20, 352–354.

Cannon, W. B. (1929). *Bodily changes in pain, hunger, fear and rage* (2nd edn.). New York: Appleton.

Caporael, L. R., Lukaszewski, M. P., & Culbertson, G. H. (1983). Secondary baby talk: Judgments by institutionalized elderly and their caregivers. *Journal of Personality and Social Psychology*, 44, 746–754.

Carver, C. S. & de la Garza, N. H. (1984). Schema-guided information search in stereotyping of the elderly. *Journal of Applied Social Psychology*, 14, 69–81.

Carver, C. S., Gibbons, F. X., Stephan, W. G., Glass, D. C., & Katz, I. (1979). Ambivalence and evaluative response amplification. *Bulletin of the Psychonomic Society*, 13, 50–52.

Carver, C. S., Glass, D. C., & Katz, I. (1978). Favorable evaluations of Blacks and the handicapped: Positive prejudice, unconscious denial, or social desirability? *Journal of Applied Social Psychology*, 8, 97–106.

Carver, C. S., Glass, D. C., Snyder, M. L., & Katz, I. (1977). Favorable evaluations of stigmatized others. *Personality and Social Psychology Bulletin*, 3, 232–235.

Carver, C. S., Scheier, M. F., & Weintraub, J. K. (1989). Assessing coping strategies: A theoretically based approach. *Journal of Personality and Social Psychology*, 56, 267–283.

Casey, M. K., Allen, M., Emmers-Sommer, T., Sahlstein, E., Degooyer, D., Winters, A. M., Wagner, A. E., & Dun, T. (2003). When a celebrity contracts a disease: The example of Earvin "Magic" Johnson's announcement that he was HIV positive. *Journal of Health Communication*, 8, 249–265.

Cash, T. F. (1995). Developmental teasing about physical appearance: Retrospective descriptions and relationships with body image. *Social Behavior and Personality*, 23, 123–129.

Chesler, M. A. (1965). Ethnocentrism and attitudes toward the physically disabled. *Journal of Personality and Social Psychology*, 2, 877–882.

Clancey, W. J. (1997). *Situated cognition: On human knowledge and computer representations*. Cambridge: Cambridge University Press.

Clore, G. L. & Jeffrey, K. M. (1972). Emotional role playing, attitude change, and attraction toward a disabled person. *Journal of Personality and Social Psychology*, 23, 105–111.

Clutton-Brock, T. H. & Parker, G. A. (1995). Punishment in animal societies. *Nature*, 373, 209–216.

Cogan, J. C., Bhalla, S. K., Sefa Dedeh, A., & Rothblum, E. D. (1996). A comparison study of United States and African students on perceptions of obesity and thinness. *Journal of Cross-Cultural Psychology*, 27, 98–113.

Colella, A. & Varma, A. (2001). The impact of subordinate disability on leader-member exchange relationships. *Academy of Management Journal*, 44, 304–315.

Coleman, L. M. & DePaulo, B. M. (1991). "Miscommunication" and problematic talk. In N. Coupland, H. Giles & J. M. Wiemann (eds.), *Uncovering the human spirit: Moving beyond disability and "missed" communications* (pp. 61–84). Thousand Oaks, CA: Sage.

Comer, R. J. & Piliavin, J. A. (1972). The effects of physical deviance upon face-to-face interaction: The other side. *Journal of Personality and Social Psychology, 23,* 33–39.

Conrad, P. (1975). The discovery of hyperkinesis: Notes on the medicalization of deviant behavior. *Social Problems, 23,* 12–21.

Cooley, C. H. (1902). *Human nature and the social order.* New York: Charles Scribner's Sons.

Copeland, J. T. (1994). Prophecies of power: Motivational implications of social power for behavioral confirmation. *Journal of Personality and Social Psychology, 67,* 264–277.

Corrigan, P., Markowitz, F. E., Watson, A., Rowan, D., & Kubiak, M. A. (2003). An attribution model of public discrimination towards persons with mental illness. *Journal of Health and Social Behavior, 44,* 162–179.

Corrigan, P. W., Demming Lurie, B., Goldman, H. H., Slopen, N., Medasani, K., & Phelan, S. (2005). How adolescents perceive the stigma of mental illness and alcohol abuse. *Psychiatric Services, 56,* 544–550.

Corrigan, P. W. & Penn, D. L. (1999). Lessons from social psychology on discrediting psychiatric stigma. *American Psychologist, 54,* 765–776.

Corrigan, P. W., River, L. P., Lundin, R. K., Wasowski, K., Campion, J., Mathisen, J., Goldstein, H., Bergman, M., Gagnon, C., & Kubiak, M. A. (2000). Stigmatizing attributions about mental illness. *Journal of Community Psychology, 28,* 91–102.

Cosmides, L. & Tooby, J. (1992). Cognitive adaptations for social exchange. In J. H. Barkow, L. Cosmides & J. Tooby (eds.), *The adapted mind: Evolutionary psychology and the generation of culture* (pp. 163–228). New York: Oxford University Press.

Costa, P., Jr., Terracciano, A., & McCrae, R. R. (2001). Gender differences in personality traits across cultures: Robust and surprising findings. *Journal of Personality and Social Psychology, 81,* 322–331.

Cottrell, C. A. & Neuberg, S. L. (2005). Different emotional reactions to different groups: A sociofunctional threat-based approach to prejudice. *Journal of Personality and Social Psychology, 88,* 770–789.

Coupland, N., Giles, H., & Benn, W. (1986). Language, communication and the blind. *Journal of Language and Social Psychology, 5,* 53–62.

Cox, S. & Gallois, C. (1996). Gay and lesbian identity development: A social identity perspective. *Journal of Homosexuality, 30,* 1–30.

Coyne, J. C., Wortman, C. B., & Lehman, D. R. (1988). The other side of support: Emotional overinvolvement and miscarried helping. In B. H. Gottlieb (ed.), *Marshaling social support: Formats, processes, and effects* (pp. 305–330). Thousand Oaks, CA: Sage Publications.

Crandall, C. S. (1994). Prejudice against fat people: Ideology and self-interest. *Journal of Personality and Social Psychology, 66,* 882–894.

(1995). Do parents discriminate against their heavyweight daughters? *Personality and Social Psychology Bulletin, 21,* 724–735.

Crandall, C. S. & Cohen, C. (1994). The personality of the stigmatizer: Cultural world view, conventionalism, and self-esteem. *Journal of Research in Personality, 28,* 461–480.

Crandall, C. S. & Coleman, R. (1992). AIDS-related stigmatization and the disruption of social relationships. *Journal of Social and Personal Relationships, 9,* 163–177.

Crandall, C. S., D'Anello, S., Sakalli, N., Lazarus, E., Wieczorkowska, G., & Feather, N. T. (2001). An Attribution-Value model of prejudice: Anti-fat attitudes in six nations. *Personality and Social Psychology Bulletin, 27*, 30–37.

Crandall, C. S. & Eshleman, A. (2003). A justification-suppression model of the expression and experience of prejudice. *Psychological Bulletin, 129*, 414–446.

Crandall, C. S., Eshleman, A., & O'Brien, L. (2002). Social norms and the expression and suppression of prejudice: The struggle for internalization. *Journal of Personality and Social Psychology, 82*, 359–378.

Crandall, C. S. & Martinez, R. (1996). Culture, ideology, and antifat attitudes. *Personality and Social Psychology Bulletin, 22*, 1165–1176.

Crandall, C. S. & Moriarty, D. (1995). Physical illness stigma and social rejection. *British Journal of Social Psychology, 34*, 67–83.

Crandall, C. S., Tsang, J. A., Harvey, R. D., & Britt, T. W. (2000). Group identity-based self-protective strategies: The stigma of race, gender, and garlic. *European Journal of Social Psychology, 30*, 355–381.

Crawford, A. M. (1996). Stigma associated with AIDS: A meta-analysis. *Journal of Applied Social Psychology, 26*, 398–416.

Crocker, J. & Major, B. (1989). Social stigma and self-esteem: The self-protective properties of stigma. *Psychological Review, 96*, 608–630.

Crocker, J., Major, B., & Steele, C. (1998). Social stigma. In D. T. Gilbert, S. T. Fiske & G. Lindzey (eds.), *The handbook of social psychology* (4th edn., Vol. 2, pp. 504–553). New York: McGraw-Hill.

Crocker, J. & Wolfe, C. T. (2001). Contingencies of self-worth. *Psychological Review, 108*, 593–623.

Crosby, F., Bromley, S., & Saxe, L. (1980). Recent unobtrusive studies of Black and White discrimination and prejudice: A literature review. *Psychological Bulletin, 87*, 546–563.

Crossley, M. (1998). 'Sick role' or 'empowerment'? The ambiguities of life with an HIV positive diagnosis. *Sociology of Health & Illness, 20*, 507–531.

Croteau, J. M. (1996). Research on the work experiences of lesbian, gay, and bisexual people: An integrative review of methodology and findings. *Journal of Vocational Behavior, 48*, 195–209.

Crystal, D. S., Watanabe, H., & Chin, W. (1997). Intolerance of human differences: A cross-cultural and developmental study of American, Japanese, and Chinese children. *Journal of Applied Developmental Psychology, 18*, 149–167.

Cummins, R. A. & Lau, A. L. D. (2003). Community integration or community exposure? A review and discussion in relation to people with an intellectual disability. *Journal of Applied Research in Intellectual Disabilities, 16*, 145–157.

Cunningham, W. A., Nezlek, J. B., & Banaji, M. R. (2004). Implicit and explicit ethnocentrism: Revisiting the ideologies of prejudice. *Personality and Social Psychology Bulletin, 30*, 1332–1346.

Dambrun, M. & Guimond, S. (2004). Implicit and explicit measures of prejudice and stereotyping: Do they assess the same underlying knowledge structure? *European Journal of Social Psychology, 34*, 663–676.

Darley, J. M. & Fazio, R. H. (1980). Expectancy confirmation processes arising in the social interaction sequence. *American Psychologist, 35*, 867–881.

Dasgupta, N. (2004). Implicit ingroup favoritism, outgroup favoritism, and their behavioral manifestations. *Social Justice Research, 17*, 143–169.

Dasgupta, N. & Greenwald, A. G. (2001). On the malleability of automatic attitudes: Combating automatic prejudice with images of admired and disliked individuals. *Journal of Personality and Social Psychology, 81,* 800–814.

D'Augelli, A. R., Hershberger, S. L., & Pilkington, N. W. (1998). Lesbian, gay, and bisexual youth and their families: Disclosure of sexual orientation and its consequences. *American Journal of Orthopsychiatry, 68,* 361–371.

Davidson, D., Cameron, P., & Jergovic, D. (1995). The effect of children's stereotypes on their memory for elderly individuals. *Merrill Palmer Quarterly, 41,* 70–90.

Davis, F. (1961). Deviance disavowal: The management of strained interaction by the visibly handicapped. *Social Problems,* 120–132.

Dawkins, R. (1976). *The selfish gene.* Oxford: Oxford University Press.

(1982). *The extended phenotype: The long reach of the gene.* Oxford: Oxford University Press.

(1989). *The selfish gene (new edition).* Oxford: Oxford University Press.

de Waal, F. B. M. (1989). *Peacemaking among primates.* Cambridge, MA: Harvard University Press.

Dear, M. (1992). Understanding and overcoming the NIMBY. *Journal of the American Planning Association, 58,* 288–300.

Deaux, K., Reid, A., Mizrahi, K., & Ethier, A. (1995). Parameters of social identity. *Journal of Personality and Social Psychology, 68,* 280–291.

Decety, J. & Chaminade, T. (2003). Neural correlates of feeling sympathy. *Neuropsychologia, 41,* 127–138.

Deffenbacher, J. L., Oetting, E. R., & DiGiuseppe, R. A. (2002). Principles of empirically supported interventions applied to anger management. *Counseling Psychologist, 30,* 262–280.

Dekker, P. & Mootz, M. (1992). AIDS as threat, AIDS as stigma: Correlates of AIDS beliefs among the Dutch general public. *Psychology and Health, 6,* 347–365.

Dettwyler, K. A. (1991). Can paleopathology provide evidence for "compassion"? *American Journal of Physical Anthropology, 84,* 375–384.

Devine, P. G. (1989). Stereotypes and prejudice: Their automatic and controlled components. *Journal of Personality and Social Psychology, 56,* 5–18.

Devine, P. G., Evett, S. R., & Vasquez-Suson, K. A. (1996). Exploring the interpersonal dynamics of intergroup contact. In E. T. Higgins & R. M. Sorrentino (eds.), *Handbook of motivation and cognition* (Vol. 3, pp. 423–464). New York: Guilford Press.

Devine, P. G., Plant, E. A., Amodio, D. M., Harmon Jones, E., & Vance, S. L. (2002). The regulation of explicit and implicit race bias: The role of motivations to respond without prejudice. *Journal of Personality and Social Psychology, 82,* 835–848.

Diener, E. & Diener, C. (1996). Most people are happy. *Psychological Science, 7,* 181–185.

Diener, E., Suh, E. K., Lucas, R. E., & Smith, H. L. (1999). Subjective well-being: Three decades of progress. *Psychological Bulletin, 125,* 276–302.

Diener, E., Wolsic, B., & Fujita, F. (1995). Physical attractiveness and subjective well-being. *Journal of Personality and Social Psychology, 69,* 120–129.

Dienstbier, R. A. (1970). Positive and negative prejudice: Interaction of prejudice with race and social desirability. *Journal of Personality, 38,* 198–215.

DiGiuseppe, R. & Tafrate, R. C. (2003). Anger treatments for adults: A meta-analytic review. *Clinical Psychology: Science and Practice, 10,* 70–84.

Dijker, A. J. (1987). Emotional reactions to ethnic minorities. *European Journal of Social Psychology, 17,* 305–325.

(2001). The influence of perceived suffering and vulnerability on the experience of pity. *European Journal of Social Psychology, 31,* 659–676.

Dijker, A. J., Kok, G., & Koomen, W. (1996). Emotional reactions to people with AIDS. *Journal of Applied Social Psychology, 26,* 731–748.

Dijker, A. J. & Koomen, W. (1996). Stereotyping and attitudinal effects under time pressure. *European Journal of Social Psychology, 26,* 61–74.

(2003). Extending Weiner's attribution-emotion model of stigmatization of ill persons. *Basic and Applied Social Psychology, 25,* 51–68.

Dijker, A. J., Koomen, W., & Kok, G. (1997). Interpersonal determinants of fear of people with AIDS: The moderating role of predictable behavior. *Basic and Applied Social Psychology, 19,* 61–79.

Dijker, A. J., Koomen, W., van den Heuvel, H., & Frijda, N. H. (1996). Perceived antecedents of emotional reactions in inter-ethnic relations. *British Journal of Social Psychology, 35,* 313–329.

Dijker, A. J. & Raeijmaekers, F. (1999). The influence of seriousness and contagiousness of disease on emotional reactions to ill persons. *Psychology and Health, 14,* 131–141.

Dijker, A. J., Tacken, M. A., & van den Borne, B. (2000). Context effects of facial appearance on attitudes toward mentally handicapped persons. *British Journal of Social Psychology, 39,* 413–427.

Dijker, A. J. M. (In prep.). Towards understanding the content and emotional implications of images of persons with mental impairments.

Dijksterhuis, A., Spears, R., Postmes, T., Stapel, D. A., Goomen, W., Scheepers, D. & van Knippenberg, A. (1998). Seeing one thing and doing another: Contrast effects in automatic behavior. *Journal of Personality and Social Psychology, 75,* 862–871.

Dindia, K. (1997). Self-disclosure, self-identity, and relationship development: A transactional/dialectical perspective. In S. Duck (ed.), *Handbook of personal relationships: Theory, research and interventions* (2nd edn., pp. 411–426). New York: John Wiley and Sons.

Dinitz, S., Dynes, R. R., & Clarke, A. C. (eds.). (1969). *Deviance: Studies in the process of stigmatization and societal reaction.* London: Oxford University Press.

Dion, K. L. & Earn, B. M. (1975). The phenomenology of being a target of prejudice. *Journal of Personality and Social Psychology, 32,* 944–950.

Dixon, J., Durrheim, K., & Tredoux, C. (2005). Beyond the optimal contact strategy. *American Psychologist, 60,* 679–711.

Dollard, J., Miller, N. E., Doob, W., Mowrer, O. H., & Sears, R. R. (1939). *Frustration and aggression.* New Haven, CT: Yale University Press.

Donnerstein, E. & Donnerstein, M. (1976). Research in the control of interracial aggression. In R. G. Geen & E. C. O'Neal (eds.), *Perspectives on aggression.* New York: Academic Press.

Doob, A. N. & Ecker, B. P. (1970). Stigma and compliance. *Journal of Personality and Social Psychology, 14,* 302–304.

Doty, R. M., Peterson, B. E., & Winter, D. G. (1991). Threat and authoritarianism in the United States, 1978–1987. *Journal of Personality and Social Psychology, 61,* 629–640.

Dovidio, J. F. & Gaertner, S. L. (1981). The effects of race, status, and ability on helping behavior. *Social Psychology Quarterly, 44,* 192–203.

Dovidio, J. F., Gaertner, S. L., & Kawakami, K. (2003). Intergroup contact: The past, present, and the future. *Group Processes and Intergroup Relations, 6,* 5–21.

Dovidio, J. F., Kawakami, K., & Beach, K. (2001). Implicit and explicit attitudes: Examination of the relationship between measures of intergroup bias. In R. Brown & S. L. Gaertner (eds.), *Blackwell handbook of social psychology* (Vol. 4: *Intergroup Relations*, pp. 175–197). Oxford: Blackwell.

Dovidio, J. F., Kawakami, K., & Gaertner, S. L. (2000). Reducing contemporary prejudice: Combating explicit and implicit bias at the individual and inter-group level. In S. Oskamp (ed.), *Reducing prejudice and discrimination* (pp. 137–163). Mahwah, NJ: Erlbaum.

(2002). Implicit and explicit prejudice and interracial interaction. *Journal of Personality and Social Psychology, 82,* 62–68.

Dovidio, J. F., Kawakami, K., Johnson, C., Johnson, B., & Howard, A. (1997). On the nature of prejudice: Automatic and controlled processes. *Journal of Experimental Social Psychology, 33,* 510–540.

Driskell, J. E. & Mullen, B. (1990). Status, expectations, and behavior: A meta-analytic review and test of the theory. *Personality and Social Psychology Bulletin, 16,* 541–553.

Druss, B. G., Marcus, S. C., Rosenheck, R. A., Olfson, M., Tanielian, T., & Pincus, H. A. (2000). Understanding disability in mental and general medical conditions. *American Journal of Psychiatry, 157,* 1485–1491.

Duchaine, B., Cosmides, L., & Tooby, J. (2001). Evolutionary psychology and the brain. *Current Opinions in Neurobiology, 11,* 225–230.

Duckitt, J. (2001). A dual-process cognitive-motivational theory of ideology and prejudice. In M. P. Zanna (ed.), *Advances in Experimental Social Psychology* (Vol. 33, pp. 41–113). San Diego, CA: Academic Press.

(2006). Differential effects of right wing authoritarianism and social dominance orientation on outgroup attitudes and their mediation by threat from and competitiveness to outgroups. *Personality and Social Psychology Bulletin, 32,* 684–696.

Duckitt, J., Wagner, C., du Plessis, I., & Birum, I. (2002). The psychological bases of ideology and prejudice: Testing a dual process model. *Journal of Personality and Social Psychology, 83,* 75–93.

Duncan, B. L. (1976). Differential social perception and attribution of intergroup violence: Testing the lower limits of stereotyping of blacks. *Journal of Personality and Social Psychology, 34,* 590–598.

Duriez, B. & Van Hiel, A. (2002). The march of modern fascism. A comparison of social dominance orientation and authoritarianism. *Personality and Individual Differences, 32,* 1199–1213.

Dutton, D. G. & Lake, R. W. (1973). Threat of own prejudice and reverse discrimination in interracial situations. *Journal of Personality and Social Psychology, 28,* 94–100.

Eagly, A. H., Ashmore, R. D., Makhijani, M. G., & Longo, L. C. (1991). What is beautiful is good, but . . .: A meta-analytic review of research on the physical attractiveness stereotype. *Psychological Bulletin, 110,* 109–128.

Edgerton, R. B. (1970). Mental retardation in non-Western societies: Toward a cross-cultural perspective on incompetence. In H. C. Haywood (ed.), *Social-cultural aspects of mental retardation* (pp. 523–559). New York: Appleton–Century–Crofts.

Eibl-Eibesfeldt, I. (1989). *Human ethology.* New York: Aldine de Gruyter.

Eisenberg, N. & Miller, P. A. (1987). Empathy, sympathy, and altruism: Empirical and conceptual links. In N. Eisenberg & J. Strayer (eds.),

*Empathy and its development* (pp. 292–316). New York: Cambridge University Press.

Ekehammar, B., Akrami, N., Gylje, M., & Zakrisson, I. (2004). What matters most to prejudice: Big Five personality, social dominance orientation, or right-wing authoritarianism? *European Journal of Personality, 18,* 463–482.

Elliot, T. R. & MacNair, R. R. (1991). Attributional processes in response to social displays of depressive behavior. *Journal of Social and Personal Relationships, 8,* 129–132.

Ellis, J. & Fox, P. (2001). The effect of self-identified sexual orientation on helping behavior in a British sample: Are lesbians and gay men treated differently? *Journal of Applied Social Psychology, 31,* 1238–1247.

Erb, H.-P., Kruglanski, A. W., Chun, W. Y., Pierro, A., Mannetti, L., & Spiegel, S. (2003). Searching for commonalities in human judgment: The parametric unimodel and its dual mode alternatives. *European Review of Social Psychology, 14,* 1–47.

Erber, J. T., Szuchman, L. T., & Prager, I. G. (2001). Ain't misbehavin': The effects of age and intentionality on judgments about misconduct. *Psychology and Aging, 16,* 85–95.

Erber, R. & Fiske, S. T. (1984). Outcome dependency and attention to inconsistent information. *Journal of Personality and Social Psychology, 47,* 709–726.

Ernulf, K. E., Innala, S. M., & Whitam, F. L. (1989). Biological explanation, psychological explanation, and tolerance of homosexuals: A cross-national analysis of beliefs and attitudes. *Psychological Reports, 65,* 1003–1010.

Ettner, S. L., Frank, R. G., & Kessler, R. C. (1997). The impact of psychiatric disorders on labor market outcomes. *Industrial and Labor Relations Review, 51,* 64–81.

Eysenck, M. W. (1992). *Anxiety: The cognitive perspective.* Hove, UK: Erlbaum.

Fábrega, H. (1997). *Evolution of sickness and healing.* Berkeley, CA: University of California Press.

Farina, A. (2000). The few gains and many losses for those stigmatized by psychiatric disorders. In J. H. Harvey & E. D. Miller (eds.), *Loss and trauma: General and close relationship perspectives* (pp. 183–207). New York: Brunner-Routledge.

Farina, A., Allen, J. G., & Saul, B. B. (1968). The role of the stigmatized person in affecting social relationships. *Journal of Personality, 36,* 169–182.

Farina, A. & Felner, R. D. (1973). Employment interviewer reactions to former mental patients. *Journal of Abnormal Psychology, 82,* 268–272.

Farina, A., Felner, R. D., & Boudreau, L. A. (1973). Reactions of workers to male and female mental patient job applicants. *Journal of Consulting and Clinical Psychology, 41,* 363–372.

Farina, A., Gliha, D., Boudreau, L. A., Allen, J. G., & Sherman, M. (1971). Mental illness and the impact of believing others know about it. *Journal of Abnormal Psychology, 77,* 1–5.

Farina, A., Sherman, M., & Allen, J. G. (1968). Role of physical abnormalities in interpersonal perception and behavior. *Journal of Abnormal Psychology, 73,* 590–593.

Farina, A., Thaw, J., Felner, R. D., & Hust, B. E. (1976). Some interpersonal consequences of being mentally ill or mentally retarded. *American Journal of Mental Deficiency, 80,* 414–422.

Farrow, T. F. D., Zheng, Y., Wilkinson, I. D., Spence, S. A., Deakin, J. F., Tarrier, N., Griffiths, P. D., & Woodruff, P. W. R. (2001). Investigating the functional anatomy of empathy and forgiveness. *NeuroReport, 12,* 2433–2438.

Fazio, R. H. (1990). Multiple processes by which attitudes guide behavior: The MODE model as an integrative framework. In M. P. Zanna (ed.), *Advances in Experimental Social Psychology* (Vol. 23, pp. 75–109). San Diego, CA: Academic Press.

Fazio, R. H. & Hilden, L. E. (2001). Emotional reactions to a seemingly prejudiced response: The role of automatically activated racial attitudes and motivation to control prejudiced reactions. *Personality and Social Psychology Bulletin, 27,* 538–549.

Fazio, R. H., Jackson, J. R., Dunton, B. C., & Williams, C. J. (1995). Variability in automatic activation as an unobtrusive measure of racial attitudes: A bona fide pipeline? *Journal of Personality and Social Psychology, 69,* 1013–1027.

Fazio, R. H. & Olson, M. A. (2003). Implicit measures in social cognition research: Their meaning and use. *Annual Review of Psychology, 54,* 297–327.

Fein, S. & Spencer, S. J. (1997). Prejudice as self-image maintenance: Affirming the self through derogating others. *Journal of Personality and Social Psychology, 73,* 31–44.

Feldman Barrett, L., Tugade, M. M., & Engle, R. W. (2004). Individual differences in working memory capacity and dual-process theories of mind. *Psychological Bulletin, 130,* 553–573.

Fichten, C. S. (1986). Self, other, and situation-referent automatic thoughts: Interaction between people who have a physical disability and those who do not. *Cognitive Therapy and Research, 10,* 571–588.

Fichten, C. S. & Amsel, R. (1986). Trait attributions about college students with a physical disability: Circumplex analyses and methodological issues. *Journal of Applied Social Psychology, 16,* 410–427.

Fichten, C. S., Amsel, R., Robillard, K., & Tagalakis, V. (1991). Thoughts about encounters between nondisabled and disabled peers: Situational constraints, states-of-mind, valenced thought categories. *Cognitive Therapy and Research, 15,* 345–369.

Fincham, F. D. & Jaspars, J. M. (1980). Attribution of responsibility: From man the scientist to man as lawyer. In L. Berkowitz (ed.), *Advances in Experimental Social Psychology* (Vol. 13, pp. 81–138). San Diego, CA: Academic Press.

Finlay, W. M. L. & Lyons, E. (2000). Social categorizations, social comparisons and stigma: Presentations of self in people with learning difficulties. *British Journal of Social Psychology, 39,* 129–146.

Fishbein, H. D. (2002). *Peer prejudice and discrimination. The origins of prejudice* (2nd edn.). Mahwah, NJ: Erlbaum.

Fisher, R., Ury, W. L., & Patton, B. M. (1991). *Getting to YES: Negotiating agreement without giving in* (2nd edn.). New York: Penguin Books.

Fisher, R. J. (1994). Generic principles for resolving intergroup conflict. *Journal of Social Issues, 50*(1), 47–66.

Fiske, A. P. (2002). Using individualism and collectivism to compare cultures – critique of the validity and measurement of the constructs: Comment on Oyserman *et al.* (2002). *Psychological Bulletin, 128,* 78–88.

Fiske, A. P., Kitayama, S., Markus, H. R., & Nisbett, R. E. (1998). The cultural matrix of social psychology. In D. T. Gilbert, S. T. Fiske & G. Lindzey (eds.), *The handbook of social psychology* (Vol. 2, pp. 915–981). New York: McGraw-Hill.

Fiske, S. T. (1998). Stereotyping, prejudice, and discrimination. In D. T. Gilbert, S. T. Fiske & G. Lindzey (eds.), *The handbook of social psychology* (Vol. 2, pp. 357–411). New York: McGraw-Hill.

Fiske, S. T., Cuddy, A. J. C., Glick, P., & Xu, J. (2002). A model of (often mixed) stereotype content: Competence and warmth respectively follow from perceived status and competition. *Journal of Personality and Social Psychology, 82*, 878–902.

Fiske, S. T. & Neuberg, S. L. (1990). A continuum model of impression formation: From category-based to individuating processes as a function of information, motivation, and attention. In M. P. Zanna (ed.), *Advances in Experimental Social Psychology* (Vol. 23, pp. 1–74). San Diego, CA: Academic Press.

Fiske, S. T. & Taylor, S. E. (1991). *Social cognition* (2nd edn.). New York: McGraw-Hill.

Fleming, A. S., Corter, C., Stallings, J., & Steiner, M. (2002). Testosterone and prolactin are associated with emotional responses to infant cries in new fathers. *Hormones and Behavior, 42*, 399–413.

Fleming, M. S., Petty, R. E., & White, P. H. (2005). Stigmatized targets and evaluation: Prejudice as a determinant of attribute scrutiny and polarization. *Personality and Social Psychology Bulletin, 31*, 496–507.

Foa, E. B. & Kozak, M. J. (1986). Emotional processing of fear: Exposure to corrective information. *Psychological Bulletin, 99*, 20–35.

Fodor, J. (2000). *The mind doesn't work that way: The scope and limits of computational psychology.* Cambridge, MA: The MIT Press.

Ford, C. V. & Sbordone, R. J. (1980). Attitudes of psychiatrists toward elderly patients. *American Journal of Psychiatry, 137*, 571–575.

Foucault, M. (1975/1977). *Discipline and punish: The birth of the prison (org. Surveiller et punir: Naissance de la prison)* (A. Sheridan, Trans.). London: Penguin.

Frable, D. E. (1993a). Being and feeling unique: Statistical deviance and psychological marginality. *Journal of Personality, 61*, 85–110.

(1993b). Dimensions of marginality: Distinctions among those who are different. *Personality and Social Psychology Bulletin, 19*, 370–380.

Frable, D. E., Blackstone, T., & Scherbaum, C. (1990). Marginal and mindful: Deviants in social interactions. *Journal of Personality and Social Psychology, 59*, 140–149.

Frable, D. E. S., Platt, L., & Hoey, S. (1998). Concealable stigmas and positive self-perceptions: Feeling better around similar others. *Journal of Personality and Social Psychology, 74*, 909–922.

Frable, D. E. S., Wortman, C., & Joseph, J. (1997). Predicting self-esteem, well-being, and distress in a cohort of gay men: The importance of cultural stigma, personal visibility, community networks, and positive identity. *Journal of Personality, 65*, 599–624.

Franco, F. M. & Maass, A. (1999). Intentional control over prejudice: When the choice of the measure matters. *European Journal of Social Psychology, 29*, 469–477.

Franklin, K. (2000). Antigay behaviors among young adults: Prevalence, patterns, and motivators in a noncriminal population. *Journal of Interpersonal Violence, 15*, 339–362.

Frazer, J. G. (1922/1993). *The golden bough: A study in magic and religion.* Ware, Herts: Wordsworth.

Friedman, M. A. & Brownell, K. D. (1995). Psychological correlates of obesity: Moving to the next research generation. *Psychological Bulletin, 117*, 3–20.

Frijda, N. H. (1986). *The emotions.* New York: Cambridge University Press.

(1993). The place of appraisal in emotion. *Cognition and Emotion, 7*, 357–387.

Furnham, A. & Murao, M. (2000). A cross-cultural comparison of British and Japanese lay theories of schizophrenia. *International Journal of Social Psychiatry, 46*, 4–20.

Furnham, A. & Ofstein, A. (1997). Ethical ideology and the allocation of scarce medical resources. *British Journal of Medical Psychology, 70*, 51–63.

Fyock, J. & Stangor, C. (1994). The role of memory biases in stereotype maintenance. *British Journal of Social Psychology, 33*, 331–343.

Gaertner, S. L. (1973). Helping behavior and racial discrimination among liberals and conservatives. *Journal of Personality and Social Psychology, 25*, 335–341.

(1976). Nonreactive measures in racial attitude research: A focus on "liberals". In P. A. Katz (ed.), *Towards the elimination of racism* (pp. 183–211). New York: Pergamon Press.

Gaertner, S. L. & Dovidio, J. F. (1986). The aversive form of racism. In J. F. Dovidio & S. L. Gaertner (eds.), *Prejudice, discrimination, and racism* (pp. 61–89). San Diego, CA: Academic Press.

(2005). Understanding and addressing contemporary racism: From aversive racism to the common ingroup identity model. *Journal of Social Issues, 61*, 615–639.

Galinsky, A. D. & Ku, G. (2004). The effects of perspective-taking on prejudice: The moderating role of self-evaluation. *Personality and Social Psychology Bulletin, 30*, 594–604.

Galinsky, A. D. & Moskowitz, G. B. (2000). Perspective-taking: Decreasing stereotype expression, stereotype accessibility, and in-group favoritism. *Journal of Personality and Social Psychology, 78*, 708–724.

Gallo, L. C., Bogart, L. M., Vranceanu, A. M., & Matthews, K. V. (2005). Socioeconomic status, resources, psychological experiences, and emotional responses: A test of the reserve capacity model. *Journal of Personality and Social Psychology, 88*, 386–399.

Gatz, M. & Pearson, C. G. (1988). Ageism revised and the provision of psychological services. *American Psychologist, 43*, 184–188.

Gergen, K. J. & Jones, E. E. (1963). Mental illness, predictability, and affective consequences as stimulus factors in person perception. *Journal of Abnormal and Social Psychology, 67*, 95–104.

Giancola, P. R. (2003). The moderating effects of dispositional empathy on alcohol-related aggression in men and women. *Journal of Abnormal Psychology, 112*, 275–281.

Giancola, P. R. & Chermak, S. T. (1998). Construct validity of laboratory aggression paradigms: A response to Tedeschi and Quigley (1996). *Aggression and Violent Behavior, 3*, 237–253.

Gibbons, F. X. (1985). A social-psychological perspective on developmental disabilities. *Journal of Social and Clinical Psychology, 3*, 391–404.

Gibbons, F. X. & Sawin, L. G. (1979). Evaluations of mentally retarded persons: "Sympathy" or patronization? *American Journal of Mental Deficiency, 84*, 124–131.

Gibbons, F. X., Stephan, W. G., Stephenson, B., & Petty, C. R. (1980). Reactions to stigmatized others: Response amplification vs sympathy. *Journal of Experimental Social Psychology, 16*, 591–605.

Gilbert, P. (2003). Evolution, social roles and the differences in shame and guilt. *Social Research, 70*, 401–426.

Goffman, E. (1963a). *Behavior in public places. Notes on the social organization of gatherings*. New York: Free Press.

(1963b). *Stigma: Notes on the management of spoiled identity*. New York: Simon & Schuster.

Gold, G. J. & Weiner, B. (2000). Remorse, confession, group identity, and expectancies about repeating a transgression. *Basic and Applied Social Psychology, 22*, 291–300.

Goldberg, R. T. (1974). Children with invisible and visible handicaps: congenital heart disease and facial burns. *Journal of Counseling Psychology, 21*, 428–432.

Goodall, J. (1986a). *The chimpanzees of Gombe: Patterns of behavior*. Cambridge, MA: Belknap.

(1986b). Social rejection, exclusion, and shunning among the Gombe chimpanzees. *Ethology and Sociobiology, 7*, 227–236.

Goode, E. (2003). The macguffin that refused to die: An investigation into the condition of the sociology of deviance. *Deviant Behavior, 24*, 507–533.

Gortmaker, S. L., Must, A., Perrin, J. M., Sobol, A. M., et al. (1993). Social and economic consequences of overweight in adolescence and young adulthood. *New England Journal of Medicine, 329*, 1008–1012.

Graham, S., Weiner, B., & Zucker, G. S. (1997). An attributional analysis of punishment goals and public reactions to O. J. Simpson. *Personality and Social Psychology Bulletin, 23*, 331–346.

Gray, P. B., Kahlenberg, S. M., Barrett, E. S., Lipson, S. F., & Ellison, P. T. (2002). Marriage and fatherhood are associated with lower testosterone in males. *Evolution and Human Behavior, 23*, 193–201.

Green, D. P., Glaser, J., & Rich, A. (1998). From lynching to gay bashing: The elusive connection between economic conditions and hate crime. *Journal of Personality and Social Psychology, 75*, 82–92.

Green, G. (1995). Attitudes towards people with HIV: Are they as stigmatizing as people with HIV perceive them to be? *Social Science & Medicine, 41*, 557–568.

Greene, M. D., Adelman, R. D., & Rizzo, C. (1996). Problems in communication between physicians and older patients. *Journal of Geriatric Psychiatry, 29*, 13–32.

Greenwald, A. G., McGhee, D. E., & Schwartz, J. L. K. (1998). Measuring individual differences in implicit cognition: The implicit association test. *Journal of Personality and Social Psychology, 74*, 1464–1480.

Griffin, B. Q. & Rogers, R. W. (1977). Reducing interracial aggression: Inhibiting effects of victim's suffering and power to retaliate. *Journal of Psychology, 95*, 151–157.

Gross, J. J. (1997). Hiding feelings: The acute effects of inhibiting negative and positive emotion. *Journal of Personality and Social Psychology, 106*, 95–103.

(1998). The emerging field of emotion regulation: An integrative review. *Review of General Psychology, 2*, 271–299.

Grossberg, S. (1980). How does the brain build a cognitive code? *Psychological Review, 87*, 1–51.

Guglielmi, R. S. (1999). Psychophysiological assessment of prejudice: Past research, current status, and future directions. *Personality and Social Psychology Review, 3*, 123–157.

Guimond, S., Dambrun, M., Michinov, N., & Duarte, S. (2003). Does social dominance generate prejudice? Integrating individual and contextual determinants of intergroup cognitions. *Journal of Personality and Social Psychology, 84*, 697–721.

Gunthert, K. C., Cohen, L. H., & Armeli, S. (1999). The role of neuroticism in daily stress and coping. *Journal of Personality and Social Psychology, 77,* 1087–1100.

Guttman, N. & Salmon, C. T. (2004). Guilt, fear, stigma and knowledge gaps: ethical issues in public health communication interventions. *Bioethics, 18,* 531–552.

Hamilton, W. D. (1964). The genetic evolution of social behaviour. *Journal of Theoretical Biology, 7,* 1–52.

(1975). Innate social aptitudes of man: An approach from evolutionary genetics. In R. Fox (ed.), *Biosocial anthropology* (pp. 133–153). London: Malaby Press.

Hanks, J. R. & Hanks, L. M. (1948). The physically handicapped in certain non-occidental societies. *Journal of Social Issues, 4*(4), 11–20.

Harmon-Jones, E., Vaughn-Scott, K., Mohr, S., Sigelman, J., & Harmon-Jones, C. (2004). The effect of manipulated sympathy and anger on left and right frontal cortical activity. *Emotion, 4,* 95–101.

Harper, D. C. (1995). Children's attitudes to physical differences among youth from western and non-western cultures. *Cleft Palate-Craniofacial Journal, 32,* 114–119.

(1999). Social psychology of difference: Stigma, spread, and stereotypes in childhood. *Rehabilitation Psychology, 44,* 131–144.

Harris, J., Piper, S., Morgan, H., McClimens, A., Shah, S., Reynolds, H., Baldwin, S., Arksey, H., & Qureshi, H. (2003). *Experiences of providing care to people with long term conditions.* York: Social Policy Research Unit, University of York.

Harris, M. B., Walters, L. C., & Waschull, S. (1991). Gender and ethnic differences in obesity-related behaviors and attitudes in a college sample. *Journal of Applied Social Psychology, 21,* 1545–1566.

Harris, M. B., Waschull, S., & Walters, L. (1990). Feeling fat: Motivations, knowledge, and attitudes of overweight women and men. *Psychological Reports, 67,* 1191–1202.

Harris, M. J., Milich, R., Corbitt, E. M., Hoover, D. W., & Brady, M. (1992). Self-fulfilling effects of stigmatizing information on children's social interactions. *Journal of Personality and Social Psychology, 63,* 41–50.

Harris, M. J., Moniz, A. J., Sowards, B. A., & Krane, K. (1994). Mediation of interpersonal expectancy effects: Expectancies about the elderly. *Social Psychology Quarterly, 57,* 36–48.

Hastorf, A. H., Northcraft, G. B., & Picciotto, S. R. (1979). Helping the handicapped: How realistic is the performance feedback received by the physically handicapped? *Personality and Social Psychology Bulletin, 5,* 373–376.

Hastorf, A. H., Wildfogel, J., & Cassman, T. (1979). Acknowledgment of handicap as a tactic in social interaction. *Journal of Personality and Social Psychology, 37,* 1790–1797.

Havinga, T. (2002). The effects and limits of anti-discrimination law in the Netherlands. *International Journal of the Sociology of Law, 30,* 75–90.

Hazer, J. T. & Bedell, K. V. (2000). Effects of seeking accommodation and disability on preemployment evaluations. *Journal of Applied Social Psychology, 30,* 1201–1223.

Heatherton, T. F., Kleck, R. E., Hebl, M. R., & Hull, J. G. (eds.). (2000). *The social psychology of stigma.* New York: Guilford.

Heaven, P. C. L. & Connors, J. R. (2001). A note on the value correlates of social dominance orientation and right-wing authoritarianism. *Personality and Individual Differences, 31,* 925–930.

Hebl, M. & Kleck, R. E. (2002). Acknowledging one's stigma in the interview setting: Effective strategy or liability? *Journal of Applied Social Psychology*, 32, 223–249.

Hebl, M. R. & Dovidio, J. F. (2005). Promoting the "social" in the examination of social stigmas. *Personality and Social Psychology Review*, 9, 156–182.

Hebl, M. R. & Kleck, R. (2000). The social consequences of physical disability. In T. F. Heatherton, R. E. Kleck, M. R. Hebl & J. G. Hull (eds.), *The social psychology of stigma* (pp. 419–440). New York: The Guilford Press.

Hebl, M. R. & Mannix, L. M. (2003). The weight of obesity in evaluating others: A mere proximity effect. *Personality and Social Psychology Bulletin*, 29, 28–38.

Hebl, M. R., Tickle, J., & Heatherton, T. F. (2000). Awkward moments in interactions between nonstigmatized and stigmatized individuals. In T. F. Heatherton, R. E. Kleck, M. R. Hebl & J. G. Hull (eds.), *The social psychology of stigma* (pp. 273–306). New York: The Guilford Press.

Heckhausen, J. & Brim, O. G. (1997). Perceived problems for self and others: Self-protection by social downgrading throughout adulthood. *Psychology and Aging*, 12, 610–619.

Hegarty, P. (2002). "It's not a choice, it's the way we're built": Symbolic beliefs about sexual orientation in the US and Britain. *Journal of Community & Applied Social Psychology*, 12, 153–166.

Heinemann, W., Pellander, F., Vogelbusch, A., & Wojtek, B. (1981). Meeting a deviant person: Subjective norms and affective reactions. *European Journal of Social Psychology*, 11, 1–25.

Helman, C. G. (1994). *Culture, health and illness* (3rd edn.). Oxford: Butterworth-Heinemann.

Hempel, C. G. (1966). *Philosophy of natural sciences*. Englewood Cliffs, NJ: Prentice-Hall.

Herdt, G. (1997). *Same sex, different cultures: Exploring gay and lesbian lives.* Boulder, CO: Westview.

Herek, G. M. & Capitanio, J. P. (1996). "Some of my best friends": Intergroup contact, concealable stigma, and heterosexuals' attitudes toward gay men and lesbians. *Personality and Social Psychology Bulletin*, 22, 412–424.

Herman, N. J. (1993). Return to sender: Reintegrative stigma-management strategies of ex-psychiatric patients. *Journal of Contemporary Ethnography*, 22, 295–330.

Hewstone, M. (2003). Intergroup contact, panacea for prejudice? *The Psychologist*, 16, 352–355.

Heyd, D. (1996a). Introduction. In D. Heyd (ed.), *Toleration: An elusive virtue* (pp. 3–17). Princeton, NJ: Princeton University Press.

(ed.). (1996b). *Toleration: An elusive virtue*. Princeton, NJ: Princeton University Press.

Hirschauer, S. (2005). On doing being a stranger: The practical consequences of civil inattention. *Journal for the Theory of Social Behavior*, 35, 41–67.

Hofmann, W., Gawronski, B., Gschwendner, T., Le, H., & Schmitt, M. (2005). A meta-analysis on the correlation between implicit association test and explicit self-report measures. *Personality and Social Psychology Bulletin*, 31, 1369–1385.

Hofmann, W., Gschwendner, T., Nosek, B. A., & Schmitt, M. (2005). What moderates implicit-explicit consistency? *European Review of Social Psychology*, 16, 335–390.

Hofstede, G. (2001). *Culture's consequences: comparing values, behaviors, institutions, and organizations across nations.* Thousand Oaks, CA: Sage.

Holcomb, H. R. (1998). Testing evolutionary hypotheses. In C. Crawford & D. L. Krebs (eds.), *Handbook of evolutionary psychology: Ideas, issues, and applications* (pp. 303–334). Mahwah, NJ: Erlbaum.

Holroyd, E. E. (2003). Chinese cultural influences on parental caregiving obligations toward children with disabilities. *Qualitative Health Research, 13,* 4–19.

Horwitz, A. V. (1990). *The logic of social control.* New York: Plenum.

Horwitz, A. V., Reinhart, S. C., & Howell-White, S. (1996). Caregiving as reciprocal exchange in families with seriously mentally ill members. *Journal of Health and Social Behavior, 37,* 149–162.

Houlette, M. A., Gaertner, S. L., Johnson, K. M., Banker, B. S., Riek, B. M., & Dovidio, J. F. (2004). Developing a more inclusive social identity: An elementary school intervention. *Journal of Social Issues, 60,* 35–55.

Hovland, C. I. & Sears, R. R. (1940). Minor studies of aggression: VI. Correlation of lynchings with economic indices. *Journal of Psychology, 9,* 301–310.

Huebner, D. M., Nemeroff, C. J., & Davis, M. C. (2005). Do hostility and neuroticism confound associations between perceived discrimination and depressive symptoms? *Journal of Social and Clinical Psychology, 24,* 723–740.

Hughes, E. C. (1945). Dilemmas and contradictions of status. *American Journal of Sociology, 50,* 353–359.

Hummert, M. L. (1994). Stereotypes of the elderly and patronizing speech. In M. L. Hummert & J. M. Wiemann (eds.), *Interpersonal communication in older adulthood: Interdisciplinary theory and research* (Vol. 173, pp. 162–184). Thousand Oaks, CA: Sage Publications.

Humphrey, N. (1997). Varieties of altruism – and the common ground between them. *Social Research, 64,* 199–209.

Ickes, W. (1984). Compositions in black and white: determinants of interaction in interracial dyads. *Journal of Personality and Social Psychology, 47,* 330–341.

Inglehart, R. & Baker, W. E. (2000). Modernization, cultural change, and the persistence of traditional values. *American Sociological Review, 65,* 19–51.

Inglehart, R., Basanez, M., & Moreno, A. (1998). *Human values and beliefs: A cross-cultural sourcebook.* Michigan: University of Michigan Press.

Ingstad, B. & Whyte, S. R. (eds.). (1995). *Disability and culture.* Berkeley, CA: University of California Press.

Jaramillo, E. (1999). Tuberculosis and stigma: Predictors of prejudice against people with tuberculosis. *Journal of Health Psychology, 4,* 71–79.

Jenkins, R. (ed.). (1998). *Questions of competence.* Cambridge: Cambridge University Press.

Johnson, A. W. & Earle, T. K. (1987). *The evolution of human societies: From foraging group to agrarian state.* Stanford, CA: Stanford University Press.

Jones, D. A. (1996). Discrimination against same-sex couples in hotel reservation policies. *Journal of Homosexuality, 31,* 153–159.

Jones, E. E., Farina, A., Hastorf, A. H., Markus, H., Miller, D. T., & Scott, R. A. (1984). *Social stigma: The psychology of marked relationships.* San Francisco: Freeman.

Jones, J. M. (1997). *Prejudice and racism.* New York: McGraw-Hill.

Jost, J. T. & Banaji, M. R. (1994). The role of stereotyping in system-justification and the production of false consciousness. *British Journal of Social Psychology, 33,* 1–27.

Jost, J. T., Glaser, J., Kruglanski, A. W., & Sulloway, F. J. (2003). Political conservatism as motivated social cognition. *Psychological Bulletin, 129,* 339–375.

Jussim, L. & Harber, K. D. (2005). Teacher expectations and self-fulfilling prophecies: Knowns and unknowns. *Personality and Social Psychology Review, 9*, 131–155.

Jussim, L., Palumbo, P., Chatman, C., Madon, S., & Smith, A. (2000). Stigma and self-fulfilling prophecies. In T. F. Heatherton, R. E. Kleck, M. R. Hebl & J. G. Hull (eds.), *The social psychology of stigma* (pp. 374–418). New York: The Guilford Press.

Jutte, X. (1994). *Poverty and deviance in the late Middle Ages*. Cambridge: Cambridge University Press.

Juvonen, J. (1991). Deviance, perceived responsibility, and negative peer reactions. *Developmental Psychology, 27*, 672–681.

Kahan, D. M. & Posner, E. A. (1999). Shaming white-collar criminals: A proposal for reform of the federal sentencing guidelines. *Journal of Law and Economics, 42*, 365–391.

Kaiser, C. R. & Miller, C. T. (2001). Reacting to impending discrimination: Compensation for prejudice and attributions to discrimination. *Personality and Social Psychology Bulletin, 27*, 1357–1367.

Karremans, J. C., Van Lange, P. A. M., & Holland, R. (2005). Forgiveness and its associations with prosocial thinking, feeling, and doing beyond the relationship with the offender. *Personality and Social Psychology Bulletin, 31*, 1315–1326.

Karris, L. (1977). Prejudice against obese renters. *Journal of Social Psychology, 101*, 159–160.

Katz, I. (1981). *Stigma: A social psychological analysis*. Hillsdale, NJ: Erlbaum.

Katz, I., Cohen, S., & Glass, D. (1975). Some determinants of cross-racial helping. *Journal of Personality and Social Psychology, 32*, 964–970.

Katz, I., Farber, J., Glass, C., Lucido, D., & Emswiller, T. (1978). When courtesy offends: Effects of positive and negative behavior by the physically disabled on altruism and anger in normals. *Journal of Personality, 46*, 506–518.

Katz, I., Glass, D. C., Lucido, D. J., & Farber, J. (1979). Harm-doing and victim's racial or orthopedic stigma as determinants of helping behavior. *Journal of Personality, 47*, 340–364.

Katz, I. & Hass, R. G. (1988). Racial ambivalence and American value conflict: Correlational and priming studies of dual cognitive structures. *Journal of Personality and Social Psychology, 55*, 893–905.

Katz, I., Hass, R. G., Parisi, N., Astone, J., & McEvaddy, D. (1987). Lay people's and health care personnel's perceptions of cancer, AIDS, cardiac, and diabetes patients. *Psychological Reports, 60*, 615–629.

Katz, J. & Mirenda, P. (2002). Including students with developmental disabilities in general education classrooms: Social benefits. *International Journal of Special Education, 17*, 25–35.

Kawakami, K., Dovidio, J. F., Moll, J., Hermsen, S., & Russin, A. (2000). Just say no (to stereotyping): Effects of training in the negation of stereotypic association on stereotype activation. *Journal of Personality and Social Psychology, 78*, 871–888.

Kelly, A. E. & McKillop, K. J. (1996). Consequences of revealing personal secrets. *Psychological Bulletin, 120*, 450–465.

Kelly, R. L. (1995). *The foraging spectrum: Diversity in hunter-gatherer lifeways*. Washington, DC: Smithsonian Institution Press.

Kemper, S. & Harden, T. (1999). Experimentally disentangling what's beneficial about elderspeak from what's not. *Psychology and Aging, 14*, 656–670.

Kent, G. (1999). Correlates of perceived stigma in vitiligo. *Psychology and Health*, 14, 241–251.

Kessler, R. C., Mickelson, K. D., & Williams, D. R. (1999). The prevalence, distribution, and mental health correlates of perceived discrimination in the United States. *Journal of Health and Social Behavior*, 40, 208–230.

King, M. B. (1989). Psychosocial status of 192 out-patients with HIV infection and AIDS. *British Journal of Psychiatry*, 154, 237–242.

Kite, M. E. & Whitley, B. E., Jr. (1996). Sex differences in attitudes toward homosexual persons, behaviors, and civil rights: A meta-analysis. *Personality and Social Psychology Bulletin*, 22, 336–353.

Kleck, R. (1968). Physical stigma and nonverbal cues emitted in face-to-face interaction. *Human Relations*, 21, 19–28.

Kleck, R., Ono, H., & Hastorf, A. H. (1966). The effects of physical deviance upon face-to-face interaction. *Human Relations*, 19, 425–436.

Kleck, R. E., Buck, P. L., Goller, W. L., London, R. S., Pfeifer, J. R., & Vukcevic, D. P. (1968). Effect of stigmatizing conditions on the use of personal space. *Psychological Reports*, 23, 111–118.

Kleck, R. E. & Strenta, A. (1980). Perceptions of the impact of negatively valued physical characteristics on social interaction. *Journal of Personality and Social Psychology*, 39, 861–873.

Kleinman, A., Wang, W.-Z., Li, S.-C., Cheng, X.-M., Dai, X.-Y., Li, K.-T., & Kleinman, J. (1995). The social course of epilepsy: chronic illness as social experience in interior China. *Social Science & Medicine*, 40, 1319–1330.

Klesges, R. C., Klem, M. L., Hanson, C. L., Eck, L. H., Ernst, J., O'Laughlin, D., Garrott, A., & Rife, R. (1990). The effects of applicant's health status and qualifications on simulated hiring decisions. *International Journal of Obesity*, 14, 527–535.

Klink, A. & Wagner, U. (1999). Discrimination against ethnic minorities in Germany: Going back to the field. *Journal of Applied Social Psychology*, 29, 402–423.

Knauft, B. M. (1991). Violence and sociality in human evolution. *Current Anthropology*, 32, 391–428.

Kosfeld, M., Heinrichs, M., Zak, P. J., Fischbacher, U., & Fehr, B. (2005). Oxytocin increases trust in humans. *Nature*, 435, 673–676.

Koty, J. (1934). *Die Behandlung der Alten und Kranken bei den Naturvölkern. [The treatment of the elderly and ill among primitive people]* Stuttgart, Germany: C. L. Hirschfeld.

Kowner, R. (2001). Psychological perspective on human development stability and fluctuating asymmetry: Sources, applications and implications. *British Journal of Psychology*, 92, 447–469.

Krauss, S. W. (2002). Romanian authoritarianism 10 years after communism. *Personality and Social Psychology Bulletin*, 28, 1255–1264.

Krebs, D. L. (1998). The evolution of moral behaviors. In C. Crawford & D. L. Krebs (eds.), *Handbook of evolutionary psychology: Ideas, issues, and applications* (pp. 337–368). Mahwah, NJ: Erlbaum.

Kreindler, S. A. (2005). A dual group model of individual differences in prejudice. *Personality and Social Psychology Review*, 9, 90–107.

Krendl, A. C., Macrae, C. N., Kelley, W. M., Fugelsang, J. A., & Heatherton, T. F. (2006). The good, the bad, and the ugly: An FMRI investigation of the functional anatomic correlates of stigma. *Social Neuroscience*, 1, 5–15.

Kropotkin, P. (1914/1955). *Mutual aid: a factor of evolution*. Boston, MA: Extending Horizons Books.

Kruglanski, A. W. & Freund, T. (1983). The freezing and unfreezing of lay-inferences: Effects on impressional primacy, ethnic stereotyping, and numerical anchoring. *Journal of Experimental Social Psychology, 19*, 448–468.

Kruskal, J. & Wish, M. (1978). *Multidimensional scaling*. Beverly Hills, CA: Sage.

Kunda, Z. & Spencer, S. J. (2003). When do stereotypes come to mind and when do they color judgment? A goal-based theoretical framework for stereotype activation and application. *Psychological Bulletin, 129*, 522–544.

Kunda, Z. & Thagard, P. (1996). Forming impressions from stereotypes, traits, and behaviors: A parallel-constraint-satisfaction theory. *Psychological Review, 103*, 284–308.

Kurzban, R. & Leary, M. R. (2001). Evolutionary origins of stigmatization: The function of social exclusion. *Psychological Bulletin, 127*, 187–208.

Lake, R. W. (2001). Locational conflict (NIMBY). In N. J. Smelser & P. B. Baltes (eds.), *International encyclopedia of the social & behavioral sciences* (pp. 9019–9024). New York: Elsevier.

Lambert, A. J. & Chasteen, A. L. (1997). Perceptions of disadvantage versus conventionality: Political values and attitudes toward the elderly versus blacks. *Personality and Social Psychology Bulletin, 23*, 469–481.

Lambert, A. J., Payne, B. K., Jacoby, L. L., Shaffer, L. M., Chasteen, A. L., & Khan, S. R. (2003). Stereotypes as dominant responses: On the "social facilitation" of prejudice in anticipated public contexts. *Journal of Personality and Social Psychology, 84*, 277–295.

Langer, E. J. & Abelson, R. P. (1972). The semantics of asking a favor: How to succeed in getting help without really dying. *Journal of Personality and Social Psychology, 24*, 26–36.

Langer, E. J., Bashner, R. S., & Chanowitz, B. (1985). Decreasing prejudice by increasing discrimination. *Journal of Personality and Social Psychology, 49*, 113–120.

Langer, E. J., Fiske, S., Taylor, S. E., & Chanowitz, B. (1976). Stigma, staring, and discomfort: A novel-stimulus hypothesis. *Journal of Experimental Social Psychology, 12*, 451–463.

Langer, E. J., Rodin, J., Beck, P., Weinman, C., & Spitzer, L. (1979). Environmental determinants of memory improvement in late adulthood. *Journal of Personality and Social Psychology, 37*, 2003–2013.

Langlois, J. H., Kalakanis, L., Rubenstein, A. J., Larson, A., Hallam, M., & Smoot, M. (2000). Maxims or myths of beauty? A meta-analytic and theoretical review. *Psychological Bulletin, 126*, 390–423.

Le Goff, J. (1984/1987). *De cultuur van middeleeuws Europa (org. La civilisation de l'Occcident Médiéval) [The culture of medieval Europe]* (R. Fagel & L. Knippenberg, Trans.). Amsterdam: Maarten Muntinga.

LeDoux, J. (1996). *The emotional brain: The mysterious underpinnings of emotional life*. New York: Simon & Schuster.

Lee, B. A., Farrell, C. R., & Link, B. G. (2004). Revisiting the Contact Hypothesis: the case of public exposure to homelessness. *American Sociological Review, 69*, 40–63.

Lee, R. B. & DeVore, I. (eds.). (1968). *Man the hunter*. New York: Aldine Publishing Company.

Lerner, J. S. & Keltner, D. (2000). Beyond valence: Toward a model of emotion-specific influences on judgment and choice. *Cognition and Emotion, 14*, 473–493.

LeVine, R. A. & Campbell, D. T. (1972). *Ethnocentrism: Theories of conflict, ethnic attitudes, and group behavior.* New York: John Wiley & Sons.

Levine, R. V., Martinez, T. S., Brase, G., & Sorenson, K. (1994). Helping in 36 U.S. cities. *Journal of Personality and Social Psychology, 67,* 69–82.

Levine, R. V., Norenzayan, A., & Philbrick, K. (2001). Cross-cultural differences in helping strangers. *Journal of Cross-Cultural Psychology, 32,* 543–560.

Levy, B. (1996). Improving memory in old age through implicit self-stereotyping. *Journal of Personality and Social Psychology, 71,* 1092–1107.

Levy, B. & Langer, E. (1994). Aging free from negative stereotypes: Successful memory in China and among the American deaf. *Journal of Personality and Social Psychology, 66,* 989–997.

Levy, B. R. & Banaji, M. R. (2002). Implicit ageism. In T. D. Nelson (ed.), *Ageism: Stereotyping and prejudice against older persons* (pp. 49–75). Cambridge, MA: The MIT Press.

Lewis, M. A. & Rook, K. S. (1999). Social control in personal relationships: Impact on health behaviors and psychological distress. *Health Psychology, 18,* 63–71.

Lindsay, P. H. & Norman, D. A. (1977). *Human information processing: An introduction to psychology* (2nd edn.). New York: Academic Press.

Link, B. G., Cullen, F. T., Struening, E. L., Shrout, P. E., *et al.* (1989). A modified labeling theory approach to mental disorders: An empirical assessment. *American Sociological Review, 54,* 400–423.

Link, B. G., Mirotznik, J., & Cullen, F. T. (1991). The effectiveness of stigma coping orientations: Can negative consequences of mental illness labeling be avoided? *Journal of Health and Social Behavior, 32,* 302–320.

Link, B. G. & Phelan, J. C. (2001). Conceptualizing stigma. *Annual Review of Sociology, 27,* 363–385.

Link, B. G., Struening, E. L., Rahav, M., & Phelan, J. C. (1997). On stigma and its consequences: Evidence from a longitudinal study of men with dual diagnoses of mental illness and substance abuse. *Journal of Health and Social Behavior, 38,* 177–190.

Linville, P. W. & Jones, E. E. (1980). Polarized appraisals of outgroup members. *Journal of Personality and Social Psychology, 38,* 689–703.

Livingston, R. W. (2002). The role of perceived negativity in moderation of African Americans' implicit and explicit racial attitudes. *Journal of Experimental Social Psychology, 38,* 405–413.

Lloyd, E. A. (1999). Evolutionary psychology: The burdens of proof. *Biology and Philosophy, 14,* 211–233.

Loftus, J. (2001). America's liberalization in attitudes toward homosexuality. *American Sociological Review, 66,* 762–782.

Looper, K. J. & Kirmayer, L. J. (2004). Perceived stigma in functional somatic syndromes and comparable medical conditions. *Journal of Psychosomatic Research, 57,* 373–378.

Lott, B. (2002). Cognitive and behavioral distancing from the poor. *American Psychologist, 57,* 100–110.

Ludlow, A. R. (1980). The evolution and simulation of a decision maker. In F. M. Toates & T. R. Halliday (eds.), *Analysis of motivational processes* (pp. 273–296). London: Academic Press.

MacLean, P. D. (1985). Brain evolution relating to family, play, and the separation call. *Archives of General Psychiatry, 42,* 405–417.

Macrae, C. N., Bodenhausen, G. V., Milne, A. B., & Jetten, J. (1994). Out of mind but back in sight: Stereotypes on the rebound. *Journal of Personality and Social Psychology, 67*, 808–817.

Maestripieri, D. (1999). The biology of human parenting: Insights from non-human primates. *Neuroscience and Biobehavioral Reviews, 23*, 411–422.

Major, B. & Crocker, J. (1993). Social stigma: The consequences of attributional ambiguity. In D. M. Mackie & D. L. Hamilton (eds.), *Affect, cognition, and stereotyping: Interactive processes in group perception* (pp. 345–370). San Diego, CA: Academic Press.

Major, B. & O'Brien, L. T. (2005). The social psychology of stigma. *Annual Review of Psychology, 56*, 393–421.

Makas, E. (1988). Positive attitudes toward disabled people: Disabled and nondisabled persons' perspectives. *Journal of Social Issues, 44*(1), 49–61.

Malloy, T. E., Albright, L., Diaz-Loving, R., Dong, Q., & Lee, Y. T. (2004). Agreement in personality judgments within and between nonoverlapping social groups in collectivist cultures. *Personality and Social Psychology Bulletin, 30*, 106–117.

Maner, J. K., Kenrick, D. T., Becker, D. V., Robertson, T. E., Hofer, B., Neuberg, S. L., Delton, A. W., Butner, J., & Schaller, M. (2005). Functional projection: how fundamental social motives can bias interpersonal perception. *Journal of Personality and Social Psychology, 88*, 63–78.

Marcus-Newhall, A., Pedersen, W. C., Carlson, M., & Miller, N. (2000). Displaced aggression is alive and well: A meta-analytic review. *Journal of Personality and Social Psychology, 78*, 670–689.

Markowitz, F. E. (1998). The effects of stigma on the psychological well-being and life satisfaction of persons with mental illness. *Journal of Health and Social Behavior, 39*, 335–347.

Marks, I. (1987). *Fears, phobias and rituals.* New York: Oxford University Press.

Mayville, E. & Penn, D. L. (1998). Changing societal attitudes towards persons with severe mental illness. *Cognitive and Behavioural Practice, 5*, 241–253.

McArthur, L. Z. & Baron, R. M. (1983). Toward an ecological approach to social perception. *Psychological Review, 90*, 215–238.

McConnell, A. R. & Leibold, J. M. (2001). Relations among the Implicit Association Test, discriminatory behavior, and explicit measures of racial attitudes. *Journal of Experimental Social Psychology, 37*, 435–442.

McCoy, S. K. & Major, B. (2003). Group identification moderates emotional responses to perceived prejudice. *Personality and Social Psychology Bulletin, 29*, 1005–1017.

McCullough, M. E., Kilpatrick, S. D., Emmons, R. A., & Larson, D. B. (2001). Is gratitude a moral affect? *Psychological Bulletin, 127*, 249–266.

McCullough, M. E., Worthington, E. L., & Rachal, K. C. (1997). Interpersonal forgiving in close relationships. *Journal of Personality and Social Psychology, 73*, 321–336.

McDougall, W. (1908/1948). *An introduction to social psychology* (29th edn.). London: Methuen.

McKenna, K. Y. A. & Bargh, J. A. (1998). Coming out in the age of the Internet: Identity "demarginalization" through virtual group participation. *Journal of Personality and Social Psychology, 75*, 681–694.

Mehnert, T., Krauss, H. H., Nadler, R., & Boyd, M. (1990). Correlates of life satisfaction in those with disabling conditions. *Rehabilitation Psychology, 35*, 3–17.

Mehrabian, A. (1972). *Nonverbal communication*. Oxford: Aldine-Atherton.

Mehta, S. & Farina, A. (1997). Is being "sick" really better? Effect of the disease view of mental disorder on stigma. *Journal of Social and Clinical Psychology, 16*, 405–419.

Menec, V. H. & Perry, R. P. (1995). Reactions to stigmas: The effect of target's age and controllability of stigmas. *Journal of Aging and Health, 7*, 365–383.

Merton, R. K. (1957). *Social theory and social structure*. New York: Free Press.

Meyer, I. H. (1995). Minority stress and mental health in gay men. *Journal of Health and Social Behavior, 36*, 38–56.

Mikulincer, M., Gillath, O., Halevy, V., Avihou, N., Avidan, S., & Eshkoli, N. (2001). Attachment theory and reactions to others' needs: Evidence that activation of the sense of attachment security promotes empathic responses. *Journal of Personality and Social Psychology, 81*, 1205–1224.

Mikulincer, M. & Shaver, P. R. (2001). Attachment theory and intergroup bias: Evidence that priming the secure base schema attenuates negative reactions to out-groups. *Journal of Personality and Social Psychology, 81*, 97–115.

Milgram, S. (1992). *The individual in a social world: Essays and experiments* (2nd edn.). New York: McGraw-Hill.

Miller, C. T. & Downey, K. (1999). A meta-analysis of heavyweight and self-esteem. *Personality and Social Psychology Review, 3*, 68–84.

Miller, C. T. & Major, B. (2000). Coping with stigma and prejudice. In T. F. Heatherton, R. E. Kleck, M. R. Hebl & J. G. Hull (eds.), *The social psychology of stigma* (pp. 243–272). New York: The Guilford Press.

Miller, C. T., Rothblum, E. D., Barbour, L., Brand, P. A., & Felicio, D. (1990). Social interactions of obese and nonobese women. *Journal of Personality, 58*, 365–380.

Miller, C. T., Rothblum, E. D., Felicio, D., & Brand, P. (1995). Compensating for stigma: Obese and nonobese women's reactions to being visible. *Personality and Social Psychology Bulletin, 21*, 1093–1106.

Miller, D. T. & Prentice, D. A. (1996). The construction of social norms and standards. In E. T. Higgins & A. W. Kruglanski (eds.), *Social psychology: Handbook of basic principles* (pp. 799–829). New York: The Guilford Press.

Miller, J. G., Bersoff, D. M., & Harwood, R. L. (1990). Perceptions of social responsibilities in India and in the United States: moral imperatives or personal decisions? *Journal of Personality and Social Psychology, 58*, 33–47.

Miller, N. (2002). Personalization and the promise of contact theory. *Journal of Social Issues, 58*, 387–410.

Miller, N., Pedersen, W. C., Earleywine, M., & Pollock, V. E. (2003). A theoretical model of triggered displaced aggression. *Personality and Social Psychology Review, 7*, 75–97.

Miller, P. A. & Eisenberg, N. (1988). The relation of empathy to aggressive and externalizing/antisocial behavior. *Psychological Bulletin, 103*, 324–344.

Molinari, E. & Riva, G. (1995). Self-others perception in a clinical sample of obese women. *Perceptual and Motor Skills, 80*, 1283–1289.

Monteith, M. J., Devine, P. G., & Zuwerink, J. R. (1993). Self-directed versus other-directed affect as a consequence of prejudice-related discrepancies. *Journal of Personality and Social Psychology, 64*, 198–210.

Monteith, M. J., Sherman, J. W., & Devine, P. G. (1998). Suppression as a stereotype control strategy. *Personality and Social Psychology Review, 2*, 63–82.

Monteith, M. J. & Voils, C. I. (2001). Exerting control over prejudiced responses. In G. B. Moskowitz (ed.), *Cognitive social psychology: The Princeton symposium on the legacy and future of social cognition* (pp. 375–388). Mahwah, NJ: Erlbaum.

Mooney, K. M., Cohn, E. S., & Swift, M. B. (1992). Physical distance and AIDS: Too close for comfort? *Journal of Applied Social Psychology, 22,* 1442–1452.

Moore, R. I. (1987). *The formation of a persecuting society: Power and deviance in Western Europe 950–1250.* Oxford: Basil Blackwell.

Moreno, K. N. & Bodenhausen, G. V. (2001). Intergroup affect and social judgement: Feelings as inadmissible information. *Group Processes and Intergroup Relations, 4,* 21–29.

Morris, C. (1946). *Signs, language, and behavior.* New York: Braziller.

Morrow, S. L., Gore, P. A., & Campbell, B. W. (1996). The application of a socio-cognitive framework to the career development of lesbian women and gay men. *Journal of Vocational Behavior, 48,* 136–148.

Moskowitz, G. B., Salomon, A. R., & Taylor, C. M. (2000). Preconsciously controlling stereotyping: Implicitly activated egalitarian goals prevent the activation of stereotypes. *Social Cognition, 18,* 151–177.

Mueller, C. W., Mutran, E., & Boyle, E. H. (1989). Age discrimination in earnings in a dual-economy market. *Research on Aging, 11,* 492–507.

Mulatu, M. S. (1999). Perceptions of mental and physical illnesses in Northwestern Ethiopia. *Journal of Health Psychology, 4,* 531–549.

Murphy, R. F., Scheer, J., Murphy, Y., & Mack, R. (1988). Physical disability and social liminality: a study in the rituals of adversity. *Social Science & Medicine, 26,* 235–242.

Murphy, S. T. & Zajonc, R. B. (1993). Affect, cognition, and awareness: Affective priming with suboptimal and optimal stimuli. *Journal of Personality and Social Psychology, 64,* 723–739.

Myers, A. & Rosen, J. C. (1999). Obesity stigmatization and coping: Relation to mental health symptoms, body image, and self-esteem. *International Journal of Obesity, 23,* 221–230.

Na, E. Y. & Loftus, E. F. (1998). Attitudes toward law and prisoners, conservative authoritarianism, attribution, and internal-external locus of control: Korean and American law students and undergraduates. *Journal of Cross-Cultural Psychology, 29,* 595–615.

Nail, P. R., Harton, H. C., & Decker, B. P. (2003). Political orientation and modern versus aversive racism: Tests of Dovidio and Gaertner's (1998) integrated model. *Journal of Personality and Social Psychology, 84,* 754–770.

Neuberg, S. L., Smith, D. M., & Asher, T. (2000). Why people stigmatize: Toward a biocultural framework. In T. F. Heatherton, R. E. Kleck, M. R. Hebl & J. G. Hull (eds.), *The social psychology of stigma* (pp. 31–61). New York: The Guilford Press.

Neuberg, S. L., Smith, D. M., Hoffman, J. C., & Russell, F. J. (1994). When we observe stigmatized and "normal" individuals interacting: Stigma by association. *Personality and Social Psychology Bulletin, 20,* 196–209.

Neubert, D. & Cloerkes, G. (2001). *Behindering und Behinderte in verschiedenen Kulturen: Eine vergleichende Analyse ethnologischer Studien [Obstruction and obstructed in different cultures: A comparative analysis of ethnological studies]* (3rd edn.). Heidelberg, Germany: Universitätsverlag C. Winter.

Neufeldt, A. H. & Mathieson, R. (1995). Empirical dimensions of discrimination against disabled people. *Health and Human Rights, 1,* 174–189.

Neumann, R., Hülsenbeck, K., & Seibt, B. (2004). Attitudes towards people with AIDS and avoidance behavior: Automatic and reflective bases of behavior. *Journal of Experimental Social Psychology, 40,* 543–550.

Nieman, Y. F., Jennings, L., Rozelle, R. M., Baxter, J. C., & Sullivan, E. (1994). Use of free responses and cluster analysis to determine stereotypes of eight groups. *Personality and Social Psychology Bulletin, 20,* 379–390.

Nisbett, R. E. & Ross, L. (1980). *Human inference: Strategies and shortcomings of social judgment.* Englewood Cliffs, NJ: Prentice-Hall.

Nosek, B. A. (2005). Moderators of the relationship between implicit and explicit evaluation. *Journal of Experimental Psychology: General, 134,* 565–584.

Nosek, B. A., Banaji, M. R., & Greenwald, A. G. (2002). Harvesting implicit group attitudes and beliefs from a demonstration Web site. *Group Dynamics: Theory, Research, and Practice, 6,* 101–115.

Oliver, M. (1990). *The politics of disablement.* Basingstoke, UK: Macmillan.

Orcutt, J. D. (1983). *Analyzing deviance.* New York: Dorsey.

Orr, E., Thein, R. D., & Aronson, E. (1995). Orthopedic disability, conformity, and social support. *The Journal of Psychology, 129,* 203–219.

Osborne, R. E. & Gilbert, D. T. (1992). The preoccupational hazards of social life. *Journal of Personality and Social Psychology, 62,* 219–228.

Oskamp, S. (2000). Multiple paths to reducing prejudice and discrimination. In S. Oskamp (ed.), *Reducing prejudice and discrimination:* (pp. 1–19). Mahwah, NJ: Erlbaum.

Page, S. (1995). Effects of the mental illness label in 1993: acceptance and rejection in the community. *Journal of Health and Social Policy, 7,* 61–68.

  (1997). Accommodating the elderly: Words and actions in the community. *Journal of Housing for the Elderly, 12,* 55–61.

  (1998). Accepting the gay person: A rental accommodation in the community. *Journal of Homosexuality, 36,* 31–40.

Panksepp, J. (1998). *Affective neuroscience: The foundations of human and animal emotion.* New York: Oxford University Press.

Panksepp, J. & Panksepp, J. B. (2000). The seven sins of evolutionary psychology. *Evolution and Cognition, 6,* 108–131.

Paolini, S., Hewstone, M., Voci, A., Harwood, J., & Cairns, E. (2006). Intergroup contact and the promotion of intergroup harmony: The influence of intergroup emotions. In R. J. Brown & D. Capozza (eds.), *Social identities: Motivational, emotional, cultural influences.* Hove, UK: Psychology Press.

Park, B. & Judd, C. M. (2005). Rethinking the link between categorization and prejudice within the social cognition perspective. *Personality and Social Psychology Review, 9,* 108–130.

Park, J. H., Jason, J., & Schaller, M. (2003). Evolved disease-avoidance processes and contemporary anti-social behavior: prejudicial attitudes and avoidance of people with physical disabilities. *Journal of Nonverbal Behavior, 27,* 65–87.

Parker, R. & Aggleton, P. (2003). HIV and AIDS-related stigma and discrimination: A conceptual framework and implications for action. *Social Science & Medicine, 57,* 13–24.

Parsons, T. (1951). *The social system.* New York: The Free Press.

Pasupathi, M., Carstensen, L., & Tsai, J. L. (1995). Ageism in interpersonal settings. In B. Lott & D. Maluso (eds.), *The social psychology of interpersonal discrimination* (pp. 160–182). New York: The Guilford Press.

Pedersen, W. C., Gonzales, C., & Miller, N. (2000). The moderating effect of trivial triggering provocation on displaced aggression. *Journal of Personality and Social Psychology, 78,* 913–927.

Peper, B. & Spierings, F. (1999). Settling disputes between neighbours in the lifeworld: An evaluation of experiments with community mediation in

The Netherlands. *European Journal on Criminal Policy and Research, 7,* 483–507.

Perez-Lopez, M. S., Lewis, R. J., & Cash, T. F. (2001). The relationship of antifat attitudes to other prejudicial and gender-related attitudes. *Journal of Applied Social Psychology, 31,* 683–697.

Perry, E. (1997). A cognitive approach to understanding discrimination: A closer look at applicant gender and age. *Research in Personnel and Human Resources Management, 15,* 175–240.

Perry, E. L., Hendricks, W., & Broadbent, E. (2000). An exploration of access and treatment discrimination and job satisfaction among college graduates with and without physical disabilities. *Human Relations, 53,* 923–955.

Persell, C. H., Green, A., & Gurevich, L. (2001). Civil society, economic distress, and social tolerance. *Sociological Forum, 16,* 203–229.

Pettigrew, T. F. (1985). New black-white patterns: How best to conceptualize them? *Annual Review of Sociology, 11,* 329–346.

(1998). Intergroup contact theory. *Annual Review of Psychology, 49,* 65–85.

Pettigrew, T. F. & Meertens, R. W. (1995). Subtle and blatant prejudice in Western Europe. *European Journal of Social Psychology, 25,* 57–75.

Pettigrew, T. F. & Tropp, L. R. (2003). *A meta-analytic test and reformulation of intergroup contact theory.* Unpublished manuscript.

(2006). A meta-analytic test of intergroup contact theory. *Journal of Personality and Social Psychology, 90,* 751–783.

Phelan, J. C. (2002). Genetic bases of mental illness: A cure for stigma? *Trends in Neurosciences, 25,* 430–431.

Phelps, E. A., Cannistraci, C. J., & Cunningham, W. A. (2003). Intact performance on an indirect measure of race bias following amygdala damage. *Neuropsychologia, 41,* 203–208.

Phelps, E. A., O'Connor, K. J., Cunningham, J. C., Gore, J. C., & Banaji, M. R. (2000). Performance on indirect measures of race evaluation predicts amygdala activation. *Journal of Cognitive Neuroscience, 12,* 729–738.

Phillips, S. T. & Ziller, R. C. (1997). Toward a theory and measure of the nature of nonprejudice. *Journal of Personality and Social Psychology, 72,* 420–434.

Phinney, J. S., Madden, T., & Santos, L. J. (1998). Psychological variables as predictors of perceived ethnic discrimination among minority and immigrant adolescents. *Journal of Applied Social Psychology, 28,* 937–953.

Piliavin, I. M., Piliavin, J. A., & Rodin, J. (1975). Costs, diffusion, and the stigmatized victim. *Journal of Personality and Social Psychology, 32,* 429–438.

Pinel, E. C. (1999). Stigma consciousness: The psychological legacy of social stereotypes. *Journal of Personality and Social Psychology, 76,* 114–128.

Pingitore, R., Dugoni, B. L., Tindale, R. S., & Spring, B. (1994). Bias against overweight job applicants in a simulated employment interview. *Journal of Applied Psychology, 79,* 909–917.

Pinker, S. (1997). *How the mind works.* London, UK: Penguin Books.

Plant, E. A. & Devine, P. G. (1998). Internal and external motivation to respond without prejudice. *Journal of Personality and Social Psychology, 75,* 811–832.

(2003). The antecedents and implications of interracial anxiety. *Personality and Social Psychology Bulletin, 29,* 790–801.

Plant, E. A., Devine, P. G., & Brazy, P. C. (2003). The bogus pipeline and motivations to respond without prejudice: Revisiting the fading and faking of racial prejudice. *Group Processes and Intergroup Relations, 6,* 187–200.

Pliner, P., Chaiken, S., & Flett, G. L. (1990). Gender differences in concern with body weight and physical appearance over the life span. *Personality and Social Psychology Bulletin, 16,* 263–273.

Poskocil, A. (1977). Encounters between blacks and white liberals: The collision of stereotypes. *Social Forces, 55,* 715–727.

Pratto, F., Liu, J. H., Levin, S., Sidanius, J., Shih, M., Bachrach, H., & Hegarty, P. (2000). Social dominance orientation and the legitimization of inequality across cultures. *Journal of Cross-Cultural Psychology, 31,* 369–409.

Pratto, F., Sidanius, J., Stallworth, L. M., & Malle, B. F. (1994). Social dominance orientation: A personality variable predicting social and political attitudes. *Journal of Personality and Social Psychology, 67,* 741–763.

Prince-Gibson, E. & Schwartz, S. H. (1998). Value priorities and gender. *Social Psychology Quarterly, 61,* 49–67.

Pryor, J. B., Reeder, G. D., Vinacco, R., & Kott, T. (1989). The instrumental and symbolic functions of attitudes towards persons with AIDS. *Journal of Applied Social Psychology, 19,* 377–404.

Pryor, J. B., Reeder, G. D., Yeadon, C., & Hesson McInnis, M. S. (2004). A dual-process model of reactions to perceived stigma. *Journal of Personality and Social Psychology, 87,* 436–452.

Pyszczynski, T., Greenberg, J., Solomon, S., Cather, C., Gat, I., & Sideris, J. (1995). Defensive distancing from victims of serious illness: The role of delay. *Personality and Social Psychology Bulletin, 21,* 13–20.

Quinn, D. M. & Crocker, J. (1999). When ideology hurts: Effects of belief in the Protestant ethic and feeling overweight on the psychological well-being of women. *Journal of Personality and Social Psychology, 77,* 402–414.

Ragins, B. R. & Cornwell, J. M. (2001). Pink triangles: Antecedents and consequences of perceived workplace discrimination against gay and lesbian employees. *Journal of Applied Psychology, 86,* 1244–1261.

Raguram, R., Raghu, T. M., Vounatsou, P., & Weiss, M. G. (2004). Schizophrenia and the cultural epidemiology of stigma in Bangalore, India. *Journal of Nervous and Mental Disease, 192,* 734–744.

Ramund, B. & Stensman, R. (1988). Quality of life and evaluation of functions among people with severely impaired mobility and non-disabled controls. *Scandinavian Journal of Psychology, 29,* 137–144.

Rand, C. S. & MacGregor, A. M. (1990). Morbidly obese patients' perceptions of social discrimination before and after surgery for obesity. *Southern Medical Journal, 83,* 1390–1395.

Ravaud, J. F., Madiot, B., & Ville, I. (1992). Discrimination towards disabled people seeking employment. *Social Science & Medicine, 35,* 951–958.

Raven, B. H. (1999). Influence, power, religion, and the mechanisms of social control. *Journal of Social Issues, 55,* 161–186.

Reinke, R. R., Corrigan, P. W., Leonhard, C., Lundin, R. K., & Kubiak, M. A. (2004). Examining two aspects of contact on the stigma of mental illness. *Journal of Social and Clinical Psychology, 23,* 377–389.

Reisenzein, R. (1986). A structural equation analysis of Weiner's attribution-affect model of helping behavior. *Journal of Personality and Social Psychology, 50,* 1123–1133.

Renick, M. J. & Harter, S. (1989). Impact of social comparisons on the developing self-perceptions of learning disabled students. *Journal of Educational Psychology, 81,* 631–638.

Rensel, J. & Howard, A. (1997). The place of persons with disabilities in Rotuman society. *Pacific Studies, 20,* 19–50.

Revenson, T. A. (1989). Compassionate stereotyping of elderly patients by physicians: Revising the social contact hypothesis. *Psychology and Aging, 4,* 230–234.

Richards, J. M. & Gross, J. J. (2000). Emotion regulation and memory: The cognitive costs of keeping one's cool. *Journal of Personality and Social Psychology, 79,* 410–424.

Richardson, S. A. (1971). Handicap, appearance and stigma. *Social Science & Medicine, 5,* 621–628.

Richeson, J. A. & Ambady, N. (2002). Effects of situational power on automatic racial prejudice. *Journal of Experimental Social Psychology, 39,* 177–183.

Richeson, J. A. & Shelton, J. N. (2003). When prejudice does not pay: Effects of interracial contact on executive function. *Psychological Science, 14,* 287–290.

Richeson, J. A. & Trawalter, S. (2005). Why do interracial interactions impair executive function? A resource depletion account. *Journal of Personality and Social Psychology, 88,* 934–947.

Richman, L. C. & Millard, T. (1997). Cleft lip and palate: Longitudinal behavior and relationships of cleft conditions to behavior and achievement. *Journal of Pediatric Psychology, 22,* 487–494.

Ridley, M. (1996). *The origins of virtue.* London: Viking.

Riesman, D., Glazer, N., & Denney, R. (1955). *The lonely crowd: A study of the changing American character* (abridged edn.). Garden City, NY: Doubleday.

Rijksvoorlichtingsdienst. (1993). *Beeldvorming rond chronisch(e) ziek(t)en: kwalitatief en kwantitatief onderzoek. [Public images of chronic illnesses and ill people: Qualitative and quantitative research]* Zoetermeer: Rijksvoorlichtingsdienst: Nationale Commissie Chronische Zieken.

Riskind, J. H. & Wahl, O. (1992). Moving makes it worse: The role of rapid movement in fear of psychiatric patients. *Journal of Social and Clinical Psychology, 11,* 349–364.

Robarchek, C. A. & Robarchek, C. J. (1998). Reciprocities and realities: World views, peacefulness, and violence among Semai and Waorani. *Aggressive Behavior, 24,* 123–133.

Roberts, A. (1979). *Order and dispute: An introduction to legal anthropology.* Harmondsworth, UK: Penguin Books.

Robins, R. W., Trzesniewski, K. H., Tracy, J. L., Gosling, S. D., & Potter, J. (2002). Global self-esteem across the life span. *Psychology and Aging, 17,* 423–434.

Rodin, J. & Langer, E. J. (1977). Long-term effects of a control-relevant intervention with the institutionalized aged. *Journal of Personality and Social Psychology, 35,* 897–902.

Rodin, J. & Slochower, J. (1974). Fat chance for a favor: Obese-normal differences in compliance and incidental learning. *Journal of Personality and Social Psychology, 29,* 557–565.

Rodin, M. & Price, J. (1995). Overcoming stigma: Credit for self-improvement or discredit for needing to improve? *Personality and Social Psychology Bulletin, 21,* 172–181.

Roehling, M. V. (1999). Weight-based discrimination in employment: Psychological and legal aspects. *Personnel Psychology, 52,* 969–1016.

Rogers, R. W. & Prentice-Dunn, S. (1981). Deindividuation and anger-mediated interracial aggression: Unmasking regressive racism. *Journal of Personality and Social Psychology, 41,* 63–73.

Room, R., Rehm, J., Trotter II, R. T., Paglia, A., & Üstün, T. B. (2001). Cross-cultural views on stigma, valuation, parity, and societal values towards disability. In T. B. Üstün, S. Chatterji, J. E. Bickenbach, R. T. Trotter II, R. Room, J. Rehm & S. Saxena (eds.), *Disability and culture: Universalism and diversity* (pp. 247–292). Seattle: Hogrefe & Huber Publishers.

Rosenberg, M. (1979). *Conceiving the self.* New York: Basic Books.

Ross, M. H. (2000). Creating the conditions for peacemaking: theories of practice in ethnic conflict resolution. *Ethnic and Racial Studies, 23,* 1002–1034.

Rossi, P. H., Freeman, H. E., & Lipsey, M. W. (1999). *Evaluation, a systematic approach* (6th edn.). Thousand Oaks, CA: Sage.

Rothbart, M. (1976). Achieving racial equality: An analysis of resistance and social reform. In P. A. Katz (ed.), *Towards the elimination of racism* (pp. 341–375). New York: Pergamon Press.

Rothblum, E. D. (1992). The stigma of women's weight: Social and economic realities. *Feminism and Psychology, 2,* 61–73.

Rothblum, E. D., Brand, P. A., Miller, C. T., & Oetjen, H. A. (1990). The relationship between obesity, employment discrimination, and employment-related victimization. *Journal of Vocational Behavior, 37,* 251–266.

Rozin, P. (1999). The process of moralization. *Psychological Science, 19,* 218–221.

Rozin, P. & Fallon, A. E. (1987). A perspective on disgust. *Psychological Review, 94,* 23–41.

Rozin, P., Markwith, M., & McCauley, C. (1994). Sensitivity to indirect contacts with other persons: AIDS aversion as a composite of aversion to strangers, infection, moral taint, and misfortune. *Journal of Abnormal Psychology, 103,* 495–505.

Ruggiero, K. M. & Taylor, D. M. (1995). Coping with discrimination: how disadvantaged group members perceive the discrimination that confronts them. *Journal of Personality and Social Psychology, 68,* 826–838.

Rumelhart, D. E. & Norman, D. A. (1988). Representation in memory. In R. J. Atkinson, R. J. Herrnstein, G. Lindzey & R. D. Luce (eds.), *Stevens' handbook of experimental psychology* (2nd edn., Vol. 2 Learning and cognition). New York: Wiley.

Rumsey, N., Bull, R., & Gahagan, D. (1982). The effect of facial disfigurement on the proxemic behavior of the general public. *Journal of Applied Social Psychology, 12,* 137–150.

Ryan, E. B., Bieman-Copland, S., Kwong See, S. T., Ellis, C. H., & Anas, A. P. (2002). Age excuses: Conversational management of memory failures in older adults. *Journal of Gerontology, 57B,* 256–267.

Ryan, E. B., Kennaley, D. E., Pratt, W., & Shumovich, M. A. (2000). Evaluations of staff, residents, and community seniors of patronizing speech in the nursing home: Impact of passive, assertive, or humorous responses. *Psychology and Aging, 15,* 272–285.

Ryan, R. M., Chirkov, V. I., Little, T. D., Sheldon, K. M., Timoshina, E., & Deci, E. L. (1999). The American dream in Russia: Extrinsic aspirations and well-being in two cultures. *Personality and Social Psychology Bulletin, 25,* 1509–1524.

Saenz, D. S. (1994). Token status and problem-solving deficits: Detrimental effects of distinctiveness and performance monitoring. *Social Cognition, 12,* 61–74.

Saetermoe, C. L., Scattone, D., & Kim, K. H. (2001). Ethnicity and the stigma of disabilities. *Psychology and Health, 16,* 699–713.

Sagar, H. A. & Schofield, J. W. (1980). Racial and behavioral cues in black and white children's perceptions of ambiguously aggressive acts. *Journal of Personality and Social Psychology, 39,* 590–598.

Santuzzi, A. M. & Ruscher, J. B. (2002). Stigma salience and paranoid social cognition: Understanding variability in metaperceptions among individuals with recently-acquired stigma. *Social Cognition, 20,* 171–197.

Saucier, D. A., Miller, C. T., & Doucet, N. (2005). Differences in helping whites and blacks: A meta-analysis. *Personality and Social Psychology Review, 9,* 2–16.

Schaller, M., Park, J. H., & Mueller, A. (2003). Fear of the dark: Interactive effects of beliefs about danger and ambient darkness on ethnic stereotypes. *Personality and Social Psychology Bulletin, 29,* 637–649.

Scheer, J. & Groce, N. (1988). Impairment as a human constant: Cross-cultural and historical perspectives on variation. *Journal of Social Issues, 44*(1), 23–37.

Schimel, J., Simon, L., Greenberg, J., Pyszczynski, T., Solomon, S., Waxmonsky, J., & Arndt, J. (1999). Stereotypes and terror management: Evidence that mortality salience enhances stereotypic thinking and preferences. *Journal of Personality and Social Psychology, 77,* 905–926.

Schlosser, K. (1952). Körperliche Anomalien als Ursache Soziale Ausstossung bei Naturvölkern. *[Physical anomalies as causes of social exclusion among primitive people] Zeitschrift für Morphologie und Anthropologie, 44,* 220–236.

Schmelkin, L. P. (1984). Hierarchy of preferences toward disabled groups: A reanalysis. *Perceptual and Motor Skills, 59,* 151–157.

(1988). Multidimensional perspectives in the perception of disabilities In H. E. Yuker (ed.), *Attitudes towards people with disabilities* (pp. 127–137). New York: Springer.

Schneider, J. W. & Conrad, P. (1980). In the closet with illness: Epilepsy, stigma potential and information control. *Social Problems, 28,* 32–44.

Schneider, M. E., Major, B., Luhtanen, R., & Crocker, J. (1996). Social stigma and the potential costs of assumptive help. *Personality and Social Psychology Bulletin, 22,* 201–209.

Schoeneman, T. J., Segerstrom, S. C., Griffin, P., & Gresham, D. (1993). The psychiatric nosology of everyday life: Categories in implicit abnormal psychology. *Journal of Social and Clinical Psychology, 12,* 429–453.

Schulz, R. & Decker, S. (1985). Long-term adjustment to physical disability: The role of social support, perceived control, and self-blame. *Journal of Personality and Social Psychology, 48,* 1162–1172.

Schwartz, S. H. (1992). Universals in the content and structure of values: Theoretical advances and empirical tests in 20 countries. In M. P. Zanna (ed.), *Advances in Experimental Social Psychology* (Vol. 25), pp. 1–65. New York: Academic Press.

(1994). Are there universal aspects in the structure and contents of human values? *Journal of Social Issues, 50*(4), 19–45.

Schwartz, S. H. & Bardi, A. (2001). Value hierarchies across cultures: Taking a similarities perspective. *Journal of Cross-Cultural Psychology, 32,* 268–290.

Schwarz, N. & Sudman, S. (eds.). (1992). *Context effects in social and psychological research.* New York: Springer-Verlag.

Schwarzer, R. & Weiner, B. (1991). Stigma controllability and coping as predictors of emotions and social support. *Journal of Social and Personal Relationships, 8,* 133–140.

Scott, M. B. & Lyman, S. M. (1968). Accounts. *American Sociological Review, 33,* 46–62.

Seefeldt, C. (1987). The effects of preschoolers' visits to a nursing home. *The Gerontologist, 27*, 228–232.

Sennett, R. (2003). *Respect in a world of inequality.* New York: W.W. Norton & Company.

Sherman, B. F., Bonanno, G. A., Wiener, L. S., & Battles, H. B. (2000). When children tell their friends they have AIDS: Possible consequences for psychological well-being and disease progression. *Psychosomatic Medicine, 62*, 238–247.

Shweder, R. A., Much, N. C., Mahapatra, M., & Park, L. (1997). The "Big Three" of morality (autonomy, community, divinity) and the "Big Three" explanations of suffering. In A. M. Brandt & P. Rozin (eds.), *Morality and health* (pp. 119–169). New York: Routledge.

Sibicky, M. & Dovidio, J. F. (1986). Stigma of psychological therapy: Stereotypes, interpersonal reactions, and the self-fulfilling prophecy. *Journal of Counseling Psychology, 33*, 148–154.

Sidanius, J. & Pratto, F. (1999). *Social dominance: An intergroup theory of social hierarchy and oppression.* New York: McGraw-Hill.

Sigelman, C., Adams, R. M., Meeks, S. R., & Purcell, M. A. (1986). Children's nonverbal responses to a physically disabled person. *Journal of Nonverbal Behavior, 10*, 173–186.

Silk, J. B. (2003). Cooperation without counting: The puzzle of friendship. In P. Hammerstein (ed.), *Genetic and cultural evolution of cooperation* (pp. 37–54). Cambridge, MA: MIT.

Silver, R. C., Wortman, C. B., & Crofton, C. (1990). The role of coping in support provision: The self-presentational dilemma of victims of life crises. In B. R. S. I. G. Sarason & G. R. Pierce (eds.), *Social support: An interactional view* (pp. 397–426). New York: Wiley.

Simon, B. (1992). Shame, stigma, and mental illness in ancient Greece. In P. J. Fink & A. Tassman (eds.), *Stigma and mental illness* (pp. 29–39). Washington, DC: American Psychiatric Press, Inc.

Simon, B., Glaessner Bayerl, B., & Stratenwerth, I. (1991). Stereotyping and self-stereotyping in a natural intergroup context: The case of heterosexual and homosexual men. *Social Psychology Quarterly, 54*, 252–266.

Simon, B., Loewy, M., Stuermer, S., Weber, U., Freytag, P., Habig, C., Kampmeier, C., & Spahlinger, P. (1998). Collective identification and social movement participation. *Journal of Personality and Social Psychology, 74*, 646–658.

Siperstein, G. N. & Leffert, J. S. (1997). Comparison of socially accepted and rejected children with mental retardation. *American Journal of Mental Retardation, 101*, 339–351.

Sitton, S. & Blanchard, S. (1995). Men's preferences in romantic partners: Obesity vs addiction. *Psychological Reports, 77*, 1185–1186.

Slochower, J., Wein, L., White, J., Firstenberg, S., & Diguilio, J. (1980). Severe physical handicaps and helping behavior. *Journal of Social Psychology, 112*, 313–314.

Slotterback, C. S. & Saarnio, D. A. (1996). Attitudes toward older adults reported by young adults: Variation based on attitudinal task and attribute categories. *Psychology and Aging, 11*, 563–571.

Smart, L. & Wegner, D. M. (1999). Covering up what can't be seen: Concealable stigma and mental control. *Journal of Personality and Social Psychology, 77*, 474–486.

Smedley, J. W. & Bayton, J. (1978). Evaluative race-class stereotypes by race and perceived class of subjects. *Journal of Personality and Social Psychology, 36,* 530–536.

Smith, E. R. & DeCoster, J. (2000). Dual process models in social and cognitive psychology: Conceptual integration and links to underlying memory systems. *Personality and Social Psychology Review, 4,* 108–131.

Snyder, M. & Haugen, J. A. (1994). Why does behavioral confirmation occur? A functional perspective on the role of the perceiver. *Journal of Experimental Social Psychology, 30,* 218–246.

Snyder, M. L., Kleck, R. E., Strenta, A., & Mentzer, S. J. (1979). Avoidance of the handicapped: An attributional ambiguity analysis. *Journal of Personality and Social Psychology, 37,* 2297–2306.

Sobal, J., Nicolopoulos, V., & Lee, J. (1995). Attitudes about overweight and dating among secondary school students. *International Journal of Obesity, 19,* 376–381.

Sobal, J. & Stunkard, A. J. (1989). Socioeconomic status and obesity: A review of the literature. *Psychological Bulletin, 105,* 260–275.

Soble, S. L. & Strickland, L. H. (1974). Physical stigma, interaction, and compliance. *Bulletin of the Psychonomic Society, 4,* 130–132.

Solomon, R. C. (1976). *The passions.* Notre Dame, IN: University of Notre Dame Press.

Solzhenitsyn, A. (1963). *One day in the life of Ivan Denisovich.* Harmondsworth, UK: Penguin Books.

Sommerhoff, G. (1974). *Logic of the living brain.* London: Wiley.

Sroufe, L. A. (1977). Wariness of strangers and the study of infant development. *Child Development, 48,* 731–746.

Stangor, C. & Crandall, C. S. (2000). Threat and the social construction of stigma. In T. F. Heatherton, R. E. Kleck, M. R. Hebl & J. G. Hull (eds.), *The social psychology of stigma* (pp. 62–87). New York: The Guilford Press.

Stangor, C., Sullivan, L. A., & Ford, T. E. (1991). Affective and cognitive determinants of prejudice. *Social Cognition, 9,* 359–380.

Stapel, D. A. & Koomen, W. (1997). Social categorization and perceptual judgment of size: When perception is social. *Journal of Personality and Social Psychology, 73,* 1177–1190.

(1998). When stereotype activation results in (counter) stereotypical judgments: Priming stereotype-relevant traits and exemplars. *Journal of Experimental Social Psychology, 34,* 136–163.

(2001). Let's not forget the past when we go to the future: On our knowledge of knowledge accessibility. In G. B. Moskowitz (ed.), *Cognitive social psychology: The Princeton symposium on the legacy and future of social cognition* (pp. 229–246). Mahwah, NJ: Erlbaum.

Steblay, N. M. (1987). Helping behavior in rural and urban environments: A meta-analysis. *Psychological Bulletin, 102,* 346–356.

Steele, C. M. & Aronson, J. (1995). Stereotype threat and the intellectual test performance of African Americans. *Journal of Personality and Social Psychology, 69,* 797–811.

Stephan, W. G., Ageyev, V., Coates Shrider, L., Stephan, C. W., *et al.* (1994). On the relationship between stereotypes and prejudice: An international study. *Personality and Social Psychology Bulletin, 20*(3), 277–284.

Stephan, W. G. & Finlay, K. (1999). The role of empathy in improving intergroup relations. *Journal of Social Issues, 55,* 729–743.

Stephan, W. G. & Stephan, C. W. (1985). Intergroup anxiety. *Journal of Social Issues, 41*(3), 157–175.

Sterelny, K. (1990). *The representational theory of mind: An introduction.* Oxford, UK: Basil Blackwell.

Stiker, H.-J. (1999). *A history of disability* (W. Sayers, Trans.). Michigan: The University of Michigan Press.

Stiles, B. (1995). Benevolence as deviant behavior: A test of the sympathy effect. *Deviant Behavior, 16,* 81–92.

Stone, D. L. & Colella, A. (1996). A model of factors affecting the treatment of disabled individuals in organizations. *Academy of Management Review, 21,* 352–401.

Storey, A. E., Walsh, C. J., Quinton, R. L., & Wynne-Edwards, K. E. (2000). Hormonal correlates of paternal responsiveness in new and expectant fathers. *Evolution and Human Behavior, 21,* 79–95.

Strack, F. & Deutsch, R. (2004). Reflective and impulsive determinants of social behavior. *Personality and Social Psychology Review, 8,* 220–247.

Strang, H. & Sherman, L. W. (2003). Repairing the harm: victims and restorative justice. *Utah Law Review, 15,* 15–42.

Strommen, E. F. (1989). "You're a what?": Family member reactions to the disclosure of homosexuality. *Journal of Homosexuality, 18,* 37–58.

Sugiyama, L. S. (2004). Illness, injury, and disability among Shiwiar forager-horticulturalists: Implications of health-risk buffering for the evolution of human life history. *American Journal of Physical Anthropology, 123,* 371–389.

Suh, E., Diener, E., Oishi, S., & Triandis, H. C. (1998). The shifting basis of life satisfaction judgments across cultures: Emotions versus norms. *Journal of Personality and Social Psychology, 74,* 482–493.

Tajfel, H. (1969). Cognitive aspects of prejudice. *Journal of Biosocial Science, Supplement 1,* 173–191.

Tajfel, H. & Turner, J. C. (1986). The social identity theory of intergroup behavior. In S. Worchel & W. G. Austin (eds.), *The psychology of intergroup relations* (pp. 7–24). Chicago: Nelson-Hall.

Takahashi, L. M. (1997). The socio-spatial stigmatization of homelessness and HIV/AIDS: Toward an explanation of the NIMBY syndrome. *Social Science & Medicine, 45,* 903–914.

Talle, A. (1995). A child is a child: Disability and equality among the Kenya Maasai. In B. Ingstad & S. Reynolds Whyte (eds.), *Disability and culture* (pp. 56–93). Berkeley, CA: University of California Press.

Taylor, C. J. (1998). Factors affecting behavior toward people with disabilities. *Journal of Social Psychology, 138,* 766–771.

Taylor, S. E., Klein, L. C., Lewis, B. P., Gruenewald, T. L., Gurung, R. A. R., & Updegraff, J. A. (2000). Biobehavioral responses to stress in females: Tend-and-befriend, not fight-or-flight. *Psychological Review, 107,* 411–429.

Tesser, A. (1993). The importance of heritability in psychological research. *Psychological Review, 100,* 129–142.

Thayer, S. (1973). Lend me your ears: Racial and sexual factors in helping the deaf. *Journal of Personality and Social Psychology, 28,* 8–11.

Thompson, T. L. (1982). Gaze toward and avoidance of the handicapped: A field experiment. *Journal of Nonverbal Behavior, 6,* 188–196.

Thompson, W. E. & Harred, J. L. (1992). Topless dancers: Managing stigma in a deviant occupation. *Deviant Behavior, 13,* 291–311.

Tiggemann, M. & Rothblum, E. D. (1997). Gender differences in internal beliefs about weight and negative attitudes towards self and others. *Psychology of Women Quarterly, 21,* 581–593.

Titley, R. W. & Viney, W. (1969). Expression of aggression toward the physically handicapped. *Perceptual and Motor Skills, 29,* 51–56.

Toates, F. (1986). *Motivational Systems.* Cambridge: Cambridge University Press.

Tobin, D. L., Holroyd, K. A., Reynolds, R. V., & Wigal, J. K. (1989). The hierarchical factor structure of the Coping Strategies Inventory. *Cognitive Therapy and Research, 13,* 343–361.

Tooby, J. & Cosmides, L. (1990). The past explains the present: Emotional adaptations and the structure of ancestral environments. *Ethology and Sociobiology, 11,* 375–424.

(1992). The psychological foundations of culture. In J. H. Barkow, L. Cosmides & J. Tooby (eds.), *The adapted mind: Evolutionary psychology and the generation of culture* (pp. 19–136). New York: Oxford University Press.

(1996). Friendship and the Banker's Paradox: Other pathways to the evolution of adaptations for altruism. In W. G. Runciman, J. M. Smith & R. I. M. Dunbar (eds.), *Evolution of social behaviour patterns in primates and man* (pp. 119–143). Oxford: Oxford University Press.

Towler, A. J. & Schneider, D. J. (2005). Distinctions among stigmatized groups. *Journal of Applied Social Psychology, 35,* 1–14.

Traniello, J. F. A., Rosengaus, R. B., & Savoie, K. (2002). The development of immunity in a social insect: Evidence for the group facilitation of disease resistance. *Proceedings of the National Academy of Sciences, 99,* 6838–6842.

Trawalter, S. & Richeson, J. A. (in press). Regulatory focus and executive function after interracial interactions. *Journal of Experimental Social Psychology.*

Triandis, H. C. (1989). The self and social behavior in differing cultural contexts. *Psychological Review, 96,* 506–520.

(1996). The psychological measurement of cultural syndromes. *American Psychologist, 51,* 407–415.

Triandis, H. C. & Gelfand, M. J. (1998). Converging measurement of horizontal and vertical individualism and collectivism. *Journal of Personality and Social Psychology, 74,* 118–128.

Trivers, R. (1985). *Social evolution.* Menlo Park, CA: Benjamin/Cummings.

Tropp, L. R. & Pettigrew, T. F. (2005). Differential relationships between intergroup contact and affective and cognitive dimensions of prejudice. *Personality and Social Psychology Bulletin, 31,* 1145–1158.

Tsang, E. (1994). Investigating the effect of race and apparent lesbianism upon helping behaviour. *Feminism and Psychology, 4,* 469–471.

Tucker, J. S. & Mueller, J. S. (2000). Spouses' social control of health behaviors: Use and effectiveness of specific strategies. *Personality and Social Psychology Bulletin, 26,* 1120–1130.

Twenge, J. M. (2000). The age of anxiety? The birth cohort change in anxiety and neuroticism, 1952–1993. *Journal of Personality and Social Psychology, 79,* 1007–1021.

Twenge, J. M. & Crocker, J. (2002). Race and self-esteem revisited: Reply to Hafdahl and Gray-Little (2002). *Psychological Bulletin, 128,* 417–420.

Ungar, S. (1979). The effects of effort and stigma on helping. *Journal of Social Psychology, 107,* 23–28.

Uvnäs-Moberg, K. (1998). Oxytocin may mediate the benefits of positive social interaction and emotions. *Psychoneuroendocrinology, 23,* 819–835.

Van Knippenberg, A. & Dijksterhuis, A. (1996). A posteriori stereotype activation: The preservation of stereotypes through memory distortion. *Social Cognition, 14,* 21–53.

Van Lange, P. A. M. (2000). Beyond self-interest: A set of propositions relevant to interpersonal orientations. In W. Stroebe & M. Hewstone (eds.), *European Review of Social Psychology* (Vol. 11, pp. 297–331). Chichester, UK: John Wiley & Sons Ltd.

Van Oudenhoven, J. P., Prins, K. S., & Buunk, B. P. (1996). Attitudes of minority and majority members towards adaptation of immigrants. *European Journal of Social Psychology, 28,* 995–1013.

Vanhemelryck, F. (2004). *Marginalen in de geschiedenis: Over beulen, joden, hoeren, zigeuners en andere zondebokken [Marginal people in history: On executioners, Jews, whores, gypsies and other scapegoats].* Leuven, Belgium: Davidsfonds.

Vanman, E. J., Paul, B. Y., Ito, T. A., & Miller, N. (1997). The modern face of prejudice and structural features that moderate the effect of cooperation on affect. *Journal of Personality and Social Psychology, 73,* 941–959.

Vrugt, A. (1990). Negative attitudes, nonverbal behavior and self-fulfilling prophecy in simulated therapy interviews. *Journal of Nonverbal Behavior, 14,* 77–86.

Wadden, T. A., Brownell, K. D., & Foster, G. D. (2002). Obesity: Responding to the global epidemic. *Journal of Consulting and Clinical Psychology, 70,* 510–525.

Wagner, U. & Zick, A. (1995). The relation of formal education to ethnic prejudice: Its reliability, validity and explanation. *European Journal of Social Psychology, 25,* 41–56.

Wainapel, S. F. (1996). Dickens and disability. *Disability and Rehabilitation, 18,* 629–632.

Waldo, C. R., Hesson McInnis, M. S., & D'Augelli, A. R. (1998). Antecedents and consequences of victimization of lesbian, gay, and bisexual young people: A structural model comparing rural university and urban samples. *American Journal of Community Psychology, 26,* 307–334.

Walker, I. & Read, J. (2002). The differential effectiveness of psychosocial and biogenetic causal explanations in reducing negative attitudes toward "mental illness". *Psychiatry, 65,* 313–325.

Walkey, F. H., Taylor, A. J., & Green, D. E. (1990). Attitudes to AIDS: A comparative analysis of a new and negative stereotype. *Social Science & Medicine, 30,* 549–552.

Walters, A. S. & Curran, M. C. (1996). "Excuse me, sir? May I help you and your boyfriend?": Salespersons' differential treatment of homosexual and straight customers. *Journal of Homosexuality, 31,* 135–152.

Walton, M. D., Sachs, D., Ellington, R., Hazlewood, A., Griffin, S., & Bass, D. (1988). Physical stigma and the pregnancy role: Receiving help from strangers. *Sex Roles, 18,* 323–331.

Weiner, B. (1995). *Judgments of responsibility: A foundation for a theory of social conduct.* New York: The Guilford Press.

Weiner, B., Perry, R. P., & Magnusson, J. (1988). An attributional analysis of reactions to stigmas. *Journal of Personality and Social Psychology, 55,* 738–748.

Weiss, M. (1997). Signifying the pandemics: Metaphors of AIDS, cancer, and heart disease. *Medical Anthropology Quarterly, 11,* 456–476.

(1998). Parents' rejection of their appearance-impaired newborns: Some critical observations regarding the social myth of bonding. *Marriage and Family Review*, 27, 191–209.

Weitz, S. (1972). Attitude, voice, and behavior: A repressed affect model of interracial interaction. *Journal of Personality and Social Psychology*, 24, 14–21.

Wertlieb, E. C. (1985). Minority group status of the disabled. *Human Relations*, 38, 1047–1063.

Westbrook, L. E., Bauman, L. J., & Shinnar, S. (1992). Applying stigma theory to epilepsy: A test of a conceptual model. *Journal of Pediatric Psychology*, 17, 633–649.

Westbrook, M. T., Legge, V., & Pennay, M. (1993). Attitudes towards disabilities in a multicultural society. *Social Science & Medicine*, 36, 615–623.

Wetle, T., Cwikel, J., & Levkoff, S. E. (1988). Geriatric medical decisions: Factors influencing allocation of scarce resources and the decision to withhold treatment. *The Gerontologist*, 28, 336–343.

Whalen, H. A. J., Shin, L. M., McInerney, S. C., Fischer, H., & Rauch, S. L. (2000). Differential response in the human amygdala to racial outgroup vs ingroup face stimuli. *NeuroReport*, 11, 2351–2355.

Wheeler, M. E. & Fiske, S. T. (2005). Controlling racial prejudice: Social-cognitive goals affect amygdala and stereotype activation. *Psychological Science*, 16, 56–63.

Wheeler, S. C. & Petty, R. E. (2001). The effects of stereotype activation on behavior: A review of possible mechanisms. *Psychological Bulletin*, 127, 797–826.

Whiten, A. (1999). The evolution of deep social mind in humans. In M. C. Corballis & S. E. G. Lea (eds.), *The descent of mind* (pp. 173–193). Oxford: Oxford University Press.

Whitley, B. E. (1990). The relationship of heterosexuals' attributions for the causes of homosexuality to attitudes toward lesbians and gay men. *Personality and Social Psychology Bulletin*, 16, 369–377.

Whitley, B. E., Jr. (1999). Right-wing authoritarianism, social dominance orientation, and prejudice. *Journal of Personality and Social Psychology*, 77, 126–134.

Whyte, S. R. (1995). Constructing epilepsy: Images and contexts in East Africa. In B. Ingstad & R. S. Whyte (eds.), *Disability and culture* (pp. 226–245). Berkeley, CA: University of California Press.

Whyte, S. R. & Ingstad, B. (1995). Disability and culture: An overview. In B. Ingstad & S. R. Whyte (eds.), *Disability and culture* (pp. 3–32). Berkeley, CA: University of California Press.

Wilder, D. A. & Shapiro, P. (1989). Effects of anxiety on impression formation in a group context: An anxiety-assimilation hypothesis. *Journal of Experimental Social Psychology*, 25, 481–499.

Williams, B. (1996). Toleration: An impossible virtue? In D. Heyd (ed.), *Toleration: An elusive virtue* (pp. 18–27). Princeton, NJ: Princeton University Press.

Wills, T. A. (1981). Downward comparison principles in social psychology. *Psychological Bulletin*, 90, 245–271.

Wilson, T. C. (1985). Urbanism and tolerance: A test of some hypotheses drawn from Wirth and Stouffer. *American Sociological Review*, 50, 117–123.

Winzer, M. A. (1997). Disability and society: Before the eighteenth century. In L. J. Davis (ed.), *The disability studies reader* (pp. 75–109). New York: Routledge.

Wispé, L. (1986). The distinction between sympathy and empathy: To call forth a concept, a word is needed. *Journal of Personality and Social Psychology, 50,* 314–321.

Wispé, L. G. & Freshley, H. B. (1971). Race, sex, and sympathetic helping behavior: The broken bag caper. *Journal of Personality and Social Psychology, 17,* 59–65.

Witt, L. A. (1989). Authoritarianism, knowledge of AIDS, and affect toward persons with AIDS: Implications for health education. *Journal of Applied Social Psychology, 19,* 599–607.

Wolpe, J. (1990). *The practice of behavior therapy.* Oxford: Pergamon Press.

Wolsink, M. (1994). Entanglement of interests and motives: Assumptions behind the NIMBY-theory on facility siting. *Urban Studies, 31,* 851–866.

Wood, J. V., Taylor, S. E., & Lichtman, R. R. (1985). Social comparison in adjustment to breast cancer. *Journal of Personality and Social Psychology, 49,* 1169–1183.

Woodburn, J. (1968). Discussions, Part II. In R. B. Lee & I. DeVore (eds.), *Man the hunter* (p. 91). New York: Aldine Publishing Company.

Ybema, J. F., Kuijer, R. G., Hagedoorn, M., & Buunk, B. P. (2002). Caregiver burnout among intimate partners of patients with a severe illness: An equity perspective. *Personal Relationships, 9,* 73–88.

Yoon, C., Hasher, L., Feinberg, F., Rahhal, T. A., & Winocur, G. (2000). Cross-cultural differences in memory: The role of culture-based stereotypes about aging. *Psychology and Aging, 15,* 694–704.

Zebrowitz, L. A., Fellous, J.-M., Mignault, A., & Andreoletti, C. (2003). Trait impressions as overgeneralized responses to adaptively significant facial qualities: Evidence from connectionist modeling. *Personality and Social Psychology Review, 7,* 194–215.

Zippay, A. (1997). Trends in siting strategies. *Community Mental Health Journal, 33,* 301–310.

Zuckerman, M., Miserandino, M., & Bernieri, F. J. (1983). Civil inattention exists – In elevators. *Personality and Social Psychology Bulletin, 9,* 578–586.

# Index

Abandonment 36, 200, 202, 332, 348, 357
Acknowledgment of deviant condition or
    stigma 44, 100, 101–102, 315, 317,
    319, 325
ADHD (attention-deficit hyperactivity
    disorder) 268–269
Affiliation loss 281–283
African-Americans 38, 55, 83, 91–92, 93,
    95–96, 98–99, 104–105, 108,
    126–128, 132, 133–134, 135–136,
    139, 140, 143, 148, 149–150, 153,
    154, 155, 156, 157, 158, 167–169,
    177–178, 179, 231, 261, 275, 285,
    287–288, 291, 294, 329, 349, 351,
    353, 355
Aggression as deviant behavior 16, 78
Aggression as response to deviance
    126–130
  in evolutionary perspective 25, 26,
    31, 34
  indirect vs. direct 125–130, 136, 156
  inhibition of (see also Forgiveness) 36,
    129, 197, 199, 349
  interracial aggression 127–128
  situational influences on 125, 130–132
  use of Taylor paradigm in research on
    125, 127, 128
  use of teacher-learner paradigm in
    research on 125, 126–127, 128
AIDS (acquired immune deficiency
    syndrome) 72, 78, 85, 89, 91, 104,
    106, 143, 155, 253, 255, 272, 315,
    320–321, 350, 360
Alcoholism 43, 74, 80, 216
Altruism (see also Care (C) system,
    Helping)
  based on kinship or inclusive fitness 26,
    33, 34–44
  based on reciprocity 35, 38–41,
    189, 201
Ambivalence (see also Automatic and
    controlled processes) 44, 95, 96,
    104, 117, 145, 157, 201, 202, 209,
    210, 228, 324

Amputation 74, 78, 284, 357
Amygdala 55, 153, 154, 155, 349, 354
Anger (see Fight-or-flight (FF) system)
Anxiety (see also Ambivalence)
  interaction anxiety 110, 144–152
Assimilation and contrast effects 42–43, 95,
    98, 99, 104, 105
Attachment security 138–139, 200, 360
Attributional ambiguity 274
Authoritarianism 166, 167, 355–356
  and rejection of deviant conditions
    166–168, 171–174
  and values 172–174, 175–176
Automatic and controlled processes (see
    also Ambivalence, Dual-process
    models)
  integrative model of automatic and
    controlled processes 114–117
  determinants of initial motivational
    state 117–120
  factors moderating influence of initial
    motivational state 120–122
  measurement of automatic processes
    152–156
  motives for controlling automatic
    processes 113–114
  variables affecting dissociation between
    156–160
"Aversive racism" 133
Avoidance (see Escape and avoidance)
Awareness of stereotypes 272

"Baby talk" 247
Beggars 38, 205
Bible 206–207
Big Five personality traits 177
Blacks (see African-Americans)
Blaming the victim 326
Blindness 9, 74, 137, 225, 229, 272
Bogus pipeline 180, 355
Burnout among caregivers 330

Cancer 70, 71, 76, 90–91, 100, 101–102, 263,
    317, 321, 330, 334, 360

To view an author index, please visit www.cambridge.org/9780521793681

Care (C) system
  relation with egalitarianism 164–178
  and emotions 49, 51–54
  evolutionary origin of 34–44
  heritability of 176
  and inhibitory relationship with FF
      system 49–51
  as neglected motive in social control 17,
      26, 63–64
  neurophysiological aspects of 56–57
  and oxytocin 57
  and parental care 35, 56
  sex differences in activation of 57
  and social control in Category 1 and 3
      societies 197–204, 208–211
Cheaters (see also Social parasitism) 26, 38,
    40, 41, 50, 62, 63, 205, 209
Child abuse 76, 80, 83, 117, 118, 347
Chronic illness (see Disability)
Civil inattention 108, 146, 147, 152, 312
Collectivism-individualism (see also
    Societies) 192–193, 213–227
Color blind perspective 10
Compensation by individuals with deviant
    conditions 276, 286
Computational psychology (see
    Mentalism)
Concealability of deviant condition
    250–253
Conservatism (see also Authoritarianism)
    166–168, 356, 361
Contact hypothesis 21, 327, 328–330,
    352, 360
  meta-analysis of studies on 327, 328, 329
  role of emotions in 328
  and ultimate goals of contact
      interventions 329–330
Contempt 43, 54, 83, 207, 260, 324
Contrast effects (see Assimilation and
    contrast effects)
Controllability (see Responsibility)
Controlled processes (see Automatic and
    controlled processes)
Coping of persons with deviant conditions
    257–267
  effects on perceivers (see also
      Acknowledgment) 100–102
  emotion-focused vs. problem-focused
      265–266
    costs of emotion-focused coping 266
  long-term coping strategies 259–267
    attribution to prejudice and
        discrimination 262–263
    group formation and membership
        260
    reduction of the deviant condition
        259–260

  social comparison 263–265
  social creativity 261–262
  and responses to specific negative
      reactions 257–258
Crime 15, 32, 34, 41, 63, 90, 94, 113, 204,
    205, 211, 316, 320
Cross-cultural psychology (see Culture)
Culture (see also Societies)
  approaches to studying cultural
      differences 168, 184–188
  cultural dimensions and categories of
      societies 170, 188–196
    collectivism-individualism 192–193,
        213–227
    complexity 193–194
    egalitarian vs. hierarchical
        organization 193
  idiosyncratic cultural influences on
      responses to deviance 227–232
    deafness 229
    homosexuality 228–229, 230
    mental illness 229
    obesity 227, 230, 236–240

Deafness 229, 289, 353
Depression (see also Mental illness) 74,
    100, 211, 243, 244,
    282, 298
Developing countries (see Western versus
    non-Western societies)
Deviance (deviant conditions) (see also
    Mental representations of
    deviance)
  active vs. passive 16, 32, 166–167, 253
  basic types of
    Type 1 (uncontrollable-active) 31
    Type 2 (controllable-active) 32
    Type 3 (uncontrollable-passive) 36
    Type 4 (controllable-passive)
        36–37
      categories of Type 4 deviance
          37–38
  complexity of 91–92
  controllability of 32
  individual-related vs. group-related
      266–267, 351
  meaning of 4–5
  multiple deviant conditions 38
  primary vs. secondary 8
  reluctance to use term of 5, 9
  and stigma 9, 234
  universal validity of classification
      of 233
  and visibility (see also Concealability)
      72, 79, 250, 348
Deviant career 9
Diabetes 77, 79, 210

Disability 15, 20, 42, 92, 100–101, 102–103, 129, 136–137, 142, 147, 148–149, 151, 168, 193, 201–202, 207, 225, 244–246, 256, 261, 293, 301, 303, 315, 319, 326, 330, 338, 339, 351
  personal relationships of physically disabled persons 245
  work and employment of physically disabled persons 245–246
Disability movement 326–327
Disclosure of deviant condition 250–257
  and closeness of relationship 254–255
  different forms of 255–256
    "beyond-control" disclosure 255
    "colored" disclosure 255
    education 256
    "normalization" disclosure 255
  and reveal-conceal dilemma 250–253
    fear of discovery 250–251
    information management 251
    situation management 251
    social isolation 252
  timing of disclosure 256
Discrimination (see also Stigmatization) 9, 249, 283–284, 290–294
  institutional discrimination 283–285
  and self-esteem 296–299
Disfigurement 44, 78, 115, 140–142, 143, 150, 224, 228, 234, 282, 284, 316, 348, 359
Disgust 44–45, 54, 83, 207
Displacement 7, 12, 33, 62, 110, 119, 130–131, 143–144, 230–231
  and economic distress 231–232
Disrespect 37, 38, 54, 96, 209
Dissociation between automatic and controlled responses (see Ambivalence, Automatic and controlled processes)
Drug addiction 43, 74, 80, 238, 336, 347
Dual-process models (see also Automatic and controlled processes) 110–124

Economic distress (see also Displacement) 181
Education (see also Socio-economic status)
  and negative responses to deviance (prejudice) 179–182
Egalitarianism (see Liberalism/egalitarianism)
Elderly (see Old age)
Emotions
  as characteristic responses to types of deviant conditions 81–84
  composite ("secondary") 51–54
  as mediators 86

relationships among 85–86
relative importance of different emotional reactions to deviance 84–85
Empathy (see Care (C) system, Pity)
Empowerment 307, 318, 326, 327, 339, 360
Epilepsy 76, 143, 207, 229, 253, 254, 274, 297, 348
Escape and avoidance 140–143
  situational influences on 143–144
Ethnic minorities 9–10, 12, 38, 77, 85, 117, 179–180, 266, 295, 298, 311, 328, 346, 361–362
Evolutionary psychology
  and approaches to social control 62–64
  and computational psychology 17, 25, 26, 60, 61, 63
  and psychological mechanisms for social control 24–25
Expectancy (see Mental representations of deviance)
Expectation-states theory 282

Family
  Allport's description of social control in 361
  and social control 14, 53, 64, 192, 193, 198
Fear (see Fight-or-flight (FF) system)
Fight-or-flight (FF) system
  relation with authoritarianism 164–178
  and emotions of anger and fear 49, 55
  evolutionary origin of 30–34
  heritability 176
  and inhibitory relationship with Care (C) system 49–51
  neurophysiological aspects of 55–56
  and social control in Category 2 societies 204–208
Forgiveness (see also Aggression, inhibition of) 36, 40, 43, 50, 53–54, 97, 105, 199, 204, 316, 319, 332, 350
Free riders (see Social parasitism)

Genes 27–29, 34, 36, 45, 65, 346
Genetic origin
  influence of information about, on responses to deviance 87
"Getting to yes" 341–342
Gossip 6, 15, 198, 200, 334
Guilt 12, 38, 53, 113, 133, 139, 145, 156, 159, 161, 206

Handicap (see Disability)
Health care, education, or promotion 12, 15, 326, 333, 334, 343
Heart disease 42, 76, 85

Helping 133–137
  assumptive/unsolicited 275
  face-to-face vs. remote contact 134–135
  individual differences in 133–134
  interracial helping 134, 135, 353
  situational influences on 137–140
Historical variation in responding to
    deviance (see Culture, Societies)
HIV (see AIDS)
Homelessness 21, 75, 77, 209, 329, 334, 335,
    336, 344
Homosexuality 72, 83, 87, 91, 128–129, 130,
    139, 148, 149, 168, 177, 179, 181,
    201, 220, 228–229, 230, 231,
    240–243, 249, 250, 252, 254, 260,
    261, 266, 282, 292, 296–297, 299,
    320, 354, 355, 358, 360
  cultural aspects of 228–229, 230
  differences in responding to gay vs.
    lesbian persons 242
  and experienced violence 240–242
  and help 242
  and work and employment 242–243
Humanitarianism-Egalitarianism 167
Hunter-gatherers (see also Societies) 10, 25,
    64, 185, 190, 199, 232, 356, 357

Ideological orientations (see also
    Authoritarianism, Social
    dominance orientation (SDO),
    Liberalism/egalitarianism) 164
Immigrant workers (see Ethnic minorities)
Implicit Association Test (IAT) 153–154,
    155, 159
Implicit measures 152–159, 160, 161, 285
Inclusive fitness (see Kin selection)
Infanticide 202, 203
Interactional difficulties of nondeviant and
    deviant persons (see also
    Ambivalence, Anxiety)
  contribution of non-deviant person
    147–152
  contribution of person with deviant
    condition 272–276
Internal representation (see Mental
    representations of deviance)
Internet 294, 359
Interventions to prevent or reduce
    stigmatization
  anger reduction 316–317
  contact with deviant persons
    327–330
  educational 320–322
  ethical aspects of 311, 331
  fear-reducing strategies 314–316,
    359–360
  influencing the C system 317–318, 319

"liking" as an effect measure of 323–324,
    329–330
meta-strategy for dealing with deviance
    340
nature of the response to influence
    308–309
negotiation 340–342
perceiver-directed 319–325
tailoring to types of deviance 313–319
  uncontrollable-active 313–316
  controllable-active 316–317
  uncontrollable-passive 317–318
  controllable-passive 318–319
tailoring to types of social control
    331–337
target-directed 325–327
ultimate goals of 310–312, 329–330

Kin selection 16, 26, 28, 35, 45–46,
    64–65, 66

Labeling (see also Stigmatization) 8, 21, 205
Lateral inhibition 49–51
Laziness (see also Social parasitism) 9, 37,
    38, 43, 75, 77, 92, 96, 99, 105, 132,
    230, 319
Leprosy 7, 205, 228, 318, 322
Liberalism/egalitarianism (see also Social
    dominance orientation) 166–167
Locational conflict 335
Long-term care 309, 310–311, 337
"Looking–glass" self 294
Lynching 231

Magical contagion 345
Mainstreaming 329
Master status 193, 201, 273
Medical model of disability 326
Medicalization 209, 316
Mentalism (see also Evolutionary
    psychology) 25, 26, 60, 61, 350
Mental disability (see Mental handicap)
Mental handicap 43, 45, 129, 201, 244, 245,
    273, 293, 309, 318, 323, 324, 329,
    343, 362
Mental illness 5, 70, 74, 75, 83–84, 87, 104,
    128, 201, 224, 229, 243–244, 253,
    286, 292–293, 294, 303, 312, 321,
    335, 339
  cultural aspects of 229
  and help 243–244
  and personal relationships 243
  and work and employment 244
Mental representations of deviance
  content
    dimensional structure of 71–76
    emotional implications of 81–84

Mental representations of deviance (cont.)
        methods to reveal 69–71, 81
    representations of individual deviant
        conditions 76–77
    effects of additional or salient
        information on perceptions 86–91
    effects of mental representations and
        behavioral information on
        information processing (see also
        Assimilation and contrast effects)
    with respect to active deviance
        104–105
    with respect to passive deviance
        98–104
Middle Ages (European) 7, 13, 38, 205,
        206, 211
Mind-brain dualism (see Mentalism)
Motivational systems (see Care (C) system,
        Fight-or-flight (FF) system)
Multidimensional scaling analysis (MDS)
        68–70, 71
    and deviant conditions 71–76, 77–80

Negotiation (see Interventions to prevent
        or reduce stigmatization)
Neural network (FF-C network) 349
    and responses to deviance 48–51
Neurophysiological aspects of social
        control (see Care (C) system,
        Fight-or-flight (FF) system)
NIMBY ("not-in-my-backyard") (see also
        Locational conflict) 335–337
Norm violations and reactions to deviance
        32, 34
Norms for expression of responses to
        deviance (see Automatic and
        controlled processes,
        Suppression)

Obesity 72, 75, 77, 92, 100, 153, 171, 220, 224,
        227, 230, 236–240, 249, 251,
        257–258, 262, 269, 273, 277, 281,
        291–292, 295–296, 300, 303, 306,
        319, 324, 339
    cultural aspects of 220, 224, 227, 230,
        236–240
    and education 239
    and help 238–239
    and personal relationships 237–238
    and work and employment 239–240
Old age 88, 93–94, 106, 168, 178, 181, 202,
        203, 229, 246–249, 269–271, 276,
        284, 288–289, 294, 301, 303,
        329, 354
    and help 248
    and personal relationships 246–248
    and work and employment 248–249

Ostracism 6, 198–199
Outcomes of having a deviant condition
        (see Self-esteem, Socio-economic
        status, Well-being)
Outgroups (see also Ethnic minorities)
        45–46, 177, 180, 208, 225, 294
Overweight (see Obesity)
Oxytocin (see also Care (C) system) 40,
        56, 57

Parent-offspring conflict 347
Performance deficits of persons with
        deviant conditions 285–290
    awareness of having the condition
        286–287
    memory of elderly people 289
    stereotype threat 287–289
Personal control of persons with deviant
        conditions 270–271
Perspective-taking 52, 140, 318, 354
Pets 57, 208
Pity (see also Care (C) system) 51
Political correctness 179, 338
Poverty 7, 38, 77, 157, 205, 207, 209, 225, 228
Power loss 282–283
Prejudice
    consistent tendency to be prejudiced
        177–178
    educational differences in 179–182
    individual differences in
        relation with authoritarianism
            166–168, 171–174
        relation with liberalism/
            egalitarianism 166–167
        relation with social dominance
            orientation (SDO) 174–175
    meaning of 8, 163, 346
    motivation to respond without 168–169
        internal vs. external motivation
            169, 355
    sex differences in 178–179
Priming (see also Implicit measures)
        49, 153
Protestant ethic 168, 296

Reciprocity (see also Altruism, Cheaters,
        Evolutionary psychology, Kin
        selection) 97, 100, 212, 309, 311,
        323, 329, 330, 337, 342
Rejection hierarchies
    and configurations of deviant conditions
        77–80
Religion 206–207
Repair (see also Social control) 4–6
Response amplification (see also
        Ambivalence, Assimilation and
        contrast effects) 95–104, 351

Responsibility
  influence on responses to deviance 74,
      80, 88–89, 167, 211, 220
  meaning of 31, 42–43, 54, 61, 80, 105
  onset vs. offset 42, 74, 88, 89, 101, 347–348

Scapegoating (see Displacement)
Schizophrenia (see also Mental illness) 59,
      76, 84, 173, 207, 211, 220, 229, 243,
      321, 358
Self-efficacy of persons with deviant
      conditions 282
Self-esteem of persons with deviant
      conditions 294–300
  African-Americans 294
  and discrimination and stigmatization
      296–299
    approaches to study relationships
        with self-esteem 296
    and well-being 302–303
  elderly people 294
  obese persons 295–296
  physically unattractive persons 295
Self-fulfilling prophecies 267–272
  institutional prophecies 270–271
  interpersonal prophecies
    children with ADHD 268–269
    elderly persons 269–270
    mentally ill persons 268
    obese persons 269
  and power 271–272
Self-preservation 28, 30–34
Self-regulation (see Suppression)
Sex differences
  and negative responses to deviance
      (prejudice) 178–179
  and the care system 57, 178–179
Sexual reproduction 46–47, 189, 346–347
Shaman 201, 229
Shame 41, 53, 198, 250, 361
Shaming
  public 199, 211, 333, 334
  reintegrative 332
"Sick role" 41, 43, 102, 321, 327
Smoking 14, 15, 37, 42, 72, 76, 77, 210,
      334, 339
Social control
  adaptive psychological mechanisms
      for 29
  evolution of social control 14–16, 27–30
  meaning of 4
  types of social control
    empirical distinctions between types
        14–16, 27–30
    repair 4–6
    stigmatization 6–10
    tolerance 10–14

Social dominance orientation (SDO)
  and rejection of persons with deviant
      conditions 171–174
  and relation with liberalism/
      egalitarianism 174–175
  and values 172–176
Social model of disability (see Disability
      movement)
Social parasitism (see also Cheaters) 12, 37,
      54, 199, 209, 334, 336
Societies (see also Culture)
  Category 1 (simple-egalitarian-
      collectivistic) societies 197–204
  Category 2 (moderately complex-
      hierarchical-collectivistic)
      societies 204–208
  Category 3 (very complex-egalitarian-
      individualistic) societies 208–211
Socio-economic status of persons with
      deviant conditions 290–294
  African-Americans 291
  elderly 293
  homosexuals 292
  mentally ill 292–293
  obese 291–292
  physically disabled 293
Stereotype (see Mental representations of
      deviance)
Stereotype awareness 272
Stereotype threat 287–289
Stereotyping (see Mental representations
      of deviance)
Stigma (See also Deviance (deviant
      conditions)) 234
  acknowledgment of (see
      Acknowledgment)
  consciousness of 298–299
  "courtesy" stigma (stigma-by-
      association) 345–346
  enacted vs. felt stigma 298
  endorsement by persons with deviant
      conditions 283–285
  "groupiness" of 266–267, 351
  and mass media 284
  meaning of 8
Stigmatization (see also Social control)
      6–10
  defined 6
Suppression (see also Automatic and
      controlled processes) 113, 114,
      120, 148, 150
  and adherence to social norms 170–171
  and Care (C) system 168–171
  internal vs. external motivation
      169, 355
  and "rebound" effects 148, 251
  and tolerance 12

Swiss-army-knife conception of the human mind (see also Evolutionary psychology) 25
Sympathy (see Care (C) system)
System justification 285

Tenderness (see also Care (C) system) 49
Token and performance 286
Tolerance (see also Social control) 10–14

Unemployment 75, 82, 92, 174
Urban vs. rural areas
    and influence on responding to deviance 211–212, 224, 227

Values (see also Culture, Societies)
    and goals 165
    Openness to Change vs. Conservation 165
    Self-Transcendence vs. Self-Enhancement 165
Vignettes, use in psychological research 71

Violence
    in Category 2 societies 204
    in evolutionary perspective 190
    in response to homosexuality 240–242
Visibility of deviant conditions 72, 79, 250, 348
Vulnerability cues 35, 49, 51, 88

Welfare, being on 43, 75, 96, 209, 211
Well-being (subjective) of persons with deviant conditions 301–303
    adaptation and coping 301–302
    disabled persons 301
    physical unattractiveness 301
    and self-esteem 302–303
Western versus non-Western societies 78, 171, 212–227
Wheelchair (see also Amputation, Disability) 9, 15, 42, 76, 78, 103, 118, 129, 136, 138, 142, 149, 224, 228, 245, 246, 318, 321, 338
World Values Survey (WVS) 213–220, 358

*Studies in Emotion and Social Interaction*

Other books in the series

*Emotions across Languages and Cultures: Diversity and Universals,* by
Anna Wierzbicka

*Gender and Emotion: Social Psychological Perspectives,* by
Agneta H. Fischer

*Metaphor and Emotion: Language, Culture, and Body in Human Feeling,* by
Zoltán Kövecses

*Feeling and Thinking: The Role of Affect in Social Cognition,* by
Joseph P. Forgas

*Causes and Consequences of Feelings,* by
Leonard Berkowitz

*Emotions and Beliefs: How Feelings Influence Thoughts,* by
Nico H. Frijda, Antony S. R. Manstead, and Sacha Bem

*Identity and Emotion: Development through Self-Organization,* by
Harke A. Bosma and E. Saskia Kunnen

*Speaking from the Heart: Gender and the Social Meaning of Emotion,* by
Stephanie A. Shields

*The Hidden Genius of Emotion: Lifespan Development of Personality,* by
Carol Magai and Jeanette Haviland-Jones

*The Mind and Its Stories: Narrative Universals and Human Emotion,* by
Patrick Colm Hogan

*Feelings and Emotions: The Amsterdam Symposium,* by
Antony S. R. Manstead, Nico H. Frijda, and Agneta H. Fischer

*The Social Life of Emotions,* by
Larissa Z. Tiedens and Colin Wayne Leach

*Collective Guilt: International Perspectives,* by
Nyla R. Branscombe and Bertjan Doosje

*Emotions and Multilingualism,* by
Aneta Pavlenko

*Group Dynamics and Emotional Expression,* by
Ursula Hess and Pierre Philippot